Eitan Grossman, Martin Haspelmath and
Egyptian-Coptic Linguistics in Typologica

Empirical Approaches to Language Typology

Edited by
Georg Bossong
Bernard Comrie
Kristine A. Hildebrandt
Yaron Matras

Volume 55

Egyptian-Coptic Linguistics in Typological Perspective

Edited by
Eitan Grossman, Martin Haspelmath
and Tonio Sebastian Richter

DE GRUYTER
MOUTON

ISBN 978-3-11-055513-4
e-ISBN (PDF) 978-3-11-034651-0
e-ISBN (EPUB) 978-3-11-039459-7
ISSN 0933-761X

Library of Congress Cataloging-in-Publication Data
A CIP catalog record for this book has been applied for at the Library of Congress.

Bibliographic information published by the Deutsche Nationalbibliothek
The Deutsche Nationalbibliothek lists this publication in the Deutsche Nationalbibliografie;
detailed bibliographic data are available on the Internet at http://dnb.dnb.de.

www.degruyter.com

Preface

With a rich documentation spanning over 4000 years, Egyptian-Coptic would seem a treasure trove for those whose interests combine historical linguistics and language typology, yet hitherto links across these disciplines have rarely been exploited. The most obvious examples are Loprieno's *Ancient Egyptian: A Linguistic Introduction* (Cambridge 1995) – Loprieno is, incidentally, a contributor to the present volume – and Allen's *The Ancient Egyptian Language: An Historical Study* (Cambridge 2013). While these works are overall presentations of the structure and history of Egyptian-Coptic from a modern linguistic/typological perspective, the present work concentrates on a number of specific topics where Egyptian-Coptic data and linguistic typology cast light on each other, going into much more detail than was possible in either of the overviews. The two sets of works are thus complementary. Both emphasize the importance of Egyptian-Coptic, with the longest attested history of any language, for typological and especially diachronic typological studies.

The book falls into two main parts, Propaedeutics and Studies. Propaedeutics includes a historical account of the interaction of Egyptological/Coptological and typological studies in the nineteenth century (Richter), a summary account of the genealogical affiliation, periodization, etc. of Egyptian-Coptic (essential for the understanding of the Studies) (Grossman/Richter), a typological sketch of Middle Egyptian and Coptic (Haspelmath), and a proposed Leipzig-Jerusalem transliteration of Coptic (Grossman/Haspelmath).

The Studies comprise eleven articles, all of which satisfy the prerequisite of showing how Egyptological/Coptological studies and linguistic typology can mutually illuminate one another. Collier ('Conditionals in Late Egyptian') not only advances the description and analysis of conditional constructions in Egyptian, noting the richness of the available material (though also the lacunae inevitable in a limited corpus), but also sets this squarely against the background of the typology of conditional constructions, including recent work in both linguistics and logic. Gensler ('A typological look at Egyptian *d > ʕ') notes that a sound change that has become widely accepted recently by Egyptologists lacks all typological plausibility, thus suggesting that either Egyptology or typology must be wrong. Grossman ('No case before the verb', obligatory case after the verb in Coptic) provides a reanalysis of case marking of core arguments in Coptic, with a nominative/accusative distinction in postverbal position (with both cases overtly marked) versus absence of case marking for both subject and object in preverbal position, and links this pattern to the "no case before the verb" generalization suggested for other Northeast African languages by C. König. Güldemann ('How typology can inform philology: quotative *j(n)* in Earlier Egyptian') shows how the widely accepted assumption that quotative *j(n)* must have been originally a verb is justified neither by the typological study of quoted speech markers nor by the language-internal evidence. Haspelmath ('The three adnominal possessive constructions in Egyptian-Coptic: three degrees of grammaticalization') demonstrates that what are often presented traditionally as idiosyncratic constraints on and developments in possessive constructions in Egyptian-Coptic fit in neatly with current ideas on grammaticalization. Idiatov ('Egyptian non-selective interrogative pronominals: history and typology') is interesting not only for its analysis of the lack of a 'who'/'what' distinction in earlier stages of Egyptian but also for the way in which it highlights the details against the author's typology of interrogative pronouns. Loprieno ('Typological remodeling in Egyptian language history: salience, source and conjunction') not only shows the relevance of typological considerations in his reconsideration of his own earlier analysis of the function of Egyptian *jn* (ergative? salience marker?), but also in the development of *jw* from a pragmatic through a semantic to a syntactic marker, in accord with a developmental pattern described by those working in typology and grammaticalization. Peust ('Towards a typology of poetic rhyme with observations on rhyme in Egyptian') breaks new ground by developing a theory of rhyme against a rich array of poetic examples from different languages and then sets the (late) development of rhyme in Egyptian-Coptic against this background; his claim that grammars should necessarily discuss poetic rhyme will surely generate controversy. Reintges ('The Old and Early Middle Egyptian stative: morphosyntax – semantics – typology' shows that an Egyptian verb form that has been given a number of different names, including the noncommittally opaque "pseudo-participle", is best analyzed as a stative, demonstrating how this is realized in its diathetic and aktionsart properties. Stauder ('A rare change: the degrammaticalization of an inflectional passive marker into an impersonal subject pronoun in Earlier Egyptian') provides meticulous argumentation in favor of his thesis that Egyptian evinces a rare case of degrammaticalization, with an inflectional voice marker ultimately being reinterpreted as an indefinite-personal pronoun (like French *on*, German *man*), thus adding to the small but growing literature on the relatively rare and apparently heavily constrained process of degrammaticalization. Finally, Winand ('The oblique expression of the object in Ancient Egyptian') investigates object marking from the typological perspective of differential object marking, reminding us that such marking is attested not only for definite/animate objects but also for partitive ones.

Overall this is an empirically rich, well argued, and theoretically informed set of articles showing both how Egyptian-Coptic can throw light on typological issues and how consideration of typology can advance work in Egyptian-Coptic linguistics. I recommend it to all those interested in any of Egyptian-Coptic, historical linguistics, and language typology.

Leipzig, October 2014   Bernard Comrie

Acknowledgements

The editors of this volume are thankful to the Fritz Thyssen Foundation, the Hebrew University of Jerusalem, Department of Linguistics/School of Language Sciences, and the Max Planck Institute for Evolutionary Anthropology, Department of Linguistics, for the financial support of this volume, and to Ute Terletzki and Brent Reed for their assistance with editing the manuscript of this volume.

Contents

Part I: Propaedeutics

Tonio Sebastian Richter
Early encounters: Egyptian-Coptic studies and comparative linguistics in the century from Schlegel to Finck*

"... de quelle importance l'étude du dialecte sacré des Égyptiens peut devenir pour la comparaison des langues ..." (Lepsius 1837: 89)

"Our century has witnessed many intellectual feasts in the vast region of science and art, and among these we must surely reckon the deciphering of inscriptions of bygone times which reveal to us the otherwise sealed history of Egypt, of Babylon, and of Assyria, and make us acquainted with a rich literature in hieroglyphics and cuneiform characters, part of which was written in a time when neither the Pentateuch nor the Veda had been composed. ... These cuneiform inscriptions and hieroglyphics contain no doubt the earliest records of mankind, and their value is heightened by the circumstance that they occasionally give evidence of, and throw light on, the construction of languages still living." (Oppert 1879: 2)

Abstract: From Schlegel (1808) to Finck (1910), the paths of Egyptian and comparative linguistics, despite starting out from different points of departure, crossed often. The early encounters between these two domains of linguistic study have mostly been forgotten by now, perhaps due to the fact that their protagonists went their separate ways during the following century.

This article aims to remind us that one of the earliest translations of a hieroglyphic text into a modern language was accomplished by one of the most renowned comparative linguists of the age, Wilhelm von Humboldt. Moreover, one of the earliest and most influential Egyptologists, Richard Lepsius, began as a comparative linguist and, in fact, never left either of these fields. Emerging knowledge about Egyptian-Coptic was integrated into linguistic thought quite early on and played a role in the developing field of typological classification.

This article cannot tell the whole story of early encounters between the study of Egyptian and of typological classification. Rather, it aims to sketch out some of the main figures and crucial moments of this period in linguistic thought and points to avenues of future investigation.

---

* I am grateful to Elke Blumenthal, Hans-W. Fischer-Elfert, Martin Haspelmath, Eitan Grossman, Stéphane Polis, and Wolfgang Schenkel who read and helpfully commented on earlier drafts of this paper.

1 On the threshold and one step further

Both Egyptology and linguistic approaches to the classification of languages appeared on the scene of European scholarship shortly after 1800, and their early development ran parallel to each other to some extent.

Egyptian language studies in a narrower sense did not exist before 1799, when the trilingual inscription known as the Rosetta stone was discovered. Several European scholars raced to decipher its incomprehensible Egyptian parts – the Demotic and hieroglyphic lines – on the basis of its Greek part. It took only a couple of years until, in 1802, the famous Parisian Orientalist Silvestre de Sacy (1758–1838) and his pupil, the Swedish orientalist Åkerblad (1763–1819), could offer their first tentative results, identifying the phonetic values of a number of alphabetic Demotic signs in the cartouches that were rightly suspected to contain the transcribed Greek names of Ptolemaic kings and queens (Åkerblad 1802; cf. Schenkel 2012a: 43–45, 74–78). However, the Rosetta stone was to resist scholars' efforts for another 20 years.

Before its decipherment, any serious occupation with Ancient Egyptian was limited to the analysis of single Egyptian words that were occasionally transmitted by classical authors (e.g., Jablonski 1804; Quatremère 1808; Schwartze 1843: 969–972, cf. also Wiedemann 1883). This type of evidence supported the hypothesis that at least some parts of Ancient Egyptian survived in Coptic. This hypothesis is presented as a likely assumption in the most current report of the time given in Adelung's *Mithridates* in 1812:

> "Whatever is not Greek in the Coptic language may by and large be considered Ancient Egyptian, the possibility of several modifications taken for granted." (transl. from Adelung 1806–1817.3.1: 69)[1]

The existence of Coptic, the written language of the Egyptian Christians, was known to European scholars as early as the late 15th century (Emmel 2004). It was studied more thoroughly from the mid-16th century onwards in the context of humanist scholarship, polyglot editions of the Bible, and other types of theo-

---

[1] The author of this entry was Johann Severin Vater, co-editor of the 3rd volume of *Mithridates* after Adelung's death, who gave reasons for this hypothesis ibid.: 66–67 (translated from German): "The close relation of this [i.e., the pharaonic language] to the Coptic language is evident from clearly proven explanations of many Ancient Egyptian words which are mentioned by Greek and Latin authors and could be satisfactorily explained by experts of the Coptic language. Therefore, these Ancient Egyptian words were integral part of this Coptic language, and the higher their number, the more certain is the close relationship between the one and the other".

logical work (Aufrère 1999; Krause 1998; Emmel 2004). At the time when the presumed key to understanding hieroglyphs, the Rosetta stone, came to light, Coptic was a fairly well-known and translatable language.[2]

The assumption that Coptic was related to the language underlying the hieroglyphs was to be of crucial importance for the eventual decipherment of Egyptian.[3] Once it was demonstrated to be true, the relationship between Coptic and earlier Egyptian became the basis for further achievements in understanding the grammar and lexicon of Ancient Egyptian.

Excursus I: The Genealogical Classification of Ancient Egyptian
The genealogical status of Egyptian and Coptic remained unsolved for quite a while. Coptic-Sanskrit cognates, as proposed by a certain Alter in 1799, are discussed and eventually refuted by Vater in *Mithridates* (1812.3.1: 67–68, who also discussed the relation of Coptic to Semitic and Berber languages (1812.3.1: 72–78). A point of special interest is the range of hypotheses proposing connections between Egyptian and Chinese, both in terms of genealogical relation as in De Guignes' (1721–1800) academy paper of 1758 (De Guignes 1759), Champollion's experiments in reading hieroglyphs as Chinese (Hartleben 1906.1), and Klaproth's attempt to connect Coptic to North-Western Asian languages genealogically (Klaproth 1823), as well as in 'typological' terms, such as in Silvestre de Sacy (1808); Lepsius (1834, cf. below, § 3), and Steinthal (1850 and 1860, cf. below, § 5). Attempts to substantiate the relationship of Egyptian and Semitic languages were taken by Lepsius (1836a, 1836b) and Benfey (1844). Benfey compared Semitic and Coptic pronominals as well as Semitic and (relics of) Coptic gender and number markers and came, decades before the full significance of this comparison could be appreciated (cf. below, § 8), to the conclusion "that in this respect [i.e., in

---

2 Even though its morphosyntax was far from being thoroughly analyzed before Stern 1880 (cf. below, § 8), Coptic was understood well enough, due to extant Arabic-Coptic glossaries and Coptic translations of biblical literature, to be able to separate grammatical items from lexical items and to assign approximate meanings to them. Bibliographical information on contemporary standard works on Coptic grammar and the lexicon can be found in Vater (1815: 51–52).

3 Champollion, who claimed to be as fluent in Coptic as in French, had finished a grammar and a lexicon of Coptic already in 1815, and only Silvestre de Sacy's doubts that Coptic would contribute to the knowledge of Egyptian made the Paris academy refuse their publication (Erman 1922: xxxvii–xxxviii). When Lepsius began to work on Egyptian, he started by acquainting himself with Coptic, and we see him working out a (never published) Coptic grammar early in 1835 (cf. Lepsius 1836b: 86).

terms of pronominals, gender and number marking, covered by Benfey under the term "inflectional forms" (*flexivische Formen*)] the Egyptian language and the Semitic stand on the same basis, that however these both branches of the underlying source language must have been separated and developed individually very early, long before the standardization of the most inflectional forms." (transl. from Benfey 1844: vi–vii). This conclusion is still accepted, by and large (cf. Loprieno 1986: 1–12; Schenkel 1990: 13–17, and the introduction by Grossman & Richter in this volume).[4] A genealogical link to African languages was first proposed and conceptualized in the framework of the 'Hamitic' language family by Lepsius (1863a and 1880) (cf. below, § 3).

Language classification and linguistic typology have their roots in European traditions of the philosophy of language and universal grammar (cf. Robins 1973; Plank 2001; Rousseau 2001).

In 1808, Friedrich, the younger of the Schlegel brothers (1772–1829), first noticed different degrees of grammaticalization (as one would call it now) as displayed by different languages encoding functional relations between lexemes,[5] and took this difference as a criterion for distinguishing two general types (*Hauptgattungen*) of language (cf. Rousseau 2001: 1415–1416; on Friedrich Schlegel's occupation with Egyptian cf. Grimm 2004: 15–16 and 2006: 74–76): on the one hand, the inflected, truly "organic" type, as he called it, such as Sanskrit,[6] and on the other hand, the type of language where the same functions are expressed by juxtaposed or agglutinated words, occasionally or exclusively loaded with grammatical meaning. The latter was the far less sophisticated type of language, according to Schlegel.

Shortly before, in August 1807, Jean-François Champollion (1790–1832), a 17-year-old graduate of the lycée in Grenoble, who had been obsessed with the

---

4 For a hotly debated phonological issue related to the shared roots of the Egyptian and Semitic lexicon, see Gensler's article in this volume.

5 Schlegel (1808: 45, transl. from German): "Auxiliary assignments of meaning are indicated either by internal changes of stem sounds, i.e., by inflection, or by appending discrete words inherently meaning e.g., plurality, past, future obligation, or any similar terms of relation, and these two simple cases also define the main types of all languages. All other cases are only modifications and sub-categories of these two types."

6 Cf. Schlegel (1808: 50–51, transl. from German): "In the Indic language, each root [is] ... truly what the name says, and like a living seedling, since, as relation terms are indicated by internal change, its growth is given scope for free development".

decipherment of hieroglyphs from the age of twelve,[7] had started to work out a comprehensive geographical description of Ancient Egypt. Published in 1814 under the title *L'Égypte sous les pharaons*, it was his first major contribution to the investigation of Ancient Egypt (Hartleben 1906.1: 65–66). In September 1807, Champollion went to Paris to enroll at university and was introduced to Silvestre de Sacy (Hartleben 1906.1: 72–74), the most famous orientalist of the day and "the first person [in modern times] to read any Egyptian word, albeit in a small way" (Dawson & Uphill 1995: 392).

In the same year 1807, an important contribution of Champollion's later competitor, the English physician and scientist Thomas Young (1773–1829) appeared. This contribution, however, was not yet related to hieroglyphs but rather to the physical nature of light. Only at some point after 1810 did Young became captivated by the hieroglyphs and progressed further than any of his predecessors could have boasted by then.

In 1818, Young published a vocabulary comprising 204 Egyptian words (with more or less correct meanings assigned to roughly a quarter of them)[8] and a list of 14 hieroglyphs with their presumed phonetic values.[9] In the same year, the English traveler, William John Bankes (1786–1855), took the first copy of the Abydos king list of Ramesses II (Dawson & Uphill 1995: 29; James 1997) and sent a lithographic table of it to Thomas Young, who did not profit from it as Champollion later would.

Once again in 1818, Friedrich's elder brother, August Wihelm von Schlegel (1767–1845), published his *Observations sur la langue et la littérature provençales*, which was a landmark in the emerging field of linguistic typology, due to the introduction of the two influential terms, "analytic" and "synthetic". These were chosen by Schlegel to subdivide the *inflected* type of language (in terms of his younger brother's classification).[10] Apart from the inflected type ("les langues à inflections"), August Wilhelm von Schlegel defined not just one but two other

---

7 According to Hartleben (1906.1: 33–35), Champollion's decision to conquer that field can be traced back to his visit with Joseph Fourier, who showed him his Egyptian antiquities collected during Napoléon's Egyptian campaign, when he belonged to the scientific staff.

8 According to Erman (1922: xxxii–xxxiii).

9 These lists were published in Young's entry on "Egypt" in the 1819 supplement of *Encyclopedia Britannica*, but a printed version had apparently already been circulating in 1818. Wilhelm von Humboldt recorded both of them in his library inventory of 1821/1827 on Egyptian: "Young's Hieroglyphical Vocabulary. [London 1818.] 8. Broch." (Mueller-Vollmer 1993: 410).

10 Schlegel (1818: 16, translated from French): "The languages with inflection subdivide into two classes which I will call, synthetic languages and analytic languages"; cf. also Rousseau (2001: 1416).

types of languages (Schlegel 1818: 14): those lacking any grammatical structure ("les langues sans aucune structure grammaticale") and those using affixes ("les langues qui emploient des affixes").

After years of trial, error, despair, and new approaches, Jean-François Champollion made his final breakthrough in 1822.[11] On September 17, he saw for the first time a copy of the Abydos king list. He quickly convinced himself that his way of reading Ptolemaic and Roman emperors' names held good for the reading of names of much earlier, native Egyptian pharaohs too. The mechanism of hieroglyphs used to spell out the sounds of non-Egyptian names of the Graeco-Roman period turned out to be valid from a much earlier time and could thus be taken as an essential feature of the original writing system. On 27 September 1822, Champollion read his *Lettre à M. Dacier*, an outline of some of the main points of his method and results, to the Paris Academy. In 1823, he started working out his *Précis du système hiéroglyphique*, a comprehensive introduction to the hieroglyphic writing system and its different sign functions, "phonétiques", "figuratifs", and "symboliques", as he called them (Champollion 1824a, 2nd ed. 1828). The linguistic data on which Champollion based his argument at that time was almost exclusively taken from proper names: names of Roman emperors, Ptolemaic kings, pharaohs, gods, and private persons. Grammar was only sporadically touched upon when the meanings of Egyptian proper names were to be explained. Champollion continued working on a proper grammatical description of Egyptian for the rest of his life, but only four years after his premature death at the age of 42 could his *Grammaire égyptienne, ou principes généraux de l'écriture sacrée égyptienne appliquée à la représentation de la langue parlée* appear, edited by his elder brother Jacques-Joseph Champollion (Champollion 1836).

---

11 This breakthrough and its prehistory have often been narrated, cf. e.g., Hartleben (1906: 420–425); Erman (1922); Müller (1962); Hintze (1972); Parkinson (1999); Schenkel (2003). A more sophisticated version is provided by Schenkel (2012a & 2012b).

2 Humboldt's "reception of the Champollionian turn"[12]

The two groundbreaking works by Champollion, his *Lettre* (1822) and his *Précis* (1824a), meant the accomplishment of "one of the first great European scientific projects".[13] They inaugurated a new branch of scholarship – Egyptology; and they eventually initiated an intellectual encounter between the young French scholar and Wilhelm von Humboldt (1767–1835), one of the main figures in the emerging fields of comparative linguistics and language typology.[14]

The elder Humboldt brother had retired from state service on 31 December 1819 and moved to his manor at Tegel near Berlin, where he concentrated on linguistic studies. Humboldt's intellectual platform was not so much the University of Berlin, whose co-founder and *spiritus rector* he was, but the Royal Academy of Berlin, to which he delivered his seminal papers in these years (Trabant 1994).[15]

In the first of these, *Ueber das vergleichende Sprachstudium in Beziehung auf die verschiedenen Epochen der Sprachentwicklung*, read in August 1820, Humboldt conceptualized his view on the systemic role that writing plays for languages and for the study of languages (cf. Trabant 1986 and 1990: 185–216; Messling 2009: 15–21). In several following papers, he focused on the relation between language(s) and writing systems, and was occupied by this when Champollion's works crossed his path.[16]

---

12 This phrase is quoted from Messling (2008a: 127).

13 Messling (2009: 22).

14 This encounter has been profoundly illuminated by Deichler (2004) and Messling (2005, 2008a, 2009a, and 2009b); cf. also Thouard (2009). On Humboldt within the context of 19th-century language classification, see Rousseau (2001: 1416–1425).

15 Humboldt's library contained some 20 Egyptological publications, among them Young (1819 and 1823), Champollion (1822, 1824a and 1826), Salt (1825), Spohn (1825), Seyffarth (1826a, 1826b and 1827), and several Coptic publications, among them Kircher (1636), Wilkins (1716), Scholtz & Woide (1775 and 1778), Tuki (1778), Klaproth (1823), and Zoëga (1810). These are recorded in Humboldt's "list of books belonging to the study of languages" (cf. Mueller-Vollmer 1993: 410–411: "Alt Aegyptische Sprache" and 419–420: "Coptische Sprache"). Humboldt's folder "Ueber die Hieroglyphen Schrift" (Coll.Ling.fol.26) contains 139 folios, among them Humboldt's notes related to his publication of the Berlin "lion-headed statues" (cf. Mueller-Vollmer 1993: 170–174). Humboldt's extant copy of Champollion's *Précis* (Champollion 1824a) was „von Humboldt systematisch durchgearbeitet und mit Anmerkungen und Verweisungen versehen" (Mueller-Vollmer 1993: 17).

16 According to the account given by Hartleben (1906.1: 423–442), Alexander von Humboldt, who lived in Paris and was in Champollion's audience on 27 September 1822, could proudly send the foundry proof of the first printed version of the *Lettre* to his eagerly waiting brother Wilhelm

Humboldt's gradual acquaintance and final agreement with Champollion's theories can be reconstructed from his academy papers from the years 1824–1825 as well as from his correspondence (Messling 2008a: 73–92 and 127–131).

In a letter dated 22 May 1824 to his friend Friedrich Gottlieb Welcker, Humboldt writes about his work on the paper *Ueber den Zusammenhang der Schrift mit der Sprache* (Messling 2008a: 79–82):

> "Last winter [1823/24] I started working on the different types of writing and had already dealt with the hieroglyphic ones in the only way possible, according to the ancient authors. Providentially Champollion's *Lettre à Mr. Dacier* fell into my hands, and I anticipated that none of my work would be useful and the issue would be totally different. Therefore I examined these new ideas with great accuracy and meticulousness and convinced myself, even more after the appearance of the entire system [i.e., the *Précis* published early in spring 1824], that the Champollionian discovery holds indeed and is really very important." (transl. from the quotation in Messling 2008a: 70)

As Humboldt had rightly foreseen, the acquaintance with Champollion disturbed his paper, which was never read in the academy nor otherwise published during his lifetime or even prepared for publication by himself (cf. Messling 2008a: 76–78). Only after his death was *Ueber den Zusammenhang der Schrift mit der Sprache* printed.[17] The manuscript shows how Humboldt had changed some passages on hieroglyphs, obviously to accommodate an almost finished text to the contradicting solutions suggested by Champollion, whose *Précis* is quoted twice (for details see Messling 2008a: 77 and Messling 2009a: 42).

Humboldt's first public acknowledgement of Champollion's work occurs in his paper *Ueber die phonetischen Hieroglyphen des Herrn Champollion des jüngern* (Humboldt 1903–1936.5: 78–106) read on 8 March 1824, after the *Lettre* had "fallen into his hands" but before he had seen the recently published *Précis* (Messling 2008a: 88, n. 186). At that time, Humboldt was still hesitating. Although he agrees with Champollion's phonetic interpretation of hieroglyphs in broad terms, he still raises doubts and objections concerning details of Champollion's explanations (Messling 2008: 75 and 87–92).

---

as early as the first days of November 1822. But this scenario does not seem to fit with other evidence concerning Humboldt's reception of Champollion's *Lettre*.

17 Written as an appendix to the introduction to *Über die Kawi-Sprache auf der Insel Java, nebst einer Einleitung über die Verschiedenheit des menschlichen Sprachbaues und ihren Einfluss auf die geistige Entwicklung des Menschengeschlechts*, ed. by Buschmann, Eduard. 3 vols. Berlin 1836–1839: 415–436, it was also published separately in 1836 (Humboldt 1836), and in vol. 6 (1948: 426–487) of the first collected works edition (Humboldt 1841–1852).

Humboldt's next paper *Ueber Buchstabenschrift und ihren Zusammenhang mit dem Sprachbau*, read on 20 May 1824,[18] reflects his acquaintance with the *Précis* and bears witness to his increasing confidence in Champollion's work. Although Humboldt does not quote it explicitly and conspicuously avoids talking about hieroglyphs (cf. Messling 2008a: 131 and n. 262), the few times he does mention them, he credits the Egyptians with a phonetic writing system ("Buchstabenschrift"), *e.g.*:

> "The recent Coptic language shows undeniably that also the Ancient Egyptian language had a formation that does not indicate great aptitude for language, *and still, Egypt not only possessed letter writing (Buchstabenschrift) but was even its cradle.*" (transl. from German quotation in Trabant 1994: 99)

> "The fact that Egypt possessed *letter writing* (*Buchstabenschrift*) was doubted only in recent times, when even the demotic writing was pronounced conceptual signs; otherwise there were a lot of testimonies giving evidence or suggesting this. Only the issue as to which of the Egyptian writing styles might have been the alphabetic one was debated, or its place was sought after only in the aforementioned Demotic one." (transl. from Trabant 1994: 115)

Humboldt's "Champollionian turn", to put it with Messling (2008a), becomes explicit, if not yet public, in his letter from 26 June 1824 to Champollion.[19] He attached a copy of his academy paper from 8 March and also excused himself for having wrongly criticized some of Champollion's arguments in the *Lettre* that he could only fully appreciate after having read the *Précis* (Messling 2008a: 73–75).

Humboldt's final step towards an unreserved, public agreement with Champollion's method is taken in his academy paper from 24 March 1825 *Ueber vier Aegyptische löwenköpfige Bildsäulen in der hiesigen Königlichen Antikensammlung* (cf. Deichler 2004: 17–18, 26–31; Messling 2008a: 157–173). Here Humboldt attempted to read and translate a short hieroglyphic inscription *à la Champollion* – and succeeded to his full satisfaction.

Between the spoken version from March 1825 and the printed version dated 1828,[20] Humboldt improved his comprehension of the Egyptian text by correspon-

---

18 First printed in the *Abhandlungen* of the Royal Academy from the year 1824 (Humboldt 1826: 161–188).

19 This letter was first published by Ideler (1841), and has been re-edited from the original manuscript in the Bibliothèque Nationale de France by Messling (2008a: 317–357). Champollion's reply from 12 February 1825 was first published by Ideler (1841), and is re-edited in Hartleben (1909.1: 144–166) and Messling (2008a: 358–380).

20 First printed in the *Abhandlungen* of the Royal Academy of the year 1825 (Humboldt 1828: 145–168); I translate from vol. 4, (1843: 302–333) of the second print of the Collected Works edition (Humboldt 1841–1852).

dence with Champollion; only Humboldt's part of this correspondence is extant.[21] Champollion's reply from June 1826 is reflected in many references in the printed version and is explicitly mentioned in the extensive acknowledgment, in which Champollion's generosity in giving advice and detailed information is praised.[22]

Humboldt's avowal of Champollion's merits reads as follows:

> "Without making any claim for myself to have furthered the study of the decipherment of hieroglyphs by my own discoveries (as likewise everything that could seem meritorious in the present paper is owed to Champollion alone), I made it my special concern to examine most accurately what others saw in it and to combine the study of the Coptic language according to its formation and according to the texts edited by Zoëga [i.e., Zoëga 1810] with it. Hence I gladly confess here that the way taken by Mr. Champollion seems to me the only right one; that I consider the explanations given by him ... true and firmly established; and that I undertake the confident hope that, if it is for him to continue this work for another number of years, a reliable and complete decipherment of hieroglyphic monuments will be owed to him, as far as only possible with documents of which, how ever many of them we may come to possess, a certain part ... is irretrievably lost." (transl. from Humboldt 1841–1852.4: 303)

The correspondence between Humboldt and Champollion continued until summer 1827.[23] While Humboldt's linguistic interests were turning more and more toward East and Southeast Asian languages, his opinion about the decipherment and the nature of hieroglyphs remained unchanged and obviously unchallenged by invectives against Champollion from other aspirants to the decipherment of the hieroglyphs, such as Friedrich August Wilhelm Spohn (1792–1824) and his executor Gustav Seyffarth (1796–1885) from Leipzig.[24]

---

21 Humboldt's letter to Champollion from 8 March 1826 (Messling 2008a: 381–390).

22 The text, dated from 12 June 1826 (Livorno), is not preserved or is at least not available (cf. Messling 2008a: 315).

23 The last known parts of this correspondence, Champollion's letter to Humboldt from 14 June 1827 and Humboldt's reply from 7 July 1827, are edited by Messling (2008a: 381–400).

24 Cf. Spohn (1825); Seyffarth (1826a–b); Champollion (1826); Seyffarth (1827). Unlike others, Spohn/Seyffarth did not only offer another clue but an entire counter-system. On the Spohn/Seyffarthian approach to the decipherment of the hieroglyphs, see Blumenthal (1999) and Wolze (2011). For Seyffarth's (unacknowledged) failure in a public 'decipherment competition' in 1826 in Rome, see Messling (2009b). In his *Lettre à M. le duc de Blacas d'Aulps*, Champollion himself refuted the Spohn-Seyffarthian approach (Champollion 1826). Seyffarth maintained Spohn's method of deciphering hieroglyphs until his death in 1885 at the time when the *Berliner Schule* (cf. below, § 8) was beginning to flourish. Spohn's main idea was that hieroglyphs were syllabic signs, not wrong per se, but poorly combined in his and Seyffarth's thinking with the denial of other types of signs, namely determinatives and logograms. Seyffarth's defense of Spohn's system became more and more idiosyncratic and polemic in a ridiculous anti-Champollionian way.

Once and for all, Humboldt was persuaded by his own experience – his analysis and translation of the inscriptions on the Berlin "lion-headed statues", and these make him the first successful translator of a hieroglyphic text into a modern language after Champollion himself.

3 Lepsius and the birth of Egyptology from the spirit of comparative linguistics

While Humboldt's reception of the "Champollionian turn" took slightly more than one year, its reception by a wider audience took more than a decade from the time Champollion's *Précis* was published in 1824. After Champollion had suddenly passed away in 1832 without having been able to establish an academic tradition, the person to win over a wider academic public to Champollion and to leave behind (more than to convince) the aforementioned competitors was a young comparative linguist from Germany. Carl Richard Lepsius (1810–1884) had studied classical philology, Oriental languages, and comparative linguistics under the auspices of such eminent German scholars of the day as Gottfried Hermann in Leipzig, Heinrich Ewald, Jacob and Wilhelm Grimm and Ottfried Müller in Göttingen, and August Boeckh and Franz Bopp in Berlin (cf. Ebers 1885a & b; Kammerzell 1996 and 2009). His doctoral thesis (Lepsius 1833) was devoted to the decipherment of Umbrian, at that time still an unknown ancient Italic language attested in the so-called *tabulae iguvinae*.[25] At age 22, Lepsius had studied an impressive range of Indo-European and Semitic languages, was well acquainted with the current state of comparative linguistics (however not yet with that of Egyptian studies), and was – as an honest Humboldtian! – particularly interested in the phenomenology of writing and its relation to the structure of languages and language change.

To deepen and improve his skills, Lepsius moved to Paris, the European capital of Oriental studies, in the summer of 1833 (cf. Mehlitz 2010: 25–40). His concern was Sanskrit, Italic inscriptions, and manuscript collections, and

---

25 Lepsius returned to the topic of his academic origins a few years later (Lepsius 1841). Prof. Gerhard Meiser of Halle, whom I asked about the significance of Lepsius's achievements in the fields of Umbrian language study, drew my attention to a statement by Prosdocimi 1984.1: 64: "Decisivo e definitivo è Lepsius, allievo di Müller, che nella sua dissertazione di dottorato (1833) stabilisce … tutti i valori dell' alfabeto iguvino …; sono anche associati in una più corretta prospettiva alla loro genesi, con coscienza delle distinzioni conservate nelle trafile. …. Non solo i valori di massima, ma le stesse convenzioni sono quelle accettate tutt'oggi".

certainly not Egyptian, although it is reported that he attended Jean Antoine Letronne's lectures on Egypt, in which Letronne cast doubts on Champollion's discoveries (Ebers 1885a: 65–66; Mehlitz 2010: 34 + n. 6). Later in 1833, Lepsius started working on his first publication, printed in Berlin in March 1834 under the title *Paläographie als Mittel für die Sprachforschung, zunächst am Sanskrit nachgewiesen*.[26] In this paper, Lepsius presented himself as a Sanskritist and as an up-to-date comparative linguist who knew about and shared current trends and theories:

1. Lepsius briefly touched upon the issue of the origin of language, much debated at the time, and sides with the suggestion of original *empfindungslaute* (Lepsius 1834: 4–5 and 21–22) – the "Pooh-Pooh theory" in Max Müller's terms.

2. Lepsius explained his palaeographical approach to language study (programmatically claimed in the title of his paper) with the Humboldtian[27] statement that "script, as good as language, is a perceptible dress of the thought" (Lepsius 1834: 6), and stresses the analogy of the two (cf. below).[28]

3. In the wake of the Schlegel brothers and his own teacher Franz Bopp, Lepsius's idea of languages was instinctively associated with the idea of "organic growth" (Lepsius 1834: 5), by which (some) languages, namely the Indo-European, mature to "perfection":

"Here we may point to languages, such as Chinese, and to whole language families, such as Semitic, that prematurely aged as it were, so that their perceptible body never grew to perfection, as our language family: Although the Semitic language family is acknowledged to trace back to the same source as ours originally, ... we are urged to suppose that an originally common and equally undeveloped seed has achieved a higher degree of perfection in one direction, the Indogermanic, and a lesser degree of perfection in the other, the Semitic one." (transl. from Lepsius 1834, 23)

---

26 Lepsius mentioned this work in his letter to Bunsen from 12th December 1833; the appendix (95 "Diese Blätter waren schon geschrieben, als mir durch die besondere Gefälligkeit des Herrn Eug. Burnouf zu Paris etc.") is dated (p. 101): "Paris. Januar, 1834."

27 Humboldt highly appreciated Lepsius's treatise and sent him a kind letter dated 22 April 1834, cf. Mehlitz (2010: 33).

28 In his letter to Lepsius from 22 April 1834, Humboldt noticed the closeness to his own thought about the relations between writing and language explicitly and pointed to his own academy paper on the topic, *Ueber Buchstabenschrift und ihren Zusammenhang mit dem Sprachbau*, cf. Mehlitz (2010: 33, n. 29).

Excursus II: The Inequality of Languages

Still in 1806, the introduction to Adelung's *Mithridates*, the "linguistic ency-clopedia" of the Age of Enlightenment, emphatically claimed an overall func-tional equality of human languages and explicitly argued against the notion of superior and inferior languages:

"Languages are all conditioned in the same way and built on common ground; hence each of them can get to whatever time, circumstances, and culture may require. This is why the dispute about one language's merits over another one is so useless." (transl. from Adelung 1806–1817.1: xxv)

From 1808, in the context of the prevalent Romantic world-view, the com-parison and classification of languages rested on a strongly hierarchical and evaluative (rather than descriptive) conception of language diversity.[29] This conception has been strongly criticised in the context of the "Oriental-ism" debate (Said 1978; on philology and comparative linguistics esp. 99), in which it is claimed that 19th-century Western European humanities intel-lectually anticipated and ideologically supported racism and colonialism. Markus Messling has recently argued for a more sophisticated view of "West-ern Europe" and "the 19th century" and made a good point for the exonera-tion of Humboldt from this kind of reproach[30] since his thought on the diver-sity of languages differs so considerably from that of scholars such as the Schlegel brothers (cf. Bär 2002), Bopp,[31] or Steinthal (for Steinthal's mas-

---

29 Ringmacher (2001a: 1428) attributes the plain linear hierarchy only to the first two genera-tions – Pott/Bopp and Steinthal/Schleicher – of linguists aproaching language classification, who described "die in den Sprachtypen durchlaufende Geschichte kurz und auf den Gipfelpunkt der klassischen indogermanischen Sprachen hinzielend, wie es den geschichtsphilosophischen Erwartungen ihrer Zeit entsprach". According to Ringmacher (2001a: 1428), the third generation, with G. von der Gabelentz (1840–1893) as protagonist, deviated from that "geschichtsphiloso-phischen Schematismus". Von der Gabelentz conceptualized his "Typenreihe" no longer as a single, linear, and unidirectional succession, but as a circular, repeating process (cf. von der Gabelentz 1891: 250, on the spiral course of language history ["Spirallauf der Sprachgeschich-te"]) and understood typological and genealogical classification of languages as completely in-dependent modes of comparative linguistics. In this framework, such influential conceptions as Misteli's and Finck's (cf. below, § 9) would still belong to the earlier type of linguistic typology.
30 Messling (2008a: 228–276, 2008b and 2010); cf. also van Driem (2001: 129–131) on the differ-ence between Humboldt's and Steinthal's approach and Bär (2002) for the difference between Humboldt's and W.A. Schlegel's concept of linguistic diversity; cf. already Trabant (1990: 235–235) against Aarsleff (1977).
31 On Bopp's misinterpretation of Humboldt's "Kawi work" (Bopp 1841), cf. Mueller-Vollmer (1992, 1993).

sively devaluating classification, see below, § 5). A remarkable example of lonely resistance to the prevalent hierarchical concept of language classification will be presented later in this paper (cf. below, § 7).

Still in 1833, when Lepsius was working on his *Paläographie als Mittel für die Sprachforschung*, he was more or less ignorant of Egypt and Egyptian. The only time Egyptian is mentioned here, it serves as an illustration of picture-writing (*Bilderschrift*), and thus Lepsius fell back behind the view that Humboldt had already propounded in 1825:

> "All writing emerged from pictography, as all languages from intrinsically meaningful sounds of emotion, and, as it is principally the same procedure to draw a tree or an animal on paper and stone like the Chinese or the Egyptian, or in the sand like the savage, or to describe it by gestures in the air, one has to ascribe no lesser age to writing in the broadest sense, than to language itself ... Only by special organic growth over the course of time, not by lucky discovery, could perfect alphabets for the languages develop, just as only by organic growth over the course of time could a perfect grammar develop for them. In Chinese, we find the grammar as imperfect as the writing, and purely on the basis of the use of hieroglyphs, I would ascribe a similar imperfection to the Egyptian language as to the Chinese." (transl. from Lepsius 1834: 4–5)

It is thus even more striking to find Egyptian mentioned in a positive way – in one breath with Sanskrit, instead of Chinese! – at the end of the same treatise, when Lepsius finally outlined the chances of a future "scientific palaeography":

> "If palaeography is of much lower worth for our European languages since the predominant intellectual element has restrained the material organism too much, ... it rises however to highest importance and requires the utmost scientific interest if languages are concerned whose material body is still fresh and untouched as in Sanskrit, or even still preeminent as in Egyptian. A scientific palaeography might find here its focus and ascend to a more independent rank and to higher attention if it could only take possession of this rich and already largely accessible material, and could survey and treat it under higher, especially linguistic perspectives." (transl. from Lepsius 1834: 94)

Although this passage is not part of the appendix added in January 1834, and its precise dating remains tentative, it is plausible to assume that these words were written when Lepsius was already considering embarking upon a "scientific palaeography" of Egyptian himself: In November 1833 he had received an offer by Christian Karl Josias Bunsen (1791–1860), who later wrote a seminal historiographical work on Pharaonic Egypt (Bunsen 1844–1857).[32] Bunsen, who was at the time the Prussian ambassador in Rome, invited Lepsius to Rome for the study of Umbrian, Oscan, and Etruscan inscriptions, *and* for the study of Egyptian. He raised the possibility of support for this enterprise by the Berlin academy. Lepsius, whose esteem for Egyptian was originally not very high, as has been shown, eventually replied in a letter from 11 December 1833:

> "Above all, had I really convinced myself by means of the already available sources, especially Champollion's grammar [that would appear only in 1836, cf. above], that the foundations already laid by a scrupulous and scientific treatment raised hope for further results, then I would gladly devote all my energy, time, and diligence to that issue, whose further promotion can rightly claim the most general interest, whose exploration however can be the concern of only a few beneficiaries by now."[33] (transl. from quotation in Mehlitz 2010: 31–32)

Bunsen replied with further encouragement, which helped.[34] In 1834, Lepius began studying Coptic, hieroglyphic sources, Champollion's and others' publications on hieroglyphs, and Champollion's unpublished papers. Lepsius's earliest publication reflecting his new occupation is an article on a *locus classicus* about the different scripts of the Egyptians in a 3rd-century CE Greek text by the church father Clemens of Alexandria (Lepsius 1835).

Lepsius's first attempts at combining his recent Egyptian and Coptic studies with his original interests in comparative linguistics are manifested in *Zwei sprachvergleichende Abhandlungen*, published in 1836. The earlier of the two, finished in March 1835 (Lepsius 1836b: 150), deals with numerals in different language families: Indo-European, Semitic, and (Egyptian)[35]-Coptic. As a novelty in the sample of languages studied by comparative linguists, Coptic is formally introduced and recommended by Lepsius:

> "I am happy to point here for the first time to the Coptic language as being of no small interest for the comparison of languages." (transl. from Lepsius 1836b: 85)

---

32 Seminal was, for example, Bunsen's subdivision of the political history of Egypt into the Old, Middle, and New Kingdoms.

33 Translated here from Edouard Naville's quotation in his entry in Allgemeine Deutsche Biographie, vol. 51: 661.

34 Letter from 20 January 1834, cf. Mehlitz (2010: 32).

35 In contrast to what the title suggests, not only Coptic but also hieroglyphic and Demotic spellings of numerals are dealt with (Lepsius 1836b: 88–89). However, the full range of Egyptian numerals was (and still is) available only in Coptic.

Focusing on the etymology and formation patterns of numerals, Lepsius concludes that these not only exhibit structural similarities throughout the three language families but can even be traced back genealogically to a common origin, being pronominal roots of the 1st, 2nd, and 3rd persons.[36] Lepsius sent the original manuscript to Wilhelm von Humboldt, whose particular interest in the topic he anticipated, and whose personal favour he wanted to gain, since he was hoping for financial support by the Royal Academy of Berlin. However the manuscript failed to reach its addressee alive – Humboldt had passed away on 8 April 1835; the manuscript temporarily disappeared, and, after it was sought and found, it could not be printed until 1836 (cf. Mehlitz 2010: 36). In a letter written on 30 April 1835 to Bunsen, Lepsius confessed his closeness to Humboldt's style of language studies:

> "W. v. Humboldt's death grieved me a lot, both for the personal benevolence that he showed towards me several times, and for the irrecoverable loss that linguistics sustained therefrom. In particular, he was the one by whom I hoped to be best understood in my direction of linguistics and whose judgment I had always in mind with this last work [i.e., Lepsius 1836b]." (translated from the quotation in Ebers 1885a: 102)

Lepsius's other *Sprachvergleichende Abhandlung*, read on 12 November 1835 to the Berlin Academy, deals with the arrangement of the Semitic, Indian, Ancient Persian, Ancient Egyptian, and Ethiopic alphabets, with the same intention to demonstrate "the relationship in which these ... hitherto strictly separated classes of peoples originally were" (Lepsius 1836a). In a footnote, Lepsius's increasing admiration for Champollion, already expressed in a letter to Bunsen from 14 August 1835 (cf. Mehlitz 2010: 39, n. 34.), is publicised for the first time:

> "Anybody who is still in doubt about Champollion's main discoveries, in particular his hieroglyphic alphabet, must blame himself for being ignorant of one of the most important discoveries of recent sciences; the issue itself has clearly been settled long since." (transl. from Lepsius 1836a: 58–59, n. 1)

Lepsius's first and most famous contribution to Egyptian linguistics is his letter to Champollion's pupil Ippolito Rosellini (1800–1843), finished and printed in Rome in 1837. In this seminal paper, Lepsius focused on the crucial point of early Egyptian linguistics: which of the competing methods of decipherment of the hieroglyphs was the most appropriate. Overall, Lepsius confirmed Champollion's

---

36 Lepsius's conclusion contradicted the *opinio communis*, cf. Pott (1847, 1855, 1868). However, Lepsius maintained his opinion (Lepsius 1880: xxiv).

methods and results, and partially improved on them.[37] It is generally agreed that Lepsius's *Lettre* of 1837 was the beacon by which the Champollionian approach eventually gained acceptance among a wider audience of linguists.[38]

In 1846, just back in Berlin from his groundbreaking expedition to Egypt and Nubia (1842–1845), Lepsius was appointed professor of Egyptology at the University of Berlin. The first 'Egyptologist' by profession, he never stopped working on general and comparative linguistics. His scope included mainly two fields of general linguistics, (i) phonetics and (ii) the classification of African languages.

- (i) In 1855, Lepsius published a phonetic alphabet (Lepsius 1855a), based on a general phonetic classification of linguistic sounds, for transcribing European and non-European languages in a standardized way – an early ancestor of the International Phonetic Alphabet (IPA). This work was translated into English in the same year (Lepsius 1855b). A second, considerably extended English edition appeared in 1863 (Lepsius 1863a). Due to the adoption of Lepsius's standard alphabet not only by The Church Missionary Society as the title proudly admits but also by the International Congress of Orientalists in London in 1874 (cf. Ebers 1885b: xxiv–xxvii), it was widely distributed and served as a point of departure and reference for later approaches to the standardization of phonetic transcription (cf. e.g., Heepe 1928). Many of Lepsius's publications in the following years (e.g., Lepsius 1855c, 1860, 1861, 1862a, 1862b, 1863b, 1863b, 1863c, 1866a, 1867, 1868) were devoted to several theoretical and empirical issues of phonetics and phonetic transcription.

- (ii) In the 1863 edition of Lepsius's *Standard Alphabet*, Old Egyptian, Coptic, and five other African languages are dealt with under the label of "Hamitic" languages (Lepsius 1863a: 193–208). The concept of Hamitic languages was

---

37 The improvement concerned mainly the issue of different types of hieroglyphic signs, to which Lepsius added the type of phonetic but non-alphabetic signs that he called "syllabic" (in fact the only type accepted by Spohn/Seyffarth) and the diachrony of Egyptian: Lepsius demonstrated a greater difference between Egyptian as encoded in hieroglyphs and Coptic than Champollion had been aware of; see Schenkel (1990: 17–19), Richter (2013), and below, §§ 6 and 8. For a more comprehensive account of Lepsius's part in the decipherment of hieroglyphs, see Schenkel (2012a, 2012b).

38 For an illustration of the extent and the span of time that this was felt to be an open issue, it may be worth mentioning that the Ptolemaic sacerdotal decree of Canopus, discovered by Lepsius as late as 1866 (cf. Lepsius 1866b), was appreciated by scholars as a touchstone and final proof of the reliability of the Champollionian tradition of reading hieroglyphs (cf. Ebers 1871: 22, n. 27).

a novelty at this time[39] and was therefore expounded by Lepsius in the introductory part of the book:

> "We combine with this first division [i.e., literary vs. illiterate languages] a second, referring to the use of grammatical gender. It is not accidental but quite significant, that, as far as I know without any essential exception, only the most highly civilised races – the leading nations in the history of mankind – distinguish throughout the genders, and that the *Gender-languages* are the same as those, which scientifically by linguistic reasons may be proved as decending from one original Asiatic stock. The development of peculiar forms for the grammatical genders proves a comparatively higher consciousness of the two sexes; and the distinction not only of the masculine and feminine, as in the *Semitic* and *Hamitic* languages, but also of the feminine and neuter gender, exclusively expressed in the *Japhetic* branch, is only a further step in the same direction. The formation of genders has appeared to me so characteristic of the three principal branches, that I thought it a sufficient reason, to ascribe all the African non-Semitic languages, which distinguish the genders, to the Hamitic branch, viz., – besides the old Egyptian and the Coptic – the Beja language of the Bishari (whose anchestors were the Ethiopians of Meroë), the Dankali, Somali, Galla and other neighbouring languages, al (sic) those of the Libyan tribes between the Egyptian Oases and the Canarian Islands, including the Hausa farther on to the south, and even the widely distant languages of the miserably reduced Hottentots and Bushmen, whose immigration into their actual seats is still a curious problem, considering the absolute diversity of their language from all their northern neighbours and at the same time its traces of a certain affinity with the Egyptian language." (Lepsius 1863a: 89–90)

This comment gives just a short glimpse of Lepsius's work on African languages, which was to last some forty years. Starting with a systematic collection of empirical language data during his expedition,[40] it culminated in his *Nubian Grammar* (Lepsius 1880), which included a seminal classification of African languages in the introduction (Lepsius 1880: i–cxxvi; cf. also Lepsius 1879).

In 1884, when the *Internationale Zeitschrift für Allgemeine Sprachwissenschaft* (*IZAS*) was founded, it seemed only obvious that Lepsius would be a member of the editorial board among such scholars as Georg von der Gabelentz, August Leskien, Max Müller, Hermann Paul, August Friedrich Pott, Heymann Steinthal, William Dwight Whitney, and Wilhelm Wundt.[41] Although Lepsius died on 19th

---

39 The biblical name of the Noahite Ham, applied to African peoples for a long time, was apparently first used to refer to (all) African languages in the framework of comparative linguistics by Krapf (1850) and was more narrowly used to refer to African *gender* languages by Lepsius (1863a: 89–90 and 1880: xx–xxxii) along the lines he had already outlined in Lepsius (1844).

40 Lepsius's "Ethiopian journey" as he called it, started in November 1843 from Philae and brought him up to Sannar, 280 kilometers south of Khartoum, and back to Philae by September 1844, cf. Mehlitz (2010: 126–150).

41 On the *IZAS*, see Koerner (1973) and Trabant (1990: 62–63); on its large advisory board see

July 1884 and did not live to see the first volume, his name remained on the title pages of the *IZAS* up to its 5th and last volume in 1890. The second volume, from 1885 is dedicated to Lepsius's memory and contains not only an obituary contributed by Georg Ebers, *Richard Lepsius, besonders als Linguist* (Ebers 1885b), but also a frontispiece showing his image. The other four volumes are dedicated to Wilhelm von Humboldt (vol. 1), Silvestre de Sacy (vol. 3), Franz Bopp (vol. 4), and August Friedrich Pott (vol. 5). This in itself indicates Lepsius's status in general linguistics at the time.

It is a kind of symbolic coincidence that in 1890, when the *IZAS* – the intellectual platform where Egyptology took part in the discourse on general linguistics – disappeared, Egyptian linguistics had finally changed over into a new period, the age of the *Berliner Schule*, formed around Lepsius's pupil Adolf Erman (cf. below, § 8).

4 The place of Egyptian-Coptic in post-Humboldtian language classification: General remarks

Wilhelm von Humboldt's and Richard Lepisus's double occupation with Egyptian *as well as* comparative linguistics could seem to be a rather exceptional approach. But in fact, this approach was to become established and conventionalized academically in the following decades: comparative linguists in the aftermath of Humboldt did not lose sight of Egyptian and were strongly interested in establishing its place in the genealogical and typological (or "physiological", as they would have said) classification of languages. While Humboldt's well-known interest in ancient Egyptian and his own work on hieroglyphs may have been an additional motif, the main driving forces behind this impetus were clearly of a scientific nature:

1. Genealogical language classification against the background of the hotly debated issue of the possibility and degree of a relationship between the Indo-European and the Semitic language families, to which Egyptian was (rightly) expected to contribute.

2. "Typological" language classification, i.e., classification according to what Humboldt had named the "framework" of languages (*Sprachbau*), within the theoretical horizon of Humboldt's concept of an "inner form" of languages, i.e., their being shaped by the particular world view (*Weltsicht*) of individ-

---

Koerner (1973: 41–50).

ual peoples. In a "time of a deepened comprehension of language", when languages were "no longer studied just as *vehicles* of the activity of human mind but, even more so, as one of its most important *forms*" (Benfey 1844: v), the language conveying (and shaped by) the intellectual and psychological activities of such an eminent people as the Ancient Egyptians was an issue for typological classification and could not possibly be ignored.

The latter approach (or, how it was interpreted) accounts for the specific attitude of post-Humboldtian linguists towards Egyptian. These linguists shared a positive opinion about the overall sophistication of the Egyptian language, and those who worked out systems of classification (with their unavoidable implications of hierarchy, see above, Excursus II), tended to assign Egyptian to a high position, next to the top two, the Indo-European and Semitic language families. This opinion, however, was a friendly prejudice based on extra-linguistic considerations.[42] What linguists positively knew about the syntax, morphology, and word formation of Ancient Egyptian, and could not even know until 1880, would not have allowed them to propose any classification in terms of *Sprachbau*; and what they knew about Coptic and its reduced morphology, disappointed them. Moreover, since firm ground to approaching historical linguistics of Egyptian in any proper way was still lacking (see below, § 6), the extent and the kind of differences between Coptic and hieroglyphic Egyptian could not really be grasped and were tentatively estimated to be rather insignificant. The resulting ambivalence is tangible in Carl Abel's straightforward statement:

> "Like everything Egyptian, the Coptic language is particularly worth knowing for its historical importance. Furthermore, it is one of the most primitive languages possessing a literature." (transl. from Abel 1876: 11–12)

---

42 Whitney (1867: 367–368) explicitly defended this prejudice as a sophisticated multiple-criteria approach to the evaluation of languages: "Many a tongue thus stands higher, or lower, than its morphological character would naturally indicate. The Chinese is one of the most striking instances of such a discordance; though so nearly formless, in a morphological sense, it is nevertheless placed by Wilhelm von Humboldt and Steinthal [Whitney here refers to Steinthal 1860: 70 and 327] in the higher class of 'form languages,' although with the Indo-European and Semitic, as being a not unsuitable incorporation of clear logical thought". This approach was criticized already by Finck (1901: 23, transl. from German): "The fact that, notwithstanding the unmistakable differences, attempt was made to assign the Egyptian and Chinese languages to the 'form languages' equal to Semitic and Indogermanic ones, can only be explained by the high esteem for two civilized peoples, who would have defied the connection between language perfection and mental development, if they had spoken in formless languages"; on Finck's own approach to language typology see below, § 9.

The impression of "primitivity" in terms of "physiological formation" that Egyptian and Coptic gave to linguists – no inflection, poor morphology – was counterbalanced by other criteria, such as the vague notion of their "inner form" (not visible, but deduced from its *historical* role), or the existence of a gender system. The category of gender was considered an exclusive property of Indo-European and Semitic languages,[43] and was highly esteemed for the merit of requiring agreement and thereby allowing "true synthesis".

5 The place of Egyptian-Coptic in post-Humboldtian language classification: Three examples

5.1 Steinthal 1850 and 1860

A foremost representative of this approach was Heymann Steinthal (1823–1899), (cf. Ringmacher 1996 and 2001a, Wiedebach & Winkelmann 2002). In addition to the diverse languages Steinthal had studied at the University of Berlin (1843–1847) with such celebrities as Franz Bopp and Wilhelm Grimm, he had also learned Coptic with Moritz Gotthilf Schwartze, one of the few Coptic specialists of his time (cf. Endesfelder 1988, 1990 and 2003; Irmscher 1988), and Egyptian with Lepsius. Richard Lepsius, back in Berlin after returning from his expedition in January 1846 (Mehlitz 2010: 172–185), had been appointed to the first German chair of Egyptology and had delivered his inaugural lecture in the winter term of 1846.

In fact, one of Steinthal's earliest publications was the edition of a comprehensive Coptic Grammar, although not on his own behalf but on that of his pre-

---

43 Lepsius (1863a: 89–90), who made grammatical gender a primary criterion of his classification of African languages, wrote in this vein: "It is not accidental but very significant, that, as far as I know without any essential exception, only the most highly civilized races – the leading nations in the history of mankind – distinguish throughout the genders, and that the *Gender-languages* are the same as those which scientifically by linguistic reasons may be proved to descend from one original Asiatic stock. The development of peculiar forms for the grammatical genders proves a comparatively higher consciousness of the two sexes; and the distinction not only of the masculine and feminine, as in the *Semitic* and *Hamitic* languages, but also of the feminine and neuter gender, exclusively expressed in the *Japhetic* branch, is only a further step in the same direction." The same idea is developed in greater detail in Lepsius (1880: xxii–xxv). On the existence and distribution of gender systems throughout the languages of the world see Corbett (2005, 2006).

maturely deceased teacher Schwartze (Schwartze & Steinthal 1850). In his later work, Steinthal also occasionally touched on grammatical details of Coptic (cf. Steinthal 1880). However, his fame was not based on observations of philological and grammatical niceties but rather on his panoramic view of languages and linguistics, on the philosophy of language, and eventually on the new "multidisciplinary" approach called *Völkerpsychologie* (cf. Knobloch 1988 and 2001; Wiedebach & Winkelmann 2002).

In his *Classification der Sprachen, dargestellt als die Entwickelung der Sprachidee* (Steinthal 1850) as well as in its second, thoroughly revised and renamed edition *Charakteristik der hauptsächlichsten Typen des Sprachbaus* (Steinthal 1860), Steinthal gives an account of the history of language classification up to Humboldt (Steinthal 1850: 1–49 and 1860: 1–70). Humboldt is presented as a genius partially at odds with himself, a "tragic hero" (Steinthal 1852: 3) who stopped (or died) shortly before having drawn the full and right conclusions from his own thought.[44] It is Steinthal's aim to synthesize these consequences by using Hegel as a catalyst (Steinthal 1848; cf. Trabant 1990: 60–67).[45] This synthesis is visualized in a table entitled "System of languages, as the development of the idea of language" (Steinthal 1850, 82–91), where individual languages and language families are assigned to 13 classes according to "the worthiness of the physiological principle".[46]

The resulting system constitutes a hierarchy, beginning with South-East Asian languages, which are characterized as

"the least developed, most formless languages, corresponding to the zoophytes in terms of zoology. As these mark the transition from the realm of plants to that of animals, those languages mark the borderline of human speech, being close to the dumbness of gesture language. In fact they must be called *acritae*, since any grammatical distinction is still lacking. These languages do not have any construction at all, like those animals do not have a skeleton. They consist of merely monosyllabic roots, equalling fungi and algae. Their clause formation is an analogy of the lowest mechanical procedure, the fall: One word falls onto the other one." (transl. from Steinthal 1850: 85 = Steinthal 1860: 328)

---

44 For a close reading of Steinthal's reception of Humboldt see Trabant (1983) and Ringmacher (1996). Already Pott (1852), in his review of Steinthal (1850), was irritated by Steinthal's fluctuation between high praise and criticism of Humboldt.

45 See his *Die Sprachwissenschaft Wilh. v. Humboldt's und die Hegel'sche Philosophie* 1848 (on which cf. Tabant 1990: 60–67).

46 By one criterion, "*distinction of matter and form*", Steinthal separated languages *mixing* matter and form from those (higher developed) languages that *distinguish* matter and form. By a second criterion, the "*external form*", Steinthal grouped together languages with an *imperfect* external form and those (higher developed ones) with a *perfect* external form.

And, unsurprisingly, it culminates in the praise of Indo-European languages, "the rose among the languages" (Steinthal 1850: 91). Egyptian, following the Semitic languages in the third rank, is characterised and evaluated as such:

> "As to the primarily distinguished elements of languages – noun and verb, the proper force of utterance lies in the verb, to the formation of which the mind turns first [*a reference to the V-S word order of Egyptian*], resulting in the neglect of the noun: so it is in Egyptian and Semitic. The *basic division of the substantial elements* is thus accomplished. However the *balance* between the two is not yet found. The Egyptian language would be completely misunderstood if grouped together with American languages or Chinese. It is highly organised physiologically, although the nominal relations are deficiently developed; in particular, there is a weak force of articulation and an ear totally unreceptive to pleasant sounds. This is why its external formation *resembles* lower-level languages. But as Chinese is not equal to Far-Indian, but runs parallel at a higher level, so Egyptian relates to, say, Turkish." (transl. from Steinthal 1850: 90 = 1860: 330)

While Steinthal (1860) largely remains faithful to Steinthal (1850), it is extended by a new section containing descriptions of languages arranged according to the same underlying classification but this time partially correlated to races. Egyptian appears among "the languages of the Caucasian race" or "*form* languages,"[47] which subdivide into Egyptian, Semitic languages, and the Sanskrit family:[48]

> "The Caucasian race includes the Egyptians, the Semitic, and the Sanskrit peoples ... I treat the languages of these families together as they form an absolute contrast to the languages of all other peoples ... : The latter have been presented as being *material, substantial*. Only now, with these languages, do we enter the sphere of *form*. These are the languages of the *peoples of world history* [*weltgeschichtliche Völker*], and their importance for the evolution of the human mind [*Geist*] is anticipated in their language, from which the mind [*Geist*] received the perpetual impetus towards formal conception, i.e., by which they became accustomed not just to comprehending the *content* and its *real circumstances* but also to transforming it into intellectually shaped *forms* appropriate only to the mind". (transl. from Steinthal 1860: 231–232)

The concept of *weltgeschichtliche Völker* (already found in Steinthal 1850: 88–89) left no choice as to the classification of Egyptian, despite its "lack of euphony" and overall "bare, rigid plainness" (Steinthal 1860: 232).

---

47 On Steinthal's concept of *Formsprachen*, i.e., languages distinguishing matter and form, see n. 44 and Ringmacher (2001a: 1433–1434).
48 The Caucasian race as an overarching ethnic unit is still present in Finck (1909: 7–42), who subdivided it, linguistically, into Indo-European, Hamito-Semitic, Caucasian, and Dravidian languages.

Elaborating on the traits of Egyptian, Steinthal complains about the lack of stem formation (bare roots that have to be suffixed) and about nouns and verbs being partially indistinguishable. On the other hand, he acknowledges the "purity of a grammatical form created out of the mind" and the merit of possessing a gender system and, accordingly, gender agreement and synthesis (Steinthal 1860: 232–238). His conclusion reads as follows:

> "Everywhere in Egyptian we realize the plainest rise of pure forms. The means are few but sufficient for the very essentials. The form of sounds is insufficient; the junction of affixes to stems is loose. There are no further binding forces except that the relative *n* becomes *m* before labials, and long vowels of stems are shortened if connecting to suffixes." (transl. from Steinthal 1860: 241)

The Egyptian-Coptic language data on which Steinthal based his argument reflects the work of Champollion, Lepsius, Brugsch, and Schwartze. Steinthal distinguished three phases of Egyptian corresponding to the hieroglyphic, Demotic, and Coptic writing systems, although "the principle of their formation is the same in all three periods" (Steinthal 1860: 233). This comes as no surprise, given "the conservative character, the mummy-mind of the Egyptians" (Steinthal 1860: 234).

5.2 Whitney 1867

William Dwight Whitney (1827–1894) studied Oriental philology, especially Sanskrit, in Berlin and Tübingen, held the chair of Sanskrit and comparative philology at Yale University starting in 1854, and was elected corresponding member of the Berlin Academy in 1873 (cf. Alter 2005; Silverstein in Stammerjohann 2009: 1634–1636). His lectures on language and linguistics (Whitney 1867) and on historical linguistics (Whitney 1875a) saw much success not only in the USA and England – translated by European linguists into several European languages (e.g., Whitney 1874, 1875b, 1876a, 1876b, 1877, 1881), the lectures served to popularize contemporary linguistic thought. In one of his *Twelve Lectures on the Principles of Linguistic Science* (Whitney 1867), Whitney explained Steinthal's classification of languages to a wider audience. His explanations had the merits of brevity and clarity over Steinthal's original works and might thus have experienced wider reception for that reason. Whitney accepted Steinthal's concept of *Formsprachen* (as well as the reason why Egyptian had to be counted among them) and the consequence thereof, which was the elevation of its rank in terms of the hierarchy of languages:

"Its often alleged connection with Semitic, and the antiquity and importance of the culture to which it served as instrument, would have justified us in treating it next after the Indo-European and Semitic" (Whitney 1867: 340)

He also shares Steinthal's opinion about the insignificance of diachronic differences within Egyptian-Coptic:

"The differences are comparatively slight between the old Egyptian and the later Coptic, for the exceedingly simple structure of the language has saved it from the active operation of linguistic change." (Whitney 1867: 341)

And he is convinced of the primitivity of the language, quoting the same examples that Steinthal had chosen (Steinthal 1860: 233 and 239):

"The Egyptian was a language of the utmost simplicity, or even poverty, of grammatical structure. Its roots – which... are prevailingly, though not uniformly, monosyllabic – are also its words; neither noun nor verb, nor any other part of speech, has a characteristic form, or can be traced back to a simpler radical element, from which it derives by the addition of a formative element. Some roots, as in Chinese, are either verb, substantive, or adjective – thus, *ankh*, 'live, life, alive,' *sekhi*, 'write, a writing, writer' – others are only verbs or only nouns. A word used as substantive is generally marked by a prefixed article ... it has no declension, the objective uses being indicated by prepositions. The personal inflection of the verb is made by means of suffixed pronominal endings, also loosely attached, and capable of being omitted in the third person when a noun is expressed as subject of the verb. Mode and tense are, to a certain limited extend, signified by prefixed auxiliary words. But these pronominal endings, which, when added to the verb, indicate the subject (sometimes also the object), have likewise a possessive value, when appended to nouns: thus, *ran-i* is either 'I name' or 'my name;' ... that is to say, there is no essential distinction formally made between a noun and a verb." (Whitney 1867: 342)

In contrast to the overall morphological and syntactic poverty of Egyptian, its gender system is acknowledged as a further link to higher-ranking languages:

"In the singular number of both articles and pronominal suffixes ... there is made a separation of gender, as masculine and feminine. This is a highly important feature in the structure of Hamitic speech [a term that Whitney uses with explicit reference to, and in the sense defined by, Lepsius 1863a], and the one which gives it its best claim to the title of form-language. So far it goes, it puts together the tongues of the family into one class along with the Indo-European and the Semitic. ... But, by its general character, Egyptian is far enough from being entitled to rank with the Indo-European and Semitic languages, being, rather, but a single step above the Chinese, and sometimes even less clear and free from ambiguity." (Whitney 1867: 342–343)

5.3 Oppert 1879

Gustav Salomon Oppert (1836–1908) had studied Indian languages at the Universities of Bonn, Leipzig, Berlin, and Halle, and had made a career in England (Oxford, 1860–1872) and India (Madras, 1872–1893) before he returned to Berlin in 1895.

Oppert took an independent approach to language classification in general and the classification of Egyptian in particular. This approach is worked out in Oppert (1879), Oppert's main work on the topic, and is concisely presented again in Oppert (1883) and (1884). More explicitly (and less polemically) than contemporary linguists, Oppert refers to the linguistic discourse on language classification according to *Sprachbau* from F. and A.W. Schlegel, Humboldt, Grimm, and Bopp, up to Schleicher, Pott, Steinthal, Caldwell, and Max Müller (Oppert 1879: 2–7). Taking his point of departure from tripartite classifications à la A.W. v. Schlegel and Bopp,[49] he aimed to surpass his predecessors, first by refining the existing morphological classification systems and, second, by combining their merely morphological criteria of classification with another level of classification according to a criterion called "modes of thought", also called the "psychological" or "mental" character of a language.

> "It is ... the object of this discourse to suggest a classification of languages, which, while admitting the importance of ... external marks, assigns to them only the part of characterizing the different dialects belonging to the various subdivisions by stating whether those languages are monosyllabic, agglutinative, inflectional, &c. The principle arrangement rests on the tendency displayed by a language in its peculiar *mode of thought*." (Oppert 1879: 8–9)

These modes are displayed by languages (or: dialects, as he puts it) in

> "the manner in which the different categories as gender, number, space, and time are treated in several dialects" (Oppert 1879: 8–9).

---

49 On Bopp's typological approach, see Ringmacher (2001a: 1430). Bopp distinguished (1833: 112–113 and 1868–1871.1: 204–206) 1. "languages without proper roots, without capability of composition and thus without organism, without grammar at all", 2. "languages with monosyllabic roots capable of composition, as their only way of gaining organism and grammar", and 3. "languages with bi-syllabic verbal roots and three necessary consonants as the only carriers of basic meanings, generating grammatical forms not just by composition, but also by inner modification of roots".

As a criterion independent from morphological traits, its role and significance for classification is close to Steinthal's concept of *Formsprachen*.

Oppert's refinement of the morphological level, or the "physiological (vocal) characteristics" of languages as he calls it, leads to an increase of the number of classes to ten (Oppert 1879: 23–29, 107–108):

- I   Monosyllabic
- II   Incorporative
- III   Euphonic
- IV   Euphonic inflectional
- V   Alliteral
- VI   Agglutinative
- VII   Agglutinative inflectional
- VIII Dissyllabic inflectional
- IX   Inflectional synthetical
- X   Inflectional analytical

The second level, referring to "modes of thought" or "psychological (mental) characteristics" of languages, was subdivided into two main classes: "Concrete languages" (including *a.* heterologous vs. *b.* homologous) as opposed to "Abstract languages", which are distinguished by the existence of a gender system (Oppert 1879: 68–92) and further subdivide into *a)* two-gender ("digeneous") and *b)* three-gender ("trigeneous") languages (Oppert 1879: 35–39, 1883: 17).

The resulting classification of languages and language families is arranged in a system formed by those two levels as coordinates ("Scheme of the System of Classification": Oppert 1879: 104–109, 1883: 18–19, and 1884). Egyptian is located in the upper right corner: Its "physiological (vocal)" character is taken that of a monosyllabic language.[50] In terms of "psychological (mental)" character, Egyptian is defined as an "abstract", namely a "digeneous" language. Its horizontal neighbour to the left is Chinese, also classified as a monosyllabic but "concrete" language. Its vertical neighbour in the same "abstract > digeneous" column is the Semitic family, which, however, ranks higher on the morphological scale due to the "disyllabic inflectional" type it displays.[51]

---

50 In Oppert's sample of kinship terms, exemplified by certain languages in order to illustrate their principles of word formation morphology, Egyptian seems to give evidence for one-syllable words, quite in keeping with its supposed nature of a monosyllabic language (Oppert 1879: 136): "Father *Ut*, Mother *Mu*, Boy *Si*, Girl *Set*, Son *Si*, Daughter *Set*, Brother *Sen*, Sister *Sent*."

51 In Oppert (1883, 1884), Hausa ("euphonic inflectional" / "abstract > digenous") comes between Egyptian and Semitic.

It is striking to see Oppert, although in quite different ways and terms, arriving at results quite similar to those reached by Steinthal (and Whitney).

6 Historical linguistics and grammar of Egyptian still in their infancy

If the description of Egyptian in terms of 19th-century language classification looks odd to modern eyes, one has to concede that this generation of comparative linguists was well-informed about the most current advancements in Egyptian language studies and that their failure was to a considerable extent the failure of contemporary Egyptology.[52]

One crucial point is the lack of a notion of language change for Egyptian. Champollion (1824a and 1836) had conceptualized the difference between hieroglyphic Egyptian and Coptic as the written / spoken contrast of "écriture sacrée" as opposed to "langue parlée"[53] – an efficient working hypothesis that allowed him the maximal exploitation of Coptic for the understanding of hieroglyphs.

In 1837, Lepsius had *en passant* corrected Champollion's idea that even such striking differences between hieroglyphic and Coptic Egyptian as different word order patterns of nominal phrases (noun followed by gender/number-markers *versus* article followed by noun) and different conjugation patterns (VS *versus* SV), would reflect nothing but different *orthographic conventions*.[54] But as far as I can tell Egyptian diachrony was not made an issue before 1871, when the French Egyptologist Gaston Maspero (1846–1916) provided a systematic analysis of the development of Egyptian conjugation, still traditionally subdivided into three

---

52 Certainly there were also paths of information flow without direct input from Egyptology, such as Whitney's adoption of Egyptian features from Steinthal (cf. above) and Oppert's reference to Müller (cf. below, Excursus III).

53 E.g., Champollion (1836: 50, § 72): "Les trois méthodes ou procédés fondamentaux de l'écriture sacrée, l'imitation, l'assimilation et la peinture des sons, furent appliquées à la représentation des noms communs de la langue égyptienne parlée." Cf. Schenkel (1990: 18–19).

54 Lepsius (1837: 72, translated from French): "One of the most obvious differences between the sacred dialect and the Coptic language is that the majority of grammatical affixes once suffixed to substantives and verbs are found to be prefixed in the Coptic language, a linguistic phenomenon that repetedly occurs throughout all languages." See Schenkel (1990: 18–19). On the typological change of word order in the language history of Egyptian see below, §7, and the introductory chapters by Grossman & Richter (2014, in this volume) and by Haspelmath (2014, in this volume).

phases according to writing systems, i.e., Hieroglyphic, Demotic, and Coptic (Maspero 1871).

His account is compromised by another major shortcoming in the understanding of pre-Coptic Egyptian: The ignorance of the fact that hieroglyphs, even though read as phonetic signs, represent only consonantal phonemes. Accordingly, Maspero's point of departure is the notion of an extreme lack of tenses and modes. In hieroglyphic Egyptian, he identified two verbal forms altogether, employed to express a general idea of present and past,[55] not to mention the fact that the same two forms also seemed to represent suffixed nouns, depending only on context.[56]

Excursus III: The Hidden Root-and-Pattern-Morphology of Egyptian
Since the morphological dimension of *differently vocalised forms* escaped the early Egyptologists, the lack of distinction between parts of speech in Egyptian (see also above, § 5 on Steinthal and Whitney) was something obvious to them. Max Müller, quoting Bunsen, wrote (Müller 1864.2: 84–85): "In Egyptian, as Bunsen states [ref. to Bunsen 144–1857.1: 324], there is no formal distinction between noun, verb, adjective, and particle, and a word like *an'h* might mean *life, to live, living, lively.* ... I think it shows that there was a stage in the growth of language in which that distinction which we make between the different parts of speech had not yet fixed, and when even that fundamental distinction between subject and predicate, on which all the parts of speech are based, had not yet been realized in its fullness, and had not yet received a corresponding outward expression." Oppert (1879: 23 + n.) quoted Bunsen (1844–1857.1: 271) and Max Müller (1864.2: 89.): "Originally, the incoherently uttered word comprised within itself the different variations in meaning as represented later by the different forms of speech. We observe

---

55 Maspero (1871: 1:) "... une extrême pénurie de temps et de modes, puisque temps et modes se réduisent à deux qui expriment d'une manière générale, le premier l'idée de l'action présente, la seconde l'idée de l'action passée ...". So already in Champollion (1836: 391ff. "Formation des temps du mode indicatif: I. Temps présent") and 406ff. "Formation des temps du mode indicatif: II. Formation du temps passé").
56 Maspero (1871: 121): "Au début de l'histoire, la langue égyptienne n'établit aucune différence entre le verbe et le nom. La racine, non susceptible de modification extérieure marque d'une manière générale une action ou une qualité que l'on applique à une personne ou à une chose par l'adjonction en préfixe ou en suffixe des pronoms personnels". The *origin* of the Egyptian Suffix conjugation in a suffixed nominal form (a participle rather than an abstract noun) is, by the way, still considered a likely hypothesis (cf. Schenkel 1975 and Schenkel 1990: 115–121).

this fact in Old Egyptian, in Chinese, Burmese, and other languages, where e.g., 'to live, life, alive, and a living being;' 'great, to be great, and greatness;' 'eye, sight, and to see' are expressed by the same word or sound".

Moreover, the systematic absence of a whole layer of morphological information in the graphemic representation of Egyptian hieroglyphs did not even occur to them as a possibility. A main epistemological reason for that ignorance was the erroneous attribution of *vocalic* phonetic values (a, i, u) to hieroglyphs which first and foremost represent *consonants* such as a stop (Aleph [ʔ]), a fricative (Ajin [ʕ]), and glides (*w* and *y*) by Champollion (1836) and then also by Lepsius, the undisputed authority in the field of Egyptian phonology (Lepsius 1837, 1855a, 1863a), although Hincks 1848 had already produced evidence from Egyptian spellings of Canaanite loanwords for the consonantal value of these hieroglyphs (cf. Ray 1994; Schenkel 1990: 30–31 and 2008: 410–411). It is striking to realize what consequences some slightly(!) wrong assumptions about Egyptian phonology had for the overall understanding of its word formation and morphosyntax: The absence of vowels from the written record was not noticed, leading to the misinterpretations mentioned above; fewer consonants per word were counted, reinforcing the impression of primarily monosyllabic words (instead of two- or three-consonantal roots); the phonological type of weak radicals was not recognized. Thus, the entire common ground of Egyptian and Semitic word formation remained undetected and undetectable – shortcomings overcome only by the *Berliner Schule*, see below, § 8. A good deal of the linguists' discussion about the lack of differentiation between nominal and verbal lexemes and about the poverty of verbal morphology in Egyptian is due to the Egyptologists' ignorance of that possibility. The root-and-pattern morphology of Egyptian and its root-inflecting capacity thus remained hidden to linguists who would have wished for nothing more than a sign of Egyptian bearing inflection – a tragic aspect of the story!

Over the course of time, Maspero claims, the original poverty of Egyptian syntax was gradually compensated for by the employment of auxiliaries, due to which the ambivalence of parts of speech was also reduced – a narrative of growth from crude imperfection upwards.[57] The steady improvement of Egyptian would even-

---

57 Maspero (1871 : 122) : "Dans les derniers temps, l'évolution est accomplie. La forme primitive du verbe, réservée à quelques mots seulement, a disparu de la langue, et cette élimination

tually profit from contact with Greek, due to the impact of which Egyptian would for the first time develop true modes.[58]

Maspero's approach shows, however, that the notion of language change in Egyptian had eventually become somewhat obvious to Egyptologists, and he came to the result of rather significant diachronic differences between the Egyptian language phases.

In the same year (1871), Lepsius's pupil Georg Ebers (1837–1898), professor of Egyptology at the University of Leipzig, expounded on language change in Egyptian in a public lecture about the hieroglyphic writing system held before a non-specialist audience that he nevertheless credited with having some knoweldge of Indo-European:

> "The space of time between the age of the pyramid builders and the origins of Christianity is not much smaller than the time German needed to develop from Sanskrit. But would any German speaker, even though he perfectly knew the Old Indic alphabet, succeed in understanding the writings of the Brahmans? And still such an incredible constellation can be proved to have happened with the language of Egypt. Coptic has deviated from the most archaic forms of Ancient Egyptian hardly further than Italian from Latin." (transl. from Ebers 1871: 10–11)

In contrast to his predecessors, Ebers finds it important to emphasize that whatever happened to Egyptian happened in conformity with regularities close to natural laws, and he quotes August Schleicher (1821–1868), one of the early explorers of the Indo-European *Ursprache* and forerunners of the *Leipziger*, or *junggrammatische Schule* (cf. Bynon 2001):[59]

> "What we encounter hereby, is not a coincidental, but a regular phenomenon, if the laws as established especially by Schleicher are true, according to which, first, the more persistently a people stays at the same settling places, the less it will change its language, and second, the language of a people that undertakes vivid exchange with other nations is much more easily exposed to manifold changes than that of a people living in seclusion." (transl. from Ebers 1871: 11)

---

rend désormais impossible la confusion entre le nom et le verbe. Le système de conjugaison par auxiliaires s'est agrandi et fixé."

58 Maspero (1871: 122–123): "La nécessité de traduire en langue égyptienne des textes grecs où la distinction des modes est généralement marquée, amène ... les auteurs coptes à choisir certaines formes de leur langue pour rendre certains modes du Grec et prépare ainsi les voies à la création des modes." For the recent discussion of syntactic interference of Greek and Coptic, cf. Polotsky (1950); Oréal (1999); Reintges (2001, 2004), and Hasznos (2012).

59 Schleicher was also active and influential in the field of language classification: Schleicher (1848: 6–12, 1850, 1859, 1860: 11–26); cf. Ringmacher (2001a: 1430–1432).

On the basis of these assumptions, Ebers could easily explain to his audience why Champollion was able to rely on Coptic while deciphering hieroglyphs:

> "Now, the Egyptians never left their dwelling places during their historical life, and, secluded on their fertile island between the Libyan and the Arabic mountains like an oyster in its shell, they carefully avoided any contact with other peoples in full awareness. This is why Coptic, although deviating from the most ancient Egyptian language varieties in several ways, can rightly be called the basic idiom of the hieroglyphs." (transl. from Ebers 1871: 11)

Unlike his teacher Richard Lepsius and his pupils Ludwig Stern and Adolf Erman (cf. below, § 8), Georg Ebers was not particularly close to language studies, and still he proves to be fairly well-informed about recent theories in the field of comparative linguistics.[60] These theories allowed him to argue for a rather conventional view on the issue of closeness between hieroglyphic Egyptian and Coptic.

7 Ewald on the equality of languages and the typological change from *Hinterbau* to *Vorderbau* in Egyptian

The Göttingen scholar Heinrich Ewald (1803–1875), most renowned for his work on Arabic and Hebrew, but also concerned with Sanskrit (which he had once taught to Lepsius) and a good number of other languages, published two *Sprachwissenschaftliche Abhandlungen* on word order typology (though not calling it thus). The first of these deals with the morphology of the verb in Coptic (Ewald 1861), and the other one deals with relations between the four language families *Nordisch*, *Mittelländisch*, *Semitisch*, and *Koptisch* (Ewald 1862).

In his first treatise, Ewald surprisingly challenged an article of faith held by the linguists of his day – the hierarchy of languages.

> "How often it has been, and is still heard, that one language, from its origins and by its unchangeable nature as it were, is more beautiful than the other, or one language family

---

60 Although there is no positive evidence, it is not unlikely that Ebers had made the acquaintance of Schleicher in Jena, where he was affiliated from 1862 to 1870 before he moved to Leipzig. Schleicher was not officially involved in the committees of the philosophical faculty concerned with Ebers' academic qualifications, his doctoral dissertation, or his *Habilitation*, cf. Poethke (1980).

more perfect and more capable of higher development than the other, and this or that language surely deserves priority over all others." (transl. from Ewald 1861: 7)

Against the *communis opinio*, Ewald claimed that

"it does not seem right to praise one's own language, or one's own language family over all the others and, for example, to agree with what is said so often in our days, that the Indo-European ... languages were the most perfect ones from the beginning." (transl. from Ewald 1861: 7; cf. also Ewald 1862: 38–39)

Even more surprisingly, Ewald clearly realized the ideological implications and the "political" consequences of an approach that was a scientific failure in his eyes, so that his counter-position is not based on ethical considerations but on linguistic reasons:

"If such an idea had firm ground, consequences would result therefrom which are both serious and sad in every respect. Because language is the closest and most appropriate ... as well as most unchangeable expression of the particular human mind. Consequently, if a people, or an entire family of peoples, really possessed a considerably less worthy language from the very beginning, this would be the clearest evidence for the overall lesser talent of such a people, and one would be entitled to treat them accordingly; and what would result from this goes without saying. ... However, our recent linguistics is sufficiently advanced to reduce all these ideas to nothing. All languages and language families are completely equal in terms of their highest (and eventually their only) importance, as a means of the perfectly clear expression of all thinkable thoughts of the human mind. ... Given the range of historical diversity, ... one language or language family may apply some of those means or matters (by which all of them eventually achieve the same goal) in a more elegantly proportioned, or more beautiful, or more perfect way; however, no single one holds all of these merits alone, and such readily despised languages as the ancient and modern African languages have, in several respects, significant merits over other, much higher esteemed ones."

He adds in a footnote:

"What advantages has, for example, the Egyptian even by its most diverse but always precise and consistent ways of expression for what we can express only by *and!*"[61] (transl. from Ewald 1861: 7–8)

---

61 In contrast, see Steinthal's complaint (Steinthal 1867: vi) about "languages [*such as Mandé*] that have no common ground with the scheme of categories of the philosophical grammarians and which cannot possibly be compared, in terms of inner formation, to our higher organised Indo-European languages, as it is impossible to compare an insect with a mammal".

Ewald's untimely attempt to argue against an axiomatic layer of 19th-century comparative linguistics did not remain uncontradicted. The role of the nemesis was taken by August Friedrich Pott (1802–1887).

Pott, who spent the major part of his long life as a professor of general linguistics in Halle, is a seminal, but perhaps still underestimated figure of 19th century linguistics (cf. Bense et al. 2006; Plank in Stammerjohann 2009: 1203–1205; Ringmacher 2001a). He had studied Sanskrit and comparative linguistics in Berlin with Bopp and became one of the most influential interpreters of Humboldt's linguistic heritage next to (and in hostile rivalry with) Steinthal.[62] He witnessed the course of comparative linguistics, whose doyen he was considered to be (Oppert 1879: 7), from the days of the Schlegel brothers and Humboldt up to the inauguration of the *Internationale Zeitschrift für Allgemeine Sprachwissenschaft*, to which he contributed a comprehensive overview of the entire field (Pott 1884a&b, 1885a&b, 1887a&b, 1889, 1890).[63] Pott, who dealt with an amazingly wide range of topics in his academic teaching,[64] apparently liked to supervise and to guide his colleagues, and he never avoided polemics.

Already in his works on numerals (Pott 1847, 1868), Pott had rejected Lepsius's argument in favour of a common origin of the Indo-European, Semitic, and Egyptian language families (Lepsius 1836b). In fact, affirming the fundamental diversity of language families was one of Pott's major concerns (Pott 1855).[65] It is this mission for which he was to fight "the last battle over the tower of Babel"

---

62 Both of them re-edited Humboldt's linguistic chefs d'œuvre: Pott published a second edition of the monumental introduction to the Kawi work "Ueber die Verschiedenheit des menschlichen Sprachbaues und ihren Einfluss auf die geistige Entwickelung des Menschengeschlechts" after the edition of 1836 (on its editorial history and reception, cf. Mueller-Vollmer 1991, 1992 and 1993), to which he added a likewise monumental introduction on "Humboldt und die Sprachwissenschaft", comprising 421 pages in the 1st edition (1876) and 561 pages in the 2nd edition (1880). Steinthal edited and commented on *Die sprachphilosophischen Werke Wilhelm's von Humboldt* in 1884, cf. Trabant (1990: 62–64) and Ringmacher (1996).

63 In the third volume (1887) of *Internationale Zeitschrift für allgemeine Sprachwissenschaft* Pott gave an up-to-date report "Zur Litteratur der Sprachenkunde Afrikas" (249–275), where he also commented on Egyptian (267–270) and Coptic linguistics (270–273).

64 He is said to have also taught classes on "hieroglyphics", as Egyptian linguistics was called at his time.

65 See also Pott (1886) against his favourite enemy, Carl Abel (cf. Abel 1885, 1886, 1891a&b). It would be a demanding but worthwhile enterprise to acknowledge the merits of Carl Abel (1837–1906), the author of such notorious works as *Der Gegensinn der Urworte* 1884, *Einleitung in ein aegyptisch-semitisch-indoeuropaeisches Wurzelwörterbuch* 1886 (a forerunner of the Nostratic hypothesis), and an 842-page volume from 1876 called *Koptische Untersuchungen*. His research at the intersection of comparative linguistics and Egyptology was as strongly rejected by contemporary linguists (cf. e.g., Techmer 1889) as by Egyptologists (cf. e.g., Erman 1878b and 1887).

(Leopold 1989) against Franz Philipp Kaulen (1827–1907). Kaulen was a Catholic priest and Old Testament scholar who defended the biblical account of the origin of mankind and the diversity of peoples and languages according to Genesis, on the basis of the linguistic theory of an primal relationship (*Urverwandtschaft*) of language families (Pott 1863). In this battle, Heinrich Ewald innocently came under fire (Pott 1863: 219–289). His attempt to describe the driving forces of language change cross-linguistically (cf. below) was completely misunderstood by Pott and blamed as another awkward attempt to prove the monogenesis of language families; and his plea for the equality of languages was taken as further proof of the overall inferiority of Ewald's scholarship:[66]

> "Frankly spoken, should this jumble of most contradictory terms make any sense at all, I do not grasp it. Languages which are "equal" ... in terms of rank and purpose, despite all inequality, would be like ... cats that are all grey, certainly at night only, when all differences of colors fade." (transl. from Pott 1863: 225)

In fact, Pott did double injustice to Ewald, first, by mistaking his argument and, second, by intermingling it with that of an apologetic conservatism[67] from which Ewald, one of the most honest German liberals of his time, was as far as he could be.

Ewald's aim was not to demonstrate genealogical *Urverwandtschaft* but to provide a way to compare languages without regard for their genealogical relation:

> "Given the great amount and diversity of languages, it could in previous times already seem a significant success just to correctly distinguish the ones actually interrelated and to connect them to certain language families; the issue however as to how these distinct language families relate to each other remained in the dark and it seemed entirely impossible to solve it by any cautious and prudent procedure." (transl. from Ewald 1861: 5)

---

66 Pott (1863: 287, translated from German): "On my part, I take the exact opposite for the truth. These langague families are innately and principally, by 'primordial forces' to put it with Ewald, separated from each other."

67 On the other hand, this conservatism was a theoretical stronghold against the more *zeitgeist*-oriented concept of fundamental cultural differences between humans which easily combined with the developing racial science (and scientific racism) based on biological arguments such as anthropometry. On the 19th- and 20th-century linguistic and ethnological discourse on the relation of language and race, see van Driem (2001: especially 126–128) on the contemporary linguistic debate about the Comte de Gobineau. In Pott's favour, it was he who refuted (Pott 1856), from the point of view of comparative linguistics, Arthur de Gobineau's theory of the inequality of races – the "hegemonial discourse" that Ewald had hinted at *avant la lettre*.

Ewald identified such a perspective in the observation of shared tendencies of language change that he called "language forces" (*Sprachmächte*) when he claimed

> "that everything in human language finally depends on certain forces which can be recognized and traced and which are limited in number ... but irresistible in their effect ... *Language forces* is our word for those necessities that start working as soon as the mind, whatever it wants to express linguistically, does actually express using language material ... One can justly claim that the sound knowledge of these forces, based on the knowledge and the comparison of the most diverse languages, is the strongest lever of all linguistics, and neither a single language nor human language as a whole can be subject to secure and fruitful knowledge without it" (transl. from Ewald 1861: 9–10).

What Ewald claimed was therefore not a shared *substrate* underlying different language families and connecting them *genealogically*. He rather argued for a shared set of fundamental *motivating factors*, working in all languages and connecting them *typologically*, or, to put it in modern terms, for universals of, and typological constraints on, language change.

To achieve this goal, he further claimed

> "that all languages, even those most remote from ours in terms of time and place, have to be taken into account with the same due care and that especially the hitherto most overlooked ones should eventually be studied most thoroughly" (transl. from Ewald 1861: 11).

To illustrate his claims, Ewald chose Coptic, first, for the interest it bears for the study of Ancient Egyptian[68] and, second, for the very feature for which linguists used to think of it as a primitive language – its easily analyzable morphological structure, to which Ewald applied the established term "agglutinating".[69] From features which he interpreted as fossilized remains of earlier language phases,

---

68 Ewald (1861: 11–12, translated from German): "A thorough scientific knowledge of Coptic has highest importance for us not at least for its close connection to the entire Egyptian antiquity; since without its aid we could never achieve a reliable understanding of the language of the hieroglyphs and the cursive writing styles depeloped from those. Although first steps to their decipherment are taken by now, there are many further ones still to be tried, and many of the biggest difficulties are not yet resolved".

69 Ewald (1861: 12–13, translated from German): "In the Coptic language ... these primal constituents are generally more easily traceable, even though not every element of this kind forms an easily separable word of its own as in Chinese. ... As is well known, a few decades ago, some at that time influential linguists wanted to subdivide all languages into monosyllabic, agglutinating, and inflecting ones: In these terms it would be easy to label Coptic as an agglutinating language. However I have been reluctant about this catergorization already then, and cannot endorse it even now".

Ewald inferred a development of the Egyptian language from what he called "post-structuring" (*hinterbau*) to "pre-structuring" (*vorderbau*) – a development he suspected to be a typological tendency of language change in other languages too:

"Taking a closer look at the overall formation of Coptic, there eventually occurs to us a phenomenon most significant for language history, that possibly in no other language has taken shape as perfect as in Coptic, which however is equally instructive for all of them. Very distinctive traces lead us ... to the certain assumption that Coptic in its extreme primeval time preferred the post-structuring [*hinterbau*] of words. Such a construction is very natural, it developed in the strongest way, with an amazing, almost rigid force in the Nordic [i.e., Ewald's term for Turkic, etc.) language family; in the Middle Land [*Mittelländischen*, i.e., Indo-European] languages it still represents the earliest and most solid basis of word formation; and also in the Semitic, it left strong traces of its earliest dominance. In Coptic it is almost fading away, but when observed more thoroughly, it has still left many massive traces of its former dominance, and the more isolatedly dispersed and the less considerable they are, the more undoubtedly they reveal themselves as the most ancient components of that language." (transl. from Ewald 1861: 15)

The evidence for post-structuring, *hinterbau*, is found by Ewald in phenomena of the formation of words, phrases, and clauses, such as:

1. the remains of verbal endings of the Coptic verb form called the "Stative"[70] – the very forms whose origins Adolf Erman would trace to the inflection pattern of an ancient Perfect conjugation shared by Egyptian and Semitic languages (Erman 1889a, cf. below, § 8),
2. the remains of suffixed gender and number markers which, as Ewald concludes, although in Coptic being nothing but "isolatedly dispersed and disintegrated fragments of a once productive formation" (Ewald 1861: 16), originally were a shared feature of Egyptian and Semitic languages where they are still extant,[71]
3. the remains of suffixed possessive pronominals,[72] another pattern shared with Semitic languages (Ewald 1861: 18).

Among the much more frequent, and in Coptic, only productive features of pre-structuring, *vorderbau*, "according to which the elements serving to specify the

---

70 See Reintges' contribution in this volume and Haspelmath's introduction, § 1.9.
71 Ewald (1861: 16, translated from German): "There is nothing in which Semitic and Coptic must once have paralleled each other as completely as in the formation of gender and number".
72 Cf. the contribution of Haspelmath in this volume.

verbal or nominal basic lexemes are moved to the front" (Ewald 1861: 18)[73], Ewald mentions phenomena such as:

1. SV order in all conjugation patterns (Ewald 1861: 19),
2. word formation by prefixed compound elements, such as the nominal prefix *mnt-* deriving abstract nouns and the prefix *ref-* deriving agent nouns, as opposed to the transposition of lexemes by endings or word-internal morphological change (Ewald 1861: 20)
3. the use of prepositions to indicate functional relations otherwise marked by case endings (Ewald 1861: 21)
4. prefixed articles, demonstratives, and possessive markers, leading to what Ewald calls "word chain" (*Wortkette*), as opposed to suffixed, or postposed elements with this range of functions (Ewald 1861: 21–23)
5. prefixed conjugation bases, leading to what Ewald calls "clause chain" (*Satzkette*): "the morpheme dominating the sentence draws and chains with the strongest power, as it were, the both parts of the sentence, so that the full meaning of all the words working together here becomes clear only by their mutual concatenation and their strict order" (Ewald 1861: 23–24).

Ewald's conclusions about a systemic change from *hinterbau* to *vorderbau* in the Egyptian language history were immediately denied by Pott (1863: 278). But in fact, Ewald had seen the right facts in the right way. Eighty-five years later, the Egyptologist and linguist Fritz Hintze (1915–1993) described the same process, based on the same observations, although in terms of structural linguistics and against the background of a tremendously increased text corpus and an incomparably advanced Egyptian philology (Hintze 1947 and 1950).[74] Since then, this typological notion has become common wisdom in Egyptological linguistics.[75]

---

73 "... vorderbau, nach welchem die näheren bestimmungen des als grund dienenden that- oder namenswortes nach vorne verschoben werden".

74 On Hintze as a Coptic linguist, see Funk 2003. Hintze knew and mentioned his predecessor Ewald: "Diese Verhältnisse hatte schon der Göttinger Orientalist H. Ewald geahnt" (Hintze 1947: 96).

75 Cf. Schenkel (1990: 95–96); Loprieno (1995: 5–8).

8 Solutions and dissolutions: Egyptian linguistics at the dawn of the *Berliner Schule*

The most up-to-date and most advanced pre-*Berliner Schule* report on Egyptian in terms of comparative linguistics was provided by Ludwig Stern in his seminal Coptic grammar (Stern 1880).[76] Ludwig Stern (1846–1911) had studied Romance and Oriental languages as well as Egyptology (with Heinrich Brugsch) at Göttingen. Appointed Richard Lepsius's assistant in the Egyptian department of the Berlin Royal Museum in 1874, he was originally on friendly terms with Adolf Erman but increasingly became a rival of the would-be main figure of the so-called *Berliner Schule*. In 1885, when Erman, the younger of the two, was appointed Lepsius's successor as the director of the Egyptian museum instead of him, Stern turned his back on Egyptian and moved to Celtic studies. To earn his living, he took a position as a librarian at the Berlin Royal Library, where he was finally appointed the head of the manuscripts collection in 1905 (Dawson & Uphill 1995: 404; Magen 2007 and 2013).

Stern's overall description of the character of Coptic seems to be inspired – apart from his own study – by Heinrich Ewald:[77]

"The Coptic language, written by means of the Greek alphabet, is a daughter of ancient Egyptian ... Between those two, chronologically, the Demotic is situated, whose writing system is closer to the hieroglyphic, whose forms and pronunciation are however closer to the Coptic language. While the ancient language generally persisted in the stage of isolating languages, Coptic, which tends to replace such grammatical elements which in the hieroglyphic language occur in apparent isolation by internal or preposed formations, has already developed into an overall agglutinating one. Its vocalism appears rejuvenated, as it were, and to be shaped according to new rules. ... The Coptic language greatly surpasses ancient Egyptian in certainty, adroitness, and diversity, although it constructs clauses not without long-windedness; being poor in forms, it is rich in means of distinguished expression and unsurpassed in the development of diacritic possibilities. Its vocabulary is as transparent and clear as its syntax; its phonetic laws are of exceptional regularity and strictness." (transl. from Stern 1880: 3–4)

---

76 Stern's Coptic grammar constituted tremendous progress in the knowledge of Coptic morphosyntax, and his achievements were already praised by Erman (1884: 28): "In das Chaos der koptischen Verbalstämme hat Stern Licht gebracht".
77 Ewald was expelled from the University of Göttingen and lost his permission to teach in 1868 after having opposed Prussian imperialism by refusing to swear an oath of allegiance to the Prussian king. Ludwig Stern, who studied at Göttingen from 1865–1868, might have been among his last students.

Dealing with the issue of genealogical classification, Stern groups Egyptian with the Hamitic languages, although he indicates cognates with Semitic languages:

> "There is a relationship between Egyptian, which belongs to the Hamitic family, and the Semitic languages, as is unmistakably indicated in the formation of pronominals and in a few shared roots; however Egyptian apparently separated early from its Asian siblings and followed its own path. Many Coptic words still resemble the related Semitic ones ... The overall relationship is obscured by heavy phonetic shifts and changes." (transl. from Stern 1880: 4)

The new insight into the grammar of Coptic as gained by Ludwig Stern was the bud, as it were, of the bloom of Egyptian-Coptic linguistics known under the name of the *Berliner Schule* of Egyptology (cf. Gertzen 2012; Schenkel 1990: 19–21).[78] This prosperity was in no small part due to the efforts of Stern's colleague and competitor Adolf Erman (1854–1937).[79] Erman studied Egyptology with Georg Ebers at Leipzig and with Richard Lepsius and Ludwig Stern in Berlin. In his other main subject, Semitic languages (Arabic, Assyrian, Hebrew, and Syriac), Erman was taught by Fritz Hommel (1854–1936) and Ludolf Krehl (1825–1901) in Leipzig and by Eduard Sachau (1845–1930), Eberhard Schrader (1836–1908), August Dillmann (1823–1894), and Franz Prätorius (1847–1927) in Berlin.[80] Erman's new achievements were mainly based on three interrelated approaches: 1. – a decisive turn to the study of Egyptian morphology and syntax, 2. – a more sophisticated subdivision of the linguistic history of Egyptian, 3. – an attempt to look at Egyptian in the light of Semitic languages and, consequently, to deal with it in terms of Semitic linguistics.

1. The long-established notion of the "primitiveness" of Coptic and, accordingly, of Egyptian, had prevented earlier Coptologists and two generations of Egyptian philologists from a closer look at the grammar of the language. This excuse eventually collapsed in 1880, when Stern's *Koptische Grammatik* and Erman's *Neuägyptische Grammatik* appeared.[81] In his commentary on the Old

---

78 On the Berliner Schule, see Gertzen (2012), Schenkel (1990: 19–21).

79 On Erman, see Schipper (2006); on Erman's research in Egyptian linguistics, see Satzinger (2006).

80 See Erman's autobiography (Erman 1929: 110–114), where he downplays the influence of almost all of his teachers to a degree that makes him seem a self-taught man.

81 Erman (1880: viii, translation from German): "The syntax of the Egyptian language has been doomed all along. Even Peyron, the great expert of Coptic, still held the opinion that there was hardly anything to notice about the syntax of this language, and in Schwartze's grammar where phonology takes 300 pages, not even 30 are devoted to syntax ...; up to the present day not a meager description of it has been published. And likewise dreadful is the situation of the syntax

Kingdom autobiography of *Wnj*, Erman described the poor state of Egyptian grammatical investigation that he found himself faced with:

"What would one think about a classical philologist who, translating Cicero, had no idea why sometimes conjunctive, sometimes indicative, sometimes perfect, sometimes imperfect is used, and moreover, who had hardly any awareness of this ignorance? And who could deny that we are still taking this naive attitude towards the language of the Old and Middle Kingdom?"[82] (transl. from Erman 1882: 1–2)

2. Erman's *Neuägyptische Grammatik* from 1880 was a landmark not only in grammatical exploration but also in the study of the linguistic history of Egyptian. Up to Maspero (1871, cf. above, § 6), Egyptian was traditionally subdivided into three language phases corresponding with the three writing systems Hieroglyphic/Hieratic, Demotic, and Coptic.

On the basis of linguistic features Erman subdivided the hieroglyphic section into Ancient Egyptian (*altaegyptisch*) and Late Egyptian (Erman 1878: 3: *jung-aegyptisch*, Erman 1880: *neuägyptisch*), although he was aware of the dependence of these features on both language change in time, and different linguistic registers:[83]

"While all texts written in hieroglyphs ... were called Ancient Egyptian (*altaegyptisch*) up to now, I call only the ancient classical language by this name, which is preserved as a living language in the sacred books and the earlier inscriptions; I choose however the term Late Egyptian (*neuaegyptisch*) to designate the vulgar language of the New Kingdom which I shall deal with in this work. Late Egyptian is situated roughly halfway between the sacred language, whose classical period may fall around 3000 B.C., and the Demotic-Coptic language. We encounter it as early as from the beginning of the New Kingdom; however only

---

of Ancient Egyptian".

82 In a similar vein, Erman (1878b: 764) had already written: "dass wir ... vom Aegyptischen und seiner Grammatik noch nicht viel mehr wissen, als ein Quintaner vom Latein".

83 Polotsky (1969: 465 + n. 2), pointed to Stern who seems to propose an even more sophisticated periodization already years earlier (Stern 1874: 90, translated from German): "Advanced linguistic study will come to subdivide the almost 5,000 years of the Egyptian written record into four roughly equal periods. The first period, the *Ancient* one, would span over the first six dynasties; the second, the *Middle* one, would extend until the 17th dynasty, the third, *New* one until the 26th dynasty, and the last, *Late* one up to the emperor Decius, this is to say, up to the extinction of hieroglyphic writing. In this last period, maybe already a bit earlier, the ancient Egyptian language was a dead and sacred language used like Sankrit by the Indians, Hebrew by the Jews, the language of the Qur'an by the Arabs, and Latin in the Western world." See Schenkel (1990: 8), who wonders whether Bunsen's periodization of Egyptian history could have inspired Stern's periodization.

in the 19th and 20th dynasties, that is to say, around the thirteenth and twelfth centuries B.C., do we find evidence sufficient for proper knowledge of it" (Erman 1880: 1)[84] "The many easily comprehensible texts of different genres in Late Egyptian make the task for the grammarian easier, although the right interpretation of its forms and constructions is often suggested by its closeness to Coptic." (transl. from Erman 1880: viii)

Although Erman separated Late Egyptian, "the vernacular of the New Kingdom", from Demotic, "the vernacular of the last pre-Christian centuries, written in a peculiar script", and Coptic, "the language of the Christian Egyptians, written in Greek letters" (Erman 1894: 1), he grouped all three together in contrast to what he called Ancient Egyptian [*altaegyptisch*]. This notion of closeness between New Kingdom (hieroglyphic) Egyptian and Coptic was now to replace the former concept of a consistent "hieroglyphic" Egyptian as opposed to Demotic and Coptic.[85] The range of distinctive features between the norms included in Erman's concepts of Ancient Egyptian and Late Egyptian is worked out in his seminal grammatical study (Erman 1890) on the language of Papyrus Westcar, an early 18th-dynasty manuscript recording Egyptian fairy tales which are linked by a framing narrative:

> "Without being guilty of much exaggeration, one may define the overall relation in such a way that the language of the Westcar papyrus is still walking on the paths of Ancient Egyptian, while Late Egyptian is already on the track leading to Coptic; there is a vast gulf dividing the two." (transl. from Erman 1890: 9)

Erman's concept of *Altaegyptisch*, "the most ancient language, though kept in use as a learned idiom of literature up until the Roman period" (Erman 1894: 1 and already Erman 1880 and 1890), was wider than the term *Old Egyptian*, as it is used today. It includes the two phases nowadays distinguished as *Old Egyptian* (the language of Old Kingdom texts) and *Middle Egyptian* (the "classical" language from the Middle Kingdom onwards) and corresponds thus to the modern concept of *Earlier Egyptian* (cf. Grossman's & Richter's introductory chapter in this volume). However, Erman was well aware of the linguistic peculiarities of the earliest Egyptian texts, the spells inscribed in 5th- and 6th-dynasty pyramids and

---

84 Already in the introduction to his thesis on plural formation, Erman presented a first sketch of the historical grammar of Egyptian (Erman 1878a: 1–4).

85 Cf. Erman (1878a: 2–3, translated from German): "... in almost all cases where the ways of Coptic deviate from those of Ancient Egyptian, we find the language of the 19th and 20th dynasty already there – in short, it is much closer to the most recent Egyptian idiom than to that of the ancient sacred one. [...] Would not the ancient script and orthography veil its true self, no grammarian would ever have separated it and assigned it to Ancient Egyptian".

the tomb inscriptions of contemporary high officials,[86] and distinguished them carefully from the language of Egyptian literature of the Middle Kingdom.[87] The overall picture of Egyptian diachrony as drawn by him eventually comes close to much more recent Egyptological approaches to language periodization (starting with Stricker 1945) and would look like the following:

Erman's "Altaegyptisch"		[Later Egyptian]		
Old Kingdom A.Eg.	Middle Kingdom A.Eg.	*Late Egyptian*	Demotic	Coptic

3. Assumptions about the genealogical relatedness of Egyptian-Coptic and the Semitic languages used to be limited to the notion of single cognate words, most obviously in the realm of pronominals (e.g., Rossi 1808; Vater 1812; Lepsius 1836; Benfey 1844; Schwartze 1843: 466–763; Schwartze in Bunsen 1845: 517–645; Schwartze 1850: 6–7).[88] Erman demonstrated even more far-reaching similarities, including basic features of word formation and syntax, especially in the earliest layers of the Egyptian language. Already in his *Neu-ägyptische Grammatik* he wrote:

"It will not escape experts how many analogies to Semitic the syntax even of Late Egyptian still exhibits; in Ancient Egyptian this holds true to a much higher degree." (transl. from Erman 1880: vii)

The full range of such "analogies" is worked out in a number of seminal articles that Erman published in the *Zeitschrift für Ägyptische Sprache und Altertumskunde.*

---

86 Erman (1894: vi): "... the particular features of the ancient religious literature and the inscriptions of the Old Kingdom...".

87 Erman (1894: vi, translated from German): "what might be called, the Classical language, the language of Middle Kingdom poetry and inscriptions". From this one he separates what he calls (Erman 1894: 1) "Middle Egyptian, the vernacular of the Middle Kingdom" ("das Mittelägyptische, die Volkssprache des mittleren Reiches"): The term "Middle Egyptian" as used by Erman thus refers to a sociolinguistically distinguished layer of Middle Kingdom "Ancient Egyptian".

88 And even those were doubted by some linguists, cf. e.g Whitney (1867: 343): "The Egyptian pronouns present some striking analogies with the Semitic, and from this fact, the confident conclusion has been drawn by many linguistic scholars that the two families are ultimately related ... Considering, however, the exceeding structural difference between them and the high improbability that any genuine correspondences of so special a character should have survived that thorough working-over which could have made Semitic speech out of anything like Egyptian, the conclusion must be pronounced, at least, a venturesome one".

This journal, founded in 1863 by Heinrich Brugsch and edited by Richard Lepsius from 1864, was the first academic periodical exclusively dedicated to Egyptology (cf. Gertzen 2013 and Gady 2013). Its foundation indicates the increasing autonomy of Egyptian studies within the academic frame of humanities and, collateral to this development, the gradual deviation of Egyptian linguistics from general and comparative linguistics.

In the first of his contributions (Erman 1881), Erman dealt with some linguistic peculiarities of the autobiography of the high official *Wnj*, one of the most comprehensive narrative texts extant from the Old Kingdom. These peculiarities include

- the morphological formation of a *dualis* displaying forms that partially resemble their Semitic counterparts,[89]
- an adjective marker *-j* which Erman did not hesitate to call *nisbe*, adopting the name of the functionally and morphologically similar pattern in Semitic word formation,[90]
- a type of verbal noun ending in the feminine marker *.t*, the discovery of the so-called Relative forms,[91]
- and the existence of a morphological class of verbs that Erman called *verba mediae geminatae*, again drawing upon the terminology of Semitic linguistics.[92]

Erman's most far-reaching discovery was the preservation of the old Semitic Perfect conjugation in the earliest attested layers of Egyptian (Erman 1889),[93] and its further occurrence (although in changed syntactic and functional patterns) throughout Egyptian up to the residual form known as the Coptic stative (Erman 1889 and 1894b).

---

89 Erman (1881: 44–52): "Das \\, der Dualis und die Nisbe", 46–47: "This vowel *i* plays a main role in Ancient Egyptian morphology. First, it serves the formation of the dualis; in fact, Ancient Egyptian has a dualis". See also Erman (1875).

90 Erman (1881: 49): "Even more important however than this dualis is the other paradigm marked by \\ [i.e., the hieroglyphic sign encoding of the morpheme called by Erman "vowel *i*"], which I want to call by a term taken from Semitic grammar, the nisbe".

91 Erman (1881: 53–58): "Verbalformen auf t".

92 Erman (1881: 58–66): "Verba mediae geminatae im Aegyptischen".

93 On the cognates of the Semitic perfect conjugation see esp. 80–81. Today one wonders how earlier Egyptologists could have overlooked these forms. However, many of these are not that conspicuous, and the distinctive form of the 1st person singular: *-kw* was wrongly identified by Maspero (1871: 18) with the Coptic particle *ce*. See also Schenkel (1990: 13, and 105–107). For the stative in Ancient Egyptian see Kammerzell (1991); Reintges (2006); Oréal (2009), and Reintges' article in this volume.

A synthesis of these discoveries in terms of an Egyptian and Semitic genealogical relationship was given in Erman 1892 (cf. also Schenkel 1990: 13–16). Eventually in his *Ägyptische Grammatik* (Erman 1894a), Erman dealt with the classification of verbs completely in terms of Semitic grammar:[94] He distinguished verbal classes "according to the number and quality of their consonants, the so-called radicals" (Erman 1894a: 62–63), and he identified root patterns widely corresponding to those of the Semitic verb.[95] The relation of Egyptian to African and Semitic languages was now expressed in terms of an equal distance:

> "The Egyptian language is a relative of the Semitic languages (Hebrew, Arabic, Aramaic, etc.), of the eastern African languages (Bishari, Galla, Somali, and others), and of the Berber languages of Northern Africa." (Erman 1894a: 1)

The rise of the *Berliner Schule* meant an enormous increase of professionalism in the developing discipline of Egyptology. Erman himself was fully aware of the significance of the turn triggered by his discoveries. In 1895, when he delivered his inaugural speech to the Berlin academy – the very institution to which seventy years before Wilhelm von Humboldt had introduced Champollion's "phonetic hieroglyphs" – Erman put it in terms of an ambivalent feeling of pride, guilt, and melancholy:

> "We transformed a cheerful science rich in surprises into a dull philology with uncomfortable phonetic laws and wicked syntactic rules ... What is happening to Egyptology today is the process that no science can escape ... Where are the happy days gone when every text could be translated and understood? From the time when grammar became better known to us, we have unfortunately encountered difficulties and obstacles all around that we did not even suspect before ... The age of swift results is over, and the monotonous age of work on details has begun." (transl. from Grapow 1954: 14–16)

The driving forces of professionalization inherent in and resulting from Erman's solutions to a number of crucial issues of Egyptian linguistics are part of the reason why the venerable companionship between comparative linguistics and Egyptian language studies eventually dissolved, and the latter, ennobled as an independent philological discipline, was to move on in splendid isolation.

---

94 Erman (1894: 62): "The designations of the classes are those used in the Semitic grammar".
95 Erman (1894: 62–63): "The verbs subdivide into several classes according to the quantity and quality of their consonants, the so-called *radicals*. These classes differ in their ways of inflection". Erman's pupil Kurt Sethe (1869–1934) had already used this terminology two years earlier in his doctoral thesis on *Aleph prostheticum*, Berlin 1892.

9 The new achievements of Egyptian lingustics as echoed by linguistic typology: From Misteli to Finck

The development within Egyptology also affected the attempts by comparative linguists to classify Egyptian typologically, and eventually led to the same result on their side.

In pre-*Berliner Schule* times, classifying Egyptian in terms of *Sprachbau* meant to deal with a language almost bare of grammar – "the plainest rise of pure forms", "bare, rigid plainness", as Steinthal 1860 put it. How much more demanding was this business to become when the classification of this language meant dealing with not just one grammar but with three (since 1880) or four (since 1894).

The changed, in fact terribly complicated, situation is echoed in the third edition of Steinthal's *Charakteristik der hauptsächlichsten Typen des Sprachbaues* from 1893, which the Swiss linguist, Franz Misteli (1841–1903; cf. Ringmacher 1996: 202–206 and 2001b: 1437–1438; Aschenberg 2001; Häcki Buhofer in Stammerjohann 2009: 1032–1033), published more than thirty years after the appearance of its second edition (Steinthal 1860). Compared with the previous editions (Steinthal 1850 and 1860), Misteli's revision of 1893 exhibits a number of striking changes:

1. Egyptian has changed places. It is now classified together with the Bantu languages under the type 'anreihende Sprachen' (Misteli 1893: 104–110). Although Egyptian is still awarded the title of Formsprache (Misteli 1893: 107–108), this change increased the typological distance between Egyptian and Semitic, as well as between Egyptian and the Indo-European languages. On the other hand, although Misteli partially based his work on Stern 1880, he did not follow Stern's suggestion (Stern 1880: 3–4) to distinguish different phases of Egyptian typologically and to classify pre-Coptic Egyptian as an isolating language, as opposed to Coptic as an agglutinating one. Also, Erman's new insight into the closeness of Ancient Egyptian to Semitic languages – not just genealogically, but also structurally, including evidence for verbal inflection – had no impact on Misteli's classification.[96]

---

[96] The increasing danger of dilettantism faced by approaches to general language classification from the late 19th century due to the increasing number of specialized philologies is dealt with by Ringmacher (2001b: 1436–1437).

2. The description of Egyptian (Misteli 1893: 266–301) differs significantly from the second edition and presents itself as being informed by recent Egyptological work.[97] While only Stern's Coptic grammar (Stern 1880) is referred to explicitly, the whole chapter is based on Erman's *Neuaegyptische Grammatik*, starting with Misteli's introduction to the language history of Egyptian, where Erman (1880) is quoted literally, if not explicitly.[98] While the diachronically unchanged *Sprachbau* of Egyptian, as was claimed by Steinthal, is maintained theoretically (Misteli 1893: 267),[99] in practice Misteli no longer dared to deal with Egyptian as a uniform linguistic entity. Instead, he narrows the validity of his description down to Late Egyptian (*Neuägyptisch*) and Coptic (Misteli 1893: 267), the two most easily accessible phases of Egyptian, thanks to Erman (1880) and Stern (1880).

3. The overall classification system has changed:[100] Steinthal's rather idiosyncratic terminology following the overarching concept of *Formsprachen*, even though not given up entirely, is "converted" into terms that, on the one hand, explicitly link to earlier terminological traditions of language classification (F. and A.W. Schlegel, Humboldt, Pott 1848), such as *einverleibend* 'incorporating', *wurzel-isolierend* 'root-isolating', *stamm-isolierend* 'stem-isolating', *anreihend* 'attaching', *agglutinierend* 'agglutinating', *flectierend* 'inflecting'. On the other hand, they anticipate the terminology still used by Finck 1910.

---

97 Misteli writes in his preface (ix, translated from German): "Also the specimens in the Egyptian-Coptic chapter and a good deal of the idea of it are based on well-known recent studies [an implicit reference to Stern 1880 and Erman 1880], with the exception of certain scholars who think that they can find sounds of primeval language in Egyptian [an innuendo to the work of Carl Abel]".

98 Misteli (1893: 267, translated from German): "The language of Egypt is known to us from three different periods. The Egyptian of the hieroglyphs [i.e., the first period, previous to the Demotic and Coptic periods] … can further be subdivided into Old Egyptian and New Egyptian, the first one being the "classical language extant in the holy scriptures and the earliest inscriptions" (around 3000 BCE), the latter being the "vernacular language of the New Kingdom" for which we have sufficient evidence from the 13th and 12th centuries BCE". This is obviously paraphrased from Erman (1880: 1) (cf. above, § 8).

99 Misteli (1893, 267, translated from German): "These three (or four, respectively) phases are different only with regard to phonology and to the disappearance, or spread, of the one or the other form; the principle of formation is the same in all of them."

100 In his preface, Misteli describes his aims ironically (Misteli 1893: viii, translated from German): "Once having taken up a revision of Steinthal's book, I tried to limit myself to the knowable and to the purely linguistic, although ethnopsychology still won't be left empty-handed, and doubtlessly one phrase or another will sound mystical enough". On Misteli's aims and method see also Ringmacher (2001b: 1437–1438).

Franz Nikolaus Finck (1867–1910), professor of general linguistics in Berlin (cf. Koerner 1970; Plank in Stammerjohann 2009: 459–461), contributed to language classification the first time in his concise programmatic essay *Die Klassifikation der Sprachen* (Finck 1901; cf. Daniels 1998: 195; Ringmacher 2001b: 1439–1440), where he compared the two approaches taken by Byrne 1885 (on James Byrne [1820–1897] cf. Daniels 1998: 194–195 and Ringmacher 2001b: 1438–1439) and Misteli 1893. Finck's idea of Egyptian was apparently not very clear at that time, but clear enough to approve its classification together with Bantu languages, as proposed by Misteli 1893 (Finck 1901: 17), and to criticize Steinthal's earlier treatment of Egyptian (and Chinese) in terms of *Formsprachen*.[101] Although Byrne's and Misteli's systems were developed from distant points of view and are different in several respects, Finck found them compatible to a degree that gave him confidence in their achievable convergence into, what he called, "the truth".[102]

Finck's synthesis of language classification is provided in two popular booklets, *Die Sprachstämme des Erdkreises* (Finck 1909, 3rd edition 1923) and *Die Haupttypen des Sprachbaus* (Finck 1910, 5th edition 1965), which, in some way, are the final word of 19th-century language classification (Lehmann 1969: 50–52).

The first of the two, *Sprachstämme des Erdkreises* (Finck 1909), deals with genealogical classification. Egyptian, grouped together with the *Hamito-Semitic* language family, is subdivided into *Altägyptisch*, *Mittelägyptisch*, and *Neuägyptisch*, which was still unusual in Egyptology (cf. above, § 8). Given the brevity of presentation, it is difficult to guess how Finck wanted these labels to be under-

---

101 Finck (1901: 20–21, translated from German): "As is well-known, some have tried to incorporate the Egyptian and Chinese languages – albeit acknowledging great differences – together with them [i.e., the Indo-European and Semitic languages] into the class of form languages – thereby performing quite a feat of wishful interpretation! Although Egyptian does not possess *subjective verbs* [i.e., modal verbs], although roots and suffixes are not firmly fused with each other, it is still supposed to be a form language, because "the Egyptians," as Steinthal says, "have been thinking formally, and therefore their language is formal". But who stands surety for this? And even if they had been thinking formally, does this matter for somebody who wants just to study their language? The only positive argument produced in favor of formality is the grammatical gender, so much praised with effusively eloquent words. Apart from that it is not plausible why it should be of bigger importance than any other categorial differentiation, ... it is certainly not true that the rules of congruence and thereby, true synthesis would be possible by virtue of this [i.e., the category of grammatical gender] alone".

102 Finck (1901: 15–16, translated from German): "Comparing this classification [i.e., according to Byrne] with the classification at which F. Misteli, following Steinthal, arrived via a very different route, a broad consensus gets visible which, despite all differences, raises hope for an approximation to the truth by means of a careful evaluation of merits and shortcomings on either side".

stood. It seems, however, likely that he took them from Erman and, unaware of or unwilling to follow Erman's special concept of *Middle Egyptian* (cf. above, n. 92), placed it "logically" amidst Ancient and Late Egyptian. After all, the British Egyptologist Battiscombe Gunn (1883–1950), who introduced the term *Middle Egyptian* into Egyptology, was surprised to find it anticipated in a small booklet written by a general linguist: "Who invented the term 'Middle Egyptian' in this sense I do not know; I thought myself to have been perhaps the originator of it until I found it so used in Finck, *Die Sprachstämme des Erdkreises*, 25." (Gunn 1924: ix).

Finck's second booklet, *Die Haupttypen des Sprachbaus* (Finck 1910), explains language typology, as this business was now called (following von der Gabelentz 1894; cf. Ringmacher 2001b: 1436), to a wider audience. Eight types of *Sprachbau* are distinguished: *wurzelisolierend* 'root-isolating', *stammisolierend* 'stem-isolating', *einverleibend* 'incorporating', *unterordnend* 'subordinating', *anreihend* 'attaching', *gruppenflektierend* 'group-inflecting', *wurzelflektierend* 'root-inflecting', *stammflektierend* 'stem-inflecting' (Finck 1910: 153–155). Finck expounded his typological classification by introducing one representative of each of them. Egyptian-Coptic was not selected, and we cannot know for sure to which class(es) Finck would have grouped it now.

10 Outlook

As this article aimed to show, Egyptian-Coptic was a central concern to comparative linguists throughout the 19th century. This was no longer so in the 20th century. The rise and development of structuralism and the Greenbergian approach to linguistic typology is a story completely different from the further development of Egyptian philology. Admittedly some Egyptologists, such as Hans-Jakob Polotsky (1905–1991) and Fritz Hintze (1915–1993), were well aware of contemporary trends in linguistics, quite to the benefit of their thought on Egyptian. Linguistics, however, was no longer informed by Egyptology.[103] If proof were needed, nothing could be more revealing than the conspicuous behaviour of Sir

---

103 As to the best of my knowledge, Martin Haspelmath's introductory chapter on Egyptian in this volume is the first attempt to describe Egyptian in terms of general linguistics undertaken by a general linguist after Misteli 1893. An exceptional case of reception from Egyptology is Karl Bühler (Bühler 1934: 399–402 = Bühler 2011: 453–456), who referred to the (unpublished) PhD of the Austrian Egyptologist Willy Diemke (Diemke 1934) when dealing with the grammaticalization of subordinate sentences, although despite his influence on linguists, Bühler was not a linguist himself.

Alan Gardiner (1879–1963). Offspring of the *Berliner Schule*, he was one of the most eminent Egyptian philologists and linguists of the day and the author of the most successful Egyptian grammar ever written (Gardiner 1927, 3rd edition 1957 followed by numerous reprint editions up to the present). Sometimes, however, Gardiner enjoyed himself by writing on general linguistics, and whenever doing so, he carefully switched off his internal Egyptologist – only a couple of random examples in his works on general linguistics are taken from Egyptian, while his overall argument is based on the classical languages (Gardiner 1932, 1951, 1954).

According to Antonio Loprieno, Egyptian linguistics at the dawn of the third millennium experienced a "typological turn" (Loprieno 2003: 74)[104], and this diagnosis is supported last but not least by the evidence in this volume. However, turning Lepsius's initially-quoted statement (Lepsius 1837 : 89) into a question, "de quelle importance l'étude du dialecte sacré des Égyptiens peut-elle devenir pour la comparaison des langues"?

11 References

Aarsleff, Hans. 1977. Guillaume de Humboldt et la pensée linguistique des idéologues. In: Joly, André & Stéfanini, Jean (eds.), *La grammaire générale. Des modistes aux idéologues.* Villeneuve-d'Ascq: Presses Universitaires de Lille, 217–241.

Abel, Carl. 1876. *Koptische Untersuchungen.* Berlin: Ferdinand Dümmler.

Abel, Carl. 1878a. *Zur ägyptischen Kritik.* Berlin: Liepmannssohn.

Abel, Carl. 1878b. *Zur ägyptischen Etymologie.* Berlin: Liepmannssohn.

Abel, Carl. 1884. *Über den Gegensinn der Urworte.* Leipzig: Friedrich.

Abel, Carl. 1886. *Einleitung in ein aegyptisch-semitisch-indoeuropaeisches Wurzelwörterbuch.* Leipzig: Friedrich.

Abel, Carl. 1885. Zur Frage nach den Kennzeichen der Sprachverwandtschaft. *Internationale Zeitschrift für allgemeine Sprachwissenschaft* 2: 43–53.

Abel, Carl. 1887. G*egen Herrn Professor Erman. Zwei ägyptologische Antikritiken.* Leipzig: Friedrich.

Abel, Carl. 1890a. *Aegyptisch und Indogermanisch.* Frankfurt/M.: Knaur.

Abel, Carl. 1890b. *Aegyptisch-indoeuropäische Sprachverwandtschaft.* (Einzelbeiträge zu allgemeinen und vergleichenden Sprachwissenschaft 6). Leipzig: Friedrich.

Abel, Carl. 1891a. *Offener Brief an Prof. Dr. Gustav Meyer in Sachen der ägyptisch-indogermanischen Sprachverwandtschaft.* Leipzig: Friedrich.

---

104 "As for the language features that are being studied, there has been a rather dramatic shift in the general interests of Egyptian linguistics from issues of *syntax* to issues of *typology*. ... This shift ... implies that features of the Egyptian language that were previously considered within the frame of Egyptian itself are now read in the light of general trends in the history of human language, i.e., of what linguists call *universals*."

Abel, Carl. 1891b. *Nachtrag zum offenen Brief an Prof. Dr. Gustav Meyer in Sachen der ägyptisch-indogermanischen Sprachverwandtschaft.* Leipzig: Friedrich.

Adelung, Johann Christoph. 1806–1817. *Mithridates oder allgemeine Sprachenkunde mit dem Vater Unser als Sprachprobe in bey nahe fünfhundert Sprache und Mundarten.* Berlin: Voss.

Åkerblad, Johan David. 1802. *Lettre sur l'inscription égyptienne de Rosette, adressée au C.en Silvestre de Sacy, Professeur de la langue Arabe à l'école spéciale des langues Orientales vivantes, & c.* Paris: Imprimerie de la République.

Alter, Stephen G. 2005. *William Dwight Whitney and the Science of Language.* Baltimore: The Johns Hopkins University Press.

Aschenberg, Heidi. 2001. Typologie als Charakterologie. In: Haspelmath, Martin, König, Ekkehard, Oesterreicher, Wulf & Raible, Wolfgang (eds.), *Language typology and language universals. An international handbook.* (Handbücher zur Sprach- und Kommunikationswissenschaft 20.1). Berlin/New York: De Gruyter, 266–274.

Aufrère, Sydney H. 1999. La lutte dans l'Europe des érudits pour les scalae copto-arabes… La redécouverte de la langue copte aux XVIe et XVIIe siècles. In: Aufrère, Sydney H. & Bosson, Nathalie (eds.) *Égyptes… L'Égyptien et le copte.* Lattes, 91–108.

Auroux, Sylvain, Koerner, E.F.K., Niederehe, Hans-Josef & Versteegh, Kees (eds.). 2001. *History of the Language Sciences. Geschichte der Sprachwissenschaften. Histoire des sciences du langage.* (Handbücher zur Sprach- und Kommunikationswissenschaft 18.2). Berlin/New York: De Gruyter.

Bär, Jochen. 2002. August Wilhelm Schlegels Unterscheidung des „synthetischen" und des „analytischen" Sprachbaus: Pionierleistung der Sprachtypologie oder sprachphilosophisch-literaturkritische Reminiszenz? *Historiographia Linguistica* 29: 71–94.

Benfey, Theodor. 1844. *Ueber das Verhältniss der ägyptischen Sprache zum semitischen Sprachstamm.* Leipzig: F.A. Brockhaus.

Benfey, Theodor. 1869. *Geschichte der Sprachwissenschaft und orientalischen Philologie in Deutschland.* München: J.G. Cotta

Bense, Gertrud, Meiser, Gerhard, Werner, Edeltraud (eds.). 2006. *Beiträge der Halleschen Tagung anlässlich des zweihundertsten Geburtstages von August Friedrich Pott (1802–1887).* (Hallesche Sprach- und Textforschung 9). Frankfurt/M./Berlin/Bern/Wien: Lang.

Bickel, Susanne, Fischer-Elfert, Hans-W., Loprieno, Antonio & Richter, Tonio Sebastian (eds.). 2013. *Ägyptologen und Ägyptologien zwischen Kaiserreich und Gründung der beiden deutschen Staaten. Reflexionen zur Geschichte und Episteme eines altertumswissenschaftlichen Fachs im 150. Jahr der Zeitschrift für Ägyptische Sprache und Altertumskunde.* (Beihefte zur Zeitschrift für Ägyptische Sprache und Altertumskunde 1). Berlin/New York: De Gruyter Akademie

Birch, Samuel & Wilkinson, Gardner. 1857. *The Egyptians in the time of the pharaohs: being a companion to the Crystal palace Egyptian collections. To which is added an introduction to the study of the Egyptian hieroglyphs.* London: Bradbury & Evans.

Blumenthal, Elke. 1981. *Altes Ägypten in Leipzig.* Leipzig: Karl-Marx-Universität.

Blumenthal, Elke. 1999. *Ein Leipziger Grabdenkmal im ägyptischen Stil und die Anfänge der Ägyptologie in Deutschland.* (Kleine Schriften des Ägyptischen Museums der Universität Leipzig 4). Leipzig 1999.

Bopp, Franz. 1833. *Vergleichende Grammatik des Sanskrit, Zend, Armenischen, Griechischen, Lateinischen, Litthauischen, Altslavischen, Gothischen und Deutschen. (3rd ed. 1868–1871)*. 3 vols. Berlin: Dümmler

Bopp, Franz. 1841. *Über die Verwandtschaft der malaiisch-polynesischen Sprachen mit dem Indogermanischen*, Berlin: Dümmler.

Bühler, Karl. 1934. *Sprachtheorie. Die Darstellungsfunktion der Sprache.* Jena: Fischer.

Bühler, Karl. 2011. *Theory of Language. The representational function of language.* [Sprachtheorie. Die Darstellungsfunktion der Sprache (1934). Translated by Donald Fraser Goodwin]. Amsterdam – Philadelphia: John Benjamins.

Bumann, Waltraud. 1965. *Die Sprachtheorie Heymann Steinthals dargestellt im Zusammenhang mit seiner Theorie der Geisteswissenschaft.* (Monographien zur philosophischen Forschung 39). Meisenheim am Glan: Hain.

Bunsen, Christian Karl Josias. 1844–1857. *Ägyptens Stelle in der Weltgeschichte.* 5 vols. Hamburg: F. Perthes.

Bynon, Theodora. 2001. The synthesis of comparative and historical Indo-European Studies: August Schleicher. In: Auroux, Sylvain, Koerner, E.F.K., Niederehe, Hans-Josef & Versteegh, Kees (eds.), *History of the Language Sciences. Geschichte der Sprachwissenschaften. Histoire des sciences du langage.* (Handbücher zur Sprach- und Kommunikationswissenschaft 18.3), 1223–1239.

Byrne, James. 1885. *General Principles of the Structure of Language.* London: Trübner.

Chabas, François Joseph. 1865. *Sur l'étude de la langue égyptienne.* Chalons sur-Saone.

Champollion, Jean François. 1822. *Lettre à M. Dacier relative à l'alphabet des hiéroglyphes phonétiques par M. Champollion le jeune.* Paris: Didot.

Champollion, Jean-François. 1824a. *Précis du système hiéroglyphique des anciens égyptiens, ou recherches sur les éléments de cette écriture sacrée, sur leurs diverses combinaisons, et sur les rapports de ce système avec les autres méthodes graphiques égyptiennes.* Paris : Treuttel et Würtz.

Champollion, Jean-François. 1824b. *Lettre à M. Letronne, sur l'expression phonétique de Pétéménon et de Cléopâtre, dans les hiéroglyphes de la momie rapportée par M. Cailliaud.* Paris: A. Dobée.

Champollion, Jean-François. 1826. *Lettre à M. le duc de Blacas d'Aulps ... sur le nouveau système hiéroglyphique de MM Spohn et Seyffarth.* Florence: Guillaume Piatti.

Champollion, Jean François. 1836. *Grammaire égyptienne, ou principes généraux de l'écriture sacrée égyptienne appliquée à la représentation de la langue parlée, par Champollion le Jeune, publiée sur le manuscrit autographe, par l'ordre d M. Guizot.* Paris: Typographie de Firmin Didot frères.

Corbett, Greville G. 2005. Number of Genders. In: Haspelmath, Martin, Dryer, Matthew S., Gil, David & Comrie, Bernard (eds.), *The World Atlas of Language Structure*, Oxford University Press, 126–129.

Corbett, Greville G. 2006. Gender, grammatical. In: Brown, Keith (ed.), *The Encyclopedia of Language and Linguistics.* 2nd ed. Oxford: Elsevier, 749–756.

Daniels, Peter D. 1998. Survey on languages of the world. In: Hill, Jane H., Mistry, P.J. & Campbell, Lyle (eds.), *The Life of Language. Papers in Linguistics in Honor of William Bright.* (Trends in Linguistics. Studies and Monographs 108). Berlin/New York: De Gruyter, 193–220.

Dawson, Warren R. & Uphill, Eric P. 1995. *Who Was Who in Egyptology.* 3rd ed. Bierbrier, Morris L. (ed.). London: The Egypt Exploration Society.

Deichler, Susanne. 2004. "Wörter für das Auge". Wilhelm von Humboldts Reaktion auf die Lesbarkeit der Hieroglyphen. *Göttinger Miszellen* 201: 17–31.

Di Cesare, Donatella. 1996. "Innere Sprachform": Humboldts Grenzbegriff, Steinthals Begriffsgrenze. *Historiographica Linguistica* 23: 321–346.

Diemke, Willy. 1934. *Die Entstehung hypotaktischer Sätze. Dargestellt an der Entwicklung des Relativsatzes in der Sprache der alten Ägypter*. Diss. Wien.

Driem, George van. 2001: *Languages of the Himalayas. An Ethnolinguistic handbook*. (HdO II.10). Leiden/New York/Köln: Brill.

Ebers, Georg. 1871 (1875²). *Ueber das hieroglyphische Schriftsystem. Vortrag, gehalten im Saale des Gewandhauses zu Leipzig am 17. März 1871*. (Sammlung gemeinverständlicher wissenschaftlicher Vorträge, VI.131). Berlin: Lüderitz'sche Verlagsbuchhhandlung.

Ebers, Georg. 1885a. *Richard Lepsius, ein Lebensbild*. Leipzig: Wilhelm Engelmann.

Ebers, Georg. 1885b. Richard Lepsius besonders als Linguist. *Internationale Zeitschrift für allgemeine Sprachwissenschaft* 2: i–xxxi.

Emmel, Stephen. 2004. Coptic Studies before Kircher. In: Immerzeel, M. & van der Vliet, J. (eds.), *Coptic. Studies on the Threshold of a New Millennium*. (Orientalia Lovaniensia Analecta 133.1). Leuven: Peeters, 1–11.

Endesfelder, Erika. 1988. *Die Ägyptologie an der Berliner Universität: Zur Geschichte eines Fachgebietes*. (Berichte der Humboldt-Universität 8.6). Berlin.

Endesfelder, Erika. 1990. Moritz Gotthilf Schwartze (1802–1848), erster Professor für koptische Sprache und Literatur an der Berliner Universität". In: Nagel, Peter (ed.), *Carl-Schmidt-Kolloquium an der Martin-Luther-Universität 1988*. Halle/Saale: Martin-Luther-Universität, 105–117.

Endesfelder, Erika. 2003. Die Ägyptologie an der Berliner Universität. In: Endesfelder, Erika (ed.), *Von Berlin nach Meroe. Erinnerungen an den Ägyptologen Fritz Hintze (1915–1993)*. (Asien- und Afrikastudien der Humboldt-Universität zu Berlin 3). Wiesbaden: Harrassowitz, 21–29.

Erman, Adolf. 1875. Über eine dem Dualis eigenthümliche Form des Suffix *f*. *Zeitschrift für Ägyptische Sprache und Altertumskunde* 13: 76–77.

Erman, Adolf. 1876. Über den Werth der in altägyptischen Texten vorkommenden semitischen Lehnwörter. *Zeitschrift für Ägyptische Sprache und Altertumskunde* 14: 38–42.

Erman, Adolf. 1878a. *Die Pluralbildung des Aegyptischen: Ein grammatischer Versuch*. Leipzig: Engelmann.

Erman, Adolf. 1878b. Review of Carl Abel, Koptische Untersuchungen. *Zeitschrift der Deutschen Morgenländischen Gesellschaft* 32: 763–766.

Erman, Adolf. 1880. *Neuaegyptische Grammatik*. Leipzig: Wilhelm Engelmann.

Erman, Adolf. 1881. Altägyptische Studien. *Zeitschrift für Ägyptische Sprache und Altertumskunde* 19: 41–66.

Erman, Adolf. 1882. Commentar zur Inschrift des Una. *Zeitschrift für Ägyptische Sprache und Altertumskunde* 20: 1–29.

Erman, Adolf. 1883. Die tonlosen Formen in der ägyptischen Sprache. *Zeitschrift für Ägyptische Sprache und Altertumskunde* 21: 37–40.

Erman, Adolf. 1884. Spuren eines alten Subjunktivs im Koptischen. *Zeitschrift für Ägyptische Sprache und Altertumskunde* 22: 28–37.

Erman, Adolf. 1887. Review of Carl Abel, Einleitung in ein aegyptisch-semitisch-indoeuropaeisches Wurzelwörterbuch. *Deutsche Literaturzeitung*: 1237.

Erman, Adolf. 1889. Eine neue Art der ägyptischen Konjugation. *Zeitschrift für Ägyptische Sprache und Altertumskunde* 27: 65–84.

Erman, Adolf. 1890. *Die Sprache des Papyrus Westcar. Eine Vorarbeit zur Grammatik der älteren ägyptischen Sprache.* (Abhandlungen der Königlichen Gesellschaft der Wissenschaften in Göttingen, Hist.-Phil. Kl. 36.2). Göttingen: Dieterich.

Erman, Adolf. 1892. Das Verhältnis des Aegyptischen zu den semitischen Sprachen. *Zeitschrift der Deutschen Morgenländischen Gesellschaft* 46: 93–129.

Erman, Adolf. 1894a. *Ägyptische Grammatik. Mit Schrifttafel, Litteratur, Lesestücken und Wörterverzeichnis.* (= Porta linguarum orientalium XV). Berlin: Reuther und Reinhard.

Erman, Adolf. 1894b. Ein neuer Rest der alten Flexion im Koptischen. *Zeitschrift für Ägyptische Sprache und Altertumskunde* 32: 128–130.

Erman, Adolf. 1922. *Die Entzifferung der Hieroglyphen.* (Sitzungsberichte der Preußischen Akademie der Wissenschaften zu Berlin, phil.-hist. Kl.). Berlin: xxxx, xxvii–xliii.

Erman, Adolf. 1929. *Mein Werden und mein Wirken. Erinnerungen eines alten Berliner Gelehrten.* Leipzig: Quelle & Meyer.

Ewald, Heinrich. 1861. *Abhandlung über den bau der thatwörter im Koptischen.* Göttingen: Dieterichsche Buchhandlung.

Ewald, Heinrich. 1862. *Abhandlung über den zusammenhang des Nordischen (Türkischen), Mittelländischen, Semitischen und Koptischen sprachstamms.* Göttingen: Dieterichsche Buchhandlung.

Finck, Nikolaus. 1901. *Die Klassifikation der Sprachen.* Marburg: N.G. Elwert.

Finck, Nikolaus. 1909. *Die Sprachstämme des Erdkreises.* (Aus Natur und Geisteswelt 267). Leipzig: Teubner.

Finck, Nikolaus. 1910. *Die Haupttypen des Sprachbaus.* (Aus Natur und Geisteswelt 268). Leipzig: Teubner.

Freier, Elke & Reineke, Walter F. 1988. *Karl Richard Lepsius: (1810–1884); Akten der Tagung anlässlich seines 100. Todestages, 10.–12.7.1984 in Halle.* Berlin: Akademie der Wissenschaften der DDR, Zentralinstitut für Alte Geschichte und Archäologie.

Funk, Wolf-Peter. 2003. Fritz Hintzes Beitrag zur Erforschung des Koptischen. In: Endesfelder, Erika (ed.), *Von Berlin nach Meroe. Erinnerungen an den Ägyptologen Fritz Hintze (1915–1993).* (Asien- und Afrikastudien der Humboldt-Universität zu Berlin 3). Wiesbaden: Harrassowitz, 73–76.

Gabelentz, Georg von der. 1891 (1901²). *Die Sprachwissenschaft. Ihre Aufgaben, Methoden und bisherigen Ergebisse.* Leipzig: Weigel.

Gabelentz, Georg von der. 1894. Hypologie [sic] der Sprachen, eine neue Aufgabe der Linguistik. *Indogermanistische Forschungen* 4: 1–7.

Gady, Erik. 2013. Deux décennies de relations égyptologiques franco-allemandes à travers la ZÄS. In: Bickel, Susanne, Fischer-Elfert, Hans-W., Loprieno, Antonio & Richter, Tonio Sebastian (eds.), *Ägyptologen und Ägyptologien zwischen Kaiserreich und Gründung der beiden deutschen Staaten. Reflexionen zur Geschichte und Episteme eines altertumswissenschaftlichen Fachs im 150. Jahr der Zeitschrift für Ägyptische Sprache und Altertumskunde.* (Beihefte zur Zeitschrift für Ägyptische Sprache und Altertumskunde 1). Berlin/New York: De Gruyter, 39–61.

Gardiner, Alan. 1927. *Egyptian Grammar, being an introduction to the study of hieroglyphs,* Oxford: Clarendon press.

Gardiner, Alan. 1932: *The Theory of Speech and Language.* Oxford: Clarendon press.

Gardiner, Alan. 1951: *The Theory of Speech and Language.* 2nd ed. Oxford: Clarendon press.

Gardiner, Alan. 1954: *The Theory of Proper Names. A Controversial Essay*. Oxford: University Press.

Gertzen, Thomas. 2012. *École de Berlin und Goldenes Zeitalter (1882–1914) der Ägyptologie als Wissenschaft. Das Lehrer-Schüler-Verhältnis von G. Ebers, A. Erman und K. Sethe*. Berlin/ New York: De Gruyter.

Gertzen, Thomas. 2013. "Brennpunkt" Zeitschrift für Ägyptische Sprache und Altertumskunde. Die redaktionelle Korrespondenz ihres Gründers H. Brugsch (1827–1894) mit seinen Mitarbeitern und Nachfolgern und die Bedeutung wissenschaftlicher Fachzeitschriften für die Disziplinengenese der Ägyptologie in Deutschland", in: Bickel, Susanne, Fischer-Elfert, Hans-W., Loprieno, Antonio & Richter, Tonio Sebastian (eds.), *Ägyptologen und Ägyptologien zwischen Kaiserreich und Gründung der beiden deutschen Staaten. Reflexionen zur Geschichte und Episteme eines altertumswissenschaftlichen Fachs im 150. Jahr der Zeitschrift für Ägyptische Sprache und Altertumskunde*. (Beihefte zur Zeitschrift für Ägyptische Sprache und Altertumskunde 1). Berlin/New York: De Gruyter, 63–112.

Grapow, Hermann. 1954. *Worte des Gedenkens an Adolf Erman anläßlich seines hundertsten Geburtstages am 31. Oktober 1954*. (Sitzungsberichte der Deutschen Akademie der Wissenschaften zu Berlin. Klasse für Sprache, Literatur und Kunst, 3). Berlin: Akademie.

Greenberg, Joseph H. (ed.). 1980. *Universals of language. Report of a Conference held at Dobbs Ferry, New York, April 13–15, 1961*. 2nd ed., 7th printing. Cambridge, Massachusetts, London: M.I.T. Press.

Greenberg, Joseph H. 1966. *Language Universals. With special reference to feature hierarchies* (= Janua Linguarum. Series Minor. LIX). The Hague/Paris: Mouton.

Greenberg, Joseph H. 1957. *Essays in Linguistics*. Chicago: University Press.

Grimm, Alfred. 2004. Zimmer mit Aussicht oder Wir entziffern nicht mehr, wir lesen. Eine wissenschaftsgeschichtliche Collage zur Entzifferungsgeschichte der Hieroglyphen 1800–1850. In: Burkard, Günter, Grimm, Alfred, Schoske, Sylvia & Verbovsek, Alexandra (eds.), *Kon-Texte. Akten des Symposiums "Spurensuche – Altägypten im Spiegel seiner Texte". München 2.–4. Mai 2003*. (Ägypten und Altes Testament 60). Wiesbaden: Harrasowitz, 7–35.

Grimm, Alfred. 2006. Wege – Werke – Wirkungen: Anfänge und Kritik ägyptologischer Forschung im 19. Jahrhundert. In: Schipper, Bernd Ulrich (ed.), *Ägyptologie als Wissenschaft. Adolf Erman (1854–1937) in seiner Zeit*. Berlin/New York: De Gruyter, 65–89.

De Guignes, Joseph. 1759. *Mémoire dans lequel on prouve que les Chinois sont une colonie égyptienne. Lû dans l'Assemblée publique de l'Académie Royale des Inscriptions & Belles-Lettres, le 14 Novembre 1758*. Paris: Desaint & Saillant.

Gunn, Battiscombe. 1924. *Studies in Egyptian Syntax*. Paris: Geuthner.

Hartleben, Hermine. 1906. *Champollion. Sein Leben und sein Werk*. 2 vols. Berlin: Weidmann.

Hartleben, Hermine. 1909. *Lettres de Champollion le jeune*. (Bibliothèque égyptologique contenant les œuvres des égyptologues français 30–31). Paris: Leroux.

Hasznos, Andrea. 2012. *Graeco-Coptica. Greek and Coptic Clause Patterns*. (Göttinger Orient-forschungen, IV. Reihe: Ägypten 52). Wiesbaden: Harrassowitz.

Heepe, Martin (ed.). 1928. *Lautzeichen und ihre Anwendung in verschiedenen Sprachgebieten*. Berlin: Reichsdruckerei.

Hincks, Edward. 1848. An Attempt to Ascertain the Number, Names, and Powers, of the Letters of the Hieroglyphic, or Ancient Egyptian Alphabet; Grounded on the Establishment of a New Principle in the Use of Phonetic Characters. *Transactions of the Royal Irish Academy* 21: 132–232.

Hintze, Fritz. 1947. Die Haupttendenzen der ägyptischen Sprachentwicklung. *Zeitschrift für Phonetik und allgemeine Sprachwissenschaft* 1: 85–108.

Hintze, Fritz. 1950. "Konversion" und "analytische Tendenz" in der ägyptischen Sprachentwicklung. *Zeitschrift für Phonetik und allgemeine Sprachwissenschaft* 4: 41–56.

Hintze, Fritz. 1972. *Champollion – Entzifferer der Hieroglyphen. Festvortrag zum 150. Jahrestag der Entzifferung der Hieroglyphen am 22. September 1822.* Berlin: Staatliche Museen.

Humboldt, Wilhelm von. 1822. *Über das vergleichende Sprachstudium in Bezug auf die Epochen der Sprachentwicklung.* (Abhandlungen der Königlichen Akademie der Wissenschaften 1820/21). Berlin: Druckerei der königlichen Akademie der Wissenschaften, 239–260.

Humboldt, Wilhelm von. 1825. *Über das Entstehen der grammatischen Formen, und ihren Einfluss auf die Ideenentwicklung.* (Abhandlungen der Königlichen Akademie der Wissenschaften 1822/23). Berlin: Druckerei der königlichen Akademie der Wissenschaften, 401–430.

Humboldt, Wilhelm von. 1826. *Über die Buchstabenschrift und ihren Zusammenhang mit dem Sprachbau.* (Abhandlungen der Königlichen Akademie der Wissenschaften 1824). Berlin: Druckerei der königlichen Akademie der Wissenschaften, 161–188.

Humboldt, Wilhelm von. 1828. *Über vier ägyptische, löwenköpfige Bildsäulen.* (Abhandlungen der Königlichen Akademie der Wissenschaften 1825) Berlin: Druckerei der königlichen Akademie der Wissenschaften, 145–168.

Humboldt, Wilhelm von. 1830. *Über den Dualis.* (Abhandlungen der Königlichen Akademie der Wissenschaften 1827). Berlin: Druckerei der königlichen Akademie der Wissenschaften, 161–187.

Humboldt, Wilhelm von. 1836. *Ueber die Verschiedenheit des menschlichen Sprachbaus.* Ed. by Buschmann, Johann Carl Eduard. Berlin: Dümmler.

Humboldt, Wilhelm von. 1841–1852. *Wihelm von Humboldt's gesammelte Werke.* Ed. by Brandes, Carl. Berlin: Reimer.

Humboldt, Wilhelm von. 1903–1936. *Gesammelte Schriften.* Berlin: B.Behrs Verlag, Leipzig: Friedrich Feddersen.

Ideler, Julius Ludovicus. 1841. *Hermapion sive rudimenta hieroglyphicæ veterum Aegyptorum literaturæ scripsit.* Leipzig: F.C.G. Vogel.

Irmscher, Johannes. 1988. Berlin und die Koptologie. In: Görg, Manfred (ed.), *Religion im Erbe Ägyptens. Beiträge zur spätantiken Religionsgeschichte zu Ehren von Alexander Böhlig.* (Ägypten und Altes Testament 14), 73–83.

Jablonski, Paul Ernst. 1804. Collectio et explicatio vocum Aegyptiacarum, quarum mentio apud scriptores veteres occurit. In: te Water, Jona Wilhelm (ed.), *Pauli Ernesti Jablonski opuscula quibus lingua et antiquitas Aegytiorum, difficilia librorum sacrorum loca et historiae ecclesiasticae capita illustrantur, magnam partem nunc primum in lucem protracta, vel ab ipso auctore emendata ac locupletata; edidit atque animadversiones adjecit Jona Guilielmus te Water.* Leiden: A. & T. Honkoop.

James, Thomas G.H. 1997. William John Bankes, Egypt and Kingston Lacy. In: Staehelin, Elisabeth, Jaeger, Bertrand & Hofmeier, Thomas (eds.), *Ägypten-Bilder. Akten des „Symposiums zur Ägypten-Rezeption", Augs bei Basel, vom 9.–11. September 1993.* (Orbis Biblicus et Orientalis 150), 301–312.

Jespersen, Otto. 1925. *Die Sprache. Ihre Natur, Entwicklung und Entstehung.* (Indogermanische Bibliothek, 4. Abt, 3. Bd.). Heidelberg: Carl Winter.

Kammerzell, Frank. 1991. Augment, Stamm und Endung. Zur morphologischen Entwicklung der Stativkonjugation. *Lingua Aegyptia* 1: 165–199.

Kammerzell, Frank. 1996. Lepsius, Karl Richard. In: Stammerjohann, Harro (ed.), *Lexicon grammaticorum. Who's who in the history of world linguistics*. Tübingen: Niemeyer, 563–565.

Kammerzell, Frank. 2009. Lepsius, Karl Richard. In: Stammerjohann, Harro (ed.), *Lexicon grammaticorum. Bio-bibliographical companion to the history of linguistics*. Vol. II. Tübingen: Niemeyer, 891–893.

Kircher, Athanasius. 1636. *Prodromus coptus sive agyptiacus …* Rom: Typ. Sc. Congreg. de propag. fide.

Klaproth, Heinrich Julius. 1823. *Lettre à M. Champollion le jeune relative à l'affinité du Cophte avec les langues du Nord de l'Asie et du Nord-Est de l'Europe*. Paris: Dondey-Dupré.

Klaproth, Heinrich Julius. 1823. *Asia polyglotta*. Paris: Schubert.

Klaproth, Heinrich Julius. 1832. *Examen critique des travaux de feu M. Champollion sur les hiéroglyphes*. Paris: Dondey-Dupré.

Klaproth, Heinrich Julius. 1827. *Seconde lettre sur les Hiéroglyphes adressée à M. de S*****. Paris: J.-S. Merlin.

Knobloch, Clemens. 1988. *Geschichte der psychologischen Sprachauffasssung in Deutschland von 1850 bis 1920*. Tübingen: Niemeyer

Knobloch, Clemens. 2001. Die Beziehungen zwischen Sprache und Denken: Die Ideen Wilhelm von Humboldts und die Anfänge der sprachpsychologischen Forschung. In: Auroux, Sylvain, Koerner, E.F.K., Niederehe, Hans-Josef & Versteegh, Kees (eds.), *History of the Language Sciences. Geschichte der Sprachwissenschaften. Histoire des sciences du langage*. (Handbücher zur Sprach- und Kommunikationswissenschaft 18.2). Berlin/New York: De Gruyter, 1663–1679.

Koerner, E.F. Konrad. 1970. Franz Nikolaus Finck (1897–1910): Zur 60. Wiederkehr des Todestages eines grossen Sprachwissenschaftlers aus dem Niederrhein. *Der Niederrhein* 37: 91–94.

Koerner, E.F. Konrad. 1973. *The Importance of Techmer's "Internationale Zeitschrift fuer Allgemeine Sprachwissenschaft" in the development of general linguistics*. Amsterdam: Benjamins.

Krapf, Johann Ludwig. 1850. *Outline of the Elements of the Kisuaheli Language, with Special Reference to the Kinika Dialect*. Tübingen: L.F. Fues

Krause, Martin. 1998. *Die Koptologie und ihre Forschungsgeschichte. In: Krause, Martin (ed.), Ägypten in spätantik-christlicher Zeit. Einführung in die koptische Kultur*. (Sprachen und Kulturen des Christlichen Orients 4). Wiesbaden: Reichert, 1–33.

Lehmann, Winfred P. 1969. *Einführung in die historische Linguistik*. Heidelberg: Carl Winter.

Leopold, Joan. 1989. The Last Battle over the Tower of Babel: The controversy between August Friedrich Pott and Franz Kaulen. In: Gessinger, J. & von Rahden, W. (eds.). *Theorien vom Ursprung der Sprache*. Vol. 11. Berlin/New York: De Gruyter, 548–560.

Lepsius, Richard. 1833. *De tabulis Eugubinis: dissertatio philologica*. Berolini: Academ. Scient.

Lepsius, Richard. 1834. *Palaeographie als Mittel für die Sprachforschung, zunächst am Sanskrit nachgewiesen*. Berlin: Oehmigke.

Lepsius, Richard. 1835. Über die prôta stoicheia in der Stelle bei Clemens Alexandrinus über die Schrift der Ägypter. *Rheinisches Mueum für Philologie* 4: 142–148.

Lepsius, Richard. 1836a. Über die Anordnung und Verwandtschaft des semitischen, indischen, äthiopischen, alt-persischen und alt-ägyptischen Alphabets. In: Lepsius, Richard, *Zwei sprachvergleichende Abhandlungen*. Berlin: Dümmler.

Lepsius, Richard. 1836b. Die Verwandtschaft der Zahlwörter in der indogermanischen, semitischen und der koptischen Sprache. In: Lepsius, Richard, *Zwei sprachvergleichende Abhandlungen*. Berlin: Dümmler.

Lepsius, Richard. 1837. *Lettre à M. le professeur H. Rosellini sur l'alphabet hiéroglyphique*, Roma.

Lepsius, Richard. 1841. *Inscriptiones Umbricae et Oscae*. Leipzig: G. Wigand.

Lepsius, Richard. 1844. *Zwei Reiseberichte aus Philae in Oberägypten vom 10. September 1844*. (Bericht über die zur Bekanntgabe geeigneten Verhandlungen der Königl. Preuß. Akademie der Wissenschaften zu Berlin), 373–406.

Lepsius, Richard. 1855a. *Das allgemeine linguistische Alphabet. Grundsätze der Übertragung fremder Schriftsysteme und bisher noch ungeschriebener Sprachen in europäische Buchstaben*. Leipzig: Wilhelm Besser.

Lepsius, Richard. 1855b. *Standard Alphabet for reducing unwritten languages and foreign graphic systems to a uniform orthography in European letters*. London: Seeleys

Lepsius, Richard. 1855c. *Mittheilung in Bezug auf das von ihm aufgestellte Allgemeine Linguistische Alphabet, dessen Typen ... für die Akademische Druckerei angefertigt werden sollten: [Nebst] Bericht über den akademischen Typenguß und die fortschreitende Verbreitung des allgemeinen linguistischen Alphabets*. (Monatsber. d. Kgl. Akad. d. Wiss. zu Berlin. Sitzg v. 15. Febr. u. 20. Dez. 1855), 784–788.

Lepsius, Richard. 1860. *Über die Umschrift und die Lautverhältnisse einiger hinterasiatischer Sprachen, namentlich des Chinesischen und des Tibetischen*. (Abhandlungen der Kgl. Akad. d. Wiss. zu Berlin. Phil.-hist. Abhandlungen 1860), 449–496.

Lepsius, Richard. 1861. *Über die arabischen Sprachlaute und deren Umschrift nebst einigen Erläuterungen über den harten i-Vokal in der tartarischen, slavischen und der rumänischen Sprache*. (Abhandlungen der Kgl. Akad. d. Wiss. zu Berlin. Phil.-hist. Abhandlungen 1861), 97–152.

Lepsius, Richard. 1862a. *Das ursprüngliche Zend-Alphabet*. (Abhandlungen der Kgl. Akad. d. Wiss. zu Berlin. Phil.-hist. Abhandlungen 1862), 293–383.

Lepsius, Richard. 1862b. Litterae guturales und litterae faucales. *Zeitschrift für vergleichende Sprachforschung* 11: 442ff.

Lepsius, Richard. 1863a. *Standard alphabet for reducing unwritten languages and foreign graphic systems to a uniform orthography in European letters, recommended for adoption by the Church Missionary Society*. 2nd ed. London: Williams & Norgate, Berlin: W. Hertz.

Lepsius, Richard. 1863b. *Über das Lautsystem der persischen Keilschrift*. (Abhandlungen der Kgl. Akad. d. Wiss. zu Berlin. Phil.-hist. Abhandlungen 1862), 385–412.

Lepsius, Richard. 1863c. *Über den Umfang und die Verschiedenheit der menschlichen Sprachlaute* (Berliner Monats-Berichte).

Lepsius, Richard. 1866a. Über die Umschrift des Hieroglyphischen. *Zeitschrift für Ägyptische Sprache und Altertumskunde* 4: 73–81.

Lepsius, Richard. 1866b. *Das bilingue Dekret von Kanopus in der Originalgröße mit Übersetzung beider Texte. 1.: Einleitung; Griech. Text mit Übers.; Hieroglyph. Text mit Umschr. u. Interlinearübers*. Berlin: Hertz.

Lepsius, Richard. 1867. Zu dem Artikel des Herrn Baillet (de la transcription des hiéroglyphes). *Zeitschrift für Ägyptische Sprache und Altertumskunde* 5: 70–72.

Lepsius, Richard. 1868. *Über die Anwendung des lateinischen Universal-Alphabets auf den chinesischen Dialekt von Canton und über die Berufung auswärtiger Gelehrter an eine in*

Peking zu gründende kaiserliche Lehranstalt. (Berliner Monats-Berichte 5. März 1868). Berlin.

Lepsius, Richard. 1879. *Über die Sprachgruppen der afrikanischen Völker.* (Abhandlungen der Kgl. Akad. d. Wiss. zu Berlin. Phil.-hist. Abhandlungen 1879).

Lepsius, Richard. 1880. *Nubische Grammatik: mit einer Einleitung über die Völker und Sprachen Afrikas.* Berlin: Hertz.

Loprieno, Antonio. 1986. *Das Verbalsystem im Ägyptischen und im Semitischen. Zur Grundlegung einer Aspekttheorie.* (Göttinger Orientfoschungen 4.17). Wiesbaden: Harrassowitz.

Loprieno, Antonio. 1995. *Ancient Egyptian. A Linguistic Introduction.* Cambridge: University Press.

Loprieno, Antonio. 2003. Egyptian Linguistics in the Year 2000. In: Hawass, Zahi (ed.), *Egyptology at the Dawn of the Twenty-First Century. Proceedings of the Eighth International Congress of Egyptologists Cairo, 2000. Vol. 3: Language, Conservation, Museology.* Cairo/New York: The American University in Cairo Press, 73–90.

Magen, Barbara. 2007. Ludwig Stern. Ein Gelehrter aus Hildesheim. *aMun. Magazin für Freunde der Ägyptischen Museen* 32: 56–58.

Magen, Barbara. 2013. Ludwig Stern – ein Ägyptologe zwischen Keltologie und Bibliothek. In: Bickel Susanne, Fischer-Elfert, Hans-W., Loprieno, Antonio & Richter, Tonio Sebastian (eds.), *Ägyptologen und Ägyptologien zwischen Kaiserreich und Gründung der beiden deutschen Staaten. Reflexionen zur Geschichte und Episteme eines altertumswissenschaftlichen Fachs im 150. Jahr der Zeitschrift für Ägyptische Sprache und Altertumskunde.* (Beihefte zur Zeitschrift für Ägyptische Sprache und Altertumskunde 1). Berlin/New York: De Gruyter, 155–169.

Maspero, Gaston. 1871. *Des formes de la conjugaison en égyptien antique, en démotique et en copte.* (Bibliothèque de l'école des hautes études, sciences philologiques et historiques, sixième fasc.). Paris: Librairie A. Franck.

Mehlitz, Hartmut. 2010. *Richard Lepsius: Ägypten oder die Ordnung der Wissenschaft.* Berlin: Kulturverlag Kadmos.

Messling, Markus. 2005. Bilderschrift und Schriftbilder. Jean-François Champollions anthropologisches Projekt zwischen historischem Partikularismus und zivilisatorischem Universalismus. In: Jostes, Brigitte & Trabant, Jürgen (eds.), *Historische Anthropologie der Sprache.* (Paragrana 14.1). Berlin: Akademie Verlag, 153–180.

Messling, Markus. 2008a. *Pariser Orientlektüren. Zu Wilhelm von Humboldts Theorie der Schrift. Nebst der Erstedition des Briefwechsels zwischen Wilhelm von Humboldt und Jean-François Champollion le jeune (1824–1827).* Humboldt-Studien. Paderborn/München/Wien/Zürich: Schöningh.

Messling, Markus. 2008b. Wilhelm von Humboldt and the „Orient". On Edward W. Said's remarks on Humboldt's Orientalist studies. *Language Sciences* 30.5 (=Special Issue: The History of Linguistics, ed. by Hutton, Christopher M. & Wolf, Hans G.): 482–498.

Messling, Markus. 2009a. Bild und Schrift. Wilhelm von Humboldts Kritik der Hieroglyphen. In: Tintemann, Ute & Messling, Markus (eds.), *„Der Mensch ist nur Mensch durch Sprache". Zur Sprachlichkeit des Menschen.* München: Wilhelm Fink Verlag, 37–49.

Messling, Markus. 2009b. Duell in Rom. Das Ringen um die Hieroglyphen. *Zeitschrift für Ideengeschichte* 3.4 (=Kampfzone): 17–32.

Messling, Markus. 2010. Kulturelle Repräsentation und Macht. Selbstkritik der Philologie in Zeiten ihrer Ermächtigung (Wilhelm von Humboldt, Eugène Jacquet, Jean-Pierre

Abel-Rémusat). In: Häberlein, Mark & Keese, Alexander (eds.), *Sprachgrenzen – Sprachkontakte – kulturelle Vermittler. Kommunikation zwischen Europäern und Außereuropäern (16.–20. Jahrhundert)*. Stuttgart: Steiner, 247–260.

Messling, Markus. 2012. *Champollions Hieroglyphen. Philologie und Weltaneignung*. Berlin: Kulturverlag Kadmos.

Misteli, Franz. 1893. *Charakteristik der hauptsächlichsten Typen des Sprachbaus. Neubearbeitung des Werkes von Prof. H. Steinthal (1861)*. Berlin: Dümmler.

Müller, Hans Wolfgang. 1962. Nachwort. In: Jean-François Champollion le jeune, *Lettre à M. Dacier*. (Milliaria. Faksimiledrucke zur Dokumentation der Geistesentwicklung 2). Aalen: Otto Zeller, 53–65.

Müller, Max. 1861. *Lectures on the Science of Language delivered at the Royal Institution of Great Britain in April, May, and June 1861*. London: Longman, Roberts & Green.

Müller, Max. 1864. *Lectures on the Science of Language delivered at the Royal Institution of Great Britain in February, March, April, & May, 1863*. London: Longman, Roberts & Green.

Mueller-Vollmer, Kurt. 1991. Mutter Sanskrit und die Nacktheit der Südseesprachen: Das Begräbnis von Humboldts Sprachwissenschaft. *Athenäum. Jahrbuch für Romantik* 1: 109–133.

Mueller-Vollmer, Kurt. 1992. Wilhelm von Humboldt's Introduction to the Kawi Language. *Semiotica. Journal of the International Association for Semiotic Studies* 92.1/2: 129–144.

Mueller-Vollmer, Kurt. 1993. *Wilhelm von Humboldts Sprachwissenschaft. Ein kommentiertes Verzeichnis des sprachwissenschaftlichen Nachlasses*. Paderborn: Schöningh.

Naville, Édouard. 1906. Lepsius, Karl Richard. *Allgemeine Deutsche Biographie*. Vol. 51, 659–670.

Oppert, Gustav Salomon. 1879 (1883^2). *On the Classification of Languages: a contribution to comparative philology*. Madras: Higginbotham, London: Trübner.

Oppert, Gustav Salomon. 1883. *On the classification of languages in conformity with ethnology*. London: Harrison and Sons.

Oppert, Gustav Salomon. 1884. Die Verschiedenheiten des Sprachcharakters und deren natürliche Ursache. *Zeitschrift für Ethnologie* 16: 1–16.

Oréal, Elsa. 1999. Contact linguistique. Le cas du rapport entre le grec et le copte. *Lalies* 19: 289–306.

Oréal, Elsa. 2009. Same Source, Different Outcomes? A Reassessment of the Parallel between Ancient Egyptian and Akkadian "Stative" Conjugations. *Lingua Aegyptia* 17: 183–200.

Osthoff, Hermann. 1879. *Das physiologische und psychologische Moment in der sprachlichen Formenbildung*. Berlin: Carl Habel.

Parkinson, Richard B. 1999. *Cracking codes: the Rosetta Stone and decipherment*. With contributions by W. Diffie, M. Fisher and R.S. Simpson. London: British Museum Press.

Paul, Hermann. 1920. *Prinzipien der Sprachgeschichte*. Halle: Max Niemeyer.

Plank, Frans. 2001. Typology by the end of the 18th century. In: Auroux, Sylvain, Koerner, E.F.K., Niederehe, Hans-Josef & Versteegh, Kees (eds.), *History of the Language Sciences. Geschichte der Sprachwissenschaften. Histoire des sciences du langage*. (Handbücher zur Sprach- und Kommunikationswissenschaft 18.2). Berlin/New York: De Gruyter, 1399–1414

Poethke, Günter. 1980. Ebers und Jena. *Zeitschrift für Ägyptische Sprache und Altertumskunde* 107: 71–76.

Polotsky, Hans-Jakob. 1944. *Études de syntaxe copte*. Cairo: Société d'archéologie copte.

Polotsky, Hans-Jakob. 1950. Modes grecs en copte? In: *Coptic Studies in honor of W.E. Crum*. Boston: The Byzantine Institute, 73–90.

Polotsky, Hans-Jakob. 1969. Zur altägyptischen Grammatik. *Orientalia* 38: 465–481.

Pott, August Friedrich. 1847 (1868²). *Die quinäre und vigesimale Zählmethode bei Völkern aller Welttheile. Nebst ausführlichen Bemerkungen über die Zahlwörter indogermanischen Stammes und einem Anhange über Fingernamen.* Halle: Schwetschke.

Pott, August Friedrich. 1847. Die wissenschaftliche Gliederung der Sprachwissenschaft: Eine Skizze. *Jahrbuch der freien deutschen Akademie* 1: 185–190.

Pott, August Friedrich. 1852. Zur Frage über die Klassifikation der Sprachen, dargestellt als die Entwicklung der Sprachidee. *Zeitschrift der Deutschen Morgenländischen Gesellschaft* 6: 287–293.

Pott, August Friedrich. 1855. Max Müller und die Kennzeichen der Sprachverwandtschaft. *Zeitschrift der Deutschen Morgenländischen Gesellschaft* 9: 405–464.

Pott, August Friedrich. 1856. *Die Ungleichheit menschlicher Rassen, hauptsächlich vom sprachwissenschaftlichen Standpunkte, unter besonderer Berücksichtigung von des Grafen v. Gobineau gleichnamigen Werke: mit einem Überblick über die Sprachverhältnisse der Völker, ein ethnologischer Versuch.* Lemgo, Detmold: Meyer.

Pott, August Friedrich. 1863. *Anti-Kaulen, oder mythische Vorstellungen vom Ursprunge der Völker und Sprachen. Nebst Beurtheilung der zwei sprachwissenschaftlichen Abhandlungen Heinrich von Ewald's.* Lemgo, Detmold: Meyer'sche Hofbuchhandlung.

Pott, August Friedrich. 1868. *Die Sprachverschiedenheit in Europa an den Zahlwörtern nachgewiesen.* Halle: Verlag der Buchhandung des Waisenhauses.

Pott, August Friedrich. 1876 (1880², 1883³). *Ueber die Verschiedenheit des menschlichen Sprachbaues und ihren Einfluss auf die geistige Entwickelung des Menschengeschlechts von Wilhelm von Humboldt. Mit erläuternden Anmerkungen und Excursen sowie als Einleitung: Humboldt und die Sprachwissenschaft von A.F. Pott.* Berlin: Calvary & Co.

Pott, August Friedrich. 1884a. Einleitung in die allgemeine Sprachwissenschaft. *Internationale Zeitschrift für allgemeine Sprachwissenschaft* 1: 1–68.

Pott, August Friedrich. 1884b. Einleitung in die allgemeine Sprachwissenschaft. Fortsetzung: Zur Litteratur der Sprachenkunde im Allgemeinen. *Internationale Zeitschrift für allgemeine Sprachwissenschaft* 1: 329–354.

Pott, August Friedrich. 1885a. Einleitung in die allgemeine Sprachwissenschaft. Zur Litteratur der Sprachenkunde im Besondern. I. Asien. *Internationale Zeitschrift für allgemeine Sprachwissenschaft* 2: 54–115.

Pott, August Friedrich. 1885b. Einleitung in die allgemeine Sprachwissenschaft. Zur Litteratur der Sprachenkunde im Besondern. I. Asien (Fortsetzung). *Internationale Zeitschrift für allgemeine Sprachwissenschaft* 2: 209–251.

Pott, August Friedrich. 1886. *Allgemeine Sprachwissenschaft und Carl Abel's Aegyptische Sprachstudien.* Leipzig: Wilhelm Friedrich.

Pott, August Friedrich. 1887a. Einleitung in die allgemeine Sprachwissenschaft. Zur Litteratur der Sprachenkunde im Besondern. Asien (Fortsetzung). *Internationale Zeitschrift für allgemeine Sprachwissenschaft* 3: 110–126.

Pott, August Friedrich. 1887b. Einleitung in die allgemeine Sprachwissenschaft. Zur Litteratur der Sprachenkunde Afrikas. *Internationale Zeitschrift für allgemeine Sprachwissenschaft* 3: 249–275.

Pott, August Friedrich. 1889. Einleitung in die allgemeine Sprachwissenschaft. Zur Litteratur der Sprachenkunde Amerikas. *Internationale Zeitschrift für allgemeine Sprachwissenschaft* 4: 67–96.

Pott, August Friedrich. 1890. Einleitung in die allgemeine Sprachwissenschaft (Schluß). Zur Litteratur der Sprachenkunde Australiens. *Internationale Zeitschrift für allgemeine Sprachwissenschaft* 5: 3–18.

Prosdocimi, Aldo Luigi. 1984. *Le Tavole Iguvine*. (Lingue e iscrizioni dell'Italia antica 6). Florence: Olschki.

Quatremère. Étienne. 1808. *Recherches critiques et historiques sur la langue et la littérature de l'Égypte*. Paris: Imprimerie Impériale.

Ray, John. 1994. Edward Hincks and the Progress of Egyptology. In: Cathcart, K. J. (ed.), *The Edward Hincks Bicentenary Lectures*. Dublin: Department of Near Eastern Languages, University College Dublin, 58–74.

Reintges, Chris. 2001. Code-mixing strategies in Coptic Egyptian. *Lingua Aegyptia* 9: 193–237.

Reintges, Chris. 2004. Coptic Egyptian as a Bilingual Language Variety. In: Bádenas de la Peña, Pedro, Torallas Tovar, Sofía & Luján, Eugenio R. (eds.), *Lenguas en contacto: el testimonio escrito*. Madrid, 69–86.

Reintges, Chris. 2006. The Older Egyptian Stative Revisited. *Lingua Aegyptia* 14: 115–134.

Richter, Tonio Sebastian. 2013. "… zwischen der Epoche der Pyramidenerbauer und den Anfängen des Christenthums … " Sprachwandel im ägyptischen Wortschatz und das Leipziger Projekt Database and Dictionary of Greek Loanwords in Coptic (DDGLC). *Denkströme. Journal der Sächsischen Akademie der Wissenschaften* 11: 67–80.

Ringmacher, Manfred. 1996. *Organismus der Sprachidee. H. Steinthals Weg von Humboldt zu Humboldt*. Paderborn: Schöningh.

Ringmacher, Manfred. 2001a. Die Klassifizierung der Sprachen in der Mitte des 19. Jahrhunderts. In: Auroux, Sylvain, Koerner, E.F.K., Niederehe, Hans-Josef & Versteegh, Kees (eds.), *History of the Language Sciences. Geschichte der Sprachwissenschaften. Histoire des sciences du langage.* (Handbücher zur Sprach- und Kommunikationswissenschaft 18.2). Berlin/New York: De Gruyter, 1427–1435.

Ringmacher, Manfred. 2001b. Sprachtypologie und Ethnologie in Europa am Ende des 19. Jahrhunderts. In: Auroux, Sylvain, Koerner, E.F.K., Niederehe, Hans-Josef & Versteegh, Kees (eds.), *History of the Language Sciences. Geschichte der Sprachwissenschaften. Histoire des sciences du langage.* (Handbücher zur Sprach- und Kommunikationswissenschaft 18.2). Berlin/New York: De Gruyter, 1436–1442.

Robins, Robert Henry. 1973. The History of Language Classification. In: Sebeok, Thomas A. (ed.), *Current Trends in Linguistics* II. Hague: Mouton, 3–41.

Rosellini, Ippolito. 1837. *Elementa linguae aegyptiacae vulgo copticae*. Romae.

Rossi, Ignazio. 1808. *Etymologiae Aegptiacae*. Romae.

Rousseau, Jean. 2001. La classification des langues au début du XIXe siècle. In: Auroux, Sylvain, Koerner, E.F.K., Niederehe, Hans-Josef & Versteegh, Kees (eds.), *History of the Language Sciences. Geschichte der Sprachwissenschaften. Histoire des sciences du langage.* (Handbücher zur Sprach- und Kommunikationswissenschaft 18.2). Berlin/New York: De Gruyter, 1414–1426.

Salt, Henry. 1825. *Essay on Dr. Young's and M. Champollion's Phonetic system of Hieroglyphics*. London: Longan.

Salt, Henry. 1827. *Essai sur le système des hiéroglyphes phonétiques du Dr. Young et de M. Champollion, trad. de l'anglais et augm. de notes par L. Devere*. Paris: Hingray.

Sapir, Edward. 1921. *Language. An introduction to the study of speech*. New York: Harcourt, Brace & Co.

Satzinger, Helmut. 2006. Adolf Ermans Forschungen zu Grammatik und Sprache des Alten Ägypten. In: Schipper, Bernd Ulrich (ed.), *Ägyptologie als Wissenschaft. Adolf Erman (1854–1937) in seiner Zeit*. Berlin/New York: De Gruyter, 141–149.

de Saussure, Ferdinand. 1931². *Cours de linguistique générale*. Paris: Payot.

de Saussure, Ferdinand. 1879. *Mémoire sur le système primitif des voyelles dans les langues Indo-européennes*. Leipzig: B.G. Teubner.

Schenkel, Wolfgang. 1975. *Die altägyptische Suffixkonjugation*. (Ägyptologische Abhandlungen 32). Harrassowitz: Wiesbaden.

Schenkel, Wolfgang. 1990. *Einführung in die altägyptische Sprachwissenschaft*. Darmstadt: Wissenschaftliche Buchgesellschaft.

Schenkel, Wolfgang. 1994. Die ägyptische Hieroglyphenschrift und ihre Weiterentwicklungen. In: Günther, Hartmut & Ludwig, Otto (eds.), *Schrift und Schriftlichkeit. Ein interdisziplinäres Handbuch internationaler Forschung*. (Handbücher zur Sprach- und Kommunikationswissenschaft 10.1). Berlin/New York: De Gruyter, 289–297.

Schenkel, Wolfgang. 2003. *Die hieroglyphische Schriftlehre und die Realität der hieroglyphischen Graphien*. (Sitzungsberichte der Sächsischen Akademie der Wissenschaften zu Leipzig. Phil.-hist. Kl., 138.5). Stuttgart/Leipzig: S. Hirzel.

Schenkel, Wolfgang. 2008. Review on Kevin J. Cathcart, The Correspondence of Edward Hincks. *Orientalia* 77: 408–412.

Schenkel, Wolfgang. 2012a. Die Entzifferung der Hieroglyphen und Richard Lepsius. In: Lepper, Verena M. & Hafemann, Ingelore (eds.), *Karl Richard Lepsius. Der Begründer der deutschen Ägyptologie*. Berlin: Kulturverlag Kadmos, 37–78.

Schenkel, Wolfgang. 2012b. The Decipherment of Hieroglyphs and Richard Lepsius. *The Bulletin of the Australian Centre for Egyptology* 23 (2012): 105–144.

Schipper, Bernd Ulrich (ed.). 2006. *Ägyptologie als Wissenschaft. Adolf Erman (1854–1937) in seiner Zeit*. Berlin/New York: De Gruyter.

Schlegel, Friedrich. 1808. *Über die Sprache und die Weisheit der Indier*. Heidelberg: Mohr & Zimmer.

Schlegel, August Wilhelm. 1818. *Observations sur la langue et la littérature provençales*. Paris: Librairie grecque-latine-allemande.

Schleicher, August. 1848. *Sprachvergleichende Untersuchungen*. Vol. 1: *Zur vergleichenden Sprachgeschichte*. Bonn: König.

Schleicher, August. 1850. *Linguistische Untersuchungen*. Vol. 2: *Die Sprachen Europas in systematischer Übersicht*. Bonn: König.

Schleicher, August. 1859. *Zur Morphologie der Sprache*. St. Pétersbourg: Academy of Sciences.

Schleicher, August. 1860. *Die deutsche Sprache*. Stuttgart: J.G. Cotta'scher Verlag.

Scholtz, Christian. 1775. *Lexicon Aegyptiaco-latinum ... a Maturino Veyssière la Croze indices adjecit*. C.G. Woide. Oxford: Claredon.

Scholtz, Christian. 1778. *Grammatica Aegyptiaca utriusque dialecti: quam breviavit, illustravit, edidit Carolus G. Woide*. Oxford: Clarendon.

Schwartze, Moritz Gotthilf. 1843. *Das Alte Aegypten oder Sprache, Geschichte, Religion und Verfassung des alten Aegyptens nach den altägyptischen Original-Schriften und dem Mittheilungen der nicht-ägyptischen alten Schriftsteller*. Leipzig: Barth.

Schwartze, Moritz Gotthilf. 1850. *Koptische Grammatik. Herausgegeben nach des Verfassers Tode von Dr. H.[eymann] Steinthal*. Berlin: Dümmler.

Seyffarth, Gustav. 1825. *De Hieroglyphica Aegyptiorum scriptura disserit et orationem aditialem indicit Gustavus Seyffarth*. Leipzig: G. Haack.

Seyffarth, Gustav. 1826a. *Rudimenta Hieroglyphices: accedunt explicationes speciminum hieroglyphicorum glossarium atque alphabeta.* Leipzig: Barth.

Seyffarth, Gustav. 1826b. *Beiträge zur Kenntnis der Literatur, Kunst, Mythologie und Geschichte des alten Aegypten.* 1. Heft. Leipzig: Barth.

Seyffarth, Gustav. 1827. *Brevis defensio hieroglyphice inventae a Fr. Aug. Guil. Spohn et Gustav Seyffarth.* Leipzig: Barth.

Seyffarth, Gustav. 1855. *Grammatica Aegyptiaca. Erste Anleitung zum Uebersetzen altägyptischer Literaturwerke nebst der Geschichte des Hieroglyphenschlüssels.* Gotha: Friedrich Andreas Perthes.

Silvestre De Sacy, Antoine Isaak. 1808. Recherches critiques et historiques sur la langue el la littérature de l'Égypte par E. Quatremère (Compte-rendu). *Le magasin encyclopédique* IV: 241–282.

Spohn, Friedrich August Wilhelm. 1825. *De lingua et literis veterum Aegyptiorum cum permultis tabulis lithographicis literas aegyptiorum tum vulgari tum sacerdotali ratione scriptas explicantibus atque interpretationem Rosettanae aliarumque inscriptionum et aliquot voluminum papyraceorum in sepulcris repertorum exhibentibus accedunt grammatica atque glossarium aegyptiacum edidit et absoluit Gustauus Seyffarth in Acad. Lips. prof. d.* Leipzig: Weidmann.

Stammerjohann, Harro (ed.). 1996. *Lexicon grammaticorum. Who's who in the history of world linguistics.* Tübingen: Niemeyer.

Stammerjohann, Harro (ed.). 2009. *Lexicon grammaticorum. Bio-bibliographical companion to the history of linguistics.* 2 vols. Tübingen: Niemeyer.

Steinthal, Heymann. 1848. *Die Sprachwissenschaft Wilh. v. Humboldt's und die Hegel'sche Philosophie.* Berlin: Dümmler.

Steinthal, Heymann. 1850. *Classification der Sprachen, dargestellt als die Entwickelung der Sprachidee.* Berlin: Dümmler.

Steinthal, Heymann. 1851. *Der Ursprung der Sprache im Zusammenhange mit den letzten Fragen alles Wissens. Eine Darstellung der Ansicht Wilhelm v. Humboldts, verglichen mit denen Herders und Hamanns.* Berlin: Dümmler.

Steinthal, Heymann. 1852. *Die Entwicklung der Schrift ... nebst einem offenen Sendschreiben an Herrn Prof. Pott.* Berlin: Dümmler.

Steinthal, Heymann. 1860. *Charakteristik der hauptsächlichsten Typen des Sprachbaus.* Berlin: Dümmler.

Steinthal, Heymann. 1867. *Die Mandé-Neger-Sprachen psychologisch und phonetisch betrachtet.* Berlin: Dümmler.

Steinthal, Heymann 1880. *Gesammelte kleine Schriften. I. Sprachwissenschaftliche Abhandlungen und Recensionen.* Berlin: Dümmler.

Steinthal, Heymann. 1884. *Die sprachphilosophischen Werke Wilhelm's von Humboldt, herausgegeben und erklärt von H. Steinthal.* Berlin: Dümmler.

Stern, Ludwig. 1874. Urkunde über den Bau des Sonnentempels zu On. Eine hieratische Handschrift auf Leder im Königlichen Museum zu Berlin. *Zeitschrift für Ägyptische Sprache und Altertumskunde* 12: 85–96.

Stern, Ludwig. 1880. *Koptische Grammatik.* Leipzig: T.O. Weigel.

Sternemann, Reinhard (ed.). 1994. *Bopp-Symposium 1992 der Humboldt-Universität zu Berlin. Akten der Konferenz vom 24.3.–26.3. 1992 aus Anlaß von Franz Bopps zweihundertjährigem Geburtstag am 14.9. 1991.* Heidelberg: C. Winter.

Stricker, Bruno Hugo. 1945. *De indeeling der egptische taalgeschiedenis.* Leiden: Brill.

Sutcliffe, Patricia Casey. 2004. Mithridates in Berlin. In: Tintemann, Ute & Trabant, Jürgen (eds.), *Sprache und Sprachen in Berlin um 1800*. (Berliner Klassik 3). Hannover: Wehrhahn, 141–159.

Techmer, Friedrich Heinrich Hermann. 1889. Review of Carl Abel, Einleitung in ein Ägyptisch-Semitisch-Indoeuropäisches Wurzelwörterbuch (Leipzig 1885/6). *Internationale Zeitschrift für allgemeine Sprachwissenschaft* 4: 172–176.

Thouard, Denis. 2009. Le déchiffrement de l'énigme. Humboldt, Champollion et la question de l'écriture. *Historiographia Linguistica* 36.2/3: 407–427.

Tintemann, Ute & Messling, Markus (eds.). 2009. *"Der Mensch ist nur Mensch durch Sprache"*. *Zur Sprachlichkeit des Menschen*. München: Wilhelm Fink Verlag.

Trabant, Jürgen. 1983. Ideelle Bezeichnung. Steinthals Humboldt-Kritik. In: Eschbach, Achim & Trabant, Jürgen (eds.), *History of Semiotics*. Amsterdam/Philadelphia: Benjamins, 251–276.

Trabant, Jürgen. 1986. Gedächtnis und Schrift: Zu Humboldts Grammatologie. *KODIKAS/CODE. Ars semantica. An international Journal of Semiotics* 9.3–4: 293–315.

Trabant, Jürgen. 1990. *Traditionen Humboldts*. Frankfurt/M.: Suhrkamp.

Trabant, Jürgen (ed.). 1994. *Wilhelm von Humboldt: Über die Sprache*. Tübingen/Basel: A. Francke.

Tuki, Raphael. 1778. *Rudimenta linguae Coptae*. Roma: Sacra congregatio de propaganda fide.

Vater, Johann Severin. 1812. *Mithridates oder allgemeine Sprachenkunde mit dem Vater unser als Sprachprobe in bey nahe fünfhundert Sprachen und Mundarten*. Vol. 3.1. Berlin: Vossische Buchhandlung.

Vater, Johann Severin. 1815. *Litteratur der Grammatiken, Lexica und Wörtersammlungen aller Sprachen der Erde: nach alphabetischer Ordnung der Sprachen, mit einer gedrängten Uebersicht*. Berlin: Nicolaische Buchhandlung.

Voigt, Rainer. 2001. Semitohamitische Philologie und vergleichende Grammatik: Geschichte der vergleichenden Semitohamitistik. In Auroux, Sylvain, Koerner, E.F.K., Niederehe, Hans-Josef & Versteegh, Kees (eds.), *History of the Language Sciences. Geschichte der Sprachwissenschaften. Histoire des sciences du langage*. (Handbücher zur Sprach- und Kommunikationswissenschaft 18.2). Berlin/New York: De Gruyter, 1318–1325.

Whitney, William Dwight. 1867. *Language and the Study of Language. Twelve Lectures on the Principles of Linguistic Science*. London: Trübner & Co.

Whitney, William Dwight. 1874. *Sprachwissenschaft. W.D. Whitney's Vorlesungen über die Principien der vergleichenden Sprachforschung für das deutsche Publikum bearbeitet und erweitert von Dr. Julius Jolly*. München: Ackermann.

Whitney, William Dwight. 1875a. *The life and growth of language*. London: King.

Whitney, William Dwight. 1875b. *La vie du langage*. Paris.

Whitney, William Dwight. 1876a. *Leben und Wachstum der Sprache. Deutsch von August Leskien*. (Internationale Wissenschaftliche Bibliothek 20). Leipzig: Brockhaus.

Whitney, William Dwight. 1876b. *La vita e i sviluppo del linguaggio. Traduzione e note di Francesco D'Ovidio*. (Biblioteca Scientifica Internazionale 8). Milano: Fratelli Dumolard.

Whitney, William Dwight. 1877. *Taal en taalstudie. Voorlezingen over de gronden der wetenschappelijke taalbeoefening. Volgens de derde uitgave voor Nederlanders bewerkt door J. Beckeering Vinckers*. 1st series. Haarlem: Bohn.

Whitney, William Dwight. 1881. *Taal en taalstudie. Voorlezingen over de gronden der wetenschappelijke taalbeoefening. Volgens de derde uitgave voor Nederlanders bewerkt door J. Beckeering Vinckers*. 2nd series. Haarlem: Bohn.

Wiedebach, Hartwig & Winkelmann, Annette (eds.). 2002. *Chajim H. Steinthal. Linguist and Philosopher in the 19th Century*. (Studies in European Judaism 4). Leiden: Brill.

Wiedemann, Alfred. 1883. *Die ältesten Beziehungen zwischen Aegypten und Griechenland*. Leipzig: Barth.

Wilkins, David (ed.). 1716. *Novum Testamentum Aegyptium vulgo Copticum*. Oxford: E theatro Sheldoniano.

Witzel, Wiebke. 1994. Wilhelm von Humboldts Akademie-Vorträge nach den Protokollen der Akademie. In: Trabant, Jürgen (ed.). *Wilhelm von Humboldt: Über die Sprache*. Tübingen/ Basel: A. Francke, 224–227.

Wolze, Waldemar. 2011. Der falsche Weg zu den Hieroglyphen: Gustav Seyffarth, einer der ersten deutschen Ägyptologen. *Antike Welt. Zeitschrift für Archäologie und Kulturgeschichte* 42.3. Darmstadt: von Zabern, 57–61.

Young, Thomas. 1819. Hieroglyphical Vocabulary. *Encyclopaedia Britannica Supplement*. Vol. IV.1. Edinburgh, pl. 74–77.

Young, Thomas. 1823. *An account of some recent discoveries in hieroglyphical literature and Egyptian antiquities. Including the author's original alphabet, as extended by Mr. Champollion, with a translation of five unpublished Greek and Egyptian manuscripts. By Thomas Young, M. D. F. R. S., fellow of the Royal College of physicians*. London: J. Murray.

Young, Thomas. 1826. Remarks on Professor Spohn's Essay De Lingua et Literis Veterum Aegyptiorum, edited by Professor Seyffarth, Leipzig, 1825. In a Letter to Baron William von Humboldt. *The Quarterly Journal of Science, Literature, and the Arts* 20: 159–160.

Young, Thomas. 1827. Hieroglyphical Fragments; with some Remarks on English Grammar. In a Letter to the Baron William von Humboldt. By a Correspondent. *The Quarterly Journal of Science, Literature, and the Arts* 24: 92–100.

Young, Thomas. 1855. *Miscellaneous Works of the Late Thomas Young, M.D., F.R.S. Sc. (...)*. Vol. 3: *Hieroglyphical Essays and Correspondence*, ed. by Leitch, John. London: J. Murray.

Zoëga, Georg. 1810. *Catalogus Codicum Copticorum Musei Borgiani*. Roma: Sacra congregatio de propaganda fide.

Eitan Grossman & Tonio Sebastian Richter

The Egyptian-Coptic language: its setting in space, time and culture*

Abstract: The goal of this article is to provide the non-Egyptological reader with some background information about the Egyptian-Coptic language, focusing on its genealogical affiliations and diachrony, as well as the types of texts in which the language is attested. For a typologically-oriented overview of some central aspects of Egyptian-Coptic language structures, see Haspelmath (this volume).

1 Genealogical affiliations

Egyptian-Coptic was the native language of the population of the northern Nile valley in antiquity. It is considered to represent an autonomous branch of the Afroasiatic phylum (Loprieno 1995; Voigt 1999; Hayward 2000). It is a dead language, and has been one since the 14th century or so, when its last speakers shifted to Arabic; however, it remains in use as a liturgical language. As such, Egyptian-Coptic is by definition a *text language* (Fleischman 2000). While some discussions of Egyptian-Coptic refer to "vernacular" or "spoken" varieties, it is important to stress that modern scholarship has no direct access to any form of the language as it was spoken at any stage (Kammerzell 1998; Richter 2006b).

The remote but clear relationship with the Semitic language family is visible in phonological traits as well as in shared patterns of word formation and morphosyntax (Loprieno 1995).[1] The list of accepted lexical cognates includes several hundred items (Schenkel 1990).[2] There is also evidence of a historical – but not necessarily genealogical – relationship between Egyptian-Coptic and Indo-European (Kammerzell 2005).

---

* The authors are indebted to Peter Dils, Martin Haspelmath, Stéphane Polis, and Jean Winand, who have commented on an earlier draft of this introduction.

1 On the growing awareness of the genealogical relations of Egyptian with Near Eastern and African languages in 19th-century Egyptology, cf. Richter's paper in this volume.

2 A typological discussion of a phonological issue relating to the identification of Semitic-Egyptian cognates is provided in Gensler's article in this volume.

The genealogical relation of Egyptian with African language families such as Berber, Cushitic and Chadic languages is usually not disputed. However, the precise nature of the relationships is not very clear, at least in part due to the large chronological gap between the attestation of Egyptian and the earliest attested African languages. Currently, Ancient Egyptian does not figure prominently in genealogically- or typologically-oriented areal studies of African linguistics (e.g., Heine & Nurse 2000, 2008 or Dimmendaal 2011).

Further reading: *Semitic-Egyptian relations*: Takács 2004; Militarev 2007; *Afroasiatic-Egyptian relations*: Kammerzell 1995 & 1996; Loprieno 2008; Loprieno & Müller 2012; Mendel & Claudi 1991; Peust 2004; Quack 2002; Satzinger 1999; Takács 1999–2008 & 2004; Vernus 1988 & 2000.

2 Diachrony

The Egyptian-Coptic language is attested in a vast corpus of written texts that almost uninterruptedly document its lifetime over more than 4000 years, from the invention of the hieroglyphic writing system in the late 4th millennium BCE, up to the 14th century CE. Egyptian is thus likely to be the longest-attested human language known.

Traditionally, Egyptologists distinguish two macro-phases in Egyptian-Coptic, Earlier and Later Egyptian (Loprieno 1995; Loprieno & Müller 2012, Allen 2013). "Earlier Egyptian" refers to Old and Middle Egyptian, including varieties of the latter that continued to be used until the end of Pharaonic civilization. "Later Egyptian" comprises Late Egyptian, Demotic, and Coptic. However, the non-Egyptological reader should be aware that the linguistic and sociohistorical nature of Egyptian diachrony are a matter of considerable debate. Moreover, the dates given are approximate and tend to differ somewhat from linguist to linguist.

The main distinguishing feature separating the two macro-phases is generally considered to be a sort of holistic morphosyntactic typology: Earlier Egyptian is seen as synthetic, Later Egyptian as analytic, and – eventually – agglutinating. This distinction is generally considered with respect to the noun phrase, on the one hand, and the verb phrase on the other. Moreover, some scholars have proposed "a diachronic tendency to replace VSO-synthetic structures by SVO-analytic structures" (Hintze 1947 and 1950; Loprieno 1996, 2000 and 2001; Reintges 2012)[3], although other scholars have disputed the analysis of Earlier Egyptian syntax as VSO and Later Egyptian as SVO (Shisha-Halevy 2000).

A detailed presentation is found in Kammerzell 2000: 97, reproduced as Figure 1:

PRE-OLD EGYPTIAN		32nd–27th cent. BCE
EARLIER EGYPTIAN	Old Egyptian	27th–21st, 7th cent. BCE
	Archaic Old Egyptian	27th–22nd cent. BCE
	Standard Old Egyptian	25th–21st cent. BCE
	Neo-Old Egytian	7th cent. BCE
	Middle Egyptian	23th cent. BCE–4th cent. CE
	Early Middle Egyptian	23rd–20th cent. BCE
	Classical Middle Egyptian	21st–14th cent. BCE
	Late Middle Egyptian	20th–13th cent. BCE
	Transitional Middle Egyptian	15th–12th cent. BCE
	Neo-Middle Egyptian	11th cent. BCE–4th cent. CE
LATER EGYPTIAN	Late Egyptian	14th–7th cent. BCE
	Late Egyptian I	14th–12th cent. BCE
	Late Egyptian II	13th–7th cent. BCE
	Demotic	8th cent. BCE–5th cent. CE
	Early Demotic	8th cent.–4th cent. BCE
	Middle Demotic	4th–1st cent. BCE
	Late Demotic / Old Coptic	1st cent. BCE–5th cent. CE
	Coptic	3rd–20th cent. CE
	Standard Coptic	3rd–12th cent. CE
	Late Coptic	11th–16th cent. CE
	Neo-Coptic	19th–20th cent. CE

Figure 1: Chronolectal division of Egyptian (Kammerzell 2000)

To be sure, both subdivisions of Egyptian-Coptic linguistic history are broad and imprecise. However, it is important to stress that they do capture real and sig-

---

3 On this development which was first noticed, and described as restructuring from *Hinterbau* to *Vorderbau*, by Ewald (1861 and 1862), and was integrated in a more sophisticated concept of Egyptian diachrony by Erman (1880), cf. also Richter's article in this volume, § 7–§ 8.

nificant linguistic differences between the different phases of Egyptian-Coptic, since one occasionally finds unjustified doubts about the matter in non-specialist literature.[4]

2.1 An overview of the major stages of Egyptian-Coptic

2.1.1 Old Egyptian (including Archaic Egyptian or "pre-Old Egyptian")

Archaic Egyptian, or "Pre-Old Egyptian", is the language of the earliest Egyptian texts from the Early Dynastic Period (Dynasties 1–3, roughly the first third of the 3rd millenium BCE).[5] The cultural changes culminating in the early state formation in the Nile valley during the late fourth millennium BCE provided the soil on which a native writing system, hieroglyphs, developed. While many particulars about the initial process of the turn from pictograms and symbols into representations of sounds and grammar in the late Predynastic Period (late 4th millennium BCE) are still debated (Baines 2007; Dreyer 1999; Kahl 1994; Morenz 2004; Vernus 1993), and the sound values of some early hieroglyphs are still unknown, short texts written in a fairly standardized, basically phonological script are found in the Early Dynastic Period (first third of the 3d millennium BCE). Although the newly invented device was first applied to very short textual units, such as nominal designations of items, short lists, and brief funerary formula, the earliest specimens of Egyptian language provide more evidence for lexical items than for elaborate grammar. While some scholars prefer to subsume them under the label of Old Egyptian, there are some hints of a more significant difference between the language of these documents and that of Old Kingdom texts (Kahl 2000, 2001a); particularly striking are phonological differences between Archaic or "Pre-Old

---

4 E.g., "[the distinction between Late Egyptian and Coptic is] associated with literary and graphic sources rather than with linguistic features *per se*" (Dimmendaal 2011: 70, apparently based on Hayward 2000: 78, which has a similar wording).

5 Egyptian history is traditionally subdivided into four main periods: Old Kingdom, Middle Kingdom, New Kingdom, and Late Period, with so-called 'Intermediate Periods' in between, the first Intermediate Period separating the Old and Middle Kingdoms; the second one separating the Middle and New Kingdoms, and the third one separating the New Kingdom and the Late Period. The Old Kingdom is preceded by the Pre-Dynastic and the Early Dynastic periods. The Late Period is followed by the Hellenistic (Ptolemaic), Roman, and Islamic periods. Although political developments as reflected in this periodization did affect the use of linguistic norms, there is of course no straightforward correspondence between the aforementioned chronolects and those periods.

Egyptian" and Old Egyptian (Kammerzell 1998, 2005). Archaic Egyptian language data are not dealt with in this volume, but see Gensler's article referring to a pre-archaic stage of the Egyptian language.

Old Egyptian is the language of texts of the Old Kingdom of Egypt (Dynasties 4–8, corresponding to the mid- until late 3rd millennium BCE). Old Egyptian is the first phase of the Egyptian language phase that provides us with a significant quantity of texts. However, the textual repertoire is still very limited in terms of genre and accordingly, in terms of of linguistic registers represented in the written record. Apart from some traditional textual genres, which were already fairly well-established by then – nominal designations, short lists and funerary formula – two large text corpora form the basis for our knowledge of Old Egyptian. First, the corpus of the Pyramid Texts, a collection of about 750 spells, recorded in the burial chambers of pyramids of the late 5th and 6th dynasties (ca. 2500–2200 BCE). These spells were to serve the ritual transfiguration of the dead king into a divine being able to enjoy eternal life in the beyond. Their attitude is that of the voice of a funerary priest, fixed and materialized in the medium of script to address the king and to award him eternal life by a perpetual performative speech act ("O thou [king] NN, get up, etc."). Thus the corpus of Pyramid Texts is the main sample of interlocutive (or even allocutive) speech in Old Egyptian. Most examples of constructions encoding the addressee speech role (e.g., 2nd person forms) come from this corpus. The language of the Pyramid Texts is usually considered to represent an earlier language stage than that of the other, roughly contemporary corpus of Old Egyptian texts, so-called autobiographies (Gnirs 1996; Kloth 2002). This genre of funerary texts emerged in 4th-dynasty non-royal tombs, evolving from earlier types of (oral and written) text (Assmann 1983; Baines 1999a). The autobiographies, which extol the virtues and merits of a tomb owner as if spoken by himself, developed into more sophisticated and extensive narratives during the 5th and 6th dynasties (ca. 2350–2150 BCE). Autobiographies are our main evidence for the narrative system of Old Egyptian (Doret 1986; Osing 1977; Zonhoven 2003).[6] Only little evidence of non-monumental, everyday writing is extant from the Old Kingdom, although we have specimens of, e.g., economic records related to temple administration (Posener-Kriéger 1968, 1976, 2004; Posener-Kriéger et al. 2006) and letter writing. Old Egyptian language

---

6 The most extensive of these texts, the autobiography of *Wni* (on which cf. Eyre 1994; Hofmann 2002; Richards 2004), was Adolf Erman's source when he first explored the linguistic features of Ancient Egyptian, and the morphosyntactic relations between Egyptian and Semitic languages, cf. Richter's article in this volume, § 8.

data are dealt with in the papers of Güldemann, Idiatov, Loprieno, Peust, Reintges, and Stauder in this volume.

Further reading: (*Archaic Egyptian*) *Lexicon*: Kahl 2002–2004 & 2003. *Grammar*: Kammerzell 2005; (*Old Egyptian*) *Lexicon*: Erman & Grapow 1926–1963; Hannig 2003; Schweitzer 2005; *Grammar*: Allen 1984; Doret 1986; Edel 1955–1964; Osing 1977; Schweitzer 2005; Zonhoven 2003.

2.1.2 Middle Egyptian

Middle Egyptian is the name given to the set of linguistic norms found in texts from the Middle Kingdom of Egypt (Dynasties 11–13, roughly the first third of the 2nd millennium BCE). Approximations to this norm continued to serve, in a number of varieties, as the basis of prestigious registers for purposes such as religious and funerary writing over the following two millennia up until Roman times. Middle Egyptian first emerges in texts of the First Intermediate Period (ca. 2200–1950 BCE) and the Middle Kingdom (ca. 1950–1750 BCE). It differs from Old Egyptian mainly in terms of phonology (Peust 1999; Kammerzell 2005), morphology, and lexicon, although recent work also highlights significant syntactic differences (Oréal 2010). The study of these changes is facilitated by the continuing tradition of certain textual genres, such as autobiographies and the huge funerary corpus of so-called Coffin Texts. The latter is a corpus of more than 1200 spells recorded on the inside of Middle Kingdom wooden coffins. These spells were intended to support the eternal life of non-royal persons, as the Old Kingdom Pyramid Texts did for the king. In fact, many spells from the earlier collection of the Pyramid Texts continued to be transmitted, albeit with changes, in the Coffin Texts (Bickel & Mathieu 2004). The multiple transmission of the same spells in several text types, providing a range of textual and orthographic variation and thus allowing occasionally to suspend the systemic restrictions of hieroglyphic orthography, makes the Coffin Texts a particularly important source for the study of Middle Egyptian morphology and syntax (Schenkel 1998, 1999, 2000, 2002, 2004/5, 2005, 2007, 2008, 2009; van der Molen 2000 & 2005, Vernus 1996a & 2004).

Compared to the range and diversity of written texts in the Old Kingdom, the application of writing and the textual repertoire expanded tremendously in Middle Kingdom Egypt. The spread of writing in the sphere of everyday life provides us with a fairly substantial corpus of non-literary texts, which bear evidence for linguistic registers that are less standardized, less conservative and more permeable to innovation (e.g., Allen 1994; Collier & Quirke 2002, 2006; Luft 1992). Among the innovative textual genres of the Middle Kingdom, the most

important ones are non-funerary royal texts (Blumenthal 1970), scientific trea-
tises (Clagett 1989, 1995, 1999), and – most significant for linguistic study – the
emergence of a kind of text that has been called, *cum grano salis*, Egyptian *belles-
lettres* (Assmann 1974 & 1983; Blumenthal 1996 & 1998; Parkinson 2002; Posener
1956). Unlike other textual genres of Ancient Egypt that were formerly closely
connected to delimited compartments of social practice, such as the cult of the
dead, they cannot be assigned to any clear-cut *Sitz im Leben*. Linguistically, these
"literary" or "belletristic" texts are distinctive for their reflection on and deliberate use of extravagant language (*mdw nfr* 'perfect speech' as they put it) and for
their mixing of textual genres, such as autobiographical narrative, prayer and
hymn, into text-linguistically hybrid units (Burkhard 1996; Collier 1996). Three
sub-genres of Egyptian "literature" are usually identified according to formal and
content-related criteria: teachings, discourses, and narratives (Moers 2001; Parkinson 1991 & 1996). Most standard grammars of Middle Egyptian heavily rely on
this relatively small and rather atypical corpus of texts for their examples.

Post-New Kingdom applications of an Egyptian idiom supposed to meet the
standard of Middle Egyptian are labeled by Egyptologists the term "Égyptien de
tradition", "traditional Egyptian", "Neo-" or simply "Late Middle Egyptian" (cf.
Vernus 1996b; Jansen-Winkeln 1996 & 2010). Middle Egyptian language data are
dealt with in the papers of Güldemann, Haspelmath, Idiatov, Loprieno, Peust,
Reintges, Stauder and Winand in this volume. "Égyptien de tradition" is touched
upon in Peust's paper in this volume.

Further reading: *Lexicon*: Erman & Grapow 1926–1963; Faulkner 1962; Hannig
2006; *Grammar*: Allen 2010; Borghouts 2010; Gardiner 1957; Jenni 2010; Junge
1978; Malaise & Winand 1999; Schenkel 2012.

2.1.3 Late Egyptian

Late Egyptian is traditionally considered to be a register that was elevated to the
rank of a written language during the Amarna period of the New Kingdom of
Egypt (14th c. BCE), continued to be used, alongside *Égyptien de tradition*, during
the later 2nd and earlier 1st millennium BCE (19th–25th Dynasties).

Late Egyptian differs structurally from Middle Egyptian more strikingly than
any other Egyptian language phase from its predecessor. This has often been inter-
preted as indicating a long-term gap between the norms of written and spoken
Egyptian. The relationship between Late Egyptian and various forms of Earlier
Egyptian has been conceptualized as a kind of covert diglossic situation (Jansen-
Winkeln 1995; Vernus 1996b), which became overt when typical Late Egyptian

features began to penetrate written registers, and, eventually, became consolidated as a relatively coherent system, albeit one with much internal variation. The first instances of certain "Late Egyptian" traits, such as the use of the definite article (*p3, t3, n3*) and possessive-marking by a paradigm of preposed possessive articles (cf. Haspelmath's paper in this volume) surface sporadically already in early Middle Kingdom texts (Kroeber 1970). The label "Late Egyptian" generally refers to texts of the later New Kingdom (19th–20th dynasties, corresponding to the 13th–11th century BCE) and the Third Intermediate Period (21st–25th dynasties, corresponding to the 11th–7th centuries BCE) that share a number of such traits, while otherwise representing rather different norms (Goldwasser 1999). Texts dealt with under this label include genres as different as royal inscriptions from the Amarna period (2nd half of the 14th century BCE) and the Ramesside period (19th–20th dynasties, roughly the 13th–11th century BCE), private hymns and prayers, a number of narratives and "fairy tales" (Hintze 1950–1952), literary texts of the teachings type and of the new genre of love songs, and a substantial corpus of non-literary texts, including private letters and legal documents, administrative documents and records of criminal procedures. One of the standard grammars of Late Egyptian, Černý & Groll (1984), takes a narrow approach to Late Egyptian, limiting its corpus to non-literary texts, while the majority of scholars, notably the "Liège school" of Egyptian language study (Polis & Winand 2013), take a more comprehensive approach, defining Late Egyptian as a label applying to any written registers at least partly open to the norm of everyday life texts of the time. Late Egyptian language data are dealt with in the papers of Collier, Güldemann, Haspelmath, Idiatov, Loprieno, Stauder and Winand in this volume.

Further reading: *Lexicon*: Erman & Grapow 1926–1963; Hoch 1994; Lesko 1982–1990; Winand 1999; *Grammar*: Erman 1933; Černý & Groll 1984; Junge 1999; Neveu 1998; Satzinger 1976; Winand 1992.

2.1.4 Demotic

Demotic is the name of a set of language norms whose appearance in the mid-7th century BCE (early 26th dynasty) is closely connected to the introduction of a new chancellery writing style, distinct from the hieratic cursive (cf. below §§ 5.2 and 5.3). While the other designations have been invented for (such as Old, Middle, and Late Egyptian), or applied to (such as Coptic), Egyptian language phases only in recent times, the name Demotic is an antique designation for an Egyptian writing style. It was chosen by the Greek geographer Herodotus (ca. 450 BCE) to distinguish two Egyptian writing styles, *hierá grámmata* 'sacred characters' and *demotiká grámmata* 'ordinary characters'. In the first three hundred years after its inauguration in the mid-7th century, thus still during the time of which Herodotus could have had some knowledge, Demotic (both in the sense of a distinct style of cursive writing and of a stage of the Egyptian language) was in fact a medium restricted to administrative and private day-to-day writing, i.e., "ordinary", as opposed to religious and funerary, purposes. Although it was at first reserved for administrative writing, Demotic became gradually used for literary writing (teachings, narratives) and religious texts (cf. Hoffmann & Quack 2007). The latest Demotic text, at the same time the latest datable specimen of any hieroglyph-based Egyptian script, is a visitor's inscription at the Isis temple of Philae from the year 452 CE. In the wake of the influential "Berliner Schule" of Egyptology (cf. Richter's paper in this volume, § 8) Demotic was mistakenly considered as an artificial extension of written Late Egyptian with no connection to actual language change (Grapow 1938; Stricker 1945), and its study was marginalized in Egyptology for quite a while. Johnson (1976) has strikingly shown that Demotic must be the link between Late Egyptian and Coptic, and this view has been fully corroborated more recently (Quack fc. [a]; Simpson 1996). Demotic language data are dealt with in the papers of Grossman, Idiatov, Loprieno and Winand in this volume.

Further reading: *Lexicon:* The Demotic Dictionary of the Oriental Institute of the University of Chicago: http://oi.uchicago.edu/research/pubs/catalog/cdd/; Clarysse 1987; Erichsen 1954; Johnson 1999; Vittmann; 1996; Vleeming 1987; *Grammar:* Johnson 1976 & 2000; Quack fc. (a); Simpson 1996; Spiegelberg 1925.

2.1.5 Coptic

Coptic is the last language phase (ca. 4th century CE – ca. 14th century CE) of the Egyptian-Coptic language, starting with the alphabetization of written Egyptian on the basis of the Greek script, and ending with the language shift of Egyptian native speakers to Arabic in the Middle Ages. The process of *neuverschriftung* of Egyptian during the first centuries CE, resulting in the more or less complete standardization of several Coptic dialects around 300 CE, accompanied (or partially resulted from) a major change in the domain of religion, namely, the rise and spread of Christianity in Egypt. Next to Greek, Latin, and Syriac, Coptic became one of the most important languages of ancient Christian literature. Biblical books and other early Christian texts were translated into and composed in Coptic. A substantial corpus of monastic literature, including normative writings such as homilies, sermons, and rules, as well as narratives, has come down to us. Other types of narrative include martyrdoms and miraculous stories commemorating the virtues and deeds of saints. In addition, writings of "heretical" movements, such as Manichaeism and Gnosticism, survived (often exclusively) in Coptic manuscripts. Besides its significance as a written medium of literary texts, Coptic also served as the vehicle of written communication related to everyday life. Massive finds of papyri and ostraca in Egypt have brought us many thousands of Coptic documentary texts, such as administrative records, legal documents, and private letters. These texts afford us a precious glimpse of a range of registers, including highly colloquial and informal language, as well as of the idiolectal usage of individual scribes. Coptic language data are dealt with in the papers of Grossman, Haspelmath, Idiatov, Loprieno, Peust and Winand in this volume.

Further reading: *Lexicon*: Černý 1976; Crum 1939; Förster 2002; Kasser 1964; Quack 2005; Richter 2006a; Vycichl 1983; Westendorf 1965. *Morphophonology*: Funk 2009; Vergote 1973–1983. *Grammar* (*Sahidic dialect*): Lambdin 1983; Layton 2004; Polotsky 1987/90; Reintges 2004a; Shisha-Halevy 1986 & 1988; Steindorff 1894 and 1951; Till 1955.

3 Dialects and intradialectal variation

There is little hard evidence for the written representation of distinct geographical dialects before Coptic, although it has been proposed that Earlier Egyptian reflects a northern dialect, Late Egyptian a southern one (Peust 1999: 33; Feder 2005). However, it is only in Coptic that we observe significant differences between dialects. Coptic can be divided into a dozen or so highly standardized written dialects (Funk 1988 & 1991; Kasser 1991c). The best attested Coptic dialects are Sahidic, Bohairic, Akhmimic, Fayyumic, Oxyrhynchitic (also known as Mesokemic or Middle Egyptian), and Lycopolitan (formerly "Subakhmimic"), which is in fact a group of closely-related but distinct dialects. In addition, there are a number of dialects which are sparsely attested, and are generally known by alphabetical sigla (e.g., Dialect I) rather than geographically-based names. Within a particular dialect group, subdialects are often distinguished by number, e.g., L4/L5/L6 for the three major Lycopolitan varieties. The following map (Figure 2) gives an idea of where some of these dialects likely originated, based on a study of 33 variables (Funk 1988).[7]

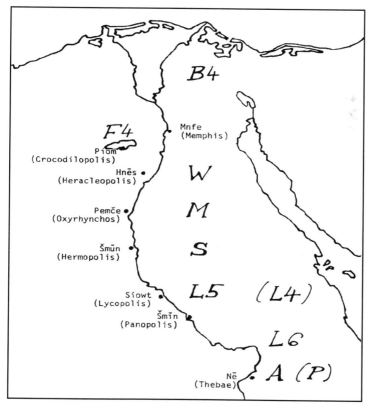

Figure 2: Coptic dialectal geography (Funk 1988)

Many literary and non-literary texts show considerable variation from the norms of the standardized dialects. Interestingly, these "destandardized" texts often show distinctive regional characteristics. For example, Sahidic texts produced in the monasteries of the Fayyum often show particular features, some of which can be attributed to the influence of the Fayyumic dialect. Documentary texts from Thebes (Nē, Thebae) are often strikingly different from comparable texts originating from Ashmunein (Šmūn, Hermopolis).

The regionalization of Egyptian written standards and the occurrence of destandardized norms are not very visible in pre-Coptic Egyptian, although recent

---

7 See Funk (1988) for important reservations about this map.

work on Demotic may shed more light on this issue. This change in the visibility of diatopic and diastratic variation might be the result of historical changes in the sociolinguistic status of Egyptian during the first millennium CE, which was that of a socially and functionally restricted, recessive language variety, used in certain milieux, for certain purposes, alongside a dominant prestige language, Greek, until the 7th century CE, followed by Arabic.

Further reading: *Bohairic dialect*: Stern 1880; Mallon 1956; Shisha-Halevy 2007. *Lycopolitan dialects*: Chaîne 1934; Nagel 1969 & 1991b; Funk 1985. *Akhmimic dialect*: Rösch 1909; Till 1928; Nagel 1991a. *Fayyumic dialect(s)*: Kasser 1991e; Till 1930. *Middle Egyptian dialect*: Quecke 1974; Funk 1981; Schenke 1978 & 1991. *Dialectal geography*: Funk 1988; Hintze 1984; Kasser 1991c, d & f.

4 Language contact

It is likely that there was never a time in which Egyptian-Coptic was not in contact with other languages. The traces of such contact can be seen throughout its history, although the transparency of the evidence varies. According to some scholars (e.g., Kammerzell 2000, 2005), Old Egyptian proper was the result of contact between languages of different genealogical stocks. Northwest Semitic loanwords are particularly visible in Late Egyptian, and to an extent, in Demotic. Peust has identified a "Napatan" variety of Egyptian from ancient Nubia, influenced by a substrate language.

From the middle of the 1st millennium BCE, due to political changes, contact-induced language change became a more prevalent tendency in Egyptian, notably its lexicon. It is Coptic that is most transparently a "language in contact", having borrowed thousands of Greek loanwords of almost all basic root-types and semantic fields (Kasser 1991g; Oréal 1999; Reintges 2001, 2004b). In the 8th and 9th centuries CE, occasional Arabic loanwords indicate incipient Coptic-Arabic contact, and later Coptic texts from the 10th and 11th centuries, the time when parts of the indigenous population of Egypt began to shift from their native language to Arabic, bear evidence of intensified borrowing from Arabic (Richter 2006a, 2009).

Interestingly, Egyptian-Coptic seems to have influenced languages of the area as well. Kammerzell (2001a, 2001b & 2001c) has suggested that Egyptian influenced West Semitic languages, and perhaps, indirectly, Indo-European languages.

Further reading: *Semitic loanwords in Egyptian*: Hoch 1994; Quack 2005; Vittmann 1996. *Non-Semitic loanwords in Egyptian*: Knigge 2004; Schneider 2004a & 2004b. *Greek-Egyptian language contact*: Feder 2004; Fewster 2002; Fournet 2009; Hasznos 2012; Papaconstantinou 2010; Peremans 1964 & 1983; Rutherford 2010; Satzinger 1984; Torallas Tovar 2010; Vierros 2012. *Greek Loanwords in Egyptian*: Almond 2010; Clarysse 1987; Dils et al. (fc.); Kasser 1966 & 1991g; Oréal 1999; Reintges 2001 & 2004b. *Egyptian Loanwords in Greek*: Fournet 1989; Torallas Tovar 2004. *Arabic loanwords in Coptic*: Richter 2006a. *Coptic substrate of Egyptian Arabic*: Behnstedt 1981; Bishai 1960, 1961, 1962 & 1964; Ishaq 1991; Lucas & Lash 2010; Vittmann 1991.

5 Writing systems

Egyptian-Coptic is attested in a number of native (Betrò 1996; Cruz-Uribe 2001; Schenkel 1984) and non-native writing systems. The most important are sketched in the following sections.

5.1 Hieroglyphs

Hieroglyphs, (a term found in classical authors such as Diodorus Siculus, Plutarch, and Clemens Alexandrinus: *hieroglyphiká* [*grámmata*] 'sacred carved letters'): The native Egyptian writing system is one of the few original, unprecedented writing systems in the history of writing, and next to the cuneiform script the most ancient one, emerging from symbolic codes as early as in the late 4th millennium BCE (Dreyer 1999; Kahl 1994; Morenz 2004). The inventory of hieroglyphic signs includes several hundreds of mostly pictorial signs, representing e.g., men, women and gods in different outfits and occupations, parts of the human body, domestic and wild animals, birds, fishes, reptiles and invertebrates and various animal body parts, plants and parts of them, items of the natural environment, and all kinds of artefacts. The standard catalogue of hieroglyphs, the sign-list of Gardiner (1957), comprises 734 signs. However, much smaller repertoires were usually sufficient to write texts. On the other hand, religious texts authored in circles of the priestly élite were complicated by unconventional uses of signs and newly-invented signs, notably the encyclopedic textual universes as carved into the walls of the temples of the Graeco-Roman period, when the number of signs rose to several thousand.

As Kammerzell and Lincke (2012) stress, Egyptian graphemes can fulfill a structured range of functions, based on two parameters: their autonomy and their meaningfulness (cf. Figure 3). Hieroglyphic signs can convey *semantic* values related to their pictorial content (*semograms*), or *phonological* values derived from a word designating the depicted item (*phonograms*), or either of both depending on usage (cf. Figure 4 and 5).

Semograms could be used as logograms, i.e., to write the word designating the depicted item. They were also part of an elaborate system of graphemic classifiers, traditionally called "determinatives" in Egyptology (Goldwasser & Grinevald 2012; Kammerzell & Lincke 2012). Classifiers were written after words (thereby serving as a word division marker) and were to assign words to semantic categories, such as "divine being", "male human being", "female human being", "animal", "bird", "fish", "place-related item", "time-related item", "foreign person/item", "vessel", "textile", "mineral", "grain", "motion verb", "violent action", etc.

Phonograms could encode one consonantal phoneme (uniliteral signs) or a sequence of two consonants (biliteral signs) or even three (triliteral signs, although many triliteral phonograms can also be interpreted as logograms). Phonograms had two main functions: to represent the elements of a consonantal skeleton of lexical and grammatical items, on the one hand (the "autonomous" function, in Kammerzell and Lincke's terms), and, as "interpretants" (traditionally called "phonetic complements"), to redundantly represent elements of sound structure already present in writing. The following figure is a schematic representation of sign functions of Egyptian graphemes:

	[+meaningful]	[−meaningful]
[+autonomous]	logograms (inaccurately: "ideograms")	phonograms (in the narrower sense)
[−autonomous]	classifiers (inaccurately: "determinatives")	interpretants ("phonetic complements")
	semograms	phonograms (in the wider sense)

Figure 3: Sign function classes in written Egyptian (Kammerzell & Lincke 2012)

An alphabetic set of uniliteral signs covering the complete (consonantal) phoneme inventory of Egyptian was available, but was never used exclusively.

Grapheme type	Gardiner, Sign-list A1: Seated man	Transcription	Meaning
Semogram: logogram	𓀀𓏤	z	'man'
Semogram: classifier	𓀀	–	'male person'
Phonogram	𓀀	.y	(suffixed pronoun 1SG.M)

Figure 4: Hieroglyphic sign Gardiner, sign-list A1, its semographic and phongraphic use

Grapheme type	Gardiner, Sign-list D21: Mouth	Transcription	Meaning
Semogram: logogram	⬭𓏤	r3	'mouth'
Semogram: classifier	–	–	–
Phonogram	⬭	r	(alphabetic sign)

Figure 5: Hieroglyphic sign Gardiner, sign-list D21, its semographic and phonographic use

5.2 Hieratic (and cursive hieroglyphs)

Hieratic (the term applied to one of the Egyptian scripts by Clement of Alexandria: *hieratikón grammátōn méthodos* 'sacerdotal script') is the conventional name of the Ancient Egyptian cursive writing. Generally based on and following the orthographic conventions of the hieroglyphic system, the individual shapes of signs have been adjusted to the needs of swift writing on papyrus with the brush-like writing utensil used by Egyptian scribes, leading to more abstract, less pictorial shapes of signs and ligatures (cf. Figure 5, third column). So-called *Cursive Hieroglyphs*, less cursive (and closer to the monumental types) than *Hieratic*, are a writing style especially used for funerary texts, such as Coffin Texts, the Book of the Dead, and royal funerary texts on the walls of the rock tombs of New Kingdom pharaohs in the Valley of the Kings.

5.3 The Demotic script

The Demotic script (to be distinguished from the language phase of the same name, cf. above, § 2.1.4) appeared in the 7th century BCE as a new chancellery script which was to replace late Hieratic (which persisted in the literary domain) in the sphere of day-to-day writing. Its Greek name is first attested in Herodotus' chapter on Egypt (*demotikà grámmata* 'ordinary characters' as opposed to *hierà grámmata* 'holy characters'); its native Egyptian name was *sẖ šꜥ.t* 'document script'. Over time it gained more functions, being used for, e.g., narrative and wisdom literature, religious and funerary texts. The main principle of the Demotic script is formal simplification of signs, with the effect of a considerable decrease in the diversity of shapes (down to about 30 or 40 basic types composed of elements such as vertical, horizontal and oblique strokes, loops, dots etc.), and accordingly, an increase in ambiguity of the meaning of single signs (cf. Figure 6, fourth column). This holds true for both of the two functional types of sign, phonograms and classifiers. The comprehensibility of Demotic is thus strongly depending on standard spellings of whole words, rather than of their components, and in fact Demotic was taught and learned word-by-word, as Demotic school exercises show.

5.4 The Coptic script

The Coptic script was the final result of a shift from hieroglyph-based Egyptian writing systems – all of them, the monumental script and its cursive decendents, still being used in the 4th century CE – firstly to a multitude of idiosyncratic Greek-based systems, the so-called Old Coptic alphabets of the first centuries CE, (Kasser 1991b; Quack fc. [b], Quaegebeur 1982; Richter 2009; Satzinger 1984), and eventually to a few standardized Coptic alphabets around 300 CE (Kasser 1991a). While Late Antiquity saw a remarkable multiplication and spread of alphabets throughout the eastern Mediterranean and beyond, usually derived from either the Greek or the Aramaic alphabet, we are mostly dealing with cases of *first alphabetization*, this is to say, the first time a spoken language was provided with a written medium and thus with the possibility of a literature of its own. *Coptic*, on the other hand, is one of the rare cases of *replacement* of an established writing system by a new one. The Coptic alphabet includes the twenty four characters of the Greek alphabet plus six (Bohairic: seven) letters derived from Demotic signs (cf. Figure 6, right column).

Gardiner, Sign list	Hieroglyphic	Hieratic	Demotic	Coptic
M8: pool with lotus flowers				ϣ (š)
I9: horned viper				ϥ (f)
F18:tusk (+ Y1: tied and sealed papyrus roll)				ϩ (h)
U28: fire drill				ϫ (č)
V31: wickerwork basket with handle				ϭ (c)
D37: forearm with hand holding a loaf (+ X1: bread)				ϯ (tⁱ)
M12: stalk and leaf of lotus				Bohairic only: ϧ (χ)

Figure 6: Palaeographical change of Hieroglyphic characters in cursive writing, and the six (Bohairic: seven) letters supplementing the 24 Greek letters of the Coptic alphabet.

5.5 Other, non-native scripts

In conjunction with cultural and language contact, Egyptian-Coptic words, phrases and even texts were occasionally transcribed in cuneiform, West Semitic writing systems, Greek, Latin, Arabic, and other scripts.

Further reading: *Hieroglyphs*: Goldwasser 1995 & 2001; Loprieno 1995: 11–27; Schenkel 1984, 1994, 2003; 2011 & 2012: 31–63. *Classifiers*: Goldwasser 2002, 2005, 2006, 2009; Goldwasser & Grinvald 2012; Goldwasser & Müller 1999; Kammerzell 1999; Kammerzell & Lincke 2012; Lincke 2011; Smoczynski 1999. *Hieratic*: Schenkel 1994. *Demotic*: Betrò 1996; Quack (fc. [a]); Schenkel 1994; Stadler 2008. *Coptic*: Felber 2008; Kasser 1991a & 1991b; Quaegebeur 1982; Richter 2009.

6 Concluding remarks

The model of two diachronic macro-phases, comprising five discrete language phases, rests on a fairly sound empirical basis, and has some practical merits. Still, it is a real simplification of linguistic reality, and some aspects of Ancient Egyptian linguistic history are hardly reflected by it. The idea of discrete diachronic stages is challenged by the heavy and long-term diglossia of written Egyptian after the Middle Kingdom. Furthermore, there is considerable internal variation and evidence for ongoing language change, both at the seams of the successive stages and *within* each of the stages. For example, studies have demonstrated that Coptic, which is generally considered to be more or less stable over its thousand-year history as a written language, clearly shows significant diachronic changes (Grossman 2007, 2010); it has also been proposed that language change is visible within Old Egyptian (Kammerzell 2005), Middle Egyptian (Doret 1986), Late Egyptian (Groll 1982; Winand 1995), and Demotic (Quack fc. [a]).

In general, recent scholarship has tended to move away from a broad holistic diachronic conception based on discrete stages, and towards a more fine-grained construction- or feature-oriented approach, combined with a heightened awareness of the importance of sociohistorical parameters for the study of variation. Such perspectives have tended to identify continuous long-term change rather than abrupt shifts or ruptures.

Whatever the empirical validity of the schemes presented above, we think it is helpful for the non-Egyptological reader to have a basic acquaintance with them, since they are used – with or without reservations – by all linguists and philologists working on Egyptian.

7 References

Allen, James P. 1984. *The Inflection of the Verb in the Pyramid Texts*. Malibu: Undena Publications.

Allen, James P. 1994. Colloquial Middle Egyptian: Some Observations on the Language of Heqanakht. *Lingua Aegyptia* 4: 1–12.

Allen, James P. 2010. *Middle Egyptian. An Introduction to the Language and Culture of Hieroglyphs*. 2nd ed. Cambridge: Cambridge University Press.

Allen, James P. 2013. *The Ancient Egyptian Language. An Historical Study*. Cambridge: Cambridge University Press.

Almond, Mathew. 2010. Language Change in Greek Loaned Verbs. *Lingua Aegyptia* 18: 19–31.

Assmann, Jan. 1974. Der literarische Text im Alten Ägypten. *Orientalistische Literaturzeitung* 69: 117–126.

Assmann, Jan. 1983. Schrift, Tod und Identität: Das Grab als Vorschule der Literatur im Alten Ägypten. In: Assmann, Aleida, Assmann, Jan & Hardmeier, Christof (eds.), *Schrift und Gedächtnis*. (Beiträge zur Archäologie der literarischen Kommunikation I). München: Fink, 64–93.

Assmann, Jan. 1999. Cultural and literary texts. In: Moers, Gerald (ed.), *Definitely: Egyptian Literature. Proceedings of the Symposium Ancient Egyptian Literature. History and Forms, Los Angeles, March 24–26 1995*. (Lingua Aegyptia Studia Monographica 2). Göttingen: Seminar für Ägyptologie und Koptologie, 1–15.

Baines, John. 1999a. Forerunners of Narrative Biographies. In: Leahy, Anthony & Tait, John (eds.), *Studies on Ancient Egypt in Honour of H.S. Smith*. (BM Occasional Publications 13). London: Egypt Exploration Society, 23–37.

Baines, John. 1999b. Prehistory of Literature: Performance, Fiction and Myth. In: Moers, Gerald (ed.), *Definitely: Egyptian Literature. Proceedings of the Symposium Ancient Egyptian Literature. History and Forms, Los Angeles, March 24–26 1995*. (Lingua Aegyptia, Studia Monographica 2). Göttingen: Seminar für Ägyptologie und Koptologie, 17–41.

Baines, John. 2007. *Visual and Written Culture in Ancient Egypt*. Oxford: Oxford University Press.

Behnstedt, Peter. 1981. Weitere koptische Lehnwörter im Ägyptisch-Arabischen. *Welt des Orients* 12: 81–98.

Betrò, Maria Carmela. 1996. *Hieroglyphics: The Writings of Ancient Egypt*. New York/Milan: Abbeville.

Bickel, Susanne & Mathieu, Bernard (eds.). 2004. *D'un monde à l'autre: Textes des Pyramides & Textes des Sarcophages (Actes de la table ronde internationale «Textes des Pyramides versus Textes des Sarcophages» IFAO – 24–26 septembre 2001)*. (Bibliothèque d'étude 139). Cairo: Institut français d'archéologie orientale, 256–258.

Bishai, Wilson B. 1960. Notes on the Coptic Substrate in Egyptian Arabic. *Journal of the American Oriental Society* 80: 225–229.

Bishai, Wilson B. 1961. Nature and Extent of Coptic phonological influence on Egyptian Arabic. *Journal of Semitic Studies* 6: 175–182.

Bishai, Wilson B. 1962. Coptic Grammatical Influence on Egyptian Arabic. *Journal of the American Oriental Society* 82: 285–189

Bishai, Wilson B. 1964. Coptic influences on Egyptian Arabic. *Journal of Near Eastern Studies* 23: 39–47.

Blumenthal, Elke. 1970. *Untersuchungen zum ägyptischen Königtum des Mittleren Reiches, Teil 1: Phraseologie.* (Abhandlungen der Sächsischen Akademie der Wissenschaften zu Leipzig, phil.-hist. Kl., 61.1). Berlin: Akademie.

Blumenthal, Elke. 1996. Die literarische Verarbeitung der Übergangszeit zwischen Altem und Mittlerem Reich. In: Loprieno, Antonio (ed.), *Ancient Egyptian Literature. History and Forms.* (Probleme der Ägyptologie 10). Leiden/New York/Köln: Brill, 105–135.

Blumenthal, Elke. 1998. Prolegomena zu einer Klassifizierung der ägyptischen Literatur. In: Eyre, Christopher (ed.), *Proceedings of the 7th International Congress of Egyptologists, Cambridge, 3–9 September 1995.* (Orientalia Lovaniensia Analecta 82). Leuven: Peeters, 173–183.

Borghouts, Joris F. 2010. *Egyptian. An Introduction to the Writing and Language of the Middle Kingdom.* Leuven: Peeters.

Burkard, Günter. 1996. Metrik, Prosodie und formaler Aufbau ägyptischer literarischer Texte. In: Loprieno, Antonio (ed.), *Ancient Egyptian Literature. History and Forms.* (Probleme der Ägyptologie 10). Leiden/New York/Köln: Brill, 447–463.

Burkard, Günter & Thissen, Heinz J. 2003. *Einführung in die altägyptische Literaturgeschichte.* (Einführungen und Quellentexte zur Ägyptologie 1). Münster/Hamburg/London: LIT Verlag.

Černý, Jaroslav. 1976. *Coptic Etymological Dictionary.* Cambridge: Cambridge University Press.

Černý, Jaroslav & Groll, Sarah Israelit. 1984. *A Late Egyptian Grammar.* 3rd, updated ed. (Studia Pohl, series maior 4). Rome: Biblical Institute Press.

Chaîne, Marius. 1934. *Les dialectes coptes assioutiques A2, les charactéristiques de leur phonétique, de leur morphologie, de leur syntaxe.* Paris: P. Geuthner.

Clagett, Marshall. 1989. *Ancient Egyptian Science. A Source Book.* Volume 1: *Knowledge and Order.* (Memoirs of the American Philosophical Society 184). Philadelphia: American Philosophical Society.

Clagett, Marshall. 1995. *Ancient Egyptian Science. A Source Book.* Volume 2: *Calendars, Clocks, and Astronomy.* (Memoirs of the American Philosophical Society 214). Philadelphia: American Philosophical Society.

Clagett, Marshall. 1999. *Ancient Egyptian Science. A Source Book.* Volume 3: *Ancient Egyptian Mathematics.* (Memoirs of the American Philosophical Society 232). Philadelphia: American Philosophical Society.

Clarysse, Willy. 1987. Greek loan-words in Demotic. In: Vleeming, Sven P. (ed.), *Aspects in Demotic Lexicography.* (Studia Demotica I). Leuven: Peeters, 9–33.

Claudi, Ulrike & Mendel, Daniela. 1991. Noun/verb distinction in Egyptian-Coptic and Mande: A grammaticalization perspective. In: Mendel, Daniela & Claudi, Ulrike (eds.), *Ägypten im afro-orientalischen Kontext: Aufsätze zur Archäologie, Geschichte und Sprache eines unbegrenzten Raumes. Gedenkschrift Peter Behrens.* (Afrikanistische Arbeitspapiere, Sondernummer). Köln: Universität zu Köln, 31–53.

Collier, Mark. 1996. The Language of Literature: On Grammar and Texture. In: Loprieno, Antonio (ed.), *Ancient Egyptian Literature. History and Forms.* (Probleme der Ägyptologie 10). Leiden/New York/Köln: Brill, 531–553.

Collier, Mark & Quirke, Stephen. 2002. *The UCL Lahun Papyri: Letters.* (British Archaeological Reports 1083). London: Archaeopress.

Collier, Mark & Quirke, Stephen. 2006. *The UCL Lahun Papyri: Accounts.* (British Archaeological Reports 1471). London: Archaeopress.

Crum, Walter E. 1939. *A Coptic Dictionary.* Oxford: Oxford University Press.

Cruz-Uribe, Eugene. 2001. Scripts: An Overview. In: Redford, Donald B. (ed.), *The Oxford Encyclopedia of Ancient Egypt*. Vol. 3. Oxford: Oxford University Press and New York/Cairo: The American University in Cairo Press, 192–198.

Depuydt, Leo. 1999. *Fundamentals of Egyptian Grammar*. Norton: Frog Publishing.

Dils, Peter, Grossman, Eitan, Richter, Tonio Sebastian & Schenkel, Wolfgang (eds.). fc., *Language contact and linguistic borrowing in Late Antiquity: the case of Coptic. Papers read on the inaugural conference of the project "Database and Dictionary of Greek Loanwords in Coptic", Leipzig, Sächsische Akademie der Wissenschaften zu Leipzig, April 2010*. (Lingua Aegyptia – Studia Monographica).

Dimmendaal, Gerrit J. 2011. *Historical Linguistics and the Comparative Study of African Languages*. Amsterdam/Philadelphia: Benjamins.

Doret, Eric. 1986. *The narrative verbal system of Old and Middle Egyptian*. (Cahiers d'Orientalisme 12). Geneva: P. Cramer.

Dreyer, Günter. 1999. *Umm el-Qaab 1. Das prädynastische Königsgrab U-j und seine frühen Schriftzeugnisse*. Mainz: Philipp von Zabern.

Edel, Elmar. 1955/1964. *Altägyptische Grammatik*. (Analecta Orientalia 34–39). Rom: Pontificium Institutum Biblicum.

Erichsen, Wolja. 1954. *Demotisches Glossar*. Kopenhagen: E. Munksgaard.

Erman, Adolf. 1880. *Neuaegyptische Grammatik*. Leipzig: Engelmann

Erman, Adolf. 1933. *Neuägyptische Grammatik*. 2nd. ed. Leipzig: Engelmann.

Erman, Adolf & Grapow, Hermann. 1926–1963. *Wörterbuch der aegyptischen Sprache*, 12 Bde., Leipzig: Hinrichs, Berlin: Akademie Verlag.

Ewald, Heinrich. 1861. *Abhandlung über den bau der thatwörter im Koptischen*. Göttingen: Dieterichsche Buchhandlung.

Ewald, Heinrich. 1862. *Abhandlung über den zusammenhang des Nordischen (Türkischen), Mittelländischen, Semitischen und Koptischen sprachstamms*. Göttingen: Dieterichsche Buchhandlung.

Eyre, Christopher. 1994. *Wni*'s career and Old Kingdom historiography. In: Eyre, Christopher, Leahy, Anthony & Leahy, Lisa Montagno (eds.), *The Unbroken Reed. Studies in the Culture and Heritage of Ancient Egypt in Honour of A.F. Shore*. (British Museum Occasional Publications 111). London: Egypt Exploration Society, 107–124.

Faulkner, Raymond O. 1962. A *Concise Dictionary of Middle Egyptian*. Oxford: Oxford University Press.

Feder, Frank. 2004. Der Einfluß des Griechischen auf das Ägyptische in ptolemäisch-römischer Zeit. In: Schneider, Thomas (ed.), *Das Ägyptische und die Sprachen Vorderasiens, Nordafrikas und der Ägäis. Akten des Basler Kolloquiums zum ägyptisch-nichtsemitischen Sprachkontakt, Basel 9.–11. Juli 2003*. (Alter Orient und Altes Testament 310). Münster: Ugarit-Verlag, 509–521.

Feder, Frank. 2005. Spuren oberägyptischer Dialekte in einem ägyptischen Text des 11.–10. Jahrhunderts v. Chr. *Hallesche Beiträge zur Orientwissenschaft* 40: 59–69.

Felber, Heinz. 2008. *Vom Demotischen zum Koptischen. In: Kootz, Anja & Pasch, Helma (eds.), 5000 Jahre Schrift in Afrika. Entstehung, Funktionen, Wandel*. (Kleine Schriften der Universitäts- und Staatsbibliothek Köln 24). Köln: Universitäts- u. Stadtbibliothek Köln, 17–22.

Fewster, Penelope. 2002. Bilingualism in Roman Egypt. In: Adams, J.N., Janse, M. & Swain, S., *Bilingualism in Ancient Society. Language Contact and the Written Text*. Oxford: Oxford University Press, 220–245.

Fleischman, Suzanne. 2000. Methodologies and Ideologies in Historical Linguistics: On Working with Older Languages. In: Herring, Susan C., van Reenen, Pieter & Schøsler, Lene (eds.), *Textual Parameters in Older Languages*. Amsterdam/Philadelphia: Benjamins, 33–58.

Förster, Hans. 2002. *Wörterbuch der griechischen Wörter in den koptischen dokumentarischen Texten*. (Texte und Untersuchungen zur Geschichte der altchristlichen Literatur 148). Berlin/New York: De Gruyter.

Fournet, Jean-Luc. 1989. Les emprunts du grec à l'égyptien. *Bulletin de la Société de Linguistique de Paris* 84: 55–80.

Fournet, Jean-Luc. 2009. The multilingual environment of Late Antique Egypt: Greek, Latin, Coptic, and Persian documentation. In: Bagnall, Roger S. (ed.), *The Oxford Handbook of Papyrology*. Oxford: Oxford University Press, 418–451.

Funk, Wolf-Peter. 1981. Beiträge des mittelägyptischen Dialekts zum koptischen Konjugationssystem. In: Young, Dwight W. (ed.), *Studies presented to Hans Jakob Polotsky*. Beacon Hill/Mass.: Eisenbrauns, 177–210.

Funk, Wolf-Peter. 1985. How closely related are the Subakhmimic Dialects? *Zeitschrift für Ägyptische Sprache und Altertumskunde* 112: 124–139.

Funk, Wolf-Peter. 1988. Dialects wanting homes: a numerical approach to the early varieties of Coptic. In: Fisiak, Jacek (ed.), *Historical dialectology: Regional and Social*. Berlin/New York/Amsterdam: Mouton de Gruyter, 149–192.

Funk, Wolf-Peter .1991. Dialects, Morphology of Coptic. In: *The Coptic Encyclopedia*. Vol. 8, 101–108.

Funk, Wolf-Peter. 2009. Methodological issues in the (morpho-)phonological description of Coptic. In: Goldenberg, Gideon & Shisha-Halevy, Ariel (eds.), *Egyptian, Semitic, and General Grammar. Studies in Memory of H.J. Polotsky*. Jerusalem: The Israel Academy of Scienes and Humanities, 70–91.

Gardiner, Alan H. 1957. *Egyptian Grammar. Being an Introduction to the Study of Hieroglyphs*. 3rd ed. Oxford: Oxford University Press.

Gnirs, Andrea M. 1996. Die ägyptische Autobiographie. In: Loprieno, Antonio (ed.), *Ancient Egyptian Literature. History and Forms*. (Probleme der Ägyptologie 10). Leiden/New York/ Köln: Brill, 191–241.

Goldwasser, Orly. 1990. On the Choice of Registers – Studies in the Grammar of Papyrus Anastasi I. In: Groll, Sarah Israelit (ed.), *Studies in Egyptology Presented to Miriam Lichtheim*. Jerusalem: Magnes Press, 120–149.

Goldwasser, Orly. 1992. Literary Late Egyptian as a Polysystem. *Poetics Today* 13: 447–462.

Goldwasser, Orly. 1995. *From Icon to Metaphor, Studies in the Semiotics of the Hieroglyphs*. (Orbis Biblicus et Orientalis 142). Fribourg: University Press.

Goldwasser, Orly. 1999. "Low" and "High" dialects in Ramesside Egyptian. In: Grunert, Stefan & Hafemann, Ingelore (eds.), *Textcorpus und Wörterbuch. Aspekte zur ägyptischen Lexikographie*. (Probleme der Ägyptologie 14). Leiden/New York/Köln: Brill, 311–328.

Goldwasser, Orly. 2001. Hieroglyphs. In: *The Oxford Encyclopaedia of Ancient Egypt*. Oxford/N.Y.: Oxford University Press.

Goldwasser, Orly. 2002. *Lovers, Prophets and Giraffes – Wor[l]d Classification in Ancient Egypt*. (Classification and categorization in Ancient Egypt 3). Wiesbaden: Harrassowitz.

Goldwasser, Orly. 2005. Where is Metaphor? Conceptual Metaphor and Alternative Classification in the Hieroglyphic Script. *Metaphor and Symbol* 20.2: 95–113.

Goldwasser, Orly. 2006. On a New Definition of Classifier Languages and Classifier Scripts. *Lingua Aegyptia 14*: 473–484.

Goldwasser, Orly. 2009. A Comparison between Classifier Language and Classifier Script: The Case of Ancient Egyptian. In: Goldenberg, G. (ed.), Goldenberg, Gideon & Shisha-Halevy, Ariel (eds.), *Egyptian, Semitic, and General Grammar. Studies in Memory of H.J. Polotsky.* Jerusalem: The Israel Academy of Scienes and Humanities, 16–39.

Goldwasser, Orly & Grinevald, Colette. 2012. What Are Determinatives Good For? In: Grossman, Eitan, Polis, Stéphane & Winand, Jean (eds.), *Lexical Semantics in Ancient Egyptian.* (Lingua Aegyptia Studia Monographica). Hamburg: Widmaier, 17–53.

Goldwasser, Orly & Müller, Matthias. 1999. The determinative system as a mirror of world organization. *Göttinger Miszellen* 170: 49–68.

Grapow, Hermann. 1938. *Vom Hieroglyphisch Demotischen zum Koptischen.* Berlin: De Gruyter.

Groll, Sarah Israelit. 1982. Diachronic grammar as a means of dating undated texts. In: Groll, Sarah Israelit (ed.), *Egyptological studies.* (Scripta Hierosolymitana 28). Jerusalem: Magnes Press, Hebrew University, 11–104.

Grossman, Eitan. 2007. Worknotes on the syntax of Nitrian Bohairic: A hitherto unnoticed circumstantial conversion. In: Bosson, Nathalie & Boud'hors, Anne (eds.), *Actes du huitième congrès international d'études coptes, Paris, 28 juin – 3 juillet 2004.* Vol. 2. (Orientalia Lovaniensia Analecta 163). Leuven/Paris/Dudley, Ma: Peeters, 711–725.

Grossman, Eitan. 2010. Periphrastic perfects in the Coptic dialects: a case study in grammaticalization. *Lingua Aegyptia* 17: 81–118.

Grunert, Stefan & Hafemann, Ingelore (eds.) 1999. *Textcorpus und Wörterbuch. Aspekte zur ägyptischen Lexikographie.* (Probleme der Ägyptologie 14). Leiden/New York/Köln: Brill.

Hafemann, Ingelore (ed.). 2013. *Perspektiven einer corpusbasierten historischen Linguistik und Philologie: Internationale Tagung des Akademienvorhabens „Altägyptisches Wörterbuch" an der BBAW, 12.–13. Dezember 2011* (Thesaurus Linguae Aegyptiae 4). Berlin: BBAW.

Hannig, Rainer. 2003. *Ägyptisches Wörterbuch I. Altes Reich und Erste Zwischenzeit.* (Hannig-Lexica 4). Mainz: Philipp von Zabern.

Hannig, Rainer. 2006. *Ägyptisches Wörterbuch II. Mittleres Reich und Zweite Zwischenzeit.* (Hannig-Lexica 5). Mainz: Philipp von Zabern.

Hasznos, Andrea. 2012. *Graeco-Coptica. Greek and Coptic Clause Patterns.* (Göttinger Orientforschungen IV.52). Wiesbaden: Harrassowitz.

Hayward, Richard J. 2000. Afroasiatic. In: Heine, Bernd & Nurse, Derek, *African languages: An introduction.* Cambridge: Cambridge University Press, 74–98.

Heine, Bernd & Nurse, Derek. 2000. *African Languages. An introduction.* Cambridge: Cambridge University Press.

Heine, Bernd & Nurse, Derek (eds.). 2008. *A Linguistic Geography of Africa.* Cambridge: Cambridge University Press.

Hintze, Fritz. 1947. Die Haupttendenzen der ägyptischen Sprachentwicklung. *Zeitschrift für Phonetik und allgemeine Sprachwissenschaft* 1: 85–108.

Hintze, Fritz. 1950. "Konversion" und "analytische Tendenz" in der ägyptischen Sprachentwicklung. *Zeitschrift für Phonetik und allgemeine Sprachwissenschaft* 4: 41–56.

Hintze, Fritz. 1950–1952. *Untersuchungen zu Stil und Sprache neuägyptischer Erzählungen.* Berlin: Akademie.

Hintze, Fritz. 1984. Eine Klassifizierung der koptischen Dialekte. In: *Studien zu Sprache und Religion Ägyptens, zu Ehren von Wolfhart Westendorf überreicht von seinen Freunden und Schülern.* Vol. 1. Göttingen: Hubert, 411–432.

Hoch, James. 1994. *Semitic Words in Egyptian Texts of the New Kingdom and Third Intermediate Period*. Princeton: Princeton University Press.

Hoffmann, Friedhelm & Quack, Joachim. 2007. *Anthologie der demotischen Literatur*. (Einführungen und Quellentexte zur Ägyptologie 4). Berlin: LIT-Verlag.

Hofmann, Tobias. 2002. Die Autobiographie des Uni von Abydos. *Lingua Aegyptia* 10: 225–237.

Ishaq, Emile Maher. 1991. Egyptian Arabic Vocabulary, Coptic Influence on. In: *The Coptic Encyclopedia*. Vol. 8, 112–118.

Jansen-Winkeln, Karl. 1995. Diglossie und Zweisprachigkeit im alten Ägypten. *Wiener Zeitschrift für die Kunde des Morgenlandes* 85: 85–115.

Jansen-Winkeln, Karl. 1996. *Spätmittelägyptische Grammatik der Texte der 3. Zwischenzeit*. (Ägypten und Altes Testament 34). Wiesbaden: Harrassowitz.

Jansen-Winkeln, Karl. 2011. Sprachgeschichte und Textdatierung. *Studien zur Altägyptischen Kultur* 40: 155–179.

Jenni, Hanna. 2010. *Lehrbuch der Klassisch-Ägyptischen Sprache*. Basel: Schwabe.

Johnson, Janet H. 1976. *The Demotic Verbal System*. (Studies in Ancient Oriental Civilization 38). Chicago: Oriental Institute.

Johnson, Janet H. 1999. The Chicago Demotic Dictionary Project. In: Grunert, Stefan & Hafemann, Ingelore (eds.), *Textcorpus und Wörterbuch. Aspekte zur ägyptischen Lexikographie*. (Probleme der Ägyptologie 14). Leiden/New York/Köln: Brill, 243–257.

Johnson, Janet H. 2000. *Thus Wrote Onchsheshonqy – An Introductory Grammar of Demotic*. (Studies in Ancient Oriental Civilization 45). 3rd ed. Chicago: Oriental Institute.

Junge, Friedrich. 1978. *Syntax der mittelägyptischen Literatursprache. Grundlagen einer Strukturtheorie*. Mainz: Philipp von Zabern.

Junge, Friedrich. 1984. Sprache. In: *Lexikon der Ägyptologie* V. Wiesbaden: Harrassowitz, 1176–1211.

Junge, Friedrich. 1985. Sprachstufen und Sprachgeschichte. *Zeitschrift der Deutschen Morgenländischen Gesellschaft*, Supplement VI. Stuttgart: Steiner, 17–34.

Junge, Friedrich. 1999. *Neuägyptisch. Einführung in die Grammatik*. 2nd ed. Wiesbaden: Harrassowitz.

Kahl, Jochem. 1994. *Das System der altägyptischen Hieroglyphenschrift in der 0.–3. Dynastie*. (Göttinger Orientforschungen 29). Wiesbaden: Harrassowitz.

Kahl, Jochem. 2000. *nb* ("jeder") als Quantitäts-Substantiv in der frühen ägyptischen Sprache. *Göttinger Miszellen* 175: 5–7.

Kahl, Jochem. 2001a. Perspektiven der Erforschung der frühen ägyptischen Schrift und Sprache. In: Popielska-Grzybowska, Joanna (ed.), *Proceedings of the First Central European Conference of Young Egyptologists. Egypt 1999: Perspectives of Research. Warsaw 7–9 June 1999*. Warsaw: Institute of Archaeology Warsaw University, 47–55.

Kahl, Jochem. 2001b. "Hieroglyphic Writing During the Fourth Millennium BC: an Analysis of Systems". *Archéo-Nil* 11, 101–134.

Kahl, Jochem. 2003. "Forschungsvorhaben «Frühägyptisches Wörterbuch»". In: Popielska-Grzybowska, Joanna (ed.), *Proceedings of the Second Central European Conference in Egyptology. Egypt 2001: Perspectives of Research. Warsaw 5–7 March 2001*. Warsaw: Institute of Archaeology Warsaw University, 75–83.

Kahl, Jochem. 2002–2004. *Frühägyptisches Wörterbuch*. Lieferung 1–3. Wiesbaden: Harrassowitz.

Kahle, Paul Eric. 1954. *Bala'izah. Coptic Texts from Deir el-Bala'izah in Upper Egypt*. Oxford/London: Oxford University Press.

Kammerzell, Frank. 1995. Afroasiatische und nicht-afroasiatische Komponenten des ägyptischen Lexikons. In: Eyre, Christopher (ed.), *Seventh International Congress of Egyptologists, Cambridge, 3–9 September 1995, Abstracts of papers*. Oxford: Oxbow, 95–96.

Kammerzell, Frank. 1996. Probleme des afroasiatischen Sprachvergleichs. Zum Hamito-Semitic Etymological Dictionary von E. Orel & O.V. Stolbova. *Indogermanische Forschungen* 101: 268–290.

Kammerzell, Frank. 1998. The sounds of a dead language. Reconstructing Egyptian Phonology. *Göttinger Beiträge zur Sprachwissenschaft* 1: 21–41.

Kammerzell, Frank. 1999. Klassifikatoren und Kategorienbildung in der ägyptischen Hieroglyphenschrift. *Spektrum – Informationen aus Forschung und Lehre* 99.3: 29–34.

Kammerzell, Frank. 2000. Egyptian possessive constructions: a diachronic typological perspective. *Sprachtypologie und Universalienforschung* 53.1: 97–108.

Kammerzell, Frank. 2001a. Die Entstehung der Alphabetreihe: zum ägyptischen Ursprung der semitischen und westlichen Schriften. In: Borchers, Dörte, Kammerzell, Frank & Weninger, Stefan (eds.), *Hieroglyphen, Alphabete, Schriftreformen: Studien zu Multiliteralismus, Schriftwechsel und Orthographieneuregelungen*. (Lingua Aegyptia Studia Monographica 3). Göttingen: Seminar für Ägyptologie und Koptologie, 117–158.

Kammerzell, Frank. 2001b. Aegypto-Germanica: Ägyptischer Wortschatz in westeuropäischen Sprachen (Teil 1). In: Schierholz, Stefan J., Fobbe, Eilika, Goes, Stefan & Knirsch, Rainer (eds.), *Die deutsche Sprache in der Gegenwart. Festschrift für Dieter Cherubim zum 60. Geburtstag*. Frankfurt/M. et al.: Peter Lang, 115–127.

Kammerzell, Frank. 2001c. Aegypto-Germanica: Ägyptischer Wortschatz in westeuropäischen Sprachen (Teil 2). *Göttinger Beiträge zur Sprachwissenschaft* 5: 39–55.

Kammerzell, Frank. 2005. Old Egyptian and Pre-Old Egyptian. Tracing linguistic diversity in Archaic Egypt and the Creation of the Egyptian Language. In: Seidlmayer, St. (ed.), *Texte und Denkmäler des ägyptischen Alten Reiches*. Berlin: Achet, 165–247.

Kammerzell, Frank & Lincke, Eliese-Sophia. 2012. Egyptian classifiers at the interface of lexical semantics and pragmatics. In: Grossman, Eitan, Polis, Stéphane & Winand, Jean (eds.), *Lexical Semantics in Ancient Egyptian* (Lingua Aegyptia Studia Monographica 9). Hamburg: Widmaier, 55–112.

Kasser, Rodolphe. 1964. *Compléments au dictionnaire copte de Crum*. (Bibliothèque d'Études Coptes 7). Le Caire: IFAO.

Kasser, Rodolphe. 1966. La penetration des mots grecs dans la langue copte. *Wissenschaftliche Zeitschrift der Martin-Luther-Universität Halle – Wittenberg* 15: 419–425.

Kasser, Rodolphe. 1991a. Alphabets, Coptic. In: *The Coptic Encyclopedia*. Vol. 8, 33–41.

Kasser, Rodolphe. 1991b. Alphabets, Old Coptic. In: *The Coptic Encyclopedia*. Vol. 8, 41–45.

Kasser, Rodolphe. 1991c. Dialects. In: *The Coptic Encyclopedia*. Vol. 8, 87–97.

Kasser, Rodolphe. 1991d. Dialects, Grouping and Major Groups of. In: *The Coptic Encyclopedia*. Vol. 8, 97–101.

Kasser, Rodolphe. 1991e. Fayyumic. In: The *The Coptic Encyclopedia*. Vol. 8, 124–131.

Kasser, Rodolphe. 1991f. Geography, Dialectal. In: *The Coptic Encyclopedia*. Vol. 8, 133–141.

Kasser, Rodolphe. 1991g. Vocabulary, Copto-Greek. In: *The Coptic Encyclopedia*. Vol. 8, 215–222.

Kloth, Nicole. 2002. *Die (auto-)biograpischen Inschriften des ägyptischen Alten Reiches: Untersuchungen zu Phraseologie und Entwicklung*. (Studien zur Altägyptischen Kultur, Beihefte 8). Hamburg: Buske.

Knigge, Carsten. 2004. Sprachkontakte und lexikalische Interferenz im ersten vorchristlichen Jahrtausend. In: Schneider, Thomas (ed.), *Das Ägyptische und die Sprachen Vorderasiens, Nordafrikas und der Ägäis. Akten des Basler Kolloquiums zumägyptisch-nichtsemitischen Sprachkontakt, Basel 9.–11. Juli 2003.* (Alter Orient und Altes Testament 310.) Münster: Ugarit-Verlag, 33–88.

Kroeber, Burkhart. 1970. *Die Neuägyptizismen vor der Amarnazeit: Studien zur Entwicklung der ägyptischen Sprache vom Mittleren zum Neuen Reich.* Bamberg: Aku.

Lambdin, Thomas O. 1983. *Introduction to Sahidic Coptic.* Macon/Georgia: Mercer University Press.

Layton, Bentley. 2004[2]. *A Coptic Grammar. With Chrestomathy and Glossary. Sahidic Dialect.* (Porta linguarum orientalium n.s. vol. 20). Wiesbaden: Harrassowitz.

Lesko, Leonard H. & Switalski Lesko, Barbara. 1982–1990. *A Dictionary of Late Egyptian.* Providence: B.C. Scribe Publications.

Lincke, Eliese-Sophia. 2011. *Die Prinzipien der Klassifizierung im Altägyptischen.* (Göttinger Orientforschungen, Reihe IV: Ägypten 38.6 = Classification and Categorization in Ancient Egypt 6). Wiesbaden: Harrassowitz.

Loprieno, Antonio. 1995. *Ancient Egyptian. A Linguistic Introduction.* Cambridge: Cambridge University Press.

Loprieno, Antonio. 1996. Linguistic variety and Egyptian literature. In: Loprieno, Antonio (ed.), *Ancient Egyptian Literature. History and Forms.* (Probleme der Ägyptologie 10). Leiden/New York/Köln: Brill, 515–529.

Loprieno, Antonio. 2000. From VSO to SVO? Word order and rear extraposition in Coptic. In: Sornicola, Rosana, Poppe, Erich & Shisha-Halevy, Ariel (eds.), *Stability, Variation and Change of Word-Order Patterns over Time.* Amsterdam/Philadelphia: Benjamins, 23–39.

Loprieno, Antonio. 2001. From Old Egyptian to Coptic. In: Haspelmath, Martin, König, Ekkehard, Oesterreicher, Wulf & Raible, Wolfgang (eds.), *Language Typology and Language Universals / Sprachtypologie und sprachliche Universalien.* (Handbücher zur Sprach- und Kommunikationswissenschaft 20.2). Berlin: De Gruyter, 1742–1761.

Loprieno, Antonio. 2003. Egyptian Linguistics in the Year 2000. In: Hawass, Zahi (ed.), *Egyptology at the Dawn of the Twenty-first Century. Proceedings of the Eighth International Congress of Egyptologists, Cairo 2000.* Cairo: The American University in Cairo Press, 73–90.

Loprieno, Antonio. 2008. Egyptian and Coptic. In: Woodard, Roger D., *The Ancient Languages of Mesopotamia, Egypt and Aksum.* Cambridge/New York: Cambridge University Press, 153–210.

Loprieno, Antonio & Müller, Matthias. 2012. Ancient Egyptian and Coptic. In: Frajzyngier, Zygmunt & Shay, Erin (eds.), *The Afroasiatic Languages.* (Cambridge Language Surveys). Cambridge: Cambridge University Press, 102–144.

Lucas, Christopher & Lash, Elliott. 2010. Contact as catalyst: The case for Coptic influence in the development of Arabic negation. *Journal of Linguistics* 46: 379–413.

Luft, Ulrich. 1992. *Hieratische Papyri aus den Staatlichen Museen zu Berlin – Preussischer Kulturbesitz/Lfg. 1: Das Archiv von Illahun.* Berlin: Akademie Verlag.

Malaise, Michel & Winand, Jean. 1999. *Grammaire raisonnée de l'égyptien classique.* (Ægyptica Leodiensia 6). Liège: C.I.P.L.

Mallon, Alexis. 1956. *Grammaire Copte. Quadrième édition revue par M. Malinine.* Beyrouth: Imprimerie catholique.

Meeks, Dmitri. 1977–1979. *Année lexicographique.* Paris: Cybele.

Meeks, Dmitri. 1999. Dictionnaires et lexicographie de égyptien ancien: méthodes et resultants. *Bibliotheca Orientalis* 56: 569–594.

Mendel, Daniela & Claudi, Ulrike (eds.). 1991. *Ägypten im afro-orientalischen Kontext: Aufsätze zur Archäologie, Geschichte und Sprache eines unbegrenzten Raumes. Gedenkschrift Peter Behrens*. (Afrikanistische Arbeitspapiere, Sondernummer). Köln: Universität zu Köln, 31–53.

Militarev, Alexander. 2007. Akkadian-Egyptian Lexical Matches. In: Miller, Cynthia L. (ed.), *Studies in Semitic and Afroasiatic Linguistics Presented to Gene B. Gragg*. (Studies in Ancient Oriental Civilization 60). Chicago: The Oriental Institute.

Moers, Gerald. 2001. *Fingierte Welten in der ägyptischen Literatur des 2. Jahrtausends v. Chr. Grenzüberschreitung, Reisemotiv und Fiktionalität*. (Probleme der Ägyptologie 19). Leiden/New York/Köln: Brill.

Morenz, Ludwig. 2004. *Bild-Buchstaben und Symbolische Zeichen: die Herausbildung der Schrift in der hohen Kultur Altägyptens*. (Orbis Biblicus et Orientalis 205). Göttingen: Vandenhoeck & Ruprecht.

Nagel, Peter. 1969. Grammatische Untersuchungen zu Nag Hammadi Codex II. In: Altheim, Franz & Stiehl, Ruth (eds.), *Die Araber in der Alten Welt*. Vol. 7, Berlin: De Gruyter, 393–469.

Nagel, Peter. 1991a. Akhmimic. In: *The Coptic Encyclopedia*. Vol. 8, 19–27.

Nagel, Peter. 1991b. Lycopolitan (or Lyco-Diospolitan or Subakhmimic). In: *The Coptic Encyclopedia*. Vol. 8, 151–159.

Neveu, François. 1998. *La langue des Ramsès. Grammaire du néo-égyptien*. 2nd ed. Paris: Khéops.

Oréal, Elsa. 1999. Contact linguistique. Le cas du rapport entre le grec et le copte. *Lalies* 19: 289–306.

Oréal, Elsa. 2010. *Les particules en égyptien ancien. De l'ancien égyptien à l'égyptien classique*. (Bibliothèque d'étude 152). Le Caire: IFAO.

Osing, Jürgen. 1976. *Die Nominalbildung des Ägyptischen*. Mainz: Philipp von Zabern.

Osing, Jürgen. 1977. Zur Syntax der Biographie des *Wnj*. *Orientalia* 46: 165–182

Osing, Jürgen. 1990. Ägyptische und koptische Lexikographie. In: *Wörterbücher – Dictionaries – Dictionnaires*. (Handbücher der Sprach- und Kommunikationswissenschaft 5.2). Berlin/New York: De Gruyter, 1679–1682.

Papaconstantinou, Arietta (ed.). 2010. *The multilingual experience: Egypt from the Ptolemies to the 'Abbâsids*. Farnham/Burlington, VT: Ashgate Publishing Company.

Parkinson, Richard B. 1991. Teachings, Discourses and Tales from the Middle Kingdom. In: Quirke, Stephen (ed.), *Middle Kingdom Studies*. New Malden, Surrey: SIA, 91–122.

Parkinson, Richard B. 1996. Types of Literature in the Middle Kingdom. In: Loprieno, Antonio (ed.), *Ancient Egyptian Literature. History and Forms*. (Probleme der Ägyptologie 10). Leiden/New York/Köln: Brill, 297–312.

Parkinson, Richard B. 2002. *Poetry and Culture in Middle Kingdom Egypt. A Dark Side to Perfection*. London/New York: Equinox.

Peremans, Willy. 1964. Über die Zweisprachigkeit im ptolemäischen Ägypten. In: *Studien zur Papyrologie und antiken Wirtschaftsgeschichte, Friedrich Oertel zum achtzigsten Geburtstag gewidmet*. Bonn: R. Habelt, 49–60.

Peremans, Willy. 1983. Le bilinguisme dans les relations gréco-égyptiennes sous les lagides. In: Van't Dack, E., Van Dessen, P. & Van Gucht, W. (eds.) *Egypt and the Hellenistic World*. (Studia Hellenistica 27). Leuven: Peeters, 253–280.

Peust, Carsten. 1999. *Egyptian Phonology. An Introduction to the Phonology of a Dead Language.* (Monographien zur Ägyptischen Sprache 2). Göttingen: Peust & Gutschmidt.

Peust, Carsten. 2004. Das Ägyptische als afrikanische Sprache. In: Schneider, Thomas (ed.), *Das Ägyptische und die Sprachen Vorderasiens, Nordafrikas und der Ägäis: Akten des Basler Kolloquiums zum ägyptisch-nichtsemitischen Sprachkontakt, Basel 9.–11. Juli 2003.* (Alter Orient und Altes Testament 310). Münster: Ugarit-Verlag, 321–407.

Polis, Stéphane. fc. Linguistic variation in Ancient Egyptian. Genres and registers in the scribal repertoires of Amennakhte son on Ipuy. In: Cromwell, Jennifer & Grossman, Eitan (eds.), *Beyond Free Variation: Scribal Repertoires from Old Kingdom to Early Islamic Egypt* (in press).

Polis, Stéphane & Winand, Jean. 2013. The Ramses project: Methodolgy and practices in the annotation of Late Egyptian Texts. In: Hafemann, Ingelore (ed.), *Perspektiven einer corpusbasierten historischen Linguistik und Philologie: Internationale Tagung des Akademienvorhabens „Altägyptisches Wörterbuch" an der BBAW, 12.–13. Dezember 2011.* (Thesaurus Linguae Aegyptiae 4). Berlin: BBAW, 81–108.

Polotsky, Hans Jakob. 1960. The Coptic Conjugation System. *Orientalia* 29 n.s.: 392–422.

Polotsky, Hans Jakob. 1987/1990. *Die Grundlagen des koptischen Satzbaus.* (American Studies in Papyrology 28–29). Decatur, Ga.: Scholars Press.

Posener, Georges. 1956. *Littérature et politique dans l'Égypte de la XIIe dynastie.* (Bibliothèque de l'Ecole pratique des hautes études 307). Paris: Champion.

Posener-Kriéger, Paule. 1968. *The Abusir Papyri.* (Hieratic papyri in the British Museum 5). London: British Museum.

Posener-Kriéger, Paule. 1976. *Les archives du temple funéraire de Néferirkarê-Kakaï: les papyrus d'Abousir.* (Bibliothèque d'Étude de l'Institut Français d'Archéologie Orientale du Caire 65). Le Caire: IFAO.

Posener-Kriéger, Paule. 2004. *I Papiri di Gebelein.* Torino: Museo Egizio.

Posener-Kriéger, Paule, Verner, Miroslav & Vymazalová, Hana. 2006. *Abusir X. The Pyramid Complex of Raneferef. The Papyrus Archive.* Prague: Czech Institute of Egyptology.

Quack, Joachim Friedrich. 2002. Zur Stellung des Ägyptischen innerhalb der afroasiatischen Sprachen. *Orientalistische Literaturzeitung* 97: 161-185.

Quack, Joachim Friedrich. 2005. Zu den vorarabischen semitischen Lehnwörtern des Koptischen. In: Burtea, Bogdan, Tropper, Josef & Younansardaroud, Helen (eds.), *Studia semitica et semitohamitica. Festschrift für Rainer Voigt anläßlich seines 60. Geburtstages am 17. Januar 2004.* (Alter Orient und Altes Testament 317). Münster: Ugarit-Verlag, 307–338.

Quack, Joachim Friedrich. fc. (a). *Demotische Grammatik.*

Quack, Joachim Friedrich. fc. (b). How the Coptic Script Came About. In: Dils, Peter, Grossman, Eitan, Richter, Tonio Sebastian & Schenkel, Wolfgang (eds.) fc., *Language contact and linguistic borrowing in Late Antiquity: the case of Coptic. Papers read on the inaugural conference of the project "Database and Dictionary of Greek Loanwords in Coptic", Leipzig, Sächsische Akademie der Wissenschaften zu Leipzig, April 2010.* (Lingua Aegyptia – Studia Monographica).

Quaegebeur, Jan. 1982. De la préhistoire de l'écriture Copte. *Orientalia Lovaniensia Periodica* 13: 125–136.

Quecke, Hans. 1974. Il dialetto. In: Orlandi, Tito, *Papiri della Università degli studi di Milano, volumo quinto: Lettere di San Paolo in copto-ossirinchita.* Milano: Istituto editoriale cisalpino, 87–107.

Quirke, Stephen. 1996. Narrative Literature. In: Loprieno, Antonio (ed.), *Ancient Egyptian Literature. History and Forms*. (Probleme der Ägyptologie 10). Leiden/New York/Köln: Brill, 263–276.

Reintges, Chris H. 2001. Code-mixing strategies in Coptic Egyptian. *Lingua Aegyptia* 9: 193–237.

Reintges, Chris H. 2004a. *Coptic Egyptian (Sahidic Dialect). A Learner's Grammar*. Köln: Köppe, 2004.

Reintges, Chris H. 2004b. Coptic Egyptian as a Bilingual Language Variety. In: Bádenas De La Peña, Pedro, Torallas Tovar, Sofía, Luján, Eugenio R. & Gallego, Maria Ángeles (eds.), *Lenguas en contacto: el testimonio escrito*. Madrid: CSIC, 69–86.

Reintges, Chris H. 2012. Macroparametric change and the synthetic-analytic dimension. The Case of Ancient Egyptian. In: Galves, Charlotte, Cyrino, Sônia, Lopes, Ruth, Sandalo, Filomena & Avelar, Juanito (eds.), *Parameter Theory and Linguistic Change*. Oxford: Oxford University Press, 132–156.

Richards, Janet E. 2004. Text and Context in late Old Kingdom Egypt: The Archaeology and Historiography of Weni the Elder. *Journal of the American Research Center in Egypt* 39: 75–102.

Richter, Tonio Sebastian. 2006a. Coptic[, Arabic loanwords in], in: Versteegh, K. (ed.), *Encyclopedia of Arabic Language and Linguistics*. Vol. I. Leiden/New York/Köln: Brill 2006, 595–601.

Richter, Tonio Sebastian. 2006b. "Spoken" Sahidic. Gleanings from non-literary texts. In: Lepper Verena, Nagel, Peter & Schenkel, Wolfgang (eds.), *"After Polotsky". Akten des Kolloquiums im Gedenken an den 100. Geburtstag von Hans Jakob Polotsky (1905–1991) in Bad Honnef bei Bonn, 9.–11. November 2005*. (= Lingua Aegyptia 14), 311–323.

Richter, Tonio Sebastian. 2009. Greek, Coptic, and the 'Language of the Hijra'. Rise and Decline of the Coptic Language in Late Antique and Medieval Egypt. In: Cotton, Hannah M., Hoyland, Robert G., Price, Jonathan J. & Wasserstein, David J. (eds.), *From Hellenism to Islam: Cultural and Linguistic Change in the Roman Near East*. Cambridge: Cambridge University Press, 402–447.

Roeder, Hubert. 2009. Erzählen im Alten Ägypten. Vorüberlegungen zu einer Erzähltheorie zwischen Literaturwissenschaft und Altertumswissenschaft. In: Roeder, Hubert (ed.), *Das Erzählen in frühen Hochkulturen, 1. Der Fall Ägypten*. (Ägyptologie und Kulturwissenschaft 1). München: Fink, 15–54.

Rösch, Friedrich. 1909. *Vorbemerkungen zu einer Grammatik der achmimischen Mundart*. Strasbourg: Schlesier und Schweikhardt.

Rutherford, Ian. 2010. Bilingualism in Roman Egypt? Exploring the Archive of Phatres of Narmuthis. In: Evans, Trevor & Obbink, Dirk (eds.), *The Language of the Papyri*. Oxford: Oxford University Press, 198–207.

Satzinger, Helmut. 1976. *Neuägyptische Studien. Die Partikel ir – Das Tempussystem*. Wiener Zeitschrift für die Kunde des Morgenlandes, Beiheft 6. Wien: Verlag des Verbandes der wissenschaftlichen Gesellschaften Österreichs.

Satzinger, Helmut. 1984. Die altkoptischen Texte als Zeugnisse der Beziehungen zwischen Ägyptern und Griechen. In: Nagel, Peter (ed.), *Graeco-Coptica. Griechen und Kopten im byzantinischen Ägypten*. Wissenschaftliche Beiträge der Martin-Luther-Universität Halle – Wittenberg 48 (I 29), Halle/Saale: Martin-Luther-Universität, 137–146.

Satzinger, Helmut. 1999. Afroasiatischer Sprachvergleich. In: Grunert, Stefan & Hafemann, Ingelore (eds.), *Textcorpus und Wörterbuch. Aspekte zur ägyptischen Lexikographie*. (Probleme der Ägyptologie 14). Leiden/New York/Köln: Brill, 367–386.

Satzinger, Helmut. 2000. Egyptian as an African Language. In: *Atti del IV Convegno Nazionale di Egittologia e Papirologia, Siracusa, 5–7 Dicembre 1997.* (Quaderni del Museo del Papiro IX). Siracusa: Istituto internazionale del papiro, 31–43.

Schenke, Hans-Martin. 1978. On the Middle Egyptian Dialect of the Coptic Language. *Enchoria* 8 (Sonderband): 43*(89)–58*(104).

Schenke, Hans-Martin. 1991. Mesokemic (or Middle Egyptian). In: *The Coptic Encyclopedia.* Vol. 8, 162–164.

Schenkel, Wolfgang. 1983. *Zur Rekonstruktion der deverbalen Nominalbildung des Ägyptischen.* (Göttinger Orientforschungen IV). Wiesbaden: Harrassowitz.

Schenkel, Wolfgang. 1984. Schrift. In: *Lexikon der Ägyptologie* V. Wiesbaden: Harrassowitz, 713–735.

Schenkel, Wolfgang. 1990. *Einführung in die altägyptische Sprachwissenschaft.* Darmstadt: Wissenschaftliche Buchgesellschaft.

Schenkel, Wolfgang. 1994. Die Hieroglyphenschrift und ihre Weiterentwicklungen. In: Günther, Hartmut & Ludwig, Otto (eds.), *Schrift und Schriftlichkeit / Writing and its Use.* (Handbücher zur Sprach- und Kommunikationswissenschaft 10.1). Berlin/New York: De Gruyter, 289–298.

Schenkel, Wolfgang. 1995. Die Lexikographie des Altägyptisch-Koptischen. In: *The lexicography of the ancient Near Eastern languages.* (Studi epigraphi e linguistici 12), 191–203.

Schenkel, Wolfgang. 1997. Ägyptisch-Koptisch: Einfahren einer linguistischen Ernte. *Orientalistische Literaturzeitung* 92: 5–25.

Schenkel, Wolfgang. 1998. Graphien der 1. Person Plural mit Personendeterminativ in den Sargtexten. *Göttinger Miszellen* 165: 91–98.

Schenkel, Wolfgang. 1999. *ś*-Kausativa, *t*-Kausativa und "innere" Kausativa: die *ś*-Kausativa der Verben I.*ś* in den Sargtexten. *Studien zur Altägyptischen Kultur* 27: 313–352.

Schenkel, Wolfgang. 2000. Die Endungen des Negativkomplements im Spiegel der Befunde der Sargtexte. *Lingua Aegyptia* 7: 1–26.

Schenkel, Wolfgang. 2002. Zur Formenbildung des prädikativen *sḏm=f* der Verben II.gem., vornehmlich nach dem Zeugnis der Sargtexte. *Göttinger Miszellen* 189: 89–98.

Schenkel, Wolfgang. 2003. *Die hieroglyphische Schriftlehre und die Realität der hieroglyphischen Graphien.* (Sitzungsberichte der Sächsischen Akademie der Wissenschaften zu Leipzig, Phil.-hist. Kl., Band 138, Heft 5). Stuttgart/Leipzig: Hirzel.

Schenkel, Wolfgang. 2004/5. Das *sḏm(w)=f*-Passiv, Perfekt vs. Futur, nach dem Zeugnis der Sargtexte. *Zeitschrift für ägyptische Sprache und Altertumskunde* 131: 173–188; 132: 40–54.

Schenkel, Wolfgang. 2005. Die ägyptische Nominalbildungslehre und die Realität der hieroglyphischen Graphien der Sargtexte. Die Nominalbildungsklassen A I 5 und A I 6. *Lingua Aegyptia* 13: 141–171.

Schenkel, Wolfgang. 2007. Zur Formenbildung des Perfekts *śčm=f / rčj=f* der Verben II.gem., vornehmlich nach dem Zeugnis der Sargtexte. *Lingua Aegyptia* 15: 203–216.

Schenkel, Wolfgang. 2008. Die ägyptische Nominalbildungslehre und die Realität der hieroglyphischen Graphien der Sargtexte II: Weitere Nominalbildungsklassen mit einer Endung -*w/y/i* (A II 5–10, A III 4–6 und A I 7/8/10). *Lingua Aegyptia* 16: 153–170.

Schenkel, Wolfgang. 2009. Prädikatives und abstrakt-relativisches *śčm.n=f*: Beobachtungen an den Verben II. gem. und ult.n im Korpus der Sargtexte. In: Goldenberg, Gideon & Shisha-Halevy, Ariel (eds.), *Egyptian, Semitic and general grammar: Studies in memory of H.J. Polotsky.* Jerusalem: Israel Academy of Sciences and Humanities, 40–60.

Schenkel, Wolfgang. 2011. Wie ikonisch ist die altägyptische Schrift? *Lingua Aegyptia* 19: 125–153.

Schenkel, Wolfgang. 2012. *Tübinger Einführung in die klassisch-ägyptische Sprache und Schrift.* Überarbeitete und erweiterte Ausgabe. Tübingen: Wolfgang Schenkel.

Schneider, Thomas (ed.). 2004a. *Das Ägyptische und die Sprachen Vorderasiens, Nordafrikas und der Ägäis. Akten des Basler Kolloquiums zum ägyptisch-nichtsemitischen Sprachkontakt, Basel 9.–11. Juli 2003.* (Alter Orient und Altes Testament 310). Münster: Ugarit-Verlag, 509–521.

Schneider, Thomas. 2004b. Nichtsemitische Lehnwörter im Ägyptischen. Umriss eines Forschungsgebietes. In: Schneider, Thomas (ed.) 2004a. *Das Ägyptische und die Sprachen Vorderasiens, Nordafrikas und der Ägäis. Akten des Basler Kolloquiums zum ägyptisch-nichtsemitischen Sprachkontakt, Basel 9.–11. Juli 2003.* (Alter Orient und Altes Testament 310). Münster: Ugarit-Verlag, 11–31.

Schweitzer, Simon D. 2005. *Schrift und Sprache der 4. Dynastie.* (Menes 3). Wiesbaden: Harrassowitz.

Shisha-Halevy, Ariel. 1986. *Coptic Grammatical Categories. Structural Studies in the Syntax of Shenoutean Sahidic.* (Analecta Orientalia 53). Roma: Biblical Institute Press.

Shisha-Halevy, Ariel. 1988. *Coptic Grammatical Chrestomathy.* (Orientalia Lovaniensia Analecta 30). Leuven: Peeters.

Shisha-Halevy, Ariel. 2000. Stability in Clausal/Phrasal Pattern Constituent Sequencing: 4000 years of Egyptian (With some Theoretical Reflections, also on Celtic). In: Sornicola, Rosana, Poppe, Erich, Shisha-Halevy, Ariel (eds.), *Stability, Variation and Change of Word-Order Patterns over Time.* Amsterdam/Philadelphia: Benjamins, 71–100

Shisha-Halevy, Ariel. 2007. *Topics in Coptic Syntax: Structural Studies in the Bohairic Dialect.* (Orientalia Lovaniensia Analecta 160). Leuven: Peeters.

Simpson, Robert S. 1996. *Demotic Grammar in the Ptolemaic Sacerdotal Decrees.* Oxford: Griffith Institute, Ashmolean Museum.

Smoczynski, Wawrzyniec. 1999. Seeking structure in the lexicon. On some cognitive-functional aspects of determinative assignment. *Lingua Aegyptia* 6: 153–162.

Spiegelberg, Wilhelm. 1925. *Demotische Grammatik.* Heidelberg: Carl Winter.

Stadler, Martin Andreas. 2008. On the Demise of Egyptian Writing: Working with a Problematic Source Basis. In: Baines, John, Bennet, John & Houston, Stephen (eds.), *The Disappearance of Writing Systems. Perspectives on Literacy and Communication.* London/Oakville: Equinox, 157–181.

Steindorff, Georg. 1894, 1904², 1930³. *Koptische Grammatik.* Berlin: Reuther & Reichard.

Steindorff, Georg. 1951. *Lehrbuch der koptischen Grammatik.* Chicago: University Press.

Stern, Ludwig. 1880. *Koptische Grammatik.* Leipzig: T.O. Weigel.

Stricker, Bruno. 1945. *De indeeling der egyptische taalgeschiedenis.* Leiden/New York/Köln: Brill.

Takács, Gábor. 1999–2008. *Etymological Dictionary of Egyptian.* (Handbuch der Orientalistik I.48. Vols. 1–3.). Leiden/New York/Köln: Brill.

Takács, Gábor (ed.). 2004. *Egyptian and Semito-Hamitic (Afro-Asiatic) Studies in Memory of Werner Vycichl.* (Studies in Semitic Languages and Linguistics 39). Leiden/New York/Köln: Brill.

Thesaurus Linguae Aegyptiae. <http://aaew2.bbaw.de/tla/>

Till, Walter C. 1928. *Achmimisch-koptische Grammatik.* Leipzig: Hinrichs.

Till, Walter C. 1930. *Koptische Chrestomathie für den fayumischen Dialekt, mit grammatischer Skizze und Anmerkungen.* (Schriften der Arbeitsgemeinschaft der Aegyptologen und Afrikanisten in Wien 1). Wien: Arbeitsgemeinschaft der Ägyptologen und Afrikanisten in Wien.

Till, Walter C. 1931, 1962². *Koptische Dialektgrammatik.* München: C. H. Beck.

Till, Walter C. 1955, 1978⁵. *Koptische Grammatik (Saïdischer Dialekt).* Leipzig: Verlag Enzyklopädie.

Torallas Tovar, Sofía. 2004. Egyptian Lexical Interference in the Greek of Byzantine and Early Islamic Egypt. In: Sijpesteijn, Petra M. & Sundelin, Lennart (eds.), *Papyrology and the History of Early Islamic Egypt.* (Islamic History and Civilization 55). Leiden/New York/Köln: Brill, 163–198.

Torallas Tovar, Sofia. 2010. Greek in Egypt. In: Bakker, E. (ed.), *A companion to the Ancient Greek language.* Oxford: Wiley-Blackwell, 253–266.

Tubach, Jürgen. 1999a. Bemerkungen zur geplanten Wiederaufnahme des Wörterbuchprojekts „Griechische Lehnwörter im Koptischen" in Halle. In: Emmel, Stephen, Krause, M., Richter, S.G. & Schaten, S. (eds.), *Ägypten und Nubien in spätantiker und christlicher Zeit. Akten des 6. Internationalen Koptologenkongresses Münster, 20.–26. Juli 1996.* Vol. 2: *Schrifttum, Sprache, Gedankenwelt.* (Sprachen und Kulturen des Christlichen Orients 6.2). Wiesbaden: Reichert, 405–419.

Tubach, Jürgen. 1999b. Griechische Lehnwörter in den koptischen Manichaica. Zur Problematik eines Lehnwortschatzes in einer Übersetzung aus einem anderen Kulturbereich. In: Grunert, Stefan & Hafemann, Ingelore (eds.), *Textcorpus und Wörterbuch. Aspekte zur ägyptischen Lexikographie.* (Probleme der Ägyptologie 14). Leiden/New York/Köln: Brill, 329–343.

Van der Molen, Rami. 2000. *A Hieroglyphic Dictionary of Egyptian Coffin Texts.* (Probleme der Äyptologie 15). Leiden/New York/Köln: Brill.

Van der Molen, Rami. 2005. *An analytical concordance of the verb, the negation and the syntax in Egyptian coffin texts.* (Handbuch der Orientalistik 77). Leiden/New York/Köln: Brill.

Vergote, Joseph. 1973, 1983: *Grammaire copte.* Vols. I–II. Leuven: Peeters.

Vergote, Joszef. 1973–1983. *Grammaire copte.* 2 vols. Leuven: Peeters.

Vernus, Pascal. 1988. L'égypto-copte. In: Perrot, Jean (ed.), *Les langues dans le monde ancien et moderne. Troisième partie: les langues chamito-sémitiques. Textes réunis par David Cohen.* Paris: Éd. du Centre national de la recherche scientifique, 161–206.

Vernus, Pascal. 1993. La naissance de l'écriture dans l'Égypte ancienne. *Archéo-Nil* 3: 75–108.

Vernus, Pascal. 1996a. La position linguistique des Textes des Sarcophages. In: Willems, Harco (ed.), *The World of the Coffin Texts. Proceedings of the Symposium Held on the Occasion of the 100th Birthday of Adriaan de Buck. Leiden, December 17–19, 1992.* (Egyptologische Uitgaven 9). Leiden: Nederlands Instituut voor het Nabije Oosten, 143–196.

Vernus, Pascal. 1996b. Langue littéraire et diglossie. In: Loprieno, Antonio (ed.), *Ancient Egyptian Literature. History and Forms.* (Probleme der Ägyptologie 10). Leiden/New York/Köln: Brill, 555–564.

Vernus, Pascal .2000. Situation de l'égyptien dans les langues du monde. In: Fauvelle-Aymar, François-Xavier, Chrétien, Jean-Pierre & Perrot, Claude-Hélène (eds.), *Afrocentrismes. L'histoire des Africains entre Égypte et Amérique.* (Collection Hommes et Sociétés). Paris: Éditions Karthala, 169–208.

Vernus, Pascal. 2004. La syntagme de quantification en égyptien de la première phase: sur les relations entre Textes des Pyramides et Textes des Sarcophages. In: Bickel, Susanne

& Mathieu, Bernard (eds.), *D'un monde à l'autre: Textes des Pyramides & Textes des Sarcophages (Actes de la table ronde internationale «Textes des Pyramides versus Textes des Sarcophages» IFAO – 24–26 septembre 2001).* (Bibliothèque d'étude 139). Cairo: Institut français d'archéologie orientale, 279–311.

Vierros, Marja. 2012. *Bilingual Notaries in Hellenistic Egypt. A Study of Greek as a Second Language.* (Collectanea Hellenistica 5). Brussel: KVAB Press.

Vittmann, Günther. 1991. Zum koptischen Sprachgut im Ägyptisch-Arabischen. *Wiener Zeitschrift für die Kunde des Morgenlandes* 81: 197–227.

Vittmann, Günther. 1996. Semitisches Sprachgut im Demotischen. *Wiener Zeitschrift für die Kunde des Morgenlandes* 86: 435–447.

Vleeming, Sven P. (ed.). 1987. *Aspects in Demotic Lexicography.* (Studia Demotica I). Leuven: Peeters.

Voigt, Rainer. 1999. Ägyptosemitischer Sprachvergleich. In: Grunert, Stefan & Hafemann, Ingelore (eds.), *Textcorpus und Wörterbuch. Aspekte zur ägyptischen Lexikographie.* (Probleme der Ägyptologie 14). Leiden/New York/Köln: Brill, 345–366.

Voigt, Rainer. 2002/2003. Die beiden Suffixkonjugationen des Semitischen (und) Ägyptischen. *Zeitschrift für Althebraistik* 15/16: 138–165.

Vycichl, Werner. 1983. *Dictionnaire étymologique de la langue copte.* Leuven: Peeters.

Wente, Edward Frank. 2001. Scripts: Hieratic. In: Redford, Donald (ed.), *The Oxford Encyclopedia of Ancient Egypt.* Vol. 3. Oxford: Oxford University Press & New York/Cairo: The American University in Cairo Press, 206–210.

Westendorf, Wolfhart. 1965. *Koptisches Handwörterbuch.* Heidelberg: Carl Winter.

Winand, Jean. 1992. *Etudes de néo-égyptien.* (Aegyptiaca Leodiensia 2). Liège: Comité International Permanent des Linguistes.

Winand, Jean. 1995. La grammaire au secours de la datation des textes. *Revue d'égyptologie* 46: 187–202.

Winand, Jean. 1999. Un dictionnaire des verbes néo-égyptiens. In: Grunert, Stefan & Hafemann, Ingelore (eds.), *Textcorpus und Wörterbuch. Aspekte zur ägyptischen Lexikographie.* (Probleme der Ägyptologie 14). Leiden/New York/Köln: Brill, 259–270.

Wilson, Penelope. 1997. *A Ptolemaic Lexikon. A Lexicographical Study of the Texts in the Temple of Edfu.* (Orientalia Lovaniensia Analecta 78). Leuven: Peeters.

Zeidler, Jürgen. 1992. Altägyptisch und Hamitosemitisch. Bemerkungen zu den Vergleichenden Studien von Karel Petrácek. *Lingua Aegyptia* 2: 189–222.

Zonhoven, Louis M.J. 2003. Some Observations on the narrative verbal systems in Old Egyptian. In: Hasitzka, Monika R.M., Diethart, Johannes & Dembski, Günther (eds.), *Das Alte Ägypten und seine Nachbarn. Festschrift zum 65. Geburtstag von Helmut Satzinger; mit Beiträgen zur Ägyptologie, Koptologie, Nubiologie und Afrikanistik.* (Wissenschaftliche Reihe 3). Österreichisches Literaturforum Krems, 183–201.

Martin Haspelmath
A grammatical overview of Egyptian and Coptic*

Abstract: This chapter presents a brief outline of the grammar of Earlier Egyptian (in the form of Middle Egyptian; Section 1) and a brief outline of the grammar of Later Egyptian (in the form of Coptic, Sahidic dialect; Section 2). This outline is intended for non-Egyptologist readers who are interested in the grammatical structure of Egyptian, so the description makes minimal use of idiosyncratic terminology. Occasionally peculiarities of Egyptian that are cross-linguistically uncommon are pointed out.

Middle Egyptian (the most-studied form of Earlier Egyptian) is written in hieroglyphic or hieratic script, which is a complex mixture of ideographic, logographic and phonographic signs. Only consonants are represented by the phonographic signs, so the vowel sounds are largely unknown (though some of them can be inferred from the representation of Egyptian names in other languages, and most importantly, from Coptic forms). Transliteration of pre-Coptic Egyptian is not practical due to the very large number of signs, so Egyptologists use a system that transcribes only the consonants.[1]

Coptic is written with Greek letters, augmented by a few consonant letters deriving from the Demotic script. The transliteration that is used here is the Leipzig-Jerusalem transliteration (see Grossman & Haspelmath 2014, in this volume).

---

* I am grateful to Bernard Comrie, Eitan Grossman, Tonio Sebastian Richter and Daniel A. Werning for helpful comments on this chapter.

1 For oral discussion of Egyptian expressions, Egyptologists generally use an artificial pronunciation that syllabifies consonant sequences with an [e] sound (e.g., *nfr* is pronounced [nefer]), that treats *j* and *w* as [i] and [u], and that treats *ꜣ* and *ꜥ* as [a] (thus, *Nfrtjtj* is pronounced as [nefertiti], and the name is also rendered in English as *Nefertiti*).

1 Salient grammatical patterns of Middle Egyptian

1.1 Consonant inventory

This chapter focuses on morphosyntax, so very little is said about phonology here. Most importantly, Middle Egyptian has the consonants in Table 1.

Table 1: Middle Egyptian consonants

p	t	t̲	k	q			
b	d	d̲	g				
f	s	š	ḫ	ḫ	ḥ	h	
	z				ʕ		
m	n	r		3			
w		j, jj					

The exact values of several of these consonants is not quite clear. For discussion of Egyptian phonology and the values of the letters used in transcription, see Schenkel (1990: ch. 2), Loprieno (1995), Kammerzell (1998), Peust (1999), Müller (2011), and Allen (2013). The special case of the consonant ʕ is discussed in detail by Gensler (2014, in this volume).

The transcription conventions used here mostly follow Loprieno (1995) and Allen (2000). Other authors follow different conventions. In particular, t̲ and d̲ are sometimes transcribed as č and č̣, j is transcribed as ỉ, jj is transcribed as y, and ʕ is transcribed as ᶜ.[2] Note that 3 is a consonant (perhaps [l], [r] or later [ʔ]).

1.2 Word order

Egyptian is a consistently right-branching language in which word order is primarily determined grammatically, or in other words, word order is fairly rigid. Right-branching (Dryer 1992) means that in syntactic phrases consisting of a non-

---

2 Reintges (2014, in this volume) uses an idiosyncratic transcription with IPA symbols: ʃ for š, x for ḫ, h for ḥ, ɣ for ḫ, ʔ for 3, dʒ for d̲, and tʃ for t̲. The problem with using IPA characters is that the actual pronunciation of these consonants is quite uncertain.

branching constituent and a branching constituent, the branching constituent follows. Thus, Egyptian has the word-order patterns in Table 2.

Table 2: Some phrase types in Middle Egyptian

phrase type	non-branching constituent	branching constituent	example
verb phrase	verb	object NP	(1)
noun phrase	noun	possessor NP	(2)
adpositional phrase	preposition	complement NP	(3)
auxiliary complex	auxiliary	verb phrase	(4)
subordinate clause	subordinator	clause	(5)

(1) *jw*   *m33-n-j*   [*nḫt-w*]
PCL   see-PRF-1SG victory-PL
'I saw the victories.' (Englund 1988: 35)

(2) *swḥ-t* [*n-t njw*]
egg-F of-F ostrich
'The egg of an ostrich' (Allen 2000: 41)

(3) *ḫnt-f*   *ntj*   *m*   [*ḥwt-nṯr*]
statue-3SGM   which.M   in   house-god
'His statue, which is in the temple.' (Allen 2000: 135)

(4) *wn-jn ḥm-f*   [*ḥr pg3   zḫ3-w*]
be-JN majesty-3SGM on   open writing-PL
'Then His Incarnation was spreading open the writings.' (A178)

(5) *m33-f* [*ntt* *št3w*   *pw*   *ʕ3*]
see-3SG that   serpent COP   big
'He saw that it was a great serpent.' (A137)[3]

---

3 "(A137)" is short for "(Allen 2000: 137)". Most of the Middle Egyptian examples cited here are from Allen's excellent grammar. Almost all the examples are attested in texts (see Allen 2000 for the sources), and only a few are constructed by the grammarian for pedagogical purposes.

In this respect, Egyptian behaves like many other Afroasiatic languages, notably like Berber and Chadic languages, and like many Semitic languages such as Arabic and Hebrew (but note that Cushitic languages as well as Ethiopic Semitic and Akkadian have different word-order patterns).

The canonical position of the nominal subject is immediately following the verb, so Egyptian is a VSO language, like Berber, Classical Arabic, and Biblical Hebrew:

(6) *jsṯ*   *gm-n*   *ḥm-f*   *r-pr*   *pn*   *m*   *ḏbt*
     PCL   find-PRF   majesty-3SGM   mouth-house   this   in   brick
     'His Incarnation found this sanctuary in brick.' (Gardiner 1957: 330)

1.3 Gender and number

Egyptian nouns are either masculine or feminine, much like nouns in Semitic, Berber, and other Afroasiatic languages. Gender is shown on agreeing personal pronouns as well as adjectives, demonstratives and other adnominal modifiers. Feminine nouns typically show the feminine gender suffix *-t*, while masculine nouns have no particular suffix.

The plural of masculine nouns generally ends in *-w*, while the plural of feminine nouns also ends in *-t* (though it is often distinguished in writing by ideographic signs).

(8) *nṯr*   'god'   *nṯr-w*   'gods'

(9) *sn-t*   'sister'   *sn-t*   'sisters'

There was also a dual number form, masculine *-wj* and feminine *-tj* (see 15b).

1.4 Reference, predication and attribution: nouns, verbs and adjectives

Most commonly, in all languages, thing-words (including words for people) are used for the function of reference, action-words are used for the function of predication, and property-words are used for the function of attribution (= nominal modification) (see Croft 1991, 2000, 2001: ch. 2). These combinations of semantic type (thing/action/property) and pragmatic function (reference/predication/attri bution) tend to be expressed in the simplest way across languages, without additional coding. Consider example (9), with a predicating action-word ('arrive'), a referential thing-word ('cause'), and an attributive property-word ('unworthy').

(9) *nj   spr-n   zp   ḥz   r   dmj*
NEG   arrive-PRF   cause   unworthy   to   harbour
'An unworthy cause cannot succeed (lit. arrive at the harbour).' (A236)

In Middle Egyptian, nouns, verbs, and adjectives are clearly distinct in these three basic constructions. Special marking is required for less usual combinations of semantic type and pragmatic function. When used referentially, action-words use the special infinitive form, which has a *-t* suffix with many verbs, thus distinguishing verbs from nouns (e.g., *pr-t* 'to go out'):

(10)   *nn   n-s   pr-t   m   jmnt*
NEG   for-3SGF   exit-INF   in   west
'Emerging from the West is not for her.' (A167)

Property-words can be used referentially like thing-words, so in this respect adjectives are noun-like, e.g.

(11)   a.   *nfr*   'a good one (masculine)'

       b.   *nfr-t*   'a good one (feminine)'

For this reason, Allen (2000: 61) claims that "all Egyptian adjectives are nouns", but this is not true, because in predicative function, property-words behave quite differently from thing-words. First of all, they do not show gender forms, so (12) has *nfr*, not *nfr-t*, even though the subject is a feminine noun. And second, clauses with a predicative noun usually require the copula *pw*, as in (13).

(12)   *nfr   ḥm-t   tn*
beautiful   woman-F   this.F
'This woman is beautiful.' (A68)

(13)   *sn-t-f   pw   tfnt*
sister-F-3SGM   COP   Tefnut
'His sister is Tefnut.' (A72)

Thus, predicative adjectives are more verb-like than noun-like, but they are also distinct from verbs in that they lack the various tense and aspect forms that we find with verbs. Thus (12) is not specified for tense and could also mean 'The woman was beautiful.'

In attributive function, adjectives are postposed and agree in gender and number:

(14) a. *z3 nfr* 'good son'

     b. *z3-t nfr-t* 'good daughter'

When nouns are used attributively, there are two possibilities: either they are preceded by the possessive marker *n(j)*, as in (15a) or (2), or they follow the possessum directly, as in (15b).

(15) a. *z3 n zj*
         son of.M man
         'the son of a man'

     b. *nswt t3-wj*
         king land-DU
         'the king of Egypt' (lit. 'of the two lands')

When verbs are used attributively, they are more like adjectives – see the discussion of participles and relative forms in § 1.11 below.

Thus, noun, verb, and adjective are clearly distinguished in Egyptian, not unlike the situation in Semitic languages or in older Indo-European languages. Adjectives are similar to verbs in predicative function and to nouns in referential function, but overall, they are clearly distinct from both.

1.5 Personal pronouns and full NPs

Earlier Egyptian does not have an agent-patient distinction in full noun phrases. There is neither accusative case nor an accusative preposition, and no ergative marking either. The verb does not agree with a full NP Subject or Object, so the alignment of full NPs is completely neutral.

(16) jm   sḫpr   [jb-j   pn]   [ḏbʕw   pn   ḏw] r-j
       NEG   create   heart-1SG this.M   reproach this.M   bad to-1SG
       'May my heart not create this bad reproach against me.' (A256)

However, agent-patient clauses with two full NPs are very rare in actual discourse: Most of the time, the agent or the patient is a personal pronoun, and these do distinguish clearly between agents and patients (or Subjects and Objects).

Table 3 shows a simplified representation of the three series of personal pronouns in Middle Egyptian: person suffixes, dependent pronouns, and independent pronouns.

Table 3: Three series of personal pronouns

		person suffixes	dependent pronouns	independent pronouns
SG	1	-j	wj	jnk
	2M	-k	ṯw	ntk
	2F	-ṯ	ṯn	ntṯ
	3M	-f	sw	ntf
	3F	-s	sj/st	nts
PL	1	-n	n	jnn
	2	-ṯn	ṯn	ntṯn
	3	-sn	sn/st	ntsn

With transitive verbs, the suffix pronouns are used as Subjects and the dependent pronouns are used as Objects, so they could be called "nominative" and "accusative" forms, respectively:

(17) m33-n-j   ʕfd-t n-t   sj3
       see-PRF-1SG   box-F of-F   Sia
       'I have seen the box of Sia.' (A232)

(18) sj3-n   wj   mjtn(w)
       recognize-PRF 1SG.DEP   scout
       'The scout recognized me.' (A226)

However, the suffix pronouns also have a variety of other functions, most notably as possessors and as complements of prepositions.

(19) *pr-f*   'his house'
      house-3SGM

(20) *n-j*   'to me'
      to-1SG

Thus, the term "nominative" does not fit in general, and the leftmost series in Table 3 is generally called "suffix pronouns". The dependent pronoun series is used not only in object function with transitive verbs, but also in subject function with predicative adjectives, e.g.

(21) *nfr* *ṯw*   *ḥnʕ-j*
      good 2SG.DEP with-1SG
      'You are good with me.' (Schenkel 2012: 112)

Thus, the term "accusative" would not fit well either. However, the use of the same pronoun forms for transitive objects and intransitive subjects is quite remarkable, and one could regard this as a kind of alignment partition: While the Subjects of (mostly dynamic) intransitive verbs are coded like transitive Subjects (thus showing nominative-accusative alignment), the Subjects of stative (intransitive) adjectives are coded like transitive Objects (thus showing ergative-absolutive alignment). This is certainly not a common situation cross-linguistically (though similar situations have been described as "agentive-inagentive" in the typological literature, see Donohue & Wichmann 2008).

Dependent pronouns are generally regarded as enclitics, as opposed to the suffixal pronouns of the first series. They may occur directly after the verb, as in (18) above and in (22), but they may also occur as subject pronouns of adverbial-predicate clauses after certain initial particles (such as *nḥmn* in 23).

(22) *ḏꜣ-n-f*   *sw*
      ferry-PRF-3SGM 3SGM.DEP
      'He ferried him.' (Gardiner 1957: 45)

(23) *nḥmn* *wj*   *mj* *kꜣ*
      surely 1SG.DEP like bull
      'I am really like a bull.' (A111)

But the contrast between "enclitic" dependent pronouns and "suffixal" pronouns is not very clear-cut, because these can sometimes occur in second position as well, e.g., following the element *jw*:

(24) *jw-f*   *m*   *ꜥt*
      PCL-3SGM in   room
      'It is in a room.' (A110)

One could say that *jw* is really a copula verb, not a particle like *nḥmn*, so that *jw-f* shows the suffix pronoun in verbal subject function, as in (17). But *jw* does not behave like a verb in other respects (it does not have different tense-aspect forms, and is negated differently), so it is generally called a particle.

Independent pronouns are mostly used in nominal predication, as in (25).

(25) *jnk*   *jt(j)-k*
      1SG.INDP father-2SGM
      'I am your father.'

1.6 Verbal arguments

A verb has either a single unflagged argument (i.e., an argument without case or adposition) or two unflagged arguments: Intransitive verbs have just a subject, and transitive verbs have a subject and an object. All other arguments are prepositional phrases. With full NPs, the order is strictly "Verb – Subject – Object – prepositional phrase". Recipient arguments of ditransitive verbs are expressed by prepositional phrases with the dative preposition *n*:

(26) *jmj*   *mrwt-k*   *n*   *t3-tmw*
      give.IMP love-2SGM to   everyone
      'Give your love to everyone.' (A187)

However, when the object is a pronoun, it precedes the full-NP subject, as seen in (18). Likewise, prepositional pronominal objects with the preposition *n* precede full-NP Objects, as seen in (27):

(27) *jmj*   *n-n*   *ḥn-t-n*   *nfr-t*
      give.IMP to-1PL outcome-F-1PL good-F
      'Give us our good outcome.' (A187)

In fact, the dative pronominal object even precedes the pronominal nonprepositional object:

(28) *jr-t*   *n-f*   *st*
     do-INF to-3SGM it
     'To do it to him' (A163)

The tendency for pronominal arguments to precede full NP arguments is very widespread in the world's languages (e.g., Dik 1997: 411).

Adverbial phrases are usually expressed by prepositional phrases as well, following the verb and its arguments.

(29) *dd-tw*   *ḥtp-nṯr*   *pn m-bȝḥ twt*   *pn*
     place-PASS offering-god this in-front statue   this
     'This offering shall be placed before this statue.' (Gardiner 1957: 353)

Topicalized phrases may occur before the verb, e.g.

(30) *m-k*   *nṯr rdj-n-f*   *ʕnḫ-k*
     behold-2SG god cause-PRF-3SGM live-2SGM
     'Behold, god has caused thee to live.' (Gardiner 1957: 115)

1.7 Noun phrase structure

Noun phrases consist of nouns plus optional modifiers which generally follow the noun, such as adjectives, demonstratives, numerals, and possessors:

(31) a. *ḥm-wt*   *nfr-t*
       woman-PL.F good-F
       'good women' (A60)

     b. *nṯr pn*
       god this.M
       'this god' (A52)

c. *dmj   wʕ*
  harbour one.M
  'one harbour' (A100)

d. *nswt t3-wj*
  king land-DU
  'the king of the two lands (= of Egypt)' (A40)

The demonstratives *pn/tn* ('this', M/F) and demonstrative *pw/tw* ('this', M/F) follow the noun, while the demonstrative *p3/t3* ('this', M/F) precedes the noun. Likewise, the determiners *kjj* 'other' and *tnw* 'each' precede the noun (*kjj sb3* 'another gate, the other gate'; *tnw rnpt* 'each year', Allen 2000: 62).

When the possessor is a personal pronoun, it is expressed by the suffix series, e.g., *pr-f* 'his house', *sn-w-t* 'your (F) brothers'.

In addition to the unmarked possessive construction, as in (31d, 34b) (and in *pr-f* 'his house'), Middle Egyptian has an "indirect" possessive construction with the genitive preposition *n/n-t/n-w* (M/F/M.PL) that agrees with the possessum in gender and number:

(32) a. *z3   n   zj*
        son(M) of.M man
        'the son of a man' (A41)

b. *ḥm-wt   n-t wr-w*
   wife-PL.F of-F chief-PL
   'the wives of the chiefs' (A41)

The contrast between the unmarked and the *n*-marked possessive constructions is discussed further in Haspelmath (2014, in this volume).

1.8 Nonverbal predication

Egyptian clauses are typically divided into verbal-predicate clauses (§ 1.9) and nonverbal-predicate clauses, and the latter are subdivided into adjectival-predicate, nominal-predicate and adverbial-predicate clauses.

We already saw that adjectival-predicate clauses are expressed by clause-initial non-agreeing adjectives followed by full NPs (cf. 12) or by dependent pronouns (cf. 21).

Nominal predicates are generally marked by the copula *pw*, as in (13) and in (33).

(33) *pḫrt pw ʿnḫ*
cycle COP life
'Life is a cycle.' (A72)

When the subject of a nominal-predicate clause is a third person pronoun, it is not expressed at all:

(34) a. *z3-j   pw*
son-1SG COP
'He is my son.' (A72)

b. *ḥm-t   wʿb pw*
wife-F   priest COP
'She is a priest's wife.' (A72)

The copula *pw* presumably derives from the demonstrative *pw* 'this(M.SG)', but it is used regardless of gender. When the predicate NP has an adjectival or indirect-possessor modifier, the copula follows the noun immediately, i.e., it is a kind of second-position enclitic that may occur inside a noun phrase:

(35) a. *t3   pw   nfr*
land COP   good
'It is a good land.' (A72)

b. *mnw   pw   n zj   nfrw-f*
monument COP   of man goodness-3SGM
'The monument of a man is his goodness.' (A73)

Nominal-predicate clauses may be copula-less when the subject is a first- or second-person pronoun (see (25) above), or when the predicate is an inalienable kinship term (e.g., *mwt-j nwt* [mother-1SG Nut] 'Nut is my mother', Allen 2000: 71).

While adjectival-predicate and nominal-predicate clauses are mostly predicate-initial, adverbial-predicate clauses have the adverbial predicate following the subject, e.g.,

(36) *ḥr-t-k*   *m*   *pr-k*
     possession-PL.F-2SGM in   house-2SGM
     'Your possessions are in your house.' (A109)

(37) a. *jw   mwt   m   ḥr-j   mjn*
        PCL death in   face-1SG today
        'Death is in my sight today.' (A110)

     b. *m-k   sw   ʕȝ   m   ʕ-j*
        lo-2SGM   3SGM.DEP here in   hand-1SG
        '(Look) he is here in my hand.' (A111)

     c. *nn   mwt-k   ḥnʕ-k*
        NEG   mother-2SGM with-2SGM
        'Your mother is not with you.' (A111)

The predicate of an adverbial-predicate clause is generally a prepositional phrase, but it may also be a simple adverb such as *ʕȝ* 'here'. The subject may be clause-initial as in (36), but it is mostly preceded by some kind of "particle" such as *jw*, *m-k* or *nn* in (37a–c). The most neutral and most frequent "particle" is *jw*, which is followed by a suffix pronoun when the subject is pronominal (cf. (24) above).

Adverbial-predicate clauses can also have the sense of nominal predication, using the preposition *m* (originally 'in'):

(38) *m-k   ṯw   m   mnjw*
     behold-2SGM   2SGM.DEP in   herdsman
     'You are a herdsman.'

1.9 Verbal predication

There are three types of verbal predication, used for different tense-aspect forms: postverbal-subject clauses, periphrastic clauses, and Stative clauses. They make use of three different types of verb forms: standard finite verb forms, infinitives, and Stative verb forms.

Postverbal-subject clauses have postverbal full-NP or pronominal subjects that follow the finite verb. Pronominal subjects are from the suffix series, so verbs and pronominal subject suffixes are often said to form the "suffix conjugation".

However, the construction with postverbal full NPs (where there is no suffix on the verb as in 39a) is no different, so this term is not very suitable.

(39) a. *ḥʕ*   *sbkw,*   *ḥq3-n-f*   *pt*
       appear Sobek rule-PRF-3SG sky
       'Sobek has appeared, he has begun to rule the sky.' (A265)

   b. *šm-k*   *ḥnʕ-sn*   *r*   *ḥnw*
      go-2SGM   with-3PL   to   home
      'You will go home with them.' (A248)

   c. *ḏd-n-f*   *ʕḥ3-f*   *ḥnʕ-j*
      say-PRF-3SGM fight-3SG with-1SG
      'He said he would fight with me.' (A253)

Postverbal-subject clauses are further discussed in § 1.10.

Periphrastic clauses have verbal predicates that consist of a preposition and an infinitive: *ḥr* + infinitive ('upon doing') and *m* + infinitive ('in doing') are used in a progressive sense, while *r* + infinitive ('to doing') is used in a future sense. As in adverbial-predicate clauses, their subject precedes the predicate, though normally some kind of particle comes first.

(40) a. *jw srj-w*   *ḥr rdj-t*   *n-k*   *jw-k*   *ḥr jt-t*
       PCL official-PL on give-INF to-2SGM PCL-2SGM on take-INF
       'The officials are giving to you and you are taking.' (A176)

   b. *m-ṯ*   *wj*   *m*   *h3-t*   *r*   *km-t*
      lo-2SGF 1SG.DEP in go.down-INF to Egypt
      '(Look) I am going down to Egypt.' (A176)

   c. *nn*   *sw*   *r*   *ḥpr*
      NEG   3SGM.DEP to become.INF
      'He will not come into existence.' (A178)

The infinitive is most typically identical to the verb stem, but with some verbs it has the suffix *-t*. Note that the pronominal object of the infinitive is often expressed as a suffix pronoun, as in (41).

(41) *nn jw-j   r   w3ḥ-t*
     NEG PCL-1SG to stop.INF-2SG.F
     'I am not going to stop you.' (A178)

Stative clauses typically have the subject before the verb as well, as in (42).

(42) a. *m-k   wj   3tp-kw   m jʕnw*
        behold-2SGM 1SG.DEP load.STAT-1SG in woe
        '(Look) I am loaded with woe.' (A204)

     b. *t3   3q-w   r   3w*
        land   ruin.STAT-3SG to entirety
        'The land is ruined entirely.' (A204)

The Stative verb forms have a special set of person-number forms, shown in sim-plified form in Table 4. These suffixes are very different from the ordinary suffixes shown in Table 3.

Table 4: Stative suffixes

SG	1	*-kw*
	2	*-tj*
	3M	*-w*
	3F	*-tj*
PL	1	*-wjn*
	2	*-tjwnj*
	3	*-wj*

The Stative is special in a number of respects: It seems to be the oldest finite verb form (with clear cognates in Semitic languages), but it is also the only one that has survived into Coptic – all the standard finite verb forms disappeared and were replaced by a variety of periphrastic forms using the Infinitive. Grammatically, the most striking peculiarity of the Stative is that the person-number suffixes act more like agreement markers than like pronouns. While the suffix pronouns are in complementary distribution with full-NP subjects in the postverbal-subject construction (*šm-f* 'he will go', *šm sn-j* 'my brother will go'), in the Stative the per-son-number suffixes generally cooccur with an overt (full-NP or pronoun) subject (*wj* in 42a, *t3* in 42b). Orthographically, what is special about the Stative is that (some of) its suffixes are normally written before the determinative of the verb, unlike all the other postverbal grammatical markers. This suggests that they are felt to be closer to the verb stem than the other markers.

Semantically, the Stative is peculiar as well because it expresses a state or (completed) past event, but with a different effect for intransitive and transitive verbs. The Stative of an intransitive verb expresses an ordinary intransitive action or state:

(43) a. *m-k*   *wj*   *jj-kw*
           behold-2SGM 1SG.DEP   come.STAT-1SG
           '(Look) I have come.' (A205)

   b. *nḥmn*   *z3-f*   *ʕq-w*   *r*   *ʕḥ*
       PCL   son-3SGM enter.STAT-3SGM to   palace
       'His son has surely entered the palace.' (A208)

But the Stative of transitive verbs expresses a passive state or completed event, as seen in (42). Such verb forms have been called "resultative" (Nedjalkov 1988). A syntactic peculiarity is that it most often occurs in a circumstantial adverbial clause. The Stative is discussed in great detail by Reintges (2014, in this volume).

1.10 Postverbal-subject clauses

Verbal-predicate clauses with postverbal subjects contain standard finite verb forms, which come in a variety of subtypes. The most clearly distinguishable subtypes are the *V-Ø* form, the *V-n* form, the *V-jn* form, and the *V-ḫr* form (as well as a few others where a consonant follows the verb stem). Only the *V-Ø* form and the *V-n* form are common, but here are examples of the rarer forms:

(44) a. *jw-jn-tw*   *r*   *smj*   *n*   *ḥm-f*
           come-JN-GENER to   report.INF   to   majesty-3SGM
           'Then one came to report to His Incarnation (i.e., the king).' (A302)

   b. *jr-ḫr-k*   *n-f*   *zp-w*   *n-w*   *wšš*
       make-HR-2SGM to-3SGM   concoction-PL of-PL   excretion
       'You have to make for him concoctions for excretion.'

The *V-n* form (also called the Perfect) is used as a past tense or perfect aspect:

(45) *rdj-n-j*   *ḥknw*   *n*   *mntw*
      give-PRF-1SG   praise   to   Montu
      'I gave praise to Montu.' (A226)

But when negated, the Perfect refers to a potential event (see also (9) above):

(46) *m-k*   *wj*   *ḥr*   *spr*   *n-k,*   *nj*   *sḏm-n-k*
      lo-2SGM   1SG.DEP   on   petition.INF   to-2SGM   NEG   hear-PRF-2SGM

      st
      3SGF.DEP
      '(Look) I am petitioning to you, but you cannot hear it.' (A235)

The simple *V-Ø* form has a variety of different uses: perfective (e.g., 47a), imperfective (e.g., 47b), and subjunctive or prospective (e.g., 47c), as well as a passive use (e.g., 47d). With some verbs, especially several frequent and irregular verbs, there are different forms for different uses, e.g., the verb *rdj/dj* has the stem *dj* with subjunctive uses (*dj-k* 'you should give') and the stem *rdj* with perfective uses (*rdj-k* 'you gave'). Thus, Egyptologists generally assume that there were at least three different *V-Ø* forms for most or all verbs, distinguished primarily by the (unwritten) vowels.

(47) a. *nj*   *k3-j*   *spr*   *r*   *ḥnw*   *pn*
          NEG   plan-1SG   arrive.INF to   capital   that
          'I did not plan to arrive at that capital.' (A265)

      b. *jw* *jr-j*   *m*   *mt-t*   *n-t* *jb*   *n*   *nb*   *rꜥ* *nb*
          PCL do-1SG   in   correctness-F   of-F heart   to   lord   day every
          'I used to act with correctness of heart for the lord every day.'
          (A267)

      c. *jr-n-f*   *t3w* *n*   *jb,*   *ꜥnḫ*   *fnḏ-w-sn*
          make-PRF-3SGM   air   to   heart   live   nose-PL-3PL
          'He has made air for the heart, so that their noses might live.'
          (A251)

> d. *ꜥꜥb   šnw-j*
> comb hair-1SG
> 'My hair was combed.' (A291)

The question of how many different verb forms there were in the postverbal-subject construction, and how they were used, has been a matter of considerable debate (see, e.g., Schenkel 1990: ch. 3).

1.11 Relative clauses

Relative clauses follow the head noun like other adnominal modifiers. When the predicate of a relative clause is a verb, Middle Egyptian uses a set of special verb forms that agree in gender and number with the head noun, as in (48).

> (48) a. *jt-w   mw-t   wnnjj-w   ḥnꜥ-j*
>   father-PL mother-PL.F [exist.REL-PL with-1SG]
>   'The fathers and mothers who existed with me.' (A327)
>
>   b. *nfr-t   nb-t   jnn-t   n   ḥm   n   nb-j*
>   good-F every-F [bring.REL-F to majesty of lord-1SG]
>   'Every good thing that was brought to the incarnation of my lord.'
>   (A328)
>
>   c. *mdw-w ḏd-w   n-sn nṯr pn*
>   word-PL [say.REL-PL to-3PL god this]
>   'The words that this god says to them.' (A349)

Egyptologists distinguish between various subtypes of "participles" used in subject relative clauses like (48a) and "relative forms" used in non-subject relative clauses like (48c). However, there are also "passive participles" as in (48b) that are semantically non-subject relative clauses as well. Like adjectives, relative verb forms can be used on their own without a head noun (e.g., *mr* 'one who loves').

The relative pronoun *ntj/ntt* (M/F) is used almost exclusively in relative clauses with non-verbal predicates (e.g., (3) in § 1.2 above).

2 Salient grammatical patterns of Coptic

2.1 Anasynthesis in Later Egyptian

Perhaps the most salient change between Earlier Egyptian (Old and Middle Egyptian) and Later Egyptian (represented here by Coptic) is the change from postposed (and probably suffixed) markers of person and tense-aspect to preposed markers, deriving from originally analytic, periphrastic expressions. Such a replacement of synthetic patterns by analytic patterns, which later become synthetic again, has long been discussed as "synthesis-analysis-synthesis" cycle (e.g., von der Gabelentz 1901, Schwegler 1990, van Gelderen 2011; for Egyptian-Coptic, see Ewald 1862, Hintze 1950, Hodge 1971, and Reintges 2012). I call this macro-process anasynthesis here. Since few languages are attested over a similarly long period, it is not quite clear whether anasynthesis is a truly universal diachronic trend, and in some language families such as Chinese and Germanic, there is not much evidence for secondary synthesis (though analysis, i.e., innovative periphrastic expression, is widely attested). However, for Egyptian-Coptic, the trend is hard to overlook. In particular, we observe the changes listed (and briefly illustrated) in (49). Here >> means 'is replaced by', and > means 'turns into'.

(49) a. postposed demonstrative >> preposed demonstrative *pei-/tei-*

           rmṯ pn >> pȝj rmṯ > pei-rôme (пєιρωмє)
           man this this man this-man
           'this man'

     b. preposed demonstrative > prefixed definite article *p-/t-*

           pȝ rmṯ > pȝ rmt > p-rôme (пρωмє)
           'this man' 'the man' 'the man'

     c. numeral 'one' > prefixed indefinite article *ou-*

           ḥfȝw wʕ >> wʕ (n) ḥfȝw > ou-hof (ογϩοϥ)
           snake one one (of) snake INDF-snake

d. ordinal numeral suffix *-nw* >> prefix *meh-*

ḥmt-nw	>>	*mḥ-ḥmt*	>	*meh-šomnt* (ме2ϣомнт)
three-ORD		fill-three		ORD-three

   'third'

e. suffixed possessive pronoun >> prefixed possessive pronoun
   (following the article)

rn-k	>>	*p3j-k*	*rn*	>	*pe-k-ran* (пекрам)
name-2SGM		DEF-2SGM	name		DEF-2SGM-name

   'your name'

f. postverbal-subject construction >> pre-subject-TAM construction

sḏm-n-f	>>	*jr-f*	*sḏm*	>	*a-f-sôtm* (а̤чсωтн)
hear-PRF-3SGM		do-3SGM	hear		PRET-3SGM-hear

   'he heard'

g. Stative construction with agreement > Stative without agreement

X st	*wḏ3-tj*		>	*st*	*wḏ3*	>	*s-ouoč* (соγох)
X she	whole.STAT-3SGF			she	whole		3SGF-whole.STAT

   'she is whole'

h. synthetic suffixed passive >> passive-like construction with 3PL
   person form

sḏm-w-f	>>	*a-u-sotm-f* (а̤γсотнч)
hear-PASS-3SGM		PRET-3PL-hear-3SGM
'he was heard'		'he was heard' ("they heard him")

i. periphrastic construction > subject-verb construction

X sw ḥr sḏm	>	*f-sôtm* (чсωтн)
he on hear		3SGM-hear
'he is hearing'		'he is hearing, he hears'

j.   suffix object pronouns (on infinitives) >> prepositional accusative[4]

s̲d̲m-n	>> sḏm	jm-n	> sôtm	mmo-n (ⲥⲱⲧⲙ ⲙⲙⲟⲛ)
hear.INF-1PL	hear.INF	in-1PL	hear	ACC-1PL

'to hear us'

In some of these changes, the analytical construction is very old (e.g., the peri-phrastic construction with ḥr in 49i, which we saw in 40a above), while in others it is newer. Thus the changes did not take place simultaneously, and it is not clear how closely they are connected. It may only be in hindsight that they seem to form a coherent group of changes. The extent to which the Coptic constructions are synthetic is not always clear, as there are no criteria for distinguishing between prefixes and proclitics in Coptic. But it is striking to see the massive reorganiza-tion of Egyptian morphosyntax over the millennia.[5]

The anasynthesis changes observed in Egyptian are of course just a manifes-tation at the macro-level of what is generally called grammaticalization. Changes of this type are widespread in all languages, and we observe anasynthesis also elsewhere, but not in the same clear way. We always observe a change from syn-thesis being replaced by analysis which then turns into synthesis, and there has been a fair amount of discussion of the unidirectional development that we see here (e.g., Haspelmath (1999), Börjars & Vincent (2009)), but even if it is not fully understood yet, it is clear that this is a widespread tendency of which Egyptian shows a particularly striking example.

2.2 Coptic sounds and stress groups

The Sahidic Coptic consonants and vowels are given in Table 5 (simplified, as everything in this chapter). (See Depuydt 1993, Peust 1999 and Funk 2009 for details on Coptic phonology.)

---

4 The new prepositional accusative with the preposition n-/mmo- coexists with the old suffixed person forms (sotm-n 'to hear us', cf. 49h above and § 2.3 below; see also Winand's article in this volume).

5 Grammaticalization is continuing in Coptic. As shown by Grossman (2009), some varieties of Coptic have a new perfect of the form: a-f-ouô e-f-sôtm 'he finished hearing' >'he has heard'.

Table 5: Coptic consonants and vowels

p	t	c	k	kʲ	?		i:			u:
b	(d)		(g)						ə	
f	s	ʃ	(x)		h		e	e:		o	o:
m	n, r						a			
w	l	j								

The sounds [p, t, k, d, g, s, m, n, r, l, e, o, a, e:, o:, i:] are written in the expected way, using the corresponding Greek letters (п, т, к, ⲇ, г, с, м, ⲛ, ⲣ, λ, ⲉ, ⲏ, ⲱ, ⲓ). [u:] is written as <ou>, as in Greek, and [i:] is written as <i> or <ei>. [w] and [j] are written as <ou> (or as <u> in the diphthongs <au>, <êu> and <eu>) and <i, ei>.

For the sounds [f, ʃ, h, x, c, kʲ], Coptic uses a set of special letters not derived from Greek, but from the Demotic script: ϥ, ϣ, ϩ, ϭ, and ϫ. In the Leipzig-Jerusalem transliteration of Coptic, ϭ and ϫ are transliterated as <c> and <č>, mostly for typographic convenience.[6]

Another special letter, ϯ, is used for [ti] (transliterated as <ti>). The Greek letters ϕ, θ, χ, ϥ, and ⲝ are also used for sequences of two segments in Sahidic Coptic: /pʰ/, /tʰ/, /kʰ/, /pˢ/, and /kˢ/, respectively. (They are transliterated as <pʰ>, <tʰ>, <kʰ>, <pˢ>, and <kˢ>, reflecting the fact that the two sounds correspond to a single letter.)

The glottal stop was apparently written by doubling the letter of the preceding vowel, e.g., *toot* /toʔt/ 'my hand', *ouêêb* /we:ʔb/ 'priest'. The schwa sound is written as <e> at the end of words (e.g., *mise* [mi:sə] 'give birth'), and is unwritten between consonants (e.g., *tootf* 'his hand', probably pronounced [toʔtəf], and *ouêêb* was probably pronounced [we:ʔəb].

There was a clear contrast between stressed and unstressed syllables in Coptic: Stressed syllables may have long vowels or the vowel [o], but unstressed syllables were apparently confined to the vowels [a] and [ə]. Where unstressed <e>, <i> and <ou> occur in writing, they were probably pronounced as [ə], [(ə)j], and [(ə)w] (Loprieno 1995: 50).

Stress is not marked in Coptic writing, but it can be inferred from a number of vowel alternations where a long vowel appears to alternate with schwa, e.g.,

---

6 It is not quite clear how ϭ <c> and ϫ <č> were actually pronounced. The values [c] and [kʲ] are from Loprieno (1995: 40), but in view of the similarity between the two, this is not very likely. Layton (2004: 13) gives [kʲ] for ϭ and [tʃ] for ϫ.

eire [ˈiːrə] 'do' (ⲉⲓⲣⲉ)   vs. *r-nobe* [ər-ˈnobə] '(do) sin' (ⲣⲛⲟⲃⲉ)
nouče [ˈnuːkʲə] 'throw, put' (ⲛⲟⲩϫⲉ)   vs. *neč-êrp* [nəkʲ-ˈeːrəp] 'put wine'
                                                 (ⲛⲉϫⲏⲣⲡ)

The stress pattern that can be inferred from vowel patterns allows us to identify a prosodic constituent "stress group" (called "bound group" in Layton 2004: 22). A stress group consists of a noun or a verb root (always stressed on the last non-schwa syllable) preceded by a series of unstressed, phonologically dependent ("clitic") elements which are typically grammatical morphemes, e.g.

(50)   a.   ⲡⲉⲕⲣⲁⲛ
          pe-k-ran   [pə-k-rán]
          DEF.M-2SGM-name
          'your name'

      b.   ϩⲙⲡⲙⲉϩϣⲟⲙⲛⲧ
          hm-p-meh-šomnt   [həm-p-məh-ʃómənt]
          in-DEF.M-ORD-three
          'in the third'

      c.   ⲟⲩⲣⲉϥⲣⲛⲟⲃⲉ
          ou-ref-r-nobe   [w-rəf-ər-nóbə]
          INDF-AGT-do-sin
          'a sinner'

      d.   ⲉⲩⲛⲧⲥⲟⲩϣⲉⲉⲣⲉ
          e-unt-s-ou-šeere   [ə-wənt-əs-w-ʃéʔrə]
          REL-have-3SGF-INDF-daughter
          'who had a daughter'

      e.   ⲙⲛⲛⲉⲧⲉⲛⲧⲛⲛⲁⲩ   ⲉⲣⲟⲟⲩ
          mn-n-ete-n-tn-nau   *ero-ou*   [mən-n-ətə-n-tən-náw ərów]
          with-DEF.PL-REL-NEG-1PL-see to-3PL
          'and those which we do not see'

Stress groups cannot be identified with "words", however, because verb roots are sometimes unstressed and precede a stressed subject or object:

(51) a. ⲡⲉϫⲉⲓⲏⲥⲟⲩⲥ
          peče-iêsous   [pək^jə-je:sú:s]
          say-Jesus
          'Jesus said.'

    b. ⲉⲛⲉϫⲧⲉϥϭⲓⲙⲉ   ⲉⲃⲟⲗ
          e-neč-t-ef-shime   *ebol*   [ə-nək^j-t-əf-shí:mə əból]
          to-throw-DEF.F-3SGM-wife   out
          'to throw out (=divorce) his wife'

Moreover, unstressed tense-aspect and relative markers can precede a full-NP subject:

(52) a. ⲁⲡⲁⲩⲗⲟⲥ ⲛⲁⲩ ⲉⲣⲟϥ
          a-paulos nau ero-f   [a-páwlos náw əró-f]
          PRET-Paul see to-3SGM
          'Paul saw him.'

    b. ⲡⲉⲛⲧⲁⲙⲱⲩⲥⲏⲥ   ⲥϩⲁⲓ   ⲉⲧⲃⲏⲏⲧϥ
          p-ent-a-môusês   *shai*   *etbêêt-f*
          [p-ənt-a-mo:isé:s   sháj   ətbé:ʔt-əf]
          DEF.M-REL-PRET-Moses   write about-3SGM
          'the one of whom Moses wrote'

One would of course not want to say that the stress group *p-ent-a-môusês* 'the one who Moses (past tense)' is a word. There does not seem to be any use for the term "word" in Coptic, and Layton's (2004) thoughtful description of Coptic completely dispenses with the notion "word" (he confines himself to the two related notions of "morph" and "bound group", i.e., stress group).

2.3 Personal pronouns and full NPs

Coptic has two basic series of person forms, independent personal pronouns (which have been preserved from Earlier Egyptian) and bound person forms. The prefixal and suffixal bound person forms differ somewhat in their shapes.

Table 6: Three series of personal pronouns (simplified)

		independent pronouns	prefixal forms (subject)	suffixal forms (subject, object)
SG	1	anok	ti-	-i/-t
	2M	ntok	k-	-k
	2F	nto	te-	-Ø/-re
	3M	ntof	f-	-f
	3F	ntos	s-	-s
PL	1	anon	tn-	-n
	2	ntôtn	tetn-	-(t)etn
	3	ntoou	se-	-ou

The independent pronouns are mostly used in nonverbal predication and to express contrast, as in Earlier Egyptian. The prefixal forms are used as subject pronouns, while the suffixal forms can be used both as subject and as object pronouns.

There are two basic types of clause patterns: TAM-subject patterns and subject-predicate patterns. The former use the suffixal person forms, while the latter use the prefixal forms of the personal pronouns. In the subject-predicate pattern, the prefixal personal pronouns may combine directly with the verb stem, though the future tense marker *na-* comes between the subject and the verb.

(53) TAM-subject patterns

a. ⲁϥⲥⲱⲧⲙ
a-f-sôtm
PRET-3SGM-hear
'He heard'

b. ⲙⲡⲥⲙⲟⲩ
mp-s-mou
PRET.NEG-3SGF-die
'She did not die'

(54) subject-predicate patterns[7]

a. ϥⲥⲱⲧⲙ
f-sôtm
3SGM-hear
'He is hearing'

b. ⲧⲉⲛⲁⲃⲱⲕ
te-na-bôk
2SGF-FUT-go
'You will go'

---

7 What is called "subject-predicate pattern" here is often called "durative sentence pattern" in Coptic linguistics.

c. ϣⲁⲩⲕⲁⲁϥ
ša-u-kaa-f
HAB-3PL-put-3SGM
'They put it (habitually)'

c. ⲥⲉⲕⲏⲧ
se-kêt
3PL-build.STAT
'They are built'

As in Earlier Egyptian, a bound person form does not normally cooccur with a coreferential full NP, so when an NP is present, the bound person form is absent. In the TAM-subject patterns (cf. 53d), this means that the TAM marker is procliticized to the subject. This is a cross-linguistically very unusual situation, but it is explicable diachronically, as the markers derive from auxiliary verbs in a VSO pattern (cf. 49f).

(53) d. ⲁⲡⲛⲟⲩⲧⲉ   ⲥⲱⲧⲙ
          a-p-noute   *sôtm*
          PRET-DEF.M-god   hear
          'God heard'

(54) d. ⲡⲉⲧⲣⲟⲥ ⲛⲁⲃⲱⲕ
          petros *na-bôk*
          Peter   FUT-go
          'Peter will go'

While the subject precedes the verb, the object follows the verb. Thus, suffixal person forms can be easily identified as subject or object forms by position (TAM-*subj*-VERB-*obj*):

(55) a. ⲁϥⲥⲟⲧⲡⲧ
          a-f-sotp-t
          PRET-3SGM-choose-1SG
          'He chose me'

      b. ϣⲁⲛⲥⲟⲧⲙϥ
          ša-n-sotm-f
          HAB-1PL-hear-3SGM
          'We hear him (habitually)'

Full-NP objects may likewise follow the verb, with no special marking:

(56) a. ⲘⲠⲞⲨⲤⲈⲦⲘⲖⲀⲀⲨ
        mp-ou-setm-laau
        PRET.NEG-3PL-hear-anyone
        'They did not hear anyone.'

     b. ⲀϤⲔⲀⲂⲀⲢⲀⲂⲂⲀⲤ   ⲚⲀⲨ   ⲈⲂⲞⲖ
         a-f-ka-barabbas   *na-u*   *ebol*
         PRET-3SGM-put-Barabbas   to-3PL out
         'He released Barabbas for them.' (L129; Mark 15:15)

Note that special verb forms are used when a direct object immediately follows the verb. In such cases, not only the pronominal suffix, but also the full-NP object is bound to the verb (in that it belongs to the same stress group). Since the stress moves to the full-NP object, the vowel of the verb is reduced, cf. the forms in (57).

(57)

free form	bound before full NP	bound before suffxed pronoun	
sôtm	setm-	sótm-	'hear'
kôt	ket-	kót-	'build'
tamó	tame-	tamó-	'inform'
číse	čest-	část-	'raise'
sólsl	slsl-	slsôl-	'console'
eíre	r-	áa-	'do'

Reduced bound forms of verbs in a verb-object combination are quite unusual typologically, and very tight verb-object combinations such as those in (56) tend to be found only in special "object incorporation" contexts, mostly when the object is generic (as in German *Fahrrad fahren* [bicycle ride] 'to cycle'). The construction in (56) has not been treated as "incorporation" by Coptic grammarians, because it is much less constrained than typical incorporation constructions.

However, the direct-object construction in (55–56) is not the only possibility. Direct objects may also be coded by the preposition *n-/m-* (before nouns) or *mmo-* (before suffix pronouns), which earlier meant 'in'; in such cases, the free form of the verb is used. This preposition is glossed ACC (accusative) here.

(58) a. ⲦⲈⲦⲚⲚⲞⲨⲬⲈ ⲘⲘⲞϤ
      tetn-nouče mmo-f
      2PL-throw ACC-3SGM
      'you throw it' (L132; Acts 13:46)

  b. ⲀϤⲚⲞⲨⲬⲈ   ⲈⲂⲞⲖ ⲚⲚⲈⲦⲠⲚⲈⲨⲘⲀ   ⲚⲀⲔⲀⲐⲀⲢⲦⲞⲚ
      a-f-nouče   *ebol n-ne-pneuma*   *n-akat^{h}arton*
      PRET-3SGM-throw out ACC-DEF.PL-spirit ATTR-unclean
      'He cast out the unclean spirits.' (L132; Matthew 8:16)[8]

Such prepositional direct objects remind the typologists of differential object marking (cf. Lazard 2001, and for Coptic see Engsheden 2008), but the conditions for the use of *n-/mmo-* in Coptic are complex. In subject-verb patterns, prepositional direct objects seem to be virtually obligatory (Stern-Jernstedt Rule), while in TAM-subject patterns, there is variation: When the NP is non-referential, it cannot occur with a preposition (Layton 2004: 132). The latter restriction is similar to conditions on incorporation constructions, which typically exclude articles or other modifiers. See Winand (2014, in this volume) for the origins of these patterns in Middle and Late Egyptian. Grossman (2014, in this volume) discusses the generalization that Coptic shows no case-marking before the verb, only after the verb, in the context of a similar situation in other African languages.

2.4 Noun phrase structure

Definite articles (*p-/t-/n-*), indefinite articles (*ou-/hen-*), demonstratives (*pei-/tei-*), and possessive pronouns precede the noun (cf. 59), while other modifiers follow it (cf. 60).

(59) a. ⲠⲢⲰⲘⲈ
      p-rôme
      DEF.M-man   'the man'

---

8 "(L132)" is short for "(Layton 2004: 132)". All of the Coptic examples cited here are from Layton's excellent grammar. Most of the examples are attested in texts (often in the Bible, and see Layton for the sources of the other examples), but some are constructed by the grammarian for pedagogical purposes.

b. ⲧⲉⲓⲥϩⲓⲙⲉ
   tei-shime
   DEM.F-woman   'this woman'

c. ⲡⲉⲥⲣⲁⲛ
   pe-s-ran
   DEF.M-3SGF-name   'her name'[9]

d. ⲟⲩⲥϩⲓⲙⲉ
   ou-shime
   INDF.SG-woman   'a woman'

e. ϩⲉⲛϩⲉⲃⲣⲁⲓⲟⲥ
   hen-hebraios
   INDF.PL-Hebrew   'Hebrews'

(60) a. ϩⲣⲁⲁⲩ ⲛⲓⲙ
   hraau nim
   dish   any   'every dish'

b. ⲡⲣⲱⲙⲉ   ⲥⲛⲁⲩ
   p-rôme   *snau*
   DEF.M-man   two   'the two men'

c. ⲧⲅⲁⲗⲓⲗⲁⲓⲁ   ⲧⲏⲣⲥ
   t-galilaia   *têr-s*
   DEF.F-Galilee   all-3SGF   'all Galilee'

d. ⲟⲩⲣⲱⲙⲉ   ⲛⲥⲁⲃⲉ
   ou-rôme   *n-sabe*
   INDF-man   ATTR-wise   'a wise man'

---

9 A few nouns have postposed possessive pronouns, like *hêt-* 'belly' (cf. 63b below) (see Haspel-math 2014, in this volume, for further discussion).

    e. ⲡⲎⲒ   ⲘⲠⲬⲞⲈⲒⲤ
       p-êi   *m-p-čoeis*
       DEF.M-house ATTR-DEF.M-lord   'the house of the lord'

Most commonly, property-words such as *sabe* 'wise' (60d) follow a thing (or person) word that they modify, but the reverse is also possible (see Malchukov 2000 for some typological discussion):

(61) ⲞⲨⲤⲀⲂⲈ   ⲚⲢⲰⲘⲈ
      ou-sabe *n-rôme*
      INDF-wise ATTR-man   'a wise man'

And thing-words may also modify other thing-words in the same attribution construction with the attributive marker *n-*:

(62) ⲞⲨⲢⲰⲘⲈ   ⲚⲈⲰϢⲰⲦ
      ou-rôme *n-ešôt*
      INDF-man ATTR-merchant 'a man who is a merchant'

Thus, there is no obvious grammatical distinction between property-words and thing-words, and consequently Layton (2004) calls them both nouns. The only difference between words like *shime* 'woman' and words like *sabe* 'wise' is that the former has a fixed gender (namely feminine: *te-shime* [DEF.F-woman] 'the woman'), whereas *sabe* can occur with either gender: *p-sabe* 'the wise one (M)', *t-sabe* 'the wise one (F)'.

2.5 Nonverbal predication

Nonverbal predications with nominal predicates use the copula *pe* (M) / *te* (F) / *ne* (PL) when the subject is 3rd person:

(63) a. ⲠⲀⲒ   ⲠⲈ   ⲠⲀⲤⲰⲘⲀ
          pai   *pe*   *p-a-sôma*
          this.M COP.M DEF.M-1SG-body
          'This is my body.' (L217; 1 Cor 11:24)

b. ⲡⲉⲩⲛⲟⲩⲧⲉ   ⲡⲉ   ⳉⲏⲧⲟⲩ
   pe-u-noute   *pe*   *hêt-ou*
   DEF.M-3PL-god COP.M   belly-3PL
   'Their god is their belly.' (L217; Phil 3: 19)

c. ⲟⲩⲣⲉϥⲣⲛⲟⲃⲉ   ⲧⲉ
   ou-ref-r-nobe   *te*
   INDF-AGT-do-sin COP.F
   'She is a sinner.' (L209; Luke 7:39)

d. ⲟⲩⲁⲇⲓⲕⲟⲥ   ⲡⲉ   ⲡⲛⲟⲩⲧⲉ
   ou-adikos   *pe*   *p-noute*
   INDF-unjust COP.M   DEF.M-god
   'God is unjust.' (L340; Rom 3:5-6)

When the subject is first or second person, it is expressed by (a reduced form of) the independent pronoun and no copula is needed:

(64)   ⲁⲛⲅⲑⲙⳉⲁⲗ   ⲙⲡϫⲟⲉⲓⲥ
      ang-t-ʰmhal   *m-p-čoeis*
      I-DEF.F-servant   ATTR-DEF.M-lord
      'I am the handmaid of the Lord.' (Luke 1:38)

When the nonverbal predicate is a prepositional phrase or an adverb, no copula is used, and the predicate simply follows the subject:

(65) a. ⲧⲙⲉ   ⳉⲙⲡⲁⲓ
      t-me   *hm-pai*
      DEF.F-truth   in-that.M
      'The truth is in that one.' (L237)

b. ⲡⲉⲧⲣⲟⲥ   ⲙⲙⲁⲩ
      petros   *mmau*
      Peter   there
      'Peter is there.' (L237; Acts 9:38)

In such constructions, person forms are from the prefixal series:

(66) a. ⲥⲙⲙⲁⲩ
   s-mmau
   3SGF-there
   'It is there.' (L237)

b. ϯⲛⲙⲙⲁϥ ⲙⲛⲧⲉϥⲑⲗⲓϯⲥ
   t̓-nmma-f hn-t-ef-t^hlip^sis
   1SG-with-3SGM in-DEF.F-3SGM-affliction
   'I am with him in his affliction.' (L237; Psalms 90:15)

c. ϥϩⲛⲙⲡⲏⲩⲉ
   f-hn-m-pêue
   3SGM-in-DEF.PL-heaven.PL
   'He is in the heavens.' (L328)

The existential copula *oun-* (negative *mn-*) is used in existential clauses:

(67) a. ⲟⲩⲛⲁⲅⲅⲉⲗⲟⲥ
   oun-aggelos
   exist-angel
   'Angels exist.' (L381; Acts 23:8)

b. ⲙⲛⲓⲟⲩⲇⲁⲓ ϩⲓϩⲉⲗⲗⲏⲛ
   mn-ioudai hi-hellên
   NEG.exist-Jew on-Greek
   'There is neither Jew nor Greek.' (L384; Galatians 3:28)

The possessive verb-like form *ounte-* (negative *mnte-*) is used to express 'have', in a special construction verb-possessor-possessum:

(68) a. ⲟⲩⲛⲧⲉⲃⲃⲁϣⲟⲣ ⲛⲉⲩⲃⲏⲃ
   ounte-b-bašor ne-u-bêb
   have-DEF.PL-fox DEF.PL-3PL-hole

ⲁⲩⲱ ⲟⲩⲛⲧⲉⲛⲅⲁⲗⲁⲧⲉ ⲛⲧⲡⲉ ⲛⲉⲩⲙⲁⲅ
auô ounte-n-halate n-t-pe ne-u-mah
and have-DEF.PL-birds ATTR-DEF.F-sky DEF.PL-3PL-nest
'Foxes have their holes and birds of the sky have their nests.' (L305;
Luke 9:58)

b. ⲟⲩⲛⲧⲕⲡⲁⲓ ⲙⲙⲁⲩ
ount-k-pai mmau
have-2SGM-this.M there
'You have this.' (Rev 2:6)

c. ⲁⲩⲱ ⲙⲛⲗⲁⲁⲩ ⲉⲙⲛⲧϥⲥⲙⲏ
auô mn-laau e-mnt-f-smê
and NEG.exist-anyone [CIRC-NEG.have-3SGM-voice]
'And there is none that has no voice.' (1 Cor 14:10)

In this construction (and nowhere else), there may be two person suffixes in a
series:

(69) ⲙⲛⲧⲁⲩϥ
mnta-u-f
NEG.have-3PL-3SGM
'They do not have it'

2.6 Relative clauses

Relative clauses are marked by the relativizer *ete(re)-/et-/ent-* when the head
noun is definite. In almost all cases, the relativized element is represented by a
resumptive pronoun in the relative clause.

(70) a. ⲡⲉⲓϣⲁϫⲉ ⲉⲛⲧⲁϥϣⲱⲡⲉ
pei-šače ent-a-f-šôpe
this.M-saying [REL-PRET-3SGM-happen]
'This saying that has come to pass.' (L327; Luke 2:15)

    b. ⲡⲥⲓⲟⲩ   ⲉⲛⲧⲁⲩⲛⲁⲩ   ⲉⲣⲟϥ   ϩⲛⲙⲙⲁ ⲛϣⲁ

       p-siou   *ent-a-u-nau*   *ero-f*   *hn-mma* *n-ša*

       DEF.M-star [REL-PRET-3PL-see to-3SGM in-place of-rise]

       'The star that they had seen in the East.' (L326; Matthew 2:9)

    c. ⲡⲣⲱⲙⲉ   ⲉⲧⲉⲣⲉⲧⲉϥϭⲓⲝ   ⲙⲟⲟⲩⲧ

       p-rôme   *etere-te-f-cič*   *moout*

       DEF.M-man [REL-DEF.F-3SGM-hand withered]

       'The man whose hand was withered.' (L326; Mark 3:3)

This relative marker presumably derives from the Earlier Egyptian relative pronoun *ntj/ntt* (§ 1.11).

    When the head noun is indefinite, the circumstantial marker *e-/ere-* (see § 2.7) is used (see also 68c above):

(71) a. ⲟⲩⲣⲱⲙⲉ   ⲉⲁϥϫⲟ   ⲛⲟⲩϭⲣⲟϭ

       ou-rôme *e-a-f-čo*   *n-ou-croc*

       INDF-man [CIRC-PRET-3SGM-SOW ACC-INDF-seed]

       'A man who sowed seed' (L327; Matthew 13:24)

    b. ⲟⲩⲥϩⲓⲙⲉ   ⲉⲩⲛⲧⲥⲟⲩϣⲉⲉⲣⲉ   ⲙⲙⲁⲩ

       ou-shime   *e-unt-s-ou-šeere*   *mmau*

       INDF-woman [CIRC-have-3SGF-INDF-daughter there]

       'A woman who had a daughter' (L327; Mark 7:25)

Relative clauses of the first type may be readily used independently with definite articles, often in a generalized sense ('all those who...', 'whoever...').

(72) a. ⲛⲉⲛⲧⲁⲩⲟⲩⲱⲙ

       n-ent-a-u-ouôm

       DEF.PL-[REL-PRET-3PL-eat]

       'Those who ate' (L333; Mark 6:44)

    b. ⲛⲉⲧⲉⲙⲛϭⲟⲙ   ⲙⲙⲟⲟⲩ

       n-ete-mn-com   *mmo-ou*

       DEF.PL-[REL-NEG.exist-power in-3PL]

       'Those in whom there is no power' (i.e., the weak) (L337; Romans 15:1)

c. ⲡⲉⲧⲉⲩⲛⲧϥⲙⲁⲁϫⲉ   ⲉⲥⲱⲧⲙ

    p-ete-unt-f-maače   *e-sôtm*

    DEF.M-[REL-have-3SGM-ear to-hear]

    'Whoever has ears to hear' (L333; Mark 4:9)

(Relative clauses preceded by definite articles also occur in cleft constructions, cf. (75a) below.)

The relative-clause marker *ete(re)-/et-/ent-* is always clause-initial and is thus similar to relative particles in many other languages (e.g., English *that*, Spanish *que*, Indonesian *yang*). It is not pronoun-like at all, as it does not show any case or agreement. But it is different from the well-known relative particles, and typologically unusual, in that its shape varies depending on the tense-aspect form of the verb: *ent-* is used before the Affirmative Past tense *a-* (e.g., 70a–b), *ete-* is used before other tense-aspect forms (e.g., 72b), and *etere-/et-* is used in subject-verb constructions (e.g., 70c). Relative markers which are intimately bound up with tense-aspect markers are known from Indo-European languages and are called "participles", but the Coptic forms are very different in that they show no signs of nonfiniteness – the subject is expressed in much the same way in relative clauses as in independent clauses.

However, in subject-predicate patterns, the pronominal subject is expressed as a suffix on the relative marker *et-*, rather than as a prefixal form. Table 7 shows that there are some differences between the two series, especially in the 3rd person plural, but also in the 2nd singular feminine and elsewhere.

Table 7: Prefixal subject pronouns and subject forms after *et-*

		prefixal forms (subject)	subject forms after *et-*
SG	1	*ti-*	*et-i*
	2M	*k-*	*et-k*
	2F	*te-*	*et-e(re)*
	3M	*f-*	*et-f*
	3F	*s-*	*et-s*
PL	1	*tn-*	*et-n*
	2	*tetn-*	*et-etn*
	3	*se-*	*et-ou*

An example of a subject suffix after *et-* in a subject-predicate construction is (73).

(73) ⲡⲙⲁ   ⲉⲧⲛⲁⲃⲱⲕ   ⲉⲣⲟϥ
   p-ma   *et-i-na-bôk*   *ero-f*
   DEF.M-place [REL-1SG-FUt-go to-3SGM]
   'The place that I am going to' (L326; John 8:21)

This is thus a peculiar combination of a relative marker and a subject pronoun. When a full NP is used in a subject-verb construction, the form *etere-* is used (e.g., 70c).

2.7 Circumstantial and focalizing constructions

The marker *e-* or *ere-* is used both as a general subordination marker (called Circumstantial) and as a marker of focalization. In TAM-subject constructions, *e-* precedes the TAM marker, while in subject-predicate constructions, *ere-* precedes a full-NP subject and *e-* combines with the same suffixes that follow the relativizer *et-* (cf. Table 7), thus:

(74)   a.   *ne-hiome sôtp*   'the women choose'   (subject-predicate pattern)

     se-sôtp   'they choose'

   b.   *ere-ne-hiome sôtp* 'as the women choose' (circumstantial)
     e-u-sôtp   'as they choose'

   c.   *a-ne-hiome sôtp*   'the women chose'   (TAM-subject pattern)
     a-u-sôtp   'they chose'

   d.   *e-a-ne-hiome sôtp* 'as the women chose' (circumstantial)
     e-a-u-sôtp   'as they chose'

Like the relative marker, the circumstantial marker is thus closely bound up with the tense-aspect structure of the clause, and is not simply a clause-initial complementizer. Again, this kind of complexity of subordinate forms is not common cross-linguistically.

The circumstantial marker is used in various kinds of adverbial clauses (75a–b) and in certain complement clauses (76a–b). It also occurs in relative clauses with an indefinite head noun, as seen above in (71a–b).

(75) a. ⲉⲙⲛⲧⲁⲩⲓⲏⲥⲟⲩⲥ   ⲅⲁⲣ ⲙⲙⲁⲩ   ⲟⲩ
      e-mnta-u-iêsous   *gar mmau*   *ou*
      [CIRC-NEG.have-3PL-Jesus   for there]   what
      ⲡⲉⲧⲛⲁⲧⲁϫⲣⲟⲟⲩ
      p-et-na-tačro-ou
      DEF.M-[REL-FUT-strengthen 3PL]
      'For as they do not have Jesus, what (is that which) will strengthen them?' (L338)

    b. ⲁⲩⲉⲓ   ⲉϩⲣⲁⲓ ⲉⲡⲉⲙϩⲁⲟⲩ   ⲉⲁⲡⲣⲏ   ϣⲁ
      a-u-ei   *ehrai e-pe-mhaou*   *e-a-p-rê*   *ša*
      PRET-3PL-come up   to-DEF.M-tomb   [CIRC-PRET-DEF.M-sun   rise]
      'They arrived at the tomb when the sun had risen.' (L338; Mark 16:2)

(76) a. ⲙⲁⲣⲉϥⲥⲱⲧⲙ   ⲉⲡⲉⲡⲣⲟⲫⲏⲧⲏⲥ   ⲉϥϫⲱ   ⲛⲛⲁⲓ
      mare-f-sôtm   *e-pe-prop^hêtês*   *e-f-čô*   *n-nai*
      OPT-3SGM-hear   to-DEF.M-prophet   [CIRC-3SGM-say   ACC-these]
      'Let him listen to the prophet saying these (words).' (L341)

    b. ⲁⲩⲗⲟ   ⲉⲩⲙⲟⲟϣⲉ   ⲛⲙⲙⲁϥ
      a-u-lo   *e-u-mooše*   *nmma-f*
      PRET-3PL-cease   [CIRC-3PL-go.about   with-3SGM]
      'They ceased going about with him.' (L342; John 6:66)

A formally similar construction with the prefix *e-/ere-* is also used in focalizing constructions, when the main focus is not on the verb but on some other constituent, cf. the contrast between (77a) and (77b):

(77) a. ⲕϫⲓϭⲟⲗ
      k-či-col   'You are lying (lit. saying falsehoods).'
      2SGM-say-falsehood

b. ⲉⲕϫⲓϭⲟⲗ

    e-k-či-col   'You are LYING (lit. saying falsehoods).' (L354)

    FOC-2SGM-say-FALSEHOOD

(78) ⲉⲕϫⲱ   ⲙⲡⲁⲓ   ⲡⲁⲣⲟⲕ   ⲛⲁⲩⲁⲁⲕ

     e-k-čô   *m-pai*   *haro-k*   *mauaa-k*

     FOC-2SGM-say ACC-this on.behalf-2SGM alone-2SGM

     'Is it OF YOUR OWN ACCORD that you say this?' (L354; John 18:34)

(79) ⲛⲉϥⲡⲓⲥⲧⲉⲩⲉ   ⲉⲣⲟⲉⲓ ⲁⲛ ⲁⲗⲗⲁ ⲉⲡⲉⲛⲧⲁϥⲧⲁⲟⲩⲟⲉⲓ

     n-e-f-pisteue   *ero-ei an alla e-p-ent-a-f-taouo-ei*

     NEG-FOC-3SGM-believe to-1SG NEG but to-DEF.M-[REL-PRET-3SGM-

                                            send-1SG]

     'He believes NOT IN ME, but in him who sent me.' (L360)

When the tense-aspect form is the Past (*a-*), the focalizing marker is not *e-*, but *nt-*:

(80) ⲛⲧⲁϥϫⲉⲡⲁⲓ   ⲇⲉ ⲉϥⲡⲓⲣⲁⲍⲉ   ⲙⲙⲟϥ

     nt-a-f-če-pai   *de e-f-piraze*   *mmo-f*

     FOC-PRET-3SGM-say-this but [CIRC-3SGM-test ACC-3SGM]

     'But he said this (by way of) TESTING HIM.' (John 6:6)

So again, we have a marker that is tightly bound up with the tense-aspect structure of the clause, even though it expresses a pragmatic notion that has nothing to do with tense or aspect. However, such special focalizing verb forms are not uncommon in African languages.

Abbreviations

AGT	agent noun
ATTR	attributive
COP	copula
DEF	definite article
DEP	dependent pronoun
DU	dual
EXIST	existential
F	feminine
FUT	future tense
GENER	generic person
IMP	imperative
INDP	independent pronoun
INF	infinitive

M	masculine
NEG	negation
ORD	ordinal numeral
PCL	particle
PL	plural
PRF	perfect
REL	relative clause marker
SGF	singular feminine
SGM	singular masculine
STAT	stative

3 References

Allen, James P. 2000. *Middle Egyptian: An introduction to the language and culture of hieroglyphs.* Cambridge: Cambridge University Press.

Allen, James P. 2013. *The ancient Egyptian language: an historical study.* Cambridge: Cambridge University Press.

Börjars, Kersti & Vincent, Nigel. 2011. Grammaticalization and directionality: data, analysis and explanation. In: Narrog, Heiko & Heine, Bernd (eds.), *Oxford handbook of grammaticalization,* Oxford: Oxford University Press, 163–176.

Croft, William. 1991. *Syntactic categories and grammatical relations: the cognitive organization of information.* Chicago: University of Chicago Press.

Croft, William. 2000. Parts of speech as language universals and as language-particular categories. In: Vogel, Petra M. & Comrie, Bernard (eds.), *Approaches to the typology of word classes.* Berlin: Mouton de Gruyter, 65–102.

Croft, William. 2001. *Radical construction grammar: syntactic theory in typological perspective.* Oxford: Oxford University Press.

Depuydt, Leo. 1993. On Coptic sounds. *Orientalia* 62: 338–375.

Dik, Simon C. 1997. *The theory of functional grammar.* 2 vols. Berlin: Mouton de Gruyter.

Donohue, Mark & Wichmann, Søren (eds.). 2008. *The typology of semantic alignment.* Oxford: Oxford University

Dryer, Matthew S. 1992. The Greenbergian word order correlations. *Language* 68.1: 81–138.

Englund, Gertie. 1988. *Middle Egyptian: an introduction.* Uppsala: Uppsala University.

Engsheden, Åke. 2008. Differential object marking in Sahidic Coptic. In: Josephson, Folke & Söhrman, Ingmar (eds.), *Interdependence of diachronic and synchronic analyses.* (Studies in Language Companion Series 103.). Amsterdam: Benjamins, 323–344.

Ewald, Heinrich. 1861. *Abhandlung über den bau der thatwörter im Koptischen.* Göttingen: Dieterichsche Buchhandlung.

Funk, Wolf-Peter. 2009. Methodological issues in the (morpho)phonological description of Coptic. In: Goldenberg, Gideon & Shisha-Halevy, Ariel (eds.), *Egyptian, Semitic and general grammar: Studies in memory of H.J. Polotsky.* Jerusalem: The Israel Academy of Sciences and Humanities, 70–91.

Gardiner, Alan. 1957. *Egyptian grammar being an introduction to the study of hieroglyphs.* 3rd ed. London: Oxford University Press.

Gensler, Orin D. 2014. A typological look at Egyptian *d > ꜥ. In this volume.

Grossman, Eitan. 2009. Periphrastic perfects in the Coptic dialects: a case study in grammaticalization. *Lingua Aegyptia* 17: 81–118.

Grossman, Eitan. 2014. No case before the verb, obligatory case after the verb in Coptic. In this volume.

Grossman, Eitan & Haspelmath, Martin. 2014. The Leipzig-Jerusalem transliteration of Coptic. In this volume.

Haspelmath, Martin. 1999. Why is grammaticalization irreversible? *Linguistics* 37.6: 1043–1068.

Haspelmath, Martin. 2014. The three adnominal possessive constructions in Egyptian-Coptic: Three degrees of grammaticalization. In this volume.

Hintze, Fritz. 1950. Konversion und analytische Tendenz in der ägyptischen Sprachentwicklung. *Zeitschrift für Phonetik und Allgemeine Sprachwissenschaft* 4: 41–56.

Hodge, Carleton T. 1970. The linguistic cycle. *Language Sciences* 13: 1–7.

Kammerzell, Frank. 1998. The Sounds of a Dead Language: Reconstructing Egyptian Phonology. *Göttinger Beiträge zur Sprachwissenschaft* 1: 21–41.

Layton, Bentley. 2004. *A Coptic grammar: with a chrestomathy and glossary: Sahidic dialect.* 2nd ed. Wiesbaden: Harrassowitz.

Lazard, Gilbert. 2001. Le marquage différentiel de l'objet. In: Haspelmath, Martin, König, Ekkehard, Oesterreicher, Wulf & Raible, Wolfgang (eds.), *Language typology and language universals: An international handbook* Vol. 2. Berlin: De Gruyter, 873–885.

Loprieno, Antonio. 1995. *Ancient Egyptian: a linguistic introduction.* Cambridge: Cambridge University Press.

Malchukov, Andrej L. 2000. *Dependency reversal in noun-attributive constructions: towards a typology.* München: LINCOM Europa.

Müller, Matthias. 2011. Ägyptische Phonologie? Möglichkeiten und Grenzen linguistischer Modelle bei der Beschreibung des Lautsystems einer extinkten Sprache. In: Verbovsek, Alexandra, Backes, Burkhard & Jones, Catherine (eds.) 2011. *Methodik und Didaktik in der Ägyptologie.* München: Fink, 509–531.

Nedjalkov, Vladimir P. (ed.). 1988. *Typology of resultative constructions.* Amsterdam: Benjamins.

Peust, Carsten. 1999. *Egyptian Phonology: an introduction to the phonology of a dead language.* Göttingen: Peust & Gutschmidt. (available from http://digi.ub.uni-heidelberg.de/diglit/peust1999)

Reintges, Chris H. 2012. Macroparametric change and the synthetic-analytic dimension: the case of Ancient Egyptian. In: Galves, Charlotte, Cyrino, Sônia, Lopes, Ruth, Sandalo, Filomena & Avelar, Juanito (eds.), *Parameter theory and linguistic change.* Oxford: Oxford University Press, 132–156.

Reintges, Chris. 2014. The Old and Early Middle Egyptian Stative: morphosyntax, semantics, typology. In this volume.

Schenkel, Wolfgang. 1990. *Einführung in die altägyptische Sprachwissenschaft.* Darmstadt: Wissenschaftliche Buchgesellschaft.

Schenkel, Wolfgang. 2012. *Tübinger Einführung in die klassisch-ägyptische Sprache und Schrift.* Tübingen: W. Schenkel.

Schwegler, Armin. 1990. *Analyticity and syntheticity: a diachronic perspective with special reference to Romance languages.* Berlin: Mouton de Gruyter.

van Gelderen, Elly. 2011. *The linguistic cycle: language change and the language faculty.* New York: Oxford University Press.

von der Gabelentz, Georg. 1901. *Die Sprachwissenschaft, ihre Aufgaben, Methoden und bisherigen Ergebnisse.* 2nd ed. Leipzig: C. H. Tauchnitz.

Winand, Jean. 2014. The oblique expression of the object in Ancient Egyptian. In this volume.

Eitan Grossman & Martin Haspelmath

The Leipzig-Jerusalem Transliteration of Coptic

Abstract: In this article, we propose a system for transliterating Coptic, akin to those systems used for transliterating Greek, Russian, or Arabic. It is intended to serve as a standard for linguists interested in making Coptic data more accessible to non-specialists. We also discuss some questions that may arise, and provide several fully transliterated and glossed Coptic examples.

1 Introduction

In recent years, linguists working on Coptic have increasingly become interested in making the results of their research accessible to non-specialists. A major symptom of this trend is the increased transliteration and glossing of examples, even in publications in forums dedicated to Egyptian-Coptic linguistics (e.g., *Lingua Aegyptia* 19, in which transliteration and glossing were obligatory).

However, no standard transliteration system for Coptic exists, so current practice shows some idiosyncrasies and inconsistencies. In some cases, transliteration systems used are somewhere between a strict transliteration system and a phonological representation. However, transliterations are not intended to be phonological representations. In some contexts, both transliteration and phonological representation are necessary, while in others, neither is.

In this article, we propose a system for transliterating Coptic, akin to those systems used for transliterating Greek, Russian, or Arabic.

2 What's transliteration?

Transliteration is different from transcription, which aims to represent the sounds of a language. Transliteration, on the other hand, is intended to represent graphemes, units of written language. In general, the ideal transliteration system involves a one-to-one mapping of graphemes, although this is not strictly observed in all transliteration systems.

3 Why transliterate Coptic?

The first reason is that we would like linguists who are not specialists in Coptic to be able to profit from the extensive – and interesting – research being conducted on this language. Since most linguists do not read the Coptic script, it is necessary to render the Coptic text in a graphemic system that is familiar to anyone occupied with linguistics. In practice, this means a Latin-based alphabetic system. The second reason is that it is sometimes impractical to use Coptic script, e.g., when citing a Coptic example in a publication venue where Coptic fonts are not readily available, or in informal contexts such as e-mails.

Moreover, transliteration facilitates morpheme-by-morpheme glossing of examples, which aid the reader in associating parts of a text with the translation. Glosses with a morpheme breakdown are very helpful for understanding more or less how a given text works, and as such, for non-expert linguists interested in knowing something about a language. Morpheme boundaries are generally shown by hyphens, and hyphens in the Coptic script would look very peculiar.

4 Our proposal

Our proposal does not differ much from the usual practices of most Copticists.[1] It should be kept in mind that we do not have the goal of providing an accurate phonological representation of any particular variety of Coptic. Our aim is to provide a way of consistently transliterating Coptic alphabetic signs, so that the Coptic letters can be determined from the rendering with Latin letters. The proposal concerns only letters; diacritics such as the supralinear stroke will not be represented (in line with the usual practice of transliterating Coptic).

In the following Table, we give our suggested transliteration equivalents of the Coptic graphemes. Some problematic issues are discussed afterwards (§ 5).

---

1 For a summary of some transliteration practices, see Peust (1999). For an extensive discussion of the relationship between the Coptic alphabet(s) and the sounds they are thought to represent, see Kasser (1991). For two recent and systematic discussions of Coptic phonology, see Funk (2009) and Müller (2011), both of which extensively cite earlier research on Coptic phonology.

Table 1: Suggested transliteration equivalents

ⲁ	*a*	ⲙ	*m*	ⲱ	*ô*
ⲃ	*b*	ⲛ	*n*	ⲱ	*š*
ⲅ	*g*	ⳉ	*k^s*	ϥ	*f*
ⲇ	*d*	ⲟ	*o*	ϩ	*h*
ⲉ	*e*	ⲡ	*p*	ⳓ	*x*
ⲍ	*z*	ⲣ	*r*	ⲭ	*č*
ⲏ	*ê*	ⲥ	*s*	ⲋ	*c*
ⲑ	*t^h*	ⲧ	*t*	ϯ	*t^i*
ⲓ	*i*	ⲩ	*u*	ⳋ	*x'*
ⲕ	*k*	ⲫ	*p^h*	ⳝ	*ç*
ⲗ	*l*	ⳟ	*p^s*	ϭ	*ç'*

5 Possible questions

In this section we address some questions that some readers might have about our proposed transliteration.

5.1 Why aren't IPA characters used?

We have purposely chosen to avoid characters that would evoke a feeling that a phonological transcription is being given. This means preferring the traditional *š* and *č*, for example, to ʃ and tʃ. Transliteration is more like an orthography than like a transcription, and *š* and *č* are orthographic characters, rather than phonetic characters. This also means preferring *ê* and *ô* to *ē* and *ō* for Coptic ⲏ and ⲱ.

5.2 Why are you using superscript letters?

Some Coptic letters cannot be readily transliterated with a single Latin letter, because there is no Latin letter with a remotely similar value. For example, <ps> and <ti> can only be transliterated by a digraph (a combination of two Latin letters). To make it clear that the two Latin letters render a single Coptic letter, the second letter is written as a superscript. This allows one to reflect the contrast between <psi>p^s and <p.sigma>ps. Another possibility would be to use a bow, e.g., $\widehat{ks}$ for ⲝ, but this is an IPA practice with a specific meaning (affricate or diphthong). Writing superscript for aspirated plosives (t^h, p^h, k^h) is a well-established practice; only t^i, p^s and k^s will need some getting used to.

5.3 Why use *c* and *č* for ϭ and ⳉ?

Copticists have a number of different practices for rendering these letters, which stand for different sounds in different dialects. We think that the transliteration *c* for ϭ is preferable to k^j because the latter is a digraph, and *č* for ⳉ is preferable to *j*, even though this is used fairly frequently, because *j* can represent IPA *j* (the palatal glide) or English *j* (the palato-alveolar affricate).

5.4 What about abbreviations?

The Coptic script has quite a few abbreviations, usually – but not always – involving holy names, e.g., $\overline{\text{ⲭⲥ}}$ 'Christ.' We suggest that the name be transliterated fully, with the missing letters being supplied between pointed parentheses, e.g., ⲭ<ⲣⲓⲥⲧⲟ>ⲥ k^h<*risto*>*s*.

6 Presenting Coptic examples

The goal of the present article is not to provide a complete system for presenting Coptic examples, from the Coptic text all the way down to the translation, but here we will nonetheless give an idea of where transliteration fits into the presentation of examples.

While an ideal presentation would include maximal data from all levels of analysis, in most cases much less information is necessary. Thus, ideally six lines of data would ensure that the reader has full information of how to link a given Coptic example with its translation.

1.	The Coptic text	ⲡⲣⲱⲙⲉ
2.	Transliteration	*prôme*
3.	A phonological representation	*pro:mə*
4.	Analyzed text, with morpheme divisions	*p-rôme*
5.	Morpheme-by-morpheme glosses	ART.MSG-man
6.	Translation	'the man'

But of course, not all of these lines are necessary in all situations. For example, specialists in Coptic, when writing for a purely Copticist audience, might use only line 1, the Coptic text.

(1) ⲙⲡⲣϭⲱ

If, for technical reasons (e.g., in e-mails), they don't have access to the Coptic script, they might make do with line 2, a transliteration.

(2) *mprcô*

In either case, they might add line 6, a translation.

(3) ⲙⲡⲣϭⲱ
    'Don't delay'

A nonspecialist would need, minimally, lines 2 and 6, a transliteration and translation, like in example (4).

(4) *mprcô*
    'Don't delay'

But in order to appreciate how the two are related, line 5, morpheme-by-morpheme glosses, is very helpful. In many typologically-oriented works, linguists use combinations of 2, 5 and 6, or 4, 5 and 6, or a combination of 2 and 4 plus 5 and 6.

(5) Russian

 2 *piši*   *otcu!*
 5 write.IMPV father.DAT
 6 'Write to the father!'

(6) Russian

 4 *piš-i*   *otc-u!*
 5 write-IMPV father-DAT
 6 'Write to the father!'

6.1 If the transliteration allows an adequate construction of the Coptic text, why bother giving the Coptic text in the examples?

It's true that in many cases, linguists don't provide the original script. If the transliteration is precise, the original can be reconstructed on its basis, so it is redundant. However, specialists will want to see the original script, and since this is becoming easier and easier from a technological point of view, there is no reason not to cite this as well.

6.2 How does the morpheme-by-morpheme glossing work when a single letter represents sounds in two different morphemes, e.g., ⲫⲱⲃ *pʰôb* 'the thing'?

Morpheme-by-morpheme translation generally presupposes linear segmentability. Where this is not possible (e.g., in the case of ablaut, e.g., *sôtp* 'choose' vs. *sotp* 'chosen'), the glosses of the two morphemes need to be combined with a special symbol (e.g., choose\STAT for *sotp*). Where a single letter represents two sounds that belong to two different morphemes, the same problem arises. But here, an additional line (or two) for the phonological representation[2] can be used to clarify the matter, e.g.

(7a)	ⲫⲱⲃ	(1)	(7b)	ⲫⲱⲃ	(1)
	pʰôb	(2)		*pʰôb*	(2)
	p-ho:b	(3–4)		*pho:b*	(3)
	ART.MSG-thing	(5)		*p-ho:b*	(4)
	'the thing'	(6)		ART.MSG-thing	(5)
				'the thing'	(6)

However, it might be simpler and more elegant in such cases to gloss a string like ⲫⲱⲃ *pʰôb* as the\thing (or as *p-ʰôb* the-thing).

---

2 For an idea of what phonological representations of Coptic are actually thought to look like, the reader is referred to the sources mentioned in the previous footnote.

7 Some examples

The following examples present the transliteration and presentation of Coptic examples from several dialects, in order to illustrate some of the issues raised above.[3]

(8) Sahidic

ⲡⲁϣⲏⲣⲉ	ⲉⲕϣⲁⲛϫⲓ	ⲛⲛϣⲁϫⲉ
pašêre	*ekšanči*	*nnšače*
pa-šêre	*e-k-šan-či*	*n-n-šače*
POSS1SG.MSG-son	PROT1-2SGM-PROT2-take	ACC-ART.PL-word
'My son, if you accept the words		

ⲛⲧⲁⲉⲛⲧⲟⲗⲏ	ⲛⲅⲕⲟⲡⲟⲩ	ϩⲁⲧⲏⲕ
ntaentolê	*nghopou*	*hatêk*
n-ta-entolê	*n-g-hop-ou*	*hatê-k*
of-POSS1SG.FSG-commandment	CONJ-2SGM-hide-3PL	within-2SGM
of my commandment and hide them within you...' (Proverbs 2:1).		

(9) Akhmimic

ⲡⲁϣⲏⲣⲉ	ⲁⲕϣⲁϫⲓ	ⲛⲛϣⲉϫⲉ
pašêre	*akšači*	*nnšeče*
pa-šêre	*a-k-ša-či*	*n-n-šeče*
POSS1SG.MSG-son	PROT1-2SGM-PROT2-take	ACC-ART.PL-word
'My son, if you accept the words		

ⲛⲧⲁⲉⲛⲧⲟⲗⲏ	ⲕϩⲁⲡⲟⲩ	ϩⲁϩⲧⲏⲕ
ntaentolê	*khapou*	*x'ahtêk*
n-ta-entolê	*k-hap-ou*	*x'ahtê-k*
of-POSS1SG.FSG-commandment	CONJ\2SGM-hide-3PL	within-2SGM
of my commandment, and hide them within yourself...' (Proverbs 2:1).		

---

3 Abbreviations used in glosses (other than those found in the Leipzig Glossing Rules (http://www.eva.mpg.de/lingua/resources/glossing-rules.php): CONJ – conjunctive, PROT – protasis.

(10) Bohairic

ⲡⲁϣⲏⲣⲓ	ⲉϣⲱⲡ ⲁⲕϣⲁⲛϭⲓ		ⲛⲛⲁⲥⲁϫⲓ
pašêri	*ešôp*	*akšanci*	*nnasači*
pa-šêri	*ešôp*	*a-k-šan-ci*	*n-na-sači*
POSS1SG.MSG-son	COND	PROT1-2SGM-PROT2-take	ACC-POSS1SG.PL-word

'My son, if you accept my words

ⲛⲧⲉⲛⲁⲉⲛⲧⲟⲗⲏ	ⲛⲧⲉⲕⲭⲟⲡⲟⲩ	ⲛϧⲏⲧⲕ
ntenaentolê	*ntekkʰopou*	*nxêtk*
nte-na-entolê	*nte-k-kʰop-ou*	*nxêt-k*
of-POSS1SG.PL-commandment	CONJ-2SGM-hide-3PL	within-2SGM

of my commandments, and hide them within yourself...' (Proverbs 2:1)

(11) Sahidic

ⲟⲩⲥⲁⲣⲝ ⲡⲉ
ousarkˢ pe
ou-sarkˢ=pe
ART.INDEF-flesh=SBJ.MSG
'It is flesh' (John 3:6)

(12) Sahidic

ⲕⲁⲧⲁ	ⲑⲉ	ⲉⲛⲧⲁⲙⲱⲟⲩⲥⲏⲥ	ϫⲓⲥⲉ	ⲙⲫⲟϥ
kata	*tʰe*	*entamôousês*	*čise*	*mpʰof*
kata	*t-he*	*ent-a-môusês*	*čise*	*m-p-hof*
according_to	ART.FSG-way	REL-PST-Moses	raise	ACC-ART.MSG-snake

'As Moses raised the snake' (John 3:14).

(13) Bohairic

ⲙⲫⲣⲏϯ	ⲉⲧⲁⲙⲱⲩⲥⲏⲥ	ⲥⲉⲥⲡⲓϩⲟϥ
mpʰrêti	*etamôusês*	*cespihof*
mpʰrêti	*et-a-môusês*	*ces-pi-hof*
like	REL-PST-Moses	raise-ART.MSG-snake

'As Moses raised the snake' (John 3:14).

(14) Sahidic

    ⲁϥϯⲥⲃⲱ   ⲛⲁⲩ

    aftᵢsbô   *nau*

    a-f-tᵢ-sbô   *na-u*

    PST-3SG.M-give-instruction to-3PL

    'He taught them' (Matthew 5:2).

8 Final comments

We cannot stress enough that the sole aim of this transliteration system is to provide a standard that those who wish to use a standard system for rendering the Coptic letters can choose to adhere to. It is not an alternative to a phonological representation, but can be supplemented by one when a Copticist would like to make a point about phonology, or for some other reason.

We hope that this system will be adopted by Copticists who are interested in communicating the results of their research on this fascinating language to a more general audience, and also in other contexts where it is cumbersome to use Coptic letters.

9 References

Funk, Wolf-Peter. 2009. Methodological Issues in the (Morpho)Phonological Description of Coptic. In: Goldenberg, Gideon & Shisha-Halevy, Ariel (eds.), *Egyptian, Semitic, and General Grammar. Studies in Memory of H.J. Polotsky*. Jerusalem: The Israel Academy of Sciences and Humanities, 70–91.

Kasser, Rodolphe. 1991. Alphabets, Coptic. In: Atiya, Aziz S. (ed.), *The Coptic Encyclopedia*, vol. 8. New York etc.: Macmillan Publishing Company.

Müller, Matthias. 2011. Ägyptische Phonologie? Möglichkeiten und Grenzen linguistischer Modelle bei der Beschreibung des Lautsystems einer extinktenSprache. In: Verbovsek, Alexandra, Backes, Burkhard & Jones, Catherine (eds.), *Methodik und Didaktik in der Ägyptologie*. München: Fink, 509–531.

Peust, Carsten. 1999. *Egyptian phonology: an introduction to the phonology of a dead language*. Göttingen: Peust und Gutschmidt.

Part II: Studies

Mark Collier

Conditionals in Late Egyptian*

Abstract: Late Egyptian has three basic forms of conditional constructions, which can be identified by the three separate introductory markers used (*ỉr*, *ỉnn*, and *hn*), as well as by other grammatical features of the P-clause. In terms of P-clauses, attested *ỉr*-conditionals cover forward-looking conditions, present counterfactuals, closed past conditions; attested *ỉnn*-conditionals cover subjectively uncertain past and present conditions, and pre-emptive predictions of the future; attested *hn*-conditionals cover past counterfactuals. Certain aspects of the form and meaning of these conditionals are exemplified and discussed (with a focus on P-clauses) in terms which aim to link relevant Egyptological work to linguistic work on conditionals.

The principal aim of this paper is to join up a particular thread of Egyptological work on conditionals in Late Egyptian with relevant linguistic work on conditionals, and to present the material in a manner accessible to, and hopefully useful to, linguists. To narrow this topic down, this paper concentrates on Late Egyptian conditionals found in documentary texts, with a particular focus on conditionals from the two rich corpora of the later Tomb Robbery Papyri (TRP)[1] and the Late Ramesside Letters (LRL),[2] both roughly contemporary, dating from the end of the Twentieth Dynasty at the end of the New Kingdom (ca. 1080–1070 BCE).[3]

---

* My thanks to the three reviewers who provided comments on this paper.

1 The Tomb Robbery Papyri (TRP) cover a series of investigations towards the end of the Twentieth Dynasty. The group I refer to as "later", limited to those which provide examples of conditionals, comprise: P. BM EA 10052 (year 1 of the "Renaissance"); P. Mayer A (= P. National Museums Liverpool M11162) (years 1–2 of the "Renaissance"), and P. BM EA 10403 (year 2 of the "Renaissance"). The "Renaissance" era is usually dated, on the basis of (partial) data from the Abbott dockets, as starting in regnal year 19 of Ramesses XI, the last Pharaoh of the Twentieth Dynasty. The papyri were published and translated in Peet (1920) and Peet (1930).

2 The Late Ramesside Letters (LRL) centre on the two late Twentieth Dynasty Deir el-Medina scribes Dhutmose (who also appears in the later TRP) and his son Butehamun. The Nubian group are dated to a year 10, usually considered to be of the "Renaissance" era (see Wente 1967: 11–12), and thus stand close in time to the later TRP. The papyri were published in Černý (1939), with comprehensive translation and commentary in Wente (1967), and with updated translations in Wente (1990). Further documents from the group have been published by Janssen (1991, also including photographic plates of papyri transcribed in Černý 1939) and Demarée (2006).

3 Ancient Egyptian documents are typically dated by regnal years of the reigning Pharaoh (the use of an era such as the "Renaissance" era is exceptional). As such, Egyptologists usually refer to regnal year/era dates or, more generally, to collections ("dynasties") of pharaohs (such as the

Late Egyptian[4] has three basic conditional constructions,[5] which can be identified by the three distinct introductory markers deployed (as well as by other grammatical features of the P-clause[6] discussed below in the relevant section).[7]

ir-conditional

The first type of conditional is introduced by *ir*:

(1) P. BM EA 10052, 9.3–48 (Peet 1930: pl. 31):[9]

Context: The foreigner of the land survey Paykamen has been asked the standard opening interrogation question by the vizier 'How did you set about getting into the great places?', where 'places' refers to tombs. The example is Paykamen's opening response to this question as framed by the scribe:

"Twentieth Dynasty", ca. 1190–1070 BCE), or broad historical phases such as the "New Kingdom" (covering the Eighteenth to Twentieth Dynasties, ca. 1550–1100 BCE), rather than referring directly to absolute dates, which are approximate (and are here rounded).

4 The term "Late Egyptian" should be taken here to refer narrowly to the corpus as described and not simply to the broad phase of the language labelled "Late Egyptian".

5 I restrict my attention to the three most well-attested conditional constructions in Late Egyptian in their most typical forms. There are, of course, other constructions which can display conditional meaning in Late Egyptian, such as examples of imperative-conjunctive clauses with the standard paratactic conditional sense of "Wash my car and I will pay you five pounds", as well as certain additional variants to the constructions discussed.

6 I use P-clause to refer to the protasis = antecedent of a conditional and Q-clause to refer to the apodosis = consequent of a conditional. In so doing I am following Declerck & Reed (2001a: 10).

7 In presenting these three initial examples, I have deliberately drawn the examples from the same Ancient Egyptian text, P. BM EA 10052, in order to avoid issues of (broad) diachrony, genre, or the like. The examples are also part of the written record of the opening responses by three different individuals to essentially the same interrogation question asked by the Vizier.

8 P. BM EA 10052 refers to the modern designation of the ancient source, here that of the Museum in which it is kept, so P. BM EA 10052 refers to "Papyrus British Museum, Department of Ancient Egypt and Sudan (formerly E[gyptian] A[ntiquities]) inventory number 10052". The stop and range notation in 9.3–4 is to be read "page 9, lines 3 to 4".

9 Examples are presented in the following form: text reference; brief description of context; example presented utilising a standard variant of the transliteration system used in Egyptology (a system developed from a nineteenth century original, and so not strongly aligned with modern linguistic conventions); presentation of the example utilising the Leipzig Glossing Rules, including adaptions to Ancient Egyptian to be found in Di Biase-Dyson, Kammerzell, & Werning (2009); translation.

ır   ıw[10]-tw   (ḥr) gmt=ı̀   ı̀w   ptrı̀=ı̀
COND   SBRD-IMPRS [PRS] find:INF=1SG   SBRD   see:PST=1SG
qdt ḥḏ   qdt nbw m   n3   swt   ıw-tw (r)   ı̀rt
qite silver qite gold from DEF:PL places FUT-IMPRS [:FUT] do:INF
n=ı̀   sb3yt   nbt bı̀n
DAT=1SG punishment   any terrible
'If I am found to have seen a (single) qite of silver or gold from the Places,
then any form of terrible punishment will be inflicted on me.'

ı̀nn-conditionals

The second type of conditional is introduced by ı̀nn:

(2) P. BM EA 10052, 8.5 (Peet 1930: pl. 30):

Context: The servant Sekhahatyamun responds to essentially the same
standard interrogation question by the vizier as in (1) above. He says he
had nothing to do with the robberies from tombs at Thebes currently
under investigation, and then adds the following, referring to earlier robberies at Iumitru:

ı̀nn   ı̀w-tw   (r)   ḥdb=ı̀   ḥr   n3
COND FUT-IMPRS [:FUT] kill:INF=1SG because DEF:PL
(m)ꜥḥꜥ(t) n   ı̀w-(m)-ı̀trw mntw n   wn=ı̀   ı̀m
tomb   of Iumitru   3PL   DEF:PL be:REL:PST=1SG there
'If I am going to be killed because of the Iumitru tombs, then (at least)
they are the ones which I've been in.'

---

10 There are separate grammatical elements represented graphically by ı̀w in Late Egyptian
(although all are derived from the same original item in earlier Egyptian): ı̀w as a essential component of the third future tense; ı̀w as a circumstantial clause marker, which is added to the basic
tense/construction form, and so, for example, can be combined with the first present to produce
the circumstantial first present; ı̀w as an essential component of the sequential. Each of these
constructions has distinctive negation as well as other distinctive grammatical characteristics.
At first sight, particularly, when preposition markers of the infinitive are omitted (as they usually are in late Twentieth Dynasty documents) the P-clause form in exx. (1) and (2) may appear
to be indistinct. However, negation and other grammatical features (e.g., the form with different
tenses) do show them to be distinct. I assume such distinctions here, but the examples presented
in the relevant sections below provide only illustrative (rather than comprehensive) material.

ḥn-conditional

The third type of conditional is introduced by *ḥn*:

(3) P. BM EA 10052, 4.13 (Peet 1930: pl. 27):

Context: The trumpeter Amenkhau denies involvement in the robberies. He says *bpy=ỉ ptr ḫt nbt* 'I didn't see anything', and then strengthens his denial with a counterfactual conditional:

ḥn   *ptrỉ=ỉ*
COND   see:PST=1SG
wn   *ỉw=ỉ*   *(r)*   *ḏd=f*
be:PST   FUT=1SG   [:FUT]   say:INF=3SG.M
'If had seen (anything), I would say so.'

Each type will be discussed separately in the sections to follow.

1 *ỉr*-conditionals

1.1 *ỉr*-conditionals: on form

In the P-clause *ỉr* introduces a circumstantial clause marked by the general Late Egyptian circumstantial/adverbial clause marker *ỉw*.[11] The majority of attested examples display *ỉr* + circumstantial first present, as in ex. (1) above, or as in ex. (4) here, whereas the Q-clause has standard main-clause form:

ỉr + circumstantial first present

(4) P. BM EA 75019+10302, vso 4 (Demarée 2006: pl. 16):

Context: The sender of the letter is discussing certain items which the addressee has not had delivered. The sender reminds the addressee of an earlier letter in which the addressee had made a conditional promise: 'if you write again, I will have them sent to you'. The sender now calls in that promise. The quoted conditional promise is:

---

11 For a recent discussion of the form of *ỉw*-clause in P-clauses marked with *ỉr*, see Kruchten (1997). On circumstantial *ỉw*, see, for example Junge (2001: 189–195).

ir	*iw=k*	(*ḥr*)	*h3b*	*ꜥn*
COND	SBRD=2SG.M	[PRS]	send:INF	again

iw=i	*r*	*dit*	*in-tw*		*n=k*
FUT=1SG	:FUT[12]	cause:INF	bring:SBJV-INDF	DAT=2SG.M

'If you write again, I will have them sent to you.'

ir-conditionals with circumstantial first present P-clauses provide the Late Egyptian equivalent of the forward-looking conditional, in which the P-clause presents a possible but as yet unrealised event as a (pre-)condition for the realisation of the Q-clause. It will be noted that the P-clause shows something of the same "tense-backstepping" feature of English, although in Late Egyptian the P-clause form is explicitly marked as a dependent (circumstantial) clause.[13]

There are attested examples with circumstantial tenses other than the first present, although examples are limited in number:

ir + circumstantial past[14]

(5) P. BM EA 10416, vso 11–12 (Janssen 1991: pl. 17):

Context: A woman who has been sleeping with a man who is not her husband is under threat of violence. A steward has restrained those threatening violence once, but writes to the woman, pointing out the following:

y3	*ir*	*iw*	*i[n]ty(=i)*		*sn*	*m*	*p3y*		*sp*
EXLM	COND	SBRD	restrain:PST=[1SG]	3PL	in	DEM:M.SG	occasion

bn	*iw=i*	(*r*)	*inty=w*		*m*	*ky*
NEG	FUT=1SG	[:FUT]	restrain:INF=3PL	in	another

'Indeed, (even) if I have restrained them this time, I won't restrain them another (time).'

---

12 The Q-clause explicitly writes the distinctive third future *r*-prepositional marker of the infinitive. On the basis of such explicit writings (and also attested examples in *ir*-conditional Q-clauses of the distinctive third future negation), graphemically ambiguous *iw=f* INF Q-clauses without explicit preposition before the infinitive are usually taken to be third futures in Egyptology, although there are certain examples which suggest that the sequential form may also be found in such Q-clauses. I do not discuss this issue here and gloss *iw=f* INF Q-clauses as third futures.

13 Compare Declerck & Reed (2001a: 124–125) on the "Present Perspective System".

14 Two other examples, with damaged contexts, seem to have temporal meaning ('once you have done something'; cf. discussion of *ir* below) rather than conditional meaning. Here I restrict my comments to this particular example and accept the conditional meaning of the concessive.

ir + circumstantial third future

(6) P. BM EA 10418+10287, rto 3–5 (Janssen 1991: pl. 19):

Context: This short communiqué is probably connected to P. BM EA 10416 (see ex. (5) above). The recto contains two recorded quotes, but with no specified connection. The second is:

ir	*iw*	*bn*	*iw=n*	*(r)*	*gmt=s*		*r*	*qnqn=s*
COND	SBRD	NEG	FUT=1PL[:FUT]		find:INF=3SG.F		to	beat:INF=3SG.F
iw=n	*(r)*	*gm*	*rt3*	*t3y=s*		*snt*	*šrỉ,*	
FUT=1PL[:FUT]		find:INF	Ruta	POSS:F.SG=3SG.F		sister	little	
iw=n	*(r)*	*gm*	[...]-*ỉs gr,*	*ḥr=w*				
FUT=1PL[:FUT]		find:INF	[...]is also,	say=3PL				

'If we will not find her in order to beat her, we will find Ruta, her little sister, and we will find [...]is also, so they say.'

Unfortunately, this is the only clearly attested example of the circumstantial third future in a P-clause in an *ir*-conditional, but with limited surviving context.

1.2 Comments on *ir*

ir is not just used in marking conditionals (and as such differs from *inn* and *hn*, which are limited to conditional usage). *ir* is also regularly used to introduce a left-dislocated topic/setting as the immediate context or ground for a following clause.[15]

---

15 Compare the discussion in Haiman (1978). Since I am concentrating here on using the three introductory lexemes *ir*, *inn*, and *hn* to help distinguish the three Late Egyptian conditional forms, I do not discuss here whether *ir*, *ir* + circumstantial *iw*, or just circumstantial *iw* is key to the conditional meaning of what I refer to as the *ir*-conditional. In the glosses, I gloss *ir* in conditionals as "COND" for convenience and for immediate comparison with *inn* and *hn*, allowing me to gloss circumstantial *iw* separately, whereas I gloss other uses of *ir* with 'as-for' or 'when'.

ỉr + nominal

(7) P. BM EA 10c_   24 (Peet 1930: pl. 28):[16]

Context: The slave Degay is interrogated for a second day, as part of extensive testimony he gives concerning his owner, a key thief Bukhaaf. He opens with the following, and then lists a series of names:

ỉr	*p3*		*m3ʿt*	*nty*	*ỉw=ỉ*	(*r*)	*ḏd=f*
as-for	DEF:M.SG	truth		REL	FUT=1SG	[:FUT]	say:INF=3SG.M

bn	*ḏḏ(=ỉ)*		*rmṯ*	*nb*	*ỉptr=ỉ*		*ỉ-r-m*
NEG	say:SBJV=[1SG]	person		every	see:REL:PST=1SG	with

bw-ḥ3ʿ=f
Bukhaaf

'As for the truth which I'm going to tell, I may not be able to name everyone who I saw with Bukhaaf.'

ỉr + prepositional phrase[17]

(8) P. BM EA 10054, 2.4 (Peet 1930: pl. 6):

Context: The fisherman Panakhtemope confesses to having ferried thieves across the river to the west bank at Thebes (where the tombs are) a number of times. He relates the first episode and then moves on to the second, starting as follows ('they' refers to the thieves):

ḥr	*ỉr*	*n*	*rwḥ3*	*n*	*hrw 2*
Then	as_for	in	evening	of	day 2

ỉw=w	(*ḥr*)	*ỉỉ*
CORD=3PL	[:CORD]	come:INF

'Then (as for) in the evening of the second day, they came.'

ỉr is also used to mark two other forms of subordinate clauses, both with temporal meaning:

---

16 Usually, the *ỉr*-marked nominal expression is resumed pronominally in the following clause; however, as this example shows, this does not have to be the case. As such, *ỉr*-marking is akin to the pairing "As for Paris, most visitors consider it a wonderful city" and "As for Paris, the Eiffel tower is a must-see tourist attraction".

17 No example of this construction happens to appear in P. BM EA 10052. P. BM EA 10054 is another papyrus from the TRP, usually dated a generation or so earlier.

ỉr + m-ḏr sḏm=f

(9) P. BM EA 10052, 10.18 (Peet 1930: pl. 31):

Context: The slave Paynekhu describes how he came to be owned by the accused thieves, a husband and wife. Paynekhu first recounts:

ỉr   m-ḏr   ḫfy   pꜣy-nḥsy   ḥrdw
as-for when destroy:PST Paynehsy Hardai
ỉw   ms-nḥsy   bw-thꜣ-ỉmn (ḥr)   ỉnt(=ỉ)
CORD young-Nubian Butehamun [:CORD] take:INF=1SG
'When Paynehsy destroyed Hardai, the young Nubian Butehamun took me.'

(ḥr) ỉr + first present/past tense

The other principal construction with *ỉr* in Late Egyptian is a temporal correlative construction in which *ỉr*, or more commonly *ḥr ỉr*, is followed by the form known as the "first present" (here with past time reference) or, more rarely, the past tense (with pluperfect time reference) in a temporal clause ('when') to a following clause in which the tense-form is restricted to the sequential. The first present and past tense in the *(ḥr) ỉr* clause do not take the circumstantial marker *ỉw* and appear in the same form as in independent main clauses:

(10) P. BM EA 10052, 10.19–20 (Peet 1930: pl. 31):

Context: Following on from ex. (9) above, the slave Paynekhu recounts that he was bought from Butehamun by the foreigner Pentasekhnu, after which (the 'him' in the following example refers to Pentasekhnu):

ḥr   ỉr   tw-tw   (ḥr) ḥdb=f
Then when PRS[18]-IMPRS [:PRS] kill:INF=3SG
ỉw   kꜣry   kꜣr (ḥr)   ỉnt=ỉ   (r) swn(t)=ỉ
CORD gardener Kar [:CORD] take:INF=1SG [at] price=1SG
'Then, when he was killed, the gardener Kar bought me at my price.'

---

18 The Late Egyptian first present (in its basic form) with pronoun subject shows (for first and second person pronouns singular and plural, and also the impersonal suffix *-tw*) a pronoun form with a pronominal prefixed base *tw=*. Circumstantial *ỉw* and past *wn* with the first present take the pronoun subject directly as a suffix pronoun and do not co-occur with the pronominal prefix base.

1.3   *ir*-conditionals: on meaning

Conditionals are a key means of coping with uncertainties, with things not fully settled. As a backdrop to this paper, I adopt here a subjective probability approach to the understanding of conditionals, a major thread in recent philosophical work on conditionals. As such, in conditionals the Q-clause is not entertained independently but conditionally on the supposition of P as 'Q given P'.[19] Languages, of course, tend to mark the P-clause based on features of how it is being entertained. In Late Egyptian it seems that P-clause marking reflects the relationship of the P-clause epistemically to the actuality, and temporally to the present, of the use-context,[20] and it is here that I shall mostly concentrate my attention.

By meaning, as already noted, the *ir*-conditional provides the typical form of forward-looking situational conditional. That is, the P-clause provides a condition which requires the outcome of future events to be fulfilled (as such the condition covers events which are both subjectively uncertain to the user and addressee of the conditional and objectively uncertain in terms of the temporality of events in the world). The Q-clause is to be realised or activated on realisation of the P-clause, and thus again awaits the unfolding of events. As such, the P-clause provides the hypothetical contextual ground in (or mental space/possible world from) which the further realisation of the Q-clause situation is projected. Consider again ex. (1):

(11)=(1) P. BM EA 10052, 9.3–4:

> Context: The foreigner of the land survey Paykamen has been asked the standard opening interrogation question by the vizier 'How did you set about getting into the great places?', where 'places' is used to refer

---

19 In terms of probability logic, the conditional probability of (Q given P) is equal to the ratio of the probability of (P&Q) and the probability of P (the Ratio formula $\pi(Q|P) = p(P\&Q)/p(P)$, for $p(P) > 0$, where, following Bennett 2003: 51, "π" refers to conditional probability and "p" to unconditional probability). For discussion of probabilistic approaches to conditionals (particularly in terms of degrees of belief), and of the Ramsey Test, see Edgington (1995: 259–270, 2003, 2005), and the general account in Bennett (2003: 28–33, 45–59). This draws on the standard Bayesian account of conditional probability, and allows for connection to work in Cognitive Psychology; see, for example, Oaksford & Chater (2007: chapter 5). Just one thing to note in the current context: the probabilistic approach makes active use only of the assumption of the stated P (which can have positive or negative polarity, of course), and does not make active use of the unstated not-P (the "bet", as it were, is cancelled or void if the stated P is false). This seems to me to link up nicely to the exploitation of a (defeasible) conversational implicature approach to the use of negated P in reading conditional perfection into conditionals (see below).
20 I use use-context generally to cover person-to-person linguistic interaction both in speech and in letter exchanges (where the user and recipient are, of course, divorced in space and time).

to tombs. The example is Paykamen's opening response to this question as framed by the scribe:

ỉr	*ỉw-tw*	*(ḥr)*	*gmt=ỉ*		*ỉw*	*ptrỉ=ỉ*
COND	SBRD-IMPRS	[PRS]	find:INF=1SG		SBRD	see:PST=1SG

qdt	*ḥd*	*qdt*	*nbw*	*m*	*nꜣ*	*swt*	*ỉw-tw*
qite	silver	qite	gold	from	DEF:PL	places	FUT-IMPRS

(r)	*ỉrt*	*n=ỉ*	*sbꜣyt*	*nbt*	*bỉn*
[:FUT]	do:INF	DAT=1SG	punishment	any	terrible

'If I am found to have seen a (single) qite of silver or gold from the Places, then any form of terrible punishment will (surely) be inflicted on me.'

In the use-context, the status of Paykamen being found to have seen the silver and gold is objectively (and thus also subjectively) uncertain and awaits the unfolding of events to be realised or not. It is thus dependent on the temporality of occurrence (the event of the P-clause actually happening or not), as can be seen by taking the conditional out of context and artificially strengthening the meaning towards certainty through 'when' as in 'when I am found to have seen silver and gold from the places, any form of punishment will be inflicted on me'. The majority of attested examples of *ỉr*-conditionals in the corpus under study are forward-looking conditionals of this type.

There are also examples in which the P-clause is an imagined alternative state of affairs (present counterfactual) as a (counterfactual mental space/possible world) immediate context within which to couch the Q-clause:[21]

---

21 As in Iatridou (2000), the term "present counterfactual" refers to the P-clause being a counterfact to, or in conflict with, the current state of affairs (although potentially still realisable), rather than to features of tense-marking. Of course, the usual caveats on the term "counterfactual" apply.

(12)   P. Paris Bibl. Nat. 198, II (LRL no. 46), vso 6–7 (Černý 1939: 68.9–10):

Context: The letter writer shows, as he has done regularly through his
letter, his disgruntlement with the intended recipient:

ir	*iw=k*		*m*	*t3ty*			
COND	SBRD=2SG.M		as	vizier			
bn	*iw=i*	*(r)*	*h3y*		*r*	*n3y=k*	*skty*
NEG	FUT=1SG	[:FUT]	descend:INF		into	POSS:PL=2SG.M	boat

'(Even) If you were the vizier, I wouldn't get into your boats.'

Although Late Egyptian has no specific marker for counterfactual or epistemic
distancing in constructions of this type (it does not use past-tense marking, for
example), the imaginary nature of certain *ir*-conditionals, particularly those
with P-clauses with non-verbal constructions (that is, with no equivalent of the
verb 'to be' in the Late Egyptian pattern), and thus referring to non-dynamic
situations, is clear enough by sense. I will return to the concessive reading of
this conditional below.

Example 5 above, with *ir iw* + past *sdm=f* in the P-clause presents an example
of the conditional assertion of a Q-clause based on a P-clause in which the situation in the P-clause is accepted as having occurred (and again has concessive
sense):

(13)=(5) P. BM EA 10416, vs. 11–12 (Janssen 1991: pl. 17):

Context: A woman who has been sleeping with a man who is not her
husband is under threat of violence. A steward has restrained those
threatening violence once, but writes to the woman, pointing out the
following:

y3	*ir*	*iw*	*i[n]ty(=i)*		*sn*	*m*	*p3y*
EXLM	COND	SBRD	restrain:PST=[1SG]		3PL	in	DEM:M.SG
sp	*bn*	*iw=i*	*(r)*	*inty=w*		*m*	*ky*
occasion	NEG	FUT=1SG	[:FUT]	restrain:INF=3PL		in	another

'Indeed, (even) if I have restrained them this time, I won't restrain them
another (time).'

Across these usages, the P-clauses of *ir*-conditionals seem to be distanced, or
excluded or projected away, from the 'now' of the use-context, whether temporally and/or epistemically, and in the P-clause there is alignment between
subjective epistemic evaluation (the perspective of an individual's knowledge
in terms of evidence available) and the objective state of affairs, at least as

that is accepted or is thought to be knowable (in contrast with *inn*-conditional P-clauses, which directly relate to the 'now' of the use-context, and for which a distinction between subjective knowledge and the objective state of affairs is significant; see below). So, the forward-looking P-clause with circumstantial first present awaits the outcome of future events and is objectively unknowable or unverifiable 'now' (and is, of course, therefore subjectively unknowable as well); P-clauses with circumstantial non-verbal predications present imaginary or present counterfactual P-clauses, a P-clause which is distanced epistemically from actuality and accepted as a counterfact; the P-clause with a circumstantial past provides a closed condition – an accepted past occurrence.

1.4 From conditional perfection to concessive readings of *ir*-conditionals

As already noted, some of the examples above readily allow a concessive meaning (and can be translated as 'even if'), although there is no specific marker for concessive conditionals in Late Egyptian. This can be addressed by looking at meaning-construction in context for Late Egyptian *ir*-conditionals, which, as might be expected, show a range of pragmatic effects from, on the one hand, a tendency to the exclusive reading of the P-clause as a condition for the realisation of the Q-clause (conditional perfection) through, on the other hand, to examples in which the P-clause is read as an inclusive, limiting condition for the realisation of the Q-clause, particularly in the context of constructed pragmatic scales.

1.4.1 Conditional perfection

Forward-looking conditionals are those which most readily lend themselves to "conditional perfection": the tendency to perfect a conditional into an "if and only if" conditional.[22] The P. BM EA 10052 9.3–4 example of an *ir*-conditional readily lends itself to a conditional perfection reading:

---

22 The discussion here draws on Horn (2000), who treats conditional perfection in terms of conversational implicature (R-based pragmatic strengthening).

(14)=(1) P. BM EA 10052, 9.3–4 (Peet 1930: pl. 31):

> Context: The foreigner of the land survey Paykamen has been asked the standard opening interrogation question by the vizier 'How did you set about getting into the great places?', where 'places' refers to tombs. The example is Paykamen's opening response to this question as framed by the scribe:

ỉr	*ỉw-tw*	*(ḥr)*	*gmt=ỉ*	*ỉw*	
COND	SBRD-IMPRS	[PRS]	find:INF=1SG	SBRD	

ptrỉ=ỉ	*qdt*	*ḥḏ*	*qdt*	*nbw*	*m*	*nꜣ*	*swt*
see:PST=1SG	qite	silver	qite	gold	from	DEF:PL	places

ỉw-tw	*(r)*	*ỉrt*	*n=ỉ*	*sbꜣyt*	*nbt bỉn*
FUT-IMPRS	[:FUT]	do:INF	DAT=1SG	punishment	any terrible

'If I am found to have seen a (single) qite of silver or gold from the Places, then any form of terrible punishment will be inflicted on me.'

Using English as a metalanguage, the conditional perfection reading emerges as follows:

(15) 'If I can be found to have seen a (single) qite of silver or gold from the Places, then any form of terrible punishment will be inflicted on me.'

'If I cannot be found to have seen a (single) qite of silver or gold from the Places, then any form of terrible punishment will not be inflicted on me.'

'If and only if I can be found to have seen a (single) qite of silver or gold from the Places, then any form of terrible punishment will be inflicted on me.'

This seems admirably suited to the context of Paykamen's defiant response. In inviting the possibility that if he is found guilty then punishment will surely befall him, he is opening the unstated conditional perfection inference that if it turns out that he is not found to have seen the silver and gold from the tombs, he should not be punished and thus the exclusivity of the relationship between guilt and punishment that punishment should befall him if and only if he is found to have seen the silver and gold from the tombs.

In terms of sufficient and necessary conditions, standard forward-looking *ỉr*-conditionals thus include clear examples which allow, in context, an implicature strengthening the P-clause from being a sufficient condition to be capable of being entertained (at least in practical terms) as a necessary and sufficient, and thus exclusive, condition.

1.4.2 Concessive Conditionals

(16)=(12) P. Paris Bibl. Nat. 198, II (LRL no. 46), vso 6–7 (Černý 1939: 68.9–10):

Context: The letter writer shows, as he has done regularly through his letter, his disgruntlement with the intended recipient:

ỉr	*ỉw=k*		*m*	*ṯзty*			
COND	SBRD=2SG.M		as	vizier			
bn	*ỉw=ỉ*	*(r)*	*hзy*		*r*	*nзy=k*	*skty*
NEG	FUT=1SG	[:FUT]	descend:INF		into	POSS:PL=2SG.M	boat

'(Even) If you were the vizier, I wouldn't get into your boats.'

The P. Paris Bib. Nat. 198 II, vso 6–7 example does not allow conditional perfection:[23] '*if and only if you were vizier, I would not get into your boats' seems a quite wrong pragmatic strengthening of this example. That is, the P-clause does not lend itself to being read as an exclusive condition. In addition, the Q-clause, rather than being realised as a consequence of the realisation of the P-clause, holds independently of the P-clause: the imagery of 'I will not get into your boats' holds also as a comment on the addressee right now and not just in the imaginary situation of the addressee being vizier. So, the counter-factual P-clause provides just one context for the realisation of the Q-clause, a context which also includes the actual state of affairs. There is also a scalar effect through which the P-clause provides a limiting condition on the Q-clause. That is, the user of the conditional is implying that he wouldn't get into the recipient's boat (as an idiom for agreeing with his point of view) as things stand, and that would remain the case right up to and including if the recipient had the powerful status of vizier.

Although there is no formal expression of concessivity in the P-clause, nevertheless the scalar reading can be readily constructed. The recipient does not in fact hold the position of vizier and so a counterpart relationship is being projected for the addressee, linking his actual standing with the hypothetical

---

23 A widely recognised feature of concessive conditionals, cf. König (1986: 235–239) for a discussion covering territory similar to the discussion here.

positing of him being vizier. This counterpart relationship is scaled or ranked pragmatically into a partially ordered set[24] ranging from the addressee as he is to what Ekkehard König termed a "pseudo-superlative" as a limiting term in the scale,[25] here the powerful position of vizier (presumably also covering a host of unstated intermediary positions in between?). As such, the Q-clause is interpreted not just in the case of the P-clause as formally expressed, but in relation to the constructed scalar range and so the Q-clause is applicable not just in the hypothetical circumstance of the addressee being vizier, but to the addressee as he currently is right up the scale to him being vizier. The P-clause thus meets the criterion noted by Haspelmath & König (1998: 565) for scalar concessive conditionals that such concessive conditionals relate not a single P-clause, but a set of P-clauses, to a Q-clause, here a set established by implicature.

2 *înn*-conditionals

The second type of conditional is the *înn*-conditional. Here example 2 is repeated:

(17)=(2) P. BM EA 10052, 8.5 (Peet 1930: pl. 30):

> Context: The servant Sekhahatyamun responds to essentially the same standard interrogation question by the vizier as in (1) above. He says he had nothing to do with the robberies from tombs at Thebes currently under investigation, and then adds the following, referring to earlier robberies at Iumitru:

> | *înn* | *îw-tw* | *(r)* | *ḥdb=î* | *ḥr* | *n3* | *(m)ʿḥ ʿ(t)* | *n* |
> |---|---|---|---|---|---|---|---|
> | COND | FUT-IMPRS | [:FUT] | kill:INF=1SG | because | DEF:PL | tomb | of |
> | *îw-(m)-îtrw* | *mntw* | *n3* | *wn=î* | | *îm* | | |
> | Iumitru | 3PL | DEF:PL | be:REL:PST=1SG | | there | | |
>
> 'If I am going to be killed because of the Iumitru tombs, then (at least) they are the ones which I've been in.'

---

24 I refer to pragmatic scales in the sense of Fauconnier (1975), and Posets as in Hirschberg (1991). For scalar approaches to concessive conditionals, see, for example, König (1986), Kay (1990/1997) (on 'even'), Haspelmath & König (1998), Declerck & Reed (2001b: 217–230), and Iten (2005: 217–233).
25 König (1986: 236).

2.1 *ỉnn*-conditionals: on form

The P-clause is formed by the introductory marker *ỉnn*[26] followed by a clause which has the same form and meaning (including time reference) as the equivalent independent main clause without *ỉnn*; the Q-clause has standard main-clause form. Examples are provided here for past, present, and future:[27]

ỉnn + past tense (here the specific negation of the past)

(18) P. BM EA 10100 (LRL no. 30), rto 14–15 (Černý 1939: 50.16–51.2):

Context: The sender is discussing 5 serving-women he has allocated to the workmen, commenting that they are for the service of all the work-gang (with the exception, apparently, of Heramunpenaf). However, the sender is unsure whether the serving-women have actually arrived and so provides guidance for this eventuality:

ḥr   ỉnn   bwpw=tn   šsp=w
CORD COND NEG:PST=2PL   receive:INF=3PL
ỉw=tn   (r)   šm   r   p3   nty   ḥr-r-t
FUT=2PL   [:FUT]   go:INF   to   DEF:M.SG   REL   Hereret
ỉm   mtw=tn   šsp=w   n=s
there   CORD.MOD=2PL   receive:INF=3PL   from=3SG.F
'But if you haven't received them, you should go to Hereret [lit. to where Hereret is] and get them from her.'

---

26 There have been differing proposals for the etymology of *ỉnn*, but the most likely proposal (see, e.g., Depuydt 1991) is that it comes from the earlier Egyptian combination *ỉr wnn* (examples still to be found in Late Egyptian), one of the attested uses of which is to mark epistemic conditional usage. If so, the epistemic usage has grammaticalized out by Late Egyptian, as so often cross-linguistically.

27 Further examples, across a wider range of tenses and constructions, are provided in Collier (2006).

ỉnn + first present

(19)   O. Berlin P 12630, vso 1–2 (Deir el-Medine on-line):[28]

Context: A letter of complaint over non-payment by the recipient for a coffin and bed which the sender has previously provided. After resuming the history the debt briefly, the sender ends:

ỉnn	*tw=t*		*ḥr*	*dỉt*		*p3*		*ỉḫ*
COND	PRS=2SG.F		PRS	give:INF		DEF.M.SG		OX

ỉmỉ		*ỉn-tw=f*
CAUSE:IMP		bring:SBJV-IMPRS=3SG.M

ḥr	*ỉnn*	*mn*		*ỉḫ*	*ỉmỉ*		*ỉn-tw*
CORD	COND	NEG.EXIS		OX	CAUSE:IMP		bring.SBJV-IMPRS

p3		*ḥˤtỉ*	*ḥnˤ*	*p3*		*wt*
DEF.M.SG		bed	and	DEF.M.SG		coffin

'If you can provide the ox, have it sent; but if there is no ox, have the bed and coffin returned.'

ỉnn + third future (see also ex. (17)=(2) above)

(20)   P. Mayer B (= P. National Museums Liverpool M11186), 4–5 (Peet 1920: pl. P. Mayer B):[29]

Context: The thief Pais is attempting to coerce his way into a share of a robbery undertaken by other thieves. He does so by using a conditional threat to inform on the thieves to (the people of) the governor of the west (of Thebes) and the inspectors (the transliteration of this lengthy phrase is omitted and replaced with NN).

ỉr		*n3*		*ḥd*	*ỉgm=k*
as-for		DEF:PL		silver	find:REL=PST=2SG.M

ỉnn	*bn*	*ỉw=k*		*(r)*		*dỉt*		*n=ỉ*		*ỉm=w*
COND	NEG	FUT=2SG.M		[:FUT]		give:INF		DAT=1SG		from=3PL

---

28 The ostracon is usually dated to the mid-Twentieth Dynasty (reigns of Ramesses III–Ramesses IV), so around about 70–80 years before TPR and LRL; see the Deir el-Medina Database web-site.
29 P. Mayer B is a single page fragment. It concerns the robbery from the tomb of the mid-Twentieth Dynasty pharaoh Ramesses VI, and so cannot be too far in time from the other TPR.

$\textit{iw=i}$	$\textit{(r)}$	$\textit{šm}$	$\textit{r}$	$\underline{d}\textit{d=f}$		$\textit{n}$	$\textit{NN}$
FUT=1SG	[:FUT]	go:INF	to	tell:INF=3SG.M		DAT	NN

'As for the monies which you have found, if you are not going to give me (anything) from them, then I will go to tell it to NN.'

2.2 *inn*-conditionals: on meaning

The *inn*-conditional deals with conditional current subjective knowledge about P-clause situations which themselves may be in the past, present, or future – the P-clause is presented as being subjectively uncertain (usually uncertain to the user, whether in fact or as a rhetorical ploy), and the Q-clause (an assertion, an instruction, a question) is put on supposition of this subjectively uncertain P-clause.[30] For P-clauses with past or present tense, whether or not the P-clause accurately characterises the situation referred to in the P-clause is, in objective terms, open to confirmation (fact-checking):[31] the formulation in the P-clause is either a true or false characterisation of matters as they stand, and the relevant evidence is, in principle, potentially available (already or through checking) to someone (usually the addressee to whom the conditional is put).[32] Future-oriented P-clauses primarily concern current predictions of the course of events and, based on the prediction, can allow for the pre-emption of the future outcome of those events by realisation of the Q-clause ahead of, or separate from, the outcome of those events.[33] Such conditionals can be glossed with 'if it is true/the case that' and the epistemic meaning of the P-clause of the *inn*-conditional can often be

---

30 See Haegeman (2003: 319–320) for a sample listing of authors who have distinguished two sorts of "if-clauses" along what seem to be similar lines as the distinction between *ir-* and *inn-* conditionals here, although there seem to be issues at the level of detail (see, for example, Edgington (2003: 394–396) for critical comments on deploying causality as a means of distinguishing a class of conditionals), and on whether terminologies and analyses apply to P-clauses or connections between P- and Q-clauses (such as Sweetser 1990's influential distinction between "content", "epistemic", and "speech-act" conditionals). My usage has a lineage within Egyptology which stretches back to work by the linguist and Copticist Wolf-Peter Funk (cf. Funk 1985; and also Depuydt 1999, who grounds his work in that of Boole), albeit that my account differs in detail.

31 Egyptologists have often noted that the P-clause in such a conditional overlaps in its properties with yes/no questions; see, for example, Junge (2001: 266). Compare Declerck & Reed (2001a: 91–92).

32 Cf. particularly Funk (1985: 375–376) and Kaufmann (2005: 186).

33 Cf. Nieuwint (1986); Dancygier (1998: 116–120); Dancygier & Sweetser (2005: 87–89).

brought out by taking the conditional out of context and artificially strengthening towards certainty through using 'since' or 'because'. Thus example (17)=(2) can be strengthened to (in this example this also happens to work in context):

(21) 'Since I am going to be killed because of the Iumitru tombs, then (at least) they are the ones I've been in.'

Ordinarily in *ỉnn*-conditionals, there is presumed to be a distinction, or asymmetry, in the subjective knowledge of the user and addressee of the conditional. Most commonly, users position themselves as being currently uncertain about the P-clause, and then follow through with a Q-clause based on supposition of the P-clause; the user seems ordinarily to expect the addressee to have a clearer body of knowledge about the P-clause situation and thus to be able to activate the Q-clause or not on the basis of this knowledge (e.g., to accept or reject an assertion, to carry out an instruction, to answer a question). Of course, as in English, users can adopt this stance as a rhetorical ploy, e.g., as a means to guide the addressee towards a particular conclusion. See ex. 22 below.

    ỉnn-conditionals can have P-clauses which can be read counterfactually, or epistemically distanced (higher degree of hypotheticality), as something which is offered up as being possible but which, in the following example, can be ruled out, although there is no explicit marking of unlikelihood or counterfactuality:

(22) P. BM EA 10375 (LRL no. 28), vso 1 (Černý 1939: 46.16–47.1):

Context: The scribe Butehamun is stressing to the general Payankh, his lord, that the workgang are carrying out all the tasks of the lord as diligently as they can even in the face of problems. He reinforces this with the following conditional claiming that they would inform the general were they not (and Payankh can see for himself that they are not informing the lord of this in their letter – just the opposite).

ỉnn	*bn*	*ỉ-ỉr=n*	*bзk*	*n=k*
COND	NEG	THMZ=1PL	work:INF	DAT=2SG.M
m	*ỉb*	*ḥзty=n*		
with	heart-force	heart=1PL		
ỉw=n	*(r)*	*hзb*	*r*	*dỉt*	*ꜥm*
FUT=1PL	[:FUT]	send:INF	to	CAUSE:INF	know:SBJV

> p3y=n   nb
> POSS:M.SG=1PL   lord
> 'If we were not working for your heart and soul, we would write to let
> our lord know.'

This is an example of an *inn*-conditional deployed by the user to try to steer the addressee towards a particular view: the content of the P-clause is not subjectively uncertain to the user, but is subjectively uncertain to the addressee. Butehamun obviously has a clear stance on whether the workmen are working heart and soul for their general (whether a truthful stance or not). He presents a conditional in which the general can reason out (by *modus tollens* reasoning) an answer to this for himself (or at least reason out Butehamun's version of the answer) based on the conditional as presented.

3 *hn*-conditionals

Finally, the third type of conditional is the *hn*-conditional:

(23)=(3) P. BM EA 10052, 4.13 (Peet 1930: pl. 27):

> Context: The trumpeter Amenkhau denies involvement in the robberies. He says *bpy=i ptr ḫt nbt* 'I didn't see anything', and then strengthens his denial with a counterfactual conditional:
>
> hn   ptri=i
> COND   see:PST=1SG
> wn   iw=i   (r)   dd=f
> be:PST FUT=1SG [:FUT] say:INF=3SG.M
> 'If had seen (anything), I would say so.'

This example expresses past counterfactual conditional meaning. The term "counterfactual" has, of course, come under criticism, even for patterns of this sort,[34] and examples exist from well-studied languages, such as English, in which the relevant P-clause tense-marking pattern need not have strictly counterfactual meaning. However, counterfactual meaning is typical, even if this is pragmatic and not essential, and, for Late Egyptian, the range of attested examples

---

34 For example, Comrie (1986: 89–91).

do display past counterfactual meaning, whereas the type of example which might show whether this pattern necessarily expresses counterfactuality or not is lacking from the available dataset.

3.1 *hn*-conditionals: on form

The P-clause is formed by the marker *hn* followed by the ordinary past tense (the past *sḏm=f* form as in ex. (23) above). Examples can also be found in which the past tense carries a further past tense marker (thus providing a "pluperfect" tense-form). For example, the counterfactual strengthening of denial found in ex. (23) occurs a number of times across the written versions of the testimonies in the later TPR, including the following variant from P. BM EA 10403:

(24) P. BM EA 10403, 3.29 (Peet 1930: pl. 37):

> Context: The townswoman Shedehnakhte denies seeing anything to do with the thefts during the time she worked in the house of the accused thief Tetisheri. She says *bpy=ỉ ptr* 'I didn't see (anything)' and then strengthens this with the following counterfactual conditional:

> | *hn* | *wn* | *ptr=ỉ* | |
> |------|------|---------|---|
> | COND | AUX:PST | see:PST=1SG | |
> | *wn* | *ỉw=ỉ* | *(r)* | *ḏd=f* |
> | be:PST | FUT=1SG | [:FUT] | say:INF=3SG.M |
>
> 'If I had seen, I would say so.'

Returning to the general form of the *hn*-conditional, the Q-clause (here a counterfactual Q-clause) also shows distinctive marking, being composed of the third future (*ỉw=f r sḏm*, which has the specific negation *bn ỉw=f r sḏm*) preceded by the past marker *wn*. The past marker *wn* appears in all surviving examples of counterfactual Q-clauses with the third future and so appears not to be optional (so *wn ỉw=f r sḏm*, with the specific negation *wn bn ỉw=f r sḏm*); see also ex. 26 below. In fact, the *wn* + third future construction can be used outside of conditionals to express a counterfactual state of affairs:[35]

---

[35] For forms marked both for "potentiality" and "past" as the most common forms for single-clause counterfactual constructions, see Van Linden & Verstraete (2008: esp. 1870–1872).

(25) P. Turin 2021, rto 3.4 (Allam 1973a: 117):[36]

Context: The priest Amenkhau states that he is providing for his second wife Anksunedjem, and also that he is providing for his children from a previous marriage. In particular, they are not omitted from anything which he brought in with their mother. He then adds the following, after which he notes that he is precluded by the word of Pharaoh from doing this:

ỉw	*wn*	*ỉw=ỉ*	*(r)*	*dỉt*	*n=w*	*m*	*p3*
SBRD	be:PST	FUT=1SG	[:FUT]	give:INF	DAT=3PL	from	DEF:M.SG

ỉn=ỉ   *ỉ-r-m* *ꜥnḫ-n-nwt* *ỉnk-sw-nḏm*
bring:REL:PST=1SG   with townswoman Anksunedjem

'I would give them from what I have brought in with the townswoman Anksunedjem.'

3.2 *hn*-conditionals: on meaning

As already noted, the *hn*-conditional covers the core ground of past counterfactual conditionals – the positing of an alternate P-clause past state of affairs from that which did obtain as a condition for the realisation of the Q-clause. In attested examples in documentary texts, the counterfactual P-clause differs only in limited particulars from actuality,[37] and the *hn*-conditional is deployed for its contribution to the current discourse, which is usually centred on actuality, thus with interplay between counterfactuality and (f)actuality. For example:

---

36 P. Turin 2021, with additional fragments P. Geneva D409, dates to the late Twentieth Dynasty (and mentions certain individuals, such as the Deir el-Medina scribe Dhutmose, known from both the later TPR and the LRL). For transcription and photographs, see Allam (1973a: 112–119); for German translation, see Allam (1973b: 320–327).

37 The limited or constrained alteration to actuality in order to construct the counterfactual space reflects something of the (admittedly more stringent) conditions on closest possible world discussed at length and in detail in the philosophical literature, a discussion going back to Lewis (1973). See Bennett (2003: chapters 10–16) and Edgington (2008) for recent discussions.

(26)   Wenamun (P. Pushkin Museum 120), 2.29–30 (Gardiner 1932: 69.15–16):[38]

Context: The ruler of Byblos Tjekerbaal has pointed out to the Egyptian representative Wenamun that previous Egyptian rulers used to pay for the timber provided from the Lebanon for the sacred bark of Amun. Wenamun counters by asserting that everything belongs to the god Amun. He then takes up the point about earlier rulers. 'As for your saying that previous rulers used to have silver and gold sent, if they had had life and health, they would not have had these things sent. They did send these things — but only instead of life and health — to your ancestors. But Amen-Re King of the Gods, he is the master of life and health'.

hn	*wn-(m)-dỉ=w*	*ʿnḫ snb,*		
COND	PST-POSS[39]=3PL	life health		
wn	*bn*	*ỉw=w*	*(r)*	*dỉt*	*ỉn-tw*
be:PST	NEG	FUT=3PL	[:FUT]	cause:INF	bring:SBJV-IMPRS
n3	*3ḫt*			
DEF:PL	things			

'If they had had life and health, they would not have had these things [= gold and silver] sent.'

Here Wenamun points out that previous rulers of Egypt had to pay because they were not the determiners of life and health, as part of his point that he, Wenamun, is a representative of the god Amun, not of a temporal ruler, and the god is the determiner of life and health. In the conditional, a counterpart for the previous rulers is projected into a counterfactual space and assigned the (counterfactual) property of the ability to determine life and health, and then the consequence of this altered state of affairs is explored based on this supposi-

---

38 The *Report of Wenamun* (a modern title) is a literary text (or at the very least an embellished literary version of a report), and probably dates a good few decades or more later than other material dealt with in this paper. However, it has long been recognised in Egyptology that the form of its language finds close parallel in late Twentieth Dynasty documentary Late Egyptian. For publication of hieroglyphic transcription, see Gardiner (1932); for photographs of the original hieratic, see the end plates to Schipper (2005); for recent English translation, see Wente in Simpson (2003: 116–124); for arguments for a dating to the mid-Twenty-first Dynasty to early Twenty-second Dynasty, see Winand (2011).

39 The possession construction in this example is comprised of the auxiliary *wn* followed by a prepositional phrase meaning etymologically 'in the hand of'. See Černý & Groll (1975/1993: 395) for brief discussion of time indication with the possession construction.

tion – that they would not have had to pay. Wenamun then returns to actuality within which space he asserts that Amun is the master of life and health (and thus has counterpart properties to the counterfactual P-clause). He thus implies (on the basis of a scalar ranking with Amun ranking above temporal rulers) that the stated consequence in the counterfactual should hold for Amun in "factual" space (without explicitly having to state that this is so):[40]

Factual	Counterfactual	Factual
Previous rulers	Previous rulers	The god Amun
- control life and health	+ control life and health	+ control life and health
+ Pay for timber	- Pay for timber	(- Pay for timber)

4 Conclusion

The three different conditional patterns in Late Egyptian have distinctive forms and meanings, in which P-clause marking is key. In the *ir*-conditional, the P-clause is distanced from the actuality of the use-context and subjective, and objective (un)certainty are not distinguished: forward-looking P-clauses await the outcome of the future course of events; present time-reference P-clauses are accepted as counterfactual; past P-clauses are accepted as closed conditions. In the *inn*-conditional, the P-clause is presented as subjectively uncertain in the use-context, although a past or present P-clause could, in principle, objectively be resolved as to whether it is right or wrong, should relevant evidence be available (e.g., to the addressee); a future P-clause is predictive, allowing for the possibility of the pre-emption of the predicted or intended event. In the *hn*-conditional, the P-clause is again excluded from the actuality of the use-context, both temporally and epistemically, as a past counterfactual.

Direct comparison can be made across all three types of Late Egyptian conditional in the case where the P-clause for each displays the standard past-tense form (the past *sḏm=f*). In this case, each type displays a clear distinction of meaning (albeit that the surviving sample set for *ir iw sḏm=f* with conditional meaning is rather small):

---

40 This seems amenable to a treatment along the lines of Fauconnier (1997: chapters 4–5).

ỉr-conditional with past *sḏm=f* in the P-clause

(27)=(5) P. BM EA 10416, vso 11–12 (Janssen 1991: pl. 17):

> Context: A woman who has been sleeping with a man who is not her husband is under threat of violence. A steward has restrained those threatening violence once, but writes to the woman, pointing out the following:

y3	ỉr	ỉw	ỉ[n]ty(=ỉ)		sn	m	p3y	sp
EXLM	COND	SBRD	restrain:PST=[1SG]		3PL	in	DEM:M.SG	occasion

bn	ỉw=ỉ	(r)	ỉnty=w			m	ky
NEG	FUT=1SG	[:FUT]	restrain:INF=3PL			in	another

> 'Indeed, (even) if I have restrained them this time, I won't restrain them another (time).'

In this *ỉr*-conditional, the past event in the P-clause is treated as closed, as something which is accepted/treated simply as having happened.

ỉnn-conditional with past *sḏm=f* in the P-clause

(28) P. Mayer A (= P. National Museums Liverpool M11162), 2.15 (Peet 1920: pl. Mayer A page 2):

> Context: The priest Nesamun is being interrogated in place of his father Paybaki. He admits his father was involved in the thefts but says that he doesn't know any of the details. He does, however, know of 3 men who were also involved. He names them and then says:

ỉnn	nw-tw		nbw
COND	obtain:PST-IMPRS		gold

mntw	n3	nty		rḫ
3PL	DEF:PL	REL[PRS:3PL]		know.RES[-3PL][41]

> 'But if gold (really) was obtained, then they are the ones who know.'

In this *ỉnn*-conditional, the user positions himself as being subjectively uncertain as to whether or not gold actually was obtained from the robbery, but this

---

41 The verb, *rḫ* 'know' is in the stative (or resultative) form, the principal alternative form of the verb in the first present (alongside *ḥr* + infinitive).

could, in principle, be determined through relevant evidence, and he names three accomplices of his father who can confirm this. As such, the user distances himself nicely from the thefts.

hn-conditional with past *sḏm=f* in the P-clause

(29) = (3) P. BM EA 10052, 4.13 (Peet 1930: pl. 27):

> Context: The trumpeter Amenkhau denies involvement in the robberies. He says *bpy=i ptr ḫt nbt* 'I didn't see anything', and then strengthens his denial with a counterfactual conditional:

> | *hn* | *ptrỉ=ỉ* | | |
> |------|----------|---|---|
> | COND | see:PST=1SG | | |
> | *wn* | *ỉw=ỉ* | *(r)* | *ḏd=f* |
> | be:PST | FUT=1SG | [:FUT] | say:INF=3SG.M |
>
> 'If had seen (anything), I would say so.'

In this *hn*-conditional, the past event in the P-clause is treated as a counterfactual, that is, as an event contrary to what is asserted actually to have taken place. The counterfactual meaning and counterfactual marking also extends to the counterfactual Q-clause.

5 References

Allam, Schafik. 1973a. *Hieratische Ostraka und Papyri: Transkriptionen aus dem Nachlaß von J. Černý.* (Urkunden zum Rechtsleben im Alten Ägypten 1). Tübingen: private publication by the author. Plate volume accompanying the following entry.

Allam, Schafik. 1973b. *Hieratische Ostraka und Papyri aus der Ramessidenzeit.* (Urkunden zum Rechtsleben im Alten Ägypten 1). Tübingen: private publication by the author.

Bennett, Jonathan. 2003. *A Philosophical Guide to Conditionals.* Oxford: Oxford University Press.

Černý, Jaroslav. 1939. *Late Ramesside Letters.* (Bibliotheca Aegyptiaca 9). Brussels: Fondation Égyptologique Reine Élisabeth.

Černý, Jaroslav & Groll, Sarah Israelit. 1975/⁴1993. *A Late Egyptian Grammar.* (Studia Pohl: Series Maior 4). Rome: Biblical Institute Press. The revisions through to the fourth edition are mostly corrections and additional paragraphs.

Collier, Mark. 2006. The lure of alterity: *ỉnn* conditionals in Late Egyptian. *Lingua Aegyptia* 14: 181–198.

Comrie, Barbara. 1986. Conditionals: A typology. In: Traugott, Elisabeth Closs, ter Meulen, Alice, Reilly, Judy S. & Ferguson, Charles A. (eds.), *On Conditionals*. Cambridge: Cambridge University Press, 77–99.

Dancygier, Barbara. 1998. Conditionals and Prediction: *Time, Knowledge and Causation in Conditional Constructions*. (Cambridge Studies in Linguistics 87). Cambridge: Cambridge University Press.

Dancygier, Barbara & Sweetser, Eve. 2005. *Mental Spaces in Grammar: Conditional Constructions*. (Cambridge Studies in Linguistics 108). Cambridge: Cambridge University Press.

Declerck, Renaat & Reed, Susan. 2001a. *Conditionals: A Comprehensive Empirical Analysis*. (Topics in English Linguistics 37). Berlin: De Gruyter.

Declerck, Renaat & Reed, Susan. 2001b. Some truths and nontruths about *even if*. *Linguistics* 39.2: 203–255.

Demarée, Robert J. 2006. The Banks Late Ramesside Papyri (British Museum Research Publications 155). London: The British Museum.

Depuydt, Leo. 1991. Late Egyptian *ỉnn* and the conditional clause in Egyptian. *Journal of Egyptian Archaeology* 77: 69–78.

Depuydt, Leo. 1999. Condition and premise in Egyptian and elsewhere and the laws of thought in expanded Boolean algebra. *Zeitschrift für Ägyptische Sprache und Altertumskunde* 126: 97–111.

Di Biase-Dyson, Camilla, Kammerzell, Frank & Werning, Daniel A. 2009. Glossing Ancient Egyptian. Suggestions for adapting the Leipzig Glossing Rules. *Lingua Aegyptia* 17: 343–366.

Edgington, Dorothy. 1995. On conditionals. *Mind* 104: 235–329.

Edgington, Dorothy. 2003. What if? Questions about conditionals. *Mind & Language* 18.4: 380–401.

Edgington, Dorothy. 2005. Ramsey's legacies on conditionals and truth. In: Lillehammer, Hallvard & Mellor, D. H. (eds.), *Ramsey's Legacy*. (Mind Association Occasional Series). Oxford: Oxford University Press, 37–52.

Edgington, Dorothy. 2008. Counterfactuals. *Proceedings of the Aristotelian Society* 108.1: 1–21.

Fauconnier, Gilles. 1975. Pragmatic scales and logical structure. *Linguistic Inquiry* 6.3: 353–375.

Fauconnier, Gilles. 1997. *Mappings in Thought and Language*. Cambridge: Cambridge University Press.

Funk, Wolf-Peter. 1985. On a semantic typology of conditional sentences. *Folia Linguistica* 19: 365–413.

Gardiner, Alan H. 1932. *Late-Egyptian Stories*. (Bibliotheca Aegyptiaca 1). Brussels: Fondation Égyptologique Reine Élisabeth.

Haegeman, Liliane. 2003. Conditional clauses: External and internal syntax. *Mind & Language* 18.4: 317–339.

Haiman, John. 1978. Conditionals are topics. *Language* 54: 564–589.

Haspelmath, Martin & König, Ekkehard. 1998. Concessive conditionals in the languages of Europe. In: van der Auwera, Johan (ed.), *Adverbial Constructions in the Languages of Europe*. (Empirical Approaches to Language Typology 20, EUROTYP 3). Berlin: De Gruyter, 563–640.

Hirschberg, Julia B. 1991. *A Theory of Scalar Implicature*. (Garland Outstanding Dissertations in Linguistics Series). Garland: New York.

Horn, Laurence R. 2000. From *if* to *iff*: Conditional perfection as pragmatic strengthening. *Journal of Pragmatics* 32: 289–326.

Iatridou, Sabine. 2000. The grammatical ingredients of counterfactuality. *Linguistic Inquiry* 31.2: 231–270.

Iten, Corinne. 2005. *Linguistic Meaning, Truth Conditions and Relevance: The Case of Concessives*. (Palgrave Studies in Pragmatics, Language and Cognition). Houndsmill: Palgrave Macmillan.

Janssen, Jacobus J. 1991. *Late Ramesside Letters and Communications*. (Hieratic Papyri in the British Museum 6). London: British Museum Press.

Junge, Friedrich. 2001. *Late Egyptian Grammar: An Introduction*. Oxford: Griffith Institute.

Kaufmann, Stefan. 2005. Conditional predictions: A probabilistic account. *Linguistics and Philosophy* 28: 181–231.

Kay, Paul. 1990. 'Even'. *Linguistics and Philosophy* 13: 59–111. Reprinted in Kay, Paul. 1997. *Words and the Grammar of Context*. (CSLI Lecture Notes 40). Stanford: CSLI Publications, 49–98.

König, Ekkehard. 1986. Conditionals, concessive conditionals and concessives: Areas of contrast, overlap and neutralization. In: Traugott, Elisabeth Closs, ter Meulen, Alice, Reilly, Judy S. & Ferguson, Charles A. (eds.), *On Conditionals*. Cambridge: Cambridge University Press, 229–246.

Kruchten, Jean-Marie. 1997. About *iw* and *wn(n)* in Late Egyptian. *Zeitschrift für Ägyptische Sprache und Altertumskunde* 124: 57–70.

Lewis, David. 1973. *Counterfactuals*. Oxford: Blackwell.

Nieuwint, Pieter. 1986. Present and future in conditional protases. *Linguistics* 24: 371–392.

Oaksford, Mike & Chater, Nick. 2007. *Bayesian Rationality: The Probabilistic Approach to Human Reasoning*. (Oxford Cognitive Science Series). Oxford: Oxford University Press.

Peet, T. Eric. 1920. *The Mayer Papyri A & B, Nos. M. 11162 and M. 11186 in the Free Public Museums, Liverpool*. London: Egypt Exploration Society.

Peet, T. Eric. 1930. *The Great Tomb-Robberies of the Twentieth Egyptian Dynasty*. 2 vols. Oxford: Oxford University Press.

Schipper, Bernd U. 2005. *Die Erzählung des Wenamun: Ein Literaturwerk im Spannungsfeld von Politik, Geschichte und Religion*. (Orbis Biblicus et Orientalis 209). Fribourg: Academic Press, and Göttingen: Vandenhoeck & Ruprecht.

Simpson, William K. (ed.). 2003. *The Literature of Ancient Egypt: An Anthology of Stories, Instructions, Stelae, Autobiographies, and Poetry*. 3rd ed. Yale University Press: New Haven & London.

Sweetser, Eve. 1990. *From Etymology to Pragmatics: Metaphorical and Cultural Aspects of Semantic Structure*. (Cambridge Studies in Linguistics 54). Cambridge: Cambridge University Press.

Van Linden, An & Verstraete, Jean-Christophe. 2008. The nature and origins of counterfactuality in simple clauses: Cross-linguistic evidence. *Journal of Pragmatics* 40: 1865–1895.

Wente, Edward F. 1967. *Late Ramesside Letters*. (Studies in Ancient Oriental Civilization 33). Chicago: University of Chicago Press.

Wente, Edward F. 1990. *Letters from Ancient Egypt*. (Writings from the Ancient World 1). Atlanta, GA: Scholars Press.

Winand, Jean 2011. The Report of Wenamun: A journey in ancient Egyptian literature. In: Collier, Mark & Snape, Steven (eds.) *Ramesside Studies in Honour of K. A. Kitchen*. Bolton: Rutherford Press, 541–559.

Web-sites

Deir el-Medina Database: <http://www.leidenuniv.nl/nino/dmd/dmd.html>. For bibliography and comments on Deir el-Medina texts (but does not include the tomb robbery papyri).

Deir el-Medine on-line: <http://obelix.arf.fak12.uni-muenchen.de/cgi-bin/mmcgi2mmhob/mho-1/hobmain/>. Includes on-line publication of Late Egyptian texts in the Berlin Museum.

Orin D. Gensler

A typological look at Egyptian *d > ʕ

Abstract: The "Neuere Komparatistik" in Egyptology has enthusiastically adopted Rössler's tour-de-force internal reconstruction of Egyptian consonant-ism, including (inter alia) the Egyptian development *d > ʕ. This paper examines this change critically under a typological lens. The change, a huge phonetic jump to a highly marked consonant, is radical and unprecedented in the world; cross-linguistically, pharyngeals sometimes develop from uvulars or from emphatic laterals, but not from a plain alveolar. Egyptologists have ignored or glossed over the issue. The paper presents the problem, lays out attested crosslinguistic paths of pharyngeogenesis, examines other possible paths of pharyngeogenesis, and criticizes the methodology of the Neuere Komparatistik. The issue is crucial to comparative Afroasiatic, as it redefines what is to count as a "cognate set".

1 Presentation of the problem

The "arm" hieroglyph ⸺ has, by common consensus, the pharyngeal value [ʕ] in attested Egyptian. We know this directly from transcriptions of Semitic words into and from Egyptian: Semitic words with ʕ are uniformly rendered in Egyptian with the arm hieroglyph, and Egyptian words with the arm hieroglyph are rendered in Semitic with ʕ (see e.g., Hoch 1984, Rössler 1971: 275). In the various attempts to build Afroasiatic cognate sets involving Egyptian data, this arm hieroglyph has traditionally been put into correspondence with Semitic ʕayin and Afroasiatic *ʕ.

For the last 30 years or so, a growing body of Egyptologists, especially in Germany, have argued for a different etymological equation: the Egyptian ʕ does not go back to Afroasiatic *ʕ, but rather reflects an original Afroasiatic **voiced dental** (*d, *z, *ð), which all collapsed together and changed into ʕ. This so-called "Neuere Komparatistik" is based on the groundbreaking work of Otto Rössler (1971), who in turn drew upon the equally groundbreaking work of Green-berg ([1950] 1990).

Greenberg firmly established that, in the triconsonantal roots of the Semitic languages, the component consonants making up a root are subject to various cooccurrence constraints. Notably, a root almost never has two non-identical con-sonants made at the same point of articulation – that is, we do not find roots con-taining two labials, two velars, etc. Rössler noted similar incompatibility restric-tions in Egyptian. Yet a close look at these Egyptian incompatibilities reveals something very strange. In Egyptian roots, the arm hieroglyph (traditionally the pharyngeal ʕ) does not cooccur with dentals. And conversely, this hieroglyph does cooccur unproblematically with the pharyngeal ḥ.

Rössler's conclusion, a brilliant tour-de-force of internal reconstruction, was that the arm hieroglyph was originally not a pharyngeal. Rather, it was originally a dental, which only later became a pharyngeal ʕ – schematically *d > ʕ, the change which gives the present paper its title. This would explain both of the above cooccurrence constraints beautifully: the arm hieroglyph does not cooccur with dentals because it itself was originally a dental, and it can easily cooccur with pharyngeals because it was originally not a pharyngeal. This is just one item of many in Rössler's thoroughgoing reconceptualization of the sound values of the alphabetic hieroglyphic signs of Egyptian. Rössler (1971: 278) presents his approach as creating a "cosmos" out of a "chaos", as creating a symmetrical and orderly consonant system quite similar to the Semitic one.

For a typologist, the proposed change is astonishing. Typically, sound changes are **small** and **natural** changes, so that the old and new sounds are quite similar (differing e.g., in one distinctive feature). But Rössler's change is huge, and very strange. If one were to seek two maximally different sounds in the inventory of Egyptian, one could hardly find a better pair than /d/ and /ʕ/. The only feature they have in common is voicedness. Their place of articulation differs greatly: the sound migrates from one extreme of the mouth to the other. The manner differs as well: a stop becomes a fricative. And a highly unmarked sound (d) becomes a highly marked sound (ʕ). These issues are not addressed by the "Neuere Komparatistik"; indeed, they hardly seem to have been perceived as a problem at all.

Now it surely does happen that "weird" sound changes sometimes occur in linguistic diachrony. The classic example is the change of Proto-Indo-European *dw > Armenian *erk* (Meillet 1967: 18, 46–47, 129–130; see also Hock 1991: 583–584). But Meillet carefully notes that this change has an inner-Armenian rationale which motivates it. He comments, tellingly, that some kind of explanation is methodologically necessary if such an odd change is to be accepted: "A correspondence which could not be explained in such a way **would be suspect**" (1967: 47). Interestingly, this change is not universally accepted by Indo-Europeanists (Schmitt 2007: 71, 77). Contrast the situation in Egyptology. Meillet's methodological stricture is ignored: the change d > ʕ is accepted uncritically by most or much of the field, with little or no serious attempt to motivate it qua sound change, and little apparent awareness that such a motivation is needed in the first place.

Indeed, the "Neuere Komparatistik" treats the change in question as if it were nothing special, i.e., a perfectly natural and normal sound change like any other normal sound change. Here are four representative quotes:

"Und dass es [das ägyptische ʕ] phonetisch dem orientalischen ʕayn ... so ähnelt, das ist auch nicht so verwunderlich, wie es zunächst scheint. Ein ʕayn [in heutigen Sprachen] ... ist ja nichts anderes als die allereinfachste, allerärmlichste Form eines spirantischen Stimmhaften, gewissermaßen reiner spirantischer Stimmton, die typische [sic!] Verfallsform von Konsonanten. Es ist sehr gut vorstellbar, dass u.U. jeder beliebige stimmhafte Laut zu ʕayn degenerieren kann. Im Ägyptischen hat eine solche Entwicklung sämtliche stimmhaften apikalen Präpalatalen ergriffen, im orientalischen Semitisch die hintersten stimmhaften Postpalatale." (Rössler 1971: 276–277)[1]

"A shift of dental stop to /ʕ/ is attested in Aramaic which clarifies that such a development is possible." (Peust 1999: 100)

"... voiced *d, *z, and *ð develop into the pharyngeal phoneme /ʕ/, probably going through an intermediate stage with pharyngealized lateral: *d, *z, *ð (> * ɫ) > /ʕ/. [FTN] See the comparable evolution from Proto-Sem. *ḍ > Aram. <q>, later <ʕ>." (Loprieno 1995: 31)

"Thus, Rössler's etymologies relating the arm hieroglyph to Semitic /d/ are quite consistent with our previous assumptions: by loss of distinctive features an original voiced dental stop /d/ became a neutral consonant possessing only one marked feature, [+voice]. This process of weakening is not uncommon in natural languages, compare for instance realizations like [mæːʔm] or [mæːʕm] ... for *madam* ... in certain varieties of Modern English." (Kammerzell 1998: 30)

Rhetorically, these quotations convey the impression of reasonable common sense. Hence it is not out of place to examine them more closely before proceeding, for they all embody a number of serious misunderstandings. Most basically, none of these quotes displays any awareness that pharyngeals are among the most unusual sounds in the world – highly marked and impressionistically "difficult" to non-native speakers. Pace Rössler, a pharyngeal is not just "pure spirantal voicing". There also is a constriction at the pharynx or epiglottis (Ladefoged & Maddieson 1996: 37, 167), which is what makes the sound unusual. Kammerzell describes the output of the change d > ʕ as a "neutral consonant", as if it were a very unmarked sound ("possessing only one marked feature"). Again, this ignores the highly marked pharyngeal constriction.

---

1 And that it [Egyptian ʕ] should phonetically resemble the oriental ʕayn ... is not as surprising as it might appear at first glance. An ʕayn [in modern spoken languages] is nothing more than the simplest, most impoverished form of a voiced spirant, in a sense "pure spirantal voicing", the typical [sic!] product of consonantal degeneration. It is perfectly conceivable that, on occasion, any voiced sound could degenerate into ʕayn. In Egyptian such a development targeted all the voiced apical prepalatals; in oriental Semitic, the furthest-back voiced postpalatals. (My translation, OG)

The quotes by Peust and Loprieno misrepresent the Semitic data. The Semitic phoneme conventionally transcribed *ḍ and called "*ḍad*" (its name in Arabic) did indeed change into a pharyngeal ʕ in Aramaic. But *ḍad* is anything but a run-of-the-mill, representative dental, as Peust's quote would seem to imply, and the fact that *ḍad* undergoes a particular sound change is no basis for assuming that "any old dental" plausibly should undergo the same change. The sound *ḍad* is an emphatic sound, with secondary velar or pharyngeal articulation. The Arabs, aware of its uniquely difficult nature, proudly called themselves the "people of the *ḍad*". Based on the lateral-like phonetic description by the great early Arabic grammarian Sibawaih, and on its realization as /l/ or /ld/ in some borrowings from Arabic (e.g., Arabic *al-qāḍī* 'judge' > Spanish *alcalde* 'mayor'), Semitists consider this sound to have originally been (roughly) a voiced emphatic fricative lateral in Arabic and in Proto-Semitic (Steiner 1977: 57). Thus, when *ḍad* changed into a pharyngeal in Aramaic, it was certainly not by virtue of its dentalness but because of its emphatic and lateral nature, which made it acoustically similar to ʕ*ayin*. Similarly, Loprieno is wrong to suggest that a garden-variety dental (*d, *z, *ð) would plausibly have passed through an intermediate stage as a pharyngeal-ized lateral (why?). The *ḍad* itself never "passed through" such a stage; rather, this was its phonetic nature from the very beginning. One cannot simply propose, as if it were the most ordinary thing in the world, that a garden-variety dental should pass through such a stage: easy sounds do not normally turn into highly marked, difficult sounds "for no reason".

Rössler's quote also embodies another problem. He presents two cases of "pharyngeogenesis" (see below) as if they were obviously parallel:

1. Semitic: "the furthest-back postpalatals" become pharyngeals. This can only refer to the merger in some Semitic languages between the Proto-Semitic uvular and pharyngeal fricatives; thus in Hebrew,

| Proto-Semitic *ʕ, *ʁ | merge to | ʕ | (voiced) | and |
| Proto-Semitic *ħ, *χ | merge to | ħ | (voiceless). | |

This is a very small change in point of articulation (uvular to pharyngeal). Moreover, the change does not involve the **creation** of a pharyngeal, but the merger of a different phoneme with an already-existing pharyngeal.

2. Egyptian: allegedly, "voiced apical prepalatals" became pharyngeals. This would be a very large change in point of articulation (dental to pharyngeal), and moreover would create a brand-new pharyngeal that did not exist before.

Rössler's choice of terminology here is tantamount to a rhetorical sleight-of-hand. The use of the word "postpalatals" for "uvulars", and of "prepalatals" for "dentals", makes the two cases appear to be minor variants on a single theme:

a "palatal" of some sort (pre-, post-) becomes a pharyngeal. In reality there are huge differences between the two cases, as just explained.

In brief, the proposed change of dental to pharyngeal is anything but obvious or well-motivated, and the above quotes gloss over the very real difficulty. The purpose of the present paper, accordingly, is to investigate the proposed change d > ʕ in typological perspective. I must emphasize that although the critical tone of the paper will be evident, it is not intended to be a full critique of the Neuere Komparatistik; to do that would require the full breadth of knowledge of an Egyptologist, which I do not have. Rather, I mean to highlight a central aspect of the change which has been accorded only the most superficial attention heretofore.

2 Pharyngeals and pharyngealization in the languages of the world

My starting point in the typological investigation is Maddieson's map "Presence of Uncommon Consonants" (2005), a chapter of the *World Atlas of Language Structures* (*WALS*), which displays very rare sounds in the languages of the world. Of 566 languages displayed on the map, just 24 are listed as having pharyngeals. Similarly, in Maddieson's (1984) summary charts of the 317 phoneme systems which comprise the UCLA Phonological Segment Inventory Database (UPSID), only 13 languages have voiceless pharyngeal fricatives and 8 have voiced pharyngeals (1984: 233). This is empirical confirmation that pharyngeals are indeed a rare and marked phonation type in the world.

Where do pharyngeals come from? For the languages listed by Maddieson (2005), I was able to check most (unfortunately not all) of the sources for the respective languages. Often pharyngeals in a language simply reconstruct as such to the protolanguage, in which case the ultimate origin of the pharyngeal is moot. But there are some cases of "pharyngeogenesis". In the following I go through the 24 languages mentioned by Maddieson (2005), with brief discussion of the origin of the pharyngeal. In some cases I was not able to ascertain the origin of the pharyngeal; these are marked below as "[not checked]". Since the concern of this paper is with the voiced pharyngeal, languages that have only a voiceless pharyngeal will be given only brief mention.

- (A) Pacific Northwest Coast:
    - Nootka (Wakashan): Pharyngeals originate from earlier **uvular** ejectives and fricatives (Jacobsen 1969).
    - Squamish (Central Salish) [not checked]; also Interior Salish. In Interior Salish, the pharyngeals are apparently reconstructible (Kuipers 1981, 2002: 3–4; Kinkade 1967: 233), or arise from **uvular** sonorants (Thompson 1979: 723).
- (B) Brao (Bahnaric; Mon-Khmer): only voiceless pharyngeal (Keller 1976: 7–8).
- (C) Atayal (Formosan; Austronesian), also other Formosan languages: Apparently only the voiceless pharyngeal ħ is at issue (Maddieson 1984: 337; Rau 1992: 18, 20).
- (D) Caucasus:
    - Northwest Caucasian: Abkhaz (Hewitt 1989: 258), Kabardian (Colarusso 1992: 11): both ħ and ʕ, but Kabardian ʕ only in Arabic loans, baby talk, and interjections. Pharyngeals (voiced and voiceless) are presented as reconstructible to Common Northwest Caucasian and to Proto-Circassian by Chirikba (1996: 289, 297, 321–324).
    - Northeast Caucasian [= Nakh-Daghestanian]: Ingush, Avar, Archi, Rutul, Hunzib, Lak, Tsova-Tush. Pharyngeals are reconstructible; also the **ejective lateral** gives rise to ʕ in Nakh (Nichols 2003: 218–219, cf. Nichols 1999: 7).
- (E) Kurdish (Iranian): originally in Arabic loans, then spread into words of Iranian origin (McCarus 1997: 694–695).
- (F) Nenets (Samoyedic; Uralic) [not checked]
- (G) Afroasiatic
    - Cushitic: Somali, Dahalo, Iraqw (and numerous others). The pharyngeals are reconstructible (Sasse 1979; Ehret 1987).
    - Berber: Tashlhiyt, Middle Atlas (and Berber generally). Pharyngeals occur mostly in Arabic loanwords (Kossmann 1999: 246–248).
    - Semitic: Arabic, Soqotri, Tigre (and numerous others). Pharyngeals are reconstructible as such. They also arise from a merger with **uvular fricatives** in several languages, and from a proto-**emphatic lateral** in Aramaic.
- (H) Tama (Eastern Sudanic; Nilo-Saharan): only voiceless ħ (Maddieson 1984: 305). The description given by Bender (2005: 7) does not indicate any pharyngeal at all.

The conclusion of this brief survey is that secondarily created pharyngeals in the WALS sample come from **uvulars** and from **emphatic** (or **ejective**) **laterals**. In the case of uvulars, the place of articulation is adjacent to that of pharyngeals.

In the case of emphatic laterals, the combination of laterality and emphasis/ejectivity plausibly either itself involves pharyngealization, or creates an acoustic impression similar to that of pharyngeals.

Interestingly, none of the above attested paths involves the particular type of pharyngeogenesis suggested by Rössler and Kammerzell (see sec. 1): the loss of all articulatory features in the suprapharyngeal region of the mouth. This process, called **debuccalization**, is surveyed in detail by Fallon (2002: 123–202). As he defines the term, debuccalization is "the loss of primary supraglottal articulation with retention of, or replacement by, a glottal gesture such as [h] or [ʔ]" (123) – in other words, the removal of all oral-cavity features of a segment, leaving behind a maximally unmarked, default glottal. This kind of change, which is not unusual crosslinguistically, is certainly what Rössler and Kammerzell were aiming at. But there is a crucial difference. Debuccalization results in an unmarked glottal segment "such as [h] or [ʔ]". It involves the removal of features, not the addition of features, and in particular not the addition of a highly marked articulation such as a pharyngeal constriction. In the discussion I have seen, the output of debuccalization is never a pharyngeal. (Fallon (2002: 132) reports formalizations where a feature specification [pharyngeal] is stipulated for glottals; this, however, is a question of formalism and has nothing to do with the phonetic nature of the glottals as (non-)pharyngeals.) One might perhaps imagine a voiced *h*-sound as a conceivable output ([ɦ]); this, however, is just as rare as pharyngeal fricatives (13 languages in Maddieson's 317-language UPSID database (1984: 234)). Indeed, the problem seems to me a fundamental one: the output of debuccalization should be a maximally unmarked segment, yet an ʕ*ayin* (or anything acoustically similar to it) cannot in any sense be taken as "unmarked".

3 How might a change d > ʕ come about?

The previous section has presented an empirical survey of **actual** (or reconstructed) paths of pharyngeogenesis. The present section is speculative: drawing partly on the above empirical results, it presents a tentative survey of **possible** paths of pharyngeogenesis. An important point is that an unnatural-looking phonetic change can readily be the cumulative result of multiple natural changes. Thus the change d > ʕ might have arisen by a multi-stage process of some sort. What kind of process is imaginable? I will discuss briefly various possibilities I can think of.

- (a) d > ʔ > ʕ. The first scenario involves the above-mentioned debuccalization channel as a first step. As Fallon explains, debuccalization typically occurs syllable-finally; also, debuccalization typically (but not always) targets glottalized segments. Neither of these strictures conforms to the situation in Egyptian. In Egyptian, /d/ is not a glottalized segment; and the arm hieroglyph occurs in all positions, not just (nor even preferentially) syllable-finally. Of course, neither stricture is an absolute; debuccalization still might have occurred in Egyptian. But then this would have had to be followed by spontaneous pharyngealization – not in a scattering of words, or as an assimilation phenomenon (in Tigre, ʕ and ʔ alternate freely when followed by a laryngeal or emphatic sound (Raz 1983: 5)), but across-the-board. There may conceivably be precedents for such a change, but I do not know of any.
- (b) d > ʕ. According to this scenario, the /d/ would have debuccalized directly to a pharyngeal. As discussed at the end of the previous section, this is unlikely a priori and apparently empirically unattested.
- (c) d > ð > ɣ (> ʁ) > ʕ. On this scenario, the dental would have lenited to a fricative, then moved backwards by stages in the mouth. All (or almost all) of the individual changes are plausible and attested:
    - (c–i) A change from ð > ɣ is attested e.g., over the history of Irish. Lenited /d/ is ð in Old Irish, but ɣ in Modern Irish, merging with lenited /g/:

Old Irish:	Plain	Lenited
	d	ð (becomes ɣ in Modern Irish)
	g	ɣ

    - (c–ii) A change from ɣ > ʁ is not directly known to me, but the voiceless equivalent x > χ seems to be attested in the Swiss German pronunciation of <ch>: Standard German [x], Swiss German [χ]. This stage in the progression may be optional, however; see next point.
    - (c–iii) A change from velar to glottal position is attested in German (PIE *k > German h, cf. centum vs. hundert); or in the Vannetais dialect of Breton, where Primitive Breton x, h, ɣ merge to yield [ɦ] (Jackson 1986: 72). But does a velar ever directly become a pharyngeal?
    - (c–iv) As noted above, the change ʁ > ʕ is attested in several Semitic languages (e.g., Hebrew), the result of a merger of uvular and pharyngeal fricatives.
- (d) d > emphatic lateral > ʕ. The second step in this process occurs in Aramaic, as already noted above. But the first step seems totally unmotivated and unparalleled crosslinguistically.
- (e) Perhaps the original phonetic value of the arm hieroglyph was not [d] but some kind of dental emphatic (ṭ)? A change from an emphatic to a pharyngeal would not be unreasonable. The problem here is that the Rössler

school assigns the "emphatic dental" value to a different hieroglyph, viz., the "hand" hieroglyph (traditional *d*).

– (f) Perhaps the output of the process was actually not a pharyngeal but something like a "strong glottal stop" (Peust 1999: 100). The problem here is the absolutely consistent rendering of Semitic ʕ by the arm hieroglyph, and (as far as I know) vice versa. This argues for a true pharyngeal articulation in attested Egyptian, not a "strong glottal stop". (Nor is it clear what would be meant by a "strong" glottal stop, as opposed to a normal glottal stop.)

4 Reflections on method

The reanalysis proposed by the "Neuere Komparatistik" invites a number of comments on method. Rössler's reanalysis is an internal reconstruction within a single language L (Egyptian). As such, it is vulnerable in the same way as any internal reconstruction. An internal reconstruction back-projects a neat, logical, esthetic and above all regular pattern that the language **should** have originally had **if** it had developed "sensibly". But languages do not always develop sensibly, logically, or coherently, and earlier stages are not always more regular than later stages. No internal reconstruction can ever have the concrete reliability of a comparative reconstruction, where data from several languages mutually buttress each other. Therefore, good method would seek some sort of confirmation of the internal reconstruction. What might such a confirmation look like?

The most obvious route to confirmation of an internal reconstruction would involve an appeal to comparative reconstruction outside of the language L. But in Afroasiatic this is almost impossible. Owing to its great time depth, Afroasiatic sound correspondences are not well established, the number of secure cognate sets is not large, and posited "cognate sets" often involve highly imaginative and impressionistic leeway in semantic correspondences. The reconstructions and the cognate sets of Ehret (1995) and of Orel & Stolbova (1995) are often extremely different. In Afroasiatic one cannot ground a cognate set by appealing to established regular sound correspondences, since a "regular sound correspondence" is only as reliable as the cognates it is based on. And indeed, for Egyptian vis-a-vis the rest of Afroasiatic, the issue is precisely **what** should constitute a cognate set, and which sounds should be set into correspondence with each other in setting up etymological equivalencies across the languages. Positing different sound correspondences will generate different, competing sets of alleged cognates, and evaluating which of these competing sets is "better" is often tricky in the extreme, subjective, and "unscientific".

In the present case, both sides in the debate – the traditionalists and adherents of the Rössler school – offer different etymologies (involving different sound correspondences) as "proof" of their respective stances. Each side criticizes the etymologies of the other, and each side is sure that its etymologies are more numerous and better. Thus Takács (1999) asserts, from the traditionalist perspective, that "the etymological material proving Eg. ʕ = Sem. * ʕ /* γ has grown since 1985 (much more rapidly than the arguments for Eg. ʕ = Sem. *d)" (1999: 342). And the Neuere Komparatistik presents numerous etymologies of its own; see e.g., the list in Schneider (1997). The upshot is that any attempt to ground the Rösslerian reanalysis in comparative Afroasiatic data is unlikely to be convincing.

A second way to check the internal reconstruction is to seek relevant language-internal philological data. Egyptologists have sought confirmation by this route, notably pointing out a number of doublets within Egyptian where a spelling alternation of <d> ~ <ʕ>, with <d> representing the emphatic dental /ṭ/ (i.e., the "hand" hieroglyph), can be observed in identical or (near)-synonymous words (see e.g., Zeidler 1992: 207–210). I lack the expertise to respond to this here. A third avenue considers the phonetic naturalness of the proposed reformulation: does the reconstruction invoke paths and language states that linguists would consider natural? Fourth and finally, the reconstruction can be checked by an appeal to typology: does the reconstruction invoke paths and states that are well attested in the world, or even that are attested at all? In this paper I have examined the problem from the third and fourth perspective.

Another approach to the problem would be to consider whether the facts might be explained in some alternative way. Here I will address one aspect of Rössler's argument: the quite common cooccurrence of the two pharyngeals ʕ and h. For Rössler, this compatibility provides powerful support for the notion that the ʕ could not originally have been a pharyngeal; if it were, it should have been incompatible with another pharyngeal (1971: 277). But this presupposes that in fact there existed an incompatibility constraint at the pharyngeal position. And this seems to me a very vulnerable claim (cf. also Petráček 1988, as mentioned in Zeidler 1992: 203–204). Proto-languages, like any language, can evince symmetrical or asymmetrical, esthetic or unesthetic patterns. There is no a priori reason to prefer (or disprefer) an "esthetic" reconstruction of pre-Egyptian where the incompatibility constraint applies neatly and symmetrically at every point of articulation; the constraint could perfectly well have failed to hold at the pharyngeal position. And one need not look far to find a good reason for this to be the case specifically for pharyngeals, as opposed to (say) alveolars or velars. Pharyngeal or pharyngealized articulation could readily spread out from a single segment to become a suprasegmental prosody, whose domain was all or part of a root (cf. the "emphasis harmony" found as a prosody in some Arabic dialects). If so, this would actively **foster** the cooccurrence of two pharyngeals in the same root, sometimes as an archaic retention, sometimes as an assimilatory innovation – just the reverse of Rösslerian incompatibility. (Similar processes happen in other languages regarding other points of articulation: a palatalization prosody, a labialization prosody, etc.)

A different approach would be to relax the insistence on monogenesis. It could be that the Egyptian ʕ does not have one single unitary origin, but represents (as in several Semitic languages) a merger of two different pre-Egyptian sounds: in this case, both original *d and original *ʕ. This allows the possibility that, of the Egyptian words with ʕ, some could have come from *d (as proposed by the Neuere Komparatistik) and some could have come from pre-Egyptian, Afroasiatic *ʕ. This does not in itself solve or even address the central crux (why should *d > ʕ at all?); but it does contribute to resolving three subproblems. First, as just noted, the approach allows one to have one's etymological cake and eat it too: one can accept the new etymology *d > ʕ for some cases of Egyptian ʕ, without being required to jettison the entire set of "traditional" etymologies in which Egyptian ʕ arguably comes from Afroasiatic *ʕ. Second, in terms of pharyngeogenesis, it seems to me easier to accept a scenario whereby a non-pharyngeal sound **merges** with an existing pharyngeal, as opposed to a scenario where a voiced pharyngeal, *ex nihilo*, enters a system which previously had none. And third, it frees us from having to posit the strange absence of *ʕ in earliest Egyptian, despite the highly probable existence of *ʕ in pre-Egyptian Afroasiatic (reconstructible on the strength of Semitic, Cushitic, and probably Berber) and its certain existence in later "standard" Egyptian. That is, we need not posit the strange back-and-forth scenario

Afroasiatic	→	earliest Egyptian	→	standard Egyptian
*ʕ		no ʕ		ʕ

Such a reversal is intuitively unsatisfying: why should the Afroasiatic pharyngeal, despite being found in all the neighboring Afroasiatic groups, have disappeared totally in earliest Egyptian, only to reemerge in full-blown form later?

Or one might approach the problem from a graphic perspective. It is possible that in earliest Egyptian hieroglyphic writing, a given alphabetic graphy could have represented not one but two consonant phonemes of the language. Arguably, this was the case in Hebrew with the letter ʕ*ayin*, which many scholars (drawing on Greek and Latin transcriptions) feel to have represented both a pharyngeal /ʕ/ and a uvular fricative /ʁ/, preserved (so it is argued) as distinct phonemes in Biblical Hebrew. One may hypothetically posit the same thing in earliest Egyptian. The pharyngeal phoneme would then have preserved the original Afroasiatic *ʕ, while the uvular phoneme – arguably – could represent a development of Afroasiatic *d, according to the scenario laid out in section 3(c). As opposed to a full-blown development *d > ʕ, this development from *d > ʁ is more modest and hence in principle easier to accept. Only later would the posited early Egyptian /ʁ/ have merged phonetically with the pharyngeal /ʕ/, so that the earlier graphemic artifact thereby became a phonetic reality. This provides two possible etymological sources for Egyptian words written with the arm hieroglyph. (My thanks to Ya'ar Hever for this idea, which I hope I have rendered accurately.)

I conclude this discussion of methodology by comparing the case of Egyptian *d > ʕ to perhaps the best-known case of radical phonetic reconceptualization in a protosystem: the "Glottal Theory" in Indo-European (Gamkrelidze & Ivanov 1995.I: 5–19). Three different manner-of-articulation series (I, II, III) have been reconstructed for Proto-Indo-European, but their phonetic values have been interpreted in two quite different ways:

	I	II	III
Traditional	d	dh	t
Glottal Theory (new)	t'	d(h)	t(h)

(similarly with labials and velars). Three main reasons are offered for the Glottal Theory:

- (a) Proto-Indo-European *b occurs only in a very small number of words. This rarity is strange if *b is truly a voiced segment; but it makes good sense if the alleged *b was really an ejective stop *p', inasmuch as labials are not infrequently absent in ejective series crosslinguistically (Maddieson 1984: 103; Greenberg [1970] 1990: 125–126).
- (b) There is a cooccurrence constraint on stops that occur within the same root: two consonants of series I do not cooccur. This makes no sense if series I is a voiced series, but makes quite good sense if series I is ejective, with numerous parallels crosslinguistically (Gamkrelidze & Ivanov 1995.I: 17–18).
- (c) As emphasized by Gamkrelidze & Ivanov, the traditional system (voiced, voiceless, voiced aspirate) is said to be unparalleled in the world, which would greatly reduce its plausibility as a reconstructed system for Proto-Indo-European. More recently, such a system has been found to occur in the Kwa language Mbatto of West Africa (Stewart 1989: 231–239, cited by Comrie in several articles). But despite the attestation, the system remains an extreme rarity in the world, and concomitantly risky as a postulated Proto-Indo-European reconstruction.

When we compare the Egyptian and the Indo-European revisions of the consonant systems from a methodological point of view, the two cases are inverse in almost every respect, and always to the disadvantage of the Egyptian reconstruction.

For Indo-European:
- On **family**-internal comparative grounds, the traditional system presents difficulties
- Drawing on typological knowledge, do a reformulation for the entire Indo-European family
- Typological (non-)existence check: assert that the traditional system has no parallel in the world (falsified; but still extremely rare)
- Reformulation has **no** effect on etymological equations of Indo-European
- Indo-European is safely reconstructed; sound correspondences are plentiful and (mostly) quite secure
- Revision continues to be hotly debated (Clackson 2007: 45–48)

For Egyptian:
- On **language**-internal non-comparative grounds, the traditional system presents difficulties
- Not drawing on typological knowledge, do a reformulation for the one language in question
- No typological existence check: does the proposed change *d > ʕ have any parallels?
- Reformulation has an **enormous** effect on etymological equations of Afroasiatic
- Afroasiatic (though certainly a reality) has not been safely reconstructed; sound correspondences and cognates are debated and are not at all secure
- Revision tends to be accepted with little debate

In summary, the proposed change in Egyptian is much more drastic than that proposed for Indo-European, has a vastly greater impact on comparative reconstruction, has a less solid (because non-comparative) empirical base, and is much less "controllable" – and yet has been embraced in a far more uncritical way. Egyptologists should be uneasy about this state of affairs.

Unfortunately, the issue is not merely academic. Comparative Afroasiatic lexical studies and reconstruction urgently need the input from ancient Egyptian, just as comparative Indo-European lexical studies need input from (e.g.) ancient Sanskrit and Hittite. But as long as there is no consensus on how to treat the Egyptian data, and how it should be set into correspondence with the other languages, Egyptian cannot really help much in the lexical reconstruction of Afroasiatic.

I must stress in conclusion that the arguments in this paper do not necessarily mean that the "Neuere Komparatistik" must be wrong. They only indicate that it has been accepted too facilely. The present issue belongs to the most fascinating class of problems in historical linguistics: cases where two good methodologies yield inverse results. Which do you trust more, internal reconstruction, or typology and naturalness? And why? To my mind this remains an open question, and there may well be a way to reconcile the two methodologies.

But no matter how the issue is resolved, the typological dimension of the problem needs to be taken much more seriously. Egyptologists need to realize that the Rösslerian stance is far more radical than it has been considered to be. It is radical not just within the traditional family-specific framework of Egyptian-Semitic (or Egyptian-Afroasiatic) etymological comparison, but also and much more deeply within the world of general linguistics. An unprecedented and a priori astonishing sound change is being posited purely on the basis of internal reconstruction, as if the internal reconstruction were endowed with the ineluctable force of an algebraic theorem. I do not think that most historical linguists working with other language families would be comfortable accepting such a sweeping conclusion.

Both Egyptologists and typologists need to be aware of the problem of the arm hieroglyph, for no matter how it is resolved, it will have major consequences for one or the other discipline. If typology overrules internal reconstruction, then Egyptologists will need to seek some other approach to Rössler's very persuasive cooccurrence data. If internal reconstruction overrules typology, then Egyptologists will somehow have to make the implausible change plausible – while the broader world of general linguistics and typology (and not just the world of Egyptology) will have to come to terms with the notion that internal reconstruction can be a sufficient basis for positing a unique and thoroughly remarkable sound change. Ideally, a convincing middle way should be sought and found.

5 References

Bender, M. Lionel. 2005. *The East Sudanic languages: Lexicon and phonology*. Carbondale, IL: Southern Illinois University.

Chirikba, Viacheslav A. 1996. *Common West Caucasian*. Leiden: Research School CNWS.

Clackson, James. 2007. *Indo-European linguistics: An introduction*. Cambridge: Cambridge University Press.

Colarusso, John. 1992. *A grammar of the Kabardian language*. Calgary: University of Calgary Press.

Ehret, Christopher. 1987. Proto-Cushitic reconstruction. *Sprache und Geschichte in Afrika* 8: 7–180.

Ehret, Christopher. 1995. *Reconstructing Proto-Afroasiatic*. Berkeley & Los Angeles: University of California Press.

Fallon, Paul D. 2002. *The synchronic and diachronic phonology of ejectives*. New York: Garland.

Gamkrelidze, Thomas V. & Ivanov, Vjacheslav V. 1995. *Indo-European and the Indo-Europeans*. Translated by Johanna Nichols. 2 vols. Berlin: De Gruyter.

Greenberg, Joseph H. 1950 [1990]. The patterning of root morphemes in Semitic. *Word* 6: 162–181. [Reprinted in Denning, Keith & Kemmer, Suzanne (eds.). 1990. *On language: Selected writings of Joseph H. Greenberg*. Stanford: Stanford University Press, 365–387.]

Greenberg, Joseph H. 1970 [1990]. Some generalizations concerning glottalic consonants, especially implosives. *International Journal of American Linguistics* 36: 123–145. [Reprinted in Denning, Keith & Kemmer, Suzanne (eds.). 1990. *On language: Selected writings of Joseph H. Greenberg*. Stanford: Stanford University Press, 119–149.]

Haspelmath, Martin, Dryer, Matthew S., Gil, David & Comrie, Bernard (eds.). 2005. *The world atlas of language structures* [WALS]. Oxford: Oxford University Press.

Hewitt, Brian G. 1989. *Abkhaz*. London: Routledge.

Hoch, James E. 1994. *Semitic words in Egyptian texts of the New Kingdom and Third Intermediate Period*. Princeton: Princeton University Press.

Hock, Hans Henrich. 1991. *Principles of historical linguistics*. 2nd ed. Berlin: De Gruyter.

Jackson, Kenneth Hurlstone. 1986. *A historical phonology of Breton*. Dublin: Institute for Advanced Studies.

Jacobsen, William H., Jr. 1969. Origin of the Nootka pharyngeals. *International Journal of American Linguistics* 35: 125–153.

Kammerzell, Frank. 1998. The sounds of a dead language: Reconstructing Egyptian phonology. *Göttinger Beiträge zur Sprachwissenschaft* 1: 21–41.

Keller, Charles E. 1976. *A grammatical sketch of Brao*. MA thesis, University of North Dakota.

Kinkade, M. Dale. 1967. Uvular-pharyngeal resonants in Interior Salish. *International Journal of American Linguistics* 33: 228–234.

Kossmann, Maarten. 1999. *Essai sur la phonologie du proto-berbère*. Cologne: Rüdiger Köppe.

Kuipers, Aert H. 1981. On reconstructing the Proto-Salish sound system. *International Journal of American Linguistics* 47: 323–335.

Kuipers, Aert H. 2002. *Salish eymological dictionary*. (University of Montana Occasional Papers in Linguistics 16). Missoula, MT: University of Montana.

Ladefoged, Peter & Maddieson, Ian. 1996. *The sounds of the world's languages*. Oxford: Blackwell.

Loprieno, Antonio. 1995. *Ancient Egyptian*. Cambridge: Cambridge University Press.

Maddieson, Ian. 1984. *Patterns of sounds*. Cambridge: Cambridge University Press.

Maddieson, Ian. 2005. Presence of uncommon consonants. In: Haspelmath, Martin, Dryer, Matthew S., Gil, David & Comrie, Bernard (eds.), *The world atlas of language structures* [WALS]. Oxford: Oxford University Press, 82–85.

McCarus, Ernest N. 1997. Kurdish phonology. In: Kaye, Alan S. (ed.), *Phonologies of Asia and Africa*, Vol. 2. Winona Lake, IN: Eisenbrauns, 691–706.

Meillet, Antoine. 1967. *The comparative method in historical linguistics*. Translated by Gordon B. Ford. Paris: Champion.

Nichols, Johanna. 1999. The historical geography of pharyngeals and laterals in the Caucasus. *Berkeley Linguistics Society* 25 S: 1–13. (Special session on Caucasian, Dravidian, and Turkic linguistics)

Nichols, Johanna. 2003. The Nakh-Daghestanian consonant correspondences. In: Holisky, Dee Ann & Tuite, Kevin (eds.), *Current trends in Caucasian, East European and Inner Asian linguistics*. Amsterdam: Benjamins, 207–264.

Orel, Vladmir & Stolhova, Olga V. 1995. *Hamito-Semitic etymological dictionary*. Leiden: Brill.

Petráček, Karel. 1988. *Altägyptisch, Hamitosemitisch und ihre Beziehungen zu einigen Sprachfamilien in Afrika und Asien. Vergleichende Studien*. Prague: Univ. Karlova.

Peust, Carsten. 1999. *Egyptian phonology*. Göttingen: Peust & Gutschmidt.

Rau, Der-Hwa Victoria. 1992. *A grammar of Atayal*. PhD dissertation, Cornell University.

Raz, Shlomo. 1983. *Tigre grammar and texts*. Malibu: Undena Publications.

Rössler, Otto. 1971. Das ägyptische als semitische Sprache. In: Altheim, Franz & Stiel, Ruth (eds.), *Christentum am Roten Meer*, Vol. 1. Berlin: De Gruyter, 263–326.

Sasse, Hans-Jürgen. 1979. The consonant phonemes of Proto-East-Cushitic: A first approximation. *Afroasiatic Linguistics* 7.1: 1–67.

Satzinger, Helmut. 1999. Egyptian ʕayin in variation with d. *Lingua Aegyptia* 6: 141–151.

Schenkel, Wolfgang. 1990. *Einführung in die altägyptische Sprachwissenschaft*. Darmstadt: Wissenschaftliche Buchgesellschaft.

Schenkel, Wolfgang. 1993. Zu den Verschluss- und Reibelauten im Ägyptischen und (Hamito) Semitischen. *Lingua Aegyptia* 3: 137–149.

Schmitt, Rüdiger. 2007. *Grammatik des Klassisch-Armenischen mit sprachvergleichenden Erläuterungen*. 2. Aufl. Innsbruck: Innsbrucker Beiträge zur Sprachwissenschaft.

Schneider, Thomas. 1997. Beiträge zur sogenannten „Neueren Komparatistik". *Lingua Aegyptia* 5: 189–209.

Steiner, Richard C. 1977. *The case for fricative-laterals in Proto-Semitic*. New Haven: American Oriental Society.

Stewart, John M. 1989. Kwa. In: Bendor-Samuel, John (ed.), *The Niger-Congo languages*. Lanham, MD: University Press of America, 217–245.

Takács, Gábor. 1999. *Etymological dictionary of Egyptian*. Vol. 1: *A phonological introduction*. Leiden: Brill.

Thompson, Laurence C. 1979. Salishan and the Northwest. In: Campbell, Lyle & Mithun, Marianne (eds.), *The languages of Native America*. Austin: University of Texas Press, 692–765.

Voigt, Rainer. 2003. Lautwandel im Ägyptischen. *Lingua Aegyptia* 11: 201–218.

Zeidler, Jürgen. 1992. Altägyptisch und Hamitosemitisch. Bemerkungen zu den *Vergleichenden Studien* von Karel Petráček. *Lingua Aegyptia* 2: 189–222.

Eitan Grossman

No case before the verb, obligatory case after the verb in Coptic*

Abstract: This paper presents a hitherto unnoticed fact about the coding of grammatical relations in Coptic: while postverbal core arguments must be overtly case-marked (or "flagged"), preverbal core arguments are never case-marked. This feature extends the "no case before the verb in northeastern Africa" generalization (König 2008; 2009) to the northeastern Mediterranean. Moreover, the analysis presented here reveals Coptic to be another case of an uncommon system of core argument marking, namely, "marked S/A vs. marked P".

1 No case before the verb in Coptic

Despite the fact that Coptic is a well described and abundantly attested language, with a dozen or so dialects (Funk 1988), a simple yet important feature of its grammatical structure has gone unremarked in grammatical descriptions: there are no core case distinctions before the verb, and postverbal core arguments must be case-marked.[1] This feature extends König's (2008; 2009) "no case before the verb in northeastern Africa" generalization geographically to the northeast Mediterranean. It also extends it genealogically, adding Egyptian-Coptic to Berber as Afroasiatic languages with this feature.[2] Finally, Coptic corroborates König's generalization, according to which "if there is no case distinctions before the verb, then preverbal participants occur in the morphologically unmarked form" [i.e.,

* This paper grew out of joint work by the author and Giorgio Iemmolo (Zurich), funded in part by the Swiss National Science Foundation (Grant IZKOZ1_146024). I would like to thank Denis Creissels, Zygmunt Frajzyngier, Tom Givón, Tom Güldemann, Martin Haspelmath, Christa König, Sebastian Richter, Ewa Zakrewska, Yael Ziv and other participants in the Association for Linguistic Typology 10th Biennial Conference (Leipzig 2013) for their helpful comments and criticism.
1 I assume here a broad definition of the comparative concept "case marker", roughly corresponding to the notion "flag", "relator", or "dependent-marker". Such definitions are common in typological studies of case (e.g., Haspelmath 2008; Siewierska & Bakker 2008), and it is in this sense that the term "case" is used in this paper.
2 Whether Berber "states" ought to be described in terms of case is disputed; see Mettouchi & Frajzyngier (2013) on Kabyle, as well as Arkadiev's reaction (fc).

the morphosyntactically simplest form, EG] (2008: 281), but extends it to languages which do not have ergative or marked-nominative coding.

The structure of this paper is as follows: in § 2, I present a bare-bones account of the encoding of grammatical relations in Coptic[3] and in § 3 some frequency data. In § 4, I argue that Coptic does not have a marked nominative system. In § 5, I provide a brief note on diachrony, and in § 6, König's "no case before the verb" generalization in African languages is briefly sketched. All examples, unless noted otherwise, are taken from the earliest documentation of Bohairic, the northernmost Coptic dialect (Grossman 2009a).

2 Encoding grammatical relations in Coptic: indexing and case-marking

Grammatical relations are language-specific categories, often (but not exclusively) encoded by means such as indexation ("agreement"), flagging ("case"), and linear order (Frajzyngier & Shay 2003; Payne 2013). Behavioral properties, e.g., control of reflexivization, will not be dealt with here.

Grammatical relations in Coptic are encoded by means of four main strategies: indexation, argument incorporation, case marking, and linear order. In this section, I refer only to main (i.e., non-subordinate) intransitive and monotransitive[4] verbal clauses of a particular construction type, the so-called "non-durative pattern" or "tripartite conjugation" (Polotsky 1960). This morphosyntactic[5] construction type comprises up to four "slots":

---

3 A more detailed account of Coptic grammatical relations, in the context of Differential Subject Marking, is given in Grossman & Iemmolo (2014+). The present article provides only enough background in order to substantiate the claim about case-marking and linear order.

4 This is intended to exclude ditransitives, on the one hand, and bivalent intransitives, on the other. Transitive clauses are defined according to Haspelmath (2011b) and Lazard (2002): broadly, a monotransitive clause is a bivalent clause that has A and P as its core arguments; intransitives can be either monovalent (one argument) or bivalent, if the arguments are not A and P. In turn, A and P are defined, respectively, as "the argument of the major two-argument construction that represents the agent when the construction expresses an action" and "the argument of the major two-argument construction that represents the patient when the construction expresses an action" (Haspelmath 2011b).

5 I use the term "morphosyntactic" instead of "morphological", since the latter assumes that the notion "word" is well defined, either as a cross-linguistic comparative concept or as a descriptive category of Coptic (Haspelmath 2011a). For the description of Coptic, the term "bound group" (Layton 2004) is more than adequate.

Table 1: The constructional scheme of a Coptic verb

TAM auxiliary	A/S expression	lexical verb	P expression
a	*f*	*tʰamio*	*f*
PST	3SGM	create	3SGM
'He created him.'			

This is a fairly simplified representation of the structure of the verb, since the TAM auxiliaries can be discontinuous (e.g., the future marker *e...e*), lexical arguments can occur in the A/S and P slots, and both preverbal and postverbal lexical arguments are very frequent in discourse. However, it is important to keep this basic structure in mind, since it is to this construction (rather than the lexical verb) that I refer when I use the terms "verb (V)", "preverbal" or "postverbal."

2.1 Argument Indexing

Intransitive clauses have a maximum of one argument index (ex. 1); in monotransitive clauses, one or two arguments can be indexed on the verb (ex. 2). There is no implicational relationship between A and P indexing, since an A index can occur without a P index, and vice versa (see 2.5 below).

(1) ⲁⲓⲭⲱⲡ
    a-i-kʰôp   **S**
    1SG-hide
    'I hid' (Early Bohairic, Genesis 3:10).

(2) ⲁϥⲑⲁⲙⲓⲟϥ
    a-f-tʰamio-f   **A+P**
    PST-3SGM-create-3SGM
    'He$_1$ created him$_2$' (Early Bohairic, Genesis 1:27).

In terms of alignment, indexing is mixed accusative-neutral, depending on a complex set of phonological and morphosyntactic factors, which are irrelevant to the present discussion. Example (2) shows neutral alignment (A=P) in indexing for this particular constellation of verbal construction, tense, and person. Example (3) shows accusative alignment in indexing: the 1SG A index (*-i*), which is the same as the 1SG S index (cf. ex 1 above), differs from the 1SG P index (*-t*).

(3) ⲉⲓⲧⲱⲛⲧ
    e-i-e-tôn-t   **S=A≠P** (cf. ex. 2)
    FUT1-1SG^A-FUT2-raise-1SG^P
    'I will raise myself up' (Early Bohairic, Nahum 3:5).

2.2 Argument Incorporation

Both lexical subjects (A/S) and objects (P) can be incorporated into the verb,[6] but it is rare for both lexical A and P to be incorporated into the same verb. Incorporated P arguments are bound to the lexical verb, which often shows a prosodically reduced form. This prosodically reduced verb form cannot occur as a free morpheme. For example, in examples (6–8), the forms of the lexical verbs without incorporated P are, respectively *čimi*, *kʰô*, and *tʰamio*.

(4) **S-incorporation**

    ⲁⲣⲟⲟⲩϩⲓ   ϣⲱⲡⲓ
    a-roouhi   *šôpi*
    PST-evening   become
    'It became evening' (Early Bohairic, Genesis 1:8).

(5) **A-incorporation**

    ⲁϥϯ   ⲑⲁⲙⲓⲟ   ⲛⲛⲓⲑⲏⲣⲓⲟⲛ
    a-pʰ[nou]tⁱ *tʰamio* *n-ni-tʰêrion*
    PST-G[o]d   create   ACC-DEF.PL-beast
    'God created the beasts' (Early Bohairic, Genesis 1:25).

---

6 The term "incorporation" is used somewhat unconventionally here, since the arguments bound within the morphosyntactic verb can be referential noun phrases as well as "bare" noun lexemes. In this respect, Coptic differs from constructions described as "incorporation" in other languages, but is similar to the way that Boumaa Fijian has been described by Dixon (1988); see also Aikhenvald (2007). On the other hand, Coptic unambiguously treats the verb and the object as a single bound group, by use of a prosodically-reduced verb form that cannot occur on its own. As such, the incorporation analysis will be retained here.

(6) **P-incorporation**

ⲘⲠⲞⲨϪⲈⲘⲂⲞⲎⲐⲞⲤ ⲆⲈ   ⲚⲚⲀⲆⲀⲘ

*mp-ou-čem-**boêtʰos**=de*   *nn-adam*

PST.NEG-3PL-find-helper=CONN ACC-Adam

'A helper was not found for Adam' (Early Bohairic, Genesis 2:20).

(7) **A+P-incorporation**

ⲀⲠϬⲤ   Ⲫϯ   ⲬⲀⲞⲨⲘⲎⲒⲚⲒ   ⲚⲔⲀⲒⲚ

a-pc[oi]s   *pʰ[nou]tⁱ*   *kʰa-**ou-mêini***   *n-kain*

PST-the.L[or]d G[o]d   put-INDEF.SG-mark ACC-Cain

'The L[or]d G[o]d put a mark on Cain' (Bohairic, Genesis 4:15).

(8) ⲀⲪϯ   ⲐⲀⲘⲒⲈϮⲪⲈ

*a-**pʰ[nou]tⁱ***   *tʰamie-tⁱ-pʰe*

PST-G(o)d   create-DEF.M-heaven

'God created the world' (Early Bohairic, Genesis 1:1).

2.3 Case-marking

Coptic is not traditionally described in terms of case marking. Nonetheless, Coptic has adpositions and other flags that code grammatical relations. As noted above, I assume here a broad definition of the comparative concept "case marker", roughly corresponding to the notion "flag", "relator", or "dependent-marker".

Non-incorporated postverbal lexical subjects (S/A) and objects (P) must be overtly case-marked. The accusative marker (*n-*) is seen in example (9),[7]

(9) **Accusative**

ⲀϤϪⲒ   ⲚⲞⲨⲔⲀϨⲒ   ⲈⲂⲞⲗ

a-f-či   ***n**-ou-kahi*   *ebol*

PST-3SGM-take   ACC-INDEF.SG-earth out

'He took earth' (Early Bohairic, Genesis 2:7).

---

7 The accusative case marker was grammaticalized from a highly polyfunctional preposition associated with LOCATIVE, INSTRUMENT, SOURCE, and a number of other functions. See Winand (2014, in this volume) for a discussion of its sources.

The opposition between object incorporation and accusative case marking is generally seen as a case of Differential Object Marking motivated by the interaction of referentiality and topicality rather than, e.g., animacy or definiteness (e.g., Engsheden 2008; Grossman 2009b; Winand 2014, in this volume).

The nominative marker *nče* (*nci* in other dialects, e.g., Sahidic) is found in example (10).

(10) **Nominative**

ⲁⲩⲭⲟⲡⲟⲩ	ⲛϫⲉⲁⲇⲁⲙ	ⲛⲉⲙⲧⲉϥⲥϩⲓⲙⲓ
a-u-kʰop-ou	***nče-adam***	*nem-tef-shimi*
PST-3PL-hide-3PL	**NOM**-Adam	with-his.F-woman

'Adam and his wife hid' (Early Bohairic, Genesis 3:8).

Few if any Copticists have described *nci/nče* as a nominative marker. It has typically been described as a preposition (Layton 2004), extrapositive subject marker (Loprieno 2000), or focus marker (Reintges 2004). However, it does not have other properties typically associated with prepositions in Coptic, and it is not strongly associated with focus in most dialects. The descriptive label "extrapositive" (or perhaps "postpositive") subject marker would be adequate, but it is perhaps better to have a more specific label. The term "nominative" seems appropriate enough, since *nci/nče* is highly grammaticalized for a particular function, marking postverbal lexical A/S arguments, and has a high token frequency, which indicates that it is not just an "afterthought marker", along the lines of English "namely" or Seneca *neh*.[8]

The co-occurrence of both lexical NOM and lexical ACC is possible but relatively rare:

(11)

ⲁϥⲑⲁⲙⲓⲟ	ⲛϫⲉⲫϯ	ⲙⲡⲓⲧⲁⲭⲣⲟ
a-f-tʰamio	***nče-pʰ[nou]tⁱ***	***m-pi-tačro***
PST-3SGM-create	**NOM**-G[o]d	**ACC**-DEF.S-firmament

'ᴺᴼᴹGod created ᴬᶜᶜthe firmament' (Early Bohairic, Genesis 1:7).

This rarity stems from the nature of discourse: transitive clauses with more than one lexical core argument tend to have low text frequency across languages (DuBois 1987).

---

8 I was made aware of this marker, which looks like a candidate for antitopic marker status, by Wallace Chafe in a lecture (Leipzig, 12/8/2013).

2.4 Preverbal lexical arguments and case-marking

Preverbal lexical arguments are not case-marked.

(12) **Preverbal S**

ⲁⲃⲉⲗ ⲇⲉ   ⲁϥϣⲱⲡⲓ
Abel=de   *a-f-šôpi*
Abel=CONN PST-3SGM-become
'Abel became...' (Early Bohairic, Genesis 4:2).

(13) **Preverbal A**

ⲁⲇⲁⲙ ⲇⲉ   ⲁϥϯⲣⲁⲛ   ⲉⲛⲓⲧⲉⲃⲛⲱⲟⲩ
Adam=de   *a-f-tⁱ-ran*   *e-ni-tebnôou*
Adam=CONN PST-3SGM-give-name ALL-the.PL-animals
'And Adam named the animals' (Early Bohairic, Genesis 2:20).

The following example shows that the absence of case marking is not limited to proper names.

(14) **Preverbal P**

ⲡⲓⲭⲁⲕⲓ ⲇⲉ   ⲁϥϯⲣⲉⲛϥ   ϫⲉⲡⲉⲭⲱⲣϩ
pi-kʰaki=de   *a-f-tⁱ-ren-f*   *če-pi-ečôrh*
DEF.M-darkness=CONN PST-3SGM-give-name-3SGM QUOT-DEF.M-evening
'The darkness, he named it "evening"' (Early Bohairic, Genesis 1:5).

Preverbal lexical arguments are often marked topics (ex. 15), but they can occasionally be focal as well (ex. 16). Interestingly, topical preverbal arguments tend to be accompanied by the particle *de*, while focal preverbal arguments tend to be directly followed by the verb.

(15) ⲁⲇⲁⲙ ⲇⲉ   ⲁϥⲥⲟⲩⲉⲛⲧⲉϥⲥϩⲓⲙⲓ
Adam=de   *a-f-souen-tef-shimi*
Adam=CONN PST-3SGM-know-his-woman
'As for Adam, he knew his wife' (Early Bohairic, Genesis 4:1).

(16) ⲚⲒⲘ ⲀϤⲦⲀⲘⲟⲔ
nim a-f-tamo-k
who PST-3SGM-inform-2SGM
'Who told you?' (Early Bohairic, Genesis 3:11).

2.5 Interim summary

Coptic has three[9] main strategies for coding lexical A/S:

Table 2: Indexing and case for lexical A/S

	Indexing	Case
Incorporated A/S	no	no
Preverbal A/S	yes	no
Postverbal A/S	yes	yes

Coptic also has three main strategies for coding lexical P:

Table 3: Indexing and case for lexical P

	Indexing	Case
Incorporated P	no	no
Preverbal P	yes	no
Postverbal P	no	yes

Several generalizations can be made:
1. All postverbal core arguments must be case-marked.
2. Preverbal and incorporated core arguments are never case-marked.
3. All preverbal core arguments, as well as postverbal subjects, entail indexing.
4. There is no implicational relationship between A and P indexing; all combinations of A and P indexes and lexical arguments are possible:

---

9 There are other, relatively infrequent, construction types, but they will be ignored here.

Table 4: Co-occurrence of A/P indexes and lexical arguments

	Indexed P	**Incorporated P**
Indexed A	a-f-tʰamio-f	a-f-tʰamie-tʰ-pe
	PST-3SGM-create-3SGM	PST-3SGM-create-DEF.F-heaven
	'He created him.'	'He created heaven.'
Incorporated A	a-pʰ[nou]tⁱ tʰamio-f	a-pʰ[nou]tⁱ tʰamie-tʰpe
	PST-G[o]d create-3SGM	PST-G[o]d create-DEF.F-heaven
	'God created him.'	'God created heaven.'

Similarly, all combinations of incorporation and case marking are possible for lexical noun phrase core arguments.

Table 5: Co-occurrence of case-marking and incorporation for lexical NP arguments

	Case-marked P	**Incorporated P**
Case-marked A	Ex. 11	a-u-el-ôni nče-ni-ouidai
		PST-3PL-throw-stone NOM-DEF.PL-Jew
Incorporated A	Ex. 5	Ex. 8

All in all, Coptic can be described as having both Differential Subject Marking and Differential Object Marking, which is in itself rare. Coptic Differential Argument Marking is also of a relatively rare type, in which overt case marking alternates with argument incorporation (Grossman & Iemmolo 2014+). Differential Subject Marking in Coptic is triggered by information structure: in the Bohairic dialect, preverbal subjects tend to be contrastive or shifted topics; incorporated subjects tend to be relatively "inert" in terms of topicality, with little backward or forward topicality in texts, or otherwise globally accessible referents (God, evening, morning); postverbal subjects tend to be highly accessible (Ariel 1990), already active in the discourse.[10] This last observation is discussed in the next section.

---

10 For details and argumentation, see Zakrzewska (2006); Shisha-Halevy (1986, 2007); and Grossman & Iemmolo (2014+). Loprieno (2000) proposes that postverbal subjects are rhematic, and Reintges (2004) considers that they are focal. In fact, these views are not necessarily contradictory, since Reintges (2004) deals with Sahidic, in which postverbal subjects are more frequently new referents. This, however, is very rare in Bohairic.

2.6 Linear order

Coptic is usually characterized as having basic SVO order, although this description is somewhat controversial. While a description of word order in Coptic is well beyond the scope of this paper, some relevant facts should be mentioned.

1. The order of indexes on the verb is distinctive: an A index always precedes a P index. The order is always A-V^{lex-P}.[11]
2. The order of incorporated core arguments is also distinctive; it is always A-V^{lex-P}.
3. Lexical A, no matter its position, almost always precedes lexical P. One type of exception is when the lexical object is preverbal and the lexical subject is postverbal, e.g.

(17) ⲛⲁⲓ ⲇⲉ   ⲁϥϫⲟⲧⲟⲩ   ⲛϫⲉⲓⲏⲥ
      nai=de   *a-f-čot-ou*   *nče-iê[sou]s*
      DEM.PL=CONN   PST-3SGM-say-3PL   NOM-Jesus
      'As for these things, Jesus said them...' (Early Bohairic, John 12: 36).

This construction type, however, is very rare in discourse.

There are also rare examples in which postverbal lexical P precedes lexical A:

(18) ⲁϥϫⲓ ⲇⲉ   ⲛⲛⲓⲱⲓⲕ   ⲛϫⲉⲓⲏⲥ
      a-f-či=de   *n-ni-ôik*   *nče-iê[sou]s*
      PST-3SGM-take=PTCL   ACC-DEF.PL-bread   NOM-Je[su]s
      'Then Jesus took the loaves of bread' (Early Bohairic, John 6: 11).

However, all in all, lexical A overwhelmingly tends to precede lexical P.

Linear order alternations in Coptic, as in many languages, are motivated by information-structural factors, and as such, linear order is a "coding means" in the sense of Frajzyngier & Shay (2003) and Frajzyngier (2011). As noted above, preverbal arguments are typically contrastive or shifted topics, although, they can occasionally be focal. Postverbal A/S arguments in Coptic, at least in some dialects, e.g., Bohairic, are generally identifiable/accessible (Zakrzewska 2006; Grossman & Iemmolo 2014+).

For example, in (18), 'Cain' occurs in the first clause; in the second clause, 'Cain' is already accessible, and occurs postverbally with NOM-marking.

---

11 In terms of linear order, this construction has nominative-accusative alignment, even if the person indexes themselves are neutrally aligned.

(19) ⲁⲡϭⲥ   ⲫϯ   ⲭⲁⲟⲩⲙⲏⲓⲛⲓ   ⲛⲕⲁⲓⲛ
      a-pc[oi]s *pʰ[nou]tⁱ* *kʰa-ou-mêini* *n-kain*
      PST-the.Lord G[o]d put-INDEF.SG-sign ACC-Cain
      'The Lord G[o]d marked Cain.'

      ⲁϥⲓ ⲇⲉ   ⲛⲭⲉⲕⲁⲓⲛ   ⲉⲃⲟⲗ ϩⲁⲡϩⲟ   ⲙⲫϯ
      a-f-i=de   **nče-kain** *ebol* *ha-p-ho*   *m-pʰ[nou]tⁱ*
      PST-3SGM-come=CONN **NOM**-Cain out from-DEF.M-face of-G[o]d
      '(and) Cain came away from the Lord's presence' (Bohairic, Genesis 4:
      15–16).

In the Biblical story of Jonah, the ship bearing the runaway is rocked by a storm,
which frightens the sailors. Jonah admits that the storm is his fault.

(20) [ⲉ]ⲑⲃⲏⲧ   ϥϣⲟⲡ   ⲛⲭⲉⲡⲁⲓϩⲱⲓⲙⲓ
      [e]tʰbêt   *f-šop*   **nče-pai-hôimi**
      [b]ecause.1SG 3SGM-exist **NOM**-DEM.M-wave
      'Because of me this wave exists' (Early Bohairic, Jonah 1:12).

The NOM-marked subject is the current discourse topic, and as such, is identifiable.

   In the following example, Jesus and an official are discussing the latter's ill
son, and Jesus says:

(21) ϥⲟⲛⲃ   ⲛⲭⲉⲡⲉⲕϣⲉⲣⲓ
      f-onx   **nče-pek-šêri**
      3SGM-alive **NOM**-your-son
      'Your son is alive' (Early Bohairic, John 4:50).

Highly identifiable/accessible postverbal arguments are sometimes called *antitopics* (Chafe 1976). Antitopics, according to Lambrecht (1981), tend to have the
following cluster of properties: (1) postverbal position; (2) indexed via pronominal affixes/clitics; (3) case-marked and integrated into clausal syntax, i.e., are not
clause-external; (4) identifiable (textually, frame-evoked, inferable, following
Prince 1981), i.e., they do not introduce new topics. Postverbal subjects in Coptic,
at least in the dialect discussed here, have all of these properties.

3 Frequency

To date, there are no extensive studies of the relative frequency of the various constructions in discourse, other than Zakrzewska (2006), which provides raw frequency data for around 700 narrative clauses in a single corpus of later (ca. 9th century) Bohairic.

Table 6: Subject encoding in later Bohairic

A/S-incorporation	Preverbal A/S	Postverbal A/S (nom)
31.5%	25.7%	42.8%

Note that nearly 70% of clauses have non-incorporated subjects, and nearly half of the tokens have postverbal NOM-marked subjects.

Two small samples of Early Bohairic were examined. In the first, taken from Genesis (Papyrus Bodmer III), all clauses were analyzed, with the following results:

Table 7: Subject encoding in Genesis 1:1–4:3 in all clauses

	Incorporation	Preverbal	Postverbal	Index only	Other
Number	68	12	29	79	80
%	25.373	4.478	10.821	29.477	29.851

For clauses with lexical subjects, one sees that incorporated subjects amount to nearly 70% of all tokens, with preverbal and postverbal subjects far less frequent.

Table 8: Subject encoding in Genesis 1:1–4:3 in clauses with lexical S/A

	Incorporation	Preverbal	Postverbal	Total
Number	68	12	29	109
%	62.385	11.009	26.606	100

However, this has to do with the nature of the text examined: in the first 200 clauses or so of Genesis, God is the only actor, so there is little need for formal devices that mark shifted or contrastive topics (e.g., left-dislocation), or that keep track of alternating subject referents (e.g., postverbal NOM-marked antitopics).

A second sample, from the Gospel of John, was looked at, first counting all clauses, then only clauses with lexical subjects.

Table 9: Subject encoding in the Gospel of John 18:1–19:16 in all clauses

	Incorporation	Preverbal	Postverbal	Index only	Other
Number	10	20	36	71	99
%	4.237	8.474	15.255	30.085	41.949

Table 10: Subject encoding in the Gospel of John 18:1–19:16 in clauses with lexical S/A

	Incorporation	Preverbal	Postverbal	Total
Number	10	20	36	66
%	15.152	30.303	54.545	100

In John (18:1–19:16), the frequencies resemble those found by Zakrzewska (2006) for later Bohairic, with postverbal subjects even more frequent (more than half of tokens of clauses with lexical subjects). This is probably due to the high density of actors (e.g., Jesus, Pilate, the Jews, various disciples, the priests), who have to be kept track of in narrative by formal devices. Importantly, all of the actors are identifiable/accessible in this chunk of text, which accounts for the high frequency of postverbal NOM-marked subjects as opposed to preverbal subjects.

4 Does Coptic have a "marked-nominative" system?

According to König (2008; 2009), the vast majority of African languages with "no case before the verb" have either ergative or "marked nominative" coding. Marked nominative constructions are those in which S and A are encoded by the same means, differing from that of P, but unlike other nominative-accusative constructions, the accusative is the morphologically and functionally "unmarked" form. In this context, "unmarked" means that accusatives are less morphosyntactically complex than nominatives ("morphologically unmarked"), on the one hand, and that accusatives are used in more contexts ("functionally unmarked"). König attributes special importance to the citation form, which in marked nominative systems is the accusative.

Coptic is formally similar to marked nominative systems, in that the nominative is the most functionally restricted case, both syntactically and pragmatically, and tends to occur postverbally in many marked nominative systems. On the other hand, it differs from most marked nominative systems in that *both* the

NOM and the ACC are restricted, in terms of function, relative to the zero-marked (unmarked or "bare") form. Moreover, neither the NOM nor the ACC is the citation form ("absolute" or "designative" case, Creissels 2009), like Japanese, Korean, and Kanuri. Of course, another major difference is the tripartite distinction between preverbal, postverbal, and incorporated subjects, which is atypical of marked nominative systems. The following Table gives an idea of the functions of the three forms:

Table 11: Functions of case markers in Coptic

Case		Function
NOM (*nče-*)	(a)	post-verbal A/S
ACC (*n-*)	(b)	post-verbal P, some adverbials, secondary predicates
unmarked	(c)	citation form
	(d)	vocative
	(e)	following prepositions
	(f)	incorporated S/A/P
	(g)	preverbal S/A/P
	(h)	nominal predications
	(i)	following derivational affixes

As such, Coptic cannot be described as having a marked nominative system, but rather as having an "uncommon pattern of accusative core marking", namely "marked S/A vs. marked P" (Creissels 2009: 453). On the other hand, Coptic does share with many languages with marked nominative systems the property of a basically pragmatic or information-structural basis for the occurrence of case markers. However, this is not exclusive to marked nominative systems: in some languages, postverbal subjects tend to refer to identifiable or accessible entities in discourse,[12] while preverbal subjects have a marked information-structural status, e.g., focus, on the one hand, or contrastive or shifted topic, on the other. What is particular about the Coptic system, and appears to be a cross-linguistic *rarum* is the fact that postverbal subjects have a strong association with antitopic status *and* are obligatorily coded by a highly grammaticalized case marker.

---

12 Such languages include Syriac Aramaic (Goldenberg 1983), Biblical Hebrew (Givón 1977), Ojibwa (Tomlin & Rhodes 1992), Mohawk (Mithun 1996), French (Lambrecht 1981), Chamorro (Cooreman 1992), and Sandawe (Eaton 2010). However, to the best of my knowledge there are no cross-linguistic studies of antitopics.

It is likely that an explanation for this association between nominative marking and highly accessible lexical noun phrase referents is another instantiation of a general trend: overt case marking, at least at early stages of grammaticalization, marks unexpected associations between grammatical role and information-structural properties of referents. For example, Iemmolo (2010) argues that differential object marking tends to arise in the context of topical P, since direct objects tend to be new (or "focal"). Similarly, numerous studies of "optional" ergative marking point out that "optional" ergative markers are strongly associated with focal A (e.g., Hyslop 2010; McGregor 2006; Verstraete 2010). This makes sense, since A referents overwhelmingly tend to be highly accessible (Du Bois 1987). In the present context, lexical noun phrases tend to refer to low-accessibility referents, so the occurrence of highly accessible referents as lexical noun phrases would be an unexpected association, and therefore would be prone to being marked overtly. While a number of languages exploit word order to mark this unexpected association (e.g., French and Ojibwa), Coptic seems to be unusual in using case marking.

5 A brief word on the diachrony of Differential Subject Marking in Coptic[13]

Of the three constructions discussed here – subject incorporation, preverbal subjects, and postverbal nom-marked subjects – the subject incorporation construction represents the most frequent construction of Earlier Egyptian, a largely VS language. In Earlier Egyptian, person markers and lexical noun phrases were in complementary distribution within the same clause, attaching directly to verb stems. As such, person markers are "pronominal" in the narrow sense, or "proindexes" in the sense of Haspelmath (2013), i.e., "person indexes" that cannot co-occur with conominals in the same clause.

In Later Egyptian, there began to emerge numerous periphrastic and auxiliary constructions, to which subject expressions attached, followed by lexical

---

13 Differential Object Marking in Egyptian-Coptic, which began to emerge in Late Egyptian, developed from the convergence of a number of constructions, including an antiapplicative construction and a partitive-object construction. The accusative marker itself developed from the highly polysemous preposition *m*, which codes instrument, source, location, and a range of other functions. See Winand (2014, in this volume) for further details of the diachrony of the accusative marker from Late Egyptian to Coptic.

verbs. Coptic TAM auxiliaries represent, for the most part, highly grammaticalized descendants of these auxiliaries.

Demotic (Johnson 1976: 97)

(22) *bw.ir-msḥ*   *ṯзy*   *rmt*   *n-dmy*
     AOR.NEG-crocodile   catch man   MOD-town
     'A crocodile does not/cannot catch a local man.'

(23) *bw.ir-f-ḥpr*
     AOR.NEG-3SGM-exist
     'It does not/cannot happen.'

Coptic (Shisha-Halevy 1988: 97)

(24) ⲙⲉⲣⲉⲡⲉϥϩⲏⲧ   ϩⲓⲛⲏⲃ ⲛⲟⲩⲙⲉ
     mere-pef-hêt   *hinêb noume*
     AOR.NEG-his-heart   sleep really
     'His heart cannot really sleep.'

(25) ⲙⲉⲕϩⲱⲡ   ⲉⲣⲟⲟⲩ
     me-k-hôp   *ero-ou*
     NEG.AOR-2SGM-hide   ALL-3PL
     'You cannot hide from them.'

As a result of these grammaticalization processes, lexical noun phrase subjects
and person indexes became "trapped" within the verbal syntagm, rather than at
its rightmost edge.

Since Earlier Egyptian, preverbal lexical subjects could be right-dislocated or
topicalized, as an alternative order. However, there is no comparative frequency
data for preverbal subjects in Earlier and Later Egyptian.

In contrast to the previous two constructions, the postverbal nominative
marker is largely an innovation of Coptic, with vanishingly few examples in the
previous stage of the language, Demotic. Another marker, written variously *in*, *n*,
or *m*, was relatively infrequent (Mattha 1947). The frequency of postverbal subjects is vastly greater in Coptic than in any previous stage of the language.

The implications of these processes for understanding the history of the
encoding of grammatical relations in Egyptian are significant. In a recent decon-
struction of the concept of agreement, Haspelmath (2013) argues that the term
"index" is more appropriate for describing bound person markers. The proposed
typology of bound person markers distinguishes between three main types:

1. Pro-indexes: indexes that cannot co-occur with conominals
2. Cross-indexes: indexes with optional conominals
3. Gramm-indexes: indexes with obligatory conominals

In the latest stages of Egyptian-Coptic, one witnesses a sharp increase in the co-occurrence of person indexes and conominals, or in other words, a shift from pro-indexes to cross-indexes, due to a rise in the frequency of preverbal and post-verbal lexical arguments. However, since indexes can occur without conominals in all stages of Coptic (ca. 30% in the corpora checked here), there is no stage of the Egyptian-Coptic language in which one can speak of gramm-indexes.

Nonetheless, one observes a diachronic tendency for index + conominal as a discourse preference or "soft constraint", realized by the high text frequency of such constructions vis-à-vis subject incorporation.

6 No case before the verb in northeast Africa

Despite Africa's reputation as a caseless continent, König (2008; 2009) has argued that many African languages should in fact be described as case languages, whether case is realized by bound forms, free forms, or tone. This characterization assumes a broad definition of the comparative concept "case marker", similar to that adopted here

Northeast Africa, with Berber as a possible geographical outlier, is characterized by a robust generalization: preverbal core arguments show no case distinctions; the form that occurs preverbally is "always in one case form only, namely, the morphologically most unmarked one" (König 2008: 240). This generalization holds regardless of alignment type, since it holds for both "marked nominative" (e.g., Turkana, Nilo-Saharan) and ergative systems (e.g., Shilluk, Nilo-Saharan).

In Päri (West Nilotic, Nilo-Saharan), which has a split ergative/ marked-nominative case system, pre-verbal A and P are in the absolute form, which does not have an overt case marker. On the other hand, post-verbal A and P show overt case markers.

(27) Päri (West Nilotic, Nilo-Saharan; Andersen 1988)

  (a) rìŋó ŋôl ùbúrr-ì ŋɔ́l-ɔ̀
       meat cut Ubur-ERG cut-SUF
       'Ubur will cut the meat.'

(b) *ùbúr ŋùt-ò*   *kí rìŋó*
    Ubur cut.CF.AP-SUF OBL meat
    'Ubur will cut the meat.'

König's generalization trivially does not apply to the majority of accusative languages of northeastern African languages in her sample, since all but one of her accusative languages are verb-final; this fact renders the generalization irrelevant, since if the "no case before the verb" generalization were to hold for a verb-final language, it would not be considered a case language.

In many of the languages in König's sample, linear order is motivated by the information structural properties of referents in discourse. In Dinka (West Nilotic, Nilo-Saharan, Andersen 1991; 2002), Nandi (Kalenjin, South Nilotic, Nilo-Saharan, König 2008: 260), Chai (Southeast Surmic, Nilo-Saharan, König 2008: 247), and Datooga (South Nilotic, Nilo-Saharan, König 2008: 261), preverbal arguments are topical. On the other hand, in Toposa (East Nilotic, Nilo-Saharan), Maa (East Nilotic, Nilo-Saharan, König 2008: 262; Payne 2013), and Tennet (König 2008: 262), preverbal arguments are generally focal. In Turkana (Nilo-Saharan), preverbal position can accommodate both topical and focal arguments (Dimmendaal 1983: 408; König 2008: 259). In Shilluk (Nilo-Saharan), it is postverbal arguments that are focal (König 2008: 243).

Kanuri (Saharan, Bondarev et al. 2011) Differential Subject Marking is motivated by the interaction of semantic and pragmatic features. The "nominative" marker *–ye* "is admissible providing they represent addressee-old information and occur with either transitive verbs/clauses or (if human) intransitive active verbs/clauses" (Bondarev et al. 2011).[14] This description is similar to that proposed for Coptic in this article.

7 Concluding remarks

As mentioned in the introduction, the goal of this article is a modest one: to draw attention to a grammatical feature that has hitherto gone unmentioned in most descriptions of Coptic: no case before the verb, obligatory case after the verb, although the Coptic facts would better be described as 'obligatory case after the verb, no case anywhere else'. From an areal point of view, this is not unexpected: Coptic closes the geographical gap, so to speak, between the main cluster of

---

14 I would like to thank Denis Creissels for pointing out to me the relevance of Kanuri, and Dmitry Bondarev for sharing his work on the language with me.

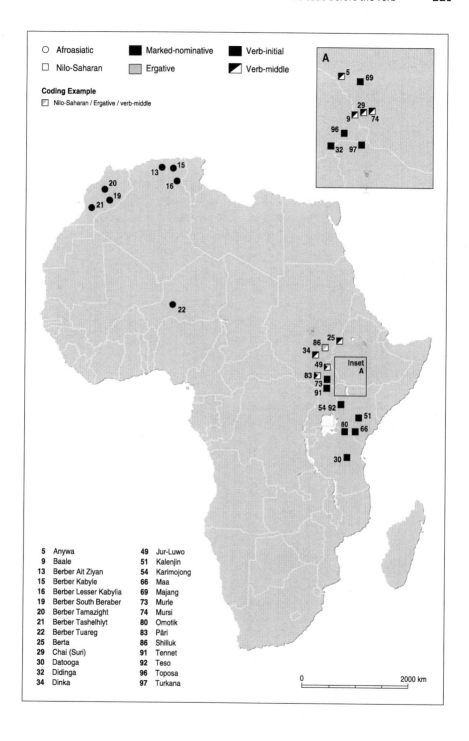

Legend:
- ○ Afroasiatic
- □ Nilo-Saharan
- ■ Marked-nominative
- (grey) Ergative
- ■ Verb-initial
- ◪ Verb-middle

Coding Example
- ◪ Nilo-Saharan / Ergative / verb-middle

5	Anywa	49	Jur-Luwo
9	Baale	51	Kalenjin
13	Berber Ait Ziyan	54	Karimojong
15	Berber Kabyle	66	Maa
16	Berber Lesser Kabylia	69	Majang
19	Berber South Beraber	73	Murle
20	Berber Tamazight	74	Mursi
21	Berber Tashelhiyt	80	Omotik
22	Berber Tuareg	83	Päri
25	Berta	86	Shilluk
29	Chai (Suri)	91	Tennet
30	Datooga	92	Teso
32	Didinga	96	Toposa
34	Dinka	97	Turkana

0   2000 km

languages in which preverbal core arguments are not overtly flagged, in north-eastern Africa, and North African Berber languages, which have until now been considered a geographical outlier. This can be seen from König's map of "no case before the verb" languages in Africa (2008: 274).

Since this feature is so striking, it is interesting to consider why it has not been explicitly mentioned in descriptions. It may be due, at least in part, to the fact that many descriptions of Coptic do not gloss examples, so there is little need to decide on labels for descriptive categories. It probably also has something to do with the fact that Coptic is not typically described as a case language.

What is interesting about the Coptic case system is not the association of postverbal subjects with antitopic status, since this seems to be cross-linguistically well attested. Nor is it its three-way case system with overt nominative and accusative, neither of which is the citation form; similar systems are attested, albeit rarely, in, e.g., Korean, Japanese, and Kanuri. Nor is it the "no case before the verb, obligatory case after the verb" feature, which is typical of the broad area in which Coptic was spoken. Rather, it is the particular constellation of these features: an overt nominative marker which differs from both the accusative and the citation form, and which obligatorily marks highly accessible postverbal subjects.

Abbreviations
The glossing conventions here are in accordance with the Leipzig Glossing Rules, and the transliteration follows the Leipzig-Jerusalem transliteration system (Grossman & Haspelmath 2014, in this volume). The following are language-specific glosses.

AOR	aorist verb form
CONN	connecting particle
MOD	modifier marker

8 References

Aikhenvald, Alexandra. 2007. Typological distinctions in word-formation. In: Shopen, Timothy (ed.), *Language Typology and Syntactic Description*. Vol. 3, *Grammatical Categories and the Lexicon*. 2nd ed. Cambridge: Cambridge University Press.

Andersen, Torben. 1988. Ergativity in Pari, a Nilotic OVS language. *Lingua* 75: 289–324.

Andersen, Torben. 1991. Subject and topic in Dinka. *Studies in Language* 15: 265–94.

Andersen, Torben. 2002. Case inflection and nominal head marking in Dinka. *Journal of African Languages and Linguistics* 23: 1–30.

Ariel, Mira. 1990. *Accessing Noun-Phrase Antecedents*. London/New York: Routledge.

Arkadiev, Peter. fc. The Kabyle "state" distinction: dependent-marking after all? A commentary on Mettouchi & Frajzyngier 2013. Ms. available http://www.academia.edu/4698192/ THE_BERBER_STATE_DISTINCTION_DEPENDENT_MARKING_AFTER_ALL_A_COMMENTARY_ ON_METTOUCHI_and_FRAJZYNGIER_2013

Bondarev, Dmitry, Jaggar, Philip J., Löhr, Doris & Tijani, Abba I. 2011. Differential subject marking in Kanuri: agentivity, pragmatics, and split-intransitive. In: Löhr, Doris, Rothmaler, Eva & Ziegelmeyer, Georg (eds.), *Kanuri, Borno and Beyond: Current Studies on the Lake Chad Region*. (Topics in Interdisciplinary African Studies 22). Köln: Rüdiger Köppe, 27–57.

Chafe, Wallace. 1976. Givenness, contrastiveness, definiteness, subjects, topics and point of view. In: Li, Charles N. (ed.), *Subject and topic*. New York: Academic Press, 25–55.

Cooreman, Ann. 1992. The pragmatics of word order variation in Chamorro narrative text. In: Payne, Doris L. (ed.), *Pragmatics of Word Order Flexibility*. Amsterdam: John Benjamins, 243–263.

Creissels, Denis. 2009. Uncommon patterns of core term marking and case terminology. *Lingua* 119: 445–459.

Dimmendaal, Gerrit. 1983. Turkana as a verb-initial language. *Journal of African Languages and Linguistics 5*: 17–44.

Dixon, Robert M.W. 1988. *A Grammar of Boumaa Fijian*. Chicago/London: University of Chicago Press.

Du Bois, John. 1987. The Discourse Basis of Ergativity. *Language* 63: 805–855.

Eaton, Helen. 2010. Information structure marking in Sandawe texts. In: Fiedler, Ines & Schwarz, Anne (eds.), *The Expression of Information Structure: A documentation of its diversity across Africa*. Amsterdam/Philadelphia: John Benjamins, 1–34.

Engsheden, Åke. 2008. Differential Object Marking in Coptic. In: Josephson, F. & Söhrman, I. (eds.), *Forms and Functions: Aspect, Tense, Mood, Diathesis and Valency*. Amsterdam: John Benjamins, 323–344.

Frajzyngier, Zygmunt. 2011. Les functions de l'ordre lineaire. *Bulletin de la Société Linguistique de Paris* CV.1: 7–37.

Frajzyngier, Zygmunt & Shay, Erin. 2003. *Explaining language structure through systems interaction*. Amsterdam/Philadelphia: John Benjamins.

Funk, Wolf-Peter. 1988. Dialects wanting homes: a numerical approach to the early varieties of Coptic. In: Fisiak, Jacek (ed.), *Historical dialectology: Regional and Social*. Berlin/New York/Amsterdam: Mouton de Gruyter, 149–192.

Givón, Talmy. 1977. The Drift from VSO to SVO in Biblical Hebrew: the Pragmatics of Tense-Aspect. In: Li, Charles N. (ed.), *Mechanisms of Syntactic Change*. Austin: University of Texas Press, 184–254.

Good, Jeff. 2010. Topic and focus fields in Naki. In: Fiedler, Ines & Schwarz, Anne (eds.), *The Expression of Information Structure: A documentation of its diversity across Africa*. Amsterdam/Philadelphia: John Benjamins, 35–67.

Goldenberg, Gideon. 1983. On Syriac Sentence Structure. In: Sokoloff, Michael (ed.), *Arameans, Aramaic, and the Aramaic Literary Tradition*. Ramat Gan: Bar-Ilan University Press, 97–140.

Grossman, Eitan. 2009a. *Studies in Early Bohairic Syntax*. PhD thesis. Hebrew University of Jerusalem.

Grossman, Eitan. 2009b. Periphrastic Perfects in the Coptic Dialects: A Case Study in Grammaticalization. *Lingua Aegyptia* 17: 81–118.

Grossman, Eitan & Iemmolo, Giorgio. 2014+. A rare case of differential marking on A/S: the case of Coptic. Paper presented at the Association for Linguistic Typology 10th Biennial Conference, Leipzig 2013.

Haspelmath, Martin. 2008. Terminology of Case. In: Malchukov, Andrej & Spencer, Andrew (eds.), *The Oxford Handbook of Case*. Oxford: Oxford University Press, 505–517.

Haspelmath, Martin. 2011a. The indeterminacy of word segmentation and the nature of morphology and syntax. *Folia Linguistica* 45.2: 31–80.

Haspelmath, Martin. 2011b. On S, A, P, T, and R as comparative concepts for alignment typology. *Linguistic Typology* 15: 535–567.

Haspelmath, Martin. 2013. Argument indexing: a conceptual framework for the syntactic status of bound person forms. In: Bakker, Dik & Haspelmath, Martin (eds.), *Languages across boundaries: Studies in memory of Anna Siewierska*. Berlin: Mouton de Gruyter.

Haspelmath, Martin. 2014. A grammatical overview of Egyptian and Coptic. This volume.

Hyslop, Gwendolyn. 2010. Kurtop case: the pragmatic ergative and beyond. *Linguistics of the Tibeto-Burman area* 33.1: 1–40.

Iemmolo, Giorgio. 2010. Topicality and differential object marking: evidence from Romance and beyond. *Studies in Language* 34.2: 239–272.

Johnson, Janet H. 1976. *The Demotic Verbal System*. (Studies in Ancient Oriental Civilization 38). Chicago: Oriental Institute.

König, Christa. 2008. *Case in Africa*. Oxford: Oxford University Press.

König, Christa. 2009. Marked Nominatives. In: Malchukov, Andrej & Spencer, Andrew (eds.), *The Oxford Handbook of Case*. Oxford: Oxford University Press, 534–548.

Lambrecht, Knud. 1981. *Topic, Antitopic, and Verb Agreement in Non-Standard French*. Amsterdam: John Benjamins.

Layton, Bentley. 2004. *A Coptic Grammar. Sahidic Dialect*. Wiesbaden: Harrassowitz.

Lazard, Gilbert. 2002. Transitivity revisited as an example of a more strict approach in typological research. *Folia Linguistica* 36.3–4: 141–190.

Loprieno, Antonio. 2000. From VSO to SVO? Word Order and Rear Extraposition in Coptic. In: Sornicola, Rosanna, Poppe, Erich & Shisha-Halevy, Ariel (eds.), *Stability, Variation and Change of Word Order Patterns over Time*. Amsterdam/Philadelphia: John Benjamins, 23–39.

Mattha, Girgis. 1947. The Origin of the Explanatory Particles n and *nci/nče*. *Bulletin de l'Institut Français d'Archéologie Orientale* 45: 61–64.

McGregor, William. 2006. Focal and optional ergative marking in Warrwa (Kimberley, Western Australia). *Lingua* 116: 393–423.

Mettouchi, Amina & Frajzyngier, Zygmunt. 2013. A previously unrecognized typological category: The state distinction in Kabyle (Berber). *Linguistic Typology* 17: 1–30.

Mithun, Marianne. 1996. The Mohawk language. In: Maurais, Jacques (ed.), *Quebec's Aboriginal Languages: History, Planning and Development*. Clevedon/Avon, England: Multilingual Matters, 159–173.

Payne, Doris L. 1992. Nonidentifiable information and pragmatic order rules in 'O'odham. In: Payne, Doris L. (ed.), *Pragmatics of Word Order Flexibility*. Amsterdam: John Benjamins, 137–167.

Payne, Doris L. 2013. Grammatical Relations and Alignment. In: Luraghi, Silvia & Parodi, Claudia (eds.), *Bloomsbury Companion to Syntax*. London/New Delhi/New York/Sydney: Bloomsbury, 218–239.

Polotsky, Hans Jakob. 1960. The Coptic Conjugation System. *Orientalia* 29: 392–422.

Prince, Ellen. 1981. Toward a Taxonomy of Given-New Information. In: Cole, Peter (ed.), *Radical Pragmatics*. New York: Academic Press, 223–254.

Reintges, Chris. 2004. *Coptic Egyptian (Sahidic Dialect)*. Köln: Rüdiger Köppe.

Shisha-Halevy, Ariel. 1986. *Coptic Grammatcial Categories. Structural Studies in the Syntax of Shenoutean Sahidic*. Roma: Pontificium Institutum Biblicum.

Shisha-Halevy, Ariel. 1988. *Coptic Grammatical Chrestomathy*. Leuven: Peeters.

Shisha-Halevy, Ariel. 2007. *Topics in Coptic Syntax: Structural Studies in the Bohairic Dialect*. Leuven/Paris/Dudley, MA: Peeters.

Siewierska, Anna & Bakker, Dik. 2008. Case and alternative strategies. In: Malchukov, Andrej & Spencer, Andrew (eds.), *Handbook of Case*. Oxford: Oxford University Press, 290–303.

Tomlin, Russell S. & Rhodes, Richard A. 1992. Information distribution in Ojibwa. In: Payne, Doris L. (ed.), *Pragmatics of Word Order Flexibility*. Amsterdam: John Benjamins, 117–135.

Verstraete, Jean-Christophe. 2010. Animacy and information structure in the system of ergative marking in Umpithamu. *Lingua* 120: 1637–1651.

Winand, Jean. 2014. The Oblique Expression of the Object in Ancient Egyptian. This volume.

Zakrewska, Ewa 2006. The Hero, the Villain and the Mob: Topicality and Focality in Bohairic Narrative Discourse. *Lingua Aegyptia* 14: 325–346.

Tom Güldemann

How typology can inform philology: quotative *j(n)* in Earlier Egyptian*

Abstract: Egyptian displays a quite versatile element *j(n)*. In its frequent use as a quotative marker in reported discourse, it has simply been treated as a verb 'say'. However, according to a cross-linguistic study by Güldemann (2008) quotative indexes are frequently not expressions based on speech verbs and structures like, e.g., *(s)he said* are often not the starting point of further grammaticalization; a number of other quotative structures turn out to be subject to change more frequently. These findings also throw new light on the history of quotative *j(n)* in Earlier Egyptian. One can make a good case for the hypothesis that quotative indexes based on *j(n)* originate in a non-verbal identificational clause 'it is ...' which only later assumed more predicate-like properties. This hypothesis also provides a better unified account for the non-quotative functions of *jn*. This paper thus demonstrates that diachronic typology can fruitfully inform historical philology.

1 Egyptian *j(n)* as a grammatically versatile element

1.1 Quotative *j(n)* through Egyptian history

Since early on, Egyptologists have been concerned with the element *j(n)* in its very frequent use as a marker of reported speech. That is, it is the structural nucleus of a "quotative index" which I define as the expression used by the reporter to signal in his/her discourse the occurrence of an adjacent reported discourse (see Güldemann 2008: 10–15). Faulkner (1935) in his detailed historical treatment of *j(n)* views it like most other scholars as a speech verb 'say'. He argues that it is attested in several conjugational forms: securely in the *infinitive*,[1] the *old*

---

* My thanks go to the editors of this volume, Guy Deutscher, Orin Gensler, Birgit Jordan, Wolfgang Schenkel, and especially Andréas Stauder for commenting on earlier drafts of this paper and helping me with their philological expertise.
1 Throughout the article I will use italics for philological terms.

perfective/stative, the *sḏm-n-f* form, and the *sḏm-f* form; and possibly also in the *relative* and *imperative*. While this range of verbal categories might suggest that it is indeed a canonical verb lexeme, it is functionally restricted to direct reported discourse constructions and is not used as a normal speech verb 'say' outside this context. Example (1) shows a typical occurrence of *j(n)* (glossed here as "quotative (marker)") in a quotative index that follows the quote.

(1) {*m*   *twt*   *n-f*}   ***jn***   ***psḏ-(tj)***   ***wr-t***
     {who resemble:PAP for-3M.S}   Q:PST Ennead-F.D be.great:PAP-F
     ˤ₃-t
     be.great:PAP-F
     "Who is like him?" said the Two Great and Powerful Enneads. (Kammerzell & Peust 2002: 302; Pyr. 1689cM)

Another remarkable property of *j(n)* is that it is actually not used in all conjugation forms but is part of a stem paradigm formed by it and two other suppletive counterparts, together called *parenthetic (verb)s* (cf., e.g., Gardiner 1957: 347–348; Allen 2000: 312–314). The other two elements, *ḥr* and *k₃*, are equally translated simply as 'say' but assigned to other TAM values; they are illustrated in (2) and (3).

(2) {*j.dr-f*   *dw-t*   *jr-t-k*   *Pjpj*   *pw*}
     {remove:SUBJ-3M.S   evil:PAP-F   against-ADJR:F-2M.S   PN   DEM}
     ḥr   ***(J)tm(w)***
     Q:PRS Atum
     "He shall remove the evil which is against you, o Pijaapij", says Atum. (Kammerzell & Peust 2002: 302; Pyr. 840cP)

(3) {*jn-m*   *j.jr*   *n-k*}   ***k₃-sn***
     {TF-who   act:PAP   for-2M.S}   Q:FUT/POT-3P
     "Who is the one who acts for you?", they may ask. (Kammerzell & Peust 2002: 303; in Pyr. *1942a–cNtb)

The functional restriction of *j(n)* to reported discourse and its limited conjugational paradigm involving stem suppletion suggest that it is not a speech verb like English *say*, French *dire*, etc. but rather a defective verb specialized to a particular context, a so-called "quotative verb (QV)" in terms of Güldemann (2008) – a characterization which also applies to *ḥr* and *k₃*. The tripartite stem paradigm in quotative verb forms in Earlier Egyptian (subsuming Old and Middle Egyptian), together with their commonly associated TAM features, is given in Table 1.

Table 1: The quotative verb paradigm in Earlier Egyptian

Form	TAM value	Syntactic distribution
k3-	Future	before suffix pronoun
ḥr(-)	Present	before noun and suffix pronoun
jn(-)	Preterite	before noun and plural suffix pronoun
j-	Stative	before singular suffix pronoun

Several authors (e.g., Faulkner 1935: 187–188; Kammerzell & Peust 2002: 303) have observed that the same suppletive verb paradigm has served as input for auxiliary periphrases which function as clause operators, including the marking of interclausal contingency (see especially Depuydt 1989); whereby, according to Faulkner (1935: 187), the auxiliation of *jn* and *ḥr* may have been modelled on *k3*. The major functions identified are summarized in Table 2. Güldemann (2005: 134–135) argues that this process is a variation on a typologically more common theme whereby semantically generic items grammaticalize in parallel (as two separate processes) into quotative markers and auxiliaries; that is, the quotative function is not necessarily a precondition for the auxiliation process.

Table 2: The quotative verb paradigm as the source of auxiliary periphrases

Form	Function in simple clause	Function in clause linkage
stem-*k3*	Potential	Future/irrealis in conditional apodosis
stem-*ḥr*	Obligation	Aorist/realis in conditional apodosis
stem-*jn*	Narrative	Consecutive

The element *j(n)* (like *ḥr* and *k3*), as the structural nucleus of the quotative index, is intimately associated with the expression of the "speaker"-referent of the quote. Three simple and two more complex patterns can be identified.

a. [*jn* Speaker.noun]   (cf. (1) and the two first tokens of (4))
b. [*jn*-Speaker.suffix]   (only 3rd plural/dual)
c. [*j*-Speaker.suffix]   (only singular) (cf. the two last tokens of (4))
d. [*j(n)*-Speaker.suffix Speaker.noun]
e. [*j(n)*-Speaker.suffix *jn* Speaker.noun]

Apart from the fact that quotative indexes containing *j(n)* can be accompanied by a prepositional phrase referring to the addressee of the quote, their overall morphosyntax follows two major patterns. The simpler structure has quotative *j(n)* either after the quote, as illustrated in (1) above, or inserted within the quote in a kind of clause-second position.

As shown in schema (I) and illustrated in (4), multiple occurrences of *j(n)* are possible in one and the same reported discourse construction; both quotes in (4) display the first quotative index after the vocative nominal and the second one after the main utterance. This versatile behavior of *j(n)* yields a range of order types: quotative indexes are postposed, intraposed, or combine intraposition with postposition.

(I) [{QUOTE} *j(n)*-SPEAKER {QUOTE} (*j(n)*-SPEAKER)]

(4) {*m'w-t(-j)*}   ***jyn*** [sic] ***Pjpj Nfr.k₃.Rᶜ(w)***
{mother-F-1S} Q:PST   PN
"My mother!" said Pijaapij Nafirkkarliiduw,

{*jm   n(-j   mnd̲-t   snq(-j)   sw*}   ***jyn   Pjpj Nfr.k₃.Rᶜ(w)***
{give:IMP for-1S breast-2F.S suck:SUBJ-1S 3M.S} Q:PST PN
"give me your breast that I may suck it" said Pijaapij Nafirkkarliiduw.

{*z₃(-j)*} *j-t*   ***jr   Pjpj Nfr.k₃.Rᶜ(w)***
{son-1S} Q:STAT-3F.S to   PN
"My son" said she to Pijaapij Nafirkkarliiduw,

{*m   n-k   mnd̲(-j)   snq   sw*}   ***j-t***
{take:IMP for-2M.S breast-1S suck:IMP 3M.S} Q:STAT-3F.S
"take my breast and suck it," said she. (after Kammerzell & Peust 2002: 301; Pyr. 911b–912aN)

Regarding the second pattern of intraposed quotative indexes with *j(n)*, Kammerzell & Peust (2002: 302) write as follows:

> "Sporadically, an inflected form of *j-* 'say' [= *j(n)*] is inserted into direct speech, which is preceded by [the speech verb 'say'] *d̲d-*. Whether this fairly tautological aggregation of quotation signals reflects actual usage of spoken Old Egyptian or should rather be considered a specific device of certain religious texts cannot be decided. Be that as it may, ... cases of double quotation index ... display a diction that is repetitive to some extent not only in respect of embedding marks."

In other words, the above simple pattern [*j(n)* Speaker] is combined with a second phrase that contains the speech verb *d̲d* 'say' within a so-called "bipartite" structure (see Güldemann 2008: 118–141) and occurs before the quote, as schematized in (II) and illustrated in (5).

This type of quotative index involves a circumpositional structure or alternatively a combination of preposed and intraposed material.

(II) [*ḏd*-SPEAKER {QUOTE} *j(n)*-SPEAKER ({QUOTE})]

(5) *wjj   Rʿ(w)* **nw   rf   ḏd-n-k**   ***Rʿ(w)*** {*ḥwj z3(j)*}
EXCL PN   DEM TF   say:REL-PST-2M.S   PN   {be it that my son}
O Re, this is just what you have said, Re: "Be it that my son",

j-t   **tw   *Rʿ(w)*** {*b3j sḥmj w3śj*}
Q:STAT-2M.S 2M.S PN   {is besouled, is mighty, is strong}
so you said, you, Re, "is besouled, is mighty, and is strong!" (Kammerzell
& Peust 2002: 302; Pyr. 886a–bP)

The typological study by Güldemann (2008: 118–41) demonstrates that bipartite structures combining a speech verb with a grammaticalized quotative marker are cross-linguistically very common and need not be considered to be an idiosyncrasy of particular text types of Earlier Egyptian. That is, the Egyptian pattern in (II) can be compared to an equally bipartite English phrase *(s)he said that* except that, as opposed to English, it is not restricted to indirect reported discourse and the speech verb *ḏd* and the grammatical element *j(n)* are not adjacent.

J(n) in early Later Egyptian (which as a whole subsumes Late Egyptian, Demotic, and Coptic) displays a quite different profile, as summarized by Faulkner (1935: 184):

> "Late Egyptian uses *jn* 'say' in a manner somewhat different from the older stages of the language, inasmuch as a pronominal dative of the person addressed is usually, though not invariably, appended, and *ḥr ḏd* 'speaking' is often added as well. Further, while in the older language *jn* generally has the nominal subject expressed in one way or another ..., and the pronominal subject without further addition ... is relatively rare, the reverse holds good of Late Egyptian, the indication of the nominal subject (always with *m* or *n* 'namely' ...) being in the minority. It should also be observed that in Late-Egyptian texts *jn* is invariably written ... with [the] determinative [for 'speak']. Yet another point of difference between Old and Middle Egyptian on the one hand, and Late Egyptian on the other, is that in the former only the suffixes 3rd plural or dual are found with [*jn*], whereas in Late Egyptian [*jn* with determinative] is found with suffixes of all persons, singular and plural, with the exception of the 2nd fem[inine]. sing[ular]."

Compare in this respect Table 3 which displays the quotative paradigms in Earlier and Later Egyptian as well as two series of pronominal forms which partly play a role in the quotative indexes (for pronouns, see Gardiner 1957: 45/§ 43, 39/§ 34, 53/§ 64 and Loprieno 1995: 63–66). The comparison of the quotative forms shows that the later paradigm no longer shows a difference between old perfective/stative in the singular and a *sḏm-n-f* form in the plural but has a regular series based on the *n*-stem followed by a suffix pronoun.

Table 3: Pronouns and quotative forms in Egyptian

Person Gender Number	Dependent pronoun	Suffix pronoun	Quotative in Earlier Egyptian (Allen 1984: 109–12/§ 206–9)	Quotative in Later Egyptian (Erman 1933: 357/§ 714)
1S	*wj*	*-j*	*j-kj*	*j-n-j*
2F.S	*ṯn*	*-ṯ*	*j-t(j) ṯn*	-
2M.S	*ṯw*	*-k*	*j-t(j) ṯw*	*j-n-k*
3F.S	*sy*	*-s*	*j-t(j) (jn* Nominal)	*j-n-s*
3M.S	*sw*	*-f*	*j-(j) jn* Nominal	*j-n-f*
1P	*n*	*-n*	-	-
2P	*ṯn*	*-ṯn*	-	-
3P	*sn, (st)*	*-sn, (-w)*	*j-n-sn ((jn)* Nominal)	*j-n-w*
Noun			*jn* Nominal	-

The major conclusion to be drawn from the above quote and Table 3 is that the incidence of personal endings on *j(n)* referring to the speaker has increased and become conjugationally regular, while the pattern of bare *jn* followed by a nominal reference to the speaker has lost in salience. In other words, the frequency of *j(n)*-forms which are most verb-like is higher in younger than in older chronolects of Egyptian.

Another difference of quotative indexes in Later Egyptian has been noted by Kammerzell & Peust (2002: 304–305), namely that the speech verb *ḏd* 'say' has also become more frequent. The major relevant structures of such quotative indexes in Later Egyptian are schematized below: besides the bipartite quotative-index pattern (II) with *j(n)* one now finds also the new patterns (III)–(V) which lack *j(n)* altogether. The overall salience of quotative indexes with *ḏd* implies that Pattern (I) with bare *jn* has decreased in frequency.

(II)	[*ḏd*-SPEAKER	{QUOTE} *j(n)*-SPEAKER ({quote})]	
(III)	[*ḏd*-SPEAKER	{QUOTE}]	
(IV)	[*ḏd*-SPEAKER COMPLEMENTIZER	{QUOTE}]	
(V)		[{QUOTE} *ḏd*-SPEAKER]	(rare)

1.2 A case for identificational *jn* in Egyptian

After outlining the basic facts of *j(n)* as a marker of quotations, I will turn to a particle with a largely similar form *jn* which is attested early on in a variety of other grammatical functions. The only obvious common denominator of these *jn*s, which don't have any similarity with a verb, is their scope over a constituent immediately following them. The major contexts are:

(I)   [*jn* Noun (phrase)]
(II) [*jn* Pronoun]
(III) [*jn* Clause]

Like Loprieno (1988: 77–98) and Reintges (1997: 159–184, 196–211; 1998) I will propose here a unified account of all the different uses of this *jn*. The major difference between my analysis and theirs is that I consider the primary function of *jn* to be that of an identificational or presentational particle, functionally identical with but syntactically different from English 'it/this/that/there is', which is based on a true copula verb preceded by a pronominal element. This proposal avoids some unnecessarily complex syntactic accounts associated with the earlier analyses, especially the one viewing *jn* in all contexts as a focus marker.

The first of the three groups of *jn*-uses involves a nuclear constituent of the structure [*jn* NOMINAL] which is always part of a more complex structure. One such structure can be characterized as a bipartite cleft-like sentence (Gardiner 1957: 175–176/§ 227.2+3; Callender 1971; Reintges 1997: 168–172; 1998). Here, *jn* precedes a noun which is syntactically exposed in a non-canonical position at the beginning of the sentence and followed by an out-of-focus clause containing the proposition; this can be schematized as: [[*jn* NOMINAL] (Background).clause]. This construction serves to mark contrastive focus on nominal constituents (called here term focus in line with Dik 1997) and is also used regularly with initial content-question words; both contexts are illustrated in the quotes of example (3) above. There are also cases of this construction where a functional analysis in terms of term focus is not satisfactory. These cases cannot be dealt with here; suffice it to say that a similar polyfunctionality of cleft-like sentences has been reported from other languages, whereby the non-focus uses are analyzed as entity-central thetic statements (cf. Sasse 1987; Güldemann 2010). Whatever the ultimate solution here, the use of *jn* in all these cleft-like structures can be derived transparently from an original function as a non-verbal identificational or presentational marker, quite parallel to Diessel's (1999: 148–149) scenario for the emergence of focus markers from demonstrative identifiers. This hypothesis thus deviates from Reintges' (1997: 165–168; 1998) proposal, who argues that *jn* was originally a true verbal copula 'be' with a phonologically null expletive pronoun.

The assumption that *jn* originates in an identificational or presentational marker is corroborated indirectly by another sentence pattern involving a constituent [*jn* Nominal]. Here a particle *jn* precedes the agent nominal in passive sentences so that *jn* has also been characterized as an agentive preposition (Gardiner 1957: 42/§ 39, 176/§ 227.4, 128–129/§ 168).[2] The sentence structure [Passive. clause [*jn* Agent.nominal]] is illustrated in (6).

(6) *ḏd-tw*   *r*   *pn*   *ỉn*   *s*
    say-PASS utterance DEM AGENT man
    This utterance is (to be) said by a man. (Gardiner 1957: 42)

That this agentive *jn* is very likely to be derived through a grammaticalization process from the identificational *jn* treated previously can be argued on typological grounds because of clear parallels in other languages where this analysis is synchronically still transparent. Several cases can be cited from Bantu languages, one such language being Tswana.[3] Example (7) first demonstrates the pattern of simple identificational clauses.

(7) Tswana (Bantu, Niger-Congo)

    a. *ké-nna*
       ID-1S
       It is I.

    b. *ké-kgôsi*
       ID-chief
       It is a chief. (Cole 1955: 313, 315)

That the same structure is involved in agent noun-phrases is clearly stated by Cole (1955: 368) in the following quote and illustrated in (8):

> "Agentive adverbs, indicating the agent of an action, are formed from substantives by prefixing *ké-*, which conveys the significance of the English 'by'. Agentive adverbs are used exclusively after passive verbs, and are identical in formation with the simple impersonal copulative of identificative type."

---

2 There is a less frequent alternative with *ḥr* 'on' (Gardiner 1957: 42/§ 39, 128/§ 167).
3 Cf. also Abels & Muriungi (2006: 5) and Lanham (1955: 141, footnote 1) for parallel cases in Tharaka and Tonga-Inhambane, respectively.

(8) a. *thôlô   yônê e-bolailwê   ké-nna*
kudu.9   9:PRO 9-kill:PST:PASS   AGENT/ID-1S
The kudu, as for it, was killed by me.

b. *ke-rom-ilwê   ké-kgôsi*
1S-send-PST:PASS   AGENT/ID-CHIEF
I have been sent by the chief.   (Cole 1955: 368)

The case of agent marking in Egyptian passives can be analyzed in a parallel fashion: identificational *jn*, like identificational *ké* in Tswana, has come to be used in a kind of secondary predicate; this marks an agent participant of passive clauses that is syntactically peripheral but, vis-à-vis a topical subject agent, pragmatically more prominent. It is unclear but of secondary importance here whether or not this agentive use of *jn* was actually grammaticalized to the extent that speakers of Egyptian no longer perceived it to be related to its identificational predecessor.

Starting out from his analysis of *jn* as a focus marker, Reintges (1997: 159–184, 196–211; 1998) has argued for a similar derivation of agentive *jn:* "agentive passives are biclausal configurations which are composed of an agentless passive and a truncated cleft-sentence" (1997: 172), whereby *jn* foregrounds the identity of the agent referent. Again, the present analysis of *jn* as an identificational marker turns out to be simpler. It can account on the one hand for exposing a nominal in a cleft discussed previously and on the other hand for simply identifying a non-topical agent nominal in the passive structure at issue here. At the same time, in the passive context it does not imply any kind of omission of an underlying out-of-focus clause from a complex focus cleft structure (note that there is also no evidence for such a "truncation" in the parallel structure of relevant Bantu languages, as shown in (8)).

In a third context, the constituent [*jn* Nominal] is found to be simply inserted in different types of clauses, identifying a certain participant. This is exemplified in (9) and (10).

(9) *ìn   ìwꜥ-(ì)   pw   ...swt rdì n-ì s(y)*
ID   heir-1S   DEM   he has given it to me
it is this (my) heir ... he has given it to me (Gardiner 1957: 176; LAC.TR. 47,35–6)

(10) *smn-s wỉ*   **ỉn**   **ꜣst** *ḥr*   *ꜣkr*
she establishes me   ID   Isis on   earth
she establishes me, does (lit. by) [rather: that/it is] Isis, on Earth (Gardiner 1957: 176; LAC.TR. 43,5.)

While Gardiner (1957: 176/§ 227.5) views this context as an "extension of the prepositional [i.e., agentive] use of *ỉn*", I venture that one is confronted here with its most basic identificational function, which sometimes is even seen in his own original translation, as in (9).

After arguing for the underlying structural unity of [*ỉn* Nominal]-constructions, I turn to the second morphosyntactic pattern of *ỉn* which can be characterized as [*ỉn*-Pronoun]. That is, *ỉn* can be identified as a kind of initial "stabilizer" in complex *independent* pronouns which also involve the suffix pronouns. Table 4 shows major pronominal paradigms for comparison, except for dual forms which are not relevant for the present discussion (cf. Gardiner 1957: 45/§ 43, 39/§ 34, 53/§ 64, 100/§ 125; Loprieno 1995: 63–66).

Table 4: Pronominal elements in Earlier Egyptian

Category	Stative	Independent or Stressed	Suffix	Dependent or Clitic
1s	-kj	jn-k	-j	wj
2F.S	-tj	(j)n-t-t	-t	tn
2M.S	-tj	(j)n-t-k	-k	tw
3F.S	-tj	(j)n-t-s	-s	sj
3M.S	-j	(j)n-t-f	-f	sw
1P	-wjn	jn-n	-n	n
2P	-twjn	(j)n-t-tn	-tn	tn
3P	-wj/-tj	(j)n-t-sn	-sn	sn, (st)

That the independent pronouns are structurally parallel to the pattern [*ỉn* Nominal] is suggested partly by their formal similarity; it is first of all obscured by the medial *t*-element (see Kammerzell (1991) for an attempt to explain this as the result of analogy with and generalization of the similar *t(j)* in the stative endings, as shown in the leftmost column of Table 4). The more striking affinity relates to the fact that the pronoun series replaces paradigmatically the constituent [*ỉn* Nominal] in all contexts outlined above except for the passive. In other words, *ỉn* in independent pronouns can be equally viewed as originating in a marker meaning 'it/that/there is', the difference being that this phrasal constituent, when involving pronouns, developed further to a plain nominal constituent without assertive identificational force.

The third basic structural context of the particle *jn* is [*jn* Clause]. This is especially salient in polar questions (Gardiner 1957: 175/§ 227.1, 403–404/§ 492–494) but is also attested in emphatic declaratives (cf. Reintges 1997: 163–164; 1998).[4] While the relation of this *jn* to identificational *jn* may appear less obvious, even here a link can be made as soon as one considers that both polar questions and emphatic declaratives focus on the truth value of an utterance, as also pointed out by Reintges (ibid.). While I cannot cite a case outside Egyptian where an identificational marker has been recruited to mark this function specifically in questions, it is attested in its affirmative declarative counterpart; Güldemann (1996), for example, shows in several Bantu languages that clause-initial identificational and presentational markers can have scope over an entire clause, which can be paraphrased as 'It is (the case) that …', and in this use have come to encode predication focus involving in particular truth value-focus. It is thus not far-fetched to hypothesize that a similar process has happened with identificational *jn* in Egyptian – the major difference being that it seems to have been more salient in the interrogative counterpart of the type 'Is it (the case) that …?'.

1.3   The history of *jn* in previous accounts

The Egyptological linguistic tradition has proposed three main historical hypotheses about the origin of quotative indexes with *j(n)*. Erman & Grapow (1926–31) simply consider the stem *j(n)* to be a normal speech verb 'say', implying that the quotative indexes are phrases of the pattern [X say]. Gardiner (1957: 347–348/§ 436) views the *jn*-forms as reduced from a full verb form of the type *ḏd-jn-f* based on *ḏd* 'say', resulting from the omission of the main verb. While the two previous hypotheses cannot account satisfactorily for the stem alternation between *jn* and *j*, Faulkner (1935), following Sethe, argues that the original form was a speech verb *j* 'say' and the *jn*-stem represents the *sḏm-n-f* form of this verb. While the three analyses differ in detail, they all have in common that *j* / *jn* has an exclusively verbal source.

With respect to the deeper history of *j(n)* and in particular the relation between the quotative and identificational functions, at least three hypotheses can be identified. Faulkner (1935) tries to account for the polyfunctionality of *jn*

---

4 According to E. Grossman, a similar situation holds for the proclitic *pe* in Coptic: it is also used in questions (with a clear negative implication) as well as in emphatic affirmative declaratives.

exclusively from within Earlier Egyptian: *j* 'say', as the ultimate source, first developed to *jn* 'say', which in turn yielded the other more grammaticalized functions of *jn* as an auxiliary, a term focus marker, an agent preposition, and a pronoun base. Suffice it to say that this scenario has no clear cross-linguistic parallels, nor are the individual steps towards the different grammatical functions motivated plausibly in functional and morphosyntactic terms.

Petráček's (1983) quite different scenario fares better in this respect, even though it considers data from all over Afroasiatic which are necessarily less certain in terms of historical-comparative principles. According to his hypothesis, the starting point was an old perception verb **N* 'see'. In a first step, 'see' developed via a kind of presentational marker parallel to French *voici/voilà* to a copula **N* 'be'. This copula in turn is assumed to be the predecessor of **N* as a focus marker, agent marker, and pronoun base. While the two scenarios differ greatly, there is again a common denominator between the two in that the grammatical elements are derived from lexical items, either from 'say' or from 'see'.

"A new – in some of its far reaching conclusions not utterly convincing – hypothesis on the origin of *jn*-" (Kammerzell & Peust 2002: 303), which also assumes a deeper historical perspective, namely Pre-Proto-Afroasiatic, has been proposed by Chetveruchin (1988). Against the Egyptological and, for that matter, general linguistic canon, he argues for the reversed directionality from a grammatical element to a quotative/speech verb:

> "At so archaic a stage [Pre-Proto-Afroasiatic] it is hardly to expect a successive formal division of semantemes in parts of speech, quite the contrary, a marked degree of functional interchange lability may be well supposed. This accepted, it would be reasonable to admit some root-morphemes meaning 'to see' and 'to say' being worked out of something like deictic bases in the course of nomination process: 'lo/here/this/now' (an object being at a certain distance from the speakers, or some event, process, action, just attracting attention of the speakers) > 'to point out at' > 'to nominate/to inform' > 'to speak of' > 'to say'; 'to point (out) at' > 'to look at' > 'to see'." (Chetveruchin 1988: 82)

> "To sum up, we would like to show that the deictic material should be in no case neglected while reconstructing the lexico-grammatical development of the [Egyptian] language." (Chetveruchin 1988: 84)

I will come back to the history of Egyptian *j(n)* in general and Chetveruchin's hypothesis in particular after the following section, where I discuss cross-linguistic data of relevance for the general history of quotative indexes.

2 Quotative sources from a typological perspective

The traditional ideas that (a) a quotative index comprises a verbal predicate based on a speech verb and that (b) grammatical function words develop from lexical items, are certainly plausible in principle and have securely attested precedents in other languages. Nevertheless, I will now argue that in the particular case of Egyptian *j(n)* they do not yield the best historical account of how its different functions are related to each other.

This new approach is based in particular on the results of a crosslinguistic study of 39 African languages (Güldemann 2008) in which a corpus of more than 3200 tokens of quotative indexes with direct quotes were analyzed in synchronic and diachronic terms, supplemented by extensive data on quotative indexes in other African and non-African languages. The results which are most relevant for a historical evaluation of Egyptian *j(n)* will be presented in the following (the reader is referred to the above source for more details).

2.1 Basic morphosyntactic types of quotative indexes

A first general outcome of the cross-linguistic investigation of quotative indexes is a morphosyntactic typology of these structures; it relates to the structure of normal verbal clauses in that a particular quotative index pattern is characterized by the way it is similar to or differs from it. The four main types that I distinguish are listed below.

(I)   Monoclausal (simplex) quotative index
(II) Monoclausal bipartite quotative index
(III) Biclausal bipartite quotative index
(IV) Non-clausal quotative index

The structure least marked in comparison to a canonical verbal clause is the monoclausal quotative index. The usual subtype is based on a speech verb, focusing on the event representation, as in (11). However, monoclausal quotative indexes also commonly recruit non-speech verbs, as in (12). These include so-called quotative verbs, which are functionally restricted to this grammatical expression and lack a transparent lexical meaning outside reported discourse.

(11) English (Germanic, Indo-European)

   He **said** to me, {Come back tomorrow!}

(12) Lamba (Bantu, Niger-Congo)

   aŵa-ku-mushi **ka-ŵema**   *ŵonse*   {*tukalipile ...*}
   2-LOC-village   THET-2:start 2:all   {let us pay ...}
   All the people of the village started off (saying), "Let us pay ..." (Madan 1908: 62)

In the second basic type, a monoclausal bipartite quotative index, a simple clausal structure is elaborated by a grammaticalized particle which regularly indicates the presence of a quote, as does *ká* (derived from a deictic) in (13) and *ti* (from 'like') in (14); such an element is commonly called a quotative marker or complementizer.

(13) Mwaghavul (Chadic, Afroasiatic)

   {*là!*} **ká** *xə̀n* **m̀ná-ná-tà**
   {go!} Q 3P say-3S-?
   They told him to go [lit.: they said like this, "Go!"] (Frajzyngier 1996: 130)

(14) Namibian Khoekhoe (Khoe, Khoe-Kwadi)

   o-s   *ge*   {*//nās ge sada îsa ge hapu kaikhoesa*
   then-3F.S.SBJ DECL {that is the woman who ate our mother
   o tita ge saita}   **ti** *go* **mî**
   and I am your elder sister}   Q PST say
   then she said like, "That is the woman who ate our mother, and I am your elder sister"
   (Und sie sagte: "Das ist die Frau, die unsere Mutter gefressen hat, und ich bin eure ältere Schwester." Schmidt 1994: 140)

The third type, a biclausal bipartite quotative index, also consists of a basic clause and an additional conventionalized constituent orienting the audience towards the presence of the quote; this quote orienter, however, is clause-like; hence the term biclausal. This structure is illustrated in (15) with a secondary predicate based on the quotative verb *ní* and (16) with a converb form of 'say'.

(15) Yoruba (Defoid, Niger-Congo)

*Adé **takú** ó **ní** {èmi ò lo}*
PN refuse3S QV {I won't go}
Ade refused and (he) said, "I won't go" (Bamgboṣe 1986: 90)

(16) Lezgian (Lezgic, Nakh-Daghestanian)

*gadadi   {zun k'wale amuq'da} **laha-na   haraj-na***
boy:ERG   {I will stay at home} say-PFV.CONV scream-PST
The boy screamed [lit.: screamed saying]: "I will stay at home!"
(Haspelmath 1993: 355)

Finally, a quotative index quite frequently displays a structure which appears reduced with respect to normal verbal clauses of a language; this is called a non-clausal quotative index, in the narrow sense of non-verbal. One non-clausal pattern is quote-oriented and often contains a quotative marker or complementizer without any verb, as in (17) based on *ká*, which has already been shown to also occur in the bipartite structure in (13).

(17) Mwaghavul (Chadic, Afroasiatic)

{*là!*} ***ká** mbítsà ndá tsí*
{go!} Q PN   COM 3S
Mbitsa told him to go [lit.: Mbitsa with him like this, "Go!"] (Frajzyngier 1996: 132)

Another subtype of non-clausal quotative index can be said to focus first of all on the representation of the speaker (or less frequently the addressee). This can be shown in Egyptian itself; cf. (18) for a recurrent quotative index of Old Egyptian.

(18) {*ꜥbꜣ Stš mꜣꜥw Wsir!*}   ***m-rʾ-nṯr-(w)***
       {Seth is sacrificed, Osiris is justified!} in-mouth-god-P
       "Seth is sacrificed, Osiris is justified!" is in the mouth of the gods ...
       (Kammerzell & Peust 2002: 304; Pyr. 1556[P])

2.2 Different origins of nuclear elements of quotative indexes

After outlining a formal classification of quotative indexes, I turn to a second major result of my typological study which refers to the range of elements which, apart from lexically opaque quotative markers, are recruited in this expression type. The most important conclusion here is that speech verbs are far less salient as the nucleus of quotative indexes than is commonly assumed. The full range of element types encountered recurrently in quotative indexes is listed below, followed by representative examples for all elements other than speech verbs:

a. Generic speech verbs   cf. *say* in (11)
b. Generic verbs of equation, inchoativity, and action   cf. *la'asot* 'do' in (19)
c. Markers of similarity and manner   cf. *like* in (20)
d. Quote-referring pronominals   cf. *ninε* 'this' in (21)
e. Speaker-referring pronominals   cf. *ɓón* 'they' in (22)
f. Markers of focus and presentation   cf. *ba* 'just' in (23)

(19) Colloquial Hebrew (Semitic, Afroasiatic)

*az   ha-mahabúl-a   ha-zòt   **osá**   l-i   {...}*
SO   DEF-fool-F.S   DEF-DEM.F.S   do:F.S.PRS   DAT-1S
So that idiot (f) goes: "... [lit.: does to me] (Zuckermann 2006: 475)

(20) Colloquial English (Germanic, Indo-European)

*And he was **like**, {Oh, I can DO it!}*

(21) Adioukrou (Kwa, Niger-Congo)

*Mel **ninε**   {òw aŋa}*
PN   this   {come here}
Mel said, "Come here." (Hill 1995: 93)

(22) Tikar (Bantoid, Niger-Congo)

ɓón   {...}
2Q.PRO
they (said), "... (Stanley 1982: 33)

(23)　Colloquial Swedish (Germanic, Indo-European)

> *Anki   å   Malin   **ba**   {öh jävla hippie}*
> PN   and   PN   just   {oh bloody hippie}
> Anki and Malin said "Oh bloody hippie" (Eriksson 1995: 19)

2.3 Speaker-oriented quotative indexes and their possible historical development

Among the major structural possibilities of quotative indexes outlined in § 2.1 and § 2.2 one subtype is of particular relevance for an evaluation of Egyptian *j(n)*, namely a non-clausal quotative index which uses a foregrounding element that focuses on the identity of the speaker. Prototypically these are short clauses of the type 'it/there is X', which combine an identificational or presentational marker with a speaker nominal. This cross-linguistically recurrent pattern is discussed extensively by Güldemann (2012b), to which the reader is referred for more details. Compare first two examples from such geographically and genealogically diverse languages as Portuguese and Tongan.

(24)　Colloquial Portuguese (Romance, Indo-European)

> ***aí*   *os*   *gajos* {...}**
> there these guys
> then/there these guys were/said like, "...

(25)　Tongan (Polynesian, Austronesian)

> {*alu atu!*}   ***ko* *Sione***
> {go away!}   ID   PN
> "Go away!" said John. [lit.: it is John] (J. Broschart p.c.)

A third even more remarkable case is represented by Tonga-Inhambane (not to be confused with 'Tongan'), because there are robust indications that an identificational structure 'it is' has come to be reanalyzed as a verbal constituent in taking on formal signs of a canonical verb lexeme. Lanham (1955: 139–140) characterizes the crucial quotative element *kh-* as follows:

"Another defective verb stem of considerable interest is that signifying 'say' or 'think'. The forms in which this monosyllabic stem appears are highly irregular and there is some doubt as to the true form of the stem ... This stem, which consists of *kh-* plus an unidentified vowel, always fuses with a succeeding absolute pronoun or demonstrative pronoun functioning as such, and forms a single unit with it, and this unit appears as the stem in any predicate. The original vowel of the stem is difficult to determine because it disappears in this process of fusion, but it is probable that it was the regular suffix *-a*. ... The stems *kheni, khuwe, khawo, khigyo, khuwo, khijo*, etc., do not permit of any suffixal inflexion, but are found in various tense and mood forms with prefixal inflexional elements. [cf. (27)] ... These forms, consisting of verb stem plus absolute pronoun, are units of high frequency in ordinary speech and are quite often found without any concords or prefixes whatsoever. [cf. (28–30) below] ..."

As example (26) shows, *kh-* can display normal verb prefixes so that it is classified as a verb but lacks normal verb suffixes, because it ends in a pronominal suffix agreeing with the speaker/subject – this somewhat tautologically, because the speaker is already encoded before the stem.

(26)   Tonga-Inhambane (Bantu, Niger-Congo)

      *si-rengo   si-ngu-**kh**-iso* {...}
      8-animal 8-PRS-QV-8PRO
      the animals say, "... (Lanham 1955: 139)

While the possible presence of verbal prefixes is crucial for *kh*'s classification as a verb, it can also be used without this morphology, as in (27), where it is glossed accordingly just as a quotative marker; note that the cross-reference suffix cannot be dropped.

(27)   **kh**-*iso*   {*khumani ahipalago*}
      Q-8PRO   {who is it that defeats us?}
      They [animals] said, "Who is it that defeats us ..." (Lanham 1955: 140)

The overall profile of the *kh*-predicative in Tonga-Inhambane is quite comparable to quotative *j(n)* in Egyptian in the sense that it is restricted to reported discourse and displays morphological irregularities compared to normal verbs. For both elements the best analysis is that of a formally defective quotative verb. Recall also that, like Egyptian *jn*, the *kh*-forms are used to mark agents in passive.

There is yet another parallel between the two elements in quotative indexes: both can be combined with a canonical complement-taking verb of speech, cognition, perception etc., thus yielding a bipartite quotative index and assuming also the function of a complementizer (Lanham 1955: 224–225). Thus compare (5) above from Egyptian with (28) from Tonga-Inhambane; the major, but in this context secondary, difference between these examples is that in the former the two elements of the bipartite structure are interrupted by (parts of) the quote while in the latter they form one unitary constituent.

(28) *nyamayi adi-wujisa* **kh**-*uye* {...}
      woman.1 1:PST-ASK Q-1PRO
      The woman asked saying, "... (Lanham 1955: 140)

The observation most crucial for the historical evaluation of Egyptian *j(n)* is the etymological origin of quotative *kh-* in Tonga-Inhambane. There is robust evidence that this element ultimately derives from an identificational particle *kha* preceding a nominal; only in the context of quotative indexes did it acquire secondarily verbal prefix morphology. Compare first the formal identity of the prefixless quotative complex *kh*-Pronoun with the identificational pronouns illustrated in Table 5 by means of a partial paradigm, whereby both forms can be regularly derived from an original form *kha* which was cliticized to an independent pronoun.[5]

Table 5: Quotative and identificational pronoun paradigms in Tonga-Inhambane (Lanham 1955: 139, 188)

Person-inflected quotative		Identificational form of (demonstrative) pronoun		
(-)*kheni*	'I say, "...'	*kheni*	'it is I'	(< *kha-ini*)
(-)*khuwe*	'you say, "...'	*khuwe*	'it is you'	(< *kha-uwe*)
(-)*khawo*	'they say, "...'	*khawo*	'it is they'	(< *kha-awo*)

The assumption that the person-inflected quotative was originally [*kha*-Pronoun] is corroborated by the existence of alternative quotative indexes where *kha* is used as an uninflected particle before bare nouns as in (29).

(29) {*nyinguhongola*} **kha** *Rasi*
      {I am going} Q PN
      "I am going" says Rasi (Lanham 1955: 140)

---

5 Note that the identificational proclitic *kh-* before bare nouns no longer surfaces as *kha* but *khu* or *khi* (Lanham 1955: 187–188). This phenomenon can be explained as the result of secondary changes of vowel assimilation and subsequent analogical leveling within the paradigm, possibly compounded by competition from a phonetically similar proclitic *kha* of negative identification.

This means that quotative indexes with *khV* plausibly originate in an identificational structure [*kha* Nominal] 'it is ...'; this has cognates in other Bantu languages. Accordingly, the forms [Verb.prefixes-*kh*-Pronoun.suffix] would, pace Lanham (1955), have emerged secondarily by means of analogical attachment of verb prefixes to the non-verbal pronoun-inflected paradigm. While this kind of "verbification" is a surely remarkable process, it is attested independently in the language with ideophones which are originally equally uninflected (Lanham 1955: 218–220). The full process of morphological change which *kha* underwent in the quotative context can be sketched as follows:

[*kha* Free.nominal] > [*kha*-Pronoun] > [Verb.prefixes-*kha*-Pronoun]

A largely parallel historical scenario is also proposed by Güldemann (2008: 368–369) for the emergence of the modern quotative verb *cêe* in Hausa. Finally, there are examples in other languages for the acquisition of morphosyntactic and semantic features of a verb within the grammatical structure of a quotative index, which are dealt with by Güldemann (2008: 381–395), which in turn can be embedded in a more general process of relexicalization within grammatical constructions (see Güldemann 2012a).

3 A different historical look at Egyptian *j(n)*

3.1 A new scenario for quotative *j(n)*

Having assembled data to the effect that an identificational marker can be recruited as the nucleus of a major type of quotative index and can in this context change in the course of time from a non-verbal element towards a more verb-like predicate, the relation between the two major domains of use of Egyptian *j(n)* can be reconsidered. While most previous scholars, if at all entertaining a relation between the two, have assumed that the quotative function has precedence and is the source of the use as an identificational or focus marker, I argue that the scenario should be reversed, parallel to the development that can be reconstructed, for example, for quotative *(-)kh-* in Tonga-Inhambane. While this hypothesis agrees with Chetveruchins basic directionality (cf. § 1.3 above), it is based on a wider typological perspective and synchronic and historical parallels in other languages, thus avoiding rather vague and speculative ideas about early lexical structure in Pre-Proto-Afroasiatic.

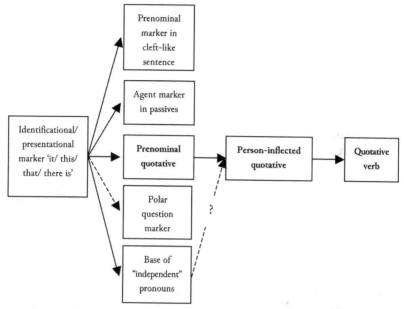

Figure 1: Semantic map of grammaticalization history of Egyptian *j(n)*

Concretely, *jn* is assumed to have started out as an identificational /presentational marker 'it/this/there is' and underwent parallel grammaticalization in a number of different constructions yielding ultimately quite distinct functions. The difficulty in relating them to each other was first of all due to the fact that this polyfunctionality was already fully established in Earlier Egyptian, so that the possibility of developing the present hypothesis had to await the availability of more transparent non-Egyptian data. The proposed semantic map for the history of Egyptian *j(n)*, which takes up separate ideas by Petráček (1983) and Chetveruchin (1988), is given in Figure 1.

The proposed unified origin of *jn* explains in a straightforward way the phonological and morphosyntactic parallels between its quotative and other structures with bare nouns, which has been observed by previous scholars:

> "It is not an occasional coincidence at all, that it is impossible here to draw a clear-cut boundary between the Egyptian verb 'to say' and the nota agentivi *jn*. Just the opposite, it is between these forms that the closest affinity does manifest itself, as nowhere else." (Chetveruchin 1988: 79)

In functional terms, too, all three contexts where *jn* occurs (originally) before a noun – viz., in clefts, passives, and, as reconstructed here, quotative indexes – show a common denominator even after their considerable divergence after grammaticalization. That is, they all share that the referent in the scope of *jn* is prototypically non-topical and in some way salient in pragmatic terms, and has an agent-like semantic role. According to A. Stauder (p.c.), this even holds for *jn*-clefts, because semantic roles other than from the agent-role complex, when under contrastive focus, usually require a different type of cleft without *jn*.

Recall that under my analysis of the quotative indexes with *jn* in (1) and (4) above as 'it/there is X' this original nuclear structure lacks a representation of the speech event itself but focuses exclusively on the reference of the speaker. This observation also ties in nicely with cross-linguistic findings in the sense that this Egyptian construction turns out to be just another exemplary case of a more general phenomenon regarding quotative indexes in direct reported discourse constructions; that is, the presentation of the speaker is by far their most frequent, hence central, element.[6] Thus, the statistical hierarchy of semanto-syntactic components of quotative indexes in my corpus of more than 3200 tokens from 39 diverse African languages (see Güldemann 2008: 142–146) turned out to be as follows:

Speaker (92%) > Quote orientation (71%) > Event (50%) > Addressee (31%)

Note the highly regular speaker representation against the low 50%-appearance of a verb expressing speech or cognition.

It was only in later stages of Egyptian that the occurrence of event-referring verbs increased in frequency and a bipartite structure with quotative *jn* and the verb *ḏd* 'say', as illustrated in (5) above, was used regularly. Kammerzell & Peust (2002: 304) write:

> "Summarizing the situation in Old Egyptian, we can state that there are various types of embedding reported speech …, particularly in the Pyramid Texts. Statistically, this corpus shows a certain preference for the usage of the quotation index *j-* [a.k.a *j(n)*] inserted after or within the reported text, while the matrix verb *ḏd* 'say' does not occur as often as one might expect, considering that this was by far the most frequent quotation index of Egyptian as a whole [that is, in later periods]."

---

6 This finding is even corroborated by the earliest attested form of reported discourse ever recorded and still attested in a human language, namely Old Egyptian itself (Kammerzell & Peust 2002: 294–297): here, the quotative index is nothing but the naming and pictorial representation of the speaker. As the authors note, this also has a nice parallel in a more modern but iconically similar medium, namely comic strips, where reported discourse is given in a "speech balloon" which is associated with the head of the speaker.

A second, diachronically younger type of bipartite quotative index is described by Faulkner (1937: 185). This now uses the more verb-like *j(n)* as the main predicate and adds *ḏd* 'say' in a prepositional phrase.

> "A curious aspect of the Late-Egyptian usages of *ỉn* 'say', 'said' is the tendency to append a tautologous (*ḥr*) *ḏd*, the full expression reading literally 'so said he, speaking'. … It is possible that a feeling may have arisen that it was desirable to reinforce *ỉn* 'said' by the better-known and less ambiguous *ḏd*, so that (*ḥr*) *ḏd* came to be appended to *ỉn-f*, etc., even when the context did not require it."

(30) {…} *jn-f*   (*ḥr*) *ḏd*   *n-f*
      Q:PST-3M.S   on   speak to-3M.S
    …", so said he to him (after Faulkner 1937: 185; d'Orbiney, 2, 4)

It must be stressed again that the increasing co-occurrence of *jn* and *ḏd* is not necessarily "tautological" and "repetitive" (Kammerzell & Peust 2002: 302). It may well reflect the typologically recurrent emergence of a clausal bipartite quotative index, which combines overt event representation (by *ḏd*) with non-tautological quote orientation (by *jn*), out of an older and simpler quotative index. The emergence of the two constructions described in the above quotes can be schematized as follows:

[{QUOTE} 'it is SPEAKER'] >   [*ḏd*-SPEAKER   {QUOTE} 'Q SPEAKER']
[{QUOTE} 'it is SPEAKER'] >   [{QUOTE} 'QV-SPEAKER' '(on) *ḏd*(ing)']

Note, however, that Jordan (2009, chapter 3.2) argues that even in Later Egyptian texts the quotative indexes involving *j(n)* still focused on the authorship of the original quoted text, that is, on the specific speaker referent. Under the present analysis, this phenomenon can be explained naturally as a variant of what Hopper (1991: 28–30) called "persistence" with reference to grammaticalization; this idea can be generalized for language change as a whole and would concern here a functional property of a construction, possibly even involving the reverse development of lexicalization.

While the assumed partial verbification of *jn* implied by the present hypothesis appears to be a more drastic and quite remarkable change at first glance, it should be noted that clear precedents for parallel phenomena exist elsewhere (see Güldemann 2012a for more discussion). Compare as just one example the reanalysis of an earlier obligation construction in Vulgar Latin [*est opus* Infinitive] towards the fully inflected verbs *estovoir* 'must' in Old French and *stuẹr* '*must*' in Modern Rhaeto-Romance (Bernardi et al. 1994: 861).[7] According to E. Grossman (p.c.), there is even another directly relevant case in Egyptian itself: the Coptic quotative marker *peče-/peča*, grammaticalized from *pзy dd-f*, also came to be assimilated to the verbal system, due to the formal identity of the possessive personal endings and those associated with finite verbs.

An important question to answer is why verbification should happen in the first place. For one thing, *jn* is a kind of default quotative marker and can be viewed as the predicator element of the structure [*jn* Nominal$_x$] 'It is X'. This short expression refers to a speech event, even if only by virtue of its collocation with a quote. It is thus possible that the phrase was increasingly perceived as a verbal clause 'said X', in line with the normal VS word order of Egyptian. In fact, *jn* followed by a noun is identical on the surface with a simple verbal clause [Verb Nominal$_x$] 'X VERBed' and thus cannot be distinguished conclusively from canonical *sdm-n-f* forms (cf. Allen 1984: 112). In general it is conceivable that there was a certain pressure to streamline quotative indexes based on *jn* with normal verbal clauses that represent a state of affairs. This would have concerned in particular the expression of predication operators referring to tense, aspect, etc. and of the pronominal subject.

Regarding tense-aspect features, recall from § 1.1 the only distinction between preterite *jn* and *stative j*. According to W. Schenkel and A. Stauder (p.c.), *jn* in fact quite often does not have past reference so that the distinction between the two stems cannot easily be explained just in terms of time reference. Instead identificational *jn* as such is neutral to tense-aspect and this was initially also the case when encroaching on the quotative domain. However, as soon as it came to be viewed as a verbal element, its etymological final *n* was reanalyzed as the preterite tense-aspect marker *n* by analogy with a canonical *sdm-n-f* form. This explains naturally the predominant but not exclusive past reference of *jn*.

Under this hypothesis, the simpler *stative* forms in *j* without final *n* could be a back formation arising also by analogical leveling. It would be important to investigate any evidence to the effect that forms in bare *j* appear later than those in *jn*. This hypothesis does, however, not explain why *stative j* is restricted to the singular. In this respect, the possible role of *n* as a sign of plural subject reference should be taken into account in future research. It is, of course, possible that the *stative* quotative forms in *j* actually go back to an old verb. However, even in this case it would have to be admitted that identificational-quotative *jn* fed the emergence of a fuller and more regular verbal quotative paradigm in Later Egyptian.

---

7 Thanks to M. Jenny for drawing my attention to this fact.

It is not clear yet whether the regular use of the determinative for 'speak' with quotative *j(n)*, which only occurs in Late Egyptian (see the quote by Faulkner in § 1.1), is a sign of its secondary status as a verb. But it should be investigated whether gaining the property of being determined by a graphemic classifier could reflect lexicalization. This would be in line with E. Grossman's (p.c.) observation that grammaticalization, the reverse of lexicalization, is usually indicated in Egyptian by a loss of graphemic classifiers.

With respect to the partial regularization of pronominal subject marking on quotative *j(n)*, the independent pronouns based on identificational *jn* (cf. § 1.2) might also have served to a certain extent as a model for the emerging fuller series of the quotative *jn* forms. In Table 6, the relevant paradigms can be compared. It can be seen that the singular quotative forms in Later Egyptian have become more similar to the relevant pronouns.

Table 6: The partial formal relation between identificational forms and Later Egyptian quotatives

Person Gender Number	Quotative in Earlier Egyptian (Allen 1984: 109–12/§ 206–9)	Identificational form (= independent pronouns)	Quotative in Later Egyptian (Erman 1933: 357/§ 714)
1s	*j-kj*	*jn-k*	*j-n-j*
2f.s	*j-t(j)*	*(j)n-t-t*	-
2m.s	*j-t(j)*	*(j)n-t-k*	*j-n-k*
3f.s	*j-t(j)*	*(j)n-t-s*	*j-n-s*
3m.s	*j-(j)*	*(j)n-t-f*	*j-n-f*
1p	-	*jn-n*	-
2p	-	*(j)n-t-tn*	-
3p	*j-n-sn*	*(j)n-t-sn*	*j-n-w*
Noun	*jn* Nominal	*jn* Nominal	-

That the assumed process of verbification of quotative *jn* actually never achieved the final state of a fully regular speech verb is evident at its status as a defective verbal lexeme within the quotative paradigm (see § 1.1). According to A. Stauder (p.c.), *jn* even behaves partly differently when compared to its suppletive counterparts *ḥr* and *k3*, which is likely to be related to their different part-of-speech origin. While *ḥr* and *k3* had given rise to analytical constructions (*ḥr-f sḏm-f*, *k3-f sḏm-f*, etc.) by early Middle Egyptian, no similar *jn*-headed constructions (**jn-f sḏm-f*) developed (cf. Vernus 1990). Similarly, while *ḥr* and *k3* were already combined with the impersonal morpheme *tw* in Middle Egyptian, *jn.tw* constructions are found only in Late Egyptian, and then only sporadically. Overall, the present hypothesis actually accounts in a natural way for the very fact that *j(n)* is as defective as a verb as it is throughout its existence in Egyptian.

3.2 Akkadian *enma/umma* – a parallel in the neighborhood

It should be mentioned in this context that the hypothesized development of the non-verbal identificational *jn* in Egyptian towards a fully-grown quotative marker appears to be embedded nicely within its narrow historical and geographical context. A quite similar phenomenon can arguably be observed in the contemporaneous language Akkadian with which Egyptian was in contact until its Demotic stage. First, Akkadian also attests a historical development from a non-clausal (aka non-verbal) quotative index based on a particle *enma/umma* towards a monoclausal bipartite quotative index in which this particle follows a speech predicate. Moreover, the origin of this particle is according to Güldemann (2008: 55–56, 364–365; 2012b) virtually identical with that proposed for Egyptian *jn*.

The oldest stage of Early Old Babylonian is illustrated first. Here the particle *enma*, which later gave way to the slightly different *umma*, precedes the nominal referring to the speaker in nominative case in a non-clausal quotative index which precedes the direct quote:

(I) [*enma/umma* SPEAKER (*ana* 'to' ADDRESSEE) {QUOTE}]

    (31) **umma** *anāku-ma* {…}
         Q   1S-EMPH
         I said "… (Deutscher 2000: 72)

In Later Old Babylonian this phrase came to be elaborated regularly by an initial speech predicate yielding a bipartite quotative index, as shown in the schema and example below.

(II) [SPEECH.VERB *umma* SPEAKER {QUOTE}]

    (32) *pîqat*   *nappāhū iqabbû-kum*   **umma** *šunu-ma* {…}
         perhaps smiths   they.say-to.you Q   3P-EMPH
         perhaps the smiths might say to you "… (Deutscher 2000: 77)

In the much later stage of Neo-Babylonian, the bipartite construction had become grammaticalized to such an extent that the pattern also expanded into indirect reported discourse and the speaker nominal was no longer obligatory, also because the referent was already expressed in the speech verb. Compare in this respect schema (III) and example (34).

(III) [SPEECH.VERB *umma* {QUOTE}]

    (33) *ašāl-šu*   ***umma*** {...}

        I.asked-him Q

        I asked him "... (Deutscher 2000: 83)

In addition to the generally parallel development from a non-clausal towards a mono-clausal bipartite quotative index in Egyptian and Akkadian, an even more significant similarity, I argue, exists regarding the ultimate source of the particle, which served as the nucleus of the non-clausal quotative index. Different hypotheses on the origin of *enma* have been proposed in the literature and have recently been discussed by Deutscher (2000: 68–70):[8] von Soden (1965–1981.1: 218) views *enma* as being composed of two morphemes; initial *en* and final emphatic *ma*. The crucial first item is said to be related to such presentational focus particles as Ugaritic *hn* and Hebrew *hinnēh*. Baumgartner (1974) tries to make an etymological connection of Akkadian *enma* to Hebrew *n'um* 'speech'. Finally, Deutscher himself (2000: 70) entertains an origin of *enma* in an utterance verb, potentially related to the Hebrew *n'm* 'deliver a speech'.

While Deutscher does not favour von Soden's hypothesis, he must acknowledge that the two available alternatives to view the constituent [*enma* + SPEAKER] in Early Old Babylonian as, or as derived from, a genitival structure 'speech of X', as per Baumgartner, or a predicative clause '(what) X said/spoke', as per himself, faces several language-internal and comparative problems. The major reasons for his proposal are twofold. First, under several additional assumptions a structural parallel would arise to a quotative formula in the substrate language Sumerian. Second, he assumes that "the usual source for quotative particles is verbs of speech." Recall, however, from § 2 that Güldemann (2008) does not support this view, this even more so for activity-oriented utterance verbs like the Hebrew item entertained as a potential cognate.

---

8 Saxena (1995: 360) has erroneously taken *umma*'s translation equivalent 'so, like this' (< German 'folgendermaßen') as its actual meaning; this erroneous analysis need not be discussed further (cf. Deutscher 2000: 68–70).

Instead, a good case can be made from within Semitic linguistics that Akkadian *en* is a cognate of Arabic *'inna/'anna*, Hebrew *hinnēh*, Ugaritic *hn*, and related forms in South Arabian and Ethiosemitic,[9] which are all involved in both presentational/focus constructions and quotative indexes/complementizers (Deutscher 2000: 70, FN-25; von Soden 1995: 221) and this ties in nicely with the typical origin of quotative markers. That is, von Soden's etymology that *enma* derives from **en-ma* [Presentational particle + Focus enclitic] has much in its favor: it can explain the morphosyntax of the oldest quotative form in Akkadian as reflecting a clause 'it/there is SPEAKER'; it is supported by comparative evidence from Semitic; and it conforms well to crosslinguistic precedents. (Note that the early change from *enma* to *umma* remains unexplained under any hypothesis.)

Recall that Petráček (1983) even performs a cross-Afroasiatic comparison regarding all the elements referred to above in proposing to reconstruct a presentational marker **N* 'there/this is'. If this were to be substantiated by future research, Akkadian *en* and Egyptian *jn* could even be related etymologically.[10]

That the quotative indexes [*enma* SPEAKER] in Akkadian and [*jn* SPEAKER] in Egyptian are semantically and structurally virtually identical might also have a very concrete historical aspect to it in the sense that direct language contact might have played a role in this parallelism. This is even more suggestive as soon as one compares the historical developments in the quotative indexes of Egyptian and Akkadian according to their different chronolects. Table 7 demonstrates first the close similarity of the different sequential stages of quotative development.

---

9 The fact that the forms here occur with object pronouns has provoked the assumption that the prenominal element must originally have been a verb. This is, however, not conclusive because non-subject pronouns may also be triggered by other grammatical contexts not involving verbs. According to Gensler (p.c.), it is also noteworthy that several common particles, including the presentational ones at issue, take accusative case in Semitic, Egyptian, and Berber, which might be related to the existing hypothesis that early Afroasiatic had a marked-nominative case system. **10** It goes beyond the topic of this paper to explore whether elements occurring in quotative indexes of other Afroasiatic languages are related to the cognate set entertained here. However, given that non-speech verbs frequently occur in quotative indexes and that quotative and generic speech verbs can be at the END point of language change involving the domain of reported discourse constructions, it is noteworthy that a potentially related form in Tamajeq (Güldemann 2008: 605) and other Berber languages (C. Naumann p.c.) is both a generic speech verb and the default verb in quotative indexes, and that a form *an* in Bedauye (Güldemann 2008: 306, 486) is both a generic copulative verb 'be' and a quotative verb.

Table 7: Frequency shift in Earlier Egyptian and Akkadian from non-clausal quotative indexes to monoclausal (bipartite) quotative indexes (simplified)

Egyptian			Akkadian	
(1)	[QUOTE [*jn* SPEAKER]	(QUOTE)]	[[*enma/umma* SPEAKER]	QUOTE]
(2) [VERB	QUOTE [*jn* SPEAKER]	(QUOTE)]	[VERB [*umma* SPEAKER]	QUOTE]
(3) [VERB	(COMPLEMENTIZER)	QUOTE]	[VERB *umma*	QUOTE]

Stage (1) represents the initial non-clausal pattern in which the bare speaker nominal is focused on by means of an identificational/presentational marker. Stage (2) is the mono-clausal bipartite pattern in which the original structure is elaborated by means of a canonical verbal predicate referring to a speech event. The major difference between the two languages is that the earlier presentational marker develops to a person-inflected verb-like element in Egyptian but remains an invariable particle in Akkadian. Moreover, in the final stage (3) the earlier nucleus of the non-clausal pattern is retained in Akkadian as the grammaticalized complementizer-like element *umma*, while the *jn*-forms in Egyptian no longer figure as function words.

Table 8: Approximate temporal correlation between Egyptian and Akkadian periods

Stage	Egyptian			Akkadian	
1	Earlier	Old	2700–2100 BCE	Old Akkadian	2500–2000 BCE
2		Middle	2300 BCE–400 CE	Old Babylonian	2000–1500 BCE
3	Later	Late	1500–700 BCE	Middle Babylonian	1500–1000 BCE
		Demotic	800 BCE–500 CE	Neo-Babylonian	1000–500 BCE
		Coptic	300–1600 CE	-	

Table 8 shows the approximate contemporaneity of the major periods of Egyptian and Akkadian. The use of bipartite structures employing speech verbs took firm hold in both languages around the same time, namely by 1500 BCE, so that the shift away from predominantly non-clausal quotative indexes based on speaker-oriented identificational-presentational clauses lies between this date and the earliest attestations of the languages.

3.3 Summary

It should be stressed that the above discussion is based on a non-Egyptological perspective and needs confirmation regarding its viability in the light of more in-depth philological research. If, however, my hypotheses are not contradicted by empirical data from within Egyptian, the analytical procedure followed here has important results to offer for both specialists and general linguists.

On the one hand, the present treatment of Egyptian *jn* provides an alternative explanation of its bewildering polyfunctionality which is more in line with cross-linguistically established phenomena of diachronic typology. In other words, typology can and should inform philology in order to achieve viable historical accounts of the development of a given language, even though the rich data sources available in a language like Egyptian might sometimes suggest that these data themselves should be sufficient for providing adequate solutions.

On the other hand, Egyptian turns out to present another potential case for a heretofore neglected historical change in which a grammatical construction influences the profile of an individual linguistic sign, not only in semantic but also in morphosyntactic terms as argued in more detail by Güldemann (2012a). Insofar as identificational-presentational *jn* seems to have gained in characteristics that are typical for verbs within the context of a quotative index, one can identify a development whereby features of a grammatical construction have influenced the properties of a lexical item. In potentially providing another case of a rare type of language change which can be traced over a long time period, including subtle intermediate stages which are so often lacking in languages without deep historical records, philology in turn feeds back into typology.

Abbreviations

ADJR	adjectivizer
COM	comitative
CONV	converb
D	dual
DAT	dative
DECL	declarative
DEF	definite
DEM	demonstrative
EMPH	emphatic
ERG	ergative
EXCL	exclamation
F	feminine
FUT	future
ID	identification
IMP	imperative

LOC	locative
M	masculine
P	plural
PAP	past active participle
PASS	passive
PFV	perfective
PN	personal name
POT	potential
PRO	pronoun
PRS	present
PST	past
Q	quotative
QV	quotative verb
REL	relative
S	singular
SBJ	subject
STAT	stative
SUBJ	subjunctive
TAM	tense-aspect-modality
TF	term focus
THET	theticity

Arabic numbers = nominal agreement class or, when immediately followed by S and P, person category.

4 References

Abels, Klaus & Muriungi, Peter. 2006. The focus particle in Kĩĩtharaka. In: Fiedler, Ines & Schwarz, Anne (eds.), *Papers on information structure in African languages*. (ZAS Papers in Linguistics 46). Berlin: Zentrum für Allgemeine Sprachwissenschaft, Typologie und Universalienforschung, 1–20.

Allen, James P. 1984. *The inflection of the verb in the pyramid texts*. (Bibliotheca Aegyptia 2). Malibu: Undena Publications.

Allen, James P. 2000. *Middle Egyptian: an introduction to the language and culture of hieroglyphs*. Cambridge: Cambridge University Press.

Bamgboṣe, Ayọ. 1986. Reported speech in Yoruba. In: Coulmas, Florian (ed.), *Direct and indirect speech*. (Trends in Linguistics, Studies and Monograplhs 31). Berlin/ New York: De Gruyter, 77–97.

Baumgartner, Walter. 1974. *Hebräisches und Aramäisches Lexikon zum Alten Testament*. Leiden: Brill.

Bernardi, Rut et al. 1994. *Handwörterbuch des Rätoromanischen N–Z*. Zürich: Offizin.

Callender, John B. 1971. Notes on constructions with 'in. *Studies in African Linguistics* 2.1: 1–23.

Chetveruchin, Alexander S. 1988. Unexpected linguistic interpretation of *jn* 'say(s), said'. *Göttinger Miszellen* 104: 75–88.

Cole, Desmond T. 1955. *An introduction to Tswana grammar*. London: Longmans and Green.

Depuydt, Leo. 1989. The contingent tenses of Egyptian. *Orientalia, Nova Series* 58: 1–27.

Deutscher, Guy. 2000. *Syntactic change in Akkadian: the evolution of sentential complementation*. Oxford: Oxford University Press.

Diessel, Holger. 1999. *Demonstratives: form, function, and grammaticalization*. (Typological Studies in Language 42). Amsterdam: John Benjamins.

Dik, Simon C. (ed. by Kees Hengeveld). 1997. The structure of the clause. In: *The theory of functional grammar*, part 1. Berlin/ New York: De Gruyter.

Eriksson, Mats. 1995. A case of grammaticalization in Modern Swedish: the use of ba in adolescent speech. *Language Sciences* 17.1: 19–48.

Erman, Adolf. 1933. *Neuaegyptische Grammatik*. Leipzig: Wilhelm Engelmann.

Erman, Adolf & Grapow, Hermann. 1926–1931. *Wörterbuch der ägyptischen Sprache*. 5 vols. Leipzig.

Faulkner, Raymond O. 1935. The verb 'i 'to say' and its developments. *Journal of Egyptian Archaeology* 21: 177–190.

Frajzyngier, Zygmunt. 1996. *Grammaticalization of the complex sentence: a case study in Chadic*. (Studies in Language Companion Series 32). Amsterdam: John Benjamins.

Gardiner, Alan H. 1957. *Egyptian grammar: being an introduction to the study of hieroglyphs*. 3rd ed. Oxford: Griffith Institute, Ashmolean Museum.

Güldemann, Tom. 1996. *Verbalmorphologie und Nebenprädikationen im Bantu: Eine Studie zur funktional motivierten Genese eines konjugationalen Subsystems*. (Bochum-Essener Beiträge zur Sprachwandelforschung 27). Bochum: Universitätsverlag Dr. N. Brockmeyer.

Güldemann, Tom. 2005. Complex predicates based on generic auxiliaries as an areal feature in Northeast Africa. In: Voeltz, F. K. Erhard (ed.), *Studies in African linguistic typology*. (Typological Studies in Language 64). Amsterdam: John Benjamins, 131–154.

Güldemann, Tom. 2008. *Quotative indexes in African languages: a synchronic and diachronic survey*. (Empirical Approaches to Language Typology 34). Berlin/New York: De Gruyter.

Güldemann, Tom. 2010. The relation between focus and theticity in the Tuu family. In: Fiedler, Ines & Schwarz, Anne (eds.), *The expression of information structure: a documentation of its diversity across Africa*. (Typological Studies in Language 91). Amsterdam: John Benjamins, 69–93.

Güldemann, Tom. 2012a. Relexicalization within grammatical constructions. In: Auwera, Johan van der & Nuyts, Jan (eds.), *Grammaticalization and (inter-)subjectification*. Brussels: Koninklijke Vlaamse Academie van Belgie voor Wetenschappen en Kunsten, 65–80.

Güldemann, Tom. 2012b. Thetic speaker-instantiating quotative indexes as a cross-linguistic type. In: Alphen, Ingrid van & Buchstaller, Isabelle (eds.), *Quotatives: cross-linguistic and cross-disciplinary perspectives. Converging Evidence in Language and Communication Series*. Amsterdam: John Benjamins, 117–142.

Haspelmath, Martin. 1993. *A grammar of Lezgian*. (Mouton Grammar Library 9). Berlin/ New York: De Gruyter.

Hill, Harriet. 1995. Pronouns and reported speech in Adioukrou. *Journal of West African Languages* 25.1: 87–106.

Hopper, Paul J. 1991. On some principles of grammaticization. In: Traugott, Elizabeth C. & Heine, Bernd (eds.), *Approaches to grammaticalization*. Vol. 1. (Typological Studies in Language 19). Amsterdam: John Benjamins, 17–35.

Jordan, Birgit. 2009. *Der Sprechakt des Zitats in ausgewählten mittel- und neuägyptischen Texten*. M.A. thesis: Johannes-Gutenberg-Universität Mainz.

Kammerzell, Frank. 1991. Personalpronomina und Personalendungem im Altägyptischen. In: Mendel, Daniela & Claudi, Ulrike (eds.), *Ägypten im afro-orientalischen Kontext: Aufsätze zur Archäologie, Geschichte und Sprache eines unbegrenzten Raumes (Gedenkschrift Peter Behrens)*. (Afrikanistische Arbeitspapiere, Sondernummer 1991). Köln: Institut für Afrikanistik, Universität Köln, 177–203.

Kammerzell, Frank & Peust, Carsten. 2002. Reported speech in Egyptian: forms, types, and history. In: Güldemann, Tom & Roncador, Manfred von (eds.), *Reported discourse: a meeting ground for different linguistic domains*. (Typological Studies in Language 52). Amsterdam: John Benjamins, 289–322.

Lanham, Leonard W. 1955. *A study of Gitonga of Inhambane*. (Bantu Linguistic Studies 1). Johannesburg: Witwatersrand University Press.

Loprieno, Antonio. 1988. Der ägyptische Satz zwischen Semantik und Pragmatik: die Rolle von *jn*. *Studien zur Altägyptischen Kultur, Beiheft (BSAK)* 3: 77–98.

Loprieno, Antonio. 1995. *Ancient Egyptian: a linguistic introduction*. Cambridge: Cambridge University Press.

Madan, Arthur Cornwallis. 1908. *Lala-Lamba handbook*. Oxford: Clarendon Press.

Petráček, Karel. 1983. La copule *näw* en amharique dans une perspective chamitosémitique et africaine. In: Segert, Stanislav & Bodrogligeti, András J. E. (eds.), *Ethiopian studies dedicated to Wolf Leslau on the occasion of his seventy-fifth birthday November 14th, 1981 by friends and colleagues*. Wiesbaden: Harrassowitz, 286–295.

Reintges, Chris H. 1997. *Passive voice in Older Egyptian: a morphosyntactic study*. (Holland Institute of Generative Linguistics Dissertations 28). The Hague: Holland Academic Graphics.

Reintges, Chris H. 1998. Mapping information structure to syntactic structure: one syntax for *jn*. *Revue d'Égyptologie* 49: 195–220.

Sasse, Hans-Jürgen. 1987. The thetic/categorical distinction revisited. *Linguistics* 25: 511–580.

Saxena, Anju. 1995. Unidirectional grammaticalization: diachronic and cross-linguistic evidence. *Sprachtypologie und Universalienforschung* 48.4: 350–372.

Schmidt, Sigrid. 1994. *Zaubermärchen in Afrika: Erzählungen der Damara und Nama*. (Afrika Erzählt 2). Köln: Rüdiger Köppe.

von Soden, Wolfram. 1965–1981. *Akkadisches Handwörterbuch*. 3 vols. Wiesbaden: Harrassowitz.

von Soden, Wolfram (with Mayer, Werner R.). 1995. *Grundriss der akkadischen Grammatik*. (Analecta Orientalia 33). Rome: Pontificium Institutum Biblicum.

Stanley, Carol. 1982. Direct and reported speech in Tikar narrative texts. *Studies in African Linguistics* 13.1: 31–52.

Vernus, Pascal .1990. Future at issue. tense, mood and aspect in Middle Egyptian: studies in syntax and semantics. *Yale Egyptological Studies* 4: 61–114.

Zuckermann, Ghil'ad. 2006. Direct and indirect speech in straight-talking Israeli. *Acta Linguistica Hungarica* 53.4: 467–481.

Martin Haspelmath

The three adnominal possessive constructions in Egyptian-Coptic: Three degrees of grammaticalization*

Abstract: This article gives an overview of the development of the three main adnominal possessive constructions of Egyptian-Coptic: the Direct Possessive Construction (which has no overt possessive marker), the Short Possessive Construction (which uses the genitive marker *n-* in Coptic), and the Long Possessive Construction (with the genitive marker *nte-* in Coptic). These can be seen as representing three layers of grammaticalization, which have parallels in many other languages. The Direct Construction is the oldest one, which we observe being gradually replaced by the Short Construction, which in turn is supplemented by the newest construction, the Long Possessive Construction. We see that the two older constructions become restricted to the most frequent contexts over time, i.e., to contexts of inalienable possession and definite noun phrases, while the newly grammaticalized forms first arise in the less usual contexts. This is typical of grammaticalization changes in general, but few other languages allow the changes to be observed over such a long period.

1 Introduction

In this paper, I describe the three different adnominal possessive constructions in the Sahidic dialect of Coptic from the perspective of grammaticalization. At least since Hodge (1970), it has been known that the history of Egyptian-Coptic provides ample evidence for what Hodge calls the "linguistic cycle", i.e., the neverending sequence of periphrasis – fusion – reduction, followed again by periphrasis – fusion – reduction, and so on (this is called anasynthesis in Haspelmath 2014, in this volume). The three adnominal possessive constructions of Coptic will be seen to represent three different stages of this process.

By "adnominal possessive construction", I mean a construction in which a noun is modified by a possessor that is part of the same noun phrase, such as *my money, Kim's mother, or the roof of the house*. I will thus not be concerned

---

* I am grateful to Eitan Grossman, Tonio Sebstian Richter and Bernard Comrie, as well as Laura Franz, for useful comments on an earlier version of this paper.

with predicative possessive constructions in which possession is predicated (as in *You have enough money,* or *This house is yours*). I use the term "possession" for adnominal kinship relations, part-whole relations, and ownership relations (cf. Koptjevskaja-Tamm 2003). The justification for treating these three semantic relations together is that many languages (including Egyptian-Coptic) code them in similar ways. Kinship and part-whole relations are not literally "possessive", and other semantic relations are also often coded in the same way in languages (e.g., *my school, your seat, her knowledge*), so a term like "association" is preferred by some linguists (e.g., Shisha-Halevy 2007a: 431–432). However, in linguistic typology, the term "possession" is widely used as a cover term for all these relationships (e.g., Seiler 1983; Heine 1997; Baron et al. 2001; Stassen 2009), and I will follow this terminology here.

In addition to discussing the best-known grammaticalization changes (periphrasis/extension of a lexical element to a grammatical function and shortening/fusion), I will also highlight the role of increasingly tight syntactic restrictions of more grammaticalized constructions, emphasizing the importance of frequency for understanding grammaticalization (cf. Bybee 2003).

Adnominal possessive constructions have been discussed in a number of specialized articles (especially Sander-Hansen 1936; Schenkel 1963; Jansen-Winkeln 2000; Egedi 2005; Egedi 2010). Doing justice to these works is beyond the scope of this paper, which focuses on the main phenomena, their cross-linguistic parallels, and their interpretation in terms of grammaticalization.

2 The three adnominal possessive constructions in Coptic

In this section, I briefly describe the three constructions in Coptic, limiting myself to the Sahidic dialect. After a general discussion of important and typical characteristics of grammaticalization in § 3, I will then discuss the diachrony and the grammaticalization of each of these constructions in some more detail in §§ 4–6. Note that the names given to these constructions (capitalized, in accordance with the principle described in Croft 2001: 50; Haspelmath 2010: § 6) are not traditional in Egyptian-Coptic linguistics and were created for ease of presentation in this paper.

2.1 The Direct Possessive Construction

The use of the Direct Possessive Construction is very restricted in Coptic, both lexically and grammatically. It only occurs (i) with a small closed set of about 20 possessum nouns which are mostly body-part terms and (ii) with pronominal possessors.

There is no overt possessive marker in this construction.[1] Pronominal possessors are expressed by person-number suffixes, as shown in the examples in (1):

(1) a. ⲣⲱⲕ
   rô-k
   mouth-2SG.M.POSS
   'Your mouth'

b. ϩⲏⲧⲥ
   hêt-s
   womb-3SG.F.POSS
   'Her womb'

Most of the body-part terms that are used in this construction actually occur primarily as relational nouns or prepositions, so the pattern in (1a–b) is not typical of body-part terms. Most body-part terms cannot use this highly restricted construction.

The person-number suffixes also occur as objects of some verb forms and as complements of prepositions, and very similar markers occur as subject person markers. When the body-part terms that occur in this construction take full-NP possessors rather than pronominal possessors, the Short Genitive has to be used (e.g., *koun-f n-braham* [bosom-3SG.M.POSS S.GEN-Abraham] 'Abraham's bosom', Layton 2004: § 138–139).

---

1 With some nouns there is both a free form and a different form combining with possessive person suffix (e.g., *tôre* 'hand', *toot=* 'hand of'). These forms are not characterized by a consistent marker.

2.2 The Short Possessive Construction

What I call the Short Possessive Construction here really comprises two subconstructions with different formal properties, the Short Genitive Construction and the Possessive-Article Construction. However, they occur under very similar circumstances and are in complementary distribution in Sahidic Coptic, so they can be regarded as subcases of a single abstract construction. This construction is the most common adnominal possessive construction. It shows almost no lexical restrictions, i.e., it can occur with almost any possessed noun, and with any possessor noun. The Short Genitive Construction is used when the possessor is a full NP, and the Possessive-Article Construction is used when the possessor is a personal pronoun. The Short Possessive Construction occurs (almost) exclusively when the possessed NP has the definite article.

In the **Short Genitive Construction** (often called "indirect genitive"), the full-NP possessor follows the possessed noun, preceded by the Short Genitive marker *n-* (*m-* before a labial consonant), as illustrated in (2):

(2) a. пхоеіс   мпні
      p-čoeis   *m-p-êi*
      DEF-lord   S.GEN-DEF-house
      'The lord of the house'

    b. псооун   мпеооу   мпноуте
      p-sooun   *m-p-eoou*   *m-p-noute*
      DEF-knowledge S.GEN-DEF-glory S.GEN-DEF-God
      'The knowledge of the glory of God'

The term "genitive" is widely used for overt markers of the possessive relation that occur in association with the possessor.[2] One might object that prepositions should not be called "genitive", because this term is reserved for case markers, but adpositional and affixal genitives are often very difficult to distinguish, so giving case names to adpositional markers is generally well-motivated (see also Haspelmath 2009).

---

2 This is fairly standard in typology now, but note that some authors continue Greenberg's (1963) usage of "genitive" in the broader sense of 'adnominal possessor' (e.g., Dryer 2005). Thus, in the earlier usage the term genitive was extended to all possessors, even if they are not overtly marked (this usage is also found in Egyptology, where the Direct Possessive Construction has often been called "direct genitive", Sander-Hansen 1936; Schenkel 1963).

In the Possessive-Article Construction, a person-number prefix precedes the possessed noun, itself preceded by the definite article:

(3) ⲡⲁⲏⲓ   ⲡⲉⲕⲏⲓ   ⲡⲉⲛϫⲟⲉⲓⲥ
     p-a-êi   *pe-k-êi*   *pe-n-čoeis*
     DEF-1SG.POSS-house   DEF-2SG.M.POSS-house   DEF-1PL.POSS-lord
     'my house'   'your house'   'our lord'

2.3 The Long Possessive Construction

The Long Possessive Construction is lexically and grammatically unrestricted, i.e., it can in principle occur with any possessed noun, and regardless of the grammatical context. Its form is invariable, using the Long Genitive marker *nte-* (before full NPs) or *nta=* (before pronominal suffixes). Some examples are given in (4a–c). In the simplest contexts, the Short Possessive Construction is preferred, but in some contexts, it cannot occur, and the Long Possessive Construction must be used. These are, in particular, possessive constructions with an indefinite possessed NP (cf. 4a), with a demonstrative modifier on the possessed NP (cf. 4b), or with an adjectival modifier on the possessed NP (cf. 4c):

(4) a.   indefinite possessed NP:

          ⲟⲩϫⲱⲱⲙⲉ   ⲛⲧⲉ   ⲫⲗⲗⲟ
          ou-čôôme   *nte*   *p-ʰllo*   (Lambdin 1983: 6)
          INDF-book   1LGEN   DEF-monk
          'A book of the monk'

     b.   demonstrative modifier on possessed NP:

          ⲡⲉⲓϫⲱⲱⲙⲉ   ⲛⲧⲉ   ⲡⲁⲥⲟⲛ
          pei-čôôme   *nte*   *p-a-son*   (Lambdin 1983: 12)
          this-book   L.GEN   DEF-1SG.POSS-brother
          'This book of my brother('s)'

c. adjectival modifier of possessed NP:

ⲡϣⲏⲣⲉ	ⲛ6ⲁⲗⲉ	ⲛⲧⲉ	ⲡⲣⲱⲙⲉ	
p-šêre	*n-cale*	*nte*	*p-rôme*	(Lambdin 1983: 12)
DEF-child	ATTR-crippled	L.GEN	DEF-man	

'The man's crippled child'

Thus, the three constructions can be arranged on a scale, as shown in Figure 1. The Direct Possessive Construction is the most restricted, and also the oldest and most grammaticalized construction, while the Long Possessive Construction is the youngest and least grammaticalized construction.

Direct	**Short**	**Long**
Possessive Construction	**Possessive Construction**	**Possessive Construction**

```
<—————————— more restricted ———————— less restricted—————————>
<—————————— older ——————————————— younger——————————>
<—————————— more grammaticalized ———— less grammaticalized————>
```

Figure 1: The three Coptic constructions arranged on a scale.

Alternatively, one could try to describe the relationship between these constructions with a term such as "prototypical" or "unmarked", but these terms are unhelpful, especially the latter. If "unmarked" means "frequent", then the Short Possessive Construction would be the unmarked pattern because it is clearly the most frequent one. If "unmarked" means "unrestricted" or "occurring by default", then the Long Possessive Construction would be the unmarked pattern because it can always occur.

3 Grammaticalization: Three key properties

To see how the synchronic properties of the three adnominal possessive constructions can be understood with reference to grammaticalization, we need to briefly review the key properties of grammaticalization changes (see, in particular, Lehmann 1995; as well as Haspelmath 1999a, 2004a, 2006, 2008a, 2008b, for more details). In the present context, the three ingredients below are the most relevant.

(i) **Extension/periphrasis:** Full words are used in a new grammatical function, e.g., a noun like *means* is used to express the instrumental role (*by means of*), or a verb like *go* is used to express future events (*I am going to do it*), or a demonstrative is used to express mere definiteness (e.g., Latin *illa civitas* 'that city' becomes Italian *la città* 'the city'). Through such an extension to a grammatical use, a new kind of periphrastic construction comes into being in the language. I have argued that this happens because speakers are sometimes "extravagant" (see Haspelmath 1999a; 2000), not because the new elements are needed to "repair" a structure that has eroded by sound change. The repair theory of extension and periphrasis has long been prevalent, especially as an explanation for the replacement of the Latin cases by Romance prepositions such as *a* (for the Dative) and *de* (for the Genitive). It has also been invoked by Egyptologists as an explanation for the rise of periphrastic constructions:

> Als [die Casusendungen] dann verloren gingen, griff man zu der nicht mißzuverstehenden Umschreibung mit *nj*. (Erman 1894: § 213)
>
> [When [the case endings] were then lost, speakers resorted to the unmistakable paraphrase with *nj*.]

Here Erman refers to the rise of the Short Genitive Construction, which he hypothesized to be due to the loss of an earlier (unattested but postulated) genitive case ending. However, if the repair theory were correct in general, we would not expect periphrases to arise while the earlier structure is still fully functional. Thus, we would not expect a new English future (*be going to*) to arise while the old *will*-future is still around, or we would not expect Modern German to develop a new prepositional genitive (with *von*) while the old genitive case still survives. The loss of the earlier pattern may well be due to the spread of the new pattern, but the rise of the new pattern cannot be triggered by the impending (or fully implemented) loss of the old pattern. Thus, extension/periphrasis must be driven by extravagance, not by the need to repair.

(ii) **Shortening/fusion:** As the new construction is adopted by more and more speakers and becomes more and more frequent, it is increasingly shortened. Speakers articulate less carefully, because a highly frequent item is also highly predictable. As a result of its phonetic reduction, the item also loses autonomy and becomes attached to another element (this is called fusion or coalescence, cf. Haspelmath 2011).

(iii) **Paradigmatic restriction:** In the course of grammaticalization, the construction, which was initially possible under all circumstances, gets restricted in various ways. A grammaticalized construction may become restricted

- to contexts not occupied by an even more grammaticalized construction ("blocking by previous occupant"),
- to contexts where it is non-redundant ("redundancy inhibition"), and/or
- to the most frequent contexts ("downsizing to core task").

Table 1 gives three typical and well-known examples of grammaticalization from English and French: the rise of the English definite article, the French clitic pronouns, and English periphrastic negation. We can use these examples to illustrate the three key ingredients that we just saw.

Table 1: Three examples and three key properties of grammaticalization

	English negation	English definite article	Latin >French clitic object pronouns
extension/ periphrasis	emphatic 'do' verb > empty negative auxiliary *I do not go > I don't go*	demonstrative > definite marker *þæt bōc > the book*	demonstrative > anaphoric pronouns *tu illum vidis > tu le vois* 'you see him'
shortening	*do not > don't*	*þæt > the*	*illum > le, illui > lui*
paradigmatic restriction	The negative *do* auxiliary is not extended to a set of high-frequency verbs which retain the old negation marking (*cannot, will not, is not, has not*, etc.)	The definite article is not extended to proper names or contexts with demonstratives (*the John, *the that book*).	The old construction is not used in rarer contexts (**il me lui présente* 'he introduces me to her', cf. *il me présente à elle*) (Haspelmath 2004b)

In English negation periphrasis, we see the auxiliary *do* extend to express negation with almost all verbs, but it does not extend to high-frequency verbs (such as *cannot, will not, has not*, etc.), where the old postverbal negation is preserved (this is thus a kind of "blocking by the previous occupant"). The definite article in English, originally a demonstrative, spread to most definite NPs, but not to proper names, where it is redundant ("redundancy inhibition"). Finally, the French clitic object pronouns, originally from Latin demonstratives, can be used in most contexts, but are banned from contexts where a recipient object and a theme object cooccur and the recipient is 3rd person, while the theme is 1st or 2nd person (sometimes called "*me-lui* constraint"). Such contexts are very rare, and in Haspelmath (2004b) I argued that this leads to their ungrammaticality. This is thus a kind of "downsizing to the core task".

Let us now look at the history of the three Egyptian possessive constructions in some more detail.

4 The Direct Possessive Construction: old and highly restricted

The Direct Possessive Construction is attested since the earliest stage of Egyptian, and due to its similarity to Semitic (and some other Afroasiatic) patterns, it is thought to be very old. While in Coptic it only occurs with pronominal possessors, in earlier Egyptian the Direct Possessive Construction (with a postposed possessor not marked morphologically, at least not in the spelling) was also possible with full-NP possessors.

4.1 Direct Possessive Construction with full-NP possessor

In Old and Middle Egyptian the construction is attested with a full-NP possessor, but it is already quite restricted. Two examples from Middle Egyptian are given in (5):

(5) Middle Egyptian (Gardiner ²1950: § 85)

    a. *ỉmy-r*   *pr*
         overseer house
         'Overseer of the house'

    b. *ḥrt-ỉb*   *nb-f*
         desire   lord-3SG.POSS
         'The desire of his lord'

The construction is restricted grammatically: as the construction is highly grammaticalized and tightly bound, nothing can intervene between the possessum and the possessor. An adjective modifying the possessum must follow the possessor, as seen in (6):

(6) Middle Egyptian (Gardiner ²1950: § 85)

> *ỉmy-r   šḥtyw   mnḫ*
> overseer fowlers efficient
> 'An efficient overseer of fowlers' (not: 'an overseer of efficient fowlers')

From early on, Egyptologists have thus compared this construction to the Semitic Status Constructus (construct state) construction. In Arabic, as in earlier Egyptian, nothing can intervene between the possessum and the possessor, and a possessum-modifying adjective has to follow the possessor:

(7) Standard Arabic

  a. *kitaab-u   r-rajul-i*
     book-NOM   DEF-man-GEN
     'The man's book'

  b. **kitaabu   qadiimu   r-rajuli*
     book   old   DEF-man
     'The man's old book'

  c. *kitaabu r-rajuli   l-qadiimu*
     book   DEF-man   DEF-old
     'The man's old book'

On the assumption that Egyptian is fairly closely related to the Semitic languages, and in view of the fact that the Status Constructus works very similarly in Akkadian, the earliest attested Semitic language, it is not unreasonable to hypothesize that the Direct Possessive Construction is directly cognate with the Semitic Status Constructus and that earlier Egyptian had genitive case suffixes, like Classical Arabic and Akkadian (cf. the Erman quotation in § 3).

In Late Egyptian, the construction becomes restricted in another way: It now occurs only with certain types of possessa: It "occurs very often when [the possessum] denotes a part of the body [or] a kinship term..." (Černý & Groll ⁴1993: § 4.5.1). A Late Egyptian example is (8):

(8) Late Egyptian

> *m   ḏr.t   šmsw   A*
> in   hand messenger A
> 'By (the) hand of (the) messenger A'

In Coptic, the Direct Possessive Construction does not exist anymore as a productive pattern, but there are certain lexicalized cases that are synchronically best regarded as nominal compounds, but that are diachronically a continuation of this construction. Till (1986: § 120) gives examples such as those in (9). (Note that the form of the possessum is reduced, compared to the free form; the corresponding free forms are *moou* 'water', *hoou* 'day', and *côôbe* 'leaf'. In this respect, too, the construction resembles the Status Constructus of some Semitic languages.)

(9) Coptic

    ⲙⲟⲩϩⲙⲙⲉ   ϩⲟⲩⲙⲓⲥⲉ   ϭⲃⲭⲟⲉⲓⲧ
    mou-hmme *hou-mise* *cb-čoeit*
    water-heat day-birth leaf-olive
    'hot water' 'birthday' 'olive leaf'

4.2 Direct Possessive Construction with pronominal possessor

With pronominal possessors, the Direct Possessive Construction is not restricted in Old and Middle Egyptian. Since the earliest time, the pronominal possessor appears to be a suffix or clitic, and it is generally assumed that the construction is cognate with the very similar older Semitic construction (cf. ex. 12 from Arabic below).

(10) Middle Egyptian (Gardiner ²1950: § 35)

    pr-f   *nïwt-sn*
    house-3SG.POSS   city-3PL.POSS
    'his house'   'their city'

It is interesting that the construction occurs also with an indefinite possessum, as in (11). Such a usage is apparently impossible in Semitic languages, where the possessed NP must be definite when the possessor is a personal pronoun (Arabic *baytu-hu*, Hebrew *bet-o* 'his house', never 'a house of his').

(11) Middle Egyptian (Gardiner [2]1950: § 115)

> ỉst   wn   ḥmt-f
> lo   exist   wife-3SG.POSS
> 'And he has a wife' (= "there is a wife belonging to him")

Restrictions begin to appear in Late Egyptian. First, from that period onward, the construction only occurs with definite possessed NPs (Černý & Groll [4]1993: § 4.2.9). The reason for this, I claim, is that possessed nouns are very frequently definite (Haspelmath 1999b). With progressive grammaticalization, constructions are often restricted to the most frequent occurrences ("downsizing to core task").

Second, in Late Egyptian, the Direct Possessive Construction is restricted to inalienably possessed nouns, especially body-part terms (Černý & Groll [4]1993: § 4.2.9; Junge [2]1999: § 2.1.2.(1)). This restriction is of course the same restriction that was noted for the Direct construction with full-NP possessors. This is a development that is not uncommon for possessive constructions, as we will see in the next subsection. It is another instance of "downsizing to core task".

4.3 Restriction of possessive constructions to inalienable contexts

It is not uncommon to observe that older possessive constructions are at some point restricted to inalienable contexts, i.e., to kinship terms and body-part terms as possessa (see Koptjevskaja-Tamm 1996; Dahl & Koptjevskaja-Tamm 1998). I have claimed that this is because inalienable nouns are very frequently possessed (Haspelmath 2006; 2008b), and as a construction is more strongly grammaticalized and experiences competition from a new, less grammaticalized construction, it often "downsizes to its core task", i.e., the expression of inalienable possession.

This development is attested, for example, in Arabic vernaculars and Maltese (Koptjevskaja-Tamm 1996), as illustrated in (12) and (13). In Maltese, a new possessive construction with ta'-/tiegħ- 'of' has arisen, and the old construction (quite analogous to the Direct construction in Egyptian) has been restricted to body-part and kinship terms. In Classical Arabic, this construction was quite unrestricted.

(12) Classical Arabic

> yad-ii   kitaab-ii
> hand-1SG.POSS   'my hand'   book-1SG.POSS 'my book'

(13) Maltese

id-i   *ktieb-i
hand-1SG.POSS 'my hand'   book-1SG.POSS 'my book'
il-ktieb   *tiegħ-i*
the-book   of-1SG 'my book'

In Old Italian, we see that a shortened version of the (postposed) possessive pronoun from Latin can be used with (inalienable) kinship terms (cf. 15), but not with other nouns such as *terra* 'earth'. For these nouns, the non-shortened independent possessive pronouns (*mia* 'mine') must be used.

(14) Latin

mulier mea 'my wife'   *terra mea*   'my land'

(15) Old Italian

moglie-ma   'my wife'   *terra-ma   'my land'
terra mia   'my land'

In most of the Oceanic languages (a branch of the Austronesian language family), possessive suffixes can only be attached to inalienable nouns. With other nouns, a kind of appositive construction with dummy nouns has to be used. There are a number of such dummy nouns, and these have come to be called "possessive classifiers" because the choice between them depends on the meaning of the noun. Although the history of these constructions is not attested, it can be inferred that the construction with the possessive suffixes is the older one, and that its limitation to inalienables is a kind of "downsizing to core task".

(16) Manam (Lichtenberk 1983: 150–151; cf. also Lichtenberk 1985)

tama-gu   *boro-gu
father-1SG.POSS 'my father'   pig-1SG.POSS   'my pig'

boro ʔana-gu
pig   POSS-1SG.POSS   'my pig'

By the term "inalienable noun", linguists generally mean body-part terms, kinship terms, and a few other inherently relational nouns ('name', 'shadow'). It does not have a clear semantic content, and in practice it refers to either the complete set of such nouns, or to the set that happens to be coded in a special way in a language. As noted by Nichols (1988), there are some languages where just kinship terms are treated in a special way, or where just body-part terms are treated specially (as is largely the case in Coptic).

5 The Short Possessive Construction: Newer but again restricted

The Short Possessive Construction, in both its subconstructions, is an Egyptian innovation and has no cognates in other Afroasiatic languages. But it is attested from early on in the history of Egyptian. Thus, from the very beginning of the attestation of the language, there is competition between several adnominal possessive constructions. Due to its age, it is not surprising that for this construction, too, we see restrictions developing after a certain time period, although initially it was unrestricted.

5.1 With full-NP possessor (Short Genitive Construction)

The Short Genitive Construction in Old and Middle Egyptian uses the Genitive marker *nj/nj-t/nj-w/nj-wt*. This marker agrees in gender and number with the possessum: masculine singular possessa take *nj*, feminine singular possessa take *nj-t*, and plural possessa take *nj-w* (masculine) or *nj-wt* (feminine).

(17) Middle Egyptian (Gardiner ²1950: § 86)

   a. *nsw*   *nj*   *Kmt*
       king(M) of[M] Egypt
       'The king of Egypt'

   b. *nỉwt*   *nj-t nḥḥ*
       city(F)   of-F eternity
       'The city of eternity'

Such genitive markers that agree in number and gender are not very common in the world's languages, but they are well-known from Bantu languages such as Swahili (cf. 18) and from Indo-Aryan languages such as Hindi (cf. 19). Spencer (2007) calls such constructions "possessum agreement constructions", because the genitive-marked possessor agrees with the possessum, and he also discusses an analogous construction in Albanian.[3]

(18) Swahili

    a. *kiti*   *ch-a*   *Hamisi*
       chair(G7) G7-GEN Hamisi
       'Hamisi's chair'

    b. *viti*   *vy-a*   *Hamisi*
       chairs(G8) G8-GEN Hamisi
       'Hamisi's chairs'

(19) Hindi

    a. *us*   *strii*   *kaa*   *beṭaa*
       that woman GEN.M son(M)
       'that woman's son'

    b. *us*   *strii*   *kii*   *bahn*
       that woman GEN.F sister(F)
       'that woman's sister'

In some Slavic languages, such as Russian, such constructions occur with a limited set of possessors (in Russian, just a class of proper nouns ending in *-a* such as *Petja, Miša, Katja*, etc., cf. Corbett 1987). See the examples in (20).

(20) Russian

    a. *Pet-in*   *dom*
       Petja-POSS.M house(M)
       'Petja's house'

    b. *Pet-ina*   *kniga*
       Petja-POSS.F book(F)
       'Petja's book'

---

3 Spencer maintains that the possession markers in these constructions are not genitive case markers, but this is based on an unusually narrow definition of "genitive" or "case".

    c.   *Pet-iny*   *deti*
        Petja-POSS.PL children(PL)
        'Petja's children'

Gardiner ([2]1950: § 86) speculates that the Genitive marker is derived by the adjective-forming suffix *-j* from the Dative preposition *n*. In any event, the construction is clearly an innovation. It does not show the same syntactic constraint requiring adjacency of possessor and possessum that we saw in the Direct Possessive Construction (cf. Jansen-Winkeln 2000: 32), so adjectives and other elements can intervene between the noun and the genitive marker:

(21) *ỉnw*   *nb* *nfr* *n*   *sḫt*
      produce all good of[M] country
      'all good produce of the country' (Gardiner [2]1950: § 86)

In Late Egyptian, the agreement on the genitive marker is lost (Junge [2]1999: 2.1.4.(3)). This is a kind of reduction, probably accompanying phonological reduction, and thus a sign of increasing grammaticalization. In Coptic, only the nasal consonant remains of this form. In § 5.3 below, we will see that new restrictions on this construction developed at this later stage.

5.2 With pronominal possessor (Possessive-Article Construction)

The Direct Possessive Construction with pronominal possessors got competition in nonliterary texts of the Middle Kingdom, and especially in Late Egyptian: a definite article developed (Loprieno 1980), and a new possessive construction arose for definite possessa (i.e., for most of them) and pronominal possessors. In this construction, the possessive suffixes appeared on the definite article, rather than on the noun.[4] Thus, in addition to the older pattern (22a), we now also find the pattern (22b).

---

4 This construction, due to its origin, is restricted to definite possessors from the beginning of its attestation. I was not able to determine how possessive constructions with indefinite possessors ('a friend of mine') were expressed in Late Egyptian.

(22)   Late Egyptian (Junge ²1999: § 2.1.1)

    a.   *prw-n*
       house-1PL.POSS
       'Our house'

    b.   *pꜣj-n*   *pr*
       the-3PL.POSS house
       'Our house'

Unlike the possessum agreement in the Short Genitive Construction, the possessive suffixes on the definite article in the Possessive-Article Construction do not have widespread parallels in other languages (but see below for a parallel from Hausa).

One possible hypothesis would be that the construction arose from the demonstrative or anaphoric use of the element *pꜣj* ('that') that also became the definite article. If *pꜣj-n* could mean 'that belonging to us, ours', then the pattern in (22b) may have arisen from an appositive construction: *pꜣj-n pr* would originally have meant 'ours, the house'. This use of *pꜣj* seems to have survived into Coptic as *pô-* (*pô-i* 'mine', *pô-k* 'yours', etc.), so the rise of the Possessive-Article Construction can be shown (from an anachronistic, Coptic perspective) as in (23).

(23)   ⲡⲁⲉⲓⲱⲧ *pa-eiôt* 'my father'   < *pôi eiôt* 'mine, (the) father'
       ⲡⲉⲥⲉⲓⲱⲧ *pes-eiôt* 'her father'   < *pôs eiôt* 'hers, (the) father'
       ⲡⲉⲛⲉⲓⲱⲧ *pen-eiôt* 'our father' < *pôn eiôt* 'ours, (the) father'
       etc.

The development of a possessive construction from a demonstrative or anaphoric pronoun combined with person-number markers is not entirely without parallels. Schuh (1990: 605) discusses the development of possessive constructions in Hausa and other Chadic languages, and proposes that the Hausa possessive marker *-n/-r* (masculine/feminine) arose from a reconstructed demonstrative *náa/táa*, as shown in (24).

(24)   a.   ˣ*náa*   'that'
       *náa-sù   'theirs' (= 'that of them')

    b.   **gídá náa-sù*   > *gídá-n-sù*
       'House, that of them' 'their house'

c. *gídá   náa   Múusáa   > gídá-n   Múusáa
house that   (of)Musa   house-POSS Musa
'House, that of Musa' 'Musa's house'

The demonstrative *náa did not at the same time become a definite article in Hausa, so the parallel with Coptic is not complete.

5.3 Restrictions on the Short Possessive Construction

Although the Short Genitive Construction (the new possessive construction with the marker *nj*) is less restricted than the Direct Construction in Old and Middle Egyptian when the possessor is a full NP, it is actually more restricted in that it does not occur when the possessor is a personal pronoun. The Short Genitive marker *nj* is not combined with (non-emphatic) personal pronouns, so that the Direct Construction does not have any competition when the possessor is pronominal. The reason for this must be sought in the fact that personal pronouns are more frequent than full NPs, so that the construction with personal pronouns is more entrenched and resistant to the establishment of a new construction ("blocking by previous occupant"). We often find that non-emphatic personal pronouns preserve earlier patterns. In the Romance and Germanic languages, the preservation of the older possessive constructions with personal pronouns, with accompanying change of the construction for full NPs, is well-known and obviously due to the same reason (cf. 25–26).

(25)   Latin   French

a. *mater Antonii* *la mère d'Antoine* 'Anthony's mother' (new)
b. *mea mater*   *ma mère*   'my mother' (old)

(26)   Old English   Modern English

a. *an cyninges þegn* *a thane of the king* (new)
b. *min cyning*   *my king*   (old)

The new prepositional construction with *di/of* is not possible with personal pronouns (**la mère de moi*, **the mother of me*).

With full-NP possessors, the Short Genitive Construction is not restricted in Old and Middle Egyptian, and as late as in the Late Egyptian period, it was apparently still possible with an indefinite possessor:

(27) w˙ ḥst   n   Kmt
      one singer of   Egypt
      'a singer of Egypt' (Junge ²1999: § 2.1.3.(3))

However, a number of restrictions developed by the Coptic stage of the language. The Short Possessive Construction (i.e., the Short Genitive Construction or the Article-Possessor Construction) cannot be used in Coptic under three conditions:

–   when the possessum is indefinite (cf. 28a)
–   when the possessum is modified by a demonstrative (cf. 28b)
–   when the possessum is modified by an adjective (cf. 28c)

(28) a. ⲟⲩϫⲟⲉⲓⲥ   ⲙ̄ⲡⲏⲓ
          ??ou-čoeis   m-p-êi   (contrasting with 2a)
          INDEF-lord   S.GEN-DEF-house
          'A lord of the house'

      b. ⲡⲉⲓϫⲱⲱⲙⲉ   ⲙ̄ⲡⲁⲥⲟⲛ
          ??pei-čôôme   m-p-a-son   (contrasting with 4b)
          this-book   S.GEN-DEF-1SG.POSS-brother
          'This book of my brother('s)'

      c. ⲡϣⲏⲣⲉ   ⲛ̄ϭⲁⲗⲉ   ⲙ̄ⲡⲣⲱⲙⲉ
          p-šêre   n-cale   m-p-rôme   (contrasting with 4c)
          DEF-child ATTR-crippled S.GEN-DEF-man
          'The man's crippled child'

Interestingly, these restrictions have parallels in some other languages, where the more grammaticalized construction can sometimes not be used under similar circumstances.

–   In English, the Preposed Genitive Construction cannot be used when the possessum is indefinite or modified by a demonstrative (cf. 29a–b) (however, with adjectives there is no problem: *the man's young child*).

(29) a. *the house's a lord, *my a book

      b. *this my brother's book, *this my book

– In Standard Arabic, the Construct State Construction cannot be used when an adjective follows the possessum immediately (cf. *kitaabu qadiimu r-rajuli* 'the man's old book' in (7) above; but Arabic can postpone the adjective). Moreover, when the possessor is definite, the possessum is obligatorily interpreted as definite (cf. 30b). When the possessum is to be interpreted as indefinite and the possessor is definite, as in (30c), it has to be replaced by a construction with the preposition *li* 'to'.

(30)   Standard Arabic (Caspari & Wright 1896–98: § 92)

    a.   *bintu*   *malik-in*
        daughter king-GEN
        'A daughter of a king'

    b.   *bintu*   *l-malik-i*
        daughter DEF-king-GEN
        'The daughter of the king' (NOT: 'a daughter of the king')

    c.   *bintu*   *li-l-malik-i*
        daughter to-DEF-king-GEN
        'A daughter of the king'

Standard Arabic also cannot use its ordinary prenominal demonstrative with a possessum (cf. 31a). In this case, the same possessive construction can be used, but the demonstrative has to be postponed (cf. 31b).

(31)   Standard Arabic (Ryding 2005: 318)

    a.   **haaðaa* *kitaabu-hu*
        this   book-3SG.M.POSS
        'this book of his'

    b.   *kitaabu-hu*   *haaðaa*
        book-3SG.M.POSS this
        'this book of his'

In Hausa (cf. 24 above), the independent possessive construction (using the possessive marker *naa*) must be used when the possessum is modified by an indefinite article (32b), or demonstrative (32c), and can be used if it is modified by an adjective (cf. 32d–e).

(32)   Hausa (Newman 2000: 301)

    a.   *gídá-n-sù*
        house-POSS-3PL
        'Their house'

    b.   *gídáa   gùdáa   náa-sù*
        house   one   POSS-3PL
        'A house of theirs'

    c.   *gídá-n   nàn náa-sù*
        house-POSS thatPOSS-3PL
        'That house of theirs'

    d.   *rìigáa   bakáa   náa-sù*
        gown   black   POSS-3PL
        'Their black gown'

    e.   *rìigá-n-sù   bakáa*
        gown-POSS-3PL   black
        'Their black gown'

–   In Romanian, the Genitive Construction (in which the possessor is in the Genitive case and follows the possessum, cf. 33) is only possible if the possessor immediately follows the possessum noun and if the possessum is definite (Grosu 1988).

(33)   *portret-ul   rege-l-ui*
      portrait-DEF king-DEF-GEN
      'The king's portrait'

In other cases, the Special Possessive Construction, using the additional possessive marker *al*, has to be used: when the possessum is indefinite (cf. 34), when the possessor is modified by a demonstrative (cf. 35), and when the possessor is modified by an adjective (cf. 36).

(34)   a.   **un portret   rege-l-ui*
          a   portrait   king-DEF-GEN

b. *un portret al   rege-l-ui*
   a   portrait POSS king-DEF-GEN
   'A portrait of the king'

(35) a. **acest   portret rege-l-ui*
        this   portrait king-DEF-GEN

      b. *acest portret al   rege-l-ui*
         this   portrait POSS king-DEF-GEN
         'This portrait of the king'

(36) a. **portret-ul   frumos rege-l-ui*
        portrait-DEF pretty king-DEF-GEN

      b. *portret-ul   frumos al   rege-l-ui*
        portrait-DEF pretty POSS king-GEN-DEF
        'The beautiful portrait of the king'

The Romanian construction shows the most complete parallel with Coptic.

Thus, although the Short Possessive Construction is innovative compared to the original Direct Possessive Construction, by the time of Coptic it is restricted in ways that cannot be accounted for via blocking by a more established construction (recall that this was the explanation for the non-extension of the Short Genitive Construction to pronominal possessors at the beginning of this subsection). The new restrictions to the most frequent contexts are a sign of increasing grammaticalization. As I argued earlier, frequency of use is crucial: in possessive constructions with a definite possessor, the possessum is most of the time definite (Haspelmath 1999b), and is much more rarely accompanied by a demonstrative than is the case with other definite NPs (the latter frequency claim needs to be substantiated in future work). The less frequent, unusual combinations now have to be expressed by an even less grammaticalized construction, the Long Possessive Construction.[5]

---

5 Another restriction on the Short Possessive Construction has been observed only for the Bohairic dialect of Coptic: Its restriction to inalienable possession (cf. Shisha-Halevy 2007b). This completely parallels the restriction of the Direct Possessive Construction to inalienables that happened already in Late Egyptian, as noted above in § 4.3.

6 The Long Possessive Construction (*nte-*)

This construction is the least grammaticalized, and the least restricted construction. It typically occurs in contexts where the Short Possessive Construction is not possible (see 4a–c). According to Egedi (2005: 144), "in the Coptic data, there is a well-observable complementary distribution between the two patterns." If so, then this would mean that the *nte*-construction is already restricted, namely to contexts not occupied by an even more grammaticalized construction (a kind of "blocking by previous occupant"). This would mean that it is already somewhat grammaticalized. However, Layton (2004: § 148) cites examples such as the following, which could be replaced by the Short Genitive Construction:

(37) a. ⲛⲁⲣⲭⲱⲛ   ⲛⲧⲉ   ⲡⲉⲓⲁⲓⲱⲛ
          n-arkʰôn   *nte*   *pei-aiôn*
          DEF.PL-ruler POSS this-age
          'The rulers of this age'

   b. ⲛⲉⲑⲏⲡ   ⲛⲧⲉ   ⲡⲛⲟⲩⲧⲉ
          ne-tʰêp   *nte*   *p-noute*
          DEF.PL-depth POSS DEF-God
          'The depths of God'

The fact that the Long Construction is possible here alongside the Short Construction means that the Long Construction is not yet strongly grammaticalized.

   The relation between the degree of grammaticalization and blocking by an existing construction can be illustrated by English. The existing construction *my book* in (38a) (prenominal word with pronominal possessor) strongly blocks the grammaticalized *N of N* construction (38b), but it only weakly blocks the less grammaticalized *N of N's* construction (38c), and it does not block the relative clause construction at all, which cannot be said to have been grammaticalized as a possessive construction.

(38) a. *my book*
          (canonical highly grammaticalized construction)

   b. **the book of me*
          (less highly grammaticalized construction, not possible)

   c. ?*the book of mine*
          (still less grammaticalized, not totally impossible)

    d.   *the book that belongs to me*
        (not grammaticalized, perfectly possible)

7 Conclusion

In Hodge's (1970) paper on grammaticalization cycles in the history of Egyptian-Coptic, he focuses exclusively on verb forms. In this paper, I hope to have shown that similar grammaticalization cycles can be observed in the domain of noun phrase syntax. We can observe three distinct layers of adnominal possessive constructions: the old Direct Possessive Construction (possibly cognate with a similar construction in older Semitic languages, and conceivably even going back to Proto-Afroasiatic), the two subconstructions of the Short Possessive Construction, and the Long Possessive Construction. In addition to the rise of new morphology (a Genitive case prefix, possessive prefixes) and the loss of old morphology (possessive suffixes, almost gone in Coptic), which are quite analogous to the more widely discussed changes in the verbal domain, we also see very interesting paradigmatic restrictions developing over the course of time. Especially the restrictions to inalienable possessa (kinship and body-part terms) and to definite possessa and possessa unmodified by demonstratives and adjectives have been discussed here and placed in a grammaticalization context, with interesting parallels in other languages noted. In particular, I have argued that these paradigmatic restrictions represent a kind of "downsizing to the core task", a restriction to the most frequent contexts in which the construction is required.

Abbreviations

ATTR	attributive marker
G	gender
L.GEN	Long Genitive
S.GEN	Short Genitive

8 References

Baron, Irène, Herslund, Michael & Sørensen, Finn (eds.). 2001. *Dimensions of possession*. Amsterdam: Benjamins.

Bybee, Joan L. 2003. Mechanisms of change in grammaticization: the role of frequency.d D. Janda, Richard D. Joseph, Brian D. (eds.), *Handbook of Historical Linguistics*. Oxford: Blackwell, 336–357.

Caspari, Carl Paul & Wright, William. 1896–98. *A grammar of the Arabic language*. 3rd ed. Cambridge: Cambridge University Press.

Černý, Jaroslav & Groll, Sarah Israelit. 1993. *A Late Egyptian Grammar*. 4th ed. Rome: Pontificio Istituto Biblico.

Craft, William. 2001. *Radical Construction Grammar*. Oxford: Oxford University Press.

Corbett, Greville G. 1987. The morphology/syntax interface: evidence from possessive adjectives in Slavonic. *Language* 63: 299–345.

Dahl, Østen & Koptjevskaja-Tamm, Maria. 1998. Alienability splits and the grammaticalization of possessive constructions. In: Haukioja, Timo (ed.), *Papers from the 16th Scandinavian Conference of Linguistics*. Turku: University of Turku, 38–49.

Dryer, Matthew S. 2005. Order of noun and genitive. In: Haspelmath, Martin, Dryer, Matthew S., Gil, David & Comrie, Bernard (eds.), *The world atlas of language structures*. Oxford: Oxford University Press. (Also online: http://wals.info)

Egedi, Barbara. 2005. Genitive constructions in Coptic. In: Kiss, Karalin É. (ed.), *Universal grammar in the reconstruction of ancient languages*. Berlin: De Gruyter, 137–159.

Egedi, Barbara. 2010. Possessive constructions in Egyptian and Coptic: Distribution, definiteness, and the construct state phenomenon. *Zeitschrift für Ägyptische Sprache und Altertumskunde* 137: 1–12.

Erman, Adolf. 1894. *Aegyptische Grammatik mit Schrifttafel, Litteratur, Lesestuecken und Woerterverzeichnis*. Berlin: Reuther & Reichard.

Gardiner, Alan. 1950. *Egyptian grammar being an introduction to the study of hieroglyphs*. 2nd ed. London: Oxford University Press.

Greenberg, Joseph H. 1963. Some universals of grammar with particular reference to the order of meaningful elements. In: Greenberg, Joseph H. (ed.), *Universals of language*. Cambridge, MA: MIT Press, 73–113.

Grosu, Alexander. 1988. On the distribution of genitive phrases in Rumanian. *Linguistics* 26: 931–949.

Haspelmath, Martin. 1999a. Why is grammaticalization irreversible? *Linguistics* 37.6: 1043–1068.

Haspelmath, Martin. 1999b. Explaining article-possessor complementarity: economic motivation in noun phrase syntax. *Language* 75.2: 227–243.

Haspelmath, Martin. 2000. The relevance of extravagance: A reply to Bart Geurts. *Linguistics* 38: 789–798.

Haspelmath, Martin. 2004a. On directionality in language change with particular reference to grammaticalization. In: Fischer, Olga, Norde, Muriel & Perridon, Harry (eds.), *Up and down the cline: The nature of grammaticalization*. Amsterdam: Benjamins, 17–44.

Haspelmath, Martin. 2004b. Explaining the ditransitive person-role constraint: a usage-based account. *Constructions* 2004. (Free online journal)

Haspelmath, Martin. 2006. Explaining alienability contrasts in adnominal possession: economy vs. iconicity. Invited talk at *the Syntax of the World's Languages* conference, Lancaster, 14–17 September 2006.

Haspelmath, Martin. 2008a. Creating economical morphosyntactic patterns in language change. In: Good, Jeff (ed.), *Language universals and language change*. Oxford: Oxford University Press, 185–214.

Haspelmath, Martin. 2008b. Frequency vs. iconicity in explaining grammatical asymmetries. *Cognitive Linguistics* 19.1: 1–33.

Haspelmath, Martin. 2009. Terminology of case. In: Malchukov, Andrej & Spencer, Andrew (eds.), *Oxford Handbook of case*. Oxford: Oxford University Press, 505–517.

Haspelmath, Martin. 2010. Comparative concepts and descriptive categories in cross-linguistic studies. *Language* 86.3: 663–687.

Haspelmath, Martin. 2011. The gradual coalescence into "words" in grammaticalization. In: Heine, Bernd & Narrog, Heiko (eds.), *The Oxford Handbook of Grammaticalization*. Oxford: Oxford University Press, 342–355.

Haspelmath, Martin. 2014. A grammatical overview of Egyptian and Coptic. In this volume.

Heine, Bernd. 1997. *Possession: Cognitive sources, forces, and grammaticalization*. Cambridge: Cambridge University Press.

Hodge, Carleton T. 1970. The linguistic cycle. *Language Sciences* 13: 1–7.

Jansen-Winkeln, Karl. 2000. Bemerkungen zum „Genetiv" im Ägyptischen. *Zeitschrift für Ägyptische Sprache* 127: 27–37.

Junge, Friedrich. 1999. *Einführung in die Grammatik des Neuägyptischen*. 2. Aufl. Wiesbaden: Harrassowitz.

Koptjevskaja-Tamm, Maria. 1996. Possessive noun phrases in Maltese: Alienability, iconicity, and grammaticalization. *Rivista di Linguistica* 8.1: 245–274.

Koptjevskaja-Tamm, Maria. 2003. Possessive noun phrases in the languages of Europe. In: Plank, Frans (ed.), *Noun Phrase Structure in the Languages of Europe*. Berlin: De Gruyter, 621–722.

Lambdin, Thomas O. 1983. *Introduction to Sahidic Coptic*. Macon, GA: Mercer University Press.

Layton, Bentley. 2004. *A Coptic grammar*. 2nd ed. Wiesbaden: Harrassowitz.

Lehmann, Christian. 1995. *Thoughts on grammaticalization*. Munich: Lincom Europa.

Lichtenberk, Frantisek. 1983. Relational classifiers. *Lingua* 60: 147–176.

Lichtenberk, Frantisek. 1985. Possessive constructions in Oceanic languages and in Proto-Oceanic. In: Pawley, Andrew & Carrington, Lois (eds.), *Austronesian linguistics at the 15th Pacific Science Congress*. (Pacific linguistics C-88). Canberra: Australian National University, 93–140.

Loprieno, Antonio. 1980. Osservazioni sullo sviluppo dell' articolo prepositivo in egiziano e nelle lingue semitiche. *Oriens Antiquus* 19: 1–27.

Newman, Paul. 2000. *The Hausa language: An encyclopedic reference grammar*. New Haven: Yale University Press.

Nichols, Johanna. 1988. On alienable and inalienable possession. In: Shipley, William (ed.), *In honor of Mary Haas*. Berlin: De Gruyter, 475–521.

Ryding, Karin. 2005. *A reference grammar of modern standard Arabic*. Cambridge: Cambridge University Press.

Sander-Hansen, Constantin Emil. 1936. Zum Gebrauch des direkten und indirekten Genitivs in der ältesten ägyptischen Sprache. *Acta Orientalia* 14: 26–54.

Schenkel, Wolfgang. 1963. Direkter und indirekter „Genitiv". *Zeitschrift für Ägyptische Sprache und Altertumskunde* 88: 58–66.

Schuh, Russell. 1990. Re-employment of grammatical morphemes in Chadic: Implications for language history. In: Baldi, Philip (ed.), *Linguistic change and reconstruction methodology*. Berlin: De Gruyter, 599–618.

Seiler, Hansjakob. 1983. *Possession as an operational dimension of language*. Tübingen: Narr.

Shisha-Halevy, Ariel. 2007a. *Topics in Coptic syntax: Structural studies in the Bohairic dialect*. Leuven: Peeters.

Shisha-Halevy, Ariel. 2007b. Determination-signalling environment in Old and Middle Egyptian: Work-notes and reflections. In: Bar, Tali & Cohen, Eran (eds.), *Studies in Semitic and general linguistics in honor of Gideon Goldenberg*. (Alter Orient und Altes Testament. Vol. 334). Münster: Ugarit Verlag, 223–254.

Spencer, Andrew. 2007. The possessum-agreement construction or Does Albanian have a genitive case? In: Radford, Andrew (ed.), *Martin Atkinson – The Minimalist Muse*. (Essex Research Reports in Linguistics). Colchester: University of Essex, Colchester, Dept. of Language and Linguistics (http://www.essex.ac.uk/linguistics/publications/errl/ERRL53. pdf)

Stassen, Leon. 2009. *Predicative possession*. Oxford: Oxford University Press.

Till, Walter. 1986. *Koptische Grammatik: Saïdischer Dialekt: Mit Bibliographie, Lesestücken und Wörterverzeichnissen*. Leipzig: Enzyklopädie.

Dmitry Idiatov

Egyptian non-selective interrogative pronominals: history and typology*

Abstract: Non-selective interrogative pronominals (NIPs) are interrogative pronominals such as *who?* and *what?* in English, that are used in non-selective contexts. In this paper, I examine NIPs throughout the recorded history of the Egyptian language from the perspective of a typology of NIPs proposed by Idiatov (2007), where NIPs are defined through their functions in terms of prototypical combinations of values. I focus on the analysis of the attested shifts in the patterns of use of different NIPs and the development of new NIPs in the course of the history of the Egyptian language. When both the formal and functional differentiation of Egyptian NIPs are considered from a broader Afroasiatic perspective, the NIP system of Egyptian appears to have evolved from a more Berber-like situation in Old and Middle Egyptian to a more Semitic/Cushitic-like situation in Late, Demotic, and Coptic Egyptian.

1 Introduction

Non-selective interrogative pronominals (NIPs) are interrogative pronominals used in non-selective contexts, where the speaker perceives the choice as free. These are forms equivalent to English *who?* and *what?*. In selective contexts, where the choice is perceived by the speaker as being restricted to a closed set of similar alternatives, selective interrogative pronominals such as English *which (one)?* are used.

In the present paper, I examine NIPs throughout the recorded history of the Egyptian language, from Old Egyptian to Coptic. Given the exclusively written nature of the available sources, I start in § 2 by discussing the challenges that the pre-Coptic Egyptian writing systems pose for the analysis of Egyptian NIPs. As to the analysis itself, I approach Egyptian NIPs from the perspective of a typology of NIPs proposed by Idiatov (2007). I briefly present this typology in § 3. This

---

* I am grateful to Jean Winand, Mark van de Velde, Johan van der Auwera, the editors and the reviewers for their comments on the previous drafts of this text. I also gratefully acknowledge the GOA (Geconcerteerde Onderzoeksactie) *Mood and Modality* project of the University of Antwerp and the project P6/44 of the Interuniversity Attraction Poles program of the Belgian Federal Science Policy for financial support.

typology is most interested in two parameters of variation in the domain of NIPs. The first parameter concerns the formal differentiation of 'who?' and 'what?' or the lack thereof in a given language. The second parameter is about the functional differentiation of 'who?' and 'what?' in languages where they are formally distinguished. I examine how Egyptian NIPs behave with respect to these two parameters in §§ 4 and 5 respectively. In both sections, I also address the question of how we can account for the attested shifts in the patterns of use of different NIPs and the development of new NIPs in the course of the history of the Egyptian language. Finally, in § 6, I consider Egyptian NIPs from a broader Afroasiatic perspective.

2 The challenges of the pre-Coptic Egyptian writing systems

The three pre-Coptic Egyptian writing systems are hieroglyphic, hieratic and demotic.[1] Roughly speaking, hieratic and (later) demotic scripts are cursive analogues of the hieroglyphic script. Although the pre-Coptic Egyptian scripts are predominantly phonetic and only partially ideographic, their usability for many kinds of linguistic research is hampered by the fact that they are almost exclusively consonantal.[2] Generally speaking, vowels (and their quality) are marked with certain regularity only in the demotic script (Lexa 1947–1951: 9), which is the latest of the three pre-Coptic Egyptian scripts. However, it is only with the Coptic script based on the Greek alphabet that vowels become fully specified in writing. It is hard to overlook the consequences that this underspecification inherent to the script may have on the strength of the claims that we can make about Egyptian. The challenge is particularly important in the case of Egyptian NIPs because

---

1 I present Egyptian examples in the traditional Egyptological transliteration, as can be found in Gardiner (2001: § 19). The letter and number given in brackets after a hieroglyphic sign, such as 𓅱 (G43), represent the codes of Gardiner's ([1957] 2001) classification of hieroglyphs traditionally used in Egyptology.

2 The only two exceptions may be represented by the signs 𓅱 (G43) and 𓇋 (M17), usually transliterated as *w* and *i ~ j* respectively. These signs, especially 𓇋 *i ~ j*, are believed to represent not only the approximants /w/ and /j/ but also "a vowel that was present in presumably an unexpected position, without necessarily indicating what vowel was present" (Callender 1975: 3). A vocalic interpretation appears to be most plausible word-initially. The double sign 𓇌 (or 𖤐), usually transliterated as *y*, is hardly found as initial letter and may represent just a graphic variation of its singleton counterpart (Callender 1975: 3, 5).

these are short words and the possibility remains that what is considered as one NIP with two meanings are in fact two NIPs with different vocalizations corresponding to two different meanings.

Nevertheless, as some indirect evidence suggests, the probability of the latter situation is actually rather low. First, although lexical homographs are usually further distinguished by means of additional signs, the so-called "determinatives", this never seems to be done for interrogative pronominals. A given interrogative pronominal is rendered with the same sign(s) whether it means 'who?' or 'what?', which strongly suggests that it is always one and the same interrogative. At the most, even if one writing does stand for more than one interrogative differing only in their vowels, any difference possibly expressed this way was not lexical, 'who?' vs. 'what?', but grammatical of some kind, e.g., difference in case, the so-called "state", focus, etc. Second, it appears that the agreement patterns associated with a presumed 'who?, what?' interrogative pronominal do not depend on whether it means 'who?' or 'what?'. Third, more than one unrelated 'who?, what?' interrogatives are recorded, which is indicative of a certain recurrent pattern in the development of Egyptian interrogative pronominals. Furthermore, for at least one of these interrogatives, *pw* (more common in combination with a particle as *pw-tr/ pw-tỉ/ ptr/ pty/ pt*), Gardiner (2001: § 497) has suggested a single source, a demonstrative *pw* 'DEM.M.SG', which implies that the writings representing the respective interrogative are also likely to have only one vocalization for both 'who?' and 'what?'. Finally, additional indirect evidence in favor of the existence of 'who?, what?' interrogatives in Egyptian is provided by the fact that such interrogatives are common in Berber (cf. Idiatov 2007: 155–180), another branch of Afroasiatic which is geographically, and probably genetically, one of the closest to Egyptian.

3 A typology of non-selective interrogative pronominals

As argued in Idiatov (2007), from a typological perspective NIPs are best defined through their functions in terms of prototypical combinations of values. Thus, 'who?' is an NIP that prototypically asks for the identification of a person and that expects a proper name as a typical answer. The interrogative 'what?' is an NIP prototypically asking for the classification of a thing and expecting a common noun as an answer. These definitions of 'who?' and 'what?' are idealizations resulting from the interaction between several parameters within a single conceptual space, as represented in Figure 1.

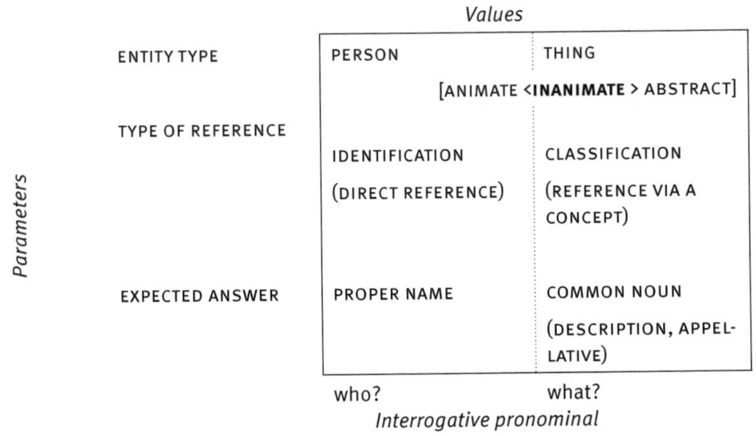

Values

		PERSON	THING
ENTITY TYPE			[ANIMATE <**INANIMATE** > ABSTRACT]
TYPE OF REFERENCE		IDENTIFICATION	CLASSIFICATION
		(DIRECT REFERENCE)	(REFERENCE VIA A CONCEPT)
EXPECTED ANSWER		PROPER NAME	COMMON NOUN
			(DESCRIPTION, APPEL-LATIVE)
		who?	what?

Parameters

Interrogative pronominal

Figure 1: Conceptual space for delimiting the prototypical functions of non-selective interrogative pronominals (Idiatov 2007: 18)

Strictly speaking, the third parameter expected answer is somewhat redundant, since its values can be defined in terms of prototypical correlates of the second parameter, i.e., type of reference. However in some cases expected answer does play an irreducible role in the choice of an interrogative pronominal, as in example (2) below.

We may call the combinations of values [person + identification (+ proper name)] and [thing + classification (+ common noun)] prototypical combinations of values with respect to the choice of a non-selective interrogative pronominal. Note that this does not imply at all that questions about classification of persons or identification of things are less natural in any sense. What this means is that the latter two kinds of questions are not prototypically associated with one of the two NIPs, viz., 'who?' and 'what?'. This is why, for instance, different languages distinguishing between 'who?' and 'what?' may opt for a different NIP in cases of such non-prototypical combinations of values. For instance, consider example (1) from Russian and its English translation where we have a non-prototypical combination of values [person + classification (+ common noun)]. I will refer to examples like (1) as KIND-questions.

Russian

(1) A   on **kto** voobšče? Doktor?
     and he **who** actually doctor
     '**What** is he actually? A doctor?'

We may say that English and Russian give preference to different parameters. That is, English prefers the TYPE OF REFERENCE, viz., what matters is that the question is about [classification]. The preference for TYPE OF REFERENCE is manifested by what we may call 'what?'-dominance, that is, in English 'what?' wins over 'who?' in the case of this particular non-prototypical combination of values. At the same time, Russian prefers the parameter ENTITY TYPE, viz., what matters is that the question is about a [person], and this preference is manifested by 'who?'-dominance, since 'who?' wins over 'what?'.

Another non-prototypical combination of values [thing + identification (+ proper name)] that I will refer to as NAME-questions is found in (2).

Kgalagadi (Niger-Congo, Bantu S30; Botswana; Kems Monaka, p.c.)

(2) [A:] *libizho* *la*   *lehelo* *lo*   *ke* ***anye?***
        G5.name AG5.CON G11.place AG11.DEM COP **who**
     [B:] *ke* *Hughunsi*
        COP PROP
     '[A:] **What** (lit.: 'who?') is the name of this place? [B:] It's Hukuntsi (a village name)'

Here again, we may say that English and Kgalagadi give preference to different parameters. Thus, English prefers ENTITY TYPE, viz., what matters is that the question is about a [thing], viz., the name of a place, whereas Kgalagadi prefers TYPE OF REFERENCE (& EXPECTED ANSWER), viz., what matters is that the question is about [identification] (& a [proper name]). The preference for ENTITY TYPE in English is manifested by 'what?'-dominance and the preference for TYPE OF REFERENCE (& EXPECTED ANSWER) in Kgalagadi is manifested by 'who?'-dominance.

Many languages treat non-human living beings similarly to humans in various respects and some also use 'who?' in questions about them, as in (3) from Russian, which can be considered a third, minor instance of a non-prototypical combination of values, viz., [animate thing + classification (+ common noun)], that I will refer to as ANIMATE-questions.

Russian

(3) **Kto** èto   tebja ukusil?
    who this you   bit
    '[Looking at a swelling on someone's hand clearly caused by an insect
    bite:] What stung you? (e.g., a wasp, a bee, etc.)'

Leaving aside some possible complications, the non-prototypical combinations
of values presented above yield the typology of 'who?'/'what?'-dominance shown
in Table 1.

Table 1: The full typology of 'who?'/'what?'-dominance in cases of non-prototypical combinations of values (Idiatov 2007: 119)

		KIND-questions	NAME-questions	ANIMATE-questions	Prominence
1	a	'who?'	'who?'	'who?'	'who?'
	b			('what?')	
2	a			'who?'	ENTITY TYPE
	b	'who?'	'what?'	('what?')	
3		'what?'	'who?'	('what?')	TYPE OF REFERENCE
4		'what?'	'what?'	('what?')	'what?'
5		'what?'	'what?'	'who?'	mixed (4/2a)
6		'what?'	'who?'	'who?'	mixed (3/2a)

It should be added that there is also a minority of languages to which the typology
presented in Table 1 does not really apply since they do not oblige their speakers
to distinguish formally between 'who?' and 'what?'. To be more precise, a lack of
differentiation between 'who?' and 'what?' in a given language implies that one
form can be used for both [person + identification (+ proper name)] and [thing +
classification (+ common noun)], which are the two prototypical combinations of
values with respect to the choice of a NIP. For considerations of space, I will not
discuss possible complications here. Let us just consider a clear example of lack
of differentiation between 'who?' and 'what?' from Poitevin, the dialect of French
spoken in the Poitou region (4).

Poitevin French

(4) a. *Qui qu'est   venu?*
     IPN REL-is   come.PST.PTCP
     'Who came?' (Mineau 1982: 255 via Rottet 2004: 173)

  b. *Qui qu'tu   manges?*
     IPN REL-2SG eat.PRS.2SG
     'What are you eating?' (Mineau 1982: 255 via Rottet 2004: 173)

To sum up, some languages do not oblige their speakers to distinguish formally between 'who?' and 'what?', although most languages do. Languages differ considerably in how they accommodate non-prototypical combinations of values.

4 Egyptian non-selective interrogative pronominals: formal differentiation of 'who?' and 'what?'

4.1 From Old Egyptian to Coptic: an overview

4.1.1 Old and Middle Egyptian

Older stages of the Egyptian language are characterized by the presence of several NIPs that are attested as both 'who?' and 'what?', viz., *m*, *pw*, and *zy*. These will be discussed in more detail in §§ 4.2.1, 4.2.2 ,and 4.2.3 respectively. Example (5) with *m* 'who?, what?' from Old Egyptian will suffice here as an illustration.

Old Egyptian

(5) a. *iri-n-i*   *m?*
     do.PFV.M-of-1SG.SUF IPN
     'What have I done? (lit.: 'The one that has been done by me (is) what?')' (Edel 1964: 517)

  b. *m   ḥwi-n-k?*
     IPN beat.REL.M-of-2SG.M.SUF
     'Whom have you beaten? (lit.: '(It is) who which has been beaten by you?')' (Edel 1964: 516)

The Old and Middle Egyptian interrogative pronominals are summarized in (6) in both transliteration and hieroglyphic script. Some rare hieroglyphic variants may be missing.

(6) Old and Middle Egyptian interrogative pronominals (based on Allen 2000; Edel 1955, 1964; Callender 1975; Gardiner 2001; Loprieno 1996; Vernus 2006)

a. *m, mỉ*   𓅓 ...   'who?, what?'

b. *pw*   'who?, what?'

    pw-tr

    pw-tỉ

    p-tr

    p-ty (p-tỉ)

    p-t

c. *ỉš-st*   'what?'

    ỉš-sy

d. *ỉḫ*   'what?'

e. *zy (zỉ), sy (sỉ)*   'which [N]?, what (kind of) [N]?' (person or thing), 'which one?, who?, what?'

    z, s

The interrogative *pw* is not attested in Old Egyptian texts (Edel 1955: 90) and is very rare in Middle Egyptian (Gardiner 2001: § 498). Nevertheless, it is believed to be old (Edel 1955: 90). According to Gardiner (2001: § 497), the interrogative *pw* stems from the demonstrative *p-w* 'M.SG-DEM'. The other, more frequent forms in (6b) result from a combination of *pw* with a particle *tr/ ty/ tỉ/ t* 'actually, forsooth, I wonder'.

The interrogative *ỉḫ* 'what?' goes back to a feminine noun (*ỉ)ḫ-t* 'thing(s), something, property' (-*t* is the feminine suffix) (cf. Gardiner 2001: § 501). The initial part *iš-* of the interrogative *iš-st/ iš-sy* 'what?' has the same origin.[3] Its final part *-st* is the dependent pronoun *st* (Allen 2000: 55), analyzed by Allen (2000: 49) as "neutral in gender and number" and referring to things ("nouns or plurals" other than those designating "living beings (people or gods)"). By analogy, the variant *-sy* is likely to be the feminine third person dependent pronoun *sy* (*sỉ*). The interrogative *iš-st/ iš-sy* 'what?' appears then to be a lexicalization of an original cleft structure 'It (she) is the thing [(that)...]?' → 'what is it (she) [(that)...]?' → 'what?'. In this respect, note that Old Egyptian questions with *iš-st/iš-sy* are commonly framed as clefts (see Edel 1964: 517), as in (7).

Old Egyptian

(7) *išst   pw   ḥm   n-n   ỉrrw-ṯn?*
    what COP indeed N-DEM do.IPFV.REL.M-2PL.SUF
    'What is it that you are doing?' (Edel 1964: 517)[4]

4.1.2 Late and Demotic Egyptian

In later stages the lack of differentiation between 'who?' and 'what?' gradually disappears either through specialization of the respective NIPs in one of the two meanings, viz., 'who?' in the case of *m* and its later derived forms and 'what?' in the case of the *pw*-based interrogatives, or through loss of the interrogative, as in the case of *zy*. Thus, consider the Late Egyptian interrogative pronominals in (8) and the Demotic Egyptian interrogative pronominals in (9).

---

3 The link between the word for 'thing' and *iš* can be supported by the fact that in Old Egyptian, *ỉḥt* was written as *ỉšt* before suffixes (Hannig 2003: 200–201). However, I am reluctant to accept Allen's (2000: 55) hypothesis that *iš-* of the interrogative *ỉšst/ỉšsy* originates in the interrogative *ỉḥ* 'what?'. Rather, *ỉḥ* 'what?' represents a later development from the same source, the noun 'thing, something'. In this respect, note that while *iš-st/iš-sy* is well attested in Old Egyptian, *ỉḥ* 'what?' is not (cf. Edel 1955: 90, 1964: 515–518). Furthermore, *ỉḥ* is also rare in Middle Egyptian, becoming common only in Late Egyptian (Gardiner 2001: § 501).

4 The masculine agreement on the verb here is controlled by the neuter demonstrative *nn*. According to Gardiner (2001: § 511, § 111), the demonstratives of the *n*-series trigger masculine (singular) agreement on "participles and relative forms".

(8) Late Egyptian interrogative pronominals (based on Černý 1978; Erman 1968; Junge 1996; Korostovtsev 1973 and Lesko & Lesko 2002–2004)

a. *nym (nîm)* 　　　　 〔hieroglyphs〕 　'who?'

　　 m 　　　　　　 〔hieroglyph〕 　'who?, what?'

b. *îḫ* 　　　　　　 〔hieroglyphs〕 　'what?'

c. *ît(î)* 　　　　　 〔hieroglyphs〕 　'which [N]?',
　　　　　　　　　　　　　　　　　　 'where?', 'which
　　　　　　　　　　　　　　　　　　 one?, who?'

d. *ptr* 　　　　　 〔hieroglyphs〕 　'what?, where?'

(9) Demotic interrogative pronominals (based on du Bourguet 1976; Johnson 2001; Lexa 1947–1951 and Spiegelberg 1925)[5]

nm, nim(e) 　　'who?'
îḫ 　　　　　 'what?', 'what (kind of) [N] (person or thing)?'[6]

The Late Egyptian interrogative *nym* (*nîm*) results from a combination of the interrogative *m(î)* with the preceding subject focus particle *în* (Gardiner 2001: § 496; Edel 1964: 515; Till 1986: 102), as in (10) and (11).

---

5 The original forms in demotic script are not provided due to difficulties with their reproduction. In Demotic data, some sources use the transliterations *a* and *e* because of their usual Coptic outcomes, ⲁ and ⲉ, (in hieroglyphic writing, these transliterations correspond to 〔M17-Z7〕 (M17-Z7) and 〔D21-Z1〕 (D21-Z1)), otherwise they are transliterated as *r* and *î(w)*, respectively (Lexa 1947–1951: 44; du Bourguet 1976: 3–4). Other transliterations that sources may differ on are ' ~ *i* and *i* ~ *y*. The latter variant in both cases is the same as in transliterations of earlier Egyptian data.

6 The attributive glosses 'which [N]?', 'what (kind of) [N]?' refer to the use of *îḫ* as the syntactic head of a genitive construction marked by *n* 'of', with the latter sometimes omitted, as in *îḫ* (*n*) *îšb3*? 'what illness?' (Spiegelberg 1925: 19).

Middle Egyptian

(10) *(i)n*   *m*   *tr*   *tw?*
SBJ.FOC IPN actually 2SG.M.DEP
'Who are you then?' (Loprieno 1996: 121), 'Who pray art thou?' (Gardiner 2001: § 496)

(11) *in*   *m*   *dd*   *sw?*
SBJ.FOC IPN say.IPFV.(M) 3SG.M.DEP
'[A:] What expresses it? [B: Twenty expresses it].' (Gardiner 2001: § 495; Callender 1975: 97)

The tendency towards the fusion of the combination *in m(i)* is already clear in Middle Egyptian. That by the Late Egyptian period this combination has already fused into a monomorphemic word is indicated by (i) the complete loss of the initial *i* of *in*, (ii) the introduction of the medial sign ⟍ (Z4) *y* (*i*) in *nym* (*nim*), which is generally believed to render the vowel *i*, (iii) the use of *nym* with prepositions, as a direct object (cf. Korostovtsev 1973: 82), or with the subject focus particle *in* (Jean Winand, p.c.).

The rare Late Egyptian interrogative *it(i)* 'which [N]?, where?, which one?, who?' is found "only in texts of refined language" (Erman 1968: 376). According to Hoch (1994: 43–44), it was borrowed from Semitic and can be reconstructed as **ē-dē< **ay-dē*, where the first part is a widespread Semitic interrogative root 'which (one)?, where?' and the second part is a demonstrative, similar for instance to the Classical Arabic demonstrative root *dā*.

4.1.3 Coptic Egyptian

In the Egyptian language of the Coptic period, the interrogatives meaning 'who?' and 'what?' are formally differentiated. Coptic interrogative pronominals are summarized in (12). In brackets, I indicate the dialect for which a given form is attested. An asterisk preceding the name of the dialect means that a given form is considered by Vycichl (1984) to be "aberrant" for this dialect.

(12) Coptic interrogative pronominals (based on Crum 1962; Lambdin 1983; Plumley 1948; Till 1961, 1986; Vycichl 1984; Jean Winand, Eitan Grossman, p.c.)[7]

a. ⲛⲓⲙ   *nim* (Bohairic, Sahidic)   'who?', 'which [N]?', what (kind of) [N]? (person or thing)', 'which (one)? (person or thing) (predicative)'

b. ⲟⲩ   *ou* (Sahidic, Bohairic)   'what?', 'what (kind of) [N] (thing)?'
   ⲟⲩⲟ   *ouo* (Akhmimic)
   ⲟⲩⲱ   *ouô* (*Sahidic)
   ⲟⲩⲁ   *oua* (*Oxyrhynchitic)
   ⲟ   *o* (Akhmimic, Lycopolitan)
   ⲱ   *ô* (Akhmimic, *Sahidic)
   ⲉⲩ   *eu* (Lycopolitan, Sahidic)

c. ⲁϣ   *aš* (Bohairic, Sahidic)   'what (kind of) [N]?, which [N]?
   ⲉϣ   *eš* (Lycopolitan, Fayyu-   (thing)', 'which one (thing)?',
   ⲉϩ'   mic)   'what? (predicative)'
   ⲁϩ'   *ex* (Akhmimic)
      ax (Proto-Theban)

The interrogative *aš* is usually assumed to go back to the pre-Coptic interrogative *íḫ* 'what?' (Vycichl 1984: 20). The interrogative *ou* must be a Coptic innovation, because it is not attested in any earlier form of Egyptian. Vycichl (1984: 228) suggests that together with a formally identical singular indefinite article, it goes back to the numeral 'one', which in Middle Egyptian was written as *w*ˁ and which in Sahidic Coptic had the forms *oua* (ᴍ) and *ouei* (ꜰ). In Coptic, the numeral is also used as an indefinite, but only about persons as '(a certain) one, a certain man/woman, someone' (Lambdin 1983: 64; Till 1986: 105–106).

When the attributive glosses 'which [N]?', what (kind of) [N]?' are used in (12), syntactically the respective interrogative pronominal functions as the head of a genitive construction marked by *n* 'of' (or its allomorph *m*), as in (13) with *nim*.

---

7 For transliterating Coptic, I use the Leipzig-Jerusalem system (Grossman & Haspelmath, this volume).

Coptic Egyptian

(13) a. *nim n-rôme*
 IPN of-man
 'which man?' or 'what (kind of) man?' (Lambdin 1983: 62; Till
 1986: 102)

   b. *nim m-prohoimion*
 IPN of-preface
 'what (kind of) preface?' or 'which preface?' (Crum 1962: 225)

The use of *nim* with this semantics as the head of the genitive construction with
non-human nouns, as in (13b), is a Coptic innovation as compared to the Late
Egyptian and Demotic data. Equally innovative are the occasional occurrences
of a predicative *nim* with a selective meaning in questions about non-humans
instead of the regular *aš*, as in (14).

Coptic Egyptian

(14) *aš / nim   gar   pe   p-noc?*
   IPN   because M.SG.COP DEF.ART.M.SG-great
   '[Fools and blind!] For which is greater, [the gold, or the temple that
   sanctifies the gold]?' (Matthew 23: 17 in Crum 1962: 225; Eberle & Schulz
   2004: 15; Till 1986: 102; Wells 2000–2006)[8]

The two new uses of *nim* in Coptic may be due to an Ancient Greek influence.
Whereas Late Egyptian *nym* (*nîm*) and Demotic *nm*, *nim(e)* functioned as exclusively human NIPs 'who?', their Coptic reflex *nim* has a much broader scope of
use, in which it bears strong resemblance to the Ancient Greek non-neuter interrogative pronominal *tis* (NON‹N›.SG.NOM). The latter is often glossed only as
'who?', but this is misleading. Its common human interpretation is really deriva-
tive of its gender specification and can be perfectly absent, as in (15) and (16),
which are parallel to the Coptic examples (13) and (14) respectively.

---

8 The use of *nim* in Matthew 23: 17 in some of its Sahidic and Bohairic versions is reported by
Crum (1962: 225). The other sources cited give only *aš*.

Ancient Greek

(15) a. *tines*   *aneres*
          IPN.NON‹N›.PL.NOM man.M.PL.NOM
          'which/what men?' (Bailly 1901: 873)

      b. *tis*   *achô*
          IPN.NON‹N›.SG.NOM sound.F.SG.NOM
          'which/what sound?' (Liddell & Scott 1940 under *tis*)

(16) *tis*   *gar*   *meizôn*   *estin*
      IPN.NON‹N›.SG.NOM because greater.M.SG.NOM be.PRS.ACT.IND.3SG
      ho   *chrusos*   *ê*   *ho*
      DEF.ART.M.SG.NOM gold.M.SG.NOM or DEF.ART.M.SG.NOM
      naos?
      temple.M.SG.NOM
      '[Fools and blind!] For which is greater, [the gold, or the temple that
      sanctifies the gold]?' (Matthew 23: 17)

The Ancient Greek examples (15) and (16) are parallel to the Coptic examples (13)
and (14) respectively. However, whereas the use of *tis* in Greek here can be readily
accounted for by its non-neuter gender specification, a similar system-internal
explanation is lacking for the use of *nim* in Coptic. Given that Ancient Greek is
otherwise well known to have exerted significant impact on Coptic, especially on
its lexicon, this is indicative of a Greek influence on the use of Coptic *nim*.

4.2 Egyptian NIPs allowing for a lack of differentiation between 'who?' and 'what?'

4.2.1 *m* 'who?, what?'

The use of *m* as 'who?' and 'what?' in Old and Middle Egyptian was illustrated
in (5), (10) and (11). As argued in § 2, there is some strong indirect evidence that
what is transliterated as *m* is indeed one and the same interrogative irrespective
of whether it means 'who?' or 'what?'. Among other things, an important piece of
evidence comes from the fact that no consistent link can be established between
one of the two meanings, viz., 'who?' or 'what?', and a given hieroglyphic writing
of the interrogative *m*. That is, the differences in its hieroglyphic form do not represent differences in its lexical meaning.

In Old Egyptian, the most typical writing of this interrogative is the bare phonogram 𓅓 *m* (G17) (Edel 1955: 90, 1964: 515–517), which would normally imply that it was realized as /m(V)/. What is relevant here is the absence of a vowel before *m* and of a second consonant at the end.[9] The presence of a final vowel or its possible quality cannot be established with certainty. In fact, it is quite possible that the transliteration *m* covers several morphosyntactically conditioned variants, such as /m/, /mi/ or /ma/. In this respect, compare the situation in Ait Ndhir Tamazight, a Northern Berber Afroasiatic language spoken in Morocco. Thus, Ait Ndhir Tamazight has an interrogative *m* 'who?, what?, which one?', which is normally used in a cleft construction in combination with the gender-number neutral demonstrative pronominal *ay* (with allomorphs *agg-* and *a*),[10] as in (17–19), and in a few contexts on its own, as in (20).

Ait Ndhir Tamazight (Penchoen 1973: 79)

(17)   *m   ay   nttannay   asəkka?*
       IPN DEM FUT.1PL.SBJ.see tomorrow
       'Whom/what shall we see tomorrow?' (lit.: 'Who/what is it that we shall see tomorrow?')

(18)   *m   aggədda   yər-taddart?*
       IPN DEM.3SG.M.SBJ.go.PFV.PTCP.SG to-house
       'Who has been to the house?' (lit.: 'Who is it who has been to the house?')

---

9 Certain (sentence-initial) "remarkable writings" ("auffälligen Schreibungen") reported for Old Egyptian by Edel (1964: 516–517), viz., 𓇋𓅓 (M17-G17) and 𓇋𓅓𓂜 (M17-G17-D35), might at first sight suggest the presence of a vowel before *m*. However, it is much more likely that they represent contractions of *in m* (where *in* is the subject focus particle) due to assimilation, viz., *im(m)* in the first case and *in(n)* in the second case. In this respect, recall that in Middle Egyptian, the subject focus marker *in* precedes the interrogative *m* so frequently, particularly in sentence-initial position, that the two ultimately end up by fusing into one morpheme (cf. § 4.1.2). Note also that an assimilation from *in m* to *im-m* or *in-n* would result in two identical consonants next to each other and in such cases there was "a strong tendency to write them but once" (Gardiner 2001: 52). In 𓇋𓅓 (M17-G17), *im(-m)*, only *m* 𓅓 (G17) would naturally be written. In 𓇋𓅓𓂜 (M17-G17-D35), *in(-n)*, however, it was probably considered more important to preserve the sign 𓅓 (G17) indicating the interrogative in order to avoid possible ambiguity. In other words, here, the sign 𓂜 (D35) is a phonetic determinative specifying the reading of the previous sign. The phonetic value of the sign 𓂜 (D35) is transliterated as *n*, whereas as an ideogram or a semantic determinative it expresses the idea of negation.
10 The allomorph *a* is used when preceding an adposition. The form *agg-* results from the fusion with the following third person singular masculine verbal subject prefix *i-*.

(19) m   a   mi iša   *lflus?*
IPN DEM to 3SG.M.SBJ.give.PFV money
'To whom did he give the money?' (lit.: 'Who is it to whom he gave the money?')

(20) m   ism-ənnəs?
IPN name-GEN.3SG
'What's his/her name? What's it called?'

However, next to *m* Ait Ndhir Tamazight also has *-mi* 'who?, what?' used in combination with prepositions, as in (21).

Ait Ndhir Tamazight (Penchoen 1973: 82)

(21) a. *ṭaddarṭ- aḏ ṭ-i-n-mi?*
house.F-this F-DEM-GEN-IPN
'Whose house is this? (lit.: 'This house is the one of who')'

b. *s-mi?*
with-IPN
'with what/whom?'

c. *xf-mi?*
on-IPN
'on what/whom?, about whom/what?'

d. *yer-mi?*
to-IPN
'to(ward) who? (to whose place?)'

e. *šəgg d-mi?*
2SG.M with-IPN
'you and who?'

Following the principles of the Egyptian hieroglyphic writing system, forms such as Ait Ndhir Tamazight *m*, *m a* and *mi* would be represented by a single hieroglyphic writing transliterable as *m*.

By the Middle Egyptian period, next to 𓅓 *m*, new writings of the interrogative become particularly common, such as 𓅓𓂟, 𓅓𓂝, 𓅔 and 𓅓𓂞, which Allen (2000: 54) transliterates as *mỉ*.[11] In the hieroglyphic script, the older bare phonogram 𓅓 *m* (G17) becomes extended with a so-called determinative, usually 𓂟 (D38) or 𓂝 (D36), sometimes 𓂞 (D37). The latter three signs can hardly be semantic determinatives here because then they normally refer to the idea of giving. Apparently, in the case of the interrogative, they function as phonetic determinatives specifying the reading of another sign (group of signs). The exact sound value of the sign 𓂝 (D36) is somewhat problematic because it is often used instead of other "forearm"-signs (D37–D44). The signs 𓂟 (D38) and 𓂞 (D37) when used as a phonogram have the value *mỉ* or *m*. In the case of the interrogative, their value is most likely *mỉ* rather than *m* and phonologically it is then /maj(V)/. The evidence for this is twofold. First, the value of the signs 𓂟 (D38) and 𓂞 (D37) as phonograms originates in their usage in the writings of an irregular imperative *ỉmỉ* 'give!' (Gardiner 2001: 454) and this imperative has survived in Demotic as *my* and in Coptic as ⲙⲁⲓ *mai*, often reduced to ⲙⲁ *ma* (Vycichl 1984: 103). Second, some vocalized Demotic writings of the reflexes of the combination of the interrogative *m(ỉ)* with the preceding subject focus particle *ỉn* (cf. § 4.1.2 and below in this section), such as *nime* (Spiegelberg 1925: 19) point at an earlier reading /maj/, which in transliteration would be *mỉ*. The Demotic final *e* normally results in Coptic ⲉ (Lexa 1947–1951: 44), also transliterated as *e* and usually assumed to be realized as /ɛ/ or /ə/. It should be kept in mind that the presumed vocalization of *mỉ*, viz., /maj(V)/, does not necessarily tell us something about the (possible) vocalization of the older form *m*.[12] In this respect, recall the

---

11 Vernus (2006: 145) mentions some rare writings that probably should be transliterated as *ỉmy* and *ỉmw*, although according to him, not all the alleged examples are certain and the exact function of these writings remains unclear. As discussed above, the initial *ỉ* is most likely to come from the subject focus marker *ỉn* (cf. footnote 10), whereas the final *y* could, in principle, also be transliterated as *ỉ* (cf. footnote 3) similarly to *mỉ*. The final *w* in *(ỉ)mw* could come from an occasional contraction of the interrogative with the following singular masculine demonstrative (and later also a copula) *pw* (cf. § 4.2.2). In this respect, note that in Old and Middle Egyptian, the phrase *m pw* 'who is it?' become lexicalized as 'someone, a certain person' (Vernus 2006: 167).

12 Although Vernus (2006: 145), referring to Albright (1926: 188), claims that at the time of the 18th dynasty, the cuneiform spelling of the interrogative *m* was *mu*, suggesting its vocalization as *mu*, the actual data presented by Albright (1926: 188) does not really warrant such interpretation. Thus, it is absolutely not obvious why the syllable *mu* in the relevant cuneiform example, viz., [*ši-na* 'two' + *aḫ* 'what?' + *mu* '?'] presumably meaning 'what is two (in Assyrian)?', should represent the interrogative in issue.

various interrogative forms and collocations used to convey the meanings 'who?' and 'what?' in Ait Ndhir Tamazight, such as *m ay* /maj/, *m a*, *m* and *mi*.

The element *i* in *mi* is likely to be related to the demonstrative root *i* mentioned by Loprieno (1996: 68).[13] Thus, the Egyptian form *mi* /maj/ could be structurally and formally similar to the Ait Ndhir Tamazight form *m ay* /maj/ 'who/what (is) it [(that)...]? ' illustrated earlier in (17). Combining interrogative pronominals with "reinforcing" deictics is quite common in other branches of Afroasiatic, especially in Berber, as illustrated here by Ait Ndhir Tamazight, and in Semitic (see, e.g., Barth 1913: 137–150; Brockelmann 1913: 196).

By the Late Egyptian period, as mentioned in § 4.1.2, the older form *m(i)* 'who?, what?' becomes largely replaced by the new form *nym* (*nim*) 'who?' which stems from a combination of the interrogative *m(i)* with the preceding subject focus particle *in* (Gardiner 2001: § 496; Edel 1964: 515; Till 1986: 102). The use of the Coptic Egyptian interrogative *nim* 'who?' is illustrated in (22) and (23).

Coptic Egyptian

(22)   *p-šêre*   *n-nim?*
       DEF.ART.M.SG-son   of-who
       'Whose son?' (Lambdin 1983: 19; Till 1986: 102)

(23)   *nim   pe   pei-rôme?*
       who   M.SG.COP   M.SG.this-man
       'Who is this man?' (Lambdin 1983: 19)

The development from the general 'who?, what?' interrogative *m* to the human 'who?' interrogative *nim* can be readily accounted for by some of the morphosyntactic peculiarities of *m*, the general patterns of the organization of information structure in Egyptian and the steering role of frequency effects. The morphosyntactic peculiarities of *m* that I have in mind refer to the fact that, morphosyntactically, *m* behaves rather like a "dependent" pronoun[14] in that it "is used mostly after other words" (Allen 2000: 54), such as a preposition (24), a genitive marker *n* 'of' (25), a verbal form (5a), or a subject focus marker *in* (10–11). It very rarely begins a sentence on its own, as in (5b).

---

13 For possible parallels of this demonstrative root in other branches of Afroasiatic, see, for instance, Barth (1913: 89–91, 115–116, 129–130) for Semitic and Frajzyngier (1985: 64–66) for Chadic.
14 In Egyptology, the term *dependent pronouns* refers to a class of pronominal elements that "are less closely attached to a preceding word than the suffix-pronouns, but can never stand as first word of a sentence" (Gardiner 2001: § 43).

Middle Egyptian

(24) a. *m-m?*
            with-IPN
            'with what?' (Gardiner 2001: § 496)

      b. *r-m?*
            to-IPN
            'to what purpose?, what for?' (Gardiner 2001: § 496)

(25) *ḫpr-n*   *mḏw m sꜣwy*   *r(ꜣ) mḏw   n   m?*
      become.PFV.(M)-of   ten   as two-thirds one tenth   of   IPN
      'Of what is ten the 23/30 part? (lit.: 'Ten has become as two-thirds (and)
      one-tenth of what?')' (Gardiner 2001: § 495; Callender 1975: 98)

To this we can add that Egyptian constituent questions are regularly built up as
focalization constructions, which can be construed as clefts (cf. Callender 1975:
96, 98; Loprieno 1996: 121). Taken together with the morphosyntactically dependent nature of *m*, this need for focalization accounts for the frequency of the
combination of *m* with the subject focus marker *ỉn*. In turn, the frequency of this
combination accounts for the fact that by the Late Egyptian period it fuses into a
monomorphemic interrogative pronominal *nym* (*nỉm*) (cf. § 4.1.2). That *nym* (*nỉm*)
becomes confined to the meaning 'who?' as compared to the earlier broader use
of *m* as 'who?, what?' can be related to the fact that *ỉn* is a subject focus marker.
Furthermore, at least in declarative sentences, according to Callender (1975: 92),
ỉn tends to mark subject focus only with specific (definite?) subjects. Subjects
tend to encode referents higher on the animacy hierarchy. Similarly, higher referentiality correlates with higher animacy. Finally, a certain role in the narrowing
of the semantics of *nym* (*nỉm*) to 'who?' should probably be attributed to the competition with the specialized 'what?' interrogatives *ỉḫ* and *ỉš-st*.

4.2.2 *pw* 'who?, what?' and related forms

As mentioned in § 4.1.1, although the interrogative *pw* is not attested in Old Egyptian texts (Edel 1955: 90) and is very rare in Middle Egyptian (Gardiner 2001:
§ 498), it is believed to be old (Edel 1955: 90). At the same time, this interrogative
root is quite common in combination with a particle *tr/ ty/ tỉ/ t* 'actually, forsooth,
I wonder', as in (6b) *pw-tr/ pw-tỉ/ ptr/ pty/ pt*.

The older form *pw* appears to be primarily used as 'who?', as in (26). Thus, Edel (1964: 518) glosses it only as 'who?'. Gardiner (2001: § 498) glosses *pw* as both 'who?' and 'what?', without providing clear examples of its use as 'what?', however.

Old Egyptian

(26) *pw sw   (i)ʕk(i)?*
      IPN 3SG.M.DEP   enter.IPFV.(M)
      'Who is he who enters?' (Edel 1964: 518; Gardiner 2001: § 498)[15]

The later combinations of this root with a particle *tr/ ty/ ti̯/ t* 'actually, forsooth, I wonder', viz., *pw-tr/ pw-ti̯/ ptr/ pty/ pt*, seem to be somewhat more commonly used as 'what?' (27–28) rather than 'who?' (29–30). By the Late Egyptian period, the *pw*-based interrogatives appear to completely lose the ability to have the human meaning 'who?'.

Middle Egyptian

(27) *p-ty   h33-t   r-f   m   sšr?*
      IPN-actually descend.IPFV.REL-F to-3SG.M.SUF as corn
      'What amount of corn can go into it?' (lit.: 'What is that which descends into it in corn?') (Gardiner 2001: § 497; Callender 1975: 97)

(28) *p-ty   n-3?*
      IPN-actually N-DEM
      'What is this/that?' (Gardiner 2001: § 111; Allen 2000: 52)

(29) *p-ty   sy   t-3   Rdḏt?*
      IPN-actually 3SG.F.DEP F.SG-DEM   PROP
      '[A:] Who is this Reddjedet? [B: She is the wife of a priest of Ra (name of a god), lord of Sakhebu, who is pregnant of three children belonging to Ra, lord of Sakhebu.]' (Gardiner 2001: exercise XXXIII)

---

15 The initial and the final *i*'s in the verb are put in brackets because they are not represented in the hieroglyphic writing that Edel gives for this example. That two *i*'s should not be present has been confirmed to me by Jean Winand (p.c.), who further comments that in some variants of the text where this example comes from the interrogative is written without the final *w*, as if it were cliticized.

(30) *p-tr*   *rf*   *sw?*
      IPN-actually FOC 3SG.M.DEP
      'Who is he?' (Gardiner 2001: § 497) or 'Who is he?, What is it?' (Callender 1975: 97)

Unlike the interrogatives *m* 'who?, what?' and *iḫ* 'what?', the interrogatives *pw, ptr* and the like always function as predicates (often of clefts) and never as objects, nor can they be headed by a preposition.

As outlined above, in the course of time the *pw*-based 'who?, what?' interrogatives appear to have shifted from primarily 'who?' to primarily 'what?'. To a large extent, this semantic evolution is likely to be accounted for by the etymology of the interrogative root *pw* and certain shifts in the use of the masculine gender. Let us start with the etymology of the interrogative root *pw*.

According to Gardiner (2001: § 497), the interrogative *pw* stems from the demonstrative *p-w* 'M.SG-DEM'. This etymology is quite plausible as it is corroborated by an apparently similar evolution that can be posited for several Northern Berber languages having the interrogative *wi(n)* 'who?', such as Kabyle Berber and Figuig *w-i* 'the one who, whoever (M.SG-INDF); who?' (Lionel Galand, p.c.; Kossmann 1997: 201) (31) or Tamezret *w-in* 'the one who, whoever (M.SG-INDF); who?' (Ben Mamou 2005: 8, 12).

Figuig (Northern Berber; Morocco; Kossmann 1997: 201)

(31) a. *w-i*   *xef-sent*   *i-jawb-en*
          M.SG-INDF   on-3SG.F   PTCP-answer.PFV-PTCP
          ad y-awey   *yelli-s*
          FUT 3SG.M.SBJ-bring.AOR   daughter-GEN.3SG
          'The one who (whoever) will answer will marry his daughter'

      b. *wi*   *ked*   *t-uṛaṛ-ed*
          who   with   2SG.SBJ-play.PFV-2SG.SBJ
          'With whom did you play?'

These *wi(n)* interrogatives can be compared to similar pronominal forms based on the root *-i* in other Northern and Southern Berber languages, such as Ait Seghrouchen *win* 'that one (M.SG)' (Northern Berber; Bentolila 1981: 53, 93) and Malian Tuareg *win* 'those ones (M.PL)' (<*w-i-en* 'M-DEM.PL-DISTANT') (Southern Berber; Heath 2005: 239–240). It is not uncommon for the forms based on the root *-i* to have non-specific or free-choice readings, as Chaouia *w-i* 'any one of these (M-DEM)' opposed to *w-a* 'exactly this (M-DEM)' (Northern Berber; Aikhenvald &

310 ── Dmitry Idiatov

Militarev 1991: 217). Often, they are then used to introduce non-specific or free-choice headless relative clauses and can be glossed as 'the one(s) who, whoever [does P]', as in (31a) or (32).

Malian Tuareg (Southern Berber; Heath 2005: 639)

(32) a. *i-dəd   osǽ-nen*
          [M]DEM-VEN go.RES-PTCP.PL
          'those (M) who (= whoever) have come'

      b. *t-i-dəd   t-osæ-t*
          F-DEM-VEN   PTCP.F.SG-go.PFV.POSITIVE-PTCP.F.SG
          'that one (F) who (= whoever) comes'

Sometimes, they can be rather interpreted as copulas 'be one that is [X]', as in (33).

Air Tuareg (Southern Berber; Galand 2002: 123)

(33) a. *ehəre-nin   i   yəggen*
          herd(M)-GEN.1SG   [M]DEM PTCP.M.SG.be.numerous.PTCP.M.SG
          'My herd is numerous (lit.: 'My herd is one that is numerous')'

      b. *tatte   t-i   n   kullu-nnəwən*
          food(F)   F-DEM   GEN   each-GEN.2PL
          'The food is of you all (lit.: 'The food is one of each of yours')'

Typically, the Berber forms based on the root *-i* are either plural, as Malian Tuareg *win* 'those ones (M.PL)', or neutral with respect to number, as in (32–33) above and (34).

Ait Ndhir Tamazight (Northern Berber; Penchoen 1973: 23)

(34) a. *w-i-nnəs*
          M-DEM-GEN.3SG
          'his/her masculine-one(s)'

      b. *w-i-s-sin*
          M-DEM-with-two.M
          'the second masculine-one(s)'

The evolution from a demonstrative to an interrogative could have started with the use of the demonstrative as introducer of (non-specific, free-choice) headless relative clauses, as in (31–32) above, and proceeded through conventionalization of stand-alone uses of such headless relative clauses accompanied by an interrogative intonation. That is, the development may have been 'The one who is the thief (is)?...' → 'Who is the thief?'. To a certain extent, this development would be analogous to the one proposed in § 4.1.1 for the Egyptian interrogative *iš-st* 'what?', viz., 'It (she) is the thing [(that)...]?' → 'what is it (she) [(that)...]?' → 'what?'.

Interestingly, the Egyptian demonstrative *p-w* 'M.SG-DEM' shows some further parallels to the Berber forms based on the root -*i*. Thus, *pw* in Egyptian has also developed copula-like uses similar to (33). Already during the Old Egyptian period ("long before the Middle Kingdom", Gardiner 2001: § 130) *p-w* 'M.SG-DEM' came to be used first as "logical subject after logical predicates consisting of a noun [...] as an equivalent for 'he', 'she', 'it' or 'they' invariable in number and gender", as in (35) and (36), and subsequently as a copula linking two nominals, as in (37)[16] (Gardiner 2001: §§ 128–130).

Middle Egyptian

(35) *RꜤ   pw*
PROP DEM
'[A: Who is he? B:] It/He/This is Ra (name of a god)' (Gardiner 2001: § 128)

(36) *ḥmt   wꜤb   pw   n   RꜤ*
wife(F) priest DEM of PROP
'[A: Who is this Reddjedet?, B:] She is the wife of a priest of Ra (name of a god)' (Gardiner 2001: § 128)

(37) *dmi̓   pw   i̓mnt*
abode COP west
'The West is an abode' (Gardiner 2001: § 130)

Somewhat similarly to the Berber use of the forms based on the root -*i* as introducers of non-specific or free-choice headless relative clauses, in Egyptian *pw* can be used to form a pseudocleft with a non-specific (or indefinite?) nominal

---

16 Eitan Grossman (p.c.) suggests that (37) should rather be analyzed as antitopic construction with *pw* being a "pronominal subject".

as the predicate, as in (38), where *pw* can be analyzed as a copula or as a relative pronominal (cf. Callender 1975: 92; Loprieno 1996: 104).

Middle Egyptian

(38) *rmṯ pw   ḥzy-n-f?*
     man COP/REL praise.PFV.(M)-of-3SG.M.SUF
     'The one whom he praised is a man' (Loprieno 1996: 104), or as Callender (1975) would translate it, 'It was a man whom he praised'

If we omit here the initial non-specific nominal and add an interrogative intonation, we get a stand-alone (non-specific, free-choice) headless relative clause used as a question, viz., 'The one whom he praised (is)?...', which would be the same construction as was suggested above as the intermediate stage on the development from a demonstrative to an interrogative pronominal in Berber. This hypothesis allows us to account straightforwardly for the aforementioned fact that unlike the interrogatives *m* 'who?, what?' and *iḫ* 'what?', the interrogatives *pw*, *ptr* and the like always function as predicates (often of clefts) and never as objects, nor can they be headed by a preposition.

The primacy of the human meaning 'who?' in the semantics of the Egyptian *pw*-based interrogatives on the earlier stages is reminiscent of the human meaning 'who?' of the *wi(n)* interrogatives in Northern Berber, which similarly appear to stem from a masculine demonstrative pronominal. For Egyptian, the primacy of 'who?' in the semantics of the Egyptian *pw*-based interrogatives on the earlier stages correlates with the fact that in Old Egyptian and to an important extent in Middle Egyptian "the sense of the English neuter ('it', 'thing')" is preferably expressed by the feminine whereas by the Late Egyptian period this function is taken over by the masculine (Gardiner 2001: § 51, § 511). That is, in Old and Middle Egyptian, the feminine is the default non-human gender, whereas the masculine is the default human gender. Such a situation is not uncommon in Afroasiatic.[17]

The later shift in the semantics of the Egyptian *pw*-based 'who?, what?' interrogatives in favor of 'what?' largely precedes the generalization of the masculine as the general default gender (both human and non-human). Therefore, the stimulus behind the shift in the semantics of the interrogative should be sought

---

17 For instance, Diakonoff (1965: 53) reports that the feminine (overtly) marked by the affix *t-* is commonly used in Afroasiatic languages for abstract notions and "socially inactive" entities (cf. also Achab 2005: 102–103 on Berber).

elsewhere. Thus, I believe that the evolution of the interrogative is largely due to another more specific change related to the use of the masculine. The change I have in mind is the gender-number neutralization of the demonstrative *p-w* 'M.SG-DEM' when, as already mentioned in this section, it came to be used first as "logical subject after logical predicates consisting of a noun [...] as an equivalent for 'he', 'she', 'it' or 'they' invariable in number and gender", as in (35) and (36), and subsequently as a copula linking two nominals, as in (37) (Gardiner 2001: §§ 128–130). First, as this change was going on already during the Old Egyptian period ("long before the Middle Kingdom", Gardiner 2001: § 130), it better corresponds in its timing to the shift in the semantics of the interrogative. Second, it affects precisely the demonstrative *p-w* 'M.SG-DEM', the presumed etymological source of the interrogative. Thus, we get an additional piece of evidence in favor of the demonstrative etymology of the interrogative, which also correlates with the exclusively predicative use of the *pw*-based interrogatives and fits the path for the development of the interrogative proposed above. It is worth mentioning here that if the semantic evolution of the interrogative was influenced by the aforementioned gender-number neutralization of the demonstrative *p-w* 'M.SG-DEM', this would imply that the development of the interrogative out of the demonstrative was still ongoing when this neutralization was introduced in the language.

By the Late Egyptian period, the *pw*-based interrogatives (i) appear to completely lose the ability to have the human meaning 'who?' and (ii) become so rare[18] that they are probably best viewed as remnants of the Middle Egyptian stage. This is likely to be due to the competition with the other, semantically more specialized interrogatives, viz., (i) the specialized human interrogative 'who?', *(i)n m*, that emerged during the Middle Egyptian period and eventually resulted in the Late Egyptian *nym* (*nỉm*) 'who?' (cf. § 4.1.1), and (ii) the specialized non-human interrogatives 'what?', *ỉš-st* and *ỉḫ*.

4.2.3 The 'who?, what?' use of *zy* (and the like)

As indicated in (6e), the interrogative *zy* is transliterated in a variety of ways in the sources, viz., *zy*, *zỉ*, *sy*, *sỉ*, *z* and *s*. However, these differences do not reflect

---

18 Thus, only one source, Lesko & Lesko (2004: 159), mentions the interrogative *ptr* for Late Egyptian. In this respect, Eitan Grossman (p.c.) points out that Lesko & Lesko (2004) is not a very reliable source and that the presumed Late Egyptian form *ptr* is more likely to be the presentative 'look, lo, behold', which evolved from the verb *ptr* 'look'.

any difference in the semantics or use of this interrogative and will therefore be ignored here.[19]

The interrogative *zy* is particularly common in attributive use as 'which [N]?, what (kind of) [N]?' (person or thing), as in (39).

Middle Egyptian

(39) *zy w3t?*
      IPN path
      'which path?' (Allen 2000: 55), '[on] what road?' (Gardiner 2001: § 499)

Given this common attributive usage, there are good chances that the final *-y* of *zy* is the same *-y* as the adjectivizing suffix *-y* (cf. Gardiner 2001: § 79). However, unlike the adjectives in *-y*, *zy* only very sporadically agrees in gender-number with the noun it modifies (cf. Vernus 2006: 146, contra Gardiner 2001: § 499).

In Old and Middle Egyptian, the interrogative *zy* also occasionally appears predicatively as 'who?' (40–41) and 'what?' (42–43) (cf. Edel 1955: 90, 1964: 518; Gardiner 2001: § 499). In some cases, *zy* can also be interpreted selectively as 'which one?' (40). Finally, Vernus (2006: 151) also provides an example of *zy* with a preposition, viz., *r zy* '[you are] to what? (i.e., 'in what direction')'.

---

19 I prefer the transliteration *zy* as the representative form of this interrogative for the following reasons. The variation between *z* and *s* in the transliterations is due to the fact that the original Old Egyptian distinction between *z* and *s* (phonologically, probably /θ/ vs. /s/, cf. Allen 2000: 16) disappeared by Middle Egyptian so that only *s* has remained, but because Egyptian orthography was rather conservative, the distinction was often still preserved in writing. As a rule, hieroglyphic writings of this interrogative use the signs —— (O34, the so-called "bolt") or 𓊃 (O35, from a combination of O34 with "walking legs" sign D54). The original phonogram value of both signs is *z*. Therefore, transliterations with *z* reflect an older reading, whereas transliterations with *s* reflect a later merger of *z* with *s*. Furthermore, this interrogative was only very rarely written with a phonogram 𓋴*s* (S29) in Middle Egyptian (Gardiner 2001: § 499). The variation between *y* and *i* in the transliterations of this interrogative appears to be a matter of interpretation, for it does not reflect any difference in hieroglyphic form. In both cases, the writing is either 𓏭 (double M17) or 𓏯 (Z4). I opt for *y* because in Middle Egyptian the two writings normally have the same transliteration value *y* (Gardiner 2001: § 20, 481, 536–537).

Old Egyptian

(40) *zi̓ pw (i̓)ḏd(i̓) i̓ri̓-f m tr?*
IPN COP/REL say.IPFV.(M) do.PFV.(M)-3SG.M.SUF in time
'Which one/Who can/would say that he can do it on time?' (Edel's
1964: 518 German translation is 'Wer ist einer, der sagen (kann), dass
er es zur (rechten) Zeit schafft?')

Middle Egyptian

(41) *ntk sy?*
2SG.M.INDEP IPN
'Who are you?' (Gardiner 2001: § 499)

(42) *sy pw mi̓w p-w ʕ3?*
IPN COP cat M-DEM great
'What is that great cat?' (Depuydt's 1999: 238 translation is 'Who is that
great cat?')

(43) *sy ty pw ʕt-y i̓pt-f?*
IPN actually COP limb-DU DEM.F.PL-3SG.M.SUF
'What are those two limbs?' (Gardiner 2001: § 499)

The lack of differentiation between 'who?' and 'what?' with the predicatively used
zy has its straightforward explanation in the attributive origins of this interrogative where it does not differentiate between humans and non-humans either.[20]

By the Late Egyptian period, the interrogative *zy* disappears from the language.

---

20 The interrogative *zy* can be compared to the French interrogative *quel* 'which [N]?, what (kind
of) [N]?', which is usually used attributively, as in *quel arbre/homme?* 'which tree/man?, what
(kind of) tree/man?', but also allows for predicative use as either 'what?' or 'who?' (cf. Riegel et
al. 2001: 395; Idiatov 2007: 247–249).

5 Egyptian non-selective interrogative pronominals: functional differentiation of 'who?' and 'what?'

The issue of functional differentiation between 'who?' and 'what?' concerns only the interrogatives that are specialized in one of the two meanings, such as *íḥ* 'what?' and *nim* 'who?'.[21] It should be mentioned that my data on the functional differentiation is rather fragmentary and more examples are needed. This is especially true for Old and Middle Egyptian. For these two earliest stages, the relevant examples (i.e., examples involving KIND-questions, NAME-questions or ANIMATE-questions as defined in § 3) that I have, involve only the interrogatives that can be used as both 'who?' and 'what?' such as *m* and *pw*-based interrogatives. This means that, strictly speaking, for the time being, it is not possible to describe Old and Middle Egyptian in terms of the typology of functional differentiation of 'who?' and 'what?' presented in § 3 and Table 1. However, we could also interpret the lack of relevant examples with the specialized non-human interrogatives 'what?', *íš-st* and *íḥ*, as an indication that the latter interrogatives were not possible in such questions. If we allow for such an interpretation, in terms of the typology of functional differentiation of 'who?' and 'what?' Old and Middle Egyptian would represent type 1 (cf. § 3), which implies the use of 'who?' in KIND-questions and in NAME-questions.

Late and Coptic Egyptian with their clear formal differentiation between 'who?' and 'what?' provide a much more rewarding domain for a study of the functional differentiation between 'who?' and 'what?'.[22] Thus, in terms of the typology presented in § 3 and Table 1, Late and Coptic Egyptian represent type 3 characterized by TYPE OF REFERENCE prominence. That is, they allow for the use of 'what?' in KIND-questions, as in (44–45), and 'who?' in NAME-questions, as in (46–47).

Late Egyptian

(44) *íḥ   ḥr   ib-k   n-n   n   ꜥꜣm.w?*
     what to   heart-2SG.M.SUF N-DEM of Asian-M.PL
     'What are these Asians for you?' (Erman 1968: 374)

---

21 This restriction is not as obvious as it may seem and is justified in the case of Egyptian only by the fact that it is a dead language for which it is impossible to get the relevant negative evidence from the native speakers. In this respect, cf. Idiatov (2009) on the use of the Mongo (Niger-Congo, Bantu C.61; DR Congo) interrogative *ná* 'who?, what?' in NAME-questions.
22 I do not consider Demotic Egyptian here due to the lack of relevant data.

Coptic Egyptian

(45) *ntk-ou-ou?*
      2SG.M-INDF.ART.M.SG-what
      'What are you?' (Lambdin 1983: 19; Till 1986: 102)

Late Egyptian

(46) *nym   rn   n   pꜣy-i̯   i̯t?*
      who   name of   my   father
      'What is the name of my father?' (Erman [1933] 1968: 376)[23]

Coptic Egyptian

(47) *nim   pe   pe-k-ran?*
      who   COP   M.SG-2SG.M.POSS-name
      'What is your name?' (Lambdin 1983: 19; Till 1986: 102)

6 Conclusion: Egyptian non-selective interrogative pronominals from the Afroasiatic perspective

By way of conclusion, let us consider the data from the different periods of the Egyptian language discussed in §§ 4 and 5 within the larger context of the Afroasiatic phylum of which Egyptian is generally held to form a separate branch.

As discussed in § 4, the older stages of the Egyptian language, Old and Middle Egyptian, have several NIPs that are attested as both 'who?' and 'what?', viz., *m, pw* and *zy,* and two mutually related specialized non-human interrogatives 'what?', viz., *i̯š-st* and *i̯ḫ.* By the Late Egyptian period, 'who?' and 'what?' become fully differentiated and this formal differentiation is maintained on all the subsequent stages. Furthermore, Old and Middle Egyptian have a bigger inventory of NIPs, many of them with largely overlapping semantics, as compared to the later stages. In both of these features, viz., a lack of differentiation between 'who?' and 'what?' and a large inventory of NIPs, Old and Middle Egyptian remarkably resemble Berber languages, especially Northern and Western Berber (cf. Idiatov

---

23 Transliteration of this example is mine because Erman gives only the hieroglyphic form.

2007: 155–180). By contrast, lack of differentiation between 'who?' and 'what?' is only sporadically attested in Semitic and Cushitic[24] and seems to be absent in Chadic. In all these groups, 'who?' and 'what?' are typically lexicalized as separate roots and the inventories of NIPs tend to be rather restricted, which is also characteristic of the later stages of the Egyptian language, viz., Late Egyptian, Demotic, and Coptic.

As far as functional differentiation between 'who?' and 'what?' is concerned, as discussed in § 5, it is difficult to characterize Old and Middle Egyptian in terms of the typology presented in § 3. Late and Coptic Egyptian represent type 3, as they allow for the use of 'what?' in KIND-questions and 'who?' in NAME-questions (cf. § 5). In this use of their NIPs, they resemble many Semitic and Cushitic languages rather than Berber. Examples (48–49a) with 'what?' in KIND-questions and (50–51) with 'who?' in NAME-questions illustrate this for Semitic.

Old Babylonian (East Semitic; Iraq; ca. 2000–1500 BCE)

(48) *mann-um*   *šum-ka?*
      who-NOM   name-2SG.M
      'What is your name?' (Izre'el & Cohen 2004: 111)

Biblical Hebrew (West Semitic, Central; Israel; ca. the first millennium BCE)

(49) a. *mi(y) šǝmɛ-χɔ?*
          who name-2SG.M
          'What is your name?' (Judges 13: 17 via Brockelmann 1913: 195;
          David Kummerow, p.c.)

      b. *ma-ššǝmɛ-χɔ?*
          what-name-2SG.M
          'What is your name?' (Genesis 32: 27 via Brockelmann 1913: 195)

---

24 The only uncontroversial examples of a lack of differentiation between 'who?' and 'what?' in these branches are the Southern Mesopotamian Arabic interrogative *man* for Semitic (cf. Ingham 1973, 1982) and the Saho (except for the Asa-Awurta and Tarua dialects) interrogative *ay* (cf. Reinisch 1890) for Cushitic.

Classical Arabic (West Semitic, Central)

(50) *fa-ma:*   *tazawwaj-ta*   *bikr-a-n*   *ʔaw*
so-what   marry.PRF-2SG.M   virgin-ACC.SG-INDF   or
tayyib-a-n?
deflowered-ACC.SG-INDF
'What (woman) have you married, a virgin or an already deflowered
one?' (Brockelmann 1913: 195)

Shehri (West Semitic, South; Oman)

(51) *emé-k*   *b-íné*   *zḥoñt?*
mother-2SG.M   with-what   come.PRF.3SG.F.SBJ
'[And he asked him,] What has your mother given birth to? [The guy
said to him, 'She has given birth to a girl...']' (Bittner 1917: 74–75)

On the whole, when both the formal and functional differentiation of 'who?' and
'what?' are considered, the NIP system of Egyptian appears to have evolved from a
more Berber-like situation in Old and Middle Egyptian to a more Semitic/Cushitic-
like situation in Late, Demotic and Coptic Egyptian. It is interesting that chronologically this shift seems to correlate with the growing interaction of Egyptians
with Semitic peoples. Thus, the Second Intermediate Period, ca. 18th–16th centuries BCE, during which the transition from Middle Egyptian to Late Egyptian
mostly occurred (or at least, is clearly manifested in the texts for the first time),
is also the period when the Semitic dynasties, the so-called Hyksos, rule over
Egypt. The end of the Middle Kingdom which immediately preceded the Second
Intermediate Period is also known for numerous Egyptian incursions in Asia and
for Asian settlers being brought to work in Egypt. Last but not least, recall in
this respect that Late Egyptian is also believed to have an interrogative of Semitic
origin, viz., *iṯ(i)* 'where?, which [N]?, which one?, who?' (cf. § 4.1.2).

Abbreviations and glossing conventions:

ACC	accusative
ACT	active
AG	agreement pattern
AOR	aorist
ART	article
COP	copula
DEF	definite
DEM	demonstrative
DEP	"dependent pronouns"
DU	dual

F	feminine
FOC	focus
FUT	future
G	gender
GEN	genitive
IND	indicative
INDEP	"independent pronouns"
INDF	indefinite
IPFV	imperfective
IPN	interrogative pronominal
M	masculine
N	neuter
NIP	non-selective interrogative pronominal
NOM	nominative
NON‹...›	non-‹...›
PFV	perfective
PL	plural
POSS	possessive
PRF	perfect
PROP	proper name
PRS	present
PST	past
PTCP	participle
REL	relative
RES	resultative
SBJ	subject
SG	singular
SUF	"suffixed pronouns"
VEN	ventive ("centripetal")

7 References

Achab, Karim. 2005. Le système de genre et son origine en berbère et en chamito-sémitique. In : Lonnet, Antoine & Mettouchi, Amina (eds.), *Les langues chamito-sémitiques (afro-asiatiques)*. Vol. 1. Paris: Ophrys, 97–128.

Aikhenvald, Aleksandra Ju. & Militarev, Aleksandr Ju. 1991. Livijsko-guančskie jazyki [Lybia-Guanche languages]. In: Diakonoff, Igor M. & Sharbatov, G. Sh. (eds.), *Jazyki Azii i Afriki [Languages of Asia and Africa]*. Vol. 4.2: *Afrazijskie jazyki [Afro-Asiatic languages]*. Moscow: Nauka, 148–267.

Albright, William Foxwell. 1926. The new cuneiform vocabulary of Egyptian words. *Journal of Egyptian Archaeology* 12: 186–190.

Allen, James Paul. 2000. *Middle Egyptian: An introduction to the language and culture of hieroglyphs*. Cambridge: Cambridge University Press.

Bailly, Anatole. 1901. *Abrégé du dictionnaire grec-français*. Paris: Hachette. http://home. tiscali.be/tabularium/bailly/index.html.

Barth, Jacob. 1913. *Die Pronominalbildung in den semitischen Sprachen*. Leipzig: Hinrichs.

Ben Mamou, El Arbi. 2005. *Dialecte berbère de Tamezret (Tunisie): Exemples berbère-français*. http://www.atmazret.info/atmazret_info/ATMAZRAT_DOCS/eddwi.pdf.

Bentolila, Fernand. 1981. *Grammaire fonctionnelle d'un parler berbère: Aït Seghrouchen d'Oum Jeniba (Maroc)*. Paris: SELAF.

Bittner, Maximilian. 1917. *Studien zur Šḫauri-Sprache in den Bergen von Ḍofâr am Persischen Meerbusen*. Vol. 3: *Zu ausgewählten Texten*. Wien: Hölder.

Brockelmann, Carl. 1913. *Grundriss der vergleichenden Grammatik der semitischen Sprachen*. Vol. 2: *Syntax*. Berlin: Reuther und Reichard.

Callender, John B. 1975. *Middle Egyptian*. Malibu: Undena.

Černý, Jaroslav. 1978. *A late Egyptian grammar*. Rome: Biblical Institute Press.

Crum, Walter Ewing. 1962 [1939]. *A Coptic dictionary*. Oxford: Clarendon.

Depuydt, Leo. 1999. *Fundamentals of Egyptian grammar*. Vol. 1: *Elements*. Norton: Frog.

Diakonoff, Igor M. 1965. *Semitoxamitskie jazyki: Opyt klassifikacii [The Semito-Hamitic languages: An essay in classification]*. Moscow: Nauka.

du Bourguet, Pierre. 1976. *Grammaire fonctionnelle et progressive de l'égyptien démotique*. Leuven: Peeters.

Eberle, Andrea & (in colloboration with) Schulz, Regine. 2004. *Koptisch: ein Leitfaden durch das Saïdische*. München: LINCOM Europa.

Edel, Elmar. 1955. *Altägyptische Grammatik*. Vol. 1. Rome: Pontificium institutum biblicum.

Edel, Elmar. 1964. *Altägyptische Grammatik*. Vol. 2. Rome: Pontificium institutum biblicum.

Erman, Adolf. 1968 [1933]. *Neuägyptische Grammatik*. Hildesheim: Olms.

Frajzyngier, Zygmunt. 1985. Interrogative sentences in Chadic. *Journal of West African Languages* 15(1): 57–72.

Galand, Lionel. 2002 [1974]. Présentation d'un parler: le touareg de l'Aïr (Introduction grammaticale). In : Galand, Lionel (ed.), *Études de linguistique berbère*. Leuven: Peeters, 117–146.

Gardiner, Alan H. 2001 [1957]. *Egyptian Grammar: Being an introduction to the study of hieroglyphs*. 3rd ed. Oxford: Griffith Institute.

Hannig, Rainer. 2003. *Ägyptisches Wörterbuch 1: Altes Reich und Erste Zwischenzeit*. Mainz am Rhein: von Zabern.

Heath, Jeffrey. 2005. *A grammar of Tamashek (Tuareg of Mali)*. Berlin: Mouton de Gruyter.

Hoch, James Erich. 1994. *Semitic words in Egyptian texts of the New Kingdom and the Third Intermediate period*. Princeton: Princeton University Press.

Idiatov, Dmitry. 2007. *A typology of non-selective interrogative pronominals*. PhD thesis. Antwerp: University of Antwerp. http://idiatov.mardi.myds.me/papers/PhD_Idiatov_2007_Final_Version+ERRATA.pdf

Idiatov, Dmitry. 2009. A Bantu path towards lack of differentiation between 'who?' and 'what?'. *Africana Linguistica* 15: 59–76.

Ingham, Bruce. 1973. Urban and rural Arabic in Khūzistān. *Bulletin of the School of Oriental and African Studies* 36(3): 533–553.

Ingham, Bruce. 1982. *North East Arabian dialects*. London & Boston: Kegan Paul International.

Izre'el, Shlomo & Cohen, Eran. 2004. *Literary Old Babylonian*. München: LINCOM Europa.

Johnson, Janet H. (ed.). 2001. *The Demotic dictionary of the Oriental Institute of the University of Chicago*. Chicago: Oriental Institute, University of Chicago. http://oi.uchicago.edu/OI/DEPT/PUB/SRC/CDD/CDD.html.

Junge, Friedrich. 1996. *Einführung in die Grammatik des Neuägyptischen*. Wiesbaden: Harrassowitz.

Korostovtsev, Mikhail A. 1973. *Grammaire du néo-égyptien*. Moscow: Nauka.

Kossmann, Maarten G. 1997. *Grammaire du parler berbère de Figuig (Maroc oriental)*. Paris: Peeters.

Lambdin, Thomas O. 1983. *Introduction to Sahidic Coptic*. Macon: Mercer University Press.

Lesko, Leonard H. & (in colloboration with) Switalski Lesko, Barbara. 2002–2004. *A dictionary of late Egyptian*. 2nd ed. Providence: Scribe Publ.

Lexa, František. 1947–1951. *Grammaire démotique*. Prague: Lexa.

Liddell, Henry George & Scott, Robert, (revised by) Jones, Henry Stuart (with the assistance of) McKenzie, Roderick. 1940. *A Greek-English lexicon*. Oxford: Clarendon Press. http://www.perseus.tufts.edu.

Loprieno, Antonio. 1996. *Ancient Egyptian: A linguistic introduction*. Cambridge: Cambridge University Press.

Mineau, Robert. 1982. *Les vieux parlers poitevins: histoire, phonétique, grammaire*. Poitiers: Brissaud.

Penchoen, Thomas G. 1973. *Tamazight of the Ayt Ndhir*. Los Angeles: Undena Publications.

Plumley, Martin J. 1948. *Introductory Coptic grammar*. London: Home & Van Thal. http://metalog.org/files/plumley/html/home.htm.

Reinisch, Leo. 1890. *Wörterbuch der Saho-Sprache*. Wien: Alfred Hölder.

Riegel, Martin, Pellat, Jean-Christophe & Rioul, René. 2001. *Grammaire méthodique du français*. Paris: Quadrige.

Rottet, Kevin J. 2004. Inanimate interrogatives and settlement patterns in Francophone Louisiana. *Journal of French Language Studies* 14.2: 169–188.

Spiegelberg, Wilhelm. 1925. *Demotische Grammatik*. Heidelberg: Winter.

Till, Walter C. 1961. *Koptische Dialektgrammatik mit Lesestücken und Wörterbuch*. 2nd revised ed. München: Beck.

Till, Walter C. 1986 [1966]. *Koptische Grammatik (Saïdischer Dialekt) mit Bibliographie, Lesestücken und Wörterverzeichnissen*. 6th ed. Leipzig: Enzyklopädie Verlag.

Vernus, Pascal. 2006. Pronoms interrogatifs en égyptien de la première phase. *Lingua Aegyptia* 14: 145–178.

Vycichl, Werner. 1984. *Dictionnaire étymologique de la langue copte*. Leuven: Peeters.

Wells, J. Warren. 2000–2006. *Sahidica: The Sahidic Coptic New Testament with parallel Greek*. http://sahidica.warpco.com.

Antonio Loprieno

Typological remodeling in Egyptian language history: salience, source and conjunction

Abstract: In this paper, I discuss the typological evolution of three Egyptian morphemes. Two of them are associated with the expression of the passive voice and indicate respectively the pragmatic function of "salience" (*jn*) and the semantic role of "source" (*m-ꜥ*). While *jn* disappears in the later stages of the language, the use of *m-ꜥ* is extended to new semantic domains, including the expression of a peripheral genitive. The third morpheme (*jw*) begins its typological development as a discourse marker and ends it as an indicator of syntactic dependency. While the entire functional array of *jw* is documented in all stages of the language, there is ample evidence for considering the typology of *jw* as an example of the discourse origin of syntactic markers.

1 Salience and source: the morphemes *jn* and *m-ꜥ*

In a paper on recent developments in Egyptian grammar studies (Loprieno 2003), I tried to explain the difference between the two known ways of signaling the agent of passive constructions in Ancient Egyptian as the remnants of a former opposition between an "ergative" and an "accusative" stage of the language. In this view, which I shall substantially correct in the present paper, the ergative construction is represented by examples such as (1), in which the agent is introduced by the morpheme *jn*:

(1) *n-zp   jr-t(j)   jꜣ-t   tn   jn*
     not-time make-PASS office-FEM   this.F AGENT
     bꜣk   nb   ḏr-bꜣḥ
     servant any since-before
     'Never before had this office been filled by any servant.' (Urk. I 103, 6)

This sentence presents an overt passive form (*jr.tj*), the promotion of the patient (*jꜣ.t tn*) to the role of syntactic subject, and the semantic agent (*bꜣk nb*) introduced by the preposition *jn*. In example (2), on the other hand, we find a different construction, intuitively closer to the strategy known in Standard European, in which the agent is introduced by the morpheme *m-ꜥ*:

(2) nn   js   gm-t-n(-j)   m-ʿ   jtj-j
    not at.all find-REL-PRET-1SG AGENT father-1SG
    'This is not what I found (performed) by my father.' (Chicago 16956)

While semantically similar, these two constructions differ sharply in their typology: the presence of a passive form of the transitive verb jrj in (1) is accompanied by the use of the marker jn 'by', limited in its prepositional use to the expression of the agent of a passive construction, whereas in (2) we find no overt predicate of the passive construction, which is introduced here by the preposition m-ʿ, which basically means 'through' (instrumental). To a certain extent, this morpheme appears to be in complementary distribution with jn, since it marks the agent of a passive predication in the presence of a pronominal agent, as in (3):

(3) jj-n(-j)   ʿrq   ø   m-ʿ-j
    come-PRET(-1SG) complete.PASS SUBJ AGENT-1SG
    'I returned after (this mission) had been completed by me.' (Urk. I 220, 7)

I have previously argued that the tendency for pronominal agents to prefer the construction with m-ʿ may have been prompted by the early grammaticalization of the compound "jn-pronoun" as an independent pronominal series (jnk, ntk, etc.) which replaced the older independent pronouns (twt, tmt, etc.) for the expression of the subject in nominal clauses. The pronominal series may have lost its ergative features before the corresponding nominal construction "jn-noun", therefore creating the need for a new specialized pattern with the preposition m-ʿ, as demonstrated by the non-paradigmatic survival of the ergative-like uses of left- or right-dislocated noun phrases introduced by jn and cataphorically resumed (4) or anaphorically preceded (5) by clitic pronouns:

(4) jn   tr   rḫ-wj   ṯw   jr-t   mrr-t
    AGENT certainly know.PTCP-how 2SG.M do-INF love-REL
    ḥzz-t   nb-k
    praise-REL lord-2SG.M
    'You certainly know how to do what your lord loves and praises.' (Urk. I 129, 5)

(5) smn-s   wj jn   3s-t ḥr 3kr
    establish.FUT -3SG.F 1SG AGENT Isis on   earth
    'She, namely Isis, will establish me on Earth.' (CT IV 27e B₁C)

Whether this hypothesis is correct or not, example (2) shows unequivocally that the preposition *m-ᶜ* was by no means limited to pronominal agents. I consider this construction closer to Standard European because having the agent in a passive construction introduced by an ablative, instrumental or locative is a typologically more similar device to the strategies adopted in the same environment by better known Indo-European languages: e.g., Greek *apó*, Latin *ab*, English *by*, German *von*, *durch*, or the Slavic instrumental case (Siewierska 1988). In fact, the preposition *m-ᶜ* exhibits an equally broad semantic spectrum, which can be best described as "source" (Stauder 2006):

(6) *n   nḥmm   sᶜḥw   N m-ᶜ-f*
    not take.FUT.PASS power   N SOURCE-3SG.M
    'The power of (King) N shall not be taken away from him.' (Pyr. § 411c)

(7) *N pj   snj   N   pj   sn-tj*
    N this release.PTCP.PRF   N   this   release-PTCP.PASS
    snj(-w)   N   m-ᶜ   jḥ-t   nb   ḏw-t
    release-pass   N   SOURCE thing-F any bad-F
    '(King) N is, has been and shall be released from all evil things.' (Pyr. 1100c–d)

(8) *ḥqr   N m-ᶜ   Šw   jb-t   N m-ᶜ   Tfnw-t*
    hunger N SOURCE Shu   thirst-F N SOURCE Tefnut-F
    'The hunger of N is caused by Shu, the thirst of N is caused by Tefnut.' (Pyr. 553a)

(9) *dbḥ-k(j)   m-ᶜ   ḥm   nj   nb-j   jn-t(j)*
    ask-PRF.1SG source majesty that.of lord-1SG bring-PASS
    n(-j)   jnr   ḥḏ   qrs   m   r3-3w
    to-1SG   stone white coffin from Turah
    'I asked the Majesty of my Lord to let me bring a coffin of white stone from Turah.' (Urk. I 99, 10–11)

(10) *[...]-n   stḫ   rḫ   m-ᶜ-j*
     [verb]-PRET Seth   know SOURCE -1SG
     'Seth ...ed to copulate with me.' (pUCL 32158 II, 3–4)

This wide array of semantic nuances harmonizes well with the use of *m-ᶜ* as marker of the agentive role which mainly concerns us here:

(11) *n*   *gm-t-n(-j)*   *js*   *pw*   *m-ᶜ*   *ḥrj-tp*
      not find-REL-PRET(-1SG) at.all this   SOURCE nomarch
      wn   *m*   *sp3-t*   *tn*   *tp-ᶜw*
      be.PTCP.PRF in   nome-F   this.F   before
      'This is not what I found (performed) by any nomarch who had been in
      this nome before.' (Urk. I 254, 10)

The dual passive typology displayed by (1)–(3) may appear due to the coexistence, in this phase of Egyptian, of two strategies for the promotion to SUBJ of an argument other than AGENT (usually OBJ). The first strategy, which is typologically closer to the ergative type that I took to characterize Egyptian at some point in prehistory (Loprieno 1995: 83–84), requires the overt use of a perfective verb form, gradually specialized in the passive use, and of a dedicated marker of the AGENT-role, i.e., the preposition *jn*, which always introduces it, whether in active (cleft sentences) or in passive clauses (as marker of the demoted agent). The second strategy is more typically "accusative": it avoids, whenever possible, the use of a strongly agentive verb form and expresses the AGENT-role, if at all, by means of an ablative or instrumental preposition such as *m-ᶜ*, literally 'with the arm (of)', which is syntactically more marginal, thus more marked, than a dedicated marker of ergativity (Dixon 1994: 56–69).

This interpretation, however, is probably not cogent and should be replaced by a more economic approach in which the unequal diachronic destiny of the two agentive patterns is read against the background of the rather different morphosyntactic origin of the two morphemes: the progressive marginalization of the particle *jn* as a marker of pragmatic salience (Loprieno 1988), as opposed to the establishment of the preposition *m-ᶜ* and its derivatives for a wide variety of semantic SOURCE-roles. The synthetic passive constructions of Earlier Egyptian become recessive in Late Egyptian, as in example (12) and disappear altogether in Demotic (Winand 1992: 299–341; Simpson 1996: 37, 148), being superseded by the use of the impersonal active third person plural or of the qualitative base, whereby the AGENT-role is introduced by the preposition *m-ᶜ* > *m-dr.t* > *m-ḏe*, as in example (13):

(12) *sw* *gm-y*   *m*   *r-ᶜ*   *wtn*   *m-ḏr.t*
      it   find-PASS.3SG.M as   work   drill.INF   SOURCE
      n3   *jṯ3-w*
      the.PL   thief-PL
      'It was found drilled by the thieves.' (pAbbott 1, 2, 16–17)

(13) jw-w   tw-s   ꜥn   m-ḏe   n3   šmꜥ-yw
      while-3.PL   worship.INF-3SG.F   also   SOURCE the.PL singer-PL
      'While she is also worshipped by the singers.' (Canopus 67).

In Coptic (Polotsky 1987–1990: 183), we find on the one hand a situation of competition, based partly on dialectal differences, partly on informational emphasis, between a passive construction in which the agent is introduced by a compound preposition ultimately connected with m-ꜥ, as in (14), and an active construction with an impersonal third person plural subject resumed by an overt subject introduced by a marker of topical prominence (Loprieno 2000) etymologically derived from a prepositional construction with the noun "shape" (ᔆnci, ᴮnče "namely" < "in shape of"), as in (15):

(14) a-u-sôbe   mmo-f   ebol-hitn   m-magos
      PRF-3PL-laugh.INF   ACC-3SG.M   AGENT   the.PL-magician
      'He was ridiculed by the magicians.' (ᔆMt 2, 16)

(15) a-u-sôbi   mmo-f   nče   ni-magos
      PRF-3PL-laugh.INF   ACC-3SG.M   TOPIC   the.PL-magician
      'The magicians ridiculed him.' (ᴮMt 2, 16)

On the other hand, the semantic fuzziness of the source-roles also underlies a further interesting syntactic evolution which led to the emergence of a genitive marker derived from m-ꜥ (Earlier Egyptian m-ꜥ > Late Egyptian m-dj > Coptic nte-) and used in presence of a looser, less direct connection between the *regens* and the *rectum*, most typically when the *regens* is unspecific or introduced by a demonstrative pronoun. Let us contrast the more grammaticalized construction (16), in which the *rectum* is preceded by the genitive marker derived from a determinative pronoun nj 'that of', with the less grammaticalized construction (17), in which the *regens* is accompanied by an adjective and the *rectum* is introduced by nte-:

(16) p-šêre   m-p-noute
      the-son   GEN-the-god
      'The son of God.' (Lk 1,35)

(17) p-šêre   n-ouôt   nte-p-noute
      the-son   GEN-unique   SOURCE-the-god
      'God's only son.' (Jo 3, 18)

It is also unnecessary to posit an ergative origin for the morpheme *jn*, since its syntactic behavior can very well be explained within the perspective of its indicating the pragmatic role of salience (SAL). The semantic similarity between a passive construction introduced by *jn* and its active counterpart where AGENT = SUBJ was also perceived by the Egyptian users themselves: in a situation of diglossia such as a sacerdotal decree, in which an Earlier Egyptian (18) and a Later Egyptian (19) version of the same text address two different circles of readers, the former presents a construction with *jn*, the latter the corresponding active form:

(18) *jr js*   *jw*   *rd*   *m-ḥꜣ-t* *jr-w*   *fꜣj*   *ḥms*
      if then come.PRS fruit in-front do-PASS carry.INF ears.of.corn
      jn   *šmꜥ-wt*
      SAL   singer-PL.F

(19) *j-jr*   *pꜣ-ḫrp*   *n*   *pꜣ-rṯ*   *pḥ*   *mtw*   *nꜣ*   *šmꜥ-yw(t)*
      do.AUX the-first of the-fruit come and.will the.PL singer-PL.F
      fy   *ḥms*   *r-ḥry*
      carry. INF ears.of.corn up
      'When the first fruits of the harvest arrive, the female singers will bear ears of corn.' (Canopus decree, Tanis dem. 68)

Thus, rather than being the remnant of an earlier ergative phase, marking the AGENT-role by means of the morpheme *jn*, as in (20) and likewise in (21b), turns out to be one of the devices of pragmatic salience, which can indeed affect personal pronouns, such as *ntsn* in (21) or *jn ṯwt* in (22), and also interrogative pronouns, such as *jn-m* in (23)–(24):

(20) *n*   *gm-t(-j)*   *js*   *pw*   *jn*   *jtj-w(-j)*
      not find-REL-1SG   at.all this SAL father-PL-1SG
      tpj-w-ꜥw
      former-PL
      'This is not what I found (performed) by my ancestral fathers at all.' (Moʿalla IV 25–26)

(21) m   rḏt   n-f   t   ḥḏ (…) ḥncprt   ntsn
     by   give.INF to-3SG.M bread   white   COM come.INF SAL.3PL
     m-s3 ḥm.k3-f (…)
     after ritualist-3SG.M
     ḥnc   rḏt   jn wcb   jmj   3bd-f   p3q
     COM   give.INF SAL priest who.is.in month-3SG.M cake
     njw   ḥ(n)q-t dwjw n   ḫntj-f
     measure   beer-F   jug   to statue-3SG.M

     'By giving him white bread (…), and then they should proceed behind
     his funerary priest (…) and then the priest who is in his monthly service
     should offer to his statue a measure of cake and a jug of beer.' (Siut I
     307–308)

(22) jn   twt js   ḫwj   znb3-w-sn   m-ḥnw
     SAL you indeed prevent.PART   fall-FUT-3PL in-inside
     c.wj-k(j)
     arm.DU-2SG.M
     'You are indeed the one who prevents them from falling into your arms'
     (Pyr. 1536a)

(23) jn-m   jnj   tw   nḏs
     SAL-WH bring.PTC.PRF   2SG.M little
     'Who brought you, little one?' (Shipwrecked Sailor 69–70)

(24) jn-m   rḏ-t(w)   mw   n   3pd   ḥḏ-t3   n
     SAL-WH give-PASS   water to   bird   white-land   to
     sf-t(j)-f   dw3w
     slaughter-PTC.FUT-3SG.M   morning
     'Who will give water to a bird at dawn if it will be slaughtered in the
     morning?' (Shipwrecked Sailor 184–186)

A contrastive analysis of (23) and (24) shows that the pragmatic force of SAL privi-
leges the expression of the AGENT-role even beyond the syntactic constraints of
the sentence, since it can lead to a neutralization of the opposition between the
active predication as in (23), where *jn-m* = AGENT = SUBJ, and the passive predication as in (24), where *jn-m* = AGENT ≠ SUBJ. The same does not hold true when the
interrogative pronoun *m* is not preceded by the marker of pragmatic salience. In
this case, *m* ≠ AGENT = SUBJ (25)–(26) or *m* ≠ AGENT = OBJ (27):

(25) m   tr   ms(-w)   n-ṯ
      SUBJ.WH   then   bear.PTC.PRF.PASS   to-2SG.F
      'Who was born to you then?' (CT VI 309j–k B1Bo)

(26) ṯwt   m   tr
      SUBJ.2SG.M   SUBJ.WH   then
      'Who are you then?' (CT III 59b)

(27) m   ḥwj-n-k
      OBJ.WH   hit-PRET-2.SG.M
      'Whom did you hit?' (pRamesseum, pl. 33)

2 The morpheme *jw* as conjunction

The second issue to be discussed in this paper is the diachronic development of probably the most famous Egyptian particle among grammarians, e.g., the conjunction *jw*. According to a widespread assumption, which is supported by much evidence, Earlier Egyptian employs *jw* 'truly' as an explicit marker of initial main sentences (28), whereas in Later Egyptian, almost symmetrically, *jw* 'while' functions as a marker of syntactic dependency (29):

(28) jw   jr-n(-j)   jd-wt   bnn-t
      truly   make-PRET-1SG   female.animal-F.PL   pregnant-F
      'I acquired pregnant female animals.' (Achmim Q 15, 1–2)

(29) jw-w   tw-s   ꜥn   m-ḏe   n3   šmꜥ-yw
      while-3PL   worship.INF-3SG.F   also   SOURCE   the   singer-PL
      'While she is also worshipped by the singers.' (Canopus 67)

While generally correct, this assumption needs to develop ad-hoc explanations for a certain number of idiosyncratic features: e.g., if the subject of the sentence is a pronoun, Earlier Egyptian seems to employ *jw* also in the dependent clause:

(30) *jw   wp-n-f*   *r3-f*   *r-j*   *jw-j*
      truly open-PRET-3SG.M mouth-3SG.M to-1SG   while -1SG
      ḥr   ḫ-t-j   *m-b3ḥ-f*
      on   belly-F-1SG in-front-3SG.M
      'He opened his mouth towards me while I was on my belly in front of
      him.' (Shipwrecked Sailor 81–83)

Lately, the present writer had attempted to read this diachronic distribution as
a gradual process leading *jw* from being a discourse marker of initiality to functioning as coordinating particle, then as coordinating conjunction and finally as
subordinating conjunction (Loprieno 2006: 41–60); in other words, I have posited
a gradual development of syntax from discourse (Givón 2009). Since some of my
arguments may have remained opaque (Schenkel 2007), it might be useful to
review some of the empirical foundations on which my claim is based.

   If one carries on reading the funerary inscription out of which (28) is quoted,
the reader's textual understanding would seem to violate the grammarian's rule
according to which the morpheme *jw* introduces initial main clauses: example
(31) – and (32), drawn from a similar context – seem to link the statements introduced by *jw* with their informational background rather than separate them as if
they were initial paragraphs:

(31) *jw   jr-n(-j)*   *jd-wt*   *bnn-t*   *jw*
      truly make-PRET-1SG female.animal-F.PL pregnant-F CONJ
      rd-n-sn   *ꜥ3*   *200*
      give-PRET-3PL   donkey 200
      'I acquired pregnant female animals and they bore 200 donkeys.'
      (Achmim Q 15, 1–2)

(32) *j(w) nn   ndm(-w)*   *jw   ḥtp-k*
      CONJ this.NEUT be.pleasant.PRF(-3SG.M) CONJ be.happy-2SG.M
      ḥr-s
      on-3SG.F
      'This is pleasant and you will be happy with it.' (Saqqara, Niankh-
      Khnum and Khnum-Hotep, W-wall, 33)

The semantic link which the morpheme *jw* seems to establish with its preceding
context is by no means a rare exception to an otherwise all-encompassing rule,
but rather a significant feature of its grammatical behavior altogether, especially
in cases such as (33), in which the main function of *jw* is that of balancing an
informational flow that has been challenged by a marker of pragmatic salience:

(33) *ntf*   *dʒr*   *ḫʒs-wt*   *jw*   *jtj-f*
SAL-3SG.M subdue.PTCP foreign.land-PL.F CONJ father-3SG.M
m-ẖnw   *ꜥḥ-f*   *smj-f*   *šꜥ-t-n-f*
in-inside palace-3SG.M report.IPV-3SG.M command-REL-PRET-3SG.M
ḫpr(-w)
happen.PRF(-3SG.M)
?'Heistheonewhosubduesforeignlands.Hisfatherremainsinhispalace,
while he reports when something he had commanded has happened'
!'He is the one who subdues foreign lands, while his father remains in
his palace. He reports when something he had commanded has happened.' (Sin. B 50)

The first of the two alternative translations given above obeys the received Egyptological rule, but it ostensibly misses the distribution of information foci: telling
the reader in the main clause that the hero's father remains in the palace while
the hero himself reports about his achievements seems to grossly violate Grice's
rule of relevance (1989: 22–40). It is the second translation, in spite of its disregard of the traditional grammatical interpretation of the role of *jw*, that fits much
better the intuitively expected informational sequence: by positing a connective function for the morpheme *jw*, it ascribes a background role to the father's
dealing while keeping the contextual attention focused on the son and his deeds.

The prevailing syntactic analysis of *jw*, therefore, should be radically questioned. In the following examples, the function of the particle seems less to mark
syntactic boundaries than to signal different degrees of informational continuity:

(34) *dm*   *(j)r-k*   *jw*   *ḫntj(-j)*   *sw*
sharpen.IMP to-2SG.M CONJ slaughter(-1SG) OBJ.3SG.M
'Sharpen (the knife): I am going to slaughter it!' (Saqqara, Mehu,
E-wall, T 237)

(35) *jmj*   *jwf*   *n*   *ḫʒ-t*   *jw*   *ẖr(j)-ḥ(ʒ)b-t* *ḥr*
give.IMP meat that.of breast-F CONJ lector.priest on
jr-t   *(j)ḫ-t*
do-INF sacrifice-F
'Bring the breast meat: the lector-priest is performing the sacrifice!'
(Saqqara, Nikau-Isesi, III, W-wall, 1)

(36) t   w*ʕb*   pw   n   wsjr   jw   n   zzj
     bread pure this   for Osiris CONJ for Zezi
     jmзḥ-w
     revere-PART.PASS
     'This is a pure loaf for Osiris and also for the revered Zezi.' (Saqqara, Ankhemʕahor, III, E-wall, 2)

(37) *wʕb(-j)*   jw   *wʕb(-j)*   n   zzj
     be.pure(-1SG) CONJ be.pure(-1SG)   for Zezi
     n   *kз-f*
     for memory-3SG.M
     'I am pure, I am pure for Zezi and for his memory.' (Saqqara, Ankhemʕahor, IV, E-wall, 2)

In order to provide a formal setting for the interpretation of the flexibility exhibited by *jw* as connective morpheme, I would like to posit a hierarchy according to which *jw* derives its syntactic status from the informational sequence within which it appears. In (38), the first *jw* marks a dependent clause connected to the preceding state of affairs, whereas the second *jw* introduces an initial dependent clause connected to the following statement, thus creating a kind of chiastic information structure:

(38) *jnk*   *ḥqз-jb*   n   *pry-t* jw_1 zj   nb
     SAL.1SG ruler-heart for crisis-F CONJ man   every
     ḥr *ḥtm*   *ʕз-f* jw_2 *jp-n*   *ḥqз*
     on shut.INF   door-3SG.M CONJ count-PRET   ruler
     jзw-t(-j)   *gm-f*   *ḥз-w*   *ḥr* *jšw-t-j*
     cattle-F(-1SG) find-3SG.M increase on possession-F(-1SG)
     'I was a truly courageous leader in critical times, while everyone else would shut his door. And when the ruler counted my cattle, he found that my possessions had increased.' (BM 1671, 9)

Particularly intriguing for the grammarian are those instances in which *jw* introduces what appears to be a clause of circumstance in spite of its being introduced by the putative marker of initiality:

(39)   *sꜥnḫ*   *n'-t-f*   *m*   *ṯꜣz-w*
      make.live.PART   city-F-3SG.M in   problem-PL
      sm   *s(j)*   *jw*   *nn wn*
      nourish.PART OBJ.3SG.F CONJ not be.PART.PRF
      'Who maintained his city alive during problematic times, who nourished it when there was nothing around.' (Hatnub 20, 8–10)

(40)   *jnk*   *jr*   *[pḥ-w]j-s*   *m*   *šd-yt*
      SAL.1SG do.PART.PRF   rearguard-DUAL-3SG.F in swamp-F
      jw   *nn rmṯ*   *ḥnꜥ-j*   *wpw-ḥr šms(-w)-j*
      CONJ not man with-1SG except attendant-PL-1SG
      'I formed her rearguard in the swamps, nobody else being with me except my own attendants.' (Hatnub 16, 5–6)

The unusual character of these examples has prompted a different explanation that conforms to the received analysis of *jw* as a morpheme marking syntactic initiality or independence (Schenkel 2007). Since these uses of *jw* seem to violate the rule, the missing main clause is taken to be cancelled in the surface structure, in accordance with an Egyptological tendency to posit zero-marking more frequently than would be called for (Winand 2009):

(41)   *jnk*   *ḥꜣ3-jb*   *n*   *pry-t*   *jw*   [ø]
      SAL.1SG ruler-heart for crisis-F this-was-at-that-time [MAIN CLAUSE]
      [zj   *nb*   *ḥr*   *ḥtm*   *ꜥꜣ-f]*
      man every on shut.INF door-3SG.M [DEPENDENT CLAUSE]
      ?'I was a truly courageous leader in critical times. (This happened at a time) when everyone else would shut his door.' (cf. ex. 38)

(42)   *sm*   *s(j)*   *jw*   [ø]
      nourish.PART OBJ.3SG.F this-was-at-that-time   [MAIN CLAUSE]
      [nn wn]
      not be.PART.PRF [DEPENDENT CLAUSE]
      ?'Who nourished it. (This happened at a time) when there was nothing around.' (cf. ex. 39)

(43) jnk   jr   [pḥ-w]j-s   m
      SAL.1SG do.PART.PRF rearguard-DUAL-3SG.F in
      šdy-t   jw   [ø]
      swamp-F this-was-at-that-time [MAIN CLAUSE]
      [nn rmṯ ḥnꜥ-j   wpw-ḥr šms(-w)-j]
      not man with-1SG except attendant-PL-1SG [DEPENDENT CLAUSE]
      ?'I formed their rearguard in the swamps. (This happened at a time)
      when nobody else was with me except my own attendants.' (cf. ex. 40)

According to this analysis, we might witness here an initial marker jw introducing
a main clause that does not exist or has been zeroed (Schenkel 2007: 170–185). It
must be admitted that this explanation does not seem to be very economical and
also leads to a semantic overload of the particle, for it would seem rather idiosyncratic to posit the existence of an underlying zero-clause without any trace in the
surface structure. It seems preferable, therefore, to disregard this explanation.

Further criticism has been expressed towards my proposal to translate jw in
the above examples as a marker of circumstance (Schenkel 2007: 190–195), since
an Earlier Egyptian circumstantial clause is usually introduced by jsṯ (44):

(44) jnk   mry   nb-f (...)   jw   jr-n-j   ꜥḥꜥw
      SAL.1SG love.PART.PRF.PASS lord-3SG.M CONJ do-PRET-1SG lifetime
      ꜥ3   m   rnp-wt   ḥr ḥm   n   N jsṯ
      long   in   year-F.PL by majesty that.of N CONJ
      t3   pn   ḥr   s-t-ḥr-f
      land   this.M under stewardship-F-3SG.M
      'I was someone loved by his lord (...) I spend a long lifetime under the
      majesty of the king, while this land was under his stewardship.' (BM
      614, 3–4)

What we are observing here are varying degrees of informational cohesion and
of grammaticalization of syntactic dependence. The difficulties created by the
common approach are evident in the following examples. The basic difference
between jsṯ and jw is that while the former is a dedicated subordinating conjunction of Earlier Egyptian without successors in the later stages of the language,
the history of jw from Earlier to Later Egyptian is characterized by a progressive
grammaticalization of its connectivity features, from an earlier independent particle ("truly, indeed") to a coordinating conjunction ("and, but") and eventually
to a subordinating conjunction ("when, while"). While one can broadly agree
with the received wisdom that in Earlier Egyptian this morpheme was not yet
fully grammaticalized and that, therefore, the instances in which jw appears to

be placed at the beginning of a portion of discourse are more frequent than those in which it does not, it is not very wise to posit for *jw* a sort of rigid functional polarity between the earlier and the later stages of the language, but rather to consider this a gradual typological evolution. Considering a linguistic continuum typologically more significant than an empirically problematic binary opposition also allows us to better deal with instances in which the presence of the particle *jw* seems to be superfluous and has led commentators to ask themselves why it appears nonetheless, as in (45)–(46):

(45)   *ḫp*   *r-f*   *sw<t>*   *nṯr-t tn*   *jw-f*   *ḏj-f*
       approach to-3SG.M   indeed   god-F this.F CONJ-3SG.M   give.IPFV-3SG.M
       ḥ3-t   *n*   *šj*
       front-F   to   lake
       'So, this goddess approached him as he was heading to the lake.'
       (Herdsman 23–24)

(46)   *njs-n-tw*   *n*   *wᶜ*   *jm*   *jsṯ*   *wj*   *ᶜḥᶜ-kw*
       call-PRET-PASS   to   one   there   while   SUBJ.1SG   stand.PRF-1SG
       sḏm-n-j   *ḫrw-f*   *jw-f*   *mdw-f*
       hear-PRET-1SG   voice-3SG.M CONJ-3SG.M   speak-3SG.M
       'One of them was summoned while I was standing; I heard his voice as
       he was speaking.' (Sin. R 24–25)

The actual reason for the presence of *jw* to introduce the circumstantial clauses in the two examples above is the topic change from the main to the dependent clause: the subject pronoun carried by the conjunction *jw* introduces the new topic and is resumed by the agreement marker in the verbal predicate. In presence of topic continuity the dependent clause is generally not introduced by a conjunction, but rather embedded in the main clause:

(47)   *nfr*   *ṯw*   *ᶜḥᶜt(j)*   *mjn*   *m*
       be.good.PART SUBJ-2SG.M stand.PERF.2SG.M today as
       ḥrw   *dw3-tj*
       Horus   netherworld-ADJ
       'You are happy, for you have stood up today as Horus of the Nether-
       world.' (CT I 311g T$_9$C)

A final point to be discussed here concerns the use of *jw* within the scope of negation. One of the arguments adduced in order to question the sporadic use of this particle as a marker of syntactic dependence in Middle Egyptian is based on my translation of *jw* as "unless" in (48):

(48)   *nn   ʿq-j*   *[r   pȝj-t]n   pr   jw   ʿḏ(-w)*
       not enter.FUT-1SG   to   this-2PL   house   CONJ   be.safe(-3SG.M)
       'I shall not enter your house unless it is safe.' (pUCL 32213, 21–22)

"Unless", so it is claimed (Schenkel 2007: 199–201), is actually rendered in the classical language by the negative particle *n-js*, as in (49), and not by the conjunction *jw*:

(49)   *nn   ḏj-j*   *ʿq-k*   *ḥr-j (...) n-js*
       not give.FUT-1SG   enter.FUT-2SG.M   on-1SG   not-indeed
       ḏd-n-k   *rn-j*
       say-PRET-2SG.M   name-1SG
       'I shall not allow you to enter next to me (...) unless you have pro-
       nounced my name.' (BD 125)

The informational horizon of the two sentences, however, and particularly the phrase affected by the negation, are quite different in (48) and (49). In (48), the scope of the negation is the predicate of the dependent clause "(your house) is safe". The morphological carrier of the semantic feature [+NEG] is still the negative particle *nn* that introduces the main clause: 'It will *not₁* (*nn*) happen that I enter your house if it is *not₁* (ø) safe.' The morpheme *jw* acts here as a sequential marker, as a conjunction expressing the contingency of the two potential situations; it is not per se a marker of [+NEG], but rather transposes this feature onto the dependent clause it governs. In (49), something very different happens: the feature [+NEG] in the second predication is not carried over by a conjunction and thus semantically implied within the informational sequence initiated by the main clause, but on the contrary overtly expressed by the dedicated marker of contrariety *n-js* (Loprieno 1995: 127–131): 'I shall *not₁* (*nn*) allow you to enter if you have *not₂* (*n-js*) pronounced my name.' We are in presence of the modality of impossibility (IRREALIS) conveyed by the preterite form *sḏm-n-f* (Polis 2009). In (48) the contextual likelihood of the two predicates taking place is identical: "entering-a-safe-house" will either take place or it will not – hence the use of the conjunction *jw*. In (49), 'allowing-to-enter' and 'pronouncing-my-name' are distinct predications which theoretically allow for a variety of real world combinations (although speaking of real world in the case of the Book of the Dead may appear somewhat audacious), e.g., that you have indeed pronounced my name, but I still do not allow you to enter – hence the use of the negative particle *n-js*. Rather than proving that *jw* cannot mean 'unless', this example actually provides supplementary evidence that this morpheme can indeed function in Middle Egyptian as marker of syntactic dependency.

The functional development of *jw*, therefore, provides an excellent example of what Givón called the genesis of syntax ex discourse (Givón 1979): from a discourse initial function ('so') through semantic connectivity ('and') to syntactic dependence ('while') in a process that gradually took place within the diachronic development of Earlier Egyptian to appear almost completely concluded in Later Egyptian:

(50)   *jw* = indeed[discourse] > and[main clause] > while[dependent clause]

Better than any theoretical discussion, example (51) can convey a sense of the typological layers that underlie the functional development of *jw*. Here, any of the three analyses could apply: *jw* could be a discourse marker introducing an independent clause, a conjunction connecting two main clauses, or a marker of syntactic dependency:

(51)   *jmj-r₃*   *s-t*   *ḥrj*   *zbj-w*   *m-ḫd*   *r*
overseer   storehouse-F   Hori   leave.PRF-3SG.M   northwards   to
t₃-mḥw jw   *b₃k-jm*   *ꜥ₃*   *wꜥ-y*
Delta   CONJ   servant-there   here   be.alone.PRF-3SG.M
'The overseer of the storehouse Hori has left northwards to the Delta, so/and/while that servant is (i.e., I am) here alone.' (pUCL 32197, 1, 9–10)

Why do I define the functional evolution leading to *jw* as subordinating conjunction as "almost completely concluded" in Later Egyptian? The reason is that Later Egyptian keeps two bound, i.e., paradigmatically restricted patterns displaying the typologically older stages of the functional history of this particle: in the so-called Future III, an "initial" *jw* is followed by a prepositional phrase with *r* 'towards' and the verbal infinitive to indicate the initial future: *jw-f r sḏm* 'he will hear' (Junge 2001: 122–128); in the so-called Sequential form, a "coordinating" *jw* is also followed by a prepositional phrase with *ḥr* 'on' and the verbal infinitive to indicate the sequential past: *jw-f ḥr sḏm* 'and he heard' (Junge 2001: 207–212). Otherwise, Later Egyptian *jw* always functions as a marker of syntactic dependency in what is called in Egyptology the circumstantial present: *jw-f ḥr sḏm* 'while he hears' (Junge 2001: 115–118). Thus, Later Egyptian exhibits on a synchronic level the entire array of the functional hierarchy captured by the three syntactic settings in (50):

(52) $jw^{\text{discourse}}$ = Future III >

   $jw^{\text{main clause}}$ = Sequential form >

   $jw^{\text{dependent clause}}$ = Circumstantial present

Thanks to its four millennia of continuously documented history, the functional evolution of Egyptian syntactic structures proves once again an ideal empirical basis for general typological investigations.

3 References

Dixon, Robert M.W. 1994. *Passive and Voice*. (Typological Studies in Language 16). Cambridge: University Press.

Givón, Talmy. 1979. From discourse to syntax: grammar as a processing strategy. In: Givón, Talmy (ed.), *Discourse and Syntax*. (Syntax and Semantics 12). New York: Academic Press, 81–112.

Givón, Talmy. 2009. *The Genesis of Syntactic Complexity*. Amsterdam: Benjamins.

Grice, H. Paul. 1989. *Studies in the Way of Words*. Cambridge/MA & London: Harvard University Press.

Junge, Friedrich. 2001. *Late Egyptian Grammar. An Introduction*. Oxford: Griffith Institute.

Loprieno, Antonio. 1988. Der ägyptische Satz zwischen Semantik und Pragmatik: die Rolle von *jn*. *Beihefte zu den Studien zur Altägyptischen Kultur* 3: 77–98.

Loprieno, Antonio. 1995. *Ancient Egyptian. A Linguistic Introduction*. Cambridge: University Press.

Loprieno, Antonio. 2000. From VSO to SVO? Word Order and rear Extraposition in Coptic. In: Sornicola, Rosanna, Poppe, Erich & Shisha-Halevy, Ariel (eds.), *Stability, Variation and Change of Word-Order Patterns over Time*. (Current Issues in Linguistic Theory 213). Amsterdam: Benjamins, 23–39.

Loprieno, Antonio. 2003. Egyptian Linguistics in the Year 2000. In: Hawass, Zahi (ed.), *Egyptology at the Dawn of the Twenty-first Century. Proceedings of the Eighth International Congress of Egyptologists, Cairo 2000*. Cairo: The American University in Cairo Press, 73–90.

Loprieno, Antonio. 2006. On fuzzy boundaries in Egyptian syntax. In: Moers, Gerald, Behlmer, Heike, Demuß, Katja & Widmayer, Kai (eds.), *jn.t ḏr.w. Festschrift für Friedrich Junge*. Göttingen: Seminar für Ägyptologie und Koptologie, 429–441.

Polis, Stéphane. 2009. *Étude de la modalité en néo-égyptien*. PhD dissertation, Université de Liège.

Polotsky, Hans Jakob. 1987–1990. *Grundlagen des koptischen Satzbaus*. (American Studies in Papyrology 27.29). Atlanta: Scholars Press.

Schenkel, Wolfgang. 2007. Die Partikel *iw* und die Intuition des Interpreten. Randbemerkungen zu A. Loprieno, "On fuzzy boundaries in Egyptian Syntax". *Lingua Aegyptia* 15: 161–201.

Siewierska, Anna. 1988. The passive in Slavic. In: Shibatani, Masayoshi (ed.), *Passive and Voice*. (Typological Studies in Language 16). Amsterdam: Benjamins, 9–23.

Simpson, Robert S. 1996. *Demotic Grammar in the Ptolemaic Sacerdotal Decrees*. Oxford: Griffith Institute.

Stauder, Andréas. 2006. *La détransitivité, voix et aspect. Le passif dans la diachronie égyptienne*. PhD dissertation, Universität Basel.

Winand, Jean. 1992. *Études de néo-égyptien, 1: La morphologie verbale*. (Aegyptiaca Leodiensia 2). Liège: C.I.P.L.

Winand, Jean. 2009. Zeros in Egyptian. Can nothing mean something? *Lingua Aegyptia* 18: 319–339.

Carsten Peust

Towards a typology of poetic rhyme*

With observations on rhyme in Egyptian

Abstract: Rhyme, like other characteristics of poetic language, belongs to the least explored fields within linguistics. I suggest that these topics would profit from being explored by linguists and that information on them should be routinely included into the grammatical description of any language.

This article attempts to outline a typology of poetic rhyme. "Rhyme" is defined as the phonetic identity of sections within text strings ("lines"). Languages vary in whether the identity is conventionally located in the beginning, the middle or the end of lines. The latter choice (end rhyme) is now the by far most common type, but its present near-global distribution seems to be the result of recent language contact.

Major typological parameters of end rhyme include the size of the sections at the line ends that are required to be identical, as well as the partition of the sound space implied in the notion of "identity", here called "rhyme phonology", which can differ from the partition of the sound space by ordinary phonology.

Finally, end rhyme in Egyptian is discussed, where this technique became current only by the Late Coptic period. Being a tradition relatively independent from the better known European rhymes, Coptic rhyme provides some exotic features which are of considerable typological interest.

1 Terminology and definitions

1.1 Rhyme and metre

Rhyme and metre are characteristics of poetic texts. The general features of rhyme and metre are largely constant for mainstream poetry of a given synchronic state of a language, although composers of poems may have some room for individual choices or alteration of the accepted rules. The investigation of these features should therefore be part of the grammatical description of a language. They have, however, rarely been objects of linguistic investigation, and grammar books typi-

---

* My thanks go to Eitan Grossman, Martin Haspelmath and one anonymous referee for valuable comments on an earlier draft of this paper.

cally fail to provide any information on rhyme and metre. There do exist some cross-linguistic or (in the widest sense) typological studies on metre (e.g., Gasparov 1996; Kiparsky 1975; Kiparsky & Youmans 1989; Küper 2002; Kuryłowicz 1976; Lotz 1960; Molino & Tamine 1982; O'Connor 1982; Stella 1995a; Watkins 1963; West 1973; Wimsatt 1972), but none of them with a world-wide approach, and none at all on rhyme, to my knowledge. What follows here cannot claim to be an exhaustive typology of rhyme, but is rather intended as a spur for further exploration of the topic and for grammar writers to collect such data for more languages than has been done so far.

Rhyme and metre are two distinct concepts. They can and should be analyzed independently from one another. Metre can appear without rhyme ("blank verse"), as in (1) from English:

(1) Now is the wínter óf our díscontént
     Made glórious súmmer bý this sún of Yórk;
     And áll the clóuds that lóur'd upón our hóuse
     In the deep bósom óf the ócean búried.
     Now are our bróws bound wíth victórious wréaths;
     Our brúised árms hung úp for mónuménts;
     Our stérn alárums chánged to mérry méetings;
     Our dréadful márches tó delíghtful méasures.
     (...)
     (William Shakespeare, King Richard the Third, beginning)

As can rhyme without metre, as in (2). (Here and in subsequent examples in this paper, the rhyming parts are underlined.)

(2) Über allen Gi<u>pfeln</u>
     Ist R<u>uh</u>,
     In allen Wi<u>pfeln</u>
     Spürest d<u>u</u>
     Kaum einen H<u>auch</u>;
     Die Vögelein schweigen im W<u>alde</u>.
     Warte nur, b<u>alde</u>
     Ruhest du <u>auch</u>.
     (Johann Wolfgang von Goethe, Ein Gleiches)

Metre will no longer be considered in what follows.

1.2 Defining rhyme

Rhyme can be defined as the phonological[1] identity of substrings of lines. A language-independent definition of what a line is will not be attempted here. In a given poetical tradition, an independent justification of the entity "line" is often provided by metre. In all languages, line breaks normally coincide with word breaks, with very few exceptions ("broken rhyme", humoristic or experimental), as in (3):

(3) The Eurydice – it concerned thee, O L<u>ord</u>:
Three hundred souls, O alas! on b<u>oard</u>,
Some asleep unawakened, <u>all un</u>-
warned, eleven fathoms f<u>allen</u>
(Gerard M. Hopkins, The Loss of the Eurydice)

I will discuss first where the identical substring is located, and then how identity is defined ("rhyme phonology"). In principle, the identity can be located in the beginning, in the middle or in the end of lines, which constitutes the three subtypes of initial rhyme, internal rhyme, and end rhyme. All these three types are attested in the world's languages.

1.3 The position of the identical segments

1.3.1 Initial rhyme

Initial rhyme (sometimes called "inverse rhyme") is not frequent but does exist. It is the norm for classical and largely still for modern Mongolian poetry.[2] I give an example from the *Sayang Sečen* (1662 CE), cited from Poppe (1970: 164), who explains: "The typical Mongolian verse consists of a quatrain, i.e., a stanza of four lines [...]. Each line of a quatrain begins with the same syllable."

(4) <u>A</u>rban nasutai dayaluyai bi
<u>A</u>liya mayui-ban ese uqaydaluyai
<u>A</u>raǰan-dur dašiyuraysan minu ünen bülüge
<u>A</u>lus buruyu sanaysan ügei bolai

---

1 With further qualifications, for which see below.
2 Very similar specimens of rhyme are found in Old Turkic texts.

Qorin nasutai dayaluyai bi
Qolčirqan mayu-ban ese medegdelügei
Qorojan-dur dašiyuraysan minu ünen bülüge
Qoortu sedkil bariysan ügei bolai
(...)

Another example of much earlier date is the *Babylonian Theodicee* (Lambert 1960: 63–91) written in the Akkadian language (ca. 1000 BCE). Each stanza contains 11 verses, all of which begin with the same segment (V, CV, VC or CVC) (as also with the same cuneiform sign). I am citing the stanza with *li-* as an example. It should be noted that this is a unique text, rhyme not being a regular feature elsewhere in Akkadian poetry.

(5) Li-'u-u$_2$ pal-ku-u$_2$ šu-e ta-šim-ti
[L]i-it-mu-um-ma ṣur-ra-ka ila ta-da-a-a-aṣ
[L]i-ib-bi ili ki-ma qe$_2$-reb šamê^e ne$_2$-si-ma
Le(LI)-e$_2$-a-us-su šup-šu-qat-ma niši^{meš} la lam-da
Li-pit qāt ^{d}a-ru-ru mit-ha-riš na-piš-ti
Li-il-li-du min$_3$-su ka-liš la HAR-ri
Li-it-tu bu-ur-šu reš-tu-u$_2$ ša$_2$-pil-ma
Li-gi-mu-ša$_2$ ar-ku-u$_2$ ma-ṣi šit-tin-šu
Li-il-lu ma-ru pa-na-a i-al-lad
Li-'u-um qar-du ša$_2$ ša$_2$-ni-i ni-bit-su
[L]i-'i-id mi-na-a pak-ki ilim-ma niši^{meš} la lam-da

1.3.2 Variations on initial rhyme: Alliteration, alphabetic acrostic

The alliterating verse of Old-Germanic and other languages could be considered a subtype of initial rhyme, although the identity is located here at the beginning of smaller segments than what is conventionally considered a "line":

(6) Hwæt we gardena in geardagum
Þeodcyninga þrym gefrunon
Hu ða æþelingas ellen fremedon
Oft scyld scefing sceaþena þreatum
Monegum mægþum meodosetla ofteah
(...)
(Beowulf, Old English, beginning)

Alliteration is also typical for Somali epic poetry, which is characterized by "alliterating (...) the initial sound of at least one word in each line (...). The alliterating sound must be the same throughout the whole poem (...). A poet must take care not to use grammatical words such as particles or pronouns for alliteration, and has to avoid repeating the same word in nearby lines." (Banti & Giannattasio 1996: 84f.).

(7) Ma sidii galowga
     Oo guluf meel ku dareemay
     Yaan gam'i waayay habeen
     Sidii aarkiyo goosha
     Oo gabnihii laga laayay
     Gurxan maygu batay
     (...)

A poetic phenomenon which used to be very common in the Eastern Mediterranean area during Late Antiquity are *alphabetic acrostics*, in which the lines begin with the letters of the alphabet in a sequence.[3] By their nature, they can only be formed in written languages and appeal to the eye more than to the ear. The earliest known examples are from Biblical Hebrew, ex. Psalm 111:

(8) ʾŌdäh jəhwāh bəkāl-lebāb   אוֹדֶה יְהוָה בְּכָל־לֵבָב
     Bəsōd jəšārīm wəʕedāh   בְּסוֹד יְשָׁרִים וְעֵדָה
     Gədolīm maʕăśē jəhwāh   גְּדֹלִים מַעֲשֵׂי יְהוָה
     Dərūšīm ləkāl-ḥäpṣēhäm   דְּרוּשִׁים לְכָל־חֶפְצֵיהֶם
     Hūd-wəhādār pāʕălō   הוֹד־וְהָדָר פָּעֳלוֹ
     Wəṣidqātō ʕomädät lāʕad   וְצִדְקָתוֹ עֹמֶדֶת לָעַד

A sportive variety on this is a Coptic reverse alphabetic acrostic, which is based on the Greek, not the Coptic alphabet (Kuhn & Tait 1996: No. 4; Sahidic dialect):[4]

---

3 I am stretching the definition of rhyme here, since alphabetic acrostics do not show identity of segments with each other, but identity with an externally defined pattern, namely the alphabet.
4 Here and throughout this paper, Coptic is given in a traditional transliteration, which should not be taken as a straightforward representation of phonemes.

(9) Ọ̄ tčot epeoou mnptaio / ntapensōtēr nagathos / kharize mmof nnefpet-
ouaab / apa biktōr mnklaudios
P̱sōtēr ōš ebol efjō mmos / jenaiatou nnentaupōt nsōou / etbetdikaiosunē
/ jetōoute tmntero nmpēue
Ḵhere nemarturos etouaab / khere nathlētēs njōōre / khere nentauji
nteklēronomia / ntmntero nmpēue
P̱hiereus napostolos paulos / ōš ebol efjō mmos / jenehoplon ntmntma-
toi / nhensarkikon anne
Ụi petsēh afjōk ebol ejōtn / ō apa biktōr mnklaudios / jeounoueiōt
naparadidou mpefšēre / auō ouson mpefson
Ṭaueid prro ōš ebol jepepsaltērion efjō mmos / jeapaiōt metamaau kaat
nsōou / pjois de pentafšopt erof
(...)

1.3.3 Internal rhyme

The idea that sections at some place in the middle of verse lines should need to be
identical may seem unexpected but is in fact realized in certain poetic traditions.
Classical Tamil poetry requires the identity of the second syllable and sometimes
subsequent elements in verse lines (here underlined). Example: Tiruvalluvar,
Thirukkural (probably early 1st millennium CE; additional tendency towards alliteration in this text) (Manickavasagam 2003: 3–7).

(10) Ak̲ara mutala eḻuttellām āti / pak̲avaṉ mutaṟṟē ulaku
Kaṟṟataṉā lāya payaṉeṉkol vālaṟivaṉ / naṟṟāḷ toḷā'ar eṉiṉ
Malarmicai ēkiṉāṉ māṇaṭi cērntār / nilamicai nīṭuvāḷ vār
Vēṉṯutal vēṇṭāmai ilāṉaṭi cērntārkku / yāṉṯum iṭumpai ila
Irulcēr iruviṉaiyum cērā iraivaṉ / poruḻcēr pukaḻpurintār māṭṭu.
Poṟivāyil aintavittāṉ poytīr oḻukka / neṟiniṉrār nīṭuvāḷ vār
Taṉakkuvamai illātāṉ tāḻcērntārk kallāl / maṉakkavalai māṟṟal aritu
Aravāli antaṉaṉ tāḻcērntārk kallāl / piravāli nīntal aritu
Kōḻil poṟiyil kuṇamilavē eṉkuṇattāṉ / tāḻai vaṇaṅkāt talai
Piṟavip peruṅkaṭal nīntuvar nīntār / iraivaṉ aṭicērā tār
(...)

Internal rhyme is also found in several Old Norse texts, e.g., Sigvatr Þórðarson,
Erfidrápa Óláfs helga (early 11th cent.; internal rhyme underlined, + alliteration
in bold type):

(11)   T<u>olf</u> frák **t**ekna <u>elf</u>ar
       T**á**llaust viðu b<u>á</u>la.
       Olli Áleifr f<u>alli</u>,
       Eirsamr konungr, þ<u>eira</u>.
       S**ví**a t<u>yggj</u>a leitk **s**<u>eggi</u>
       S**ó**knst<u>rí</u>ð<u>s</u> firum r<u>íð</u>a
       B<u>öl</u> vas **b**rátt til H<u>el</u>jar
       B**ú**it m<u>est</u> Sigars h<u>est</u>i
       (...)

2 Geographical distribution and evolution of end rhyme

2.1 Introduction

The identity of verse ends, in other words *end rhyme*, is much more common in modern times than the types described above, amounting to a practically universal distribution. I cannot demonstrate this in full breadth here, but I want to refer to the web-site http://www.mamalisa.com/ which hosts childrens' songs and nursery rhymes from all over the world, most of which display some form of end rhyme. Rhyme is also ubiquitous in texts of pop songs which are nowadays produced by mainstream cultures in most corners of the world. Judging from its modern distribution, end rhyme would seem to be universal, innate, or inherited from the world's proto-language. It was, however, largely unknown to most major literary traditions of the ancient world (Egyptian, Ancient Near Eastern languages recorded in Cuneiform writing, Classical Greek and Latin, Classical Sanskrit, Older Iranian, Classical Japanese, traditional Balto-Slavic folk verse, etc.). This suggests that end rhyme is actually a contact phenomenon which must have spread from one or few sources to the whole world only in relatively recent times.[5]

The investigation of the diachrony of end rhyme is hampered by a methodological problem. A strict borderline between rhymed texts and unrhymed texts is

---

5 An alternative explanation, which was proposed by an anonymous reviewer, could be that end rhyme used to be much more common in the past than suggested by textual evidence but was restricted to stylistical domains (such as children's or nursery language?) which were not usually put into writing.

harder to draw than one might assume. Since most human languages use grammatical affixes, the initial and/or final phonemes of sentences are not a random selection from the phoneme inventory, but certain phoneme sequences are statistically overrepresented at the sentence edges. When verse lines coincide with clauses, which is normal for most poetic traditions, verse beginnings or ends may come to be identical even if rhymes are not intentionally sought by the composer. In addition to this, the fact that parallelism and repetition in very general terms belong to the universal stylistic means of poetic language further increases the frequency of rhymes even in traditions where it is not a constitutive poetic principle. The borderline between unrhymed poetry and rhymed poetry is therefore a fluid one, and it may very well be that also the emergence of end rhyme was a fluid or stochastic process, so that a fixed time and place of origin would never have existed.

Nevertheless, I think that a differentiation between "sporadic rhyme" and "systematic rhyme" is useful at least for presentational purposes. I will use the term "sporadic rhyme" where rhymed verses occur more frequently than could be expected by chance but still belong to the inventory of optional stylistic effects, whereas "systematic rhyme" means that rhyme has become a mandatory feature of poetry. The existence of "systematic rhyme" in this sense can be affirmed if (1) a longer poem shows exceptionless rhyme, (2) a rhyme pattern (such as ABAB...) is recognizable, or (3) not only grammatical suffixes but also parts of lexical stems participate in rhyme.

So where did end rhyme originate? The famous German poet Johann Wolfgang von Goethe seems to have been on the right track when he took it to be an Oriental (as he says, Persian) invention:

Behramgur, sagt man, hat den Reim erfunden.
Er sprach entzückt aus reiner Seele Drang;
Dilaram schnell, die Freundin seiner Stunden,
Erwiderte mit gleichem Wort und Klang.
(Goethe, Westöstlicher Divan: Suleika Nameh)[6]

I will now give examples of early attestations of sporadic and/or systematic end rhyme from several regions, roughly in chronological order.

---

6 'Behramgur [a Sassanide king of Persia], they say, invented rhyme. Ecstatically he spoke, from his pure soul's inspire; and Dilaram, the darling of his hours, quickly replied with matching word and sound.'

2.2 Hittite

A fragment of a song from the time of Hattusilis Ist (16th cent. BCE) shows a repetition at the end, but the preserved portion consists of no more than three lines:[7]

(12) nesas [waspes] nesas waspes <u>tiya-mmu tiya</u>
nu-mu annas-mas katta arnut <u>tiya-mmu tiya</u>
nu-mu uwas-mas katta arnut <u>tiya-mmu tiya</u>
'[Clothes from] Nesa, clothes from Nesa bring me, bring!
My mother's (gifts) take down for me, bring me, bring!
My nurse's (gifts) take down for me, bring me, bring!' (Haas 2006: 280).

This is an example of great antiquity, but the fragment does not suffice to prove that end rhyme was a regular poetic instrument of the Hittite language, the less so as other extant Hittite poetic texts do not use rhyme.

2.3 Chinese

The Shī Jīng (詩經) "Book of Odes" (said to originate from the early 1st millennium BCE; first fragmentary manuscripts from the Han dynasty, 206 BCE–220 CE) shows clear instances of end rhyme, but with various degrees of consistency throughout the opus. One of the best examples is Ode 305 (Karlgren 1950: 265f.), the last (and latest?) one, which at present constitutes the earliest known example of clearly intentional, systematic end rhyme in the world. The rhymes are obvious but imprecise in the contemporary Mandarin pronunciation as given here. They start on the vowel of the last syllable.

(13) 撻彼殷武、奮伐荊楚、　　tà bǐ yīn w<u>ǔ</u> / fèn fá jīng ch<u>ǔ</u>
突入其阻、裒荊之旅、　　shēn rù jī z<u>ǔ</u> / póu jīng zhī l<u>ǚ</u>
有截其所、湯孫之緒。維女荊楚、yǒu jié jī s<u>uǒ</u> / tāng sūn zhī x<u>ù</u> /
　　　　　　　　　　　　　　wéi rǔ jīng ch<u>ǔ</u>
居國南鄉 、昔有成湯、　jū guó nán xi<u>āng</u> / xī yǒu chéng t<u>āng</u>
自彼氏羌、莫敢不來享、　zì bǐ dī qi<u>āng</u> / mò gǎn bú lái xi<u>ǎng</u>
莫敢不來王、曰商是常。　mò gǎn bú lái w<u>áng</u> / yuē shang shì ch<u>áng</u>
天命多辟、設都于禹之績、　tiān mìng duō b<u>ì</u> / shè dōu yú yǔ zhī j<u>ī</u>

---

7 I owe the reference to this text to Francis Breyer (Berlin).

歲事來辟、勿予禍適、稼穡匪解。 suì shì lái bì / wù yú huò shì / jià sè fěi xiè

天命降監、下民有嚴、 tiān mìng jiàng jiān / xià mín yǒu yán

不僭不濫、不敢怠遑、 bú jiàn bú làn / bú gǎn dài huáng

命于下國、封建厥福。 mìng yú xià guó / fēng jiàn jué fú

商邑翼翼、四方之極、 shāng yì yì yì / sì fāng zhī jí

赫赫厥聲、濯濯厥靈、 hè hè jué shēng / zhuó zhuó jué líng

壽考且寧、以保我後生。 shòu kǎo jū níng / yǐ bǎo wǒ hòu shēng

陟彼景山、松柏丸丸、 zhì bǐ jǐng shān / sōng bǎi wán wán

是斷是遷、方斲是虔、 shì duàn shì qiān / fāng zhuó shì qián

松桷有梴、旅楹有閑、寢成孔安。 sōng jué yǒu chān / lǚ yíng yǒu xián / qǐn chéng kǒng ān

In the reconstructions of Old Chinese pronunciation by Karlgren (1950: 266) and Baxter (1992; see his appendix "The rhyme words of the Shījīng": 745–812), the rhymes become better and sometimes appear to include consonants of the syllable onset as well. The first rhyme groups in Baxter's reconstruction:

(14) line 1–3: 武 Np(r)jaʔ = 楚 tsrhjaʔ = 阻 tsrjaʔ = 旅 grjaʔ = 所 s(k)rjaʔ = 緒 zjaʔ = 楚 tsrhjaʔ

line 4–6: 鄉 xjang = 湯 hlang = 羌 kh(l)jang = 享 xjangʔ = 王 wjang = 常 djang

line 7–8: 辟 pjek = 績 tsek = 辟 pjek = 適 drek = 解 kreks

In Karlgren's reconstruction:

(15) 武 mi̯wo = 楚 tṣʼi̯o = 阻 tṣi̯o = 旅 gli̯o = 所 ṣi̯o = 緒 dzi̯o = 楚 tṣʼi̯o

鄉 χi̯ang = 湯 tʼâng = 羌 kʼi̯ang = 享 χi̯ang = 王 gi̯wang = 常 di̯ang

辟 pi̯ĕk = 績 tsi̯ĕk = 辟 pi̯ĕk = 適 dʼĕk = 解 gʼĕg

2.4 Hebrew

The Hebrew Bible (1st millennium BCE) contains examples of sporadic rhyme, i.e., identity of verse ends at much more than random rate but with no consistency and no obvious alternation patterns. One of the best examples is Psalm 146:

(16) Halǝlū-y<u>āh</u>

    Halǝlī napšī ʾät-yǝh<u>yāh</u> / ʾăhalǝlāh yǝhyā bǝ ḥayyāy ʾăzammǝrāh
    lēlohay bǝʿōrī
    ʾAl-tibṭǝhū bindībīm / bǝbän-ʾādām šäʾeyn lō tǝšūʿ<u>āh</u>
    Teṣe rūḥō yāšūb lǝʾadmāt<u>ō</u> / bayyōm ha-hū ʾăbdū ʿăštonot<u>āw</u>
    ʾAšrē šäʾel yaʿăqob bǝʿäzr<u>ō</u> / śibrō ʿal-yǝhwāh ʾĕloh<u>āw</u>
    ʿOśäh šāmayim wāʾāräṣ / ʾät-hayyām wǝʾät-kāl-ʾăšär-b<u>ām</u>
    Haśśomer ʾĕmät lǝʿōl<u>ām</u> / ʿośäh mišpāṭ lāʿăšūq<u>īm</u>
    Noten läḥäm lārʿeb<u>īm</u> / yǝhwāh mattīr ʾăsūr<u>īm</u>
    Yǝhwāh poqeāḥ ʿiwr<u>īm</u> / yǝhwāh zoqep kǝpūp<u>īm</u>
    Yǝhwāh ʾoheb ṣadīq<u>īm</u> / yǝhwāh šomer ʾet-ger<u>īm</u>
    Yatōm wǝʾalmānāh yǝʿoded / wǝdäräk rošāʿīm yǝʿawwet
    Yimlok yǝhwāh lǝʿōlām / ʾĕlohayik ṣiyyōn lǝdor wādōr
    Halǝlū-yāh

Sporadic rhyme of this kind is generally frequent in post-biblical Hebrew liturgical texts, e.g., in Tfilat ha-Amida (thought to have been composed in the 1st century CE). Kuhn (1950) postulated that rhyme in such texts was originally exceptionless and phrases violating the rhyme are later insertions or text corruptions, a hypothesis I would not follow.

Rhyme becomes undisputably systematic by the works of Yannai, as exemplified here by his poem *Aḥar ham-midbār*, ascribed to the 6th century (from Carmi 1981: 219f.). The rather strict rhyme of the last syllable is often preceded by a section of less strict identity, which makes it difficult to determine where exactly the rhyme starts. This text is an early example of the *piyut* genre, which is characterized by both end rhyme and an alphabetic acrostic pattern:

(17) **A**ḥar ham-midbār šīr nihag ṣ<u>ōn</u> / aḥar ham-midbār hinhīg ʿammō
    kaṣṣ<u>ōn</u>
    Bǝlō raglayim rāṣ wǝ-herīṣ marʿīt<u>ō</u> / lāläkät limqōm ḥäzyōn marʾīt<u>ō</u>
    Giddūlē däšä hāyū nibrāʾ<u>īm lǝ-pānāw</u> / wǝʾaḥar kāk hāyū niblāʿīm
    <u>milpānāw</u>
    Däräk gǝdōlāh lǝ-yōm ʾāḥād <u>hillek</u> / kī ʾōheb mēšārīm yiššar lō <u>heläk</u>
    Har hā-ʾĕlohīm ʿet pī hugg<u>ā</u>ʿ / miṭṭārḥō hūnaḥ u-mīgīʿō hurg<u>ā</u>ʿ
    U-thillāh nirʾāh l<u>ō kidmūt malʾāk</u> / laʿăśōt dǝmūt<u>ō kidmūt malʾāk</u>
    Zäh lǝkī darkō ḥinnǝkō lir<u>ʾōt</u> / lihyōt bāqī bǝ-kāl marʾē mar<u>ʾōt</u>
    Ḥuzzaq libō kǝšār labbat <u>ʾeš</u> / baʿăbūr lǝlabbǝbō bǝ-kāl mīnē <u>ʾeš</u>
    Ṭāhūr bǝtūk ṭumʾāh yǝqārō hōp<u>iä</u>ʿ / gāboäḥ ʿal sǝnäh kǝbōdō hōd<u>iä</u>ʿ
    Yaʿan kī ṣārat ʿammō hī ṣār<u>ātō</u> / w-īšūʿātām hī yǝšūʿ<u>ātō</u>

2.5 Old South Arabian

The earliest known text with systematic end rhyme outside China appears to be the Sun Hymn of Saba from ca. 200 CE (Abdallāh 1988).[8] It is written in the Old South Arabian script. The text is not readily translatable, as the language is not precisely determined. According to Beeston (1994: 236–238), the text contains Old North Arabian traits as well. The text consists of 27 verses all of which terminate in -ḥk (-k being a grammatical suffix, -ḥ- belonging to the stem):

(18) Nštrn ḫyr kmhḏ hqḥk
      Bṣyd ḥnwn m'ṯ nśḥk
      Wqrnw š'b ḏqsd qsḥk
      Wlb 'lhn ḏyḥr fqḥk
      W'ylt ''db ṣl' fḏḥk
      W'yn mšqr hnbḥr wṣḥk
      Wmn ḏrm wtd' hslḥk
      Wmhś' yḫn 'ḥgy kšḥk
      (...)

2.6 Aramaic

Kuhn (1950: 30–40) provides a reconstruction of the hypothetical Aramaic original of the *Pater noster* (early 1st century CE) that has systematic end rhyme, but this is highly speculative. Many examples of early Syriac hymnody have sporadic rhyme to various degrees, as in Hebrew. The following text brings end rhyme almost to perfection, but it is largely restricted to -e and -o as grammatical suffixes and still has no regular pattern of alternation:

(19) 'Ayno bnahiro / metdakyo bneqpe
      Wmetnaṣho bzayne / wmeštapyo bdenḥe
      Wmezdahyo bziwe / wmeṣṭabto bšupre
      Maryam broz 'ayno / nuhro šro bgawo
      Wamraq ltar'ito / wšapi lmaḥšabto
      Daki lmernito / wṣalel btuluto
      Nahro da'mad ho be / brozo hpak baṭne

---

8 I owe the reference to this text to Stefan Weninger (Marburg).

ʿUbo ragyo dmay<u>o</u> / baṭne bdakyot<u>o</u>
Wyalde bzahyut<u>o</u> / w'asqe btešbuḥt<u>o</u>
Bʿubo dakyo dnahr<u>o</u> / 'ilap lbart anoš<u>o</u>
Dbeṭnat dlo gabr<u>o</u> / wyeldat dlo zarʿ<u>o</u>
Rabyat bmawhabt<u>o</u> / lmoro dmawhabt<u>o</u>
Denḥo bgaw nahr<u>e</u> / ṣemḥo bgaw qabr<u>e</u>
'Azleg briš ṭqur<u>o</u> / wadnaḥ bgaw kars<u>o</u>
W'apreg bʿuloy<u>e</u> / w'anhar bsuloqe
(...)
(Poem ascribed to Ephrem the Syrian, 4th century CE; manuscript 522
CE; Brock & Kiraz 2006: Text no. 7)

(Sporadic) rhyme and other possibly poetic sound patterns in the Syriac gospel
translation are discussed by Falla (1977).

2.7 Arabic

The Arabic *Qur'an* (early 7th century) is characterized by systematic rhyme with
the same end section typically stretching over a long sequence of lines, often a
whole Surah. Example: Surah 81 with rhyme in *-at*.

(20) Iḏā š-šamsu kuwwir<u>at</u>
      Wa-iḏā n-nuğūmu nkadar<u>at</u>
      Wa-iḏā l-ğibālu suyyir<u>at</u>
      Wa-iḏā l-ʿišāru ʿuṭṭil<u>at</u>
      Wa-iḏā l-wuḥūšu ḥušir<u>at</u>
      Wa-iḏā l-biḥāru suğğir<u>at</u>
      Wa-iḏā n-nufūsu zuwwiğ<u>at</u>
      Wa-iḏā l-mau'ūdatu su'il<u>at</u>
      Bi-'ayyi ḏanbi qutil<u>at</u>
      Wa-iḏā ṣ-ṣuḥufu nušir<u>at</u>
      Wa-iḏā s-samā'u kušiṭ<u>at</u>
      Wa-iḏā l-ğaḥīmu suʿʿir<u>at</u>
      Wa-iḏā l-ğannatu 'uzlif<u>at</u>
      ʿAlimat nafsun mā 'aḥdar<u>at</u>
      (...)

2.8 Latin

Sporadic rhyme (*homoioteleuton*) is one of the established stylistic patterns of Classical Latin literature. The intentionality of such rhymes is, however, often hard to assess. One of the most convincing passages is the following from Ovid, *Amores* I,1 (ca. 0 CE):

(21) (...)
'Nec mihi materia est numeris levioribus apta,
Aut puer aut longas compta puella comas.'
Questus eram, pharetra cum protinus ille soluta
Legit in exitium spicula facta meum,
Lunavitque genu sinuosum fortiter arcum,
'Quod' que 'canas, vates, accipe' dixit 'opus!'
Me miserum! certas habuit puer ille sagittas.
Uror, et in vacuo pectore regnat Amor.
Sex mihi surgat opus numeris, in quinque residat:
Ferrea cum vestris bella valete modis!
Cingere litorea flaventia tempora myrto,
Musa, per undenos emodulanda pedes!
(...)

The first systematic rhyme appears in Augustinus, *Psalmus contra partem Donati*, 393 CE, earliest manuscript 9th century, composed of 295 verses all of which end in *-e* or *-ae* (from Finaert & Congar 1963: 150ff.):

(22) Vos qui gaudetis de pace, modo verum iudicate.
Foeda est res causam audire et personas accipere.
Omnes iniusti non possunt regnum dei possidere.
Vestem alienam conscindas nemo potest tolerare:
Quanto magis pacem Christi qui conscindit dignus morte?
Et quis est ista qui fecit quaeramus hoc sine errore.
(...)

2.9 Celtic

The earliest known specimen of rhymed Irish poetry is Colmán mac Lénéni, *Poem for King Domnall* (dated to 565/6 by Carney 1989: 42f.; extant manuscripts are medieval). The text makes also use of alliterations (here in bold type). It has been claimed (e.g., by Stella 1995b) that Old Irish verse was the initial model for end rhyme in the other European languages.

(23)　Luin oc **e**laib / **u**ngi oc dírnaib
　　　　Crotha ban n-athech / oc **r**ódaib **r**ígnaib
　　　　Ríg oc **D**omnall / **d**ord oc aidbse
　　　　Adand oc **c**aindill / **c**alg oc mo **ch**ailg-se
　　　　Dún maic **D**aim / **d**oe ós roi
　　　　Ronn **t**art / **t**acht coi
　　　　Ó ba mac **c**léib / **c**aindlech ser
　　　　Sirt cach n-ainm / ainm gossa fer
　　　　(...)

The first examples of Welsh rhyme appear no later than those of Irish. A rhyme of a remarkably intricate pattern is used by the poet Taliesin, *Marwnad Owain ab Urien* (Parry 1962: 3f.), ascribed to the 6th century, manuscripts medieval, which also contains alliterations (in bold type).

(24)　Enaid Owain ab Urien / gobwyllid **Rh**een o'i **r**aid.
　　　　Rheged udd ae cudd tromlas / nid oedd fas ei gywyddaid.
　　　　Isgell gŵr cerddglyd clodfawr, / esgyll **gw**awr **gw**aywawr llifaid,
　　　　Cany **ch**effir **c**ystedlydd / i udd Llwyfenydd **ll**athraid.
　　　　Medel **g**alon, **g**efeilad, / Eisylud ei **d**ad a'i **d**aid.
　　　　Pan laddawdd Owain Fflamdd**w**yn / **n**id oedd fwy **n**ogyd cysgaid.
　　　　Cysgid **Ll**oegr **ll**ydan nifer / Â **ll**eufer yn eu **ll**ygaid;
　　　　A rhai ni ffoynt **h**aeach / a oeddynt **h**yach no rhaid.
　　　　(...)

2.10 German

The *Merseburger Zaubersprüche* (the only pre-Christian German text; believed to have been composed before 750 CE; manuscript 10th century) may be considered to show sporadic rhyme. Spell 1:

(25)   Eiris sazun idisi
       Sazun hera duoder.
       Suma hapt hepti<u>dun</u>,
       Suma heri lezi<u>dun</u>,
       Suma clubo<u>dun</u>
       Umbi cuoniouuidi:
       Insprinc haptban<u>dun</u>,
       Inuar uigan<u>dun</u>.

Rhyme becomes systematic in the *Liber evangeliorum* by Otfrid von Weißenburg (ca. 860 CE; note the equivalence of -*n*- and -*l*-, which is no longer valid for modern German):

(26)   Lúdowig ther sné<u>llo</u>, / thes wísduames fó<u>llo</u>,
       Er óstarrichi ríhtit <u>ál</u>, / so Fránkono kúning sc<u>al</u>;
       Ubar Fránkono l<u>ant</u> / so gengit éllu sin giw<u>alt</u>,
       Thaz ríhtit, so ih thir z<u>éllu</u>, / thiu sin giwált <u>ellu</u>.
       Thémo si íamer h<u>éili</u> / joh sálida gim<u>éini</u>,
       Druhtin hóhe mo thaz g<u>úat</u> / joh frewe mo émmizen thaz m<u>úat</u>;
       (...)

2.11 Old Norse

It was not much later that end rhyme came into use in Old Norse as well. The first example is found in Egill Skallagrímsson, *Höfuðlausn* (936 CE) (+ alliteration, in bold type):

(27)   **V**estr komk of **v**<u>er</u>, / en ek **V**iðris b<u>er</u>
       Munstrandar **m**<u>ar</u>, / Svá's **m**itt of f<u>ar</u>;
       Drók **e**ik á fl<u>ot</u> / við **í**sabr<u>ot</u>,
       Hlóðk **m**ærðar hl<u>ut</u> / **m**unknarrar sk<u>ut</u>.
       Buðumk **h**ilmi l<u>öð</u> / ák **h**róðrs of kv<u>öð</u>

Berk **Ó**ðins mj<u>öð</u> / á Engla bj<u>öð</u>;
Lofat **ví**sa v<u>ann</u>, / **ví**st mærik þ<u>ann</u>,
Hlj<u>óð</u>s biðjum **h**<u>ann</u>, / þvít **h**róðr of f<u>ann</u>.
(…)

2.12 Iranian

End rhyme is a mandatory feature of Persian poetry of the Islamic period. This was not so in earlier stages of the language. Henning (1950: 646f.) states: "(…) in the whole of the Western Middle Iranian Material so far recognized as poetical there is not a single rhyme in the strict sense. There are accidental rhymes and assonances; but the principle of the rhyme as such, the deliberate rhyme, seems to have been unknown." As the only counter-example he cites (p. 647) a passage of 12 lines in a Pahlavi text all of which end in -*ān* (the manuscript is very late, 956 CE):

(28)   Dārom andarz-ē az dānāg<u>ān</u> / az guft-ī pēšēnīg<u>ān</u>
       Ō šmāh bē wizārom / pad rāstīh andar gēh<u>ān</u>
       Agar padīrēd / bavēd sūd-ī dō-gēh<u>ān</u>
       Pad gētī vistāxw ma bēd / was-ārzōg andar gēh<u>ān</u>
       Čē gētī pad kas bē nē hišt-hēnd / nē kūšk ud xān-u-m<u>ān</u>
       (…)

The *Tārīḫ-i Sīstān* ("History of Sīstān", 1053 CE) quotes a few rhymed verses said to go back to ca. 700 BCE (cited from Elwell-Sutton 1975: 88, who tries to argue that Persian end rhyme was a native tradition not imported from Arabic):

(29)   Ābast u nabīdh<u>ast</u> / 'uṣārāt-i zabīb<u>ast</u> / u dunba farbih u pīy<u>ast</u> / sumaiya
       rūsbīdh<u>ast</u>
       Az ḫutlān <u>āmadhiya</u> / ba-rū tabāh <u>āmadhiya</u> / āvār b<u>āz āmadhiya</u> /
       bī-dil far<u>āz āmadhiya</u>

2.13 Sanskrit

Rhyme is unknown to the bulk of classical Sanskrit literature. Jayadeva, *Gīta govinda* (12th cent. CE) is considered the earliest example, or one of the earliest examples, of systematic end rhyme in this language (on this text see also Gerow 1989):

(30)   Pralayapayodhijale dhṛtavānasi v<u>edam</u>
       Vihitavahitracaritramakh<u>edam</u>
       Keśava dhṛtamīnaśarīra <u>jaya jagadīśa hare</u>
       Kṣitirativipulatare tava tiṣṭhati p<u>ṛṣṭhe</u>
       Kharaṇidharaṇakiṇacakraga<u>riṣṭhe</u>
       Keśava dhṛtakacchaparūpa <u>jaya jagadīśa hare</u>
       Vasati daśanaśikhare dharaṇī tava <u>lagnā</u>
       Śaśini kalaṅkakaleva nim<u>agnā</u>
       Keśava dhṛtasūkararūpa <u>jaya jagadīśa hare</u>
       (...)

2.14 Conclusion

We have seen that the use of end rhyme in several languages expanded considerably during their observable history, making end rhyme by now a feature with a practically global distribution. I believe that two factors have contributed to this fact: (1) Poetic principles are easily borrowed. They are almost inevitably borrowed when a powerful literary language comes into contact with a language that has not yet developed firm literary traditions. This favours a world-wide spread of a limited number of literary principles out of many more that would be possible in theory. (2) Since, typologically, inflectional suffixes are more frequent than prefixes (Dryer 2005), equal word-ends must be globally more frequent than equal word-beginnings. This made it more probable that end rhyme would prevail over other types of rhyme, as it in fact did.

It remains hard to decide whether a single origin of systematic end rhyme or rather a polygenetic origin should be assumed. For the time being, two major, perhaps independent nuclei can be recognized which have contributed to the world-wide spread of end rhyme, namely China and the Near East. The first undisputable examples of systematic end rhyme are attested from China, a country whose literacy and literature had a strong influence on several cultures of the Far East. Rhyme in the Near East, whether ultimately imported from China or not, joins a short time later, and it is from here that end rhyme entered the literary traditions of Christianity and Islam, through which it spread to most remaining regions of the globe.

It appears that, in several traditions at least, rhyme was introduced gradually during an extended period in which rhyme became more and more frequent and regularized, i.e., the emergence of rhyme was a statistical process (thus D'Angelo 1995 for Latin). This makes it difficult to determine exact migration paths.

Modern European rhyme has repeatedly, and in my view rightly, been argued to be derived from Hebrew or Semitic languages, e.g., by Kuhn (1950: 51), who also suggests that rhyme arose from identical suffixes in parallel clauses and would thus originally have been restricted to grammatical morphemes. An origin from Hebrew is also asserted by Hrushovski (1981: 62): "The rhyming system of the Hebrew *piyut* was the earliest known massive, systematic and obligatory use of rhyme in poetry, and it is very plausible that through the Christian Syriac church employing Aramaic (a cognate language to Hebrew), and via Latin liturgy, the principle of rhyme was transferred to European poetry".

Other authors prefer to believe in independent inventions (e.g., Schweikle 1967 for German). See also the contributions in Ernst & Neuser (1977) on the issue. Norden (1898.2: 810–908, appendix "Über die Geschichte des Reims"), who gives a detailed description of the rise of end rhyme in Latin and Greek, tries to take an intermediate position in arguing that rhyme exists "potentially" in all languages, being based on the idea of parallelism which he believes to be universal, but that cultural contact was needed to bring rhyme into "actual" usage.

2.15 Rhyme outside of poetry

Features more or less comparable to rhyme can be found also outside the domain of poetry. The existence of such features in a language might have facilitated the selection of the same principle for poetic use. Some miscellaneous features of this kind are the following:

– Partial reduplication, which appears as a morphological process in several languages, can be regarded as a non-poetic correlate either of initial rhyme or alliteration (Greek πείθω 'to convince', perfect participle πε-πεισμένος), of internal rhyme (Samoan *alofa* 'he loves', *alolofa* 'they love'[9]), or of end rhyme (Somali *dab* 'fire', plural *dab-ab*), depending on where the reduplica-

---

9 Cited from Moravcsik (1978: 310) where many more examples of reduplication are to be found.

tion is located. This parallelism has been commented on e.g., by Kiparsky (1975: 242f.).

- Several languages have so-called "echo compounds" (Turkish term: *mühmele*), which are formed from nouns and introduce a notion of plurality, "et cetera", or add some kind of emotional colouring. They are relatively productive in languages such as Turkish: *kitap mitap* 'books and the like' (Marchand 1952); Egyptian Arabic: *fi ṣalʾaṭ malʾaṭ* 'everywhere' (Woidich 2006: 15); Yiddish: *gelt-šmelt* 'money – who cares?'; Lezgian: *sikʾ-mikʾ* 'fox and other wild animals' (Haspelmath 1993: 109); Hindi: *pānī vānī* 'water et cetera'; Tamil: *paampu-kiimpu* 'snakes and similar reptiles'. Less prototypical examples are also found in English: *itsy-bitsy, boogie-woogie, hobson-jobson, hodgepodge, baby-shmaby* (the *shm*-type being a borrowing from Yiddish, see Spitzer 1952); German: *Hokuspokus, Kuddelmuddel, Techtelmechtel, holterdipolter*; French: *pêle-mêle*. The origin of such compounds has been claimed to lie in Dravidian (Kane 2001: 58) or Turkic (Southern 2005: 26–30) languages, but there are examples already from Hittite (*karnan marnan* 'nach besten Kräften', Haas 2006: 292) and Coptic (magical formulas such as *thalal malal*, Vycichl 1984: 103 with reference to possible Egyptian examples).
- Semantically related words may influence one another so that they acquire the same end rhyme, e.g., Bulgarian *októmbri* 'October' (with unetymological -*m*-) – *noémbri* 'November' (the same in some other Slavonic languages); French *grammaire* (irregularly < *grammatica*) – *vocabulaire*; English *female* (irregularly < French *femelle*) – *male*; Mehri *hīmel* (irregularly from the root *ymn*) 'right' – *šimel* 'left' (Brockelmann 1927: 19, who gives a lot of further examples from Semitic languages).
- It may also be mentioned that between the 11th and the 18th centuries, Arabic book titles were frequently rhymed (Ambros 1990), such as *Maǧmaʕ as-surūr wa-maṭlaʕ aš-šams wa-l-budūr* 'Assembly of Happiness, and Ascent Location of the Sun and the Moons'. Here, a genuinely poetic feature acquired an additional field of use with which it had not originally been associated.

3 Parametric variation of end rhyme across languages

Although, as we have seen, the idea of end rhyme was normally borrowed, its implementation differs greatly across languages. There are several parameters according to which rhyme rules can vary, some of which I am going to sketch in the following.

As is perhaps true for grammatical rules in general, the borderline between "grammatical" and "ungrammatical" utterances is not always a clear-cut one, which means that the attempt to describe the usage of rhyme for a language in the form of strict laws is an oversimplification. In reality, different rhymes may have a different "quality", with the worse of them being employed less frequently or only by some authors. Holtman (1996) tries to capture this fact by a description of rhyme rules in the framework of Optimality Theory (she considers data from Dutch and English only).

3.1 Rhyme phonology

I want to introduce the concept of "rhyme phonology", since the partitioning of the sound space implied by rhyme identity may differ from the partitioning of the sound space as normally practised by phonologists ("ordinary phonology"). Both ways of partitioning are distinct but may still turn out to be interrelated in some way. In particular, it seems to be typical that rhyme phonology displays mergers with respect to ordinary phonology, or, in other words, is an underdifferentiated version of ordinary phonology.

The question has been raised which linguistic level of representation provides the input for rhyme. Manaster Ramer (1994) argued that relatively abstract levels of representation are not relevant for rhyme in any language, as against Malone (1982) who took the opposite view that rhyme is based on deep phonology. I believe that this question cannot be settled before further typological research has provided data on rhyme from a wider range of languages. For the time being, I am only defending the weak formulation that "rhyme phonology" is not identical with the ordinary phonological representation.

Another approach to explain discrepancies between rhyme equivalence and ordinary phonemic analysis is taken by Baxter (1992: 88–97). He attributes them to historical factors, namely to the supposed origin of rhyme usage in either past literary traditions or other dialects. But even if this were a common pathway of how a distinct "rhyme phonology" can come into existence, it is obvious that a strictly synchronic description of rhyme usage is still necessary in its own right.

3.1.1 Underdifferentiation of vowels

In several languages, certain phonological vowel distinctions are ignored for the rhyme. Let us first examine the case of German. A minority of poets seem to distinguish rhyme vowels as in ordinary phonology (e.g., Gottfried Benn; Detlef von Liliencron; Rainer Maria Rilke).[10] However, the large majority of German poets rhyme *ü* = *i*, *ö* = *e*, /*ai*/ = /*oi*/ (but not **a* = *o*!), and most native speakers perceive such rhymes as completely acceptable. The obvious interpretation is that the feature of rounding in vowels is not relevant for rhyme phonology, and that rhyme phonology is in this respect an underdifferentiated version of ordinary phonology. Examples are abundant; I cite only one text here:

(31) Ich weiß nicht was soll es bed<u>euten</u>, /oi/
Dass ich so traurig b<u>in</u>;
Ein Märchen aus alten Z<u>eiten</u>, /ai/
Das kommt mir nicht aus dem S<u>inn</u>.
(...)
Den Schiffer im kleinen Schi<u>ffe</u>
Ergreift es mit wildem W<u>eh</u>; /ē/
Er schaut nicht die Felsenri<u>ffe</u>,
Er schaut nur hinauf in die H<u>öh</u>. /ö/
(...)
(Heinrich Heine, *Loreley*; note also the tendency towards alliteration in this text)

Some authors may, in addition, ignore vowel quantity and other subtleties (*a–o*-distinction):

---

10 Martin Stockburger (Konstanz) helped me in identifying these authors.

(32)   Ein feste Burg ist unser G<u>ott</u>, /ŏ/
Ein gute Wehr und W<u>affen</u>. /a/
Er hilft uns frei aus aller N<u>ot</u>, /ō/
Die uns jetzt hat betr<u>offen</u>. /o/
(...)
(Martin Luther, a popular hymn of the Protestant church)

In Polish, rhyme phonology does not recognize nasal vowels. They are either treated as vowel + N (word internally before stops), which is not striking because this is in agreement with their actual pronunciation. More significantly, they are treated like simple vowels in the other positions, which means that the feature of nasality is disregarded. *ą* counts as equivalent to *o(N)*. Furthermore, *i* and *y* are equivalent.

(33)   Odwraca głowę, odeszła n<u>ieco</u>,
Podniosła w niebo źren<u>ice</u>,
Nagle na oczach łezki zaśw<u>iecą</u>
I róż wystąpił na l<u>ice</u>.
(...)
Starzec ucisza, podnosi r<u>ękę</u>,
"Słuchajcie, dzieci!" – zaw<u>oła</u> –
"Powiem, od kogo mam tę pios<u>enkę</u>,
Może on był z tego si<u>oła</u>."
(...)
Idź, może znajdziesz na brzegach Ni<u>emna</u>
Tę, której już nie ob<u>aczę</u>,
Może jej piosnka będzie przyj<u>emna</u>,
Może nad listkiem zapł<u>acze</u>.
(Adam Mickiewicz, *Dudarz*)

(...)
Ot lepiej pióro wezmę i śród c<u>iszy</u>,
Gdy się bez ładu myśl pl<u>ącze</u>,
Zacznę coś pisać dla mych towarz<u>yszy</u>,
Zacznę, bo nie wiem, czy sk<u>ończę</u>.
(...)
(Adam Mickiewicz, *Do Przyjaciół*)

In Czech rhyme, vowel quantity is generally disregarded:

(34) Na stolci seděl kníže p<u>án</u>, / Vojakům kázal rozhněv<u>án</u>:
      "Již chopte páže zr<u>adné</u>, / Ať hlava jeho p<u>adne</u>!"
      To mladou kněžnou zachv<u>ělo</u> – / Jí oko mnou se zastř<u>elo</u>
      A hlava mdlá se ch<u>ýlí</u>: / "Ustaňte ještě chv<u>íli</u>!
      Ó život, což ten člov<u>ěka</u> / Jen v plaché stíny obl<u>éká</u> –
      I když jej celý pr<u>osní</u>, / Jak v růži kapku r<u>osní</u>!
      Na světlech modré obl<u>ohy </u>/ Stesk duše tá mu neb<u>ohý</u>,
      Však sotva v lesk se v<u>esní</u>, / Již mře jak kvítko l<u>esní</u>.
      Mladost, krása, láska – vš<u>e</u>, / Ach, jak to jmění prchav<u>é</u>:
      To sotva jednou zk<u>vétá</u> / A již je po všem v<u>eta</u>!
      A květu jara vonný d<u>en</u>, / Ach, jak to krátký, krátký s<u>en</u>
      (...)
      (Vítězslav Hálek, *Knížecí Soud*)

Ultimately, vowels may become completely irrelevant. This is not the norm for any European language but is occasionally found in English and French (here called "contre-assonance"):

(35) It seemed that out of battle I e<u>scaped</u>
      Down some profound dull tunnel, long since <u>scooped</u>
      Through granites which titanic wars had <u>groined</u>.
      Yet also there encumbered sleepers <u>groaned</u>,
      Too fast in thought or death to be be<u>stirred</u>.
      Then, as I probed them, one sprang up, and <u>stared</u>
      With piteous recognition in fixed <u>eyes</u>,
      Lifting distressful hands, as if to bl<u>ess</u>.
      And by his smile, I knew that sullen <u>hall</u>,
      By his dead smile I knew we stood in <u>Hell</u>.
      With a thousand pains that vision's face was <u>grained</u>;
      Yet no blood reached there from the upper <u>ground</u>
      (...)
      (Wilfred Owen, *Strange Meeting*)

(36) By the gate with star and moo<u>n</u>
      Worked into the peeled orange woo<u>d</u>
      The bronze snake lay in the su<u>n</u>
      Inert as a shoelace; dea<u>d</u>

But pliable still, his j**aw**
Unhinged and his grin crook_ed_,
Tongue a rose-colored arr**ow**.
Over my hand I hung hi_m_.
His little vermilion e**ye**
Ignited with a glassed fla_me_
As I turned him in the ligh_t_;
When I split a rock one ti_me_
The garnet bits burned like tha_t_.
Bust dulled his back to och**er**
The way sun ruins a trou_t_.
Yet his belly kept its fi**re**
Going under the chainmai_l_,
The old jewels smoldering the**re**
In each opaque belly-sca_le_:
Sunset looked at through milk gla_ss_.
And I saw white maggots coi_l_
Thin as pins in the dark brui_se_
Where innards bulged as i**f**
He were digesting a mou_se_.
Knifelike, he was chaste enou**gh**,
Pure death's-metal. The yard-man'_s_
Flung brick perfected his lau**gh**.
(Sylvia Plath, *Medallion*)

(37)   Prends ton manteau. Suspends les plaintes éter_nelles_
         Et buvons la splendeur des heures autom_nales_,
         Car la pourpre des bois environne le zè_bre_
         Qui rue et trotte et mord le feuillage et se ca_bre_.
         C'est le nouvel octobre et la sente où je ma_rche_
         Je la foulais naguère en brandissant la to_rche_
         Quand je voulais au sort attacher des en_traves_
         Et nouer à l'azur les roses de mes _rêves_.
         Et nous nous oublierons et que notre cœur _saigne_
         En regardant glisser la souplesse d'un _cygne_
         Et nous contemplerons, dédaigneux des cle_psydres_,
         Les paons de cuivre bleu dans le bronze des cè_dres_.
         (Tristan Derème, *La Verdure Dorée*, Poème no. LXXVIII)

3.1.2 Underdifferentiation of consonants

In German rhyme, consonants are normally distinguished as in ordinary phonology. A minority of authors are liberal with regard to the voiced/voiceless distinction, e.g.:

(38) Der Prolet wird in den Krieg verl<u>aden</u>
      Daß er tapfer und selbstlos f<u>icht</u>.
      Warum und für wen wird ihm nicht verr<u>aten</u>
      Für ihn selber ist es n<u>icht</u>.
      (Bertold Brecht, *Lied gegen den Krieg*)

I have found one author (dialectal, Swiss German) who systematically treats plosives and affricates sharing the same manner of articulation as equivalent:

(39) Morn han ich es wißes R<u>öckli</u>
      Und es Chränzli uf em Ch<u>öpfli</u>. (/kx/ = /pf/)
      Darf im Zug i d Chile g<u>oh</u>,
      Darf a Taufstei vürest<u>oh</u>,
      Hole dert e neue Fr<u>anke</u>,
      Goh uf d Schützematt go t<u>anze</u>. (/kx/ = /ts/)
      (Haemmerli-Marti 1950: 72)

      Summervögeli, Matten<u>ängel</u>,
      Tüend um d Meie t<u>anze</u>:
      Niedere Chrabällest<u>ängel</u>
      Lot ech lo gig<u>ampfe</u>! (/nts/ = /mpf/)
      (Haemmerli-Marti 1950: 187)

      Wenns luegt, wi wenns mi wett verscht<u>oh</u>,
      Mit sine blaue <u>Auge</u>,
      Denn chönnt de Tüfel sälber ch<u>o</u>,
      I tet keis Wörtli gl<u>aube</u>! (/g/ = /b/)
      (Haemmerli-Marti 1950: 122)

Quäcksilberfüeßli und Rubelch<u>opf</u>,
S Müli wi Blettli vom Rosechn<u>opf</u>,
S Züngli so gleitig wi s Mülir<u>ad</u>,
Auge wi Brombeeri usem H<u>ag</u> (/d/ = /g/)
(Haemmerli-Marti 1950: 210)

Storch Storch Schnibel Schn<u>abel</u>,
Bisch vom alte Chlapperi<u>adel</u>: (/b/ = /d/)
Bi de höche Piram<u>ide</u>
Hesch dis Näscht gha, lind wi S<u>ide</u>
(Haemmerli-Marti 1950: 186)

Rhyme phonology of the Arabic Qur'an, which is unique and quite different from rhyme in the classical Arabic literature, is particularly interesting and would deserve further exploration (for the time being cf. Cassels 1983, and Neuwirth 1981: 65–115). Rhyme most typically includes the last non-final vowel alongside the following segments. The rhyme phonology equates $\bar{\imath} = \bar{u}$; $m = n$; $r = l$; all voiced and emphatic obstruents are equivalent (e.g., $b = d = q = \underline{t} = \underline{s}$); but not so pairs such as $d \neq t$.[11] For reasons not yet understood, words of certain syllable structures, though common in the language, are hardly ever employed as rhyme words: $C^{\frown}CC^{\frown}$ (only accepted with geminate: *marra*); $C^{\frown}C^{\frown}C^{\frown}$ (*kataba*; only Sura 54); $C^{\frown}C^{\frown}C^{\frown}$ (*kātibu*; only Sura 37).

The following example is from Sura 50; the rhyme pattern (long high vowel + voiced/emphatic obstruent) is the same throughout the section:

(40) Wa-l-qur'āni l-maǧ<u>īd</u>
      Bal ʕaǧibū 'an ǧā'ahum munḏirun minhum faqāla l-kāfirūna hāḏā šay'un ʕaǧ<u>īb</u>
      'A-'iḏāmitnā wa-kunnā turāban ḏālika raǧʕu baʕ<u>īd</u>
      Qad ʕalimnā mā tanquṣu l-'arḍu minhum wa-ʕindanā kitābun ḥaf<u>īẓ</u>
      Bal kaḏḏabū bil-ḥaqqi lammā ǧā'ahum fa-hum fī 'amrin mar<u>īǧ</u>
      'Afa-lam yanẓurū 'ilā s-samā'i fauqahum kaifa banīnāhā wa-zayyannāhā wa-mālahā min fur<u>ūǧ</u>
      Wa l-'arḍi madadnāhā wa-'alqīnā fīhā rawāsī wa-'anbatnā fīhā min kulli zauǧi bah<u>īǧ</u>
      Tabṣiratan wa ḏikrā li-kulli ʕabdin mun<u>īb</u>

---

11 An attempt to explain this particular pattern of consonant equivalences is found in Peust (2012).

Wa-nazzalnā mina s-samā'i mā'an mubārakan fa-'anbatnā bihi
ǧannātin wa-ḥabba l-ḥaṣīd
Wan-naxla basiqātin lahā ṭalʕun naḍīd
Rizqan lil-ʕibādi wa-'aḥyaynā bihi baldatan maitan kaḏālika l-xurūǧ
Kaḏḏabat qablahum qaumu nūḥin wa-'aṣḥābu r-rassi wa-ṯamūd
Wa-ʕādun wa-firʕaun wa-'ixwānu lūṭ
(...)

In Guaraní (Paraguay), rhyme minimally includes final 'V or 'VCV, the identity of
-C- not being required. Rhyme phonology ignores vowel nasality, nasal vowels
being identified with the corresponding plain vowels. Ex.: Dario Gómez Serrato,
Pedro Marangatu Arape (from Guasch 1996: 413):

(41) Tovevéke arai ári, toguahẽke opa tet<u>ãme</u>
      El Papa rérape ohóva mbyju'ícha che ñe'<u>ẽ</u>;
      Tojuhu py'aguapýpe, Tupao kuarahy'<u>ãme</u>
      Pío doce ñahenóiva San Pedro rekovi<u>are</u>.
      Omumúiva yso sa'icha ha yvykua rupi ituj<u>úva</u>
      Pyhare ñemoñaréva mba'e pochy rembig<u>uái</u>

      Rohendúrõ ore retãme Tupao rehe oguah<u>úta</u>
      Romosẽ va'erã jaguáicha ore kuéra Parag<u>uái</u>.
      Ñande Ruvicha jahayhúva kuimba'e hete re<u>sãiva</u>
      Ko San Pedro ára guahẽvo javy'a syry va'er<u>ã</u>;
      Tojeguáke ñande róga, ha tapére ñamya<u>sãita</u>
      Ñandejára ra'arõvo, yvoty opaichag<u>ua</u>.
      (...)

Finally, some traditions go so far as to consider consonants completely irrelevant
(so-called "assonance"):

(42) Old French, e.g., Chanson de Roland, ca. 1100, beginning of the
      2nd stanza; rhyme in -*u-e-*:

      Li reis Marsilie esteit en Sarrag<u>uce</u>.
      Alez en est en un verger suz l'<u>umbre</u>;
      Sur un perrun de marbre bloi se c<u>ulchet</u>,
      Envirun lui plus de vint milie h<u>umes</u>.
      Il en apelet e ses dux e ses c<u>untes</u>:
      Oëz, seignurs, quel pecchet nus enc<u>umbret</u>:
      (...)

(43) Spanish, e.g., Ángel de Saavedra, La buenaventura (1841); rhyme in
-e-o-:

Era en punto medianoche / y reinaba hondo sil_e_nci_o_
De Medellín en la villa / sumergida en dulce su_e_ñ_o_.
Desde un trono de celajes / nacarados y lig_e_r_os_,
Cándida, apacible luna / brillaba en el firmam_e_nt_o_,
Sobre el pardo caserío / derramando sus refl_e_j_os_,
Como sobre los sepulcros / de un tranquilo cem_e_nt_e_ri_o_.
(...)

(44) German rap songs, e.g., Bushido, Bloodsport (2006); rhyme in
-/a/-/oa/-:

Es ist Bushido Bl_oo_dsp_or_t ich spreche ein M_a_chtw_or_t
Egal was ihr sagt ich ruf immer F_u_ck T_or_ch
Ich komm im BMW du kommst in nem k_a_ck F_or_d
Ich will segeln denn ich interessiere mich für Y_a_chtsp_or_t
Es ist Österreich guck ich war im Kn_a_st d_or_t
Ich hänge mit den Gees du hängst mit dem Spaßt K_or_s
Ich komm auf die Bühne jedes Mädchen m_a_cht b_oah_
Ihr habt keine Chance ihr Süßen macht euch w_a_s v_or_
Hertha BSC Berlin wir machen d_a_s T_or_
Du Schwuchtel jeden Montag singst du in nem B_a_chch_or_
Jeder quatscht mich voll Junge ich bin f_a_st _Ohr_
Guck ich bin der Pate und köpfe dein Pr_a_chth_or_se
Und ich lege deine Reste in ne B_a_ckf_or_m
Ich bin ein Osamafreund und denke du kackst _a_b Ge_or_ge
Es ist kr_a_ssc_or_e ich begeh um _a_cht M_or_d
Ersguterjunge ist Bushido Bl_oo_dsp_or_t

3.1.3 Rhyme as a criterion for hierarchizing distinctive phonological features?

It might be a promising idea to use rhyme evidence for hierarchizing distinctive features of ordinary phonology. The assumption would be that distinctions ignored in rhyme take low positions on a feature hierarchy scale. When poets differ in their amount of conflating phonological distinctions, the investigation of multiple poets' usages may result in a more elaborated hierarchy. This seems to work reasonably well for the German vowel system, where, based on the evidence presented above, a scale like the following could be suggested: (1) height /

place of articulation (always distinguished); (2) quantity (mostly distinguished); (3) rounding (rarely distinguished).

Accounts of this kind have been proposed for English (Bauschatz 2003)[12], German (Berg 1990)[13], and Turkish (Malone 1988).

3.1.4 Transitivity

Another language dependent rhyme parameter could be the question whether the rhyme relation is transitive, i.e., whether from A = B and B = C it follows that A = C. While this might seem logical and is assumed to be generally true by Baxter (1992: 89), there seem to be counter-examples such as the vowel equivalences of Bohairic Coptic rhyme treated below. I will not discuss this question in detail.

3.2 Size of identical section

After we have discussed what counts as "identical" in rhyme, the second question arises how long the sections need to be that are identical in this sense.

In many traditions, rhyme starts on the nucleus of a syllable whose selection is language-specific. This is true for German, where rhyme starts on the last stressed vowel, vowels with secondary accent included. It might be a possible alternative formulation to say that it starts on the last vowel ≠ ə.

(45) Meine Liebe, lange wie die Táube
      Von dem Falken hin- und hérgeschèucht,
      Wähnte froh, sie hab' ihr Nest erréicht
      In den Zweigen einer Gőtterlàube.
      (Gottfried August Bürger, *Liebe ohne Heimat*; secondary accents marked with accent grave)

---

12 In that work, distinctive features of consonants are hierarchized based on imperfect rhymes in a huge corpus of English poetry. It turns out that the voice distinction in fricatives is the one ignored most easily: *noise = voice*; *love = enough*.

13 Contains statistical analyses of rhymes by Wilhelm Busch. Rounding of vowels is ignored most frequently, in agreement with what has been said above.

For French, the rule is conventionally given that rhyme starts on the last vowel ≠ ə. Depending on the analysis of French accent, it might be a possible alternative formulation to say that rhyme starts on the last stressed vowel.

Poetry in Berber languages follows a similar line in that rhyme typically covers final -VC or -V. Since many words terminate in a vowel and there is no additional stress criterion, a single vowel is often the only carrier of rhyme. In the following Kabyle example (from Mammeri 2001: 343f.), the rhymes are in -i and -əɣ, with the final consonant of the first half verse sometimes being ignored because it is attached to the following word by enjambement:

(46)　Bismilləh annəbdu llsas<u>i</u> / lḥəmdulilləh a-t nəšk<u>əɣ</u>
　　　Win ibyan ur itˢmərr<u>it</u> ʃabrid n ttˢuba yənj<u>əɣ</u>
　　　Ləfwayəd yur Ṛəbbi ggwt<u>it</u> ʃɣas win ur nəby' ad ittj<u>əɣ</u>
　　　D ṣṣlatˢ yəfk a nnbi ḥəss-<u>i</u> / fk-i timəjjətˢ any<u>əɣ</u>
　　　S lḥəmd ad dək nəsmis<u>i</u> / kulyum ad dək nšəkk<u>əɣ</u>
　　　Iməns' a-k gəy d iməkl<u>i</u> / ṣṣbəḥ zik ad yəfk nəft<u>əɣ</u>
　　　Lmurəd ik ilha i tiss<u>i</u> / yif kra yəllan d lʕins<u>əɣ</u>
　　　Yif iyi kəčč udi ntrus<u>i</u> / d ššahəd n tzizwit nəy sskw<u>əɣ</u>
　　　(...)

But there are other possibilities. In Swahili, rhyme affects the last syllable (which is generally unstressed) including its onset. Example: Love song ascribed to the poet Liongo Fumo, who may have lived around 1600 (from Knappert 1979: 82):

(47)　Ewe mwana, nyamaa sili<u>e</u>
　　　Ukaliza wako mlimb<u>izi</u>.
　　　Ewe mwana nyamaa utu<u>e</u>
　　　Nikutuze nguo za Hija<u>zi</u>
　　　Nikwambike mikufu 'kupa<u>mbe</u>
　　　Na dhahabu kazi ya Shira<u>zi</u>
　　　'Kuwakie nyumba kuu yu<u>mbe</u>
　　　Ya chokaa na mawe ya ka<u>zi</u>
　　　'Kupambie kwa vyombo vya ko<u>wa</u>
　　　Waowao unyike mao<u>zi</u>.
　　　Natamani mwana kukuo<u>wa</u>
　　　Tukachinje kondoo na mbu<u>zi</u>
　　　(...)

Still other rules can be found in other languages. Amharic rhyme, as described by Leslau (1990: 158), needs to cover at least final -CV or -VC, i.e., the last two segments:

(48) mälkam säw näbbäräčč bərtukan mäsa<u>yə</u> / dägmom əndä lomi mannəm laṭat wä<u>yə</u> (Leslau No. 14)

əne wäddəšälläʷh yanči mäwdäd yä<u>tal</u> / wəha əndä qum nägär səṭṭäṭaw yanqä<u>ññal</u> (Leslau No. 9)

In Russian, the rhymed section starts on a stressed vowel as in many languages, but there is an additional requirement that it needs to cover at least two phonemes. If stress falls on a word-final vowel, the preceding consonant must therefore be included in the rhyme.

3.3 May sections longer than the minimum requirement be identical?

In some languages, rhyme must be exactly as long as the minimum requirement defined in the preceding section. It is true for German that a rhyme longer than that (so-called "rührender Reim") is not normally accepted, as prescribed already by Opitz (1624: 36): "(...) die letzte sylbe in den männlichen, und letzten zwo inn den weiblichen reimen (wie wir sie bald abtheilen werden) sollen nicht an allen Buchstaben gleiche sein". This means that *Last = Mast*, but *Last ≠ Palast*. The same is valid for English (e.g., *greed ≠ agreed*).

On the other hand, French, and probably many other languages, tolerate rhymes longer than the minimum requirement. In French, it is not only accepted, but even desirable for a large section to rhyme ("rime riche"), e.g.:

(49) Gloire du long <u>désir</u>, <u>Idées</u>,
Tout en moi s'exaltait <u>de voir</u>
La famille <u>des</u> <u>iridées</u>
Surgir à ce nouveau <u>devoir</u>.
(Stéphane Mallarmé, *Prose pour Des Esseintes*)

This may ultimately lead to a "vers holorime", although such rhymes are, of course, very difficult to construct:

(50) Dans ces meubles laqués, rideaux et dais moroses,
Où, dure, Ève d'efforts sa langue irrite (erreur!)
Ou du rêve des forts alanguis rit (terreur!)
Danse, aime, bleu laquais, ris d'oser des mots roses.
(Charles Cros, *Le Coffret de Santal*)

3.4 Restrictions against trivial rhymes

Several languages probably reject rhymes made of identical words (among them German, but here already following from restriction § 3.3; according to Baxter 1992: 89f. also true for at least some traditions of Chinese poetry).

In French, rhymes are not allowed whose rhyming portion consists of the same word or the same morpheme: *bonheur* ≠ *malheur*; *donner* ≠ *aimer*, *vendu* ≠ *résolu*. On the other hand, *perdu* = *répandu* is accepted because the rhyme includes a part of the stem in addition to the morpheme -*u*.

Rhyme between (synchronic) homonyms is accepted:

(51) Quel sera ce bienfait que je ne comprends pas?
L'illustre Josabeth porte vers vous ses pas.
(Jean Racine, *Athalie* I,1)

Note the opposite behaviour of German: spazieren = gefrieren is good in spite of morphemic identity, but spazieren ≠ stolzieren is not because of the restriction discussed in § 3.3.

3.5 Words not useable in rhyme position

It may follow from the restrictions defined in the preceding sections that certain words are unusable in rhyme position because no rhyme partners happen to exist in the language. Examples:

- English (numerous): *animal, breadth, empty, film, monster, orange, purple, sixth, …*
- German (less numerous): *falsch, Frühling, Furcht, Hoffnung, Knospe, Mensch, Schönheit, Zukunft, …*
- French (few): *belge, pauvre, quatorze, triomphe*

3.6 Additional restrictions or rules

There may be various additional requirements imposed on rhyme other than those discussed so far. I provide only a few examples; there is certainly room for further research here.

German:

- Some older authors avoided foreign words as rhyme words (or generally in poems) even where they would have matched phonetically (thus recommended e.g., by Opitz 1624: 24–27).
- It is considered good style to avoid grammatical words as rhyme words ("und", "er").

French:

- Up to the 19th century, a very archaic pronunciation was presupposed for rhyme usage. For example, -é did not rhyme with -ée, *grand* not with *sang*, *amour* not with *toujours* (details in Coenen 1998: 74–84). One interpretation could be that rhyme phonology here shows a greater differentiation than ordinary phonology. Manaster Ramer (1994: 321) takes a different view that these rules are artificial/orthographic and a description in phonological terms should not be attempted for them.

3.7 Construction of stanzas

The rhyme schemes characterizing the sequence of lines (ABAB, AABB, etc.) are another parameter which is language dependent at least to some degree. I am not going to discuss them here.

4 Rhyme in Egyptian

Although Egyptian cannot boast of a strong literary tradition of rhymed poetry, this language, which has the longest attested history of any language, does provide some observations that are valuable for a general typology of rhyme.

4.1 Alliteration

Alliteration appears sporadically in several Egyptian texts, most strikingly in Ptolemaic temple inscriptions (see Vycichl 1957 who believes in a historical connection with Somali alliteration; Guglielmi 1996: 467–481; Kurth 1994: 84f.; Watterson 1979):

(52) *ḫ3w.wt=k ḫwd m ḫ3.w n.w ḫ.t ḫm=k jm=sn ḫpry ḫ3ww m-ḫ.t=sn ḫnm=k ḫnm=sn ḫfty=k ḫr m ḫb.t=sn ḫ(3)ḫ.tj r ḫm=k*

(Edfu IV 63.14–17; Ptolemaic period; alliteration in ḫ-)

'Your altars are enriched with thousands of offerings that you may eat of them, o Winged Beetle. Spices are upon them that you may smell their odour. Your enemies are fallen upon their execution posts as you hasten to your shrine.'

Nnw: **nni** *n=k* **nnw** *ḥr* **npr.(t)**
'Nun: The flood rests on the river bank on your behalf'

Njw: **njw** *n=k* **nwy** *ḥr* **n[.]ˈḥ***ˈ
'Niu: The inundation settles down on the n... on your behalf'

Ḥḥ: **ḥḥ** *n=k* **ḥbb.t** *ḥr* **ḥnb.wt**
'Heh: Fresh water flows over the meadows on your behalf'

Šw: **š3s** *n=k* **šp** *ḥr* **šdy.w**
'Shu: The gush rushes over the fields on your behalf'

Dḥwtj: **thm** *n=k* **thm** *ḥr-dp* **t3.w**
'Thoth: The thrust (of water) thrusts over the lands on your behalf'[14]

---

14 The letter *d* in the divine name *Dḥwtj* (Greek Θουθ) was pronounced similarly or identically to *t* in the Late Period, so that both consonants are here considered as equivalent.

Ptḥ-nfr-ḥr: **pd** *n=k* **p3** *wr ḥr* **pp**
'Ptah-Neferhor: The high one (= Nile) spreads over the mud on your behalf' (Edfu II 256; subscripts on representations of gods)[15]

Slightly less impressive cases can be found already in earlier times such as the following passage, datable to the later 2nd millennium BCE, which shows an alliteration involving the two consonant sequence *wn-:*

(53) *wnwn*   'The star-observers,'
       wn.w dw3=sn Rꜥw dp t3   'who used to worship the Sun on earth,'
       wn.w jri̯=sn snṯr n nṯr.w jmj.w dw3.t 'who used to offer incense to the
                                                          gods of the netherworld,'
       wnn=sn m šms.w n nṯr pn   'will be among the entourage of this
                                                          god.' (Roulin 1996, II: 140–142)[16]

Or the following examples from as early as the Pyramid Texts (24th cent. BCE; see Firchow 1953: 217–220, and Kammerzell 2000):

(54) *ḥr* **ḥr=k** **ḥrj** *rj.t=f,* *h3i̯* **ḥr** *ṯz=k jmj n3.wt=f,* **ḥm** *n=(j)* **ḥkn.t** *m* **ḥr.wj** *sn{n}.w(j)*
       (PT 238; alliteration in **ḥ-**)
       (Spell against snakes:) 'Onto your face, you who are on your belly?; descend on your back vertebra, you who are in your thicket; retreat from me while you jubilate as the one with two faces!'

       jw **dbn**.*n=f* **p**.*tj tm.tj / jw* **pḥr**.*n=f* **jdb**.*wj* (PT 406c)
       'He traversed the entire two heavens, and he surrounded the two shores'

Longer Egyptian texts displaying a consistent pattern of alliteration, such as in Old Germanic alliterative verse, are missing, however.

---

15 I owe the reference to this text to Stefan Baumann (Tübingen).
16 I owe the reference to this text to Daniel Werning (Berlin).

4.2 Sporadic end rhyme in Earlier Egyptian?

End rhyme has been suspected in the following text containing puns on the numerals from one to ten (CT V 115h–116e; Sethe 1918; three partly conflicting manuscripts; ca. 2000 BCE):

(55) *Jṯi.n=k wʿ.t* [... wŏít] 'You took one,'

Jṯi.n=k sn.tj{wʿ.tj} [... síntj] 'you took both.'

ʿḥm.n=k s m ḏp n Ḥrw [...hárw] 'You extinguished it from the head of Horus,' (3 = *ḥmtw*)

Fd.n=k s jr=f [... jráf] 'you plucked it out from him.' (4 = *fdw*)

Ḏi m n=j [... náj] 'Give me' (5 = *djw*)

Snsn.t r ḥr=j [...ḥráj] 'something that joins my face.' (6 = *sjw*)

M sfḫḫ=k jm=s [... jmás] 'Do not dissociate from it,' (7 = *sfḫ*)

M ḥ3tb=k jm=s [... jmás] 'do not spare(?) it.' (8 = *ḥmnw*)

Sḥḏ n=k jr.t [... jírt] 'Illuminate the eye,' (9 = *psḏw*)

Ḏi n=j jr.t [... jírt] 'give me the eye!' (10 = *mḏw*)

Sethe (1918: 24) felt very confident in seeing an end rhyme here: "es kann kein Zweifel sein, daß wir es in unserem Fingerzählreim mit dem ältesten Beispiel des Reimes in Ägypten und aller Wahrscheinlichkeit nach auch dem ältesten Reime auf Erden überhaupt zu tun haben".

The Book of Caverns (ca. 13th cent. BCE) contains a sequence of 24 adjectival invocations all of which end in *-yw* or *-jw*. It is possible but hard to verify at the present state of our knowledge that they agreed also in their final vowels and would thus have constituted an end rhyme:

(56) *j nṯr.w*   'Oh you gods,'

štзy.w štзy.w   'you secret ones, you secret ones,'

sḫm.yw sḫm.yw   'you mighty ones, you mighty ones,'

ḥзt.jw ḥзt.jw   'you corpse-like ones, you corpse-like ones'

qf.yw qf.yw   'you (?) ones, you (?) ones,'

jmn.yw jmn.yw   'you hidden ones, you hidden ones,'

ḥзp.yw ḥзp.yw   'you covered ones, you covered ones,'

nnwt.jw nnwt.jw 'you idle ones, you idle ones,' (...)

(*Book of Caverns* 59.10–33, Werning 2011: 226–227)

Another account on suspected Egyptian end rhyme by Ebers (1877) was based on outdated readings and is obsolete.

4.3 End rhyme in Bohairic Coptic

Egyptian end rhyme becomes systematic only by Late Coptic, the earliest example known to me being a text in the Bohairic dialect edited by Youssef (2005; manuscript 1295 CE). This is at the same time an alphabetic acrostic:

(57) Aitōbh mmok panouti̠ / anok xa pihōb nhēki̠ / je peniōt etxen niphēoui̠
/ pha piništi nhoti̠
Bon ouhelj nran / etsapšōi nran niben / mareftoubo nje pekran / pč(ōi)
s nouon niben
Ge gar nthok ph(nou)ti / patimetouro / maresi xen ouhoti / nje tekme-
touro
Dikeos tinašōpi / eioi natthoti̠ / ešōp aišansaji̠ / pethnak marefšōpi
Ebol xen tekphe / aksaji xen pekamahi / mphrēti xen tphe / nem hijen
pikahi
Zeoš nje thmetništi̠ / nje peknai nem pekōou / penōik nte rasti̠ / mēif
nan mphoou
Ērēnē sou moi nan / ō pirefjō ebol / kha nēeteron / ph(nou)ti nan ebol
(...)

I have given an overview of end rhyme in late Bohairic texts in Peust (2009). The minimal requirement for this rhyme is only to cover the last vowel of the line including the following consonant(s), if there are any. Word stress does not play a role, so that the rhyme may be limited to posttonic syllables (as in the first line of the text above, where -*i* is unstressed), and stressed syllables may rhyme with unstressed ones. The following sets of vowels are equivalent with respect to rhyme:[17] *ou* /u/ = *ō* /o/ = *o* /ɔ/; *ō* /o/ = *o* /ɔ/ = *a* /a/; *a* /a/ = *e* /ɛ/. We observe that the rhyme equivalence is not transitive (cf. § 3.1.4 above). The only vowel which does not normally rhyme with any other vowel is *(e)i* /i/ (except for rhymes with written *ē* in Greek borrowings, which was probably likewise spoken as /i/). As opposed to the vowels, no different consonant phonemes are considered equivalent in Bohairic rhyme.

---

17 I give here both the traditional transliteration and my phonemic interpretation.

Modern scholars have not always appreciated the formal aspects of Bohairic poetry: "the rhymes are of the crudest nature (...) No attention is paid to the fall of the accent in the rhyme; if the last two letters are the same, the composer seems content. The number of feet varies, giving as fine a specimen of doggerel as could be conceived." (Engelbach 1920: 110)

As in most other languages, line boundaries almost always coincide with word boundaries. A rare counter-example is:

(58) *marenouōšt mmok je ꞮꞮthok pha piništi nōou / pčōis alla nahmen / ebol ha pipet-hōou* (Youssef 2005: 110).

4.4 End rhyme in the Sahidic Triadon

The principle that vowels matter relatively little for rhyme is brought to its extreme in the *Triadon*, the only rhymed text in the Sahidic dialect of Coptic and at the same time the latest literary work in that dialect (ed. von Lemm 1903; translation Nagel 1983; composed in the early 14th century, Nagel 1983: 22f.; bilingual Coptic-Arabic, but no rhyme in the Arabic section which is thereby proved to be secondary). This opus consists of stanzas of four lines (ca. 420 stanzas preserved). The stanzas have the rhyme pattern AAAX, BBBX, CCCX, etc., with X (each 4th line) having the same rhyme through the whole text. The analysis of the rhyme is difficult and seems to require a distinction into two categories:

1. "Narrow rhyme": This rhyme is similar to the Bohairic type. It starts on the last vowel and presupposes a rhyme phonology as in Bohairic. Here belongs the rhyme of the 4th lines, all of which terminate in -ōn, -on, or -an (stressed or unstressed). Consider the 4th lines of the strophes 692–697:

> *nthe nta nsabe meh neuhnau on*
> *auō eiōbš hn tameleia nneto nargon*
> *auō psōte ntapsukhē hn tefčom naoraton*
> *eska htēs epefnoč nna mmegan*
> *mpbaros ethorš mmon*
> *nmman nmma mmoone etsoutōn*

The same kind of rhyme is found in the first three lines of a minority of the stanzas (I cite only the rhyme words at the line ends instead of the whole lines here and in the following):

harōtn = peuouōtn = ouaatn (374)
tōs = ountas = afaas (480)
ebols = eols = pahēt ouōls (654)
etrir = nrir = neshir (676)

2. "Wide rhyme", which is longer but less restricted than narrow rhyme. This is the predominant type for the first three lines in a stanza. The rhyme starts on a syllable of which it needs to include the onset as well. On the other hand, vowels are largely irrelevant (neither quality, stress, nor position matters; single vowels = double vowels = syllabic consonants), the only recognizable restriction being that rhyme must not be based solely on syllables with unstressed /ə/ (spelled e).

iakōbos = agabos = makkabaios (317)
eršan = peršōn = nšēn (431)
mmnts črē = nečra = noučro (521)
nsetmnoueite = nneite = ntenei de (587)
eutrtōr = ntartōr = nntōrtr (596)
praše = prōše = prē ša (600)
aftašof = ntaftošf = ntaftočf (626)
tšeere = ešare = tšourē (661)
emparadosis = epparadisos = mpefpareideis (689)
afiitf = afšitf = afšbtf (698)
terēmos = eterēmos = ierēmias (701)
hnouthumos = nthe mmos = thōmas (703)

Furthermore, several sets of consonants are regarded as equivalent:

č = j = š = s:

netšōne = njaane = je janē (510)
ešōpe = ečōpe = ečepē (631)
nnetmose = tefmēse = mmēēše (652)
etsēh = etjēh = netjōh (644)

$p = b = f$:

mpenne = *noubenebene* = *noubnne* (492)
hm psat = *nrefsēt* = *nrefšōōt* (519)
enefnhētf = *etmhethotf* = *ehōtb* (457)

$k(h) = g = č$:

henkhorte = *gar te* = *noučorte* (487)
gar pe = *negraphē* = *tečrēpe* (583)

$l = r, l = n$:

neiklēma = *noukrima* = *oukluma* (511)
mmntšna = *oumnthi čla* = *ouhičlō* (526)

Finally, even the order of consonants can vary:

nneulojh = *ntejolh* = *oušolh* (483)
nentaukosf = *pentaksokf* = *eisobk* (499)
nkasma = *sigima* = *sōk mmo* (595)
peuōbš = *tefcinouōšb* = *euouōšf* (637)
nsa kham = *sekhēm* = *ngesem* (674)
aišits = *ngjits* = *etreujest* (686)
ntaubise = *apa bēsa* = *nsabē* (688)

Since *j* ϫ (= /č/) was equivalent to a cluster *t* + *š*, it can rhyme with *št*:

ehah njaj = *panjōj* = *nnšošt* (489).

Although rhyme was only a late import into Coptic from the dominant Arabic environment, the rhyme rules were adapted to the language in a very original and unique way. Coptic therefore contributes to our understanding of the typological variation of rhyme in human language no less than those languages in whose literary history rhyme occupies a much more central position.

5 References

ʿAbdallāh, Yūsuf. 1988. Der Sonnengesang von Saba. Ein Stück religiöser Literatur aus dem antiken Jemen. In: Daum, Werner (ed.), *Die Königin von Saba. Kunst, Legende und Archäologie zwischen Morgenland und Abendland*. Stuttgart: Belser, 185–194.

Ambros, Arne A. 1990. Beobachtungen zu Aufbau und Funktionen der gereimten klassisch-arabischen Buchtitel. *Wiener Zeitschrift für die Kunde des Morgenlandes* 80: 13–57.

D'Angelo, Edoardo. 1995. Problemi teorici e materiali statistici sulla rima nella poesia dattilica dell'alto medioevo. In: Stella, Francesco (ed.), *Il verso europeo. Atti del seminario di metrica comparata (4 maggio 1994)*. Firenze: Consiglio Regionale della Toscana, 129–145.

Banti, Giorgio & Giannattasio, Francesco. 1996. Music and Metre in Somali Poetry. In: Hayward, Richard J. & Lewis, I.M. (eds.), *Voice and Power: Culture of Language in North-East Africa – Essays in Honour of B.W. Andrzejewski*. London: School of Oriental and African Studies, 83–127.

Bauschatz, Paul. 2003. Rhyme and the Structure of English Consonants. *English Language and Linguistics* 7: 29–56.

Baxter, William H. 1992. *A Handbook of Old Chinese Phonology*. Berlin: De Gruyter.

Beeston, Alfred F.L. 1994. Antecedents of Classical Arabic Verse? In: Heinrichs, Wolfhart & Schoeler, Gregor (eds.), *Festschrift Ewald Wagner zum 65. Geburtstag. Band 1: Semitische Studien unter besonderer Berücksichtigung der Südsemitistik*. Stuttgart: Steiner, 234–243.

Berg, Thomas. 1990. Unreine Reime als Evidenz für die Organisation phonologischer Merkmale. *Zeitschrift für Sprachwissenschaft* 9: 3–27.

Brock, Sebastian P. & Kiraz, George A. 2006. *Ephrem the Syrian: Select Poems. Vocalized Syriac Text with English Translation, Introduction, and Notes*. Provo: Brigham Young University Press.

Brockelmann, Carl. 1927. Semitische Reimwortbildungen. *Zeitschrift für Semitistik und verwandte Gebiete* 5: 6–38.

Carmi, T. (ed.). 1981. *The Penguin Book of Hebrew Verse*. London: Penguin.

Carney, James. 1989. The Dating of Archaic Irish Verse. In: Tranter, Stephen Norman & Tristram, Hildegard L. C. (eds.), *Early Irish Literature: Media and Communication: Mündlichkeit und Schriftlichkeit in der frühen irischen Literatur*. Tübingen: Narr, 39–56.

Cassels, David A. 1983. Near-Rhyme and its Occurence in the Qur'ān. *Journal of Semitic Studies* 28: 303–310.

Coenen, Hans Georg. 1998. *Französische Verslehre. Ein Lehr- und Arbeitsbuch*. Darmstadt: Wissenschaftliche Buchgesellschaft.

Dryer, Matthew S. 2005. Prefixing versus Suffixing in Inflectional Morphology. In: Haspelmath, Martin, Dryer, Matthew S., Gil, David & Comrie, Bernard (eds.), *The World Atlas of Language Structures*, section 26. Oxford: Oxford University Press, 110–113.

Ebers, Georg. 1877. Der Klang des Altägyptischen und der Reim. *Zeitschrift für Ägyptische Sprache und Altertumskunde* 15: 43–48.

Elwell-Sutton, Lawrence P. 1975. The Foundations of Persian Prosody and Metrics. *Iran* 13: 75–97.

Engelbach, Reginald. 1920. Alphabetic Hymn in Coptic (Boheiric Dialect). *Annales du Service des Antiquités Égyptiennes* 20: 110–117.

Ernst, Ulrich & Neuser, Peter-Erich (eds.). 1977. *Die Genese der europäischen Endreimdichtung*. Darmstadt: Wissenschaftliche Buchgesellschaft.

Falla, Terry C. 1977. Poetic Features of the Peshitta Gospels. *Le Muséon* 90: 63–80.

Finaert, Guy & Congar, Yves M.-J. (eds.). 1963. *Traités anti-Donatistes*. Vol. 1 (Œuvres de Saint Augustin 28). Paris: Desclée.

Firchow, Otto. 1953: *Grundzüge der Stilistik in den altägyptischen Pyramidentexten*. Berlin: Akademie-Verlag.

Gasparov, Michail L. 1996. *A History of European Versification*. Oxford: Clarendon.

Gerow, Edwin. 1989. Jayadeva's Poetics and the Classical Style. *Journal of the American Oriental Society* 109: 533–544.

Guasch, Antonio. 1996. *El idioma guaraní. Gramática y antologia de prosa y verso*. 7a ed. Asunción: Loyola.

Guglielmi, Waltraud. 1996. Der Gebrauch rhetorischer Stilmittel in der ägyptischen Literatur. In: Loprieno, Antonio (ed.), *Ancient Egyptian Literature. History and Forms*. (Probleme der Ägyptologie 10). Leiden: Brill, 465–497.

Haas, Volkert. 2006. *Die hethitische Literatur. Texte, Stilistik, Motive*. Berlin: De Gruyter.

Haemmerli-Marti, Sophie. 1950. *Chindeliedli* (Gesammelte Werke 1). Aarau: Sauerländer.

Haspelmath, Martin. 1993: *A Grammar of Lezgian*. Berlin: De Gruyter.

Haspelmath, Martin, Dryer, Matthew S., Gil, David & Comrie, Bernard (eds.) 2005. *The World Atlas of Language Structures*. Oxford: Oxford University Press.

Henning, Walter B. 1950. A Pahlavi Poem. *Bulletin of the School of Oriental and African Studies* 13: 641–648.

Holtman, Astrid. 1996. *A Generative Theory of Rhyme: An Optimality Approach*. Diss. Utrecht.

Hrushovski, Benjamin. 1981. Notes on the Systems of Hebrew Versification. In: Carmi, T. (ed.). *The Penguin Book of Hebrew Verse*. London: Penguin, 57–72.

Kammerzell, Frank. 2000. Das Verspeisen der Götter. Religiöse Vorstellung oder poetische Fiktion? *Lingua Aegyptia* 7: 183–218 + 1 plate.

Kane, Elinor. 2001. *Echo Words in Tamil*. Dissertation Oxford.

Karlgren, Bernhard. 1950. *The Book of Odes. Chinese Text, Transcription and Translation*. Stockholm: Museum of Far Eastern Antiquities.

Kiparsky, Paul. 1975. The Role of Linguistics in a Theory of Poetry. In: Bloomfield, Morton & Haugen, Einar (eds.), *Language as a Human Problem*. Guildford: Academy of Arts and Sciences, 233–246.

Kiparsky, Paul & Youmans, Gilbert (eds.). 1989. *Phonetics and Phonology I: Rhythm and Meter*. San Diego: Academy Press.

Knappert, Jan. 1979. *Four Centuries of Swahili Verse*. London: Heinemann.

Kuhn, Karl Georg. 1950. *Achtzehngebet und Vaterunser und der Reim*. (Wissenschaftliche Untersuchungen zum Neuen Testament 1). Tübingen: Mohr.

Kuhn, Karl Heinz & Tait, William John. 1996. *Thirteen Coptic Acrostic Hymns from Manuscript M574 of the Pierpont Morgan Library*. Oxford: Griffith Institute.

Küper, Christoph. (ed.). 2002. *Meter, Rhythm and Performance – Metrum, Rhythmus, Performanz. Proceedings of the International Conference on Meter, Rhythm and Performance Held in May 1999 at Vechta*. Frankfurt: Lang.

Kurth, Dieter. 1994. Stilistik und Syntax. In: Kurth, Dieter (ed.), *Edfu: Studien zu Vokabular, Ikonographie und Grammatik*. Wiesbaden: Harrassowitz, 72–102.

Kuryłowicz, Jerzy. 1976. The Linguistic Foundations of Metre. *Biuletin Polskiego Towarzystwa Językoznawczego* 34: 63–72.

Lambert, Wilfred G. 1960. *Babylonian Wisdom Literature*. Oxford: Clarendon.

von Lemm, Oskar. 1903. *Das Triadon. Ein sahidisches Gedicht mit arabischer Übersetzung*. St.-Pétersbourg: Académie Impériale des Sciences.

Leslau, Wolf. 1990. Amharic Love Songs. *Paideuma* 36: 157–172.

Lotz, John. 1960. Metric Typology. In: Sebeok, Thomas A. (ed.), *Style in Language*. Cambridge: MIT Press, 135–148.

Malone, Joseph L. 1982. Generative Phonology and Turkish Rhyme. *Linguistic Inquiry* 13: 550–553.

Malone, Joseph L. 1988. Underspecification Theory and Turkish Rhyme. *Phonology* 5: 293–297.

Mammeri, Mouloud. 2001. *Poèmes kabyles anciens. Textes berbères et français*. Paris: Maspero.

Manaster Ramer, Alexis. 1994. Stefan George and Phonological Theory. *Phonology* 11: 317–323.

[Manickavasagam, S.] 2003. *Thirukkural (Tamil text, Paraphrase, Roman Rendering & English Translation)*. New Delhi: Richa Prakashan.

Marchand, Hans. 1952. Alliteration, Ablaut und Reim in den türkischen Zwillingsformen. *Oriens* 5: 60–69.

Molino, Jean & Tamine, Joëlle (eds.). 1982. *Introduction à l'analyse linguistique de la poésie*. Paris: Presses Universitaires de France.

Moravcsik, Edith A. 1978. Reduplicative Constructions. In: Greenberg, Joseph H. (ed.), *Universals of Human Language III: Word Structure*. Stanford: Stanford University Press, 297–334.

Nagel, Peter. 1983. *Das Triadon. Ein sahidisches Lehrgedicht des 14. Jahrhunderts*. Halle: Martin-Luther-Universität.

Neuwirth, Angelika. 1981. *Studien zur Komposition der mekkanischen Suren*. Berlin: De Gruyter.

Norden, Eduard. 1898. *Die antike Kunstprosa vom VI. Jahrhundert v. Chr. bis in die Zeit der Renaissance*, 2 Bde. Leipzig: Teubner.

O'Connor, M.P. 1982. 'Unanswerable the Knack of Tongues': The Linguistic Study of Verse. In: Obler, Loraine K. & Menn, Lise (eds.), *Exceptional Language and Linguistics*. New York: Academic Press, 143–168.

Opitz, Martin [Opitius, Martinus]. 1963. Reprint. *Buch von der Deutschen Poeterey*. Tübingen: Niemeyer. Originalausgabe Breßlaw 1624.

Parry, Thomas. 1962. *The Oxford Book of Welsh Verse*. Oxford: Oxford University Press.

Peust, Carsten. 1999. *Egyptian Phonology*. (Monographien zur Ägyptischen Sprache 2). Göttingen: Peust und Gutschmidt (also on http://digi.ub.uni-heidelberg.de/diglit/peust1999/).

Peust, Carsten. 2009. Zur Aussprache des koptischen Eta nach dem Zeugnis spätbohairischer gereimter Texte. In: Giewekemeyer, Antonia, Moers, Gerald & Widmaier, Kai (eds.), *Liber amicorum. Jürgen Horn zum Dank*. (Göttinger Miszellen Beihefte 5). Göttingen: Seminar für Ägyptologie und Koptologie, 89–98.

Peust, Carsten. 2012. Zur Aussprache der emphatischen Konsonanten im Altarabischen. *Zeitschrift der Deutschen Morgenländischen Gesellschaft* 162, 47–52.

Poppe, Nicholas. 1970. *Mongolian Language Handbook*. Washington: Center for Applied Linguistics.

Roulin, Gilles. 1996. *Le livre de la nuit. Une composition égyptienne de l'au-delà*. (Orbis Biblicus et Orientalis 147). Fribourg: Editions universitaires.

Schweikle, Günther. 1977. Reprint. Die Herkunft des althochdeutschen Reimes. Zu Otfrieds von Weißenburg formgeschichtlicher Stellung. In: Ernst, Ulrich & Neuser, Peter-Erich (eds.),

Die Genese der europäischen Endreimdichtung, 287–355. Darmstadt: Wissenschaftliche Buchgesellschaft. Originalausgabe *Zeitschrift für deutsches Altertum und deutsche Literatur* 96: 165–212.

Sethe, Kurt. 1918. Ein altägyptischer Fingerzählreim. *Zeitschrift für Ägyptische Sprache und Altertumskunde* 54: 16–39.

Southern, Mark R.V. 2005. *Contagious Couplings: Transmission of Expressives in Yiddish Echo Phrases*. London: Praeger.

Spitzer, Leo. 1952. Confusion Shmooshun. *Journal of English and Germanic Philology* 51: 226–233.

Stella, Francesco (ed.). 1995a. *Il verso europeo. Atti del seminario di metrica comparata (4 maggio 1994)*. Firenze: Consiglio Regionale della Toscana.

Stella, Francesco. 1995b. Gotescalco, La 'scuola' di Reims e l'origine della rima mediolatina. In: Stella, Francesco (ed.), *Il verso europeo. Atti del seminario di metrica comparata (4 maggio 1994)*. Firenze: Consiglio Regionale della Toscana, 159–165.

Vycichl, Werner. 1957. Der Stabreim in der ägyptischen Poesie. *Die Sprache* [Wien] 3: 216–220.

Vycichl, Werner. 1984. *Dictionnaire étymologique de la langue copte*. Leuven: Peeters.

Watkins, Calvert. 1963. Indo-European Metrics and Archaic Irish Verse. *Celtica* 6: 194–249

Watterson, Barbara. 1979. The Use of Alliteration in Ptolemaic. In: Ruffle, John, Gaballa, G.A. & Kitchen, Kenneth A. (eds.), *Glimpses of Ancient Egypt. Studies in Honour of H.W. Fairman*. Warminster: Phillips, 167–169.

Werning, Daniel A. 2011. *Das Höhlenbuch. Textkritische Edition und Textgrammatik. 2 vols., I: Überlieferungsgeschichte und Textgrammatik, II: Textkritische Edition*. (Göttinger Orient-forschungen 48). Wiesbaden: Harrassowitz.

West, Martin L. 1973. Indo-European Metre. *Glotta* 51: 161–187.

Wimsatt, William K. (ed.) 1972. *Versification. Major Language Types*. New York: New York University Press.

Woidich, Manfred. 2006. *Das Kairenisch-Arabische. Eine Grammatik*. Wiesbaden: Harrassowitz.

Youssef, Youhanna Nessim. 2005. A Coptic Psali on the Lord's Prayer and the Creed. *Bulletin de la Société d'Archéologie Copte* 44: 105–112.

Chris H. Reintges

The Old and Early Middle Egyptian Stative*

Morphosyntax • Semantics • Typology

Abstract: Ancient Egyptian represents the typologically unusual case of a language in which the dynamic–stative contrast among verbs correlates with two distinct finite verb paradigms. Building on earlier work (Reintges 2005a, 2006, 2011a), this chapter presents a refined analysis of the Stative paradigm in the early diachronic stages of the language. As an inflectional paradigm of person–number–gender forms, its most basic function is to encode subject-verb agreement within a local syntactic domain. At the same time, the Stative serves as an aspectual category, designating states that result from prior events or states irrespective of their origin. In addition to its aspectual semantics, the Stative constitutes a grammatical voice category in its own right, which indicates the affectedness of the subject referent.

1 Introduction

Ancient Egyptian has the longest written tradition of any of the world's language, with the earliest records dating back to the fourth millennium BCE. It represents an autonomous branch of the Afroasiatic language family. Ancient Egyptian language history has traditionally been subdivided into two macro-stages, each with distinct typological characteristics. The first macro-stage is represented by Earlier Egyptian and comprises Old Egyptian (2650–2000 BCE) and Middle Egyptian (2000–1300 BCE).[1] The second macro-stage is Later Egyptian and comprises

* I am indebted to the editors of the present volume, Eitan Grossman, Martin Haspelmath, and Tonio Sebastian Richter, as well as an anonymous reviewer for their detailed written comments, criticisms, and suggestions on earlier versions of this paper. I have also benefited from discussions with Edit Doron (The Hebrew University of Jerusalem) on the Ancient Egyptian Stative and related matters. None of the above-mentioned colleagues necessarily agrees with the views expressed herein. It goes without saying that all remaining shortcomings are my own responsibility.

1 The monumental corpus of the Coffin Texts (from around 2150–1990 BCE) has a complex editorial history, with one strand of tradition going back to the Pyramid Texts (Mathieu 2004), while another strand shows a tendency towards dialectal leveling and morphosyntactic innovation

Late Egyptian (1300–700 BCE), Demotic (700 BCE–400 CE), and Coptic (250–1300 CE) (see Loprieno 1995 and Grossman & Richter in this volume for a concise presentation). The present chapter offers a typologically oriented morphosyntactic study of the Old and Early Middle Egyptian **Stative** conjugation. The Stative is of particular interest for cross-linguistic comparison and morphological theory alike, as it embodies one of the functionally most versatile verbal–inflectional patterns of the language that sheds new light on the intersecting categories of agreement, aspect, and grammatical voice. More generally, it opens a window onto the complex ways in which the inflectional morphology interacts with systematic alternations in verbal semantics and the construals of states of affairs or "eventualities".[2]

The Stative first and foremost is an inflectional category of the verb, whose status is therefore comparable to that of other verbal-inflectional categories, such as tense, aspect, mood (TAM), and grammatical voice. Yet, in contrast to all other TAM and basic voice categories, the Stative is realized morphologically as a finite verb paradigm. In line with current theories of word structure, an **inflectional paradigm** represents a central unit of morphological organization and can be characterized as the set of all inflectionally related forms belonging to an individual lexical item (see, among various others, Anderson 1992: 79–80, 83–84; Carstairs-McCarthy 2001: 322–324; Stump 2001: 43–44; Joseph 2009: 46). The members of a paradigm are correlated with a particular morphosyntactic prop-

---

(Vernus 1990). The linguistic idiom of the Coffin Texts represents a halfway point between Old and Middle Egyptian. For want of a better name, it will be referred to as "Early Middle Egyptian" in this study.

2 A note on the terminology is in order here. The Stative has been labeled "pseudoparticiple" ("*Pseudopartizip*") or Old Perfective ("*ältere Flexion*") in the German Egyptological tradition. The term "pseudoparticiple" goes back to Erman's (1889) original discovery that a group of verb forms ending in a suffix *-tj* are not participles at all, but rather constitute a separate verbal paradigm (see in particular his discussion on pp. 76–78). This term is not at all felicitous, since the Ancient Egyptian Stative is inflected for number, gender, and person, which is a defining property of finite verb forms. Kouwenberg (2000: 28) makes the essentially same point for the Akkadian Stative. To highlight its resemblance with the Semitic suffix conjugation in general, and with the Akkadian Stative in particular, Gardiner (1957: 234–236 § 309 obs. 1) adopted the label "Old Perfective". However, this is an equally infelicitous term that might lead to confusion with the Perfect tense, morphologically marked by the stem-external suffix *-n*. More importantly, however, there is no compelling evidence that the Stative belongs to an older stratum of the language. For these reasons, I consider the term "Stative" to be the most appropriate and comprehensive label for this inflectional category—a label that is also most widely used in the linguistic literature (e.g.; Kratzer 2000; Mchombo 2004). An opposing view has been taken by Schenkel (1990: 108), Jansen-Winkeln (1993: 5–6, footnotes 6–7), and Oréal (2007: 376 footnote 17).

erty or combination of properties called **morphosyntactic features**. Morphosyntactic features are features which are relevant to the syntax and to syntactic processes, and which are realized by inflectional **exponents**, i.e., designated pieces of inflection. As Corbett & Baerman (2006: 231) put it, "morphosyntactic features characterize variations in morphological form which are correlated with different syntactic contexts".

Person, number, and gender represent the most typical morphosyntactic features, which are implicated in agreement-marking processes in most of the world's languages. Yet, as many linguists have observed, the notion of **agreement** and the phenomena covered by it are notoriously difficult to define. Anderson (1992: 103), for instance, writes, "Just as in the case of inflection itself, this is a quite intuitive notion which is nonetheless surprisingly difficult to delimit with precision". Yet a maximally inclusive approach would probably be to define agreement in terms of the covariance in morphosyntactic features between two or more constituents in a given phrasal or clausal domain. Crucially, the sharing of morphosyntactic features between structurally related items must be systematic. This can be seen by the fact that when one item varies so will the other. The feature–sharing view on agreement has been articulated in works by Kuroda (1988: 10), Chomsky (2000: 100–102), Wechsler & Zlatić (2003: 8–9), Corbett (2006: 4–5, 114–116), and others.

As an inflectional paradigm of person–number–gender forms, the Stative expresses subject-verb agreement as one of its most basic functions. This point is illustrated by the initial example in (1). The two correlated clauses contained in it are introduced by the adverbial subordinator *sk* 'while', followed by an enclitic subject pronoun and a Stative–inflected form of the epistemic verb *rx* 'to learn'. The two embedded clauses differ minimally with respect to the employed subject pronoun and the morphological shape of the finite verb. In the first clause, the Stative *rx-t(j)* 'you know' agrees in person and number but not in gender with the 2nd person singular masculine subject pronoun *ṯw* 'you (man)'. The covariance in person and number is morphologically manifest in the stem-final suffix *-t(j)*. In the second clause, the Stative *rx(-w)* 'knows' agrees in person and gender but not in number with the 3rd person singular masculine pronoun *sw* 'he'. The inflectional exponent of the shared person and gender features is the stem-final ending *-w* (i.e., /u/), which, due to its vocalic nature, has not been rendered in hieroglyphic writing (as indicated by parenthesis).

(1) The agreement component of the Stative paradigm: 2SG *rx-t(j)* vs. 3M
rx(-w)

m	*xm(-w)*		*Wnjs*	*nt͡r*
NEG.IMP	ignore(-GER. M.SG)		Unas.M.SG	god.M.SG
sk	*t͡w*	*rx-t(j)*	*sw*	*sk* *sw*
COMP	CL.2M.SG	learn-STAT.2SG	CL.3M.SG	COMP CL.3M.SG

rx(-w)   *t͡w*
learn-STAT.3M CL.2M.SG
'Do not ignore (King) Unas, oh God! Since he knows you and you know
him.' (Pyramid Text 327a–b/W)

Given a feature-sharing approach, the above-cited example shows that subject-
verb agreement in Stative sentences is both local and asymmetric. The agreement
relation is asymmetric in the sense that the nominal or pronominal subject acts
as the controller for the verb immediately following it. In other words, the inflectionally related forms of the Stative paradigm redundantly express the person,
number and gender specification of the preverbally placed subject constituent
(for further discussion on locality issues involved in agreement marking, see
Corbett 2006: 9).

Besides grammatical agreement, the Stative paradigm expresses two other,
equally essential meanings and functions, one of which is situation aspect (traditionally known under the German term "*Aktionsart*") and the other, grammatical
voice. **Situation aspect** refers to the typology of verbal predicates and specifies
the inherent aspectual properties of various lexical classes of verbs. The most fundamental distinction among aspectual classes of verbs, as identified by Vendler
(1967: 97–121), is that between events and states. Eventive predicates or simply
events are dynamic situations that involve some kind of change. The occurrence
of an event involves some condition when the event begins, continues, and ter-
minates. Stative predicates or **states**, by contrast, are non-dynamic situations,
which have no such clearly defined temporal boundaries. In other words, the
initial and final endpoints of a state are not part of that state, but they rather are
"distinct situations, constituting changes of state" (Smith 1991: 32).

There is some consensus in the linguistic literature that state predicates
can be further subdivided into resultant states (resultatives) and quality states
(qualitatives) (inter alia: Comrie 1976: 104; Kratzer 2000: 385–390; Embick
2004: 356–360; see also Mchombo 2004: 95–96 with particular reference to the
Chichewa Stative). **Resultant states** are states that arise as the result of a prior
event. **Quality states**, on the other hand, describe mental or physical conditions
or properties that are inherent to or acquired by the subject referent, irrespective
of their origin. The two kinds of stative differ from each other in terms of their

temporal restrictions. Resultant states emerge from the culmination of an event and are therefore in principle irreversible, meaning that the attained state could in principle hold forever after. For a result state to change, there must be another event whose corresponding state can effectively replace the previous result state. Quality states denote independently identifiable states or conditions that the subject referent has entered into or obtained. This kind of stative situation is in principle reversible and can therefore be temporally restricted and transitory. Consider in this regard the semantic contrast between the Stative–inflected verbs in examples (2a) and (2b). The 1st person singular Stative *snj-kjw* 'I am released' in (2a) has a resultative interpretation; it implies a contextually salient causing event that brought about the current "released" state of the speaking person (i.e., the deceased king). The asyndetically coordinated 2nd person singular Statives and *wr-t(j)* 'you are great' and *ʃn-t(j)* 'you are round' in sentence (2b) assert that the addressed person (i.e., the deceased pharaoh) has entered a particular condition or state, but such that there is no implication of agency responsible for that condition or state. Rather, in contrast to result states, the locus or origin of quality states is not further specified. Moreover, the attained state of being refreshed and elevated has evolved from a previous diametrically opposite state, given that expressed assertion is situated within the performative context of a funerary ritual.

(2) The aspectual semantics of the Stative: resultant states vs. quality states

    a. *snj-kjw*   *m-ʕ*   *xt*   *nb-t*
        release-STAT.1SG from-arm.M.SG thing.F.SG every-F.SG
        dȝw-t
        be.evil-PTCP.F.SG
        'I am released from all evil things.' (Pyramid Text 1100d/P)[3]

---

3 Allen's (1984: 385 § 564A) analysis of this passage as *sn=k wj* "you shall release me" must be rejected on contextual grounds, since the next clause *rmtʃ-w ntʃr-w ʕ-w(j)= tʃn yr Mrjj-n(j)-Rʕ* "oh you people and gods, your arms are under (King) Mer-ni-Re" (Pyramid Text 1101a/P) is directed towards a second person plural addressee. Due to the editorial change from first to third person singular narration, the redemption of the deceased king from all mortal sins is formulated as a passive clause in the parallel versions P and M. An intermediate stage is reflected in the N version, where the first person singular form of the primary Stative predicate *sn-k(j)* has been preserved although the added cartouche signals the shift from an interlocutive to a delocutive mode of narration. In line with Edel (1955/1964: 271–272 § 247), I interpret the graphic variant *-kjw* as a "mixed" spelling, which conflates the *-kj* and the *-kw* allomorph of the 1st person singular ending.

b. *m*   *kw*   *wr-t(j)*   *ʃn-t(j)*   *m*
   INTERJ   CL.2M.SG   be.big-STAT.2SG   be.round-STAT.2SG   in
   rn=k   *n(j)*   *ʃn*   *wr*
   name.M.SG=POSS.2M.SG   LINK.M.SG   circle.M.SG   be.big(-PTCP.M.SG)
   'Look, you are big (and)you are round in [your name of] the "Big
   Circle" (i.e., the ocean).' (Pyramid Text 629a/T)[4]

In addition to the aspectual component of its semantics, the Stative also constitutes a **grammatical voice** category in its own right. As such, it encodes alternations in the subject's participant status vis-à-vis the situation reported in the
sentence, and presents, as Klaiman (1991: 69) formulates it, the subject referent
as "the locus of the denoted situation's principal effects". To refer to the semantic
role of Stative subjects, I shall use the cover-term **affected subject**. (The interested
reader may refer to Jaggar 1988 for the original terminology and for an insightful analysis of very similar facts concerning Hausa Grade 7 verbs.) Sentence (2a)
above is an instructive example for the dual function of the Stative as an aspectual and as an "affected subject" voice category. Here the speaker is presented
as being positively affected by the state resulting from some previously occuring
releasing and loosing event. The 1st person singular *snj-kjw* 'I am released' thus
effectively renders an adjectival passive in English. In the Egyptological descriptive tradition, it has long been observed that Statives can be derived from different classes of transitive and intransitive verbs. In the present chapter, I intend
to show that transitive–based Statives may have an "active" syntax, in which
the subject and the direct object arguments are both syntactically realized. But
transitive Statives may also have a "passive" syntax, in which the Stative subject
corresponds to the logical direct object or "patient". Importantly, detransitivized
Statives with a passive syntax do not exhibit any morphological change. This
point is exemplified by the contrast between examples (3a) and (3b), in which the
selected verb *wdⁱ* 'to command' is transitive and occurs in the Stative paradigm.

---

4 Reconstructed with Pyramid Text 628b–c. Faulkner (1969: 121 note 2) regarded the description
of the deceased pharaoh as 'great and round' as a metaphor, which describes the king's authority and power as "all-embracing and universal". Oréal (2009: 196) does not adress the erroneous
ommission of *m rn=k n(j)* 'in [your name of]', which supports a quality state interpretation of
the two coordinated 2nd person singular Statives *wr-t(j)* 'you are big' and *ʃn-t(j)* 'you are round'.

(3) Active and passive uses of transitive speech-actv erbs

    a.   *wdꜣ-tj*   *mdw*   *nt͗r-w*
        command-STAT.2SG   word.M.SG   god-M.PL
        'You govern (lit. command the word of) the gods.' (Pyramid Text
        2110d/N)[5]

    b.   *wdꜣ-kw*   *ꜣ*   *ḥw*   *ꜣ*   *wj*   *jm*
        command-STAT.1SG   PCL PCL PCL CL.1SG   there
        'I am, indeed, ordered! Oh would it be, indeed,that I am there!'
        (Coffin Text IV 48d/B1C)[6]

Building on previous work (Reintges 2005a, 2006, 2011a), the present study offers a refined analysis of the Old and Early Middle Egyptian Stative, with an emphasis on paradigm structure and the intersection between agreement marking, situation aspect, and grammatical voice. One of the major claims that I shall make is that the Stative represents grammatical rather than anaphoric agreement, to use the terminology of Bresnan & Mchombo's (1986) classical paper. I shall thus depart from the traditional Egyptological view of the person, number, and gender marking as suffixal pronouns. The grammatical agreement analysis pursued here also diverges from Oréal's (2007, 2009, 2010) dual function analysis, according to which the Stative endings are sometimes used as personal pronouns and sometimes as inflectional agreement markers. The second claim concerns the portmanteau nature of the Stative paradigm, whose inflectionally related forms serve as the exponents of agreement, resultativity, and affected subject voice. On the face of it, the morphological realization of three distinct inflectional categories by a single person–number–gender marker looks like an outlandish and perplexing trait of the language's inflectional system. Kramer (2009) has challenged this view, proposing that stative–resultative aspect is expressed not as part of

---

5 See Edel (1955/1964: 285 § 590β) for the present tense reference of this example. Allen (1984: 409 § 591) maintains that this is the only example in the Pyramid Texts in which "the transitive old perfective does not have a demonstrable stative (passive) sense". However, as we shall see in in section 4.1 of this chapter, transitive–active Statives with different types of objects are attested in the corpus of the Pyramid Texts with all three grammatical persons. The interested reader may refer to Reintges (2006: 123–126) for a more detailed discussion of the indicative use of 2nd person singular Statives.

6 As pointed out by Borghouts (2010: 127 § 32.b.14, 133 § 33.b.26) the proclitic particle *ḥw* expresses an urgent wish, sometimes with an irrealis connotation, which he proposes to render as 'if only, would that'. This modal particle is frequently modified by the modal enclitic particle *ꜣ* 'indeed'.

the subject agreement marker, but rather by means of a specific stem-internal vowel melody. I shall review the issues involved and introduce some new considerations in support of my original proposal.

The organization of this chapter is as follows. Section 2 examines the organization and internal groupings of the Stative inflectional paradigm. I shall present a unifying analysis, according to which the person–number–gender markers of the Stative instantiate grammatical agreement in all syntactic contexts, i.e., even when there is no independent subject constituent in the sentence. The presence of agreement marking that distinguishes Statives from Eventives has broader consequences for the morphosyntax. Section 3 addresses two correlated morphological properties, viz., (i) the systematic absence of Stative–inflected Imperfective verb stems (e.g., *prr-tj* 'you have been coming forth') and (ii) the non-distinctiveness of lexical verb stems occurring in the Stative and the Eventive paradigm, respectively. Section 4 explores the aspectual nature of paradigmatic complexity, with a view to seeing how inflectional morphology and argument structure (valence) interact with Affected–Subjecthood on the one hand, and with the construal of situations on the other hand. This section also takes a closer look at the "passive" syntax of detransitivized Statives and the main structural differences between them and strict morphological eventive passives. Section 5 summarizes the main finding of this study and places them within a broader typological context.

2 Paradigm structure and the morphological status of subject agreement markers

Old and Early Middle Egyptian represents the typologically unusual case of a language in which a stative–resultative form is not derived by a special overt marker from a non-resultative base form. Rather, the members of the opposition, stative–resultative and non–resultative, have different finite verb paradigms (on this point, see Nedjalkov & Jaxontov 1988: 20 § 2.3.2.1). In this section, I shall take a closer look at the paradigm structure of the Old and Early Middle Egyptian Stative, with particular attention to allomorphic variation in person–number–gender markers, paradigm-internal groupings, and syncretism. **Syncretism** is a morphological phenomenon that involves the complete formal identity between two distinct inflectional exponents, or, as Spencer (1991: 45) phrases it, "a single inflected form may correspond to more than one morphosyntactic description". Syncretism arises from the mismatch between morphology and syntax. Following Baerman et al. (2005: 2) and Corbett (2006: 86), we may then say that the inflectional morphology "lets down" the syntax, in the sense that it fails to provide different realizations for all the syntactically relevant distinctions.

Another concern of this section is with the morphological category of stem–final person–number–gender endings on Stative–inflected verb forms. I shall present a uniform analysis of these exponents in terms of grammatical agreement between the subject constituent and the verbal predicate. According to this analysis, person–, number–, and gender inflections are never ambiguous between subject–agreement markers, when a full NP subject or pronoun is present, and incorporated subject pronouns, when there is no such overt subject in the sentence. As many linguists from different theoretical persuasions have pointed out, it is often difficult to find the relevant evidence to tease apart grammatical agreement from anaphoric agreement (inter alia: Ritter 1995: 406, 423; Harley & Ritter 2002: 482 footnote 1; Siewierska 2004: 121–127; Corbett 2006: 100–112). This is so because bound subject pronouns and inflectional subject agreement markers are realizations of the same set of morphosyntactic features. The two kinds of agreement can therefore not always be distinguished in terms of their morphological category, but rather only in terms of their different roles in the syntax.

2.1 Overview: Two finite verb paradigms

Akin to the well-studied Semitic languages, the Ancient Egyptian (mental) lexicon is organized around relatively abstract lexical representations (roots) and fully specified surface forms (stems), which are associated with a particular morpho-semantic pattern (see Reintges 1994 for a detailed analysis of the Egyptian root–and–pattern system). The language has two finite verb paradigms, which distinguish three persons (first, second, third), three numbers (singular, plural, dual), and two genders (masculine, feminine). They are called the Eventive and the Stative paradigm on the basis of their primary grammatical meaning. The complete person–number–gender paradigms of the Eventive and the Stative are presented in Table 1 (e.g.; Edel 1955/1964: 271–276 §§ 572–576; Allen 1984: 384–387 § 564; Borghouts 2010: 163–164 § 43a–b). In line with the philological tradition, the triliteral verb *sḏꜣm* 'to hear' has been chosen to illustrate a typical paradigm. (Syncretisms within the paradigm are indicated by enclosing the identical forms within a box.)

Table 1: The inflectional paradigms of person–number–gender forms in Old and Early Middle Egyptian

		eventive paradigm	stative paradigm
SG	3M	$sd^3m{=}f$	$sd^3m\text{-}w$, $sd^3m\text{-}jj$, $sd^3m(\text{-}w)$
	3F	$sd^3m{=}s$	
	2M	$sd^3m{=}k$	$\boxed{sd^3m\text{-}t(j),\ sd^3m\text{-}tj\ sd^3m\text{-}t^{\prime}j}$
	2F	$sd^3m{=}t^{\prime}$, $sd^3m{=}t^{\prime}n$	
	1	$sd^3m({=}j)$, $sd^3m{=}j$	$sd^3m\text{-}kj$, $sd^3m\text{-}k(j)$, $sd^3m\text{-}kw$, $sd^3m\text{-}kjw$, $sd^3m\text{-}kw$
DU	3M		$sd^3m\text{-}wjj$, $sd^3m\text{-}wj$
	3F	$\boxed{sd^3m{=}sny}$	$sd^3m\text{-}tjj$
	2	$sd^3m{=}t^{\prime}nj$, $sd^3m{=}t^{\prime}ny$	$sd^3m\text{-}tjwn$, $sd^3m\text{-}tjwnj$, $sd^3m\text{-}tjwny$
PL	3M	$\boxed{sd^3m{=}sn}$	$sd^3m\text{-}w$, $sd^3m\text{-}jj$, $sd^3m(\text{-}w)$
	3F		$sd^3m\text{-}t(j)$, $sd^3m\text{-}tj$, $sd^3m\text{-}t^{\prime}j$
	2	$sd^3m{=}t^{\prime}n$	$sd^3m\text{-}tjwn$, $sd^3m\text{-}tjwnj$, $sd^3m\text{-}tjwny$
	1	$sd^3m{=}n$	$sd^3m\text{-}wn$, $sd^3m\text{-}wjn$, $sd^3m\text{-}nw$
NP SUBJECT	M	$\boxed{sd^3m}$	$sd^3m\text{-}w$, $sd^3m\text{-}jj$, $sd^3m(\text{-}w)$
	F		$sd^3m\text{-}t(j)$, $sd^3m\text{-}tj$, $sd^3m\text{-}^{\prime}j$

To identify a particular form as syncretic, the form in question must serve as the exponent of multiple person–number–gender features. This is relatively straightforward when the syncretic pattern is found in some tense–aspect–mood (TAM) paradigms but not in others (see Baerman et al. 2005: 2; Baerman & Brown 2005: 122; Corbett 2006: 86 for further discussion and explication). In the case at hand, there is evidence for syncretisms in both finite verb paradigms.[7] But while syncre-

---

7 The allomorphic variation that we see with the Old and Early Middle Stative paradigm should strictly be distinguished from the variant spellings -*kj* and -*k*, -*tj* and -*t*, and also -*w*, -*jj*, and also zero (Ø) in the first, second, and third person singular, as shown in Table 1 of the main text. While variant spellings were traditionally recognized as instances of plene versus defective writings, such orthographic variation is now considered to be morphologically significant, most notably in Kammerzell's (1990, 1991a, 1991b) influential work. Here orthographic variation is seen as providing a diagnostic tool for the distinction of two subparadigms of the Egyptian Stative, labeled the "Perfect" and the "Pseudoparticiple". Elsewhere (Reintges 2006), I have provided a critical assessment of the Kammerzell's "Split-Stative Hypothesis" (my terminology) and revisit the evidence adduced for the purported subdivision of the Stative. Schenkel (1994) presents a semantically oriented version of the Split-Stative Hypothesis, which pays close attention to the lexical–semantic orientation of particular verbal classes as well as to the resultative and qualitative

tisms in the Eventive paradigm concern the combination of number and gender categories, the Stative paradigm also shows syncretisms of person. Let us now consider the different syncretisms in further detail:

– *Gender syncretism.* The two paradigms show gender syncretism in the 1st person singular and plural and in the 2nd person plural and dual. The gender syncretism that we see with the non-singular numbers of the Eventive paradigm conforms entirely to Greenberg's (1963: 95, 112) Universal 37 ("A language has never more gender categories in nonsingular numbers than in the singular"). Baerman et al. (2005: 61) conjecture that gender syncretism is favored in non-singular numbers since "this is precisely the context where there may be referential overlap, and hence ambiguity". In the Stative paradigm, however, gender syncretism also applies to the 2nd person singular. As a matter of fact, masculine and feminine gender is only distinguished in the third person.

– *Number syncretism.* The Stative shows a remarkable number syncretism. As far as one can tell, there is no morphological differentiation between singular and plural forms in the third person masculine and feminine, while the corresponding dual has distinct number morphology in the *-j* (var. *-jj* and *-y*) suffix.

– *Person syncretism.* The most conspicuous feature of the Stative paradigm is the syncretism between the 2nd person singular and the 3rd person feminine, whereby the two paradigmatic cells share the same exponent *-tj* (i.e., /ti/). It is worth mentioning here that the same restriction for the 2/3SG syncretism by gender can also be found with the Afroasiatic (Semitic) prefix conjugation (see Lipiński 2001: 368–377 §§ 40.16–40.36 for a particularly rich data collection). This is far too neat a pattern to be reducible to a case of "accidental homophony", as proposed in a recent paper by Harbour (2008). Rather, we seem to be dealing with a potentially significant counterexample to the

---

interpretation of Stative–inflected verb forms. The proposed opposition between a "Perfect" and a "Stative" is however almost exclusively based on the orthographic variation *-tj* vs. *-t(j)* in the Coffin Text corpus. The *-tj/-t(j)* alternation is revisited in Borghouts' (2001) grapho-phonological study, in which the plene form *-tj* is interpreted as a graphic reflex of emphatic pronunciation, and hence of information structure. It seems fair to say that the grapho-morphematic approach has only partially been successful as it has led to an inflation of morphosemantic distinctions and new paradigms for which there is no overall conclusive evidence. A more promising alternative would be to analyze orthographic variation in strictly phonological terms, i.e., as a graphic means of rendering suprasegmental units, such as emphatic pronunciation, pausal, and junctural phenomena.

cross-linguistic generalization that "TAM is not syncretic simultaneously with gender" (Baerman et al. 2005: 122).

- *Uninflectedness*. The Eventive paradigm comprises two sets of forms, for which I will use the terms **synthetic** and **analytic**, respectively (adopted from Celtic linguistics; see McCloskey & Hale 1983: 489–492). Synthetic forms are marked morphologically by a person–number–gender marker, traditionally referred to as "suffix–pronouns" (Gardiner 1957: 39 § 34). There is a single analytic form in the Eventive paradigm without such a pronominal suffix. It is important to point out in this connection that uninflectedness for person, number and gender (although not for tense, aspect, mood and passive voice) is neither the outcome of syncretism nor does it arise as a consequence of neutralization – a morphological process, where the uninflected form exposes the irrelevance of the involved morphosyntactic features for the syntax (Baerman et al. 2005: 28–33). Rather, uninflectedness in one paradigmatic cell reflects a more general property of the Eventive paradigm, whose person–number–gender markers, if present, can be identified with enclitic subject pronouns that are attached to the extended lexical verb stem. As prosodically independent constituents, full NP subjects never form a morphosyntacic unit with the verb. (We will have occasion to return to this point later on in § 2.3.1.) The Stative, in turn, is a morphologically uniform paradigm in the sense of Jaeggli & Safir (1989: 29–30). That is to say, each cell of the paradigm contains a bimorphemic word, which can be decomposed into the lexical verb stem and the person–number–gender inflection.

On the whole, there are more different person–number–gender forms in the Eventive than there are in the corresponding Stative paradigm. This asymmetry falls into place when the Eventive is analyzed as a paradigm of enclitic subject pronouns, and the Stative as an agreement paradigm with inflectional subject markers. Syncretism in agreement paradigms is cross-linguistically quite common and may in principle involve any combination of grammatical person distinctions, while person syncretisms are only marginally attested in the paradigms of personal pronouns (see Cysouw 2003: 311–315, 2010; Harley & Ritter 2002: 523 footnote 42; Baerman 2004: 808 and others).

2.2 Evidence for the loss of person markers and number neutralization

The Old and Early Middle Stative does not constitute a monolithic inflectional paradigm, but exhibits a considerable amount of allomorphic variation in various person, number, and gender distinctions. This variation is indicative of dialect mixing and ongoing morphological change. Already in the monumental corpus of the Pyramid Texts one finds clear indications for the loss of person markers and the neutralization of number distinctions. Two cases in point are the single attestation of the 1st person plural ending -*nw* and the loss of the dual–plural distinction in the 2nd person.

2.2.1 The 1st person plural endings -*nw* and -*wn*

There is only a single example of the 1st person plural ending -*nw* in the Pyramid Texts (4a). The allomorphic variant -*wn* can be found somewhat more regularly in the Old and Early Middle Egyptian documentation. Examples (4b–c) are taken from the dialogue sequences presented in late Old Kingdom scenes of daily life, while example (4d) comes from an Early Middle Egyptian magical text. Significantly, neither variant contains the dual marker -*j* and its lengthened variant -*jj*. This rules out a first person dual interpretation of the allomorphs -*nw* and -*wn*, which would include the speaker and the addressee but no other speech participant.

(4) The 1st person plural endings -*nw* and -*wn*

    a. *dȝw=f*   *n*   *ʃm=n*   *jʕb-nw*
       summon.PFV=3M.SG CL.1PL depart.PFV=1PL unite-STAT.1PL
       n=f
       with=3M.SG
       'He (the deceased king) summons us. Let's go to be united with him.'
       (Pyramid Text 1646b/N)

    b. *jw=n*   *sȝ-wn*
       AUX=1PL satisfy-STAT.1PL
       'We (group of workmen) are satisfied.' (Stele of Mehu-Akhti B: 2 [Reisner G 2375])

    c.   *s-ḏꜣʔ-wn*
        CAUS-provide-STAT.1PL
        'We are provided (with food).' (Mastaba of Gem-ni-kai, vol. I plate 18,
        2nd register from below)

    d.   *s-ḥḏꜣ*   *jr=k*   *mʔ=n*
        CAUS-be.bright(-IMP)   PCL=2M.SG   see.PFV=1PL
        t(w)t-wn
        be.complete-STAT.1PL
        'Lighten up (such that) we may all see.' (pap. Turin 54.003, recto
        24–25)

Since we are dealing with a hapax legomenon, it is impossible to decide whether
the two 1st person plural markers *-nw* and *-wn* were originally differentiated in
terms of an inclusive/exclusive opposition, with interpretations that include or
exclude reference to the addressee in addition to the speaker (for the encoding of first person plurals, see Siewierska 2004: 82–88 and the references cited
therein). In any event, there is no contextual evidence to corroborate such a distinction. Moreover, it cannot be concluded with certainty, as several Egyptologists have proposed (Edel 1955/1964: 273 § 574aa N.B; Allen 1984: 386 § 564 D;
Schenkel 1990: 105; Jansen-Winkeln 1993: 21), that the *-nw* ending allomorph is
more archaic than the more productive variant *-wn*; we may very well be dealing
with an innovative form that failed to be integrated into the paradigm of the Old
Egyptian Stative.

2.2.2 The loss of the dual–plural distinction in the second person

Another case in point for paradigm-internal morphological change is the neutralization of the dual–plural distinction in the second person. The dual number
involves a set of exactly two participants. Consequently, the interpretation of
plural number must involve a set of at least three participants. Contrary to what
is stated in Edel (1955/1964: 274 § 575), Allen (1984: 386 § 564 G), and Schenkel
(1990: 105), there is no conclusive evidence for a number opposition between 2nd
person dual and plural in the Stative. Rather, the non-singular form *-tjwn* is used
indiscriminately with dual and plural antecedents.

(5) Number syncretism in the non-singular 2nd person

    a. *ʃʔs=tʲnj*   *ḥrt*   *jʕb-tjwn*   *m*   *snkw*
        wander.PFV=2DU/PL sky.F.SG unite-STAT.2DU/PL in darkness.M.SG
        'Both of you (the deceased king and the god Atum) wander through-
        out the sky united in darkness.' (Pyramid Text 152c/W)

    b. *ḥr-tjwn*   *r*   *bʔ=j*   *pn*
        be.far-STAT.2DU/PL from soul.M.SG=POSS.1SG DEM.M.SG
        'You (group of divine personages) are to be remote from this soul of
        mine.' (Coffin Text VI 76c/B3L)

The non-singular 2nd person allomorphs *-tjwnj* and *-tjwny* are attested for the first time in the Early Middle Egyptian Coffin Texts, in which they occur in free variation with the standard, Old Egyptian variant *-tjwn*. As has already been noted by Edel (1955/1964: 73 § 163) and subsequently by Kammerzell (1991b: 189–190, 196), the two forms have been modeled after the enclitic 2nd person dual pronouns *=tʲnj* and *=tʲny* from the Eventive paradigm. The reshaping of the inflectional ending based on another ending looks like a case of cross-paradigm developments, which involve the same person–number cell but then in different paradigms (see Joseph 2009: 46–51 with particular reference to the Greek medio-passive). However, as shown by the contrast between examples (6a) and (6b), the newly created exponents *-tjwnj* and *-tjwny* can be used interchangeably as free functional variants with 2nd person plural and 2nd person dual pronouns. This clearly suggests that the dual suffix *-j* on the exponent *-tjwn* lacks semantic import and consequently fails to introduce a paradigmatic opposition between plural and dual number in the non-singular 2nd person.

(6) The non-distinctiveness of the innovative forms *-tjwnj* and *-tjwny* with
       respect to plural and dual number

    a. *m-xt=tny*   *gm-tjwny*
        COMP=CL.2.DU find-STAT.2DU/PL
        'After you two (the two hands of Horus) have been found' (Coffin Text
        II 350a/B1L)

    b. *jn*   *jw=tʲn*   *rx-tjwny*   *rdʒ-jj-t*   *P ?*
        FOC AUX=2PL learn-STAT.2DU/PL give-PASS1-PTCP.F.SG Buto.M.SG
        'Do you (groups of divine personages) know the foundation of Buto
        (toponym)?' (Coffin Text II 331d/B1L)

There are only few languages in which the inflectional paradigm manifests a dual in the third but not in the first and second person, as in the case of the Old Egyptian Stative. Siewierska (2004: 95–96) mentions two parallel cases, to wit, the independent person paradigm of Tlappanec, a language of Mexico, and the possessive prefix paradigm of the Nishel dialect of Kham, a Central Himalayan language. This atypical situation is diachronically unstable, as witnessed by the almost complete loss of the 3rd person dual endings of the Stative in the Classic Middle Egyptian period (see Reintges 2011a: 42–43 for a more detailed discussion).

2.3 Grammatical agreement vs. pronominal agreement

Having looked at the paradigm structure of the Stative and the early evidence for morphological simplification, we shall now turn to consider the morphological category and the syntactic status of the person–number–gender markers. These markers have traditionally been conceived of as incorporated subject pronouns (Allen 1984: 6 § 11, 384 § 564; Vernus 1986: 382; Schenkel 1997: 199 § 7.3.2). More recently, Oréal (2009: 193–194, 2010: 156–157) has put forward a "dual function" analysis, according to which the person–number–gender forms of the Stative are categorially ambiguous: they have a referential (anaphoric) use as incorporated subject pronouns and a non-referential use as subject–agreement markers. The purported anaphoric use of the inflectional endings is said to be a trace of their pronominal origin in a reconstructed Proto-Egyptian language stage. An early formulation of this idea can already be found in Schenkel's (1965: 48–52, 65–66) study. However, both the pronoun incorporation and the dual function analysis can be shown to face empirical difficulties. In what follows I shall present a unifying account of the Stative person–number–gender forms as inflectional subject markers. An analysis in terms of grammatical agreement not only fares well in capturing the observed syncretisms but also offers a straightforward explanation for the syntactic environments in which pronominal subjects are omissible.

2.3.1 Absence of complementarity

As has briefly been discussed above (§ 2.1), the Eventive paradigm comprises for the most part synthetic forms with pronominal clitics, while an uninflected form is selected in the context of full NP subjects. The analytic form can however still be inflected for tense, aspect, mood, and passive voice and consequently carry the relevant morphological exponent such as the Perfect tense/aspect marker -*n*.

Examples (7a–b) are meant to illustrate the complementary distribution between synthetic forms and full NP subjects.

(7) The complementarity between synthetic and analytic forms in Eventive VSO clauses

a. *jj-n*   *mʃˤ*   *pn*   *m*   *ħtp*
come-PERF   army.M.SG   DEM.M.SG   in   peace.M.SG
'This army (here) has returned in peace.'

b. *bʔ-n=f*   *tʔ*   *ħr(-y)-w*   *ʃˤw*
destroy-PERF=3M.SG   land.M.SG   upon-NOMINAL-M.PL   sand.M.PL
'It has destroyed the land of the "sand-dwellers" (i.e., Bedouins).'
(Urkunden I 103: 7–8)

The complementary distribution between full NP subjects and synthetic verb forms in the Eventive can straightforwardly be accounted for if the person–number–gender exponent is in effect identified with an enclitic subject pronoun, which competes with a related noun phrase for the post-verbal subject slot. The same distributional pattern can also be observed for non-verbal categories, two cases in point being basic prepositions (*ħr=f* [on=3M.SG] 'on him' vs. *ħr mw* [on water.M.PL] 'on water') and nominal possession (*pr=f* [house.M.SG=3M.SG] 'his house' vs. *pr Wnjs* [house.M.SG Unas.M.SG] 'house of (King) Unas'). Once again, this follows from the syntactic status of the person–number–gender exponents as pronominal arguments that occupy distinct phrasal or clausal positions.

The complementarity between independent subjects and agreement inflection has been studied extensively for the Modern Celtic VSO languages. Anderson (1982: 575–584), Doron (1988: 210–217), and Baker & Hale (1990: 295–296) argue in favour of an anaphoric agreement analysis of Breton person-number markers as incorporated subject pronouns. McCloskey & Hale (1983) present an alternative analysis of the corresponding markers in Modern Irish in terms of grammatical agreement. Although the person–number–gender exponents of the synthetic forms instantiate pronominal arguments in terms of the syntax, they behave morphologically as clitic pronouns rather than incorporated suffix pronouns. As such, they occupy the boundary between inflectional and free forms (on this point, see Siewierska 2004: 26–34, 162–163; Corbett 2006: 101–102). The morphological category of these markers becomes particularly clear in the context of complementizer cliticization. As shown by examples (8a) and (8b), the 2nd person singular masculine pronoun =*k* does not form a morphosyntactic unit with the embedded Stative verb, but rather appears to the immediate right of the finite subordinating conjunction *wnt* 'that' and the agreeing relativizing complementizer *ntj* 'that'. (Brackets demarcate the subordinated clause.)

(8) Complementizer cliticization

    a. *r   rdꜣ-t   rx-t(j)   [wnt=k   hꜣ-t(j)*
       to   give-INF learn-PASS2 COMP=2M.SG descend-STAT.2SG
       m htp   m   Jꜣm
       in peace.M.SG from Yam.M.SG
       ḥnꜥ mʃꜥ   [ntj   ḥnꜥ=k]]
       with army.M.SG COMP.REL.M.SG with=2M.SG
       '... To let (it) be known that you descended in peace from (the land of) Yam together with the army that (was) with you.' (Urkunden I 128:7–9)

    b. *ntᶠr   pw   [ntj=k*
       god.M.SG DEM.M.SG   COMP.REL.M.SG=2M.SG
       rx-t(j)   sw]
       learn-STAT.2SG CL.3M.SG
       'This god that you know' (Coffin Text V 111d/M2C)

As already noted by Shlonsky (1997:185–187), complementizer cliticization is not a possible morphological process in a language like Tamazight Berber, in which the agreement inflection is not a clitic. The same holds true for the Ancient Egyptian Stative paradigm, whose person–number–gender exponents are bound inflectional affixes. Accordingly, the 2nd person singular ending *-t(j)* on the embedded Statives *hꜣ-t(j)* 'you descended' and *rx-t(j)* 'you know' in examples (8a–b) above could not possibly be detached from the lexical verb stem and appear on the initial complementizer, to produce ungrammatical strings of the form **wnt-tj hꜣ-* and **ntj-tj rx* (for the non-detachability of the person–number–gender inflection, cf. also Borghouts 2010: 163 § 43a). Nor could the *-t(j)* suffix be doubled and appear as a subject agreement inflection both on the complementizer and on the embedded Stative, which would give rise to ungrammatical strings, such as **wnt-tj hꜣ-tj* and **ntj-tj rx-tj.*

    In comprising only inflected forms, the Stative person–number–gender paradigm does not display the complementary distribution between pronominal enclisis and full NP subjects that we have just seen for the Eventive paradigm. Despite its empirical adequacy and theoretical validity, the view that the complementary principle does not apply to the Stative paradigm has been contested by several scholars. Allen (1984: 197 § 311), for instance, maintains that "[i]n the Pyramid

Texts, the pronominal counterpart of the bare initial indicative *sḏm.f* of intransitive verbs is expressed by the (bare initial) old perfective". A slightly modified stance on this issue is taken later on, when he writes, "(...) the bare initial old perfective of intransitive verbs is a counterpart of the independent Aorist *sḏm.f* with nominal subject, for all three persons" (pg. 406 § 590). In a series of articles, Oréal (2007: 374–379, 2009: 193–198, 2010: 153–154) takes this raison d'être one step further to argue that there is a morphological gap in the paradigm of the Stative with preverbal subject NPs, which is filled in by the corresponding analytic form of the Perfective–neutral aspect of the Eventive paradigm. However, examples of the kind in (9a–b) provide prima facie evidence for the co-occurrence of preverbal nominal subjects and 3rd person agreement inflection.

(9) Co-occurrence of preverbal subject NPs and 3rd person agreement

    a.   *jb(=j)*   *nd̑m(-w)*   *<m>*   *swnt*
        heart.M.SG=1SG   be.sweet-STAT.3M   about price.F.SG
        'My heart is content about the price.' (Mastaba of Niankhchnum and Chnumhotep 42 [scene 11.3.4])

    b.   *Nwt*   *j-ḥꜥꜥ-t(j)*   *m*   *xsf*
        Nut.F.SG   AUG-cheer.PLUR-STAT.3F   about meet.INF
        Ppj   *pn*
        Pepi.M.SG   DEM.M.SG
        '(The goddess) Nut is very excited about meeting this (King) Pepi (here).' (Pyramid Text1426a/N)[8]

To maintain a dual function analysis for the person–number–gender forms of the Stative, one would have to show that simple *NP subject–Stative* sentences are functionally ambiguous. That is, the preverbal NP could either be a true nominal subject with which the finite verb shows grammatical agreement, or it could be a

---

[8] In her analysis of Pyramid Text 1426a/N (i.e., example (9b) of the main text), Oréal (2009: 194 footnote 24) disagrees with my interpretation of the verb form *j-ḥꜥꜥ-t(j)* as a Stative and the sequence *Nwt j-ḥꜥꜥ-t(j)* as a pragmatically neutral declarative clause, with the initial NP occupying the preverbal subject slot (Reintges 2005a: 39). It is proposed instead that the initial NP is to be understood as a left-dislocated topic constituent, which is anaphorically linked to the main clause via an alleged coreferential pronoun *-t(j)* – the subject marker in question ("Nut, she has rejoiced about meeting this Pepi"). However, as I shall demonstrate in the remainder of this section, NP *subject–Stative* sequences can never be analyzed as involving a left-dislocation structure with a topicalized subject NP.

topic NP related by anaphoric agreement to the incorporated subject pronoun. This is essentially the point that Bresnan & Mchombo (1987: 755–756) and Mchombo (2004: 23–24) have made in their analysis of the Chichewa subject marker and also seems to be the guiding assumption of Oréal's proposal. However, as I shall show next, there is good reason to question a pronominal agreement analysis of the person–number–gender ending of the Stative verb form when a subject NP appears preverbally.

2.3.2 The non-ambiguous status of full NP subject–Stative sentences

The first kind of evidence against a pronominal agreement analysis comes from a sentence pattern, in which the Stative verbal predicate is preceded by two lexical NPs. This pattern has come to be known as the "Broad Subject Construction" in the linguistic literature (Doron 1986; Doron & Heycock 2010). Superficially, the Broad Subject Construction looks like a left-dislocation structure but actually is an instance of a pragmatically neutral declarative clause with two nominative subjects. In Reintges (2005a: 86–87), I have proposed that the preverbal NP *jb=s* 'her heart' in the following example represents the narrow subject and the post-auxiliary NP *bʔkt tn n(j)-t Mrrj* 'this servant maid of Mereri', the broad subject. Simplifying matters somewhat, the narrow subject and the Stative-inflected verb form a semantic predicate for the broad subject, with the open position being provided by the resumptive possessive pronoun on the narrow subject. As a result, the broad subject displays properties of canonical subjects rather than those of left-dislocated topic constituents.

(10) The Broad Subject Construction with two preverbal subject NPs

jw   bʔkt   tn   n(j)-t   Mrrj
AUX   servant.F.SG   DEM.F.SG   LINK-F.SG   Mereri.M.SG
jb=s   ʕnx(-w)   r=f
heart.M.SG=3F.SG   live-STAT.3M   PCL=3M.SG
mʔʔ=s   wpwtj   n(j)   nb=s
see=3F.SG   messenger.M.SG LINK.M.SG   lord.M.SG=POSS.3F.SG
'Now, this maid servant of Mereri, her heart is alive (whenever) she sees a messenger of her lord.' (pap. Cairo CG 58043:8–9)

The second kind of evidence favouring a grammatical agreement over a pronominal agreement analysis comes from subject questions containing a Stative–inflected verb form and the interrogative pronoun *m* 'who' in preverbal position, as seen in example (11). A well-known fact about the information structure of questions is that the questioned constituent is the focus of the clause, denoting what is not presupposed as known. If the preverbal position were to be identified with an extra-clausal topic position and the person–number–gender marker, with an incorporated subject pronoun, the questioned subject would simultaneously fulfill a topic and a focus function. Such a function clash is ruled out in a language like Chichewa, as it would lead to inconsistent presuppositions about topic- and focushood (Bresnan & Mchombo 1997: 757–760).

(11)   Subject-in-situ question with Stative

   m   *twt(-w)*   *n=f ?*
   who   resemble-STAT.3M to=3M.SG
   'Who is like him?' (Pyramid Text 1689b/M)[9]

With these considerations in mind, the questioned subject must be located in the canonical preverbal subject slot and triggers 3rd person masculine agreement on the adjacent verb. There are in actual fact no compelling examples where simple Subject NP–Stative sentences must be interpreted as topicalization structures. By contrast, we find clear cases where a topic analysis of the preverbal NP must be excluded on syntactic grounds. This strongly suggests that Stative sentences with full NP subjects are never ambiguous between a simple declarative clause and a left-dislocation structure. As a subject rather than a topic constituent, the preverbal NP stands in a local relation with the Stative predicate within a single clausal domain. So this is a well-defined syntactic context in which the person–number–gender ending serves as a subject–agreement marker, which redundantly expresses the feature content of the preverbal subject NP.

2.3.3 The first/second vs. third person split in subject omissibility ("*pro*-drop")

For the grammatical agreement analysis to succeed, one needs to also show that the individual person–number–gender endings never acquire pronominal status, even when there is no independent subject in the sentence. This seems to be the gist of Oréal's proposal. Consider in this regard the following minimal

---

9 Cf. Edel (1955/1964: 516 § 1006). It may very well be the case that the interrogative sentence *m twt(-w) n=f* "Who is like him?" has a rhetorical flavour. In any event, there is a shift in perspective with respect to the person of the beneficiary from 2nd person singular (speech of the funerary priest) to 3rd person singular masculine (speech of the ennead).

sentence pair, which contains the 1st person singular Stative *jw-k(j)* 'I have come' and denotes the present location of the speaking person. Yet, the preverbal subject position is occupied by the 1st person singular clitic pronoun *w(j)* in the a-example, which is introduced by the presentative particle *m* 'look'. There is no such pronoun in the corresponding b–example, which is a pragmatically neutral declarative sentence without focus or emphasis on the anaphoric subject.[10]

(12) 1st person singular Statives with and without a corresponding personal pronoun

a. *m=k*   *w(j)*   *bs-kj*   *jw-kj*
   INTERJ=2M.SG CL.1SG install-STAT.1SG come-STAT.1SG
   'Look, I am installed. I have come.' (Pyramid Text Neith 831 [plate 32])

b. *jw-k(j)*   *yr*   *ḥnkt*   *[...] jm*
   come-STAT.1SG under offering.F.SG there
   'I have come thence [...] with an offering.' (Pyramid Text 1069c/N [P/A/E 20 = 224])

In principle two types of analysis may be envisaged for the subject omission pattern that we see with first person singular Statives. In a Lexical–Functional Grammar analysis, in which non-overt material is not posited, the person marker itself is identified with an incorporated pronoun, while the same marker expresses grammatical agreement when the sentence contains an overt nominal or pronominal subject (see Bresnan & Mchombo 1987 for subject omissibility in Chichewa and Toivonen 2000 for a related analysis of possessive pronoun dropping in Finnish). However, as Toivonen (2000: 580) herself points out, a lexical split account along these lines may be regarded as costly, insofar as the same person–number marker corresponds to two lexical entries, which are completely identical both in form and in morphosyntactic feature content. And yet, the two homophonous entries only differ from each other in one respect, namely whether they have a referential role as an incorporated subject pronoun or rather have a non-referential role as a grammatical agreement marker. No such problem arises under an alternative generative analysis, which posits covert pronominal categories. These covert pronouns are equivalent to overt pronouns as far as their syntax is concerned, with the main difference being that they are left unpronounced

---

10 I am indebted to Martin Haspelmath for clarifying this issue.

(for three representative views from different perspectives, see Doron 1988: 202; Siewierska 2004: 122; Roberts & Holmberg 2010: 2–3). Accordingly, the person–number inflection is consistently used as a subject agreement marker, which corresponds to a single lexical entry.

The ***pro*-drop parameter** covers the possibility of omitting unstressed subject pronouns in languages like Italian and Spanish as opposed to English and German. In the Government-and-Binding literature from the 1980s (Rizzi 1982, 1986; Chomsky 1982; Borer 1986; McCloskey & Hale 1983; Jaeggli & Safir 1989), the phenomenon of pronoun dropping has been related to a morphological property, in particular, to the nature of finite verb agreement and to the degree to which person and number features are discretely represented in the language's verbal–inflectional paradigms. In other words, verbal agreement must be specified beyond a certain threshold to recover the referential content of the referential content of the covert pronoun *pro*. The inclusion of a broader range of languages into the comparative research furthermore has revealed that the presence of highly structural paradigms in a language couldn't be a morphological prerequisite for the licensing of *pro*-drop. Otherwise, it would be difficult to explain why null subject pronouns are licensed in Mandarin Chinese – a language that lacks agreement inflection altogether (Huang 1984; Huang et al. 2009: 209–211). The morphological uniformity condition of Jaeggli & Safir (1989: 29–30) is intended to handle the availability of null subjects in languages with and without rich agreement. However, partial null subject languages such as Brazilian Portuguese, Finnish, Marathi, and Modern Hebrew pose an obvious problem for such an approach. In these languages, null subjects are permissible but under more restricted conditions than they are in consistent null subject languages, while the employed verbal–inflectional paradigms are otherwise morphologically uniform and distinguish most or even all person-number combinations (Holmberg et al. 2009; Vainika & Levy 1999; see also Roberts & Holmberg 2010 for a recent assessment of the *pro*-drop parameter within the Minimalist Program).

Shifting our attention back to the Old and Early Middle Egyptian situation, the first thing to observe here is that pronoun omission is not a licit option with Eventive verb forms. This can be directly related to the pronominal agreement paradigm of the Eventive, which consists of agreementless verb forms and enclitic personal pronouns. Furthermore, and perhaps more importantly, there is no alternative recovery mechanism available, which would allow null subjects to be identified by a discourse antecedent. The situation is completely different with Stative sentences, in which overt subject pronouns are omissible in the first and the second person while they cannot be so omitted in the third person. This can be seen by comparing examples (13a–d) with examples (13e–i). (Example (13f) actually comes from a Middle Egyptian text with a somewhat archaizing idiom.)

Neither the traditional view of the person–number–gender marker as an incorporated subject pronoun nor the more recent dual function analysis are apt to account for the observed person asymmetry in regard to pronoun dropping.

(13) The 1st/2nd vs. 3rd person split in the Old and Early Middle Egyptian Stative paradigm

    a. 1SG   *pr-kj*   *r=j*   *wʕb-kj*
                come.forth-STAT.1SG PCL=1SG   purify-STAT.1SG
                'I have come forth purified.' (Coffin Text VI 136o/M22C)

    b. 1PL   *s-dʒʔ-wn*
                CAUS-provide-STAT.1PL
                'We are provided (with food).' (Mastaba of Gem-ni-kai, vol. I plate 18, 2nd register from below)

    c. 2SG   *rdʒ-t(j)*   *n*   *mwt=k*   *Nwt (...)*
                give-STAT.2SG to   mother.F.SG=POSS.2M.SG Nut.F.SG
                'You are given to your mother Nut(...)' (Pyramid Text 616d/T)

    d. 2PL   *j-gr-tjwn*
                AUG-be.silent-STAT2DU/PL
                'You are to be silent!' (Mastabaof Ankh-ma-hor, 2nd room, west wall, 2nd register from below, plate 37)[11]

    e. 3M.SG *ḥmt=f*   *jr=s*   <n=>f   *st*
                wife=POSS.3M.SG make.PFV=3F.SG   for=3M.SG CL.F.SG
                sw   *qrs(-w)*   <m> *yrt-ntʲr*   *Ktktj*
                CL.3M.SG bury-STAT.3M in   necropolis Ketketi.M.SG
                'It is his wife who made it [for] him when he was buried <in> the necropolis – Ketketi.' (Junker, Gisa VI, 1943: 231–232, fig. 94)[12]

---

11 Erman (1919: 37) has already singled out the unusual presence of the *j*-augment in front of the 2nd person plural Stative *j-gr-tjwn* 'you are to be silent'. However, we should not be too surprised to find archaic or archaizing spellings in the caption of the daily life scenes in Old Kingdom mastabas. I shall return to the question of the *j*-augment (prothetic yod) in Stative–inflected verb forms at the end of this chapter (§ 4.5.2).

12 My interpretation of this admittedly difficult passage differs from the one proposed by

f. 3M.SG *sw*   *ḥms-w*   *ḥnꜥ* *jzt=f*
    CL.3M.SG sit-STAT.3M with staff.F.SG=POSS.3M.SG
    m-ẖnw   *kꜣp*
    in-inside.M.SG shelter.M.SG
    'He is sitting with his entourage inside the shelter.' (Pleasures of Fishing and Fowling B4: 1)

g. 3M.SG *sk*   *sw*   *ꜥnḫ(-w)*
    COMP CL.3M.SG live-STAT.3M
    'while he was (still) alive' (Urkunden I 21: 14)

h. 3F.SG *mwt=f*   <*rḫt*>   *njswt*
    mother.F.SG=POSS.3M.SG acquaintance.F.SG king.M.SG
    sk   *s(j)*   *ẖp-t(j)*
    COMP CL.3F.SG depart-STAT.3F
    'His mother, the king's <acquaintance>, when she passed away (lit. she departed)' (Mastaba of Kahif [G 2136], West wall, Northern false door, 1st line)

i. 3.PL *sk*   *sn*   *rḫ-jj*   *s(j)*
    COMP CL.3PL learn-STAT.3M CL.F.SG
    'while they know it' (Coffin Text VII 111j/SQ10C)

Here I propose to derive the person split in the Old and Early Middle Egyptian Stative paradigm from a **recoverability condition** on the controller of agreement. The key idea is that controller of agreement – the subject pronoun in question – can be left unpronounced if (part of) its person, number and gender features are morphologically realized on the target of agreement – the inflected verb form. This is no longer an option when the target of agreement is morphologically ambiguous. As will be recalled from the previous discussion (§ 2.1), morphologically ambiguous forms arise as a consequence of person, number, and gender

---

Grunert, *Thesaurus Linguae Aegyptiae*, lemma-no 130830, attestation 41. Firstly, note that the omission of the locative preposition *m* 'in' is also attested in the architrave inscription of the offering chapel of the Mastaba of Ka-em-neferet *qrs(-w)<=f> <m> yrt ntꜣr* "that he may be buried in the necropolis" (Hassan, Excavations at Giza II, 1930–1931: 108–109, fig.116). Secondly, the letters *s* and *t* underneath the coffin hieroglyph represent the neutral pronoun *st* 'it'. For the use of the clitic pronoun *sw* as a clause-initial subject pronoun, cf. also *sw m njwt mꜣ(w)t tn* "he (was) in this new city" (Urkunden I 292: 7).

syncretism, when one member of the paradigm realizes more than one person-number-gender cell. In such a context, the target of agreement no longer satisfies the recoverability condition. Consequently, an overt pronoun must be introduced into the structure to avoid referential ambiguity.[13] In the case at hand, the selected member of the Stative paradigm must have an explicit morphological representation of person and number features. This is obviously the case with the 1st person singular and plural forms -*kj* and -*wn* and the non singular 2nd person form -*tjwn*. In encoding gender but not number features, 3rd person agreement is less richly specified and hence, morphologically ambiguous. An analysis along these lines raises a question of why the Stative ending -*tj* licenses *pro*-drop in the context of 2nd person singular reference, in spite of the 2SG/3F person syncretism. As I have argued in related work (Reintges 2005a: 49; 2011a: 22–23), the availability of *pro*-drop in 2nd person singular contexts arises as a default option by analogy with the non-singular 2nd person ending -*tjwn*, which is ambiguous with respect to both gender and dual/plural number but crucially not with respect to person.

2.3.4 Pronoun dropping and information structure

The subject omission pattern is further complicated by the fact that other factors come into play, motivating the presence of an overt pronoun in first and second person contexts. One such factor is the information-structural status of the subject referent: first and second person pronouns cannot be left unpronounced when they fulfill a topic or focus role. Examples (14a–b) illustrate the contrastive role of independent personal pronouns, such as the first person singular pronoun *jnk* 'I' and the second person singular masculine pronoun *tʲwt* 'you'. I assume, following Frascarelli (2007: 694–695, 716–719), that freestanding pronoun share a discourse-related function (focus or contrastive topic). Accordingly, they are not placed in the preverbal subject position, but rather are located in the left periph-

---

13 A very similar contrast between 1st/2nd and 3rd person agreement with respect to the licensing of null subjects has been observed for Finnish (Vainika & Levy 1999; Holmberg 2005, 2010) and the past and future tense paradigms of Modern Hebrew (Borer 1986; Doron 1988; Ritter 1995; Shlonsky 1997, 2009). Based on Kayne's (2000: 176) proposal that "an agreement suffix having the properties of a pronoun can only be first or second person", Shlonsky (2009: 141–144) proposes that 1st and 2nd person prefixes and suffixes are pronominal clitics that occupy distinct positions. This analysis fails to acknowledge the morphological uniformity of the past and future tense paradigms, in particular, the 2SG/3F.SG syncretism in the future tense paradigm (*ti-lmad* 'you/she will study') is left unexplained.

ery of the clause. Accordingly, the preverbal subject slot must be occupied by the corresponding null pronoun.

(14) 1st/2nd person singular Statives with corresponding freestanding pronoun

    a. *jnk [ʔx]–kj*   *m*   *sꜥḥ=j*
        I   be.spirit.like.STAT.1SG in dignity.M.SG=POSS.1SG
        '(As for) me, I have become a spirit through my dignity.' (Coffin Text VII 103g/S10C)

    b. *t'wt*   *ꜥḥꜥ-tj*   *ḥr-t(j)*   *r=f*
        you.M.SG stand-STAT.2SG be.far-STAT.2SG from=3M.SG
        'You (man) are standing far away from him (the god Osiris).' (Pyramid Text 251c/W)

Another interfering factor concerns the presence of other structural elements in Stative sentence constructions, such as subordinating complementizers and auxiliary verbs, as these elements require the immediately following subject constituent to be overt. Accordingly, an overt first and second pronoun must be inserted into the preverbal subject slot of first and second person Statives. The data shown in (15a–d) illustrate the strong statistical preference for first and second person clitic pronouns to surface in temporal adverb clauses introduced by the temporal subordinators *sk* 'while' and *m-xt* 'after' (see also Zakrzewska 1990: 137–139). Yet, sentence (15c) is a notable exception, showing that the *pro*-drop option is still marginally available in 2nd person singular context.

(15) The presence of 1st/2nd person clitic pronouns in temporal adverb clauses

    a. 1SG   *sk*   *w(j)*   *ʃpss-k(j)*   *xr*   *Izzj*
            COMP CL.1.SG be.esteemed-STAT.1SG under Izezi.M.SG
            r   *mjtj(=j)*   *nb*
            (more)than equal.M.SG=POSS.1SG each.M.SG
            'While I was more esteemed under (King) Izezi than anyone of my rank' (Urkunden I 59: 13)

   b. 2SG   *sk*   *tʲw*   *xʕ-t(j)*
               COMP CL.2M.SG appear-STAT.2SG
               m *jʔbt*   *pt*
               in eastern.F.SG heaven.F.SG
               'While you appear in the eastern (side) of heaven' (Pyramid Text 1496b/P)

   c. 2SG   *sk*   *ħm rx-t(j)*
               COMP PCL learn-STAT.2SG
               mrr(=j)   *tʲw*
               love.IMPERF=1.SG CL.M.SG
               'While you, indeed, know (that) I love you' (Urkunden I 61: 14)

   d. 2PL   *m-xt tny*   *gm-tjwny*
               COMP CL.2.DU find-STAT.2DU/PL
               'After you two (i.e., hands) have been found' (Coffin Text II 350a/B1L)

Auxiliary verb constructions provide yet another context in which null pronominal subjects must be replaced by the corresponding overt pronouns. Here the unavailability of the pronoun omissibility pattern is to be sought in the morphological requirements of auxiliary verbs, which generally appear in the anaphoric agreement paradigm of the Eventive. The post-auxiliary subject pronoun does not induce a contrastive focus or topic shift interpretation, but rather signals topic continuity or familiar topichood. Such enclitic pronouns form a natural class with covert subject pronouns in terms of their information-structural properties (on this point, see also Frascarelli 2007: 695, 712–713).

(16)   The obligatory presence of 1st/2nd person pronouns in auxiliary verb constructions

   a. 1SG   *jw=j*   *rx-k(j)*   *psd̠t*
               AUX=1SG learn-STAT.1SG ennead.F.SG
               J(w)nw
               Heliopolis.M.SG
               'I know the ennead of Heliopolis.' (Coffin Text II 272a/S2P)

b. 1PL   *jw=n*   *sʔ-wn*
             AUX=1PL   satisfy-STAT.1PL
             'We (group of workmen) are satisfied.' (Stele of Mehu-Akhti B: 2 [Reisner G 2375])

c. 2SG   *j(w)=k*   *ʕnx-tj*
             AUX=2.M.SG   live-STAT.2SG
             'You are alive.' (Pyramid Text 1700/M)

d. 2PL   *jw=tⁿn*   *rx-tjwn*   *wj*
             AUX=2PL   learn-STAT.1PL   CL.1SG
             'You (plural) know me.' (Coffin Text II 24b/B1C)

The picture becomes even more complex when **impersonal** sentence constructions are taken into consideration. According to the analysis defended in the previous section (§ 2.3.3), the 3rd person masculine ending *-w/-jj* of the Stative is specified for person and gender but not for number. To avoid referential ambiguity, an overt 3rd person masculine singular or plural pronoun must be inserted in the preverbal subject slot. However, there is no such third person pronoun in the impersonal Stative sentences shown in (17a–c).

(17)   Impersonal Stative sentences with 3rd person masculine agreement

a. *jw*   *dȝw(-w)*
    AUX   be.bad-STAT.3M
    '(It) has turned out bad.' (Lepsius, Denkmäler II, plate 63)

b. *m=k*   *xpr(–w)*
    INTERJ=2M.SG   happen-STAT.3M
    'Look, (it) is done.' (Tomb of Hesi, Offering Chamber, plate 35)

c. *jw*   *sʃp(-w)*   *dȝd*   *Kʔ–rnnj*   *pn*
    AUX   be.bright-STAT.3M   speak.PFV   Ka–renni.M.SG   DEM.M.SG
    jw   *knḥ(-w)*   *dȝd*   *Kʔ–rnnj*   *pn*
    AUX   be.dark-STAT.3M   speak.PFV   Ka–renni.M.SG   DEM.M.SG
    '(It) dawns when this Ka–renni (the deceased male) (here) speaks. (It) is dusk when this Ka–renni (here) speaks.' (Coffin Text IV 29e/ Sq6C)

Null expletive pronouns, i.e., the covert counterparts of English *it* and *there*, are unexpected from a theoretical viewpoint, as they lack both semantic content and phonological realization. Yet, there is an increasing body of evidence that languages make use of such "silent dummies" (e.g., Franks 1990; Holmberg 2005). In the above example, the presence of the null expletive accounts not only for the agreement morphology of the Stative verb, which assumes a default 3rd person masculine value, but also for the absence of an overt subject constituent, which characterizes impersonal sentences. Furthermore, the null expletive pronoun has enclitic properties, requiring auxiliary support to attach itself to a verbal host.

The evidence presented in this section has shown that the subject agreement marker never acquires pronominal status itself, even when no overt personal pronoun surfaces preverbally. The most basic pattern of subject omissibility is represented by a person (1st /2nd vs. 3rd) asymmetry, which could be accounted for in terms of a morphologically conditioned recoverability condition. However, the pattern of subject omissibility turns out to be quite complex once a broader range of constructions is taken into consideration. It thus seems fair to say that the complexity of pronoun distribution poses a challenge for any analysis that treat the different person–number–gender forms of the Stative as incorporated pronouns.

3 Related morphological and syntactic properties

The presence of grammatical agreement marking that distinguishes the Stative from the Eventive paradigm has broader consequences for the morphology and the aspectual semantics. In particular, Statives and Eventives differ systematically from each other as regards their modifiability by the morphological exponents of verbal-semantic categories. While Eventive verb forms are compatible with the entire range of tense–aspect–mood (TAM) and grammatical voice markers, the corresponding Statives are subject to strict selectional restrictions. A case in point is the incompatibility of Stative agreement morphology with Imperfective verb stems. I attempt to show that the conflict actually arises between meanings rather than forms per se. A closely related topic is the question of inflectional exponence, i.e., the relation between form and content. In previous work (Reintges 1997: 98–100, 2005a: 50–52), I have analyzed the person–number–gender forms of the Stative as portmanteau morphemes, which simultaneously encode grammatical agreement and stative-resultative semantics. More recently, Kramer (2009) has advanced an alternative view, according to which stative-resultative aspect is morphologically marked by a special stem-internal vocalism. According to this decompositional analysis, the individual person–number–gender markers register a particular subject–predicate constellation, but have no independent semantics. I shall discuss the problems with this approach, which points at the possibility that the portmanteau analysis is on the right track.

3.1 The complementarity distribution between agreement and aspect morphology

As a non-deictic temporal category, *"Aktionsart"*/situation aspect is routinely grammaticalized in languages alongside viewpoint aspect. The most common aspectual viewpoints are represented by the **Perfective** and the **Imperfective**, which enter into a paradigmatic opposition with each other. According to Comrie (1976: 16), "perfectivity indicates the view of a situation as a single whole, without distinction of the various separate phases that make up that situation; while imperfectivity pays essential attention to the internal structure of the situation". This definition is slightly modified when he writes, "perfectivity involves lack of explicit reference to the internal temporal constituency of a situation, rather than denying the lack of such internal temporal constituency" (pg. 21). As pointed out by Dahl (1985: 68), the perfective–imperfective aspect opposition "differs from most other cross-linguistc TMA [Tense/Mood/Aspect] categories by not having a very clear marking relation".

The situation is more complex in Old and Early Middle Egyptian, as verbal aspect interacts with morphological classes of verbs in group-specific ways. Simplifying matters somewhat, one can basically distinguish between **bi-aspectual** verbs, which have morphologically distinct perfective and imperfective stems, and trans-aspectual or **aspect-neutral** verbs, which have only a single base stem that can be used in the perfective or in the imperfective aspect. Bi-aspectual verbs are restricted to the class of so-called "weak" verbs, which are characterized by a stem-final glide *j*. Aspect-neutral verbs typically involve the large group of "strong verbs", in which there is no such verbal classifier. Within the class of bi-aspecual verbs, the perfective–imperfective opposition in encoded by pairs of simplex and geminated stems, such as *ḥz.j* 'to praise' (Perfective aspect) vs. *ḥzz* 'to be praising' (Imperfective aspect), whereby the geminated form of the Imperfective clearly represents the marked member of the opposition, both in terms of morphology and in terms of semantic distinctiveness (i.e., absence of an aspect-neutral value). As argued in detail by Bendjaballah & Reintges (2009: 141–143), the disappearance of the stem-final glide in the Imperfective strongly suggests that this verb class marker occupies the same slot in the stem template as the geminated root consonant. The point of interest here is that only the unmarked (i.e., non-geminated) member of the aspectual opposition can be inflected for the agreement paradigm of the Stative. By contrast, there are no corresponding examples with the marked Imperfective member (*ḥzz-kj 'I am being praised') – a distributional restriction first observed by Edel (1959).

(18) 1st person singular Stative derived from simplex member of bi-aspectual verbs

> ḥz-k(j)   ḥr=s   jn   nb(=j)
> praise-STAT.1SG because.of=3F.SG FOC   lord.M.SG=POSS.1SG
> 'I was praised because of it (i.e., my vigilance) by My Lord.' (Urkunden I 255: 5)

There is good reason to believe that this selectional restriction cannot be derived from the reduplicative expression type as Statives can morphologically be derived from pluractional verb stems. **Pluractionals** designate multiple, iterative, or intensified action and are formed by the full or partial reduplication of the consonantal root. Bendjaballah & Reintges (2009: 139–143) discuss formal ways to distinguish partially reduplicated Pluractionals from Imperfective verbal stems, even though the two formation types look superficially very similar.

(19) Statives derived from fully and partially reduplicated Pluractional verb stems

> a. ḥtm   ḥr=k   jm=s
>   provide.IMP face.M.SG=POSS.2M.SG with=3F.SG
>   pd-pd(-w)
>   spread.out-PLUR-STAT.3M
>   'Provide your face with it (i.e., the eye of Horus) (such that) it (i.e., the face) is suffused (with the perfume).' (Pyramid Text 29b/W)[14]

---

14 As pointed out by Faulkner (1969: 8 footnote 4), the 3rd person masculine Stative *pd-pd(-w)* 'to be suffused' cannot take the preceding direct object NP *jrt Ḥr* 'the eye of Horus' as the antecedent, due to the mismatch in gender features, but must rather be anaphorically related to *ḥr=k* 'your face'. I furthermore assume that the Stative has a purposive-final interpretation.

b. *tꜣwt*   *wrr-tj*   *m*   *tꜣ-wr*
you.M.SG   be.great.PLUR-STAT.2SG   in
tꜣ-wr
land.M.SG-be.great(-PTCP.M.SG)
'You are very great in "Great Land" (the district of Thinis).' (Pyramid
Text 877b/P)[15]

In covering a broad spectrum of meanings, imperfective aspectual categories often
have a somewhat "polysemous" character cross-linguistically (Dahl 1985: 74). Be
that as it may, the Imperfective member of the opposition is typically used for the
description of dynamic situations that involve some kind of change. Even though
the Imperfective viewpoint presents a given situation as not having reached its
natural endpoint, the temporal interval it focuses on has a clearly defined starting point, at least under an episodic interpretation. By contrast, the Stative-resultative viewpoint imposes a non-dynamic interpretation and denotes an interval
or stretch in time without internal temporal structure and hence, lacks a clearly
defined starting and endpoint. Due to this lack of temporal boundaries, all phases
of a stative situation are essentially the same. In connection with the [±DYNAMIC]
contrast, Comrie (1976: 49) observes, "With a state, unless something happens to
change that state, then the state will continue (...). With a dynamic situation, on
the other hand, the situation will only continue if it is continually subject to a new
input of energy". Smith (1991: 32) furthermore observes that in having no dynamics, states "require external agency for change". Naturally, Imperfective stems are
excluded from the Stative paradigm, as the resulting form would specify the situation that is described both as dynamic and non-dynamic, as temporally structured
or unstructured, as agentive and non-agentive. This strongly suggests that the
observed complementarity between Imperfective verbal stems and Stative agreement inflection cannot be derived from a morphological blocking effect, but must
rather be the result of conflicting aspectual specifications.

---

15 Allen (1984: 26 § 45) argues against Edel (1955/1964: 277 § 578) that "[t]he old perfective of 2ae-
gem. ["*secundae geminatae*" or second-geminate] verbs in the Pyramid Texts is regularly formed
on the base stem". This view is difficult to accept, given that other types of partially reduplicated
Pluractionals do occur in the Stative paradigm.

3.2 Arguments against a decompositional analysis

If one views the exclusion of Imperfective verbal stems from the Stative paradigm as a significant property of the Old and Early Middle Egyptian inflectional system, then a portmanteau analysis of the person–number–gender inflections suggests itself in which stative-resultative aspect and grammatical agreement marking is fused into a single unsegmentable morph. Kramer (2009: 40–54) has put forward a competing, decompositional analysis, according to which stative-resultative aspect is morphologically realized by a stem-internal vowel pattern, while grammatical agreement marking merely registers a syntactic relation between the subject and the verbal predicate but crucially lacks semantic import. As the author formulates it with regard to the former, "a stative verb is essentially comprised of three morphemes: the stative vocalic melody, the lexical consonantal root, and an agreement affix" (pg. 41).

In what follows I would like to point out some of the empirical and theoretical problems with Kramer's decompositional analysis just outlined. The major problem with this approach is quite simply the uncertainty of the evidence. The purported Stative vocalic melody is not graphically expressed in hieroglyphic writing, but is argued for on the basis of language-internal reconstruction. Although Kramer does not discuss this further, the reconstructed /a i u/ pattern goes back to Loprieno's (1995: 77–78, 257 footnotes 130–134) understanding that the Old Egyptian Stative is "originally an inflected verbal adjective" and that its vocalism can be reconstructed accordingly as that of a participle. However, as I have shown in Reintges (2005b: 111–113), participles are derived forms of the verb marked by a particular combination of verbal and nominal features. The nominal features of participles include grammatical gender and number but crucially not grammatical person, while the verbal features include aspect, tense, and mood. Active and passive participles cannot be derived from Stative-inflected verb forms, simply because grammatical agreement cannot be replaced by nominal concord inflection. In other words, a verb form not inflected for person ceases to be a Stative. Coptic no longer has a productive process of participle formation and so the material base for internal reconstruction is rather limited. The remaining active and passive participles are, however, clearly distinct from the corresponding Statives in terms of their vowel pattern, as can be seen from examples, such as *fai* (PTCP.ACT) 'carrying' vs. *fcw* (stat) 'carried' (<*fi* 'to carry) and *mesie, emsi(e)* (PTCP.PASS) 'born' vs. *moːse* (STAT) 'to be born' (<*miːse* 'to give birth') (for additional data, see Reintges 2004a: 209–210, § 6.1.3f).

The Coptic Stative has a morphology that is unusually rich and largely unpredictable. At the root of this morphological complexity lie a variety of apophonic patterns, i.e., changes in the vowel pattern that formally distinguish Eventive and

Stative stem alternants. (The Eventive alternant will be given in the absolute state form (ABS), which is used as the citation form in Coptic dictionaries.) The most basic pattern is to be found in biliteral C_1VC_2 verbs, in which the lexically specified vowel /ɔ/ of the Eventive is replaced by the vowel /ɛ/ in the corresponding Stative, e.g., *kɔt* (ABS) 'to build' vs. *kɛt* (STAT) 'to be built'. In triliteral $C_1VC_2əC_3$ verbs, apophony is restricted to the stressed first syllable, e.g., *rɔːhət* (ABS) 'to strike' vs. *raːhət* (STAT) 'to be struck'; *nuːhəm* (ABS) 'to save' vs. *naːhəm* (STAT) 'to be saved'. In addition to apophony, the Eventive–Stative alternation in "frozen" pluractional formations is formally marked by the relocation of stress (Bendjaballah & Reintges 2009: 149–152), e.g., *fórfər* (ABS) 'to destroy' vs. *fərfɔ́r* (STAT) 'to be destroyed'. In some verb classes, the originally 3rd person masculine and feminine endings *-w* and *-t* surface in the Stative (Winand 1992: 142–143 § 253), e.g., *tⁱi* (ABS) 'to take' vs. *tⁱɛw* (STAT) 'to be taken'; *ɔːɔː* (ABS) 'to conceive' vs. *eːeːt* (STAT) 'to be pregnant'; *kto* (ABS) 'to turn' vs. *ktɛw* and *ktoit* (STAT) 'to be turned'. The apophonic patterns presented here either correspond incompletely or do not correspond at all to the reconstructed /a i u/ vocalism of the Egyptian Stative. This observation raises an important methodological concern: how could any consistent Stative vocalism could be reconstructed from such a bewildering variety of apophonic patterns? As a lexical-derivational process, the Coptic Stative has a different status from that of its Old Egyptian predecessor, which represents an inflectional category of the verb. The two kinds of Statives are therefore morphologically too different from each other to be suitable cognates for the purpose of internal reconstruction. Leaving aside these concerns for the moment, I shall now turn to the synchronic evidence in support of the hypothesis that Eventive and Stative-inflected verbs share the same lexical stem. As will be recalled from Table 1 (§ 2.1), the 3rd person masculine ending of the Stative displays an alternation between *-w*, *-j*, and zero (with graphic suppression of the inflectional vowel). Exactly the same allomorphic variation can be observed for the Passive 1 morpheme *-w*. If this analysis is on the right track, the *-w/-jj* alternation that we see with the two homophonous morphological markers in biliteral (C_1VC_2) verbs must have been triggered by the stem-internal vowel. This point is further illustrated by the following two data sets.

(19)   The *-w* / *-jj* alternation in 3M Statives and Passive 1s derived from C_1VC_2 verbs

a.   3M Statives

base form	assimilated form
rx-w (Urk. I 194: 13) 'knows'	*rx-j* (PT 1223b/M) 'knows'
dꜣr-w (PT 235a/W) 'are held off'	*pdꜣ-j* (Ti, pl.72) 'is sharpened'
s-xr-w (PT 235a/W) 'is overthrown'	*wr-j* (PT 658c/T) 'great'

b. Passive 1s

base form	assimilated form
wn-w (CT II 115c/G2T) 'is opened'	*wn-jj* (PT 1203c/P) 'is opened'
mḥ-w (PT 1205b/P) 'is filled'	*mḥ-j* (PT 1205b/N) 'is filled'
s-fx-x(-w) (CT VI 357i/B3Bo)	*s-fx-x-jj* (PT Nt 801)
'is loosened'	'is loosened'

Based on language-internal reconstruction, Quack (2003: 171–173) proposes a connection between apparently "strong" biliteral verbs and the "mediae infirmae" or "hollow" verbs in Semitic languages, so called because this morphological class is characterized by an internal glide /y/ between the first and the second root consonant (C1–y–C2). In Reintges (2004b: 66–68), I have put forward a comparable analysis, according to which biliteral verbs have the corresponding front vowel /i/ in that position (C_1–i–C_2). The stem-internal vowel is generally not rendered in hieroglyphic writing (but cf. Quack 2003: 172 for the exceptional case of *mwt* 'to die'); yet its presence can be deduced from the observed phonological effects, viz., the fronting of /u/ to /y/ of the 3rd person masculine Stative inflection *-w* and the Passive 1 formative *-w*. In view of the fact that the two homophonus morphemes can undergo the same vowel-harmonic process, one may plausibly argue that they are attached to the same vocalized form of the lexical verb stem. This leads to the overall conclusion that the person–number–gender forms of the Old Egyptian Stative are portmanteau morphemes, syncretizing grammatical agreement and stative-resultative aspect.

4 Argument structure and stative-resultative aspect across different classes of verbs

The focus of the previous two sections (§§ 2–3) has been on the morphological and syntactic properties of the Old and Early Middle Egyptian Stative. In this section, we shall turn to consider the semantic dimension of the Eventive–Stative opposition, with a view to seeing how inflectional morphology interacts with situation aspect and the construals of situations. The different aspectual values of Stative-inflected verb forms will be analyzed in terms of its similarities to and differences from the corresponding active and passive verb form of the Eventive. What I intend to show in particular is that the semantic interpretation of finite verbs can be derived both from the lexical semantics associated with the consonantal root and from the inherent aspectual meaning of the selected inflectional paradigm. In other words, the meaning alternations between Eventive-inflected and Stative-inflected verbal forms are to a large extent predictable and systematic, where the locus of semantic regularity is to be sought in the regularity of paradigmatically organized inflectional morphology. This way of looking at the paradigmatic split in the Old and Early Egyptian verbal system diverges substantially from previous accounts (e.g.; Loprieno 1995: 76; Kramer 2009: 40–41), according to which the notional categories of motion versus stasis, events and states, are part of the root's lexical information.

The following description of the Eventive–Stative opposition is based on a taxonomy of verb classes, in which valency information is considered separately from argument meanings. My point of departure is the view articulated in Grimshaw's (1990) work that argument structure cannot simply be equated with the traditional notion of valence, i.e., the number of arguments related by the predicate, but rather pertains to relations of prominence between arguments and their canonical structural realizations. Generally speaking, the most prominent argument in the argument structure of a verb will be realized as the subject, while the less prominent argument, if present, will be realized as the direct object, the indirect object, and so on (see in particular the author's résumé on pp. 4–6). As has been mentioned in the introductory section of this Chapter, the Stative paradigm constitutes a grammatical voice category in its own right, indicating that the subject referent is positively or negatively affected by the situation that is described in the sentence. As an affected-subject voice, the Stative does not necessarily involve a valence-reducing operation. On the contrary, for all intents and purposes, the transitive-active use of the Stative represents a fully grammatical option of Old and Early Middle Egyptian grammar. Considering the passive syntax of the Stative, I shall try to establish ways to distinguish in semantic terms detransitivized Statives from morphological passives, which are restricted to the Eventive paradigm.

4.1 Some problems with the traditional analysis

In what follows I shall discuss some claims made in the Egyptological literature about the syntactically restricted usage of the Old and Early Middle Egyptian Stative. I intend to show that such claims have thus far not been established with certainty. Erman (1889: 74–75, 1928: 148 § 328) and Sethe (1899 II 4–5 §§ 9–12) were the first to propose that the Stative originally had two grammatical voices ("genera verbi"): transitive-active and intransitive-passive. The transitive-active form is used to describe an action (*rdj.kwj* 'I gave'). With intransitive verbs, the passive form asserts the continuation of a state (*ᶜnḫ.kwj* 'I am alive'), while it must be interpreted as a "Passive" with transitive verbs (*śḏm.kwj* 'I am heard')

[Erman's examples and transcriptions]. In his Egyptian grammar, Gardiner (1957: 237 § 311) has taken a similar stance, writing that "There can be no doubt but that, in an early lost stage of the Egyptian language, the old perfective was a freely used narrative tense with both active and passive meanings. In historic times, however, and particularly in Middle Egyptian, this tense has become much restricted and specialized in its use". Edel (1955/1964: 269–270, § 570), adopting a more synchronic perspective, has taken the view that the active use of the Stative had already been in decline in Old Egyptian. All of the above-cited scholars have stressed the exceptional character of the Stative forms of the verb of knowledge and acquisition of knowledge *rx* 'to know', whose transitive-active use is still attested in Later Egyptian (Sethe 1899 II 4 § 10; Erman 1928: 148, § 328; Gardiner 1957: 237, § 311; Edel 1955/1964: 284, § 588).[16] Gardiner (1957: 238, § 312) and Edel (1955/1964: 284, § 590) have furthermore commented on the relative frequency of transitive-active 1st person singular Statives in the autobiographical inscriptions of the late Fifth and the Sixth Dynasties (2300–2155 BCE). This use is said to be an archaic trait of the autobiographical genre and hence, no longer fully productive.[17] However, without supporting statistical evidence, it seems rather difficult to evaluate the purported unproductivity of transitive-active Statives. All that can be said is that there is a fair amount of examples for exactly this use in the Pyramid Texts, and, as I shall demonstrate in a moment, in the closely related corpus of the Coffin Texts.

---

16 More recently, Oréal (2010: 150 footnote 38) has proposed that "the active use of the Pseudoparticiple is well attested in historical times with the verb *rḫ*, which may hint to the fact that, having undergone some sort of lexicalization due to the frequency with the meaning 'to know', it was able to resist the progressive elimination of the active interpretation of the form". The grammaticalization of Stative *rx* as a modal auxiliary 'can' with infinitival complements conforms to the crosslinguistic tendency for verbs of knowledge and acquisition of knowlegde to form particularly prominent lexical sources for modal verbs that express ability and possibility (see Reintges 2011a: 45–46, 62, 70–71 for a more detailed discussion of the diachronic process)".
17 Cf. also Oréal (2010: 152) for a restatement of the traditional view that the narrative use of 1st person singular Statives in autobiographical discourse represents an archaism: "The paucity of attestation for active transitive Pseudoparticiple with V–S order in the Pyramid Texts can be explained by the absence of narrative setting using the 1SG, which appears as the only historical context exhibiting this remnant of its Proto-Egyptian use as a perfective.

(20) The transitive-active use of the Stative in the Pyramid Texts

a. 1SG *jnk Nwt   msnt'̓t   njs-kj*
I   Nut.F.SG granary.F.SG call-STAT.1SG
rn   Wsjr   Pjpj
name.M.SG Osiris.M.SG Pepi.M.SG
'I (am) Nut, the Granary. I have called the name of Osiris Pepi.'
(Pyramid Text 786a/P)

b. 2SG *hꜣ   Nfr-kꜣ-Rꜥ   pw*
VOC Nefer-ka-Re.M.SG DEM.M.SG
wnx-tj   dꜣt=k
cover-STAT.2M.SG body.M.SG =POSS.2M.SG
'Oh (you) (King) Nefer-ka-Re (here), you should cover up yourself (lit. your body)!' (Pyramid Text 2119/N)

c. 3F   *n-jwt   mwt=k*
for-COMP.NEG mother.F.SG=POSS.2M.SG
ms-tj   t'̓w   m   rmt'̓-w
give.birth-STAT.3F CL.2M.SG among man-M.PL
'Because (of the fact) that (there is) no mother of yours (such
that) she has given birth to you among men.' (Pyramid Text
659d/T)

There is reason to believe that Pyramid Text discourse has an oral-compositional
form that manifests traditional language use (Reintges 2011b). However, this does
not carry over to the contemporaneous autobiographical inscriptions, which represent to a large extent a new literary genre. A salient feature of this genre is the
routinized usage of 1st person singular Statives as a narrative tense. Although this
possibility cannot be ruled out a priori, it seems unlikely that this stylistic innovation originated in a virtually obsolete syntactic pattern. We will have occasion to
return to this issue in the next section.

4.2 On the narrative use of 1st person singular Statives in late Old Kingdom autobiographies

The use of 1st person singular Statives as a narrative past tense has long been observed in the Egyptological literature but has, as of yet, not received an entirely satisfactory explanation. Schenkel (1971: 304) has proposed that the Stative places emphasis on the initiative of the speaker. Here I suggest a modification of this view, according to which this contextualized use of 1st person singular Stative represents a metaphorical extension of the core affectedness meaning. In other words, in expressing affected subjecthood besides grammatical agreement and "*Aktionsart*", the Stative provides a particularly suitable narrative viewpoint from which to represent the lifetime achievements of the deceased speaker. Consider in this regard the next example, which describes the speaker's holding of a high office of state. The 1st person singular Stative *jr-k(j) n=f mr ʃmʕ* 'I did for him the (office of) Overseer of Upper Egypt' appears in the concluding paragraph of a narrative segment and thus belongs to the **backgrounded** portion of the discourse that amplifies or comments on the main plot.

(21) Occurrence of first person singular Stative in backgrounded part of the discourse

> *jr-k(j)*   *n=f*   *mr*   *ʃmʕ*
> do-STAT.1SG for=3M.SG   overseer.M.SG Upper.Egypt
> *r*   *hr-t*
> according.to   be.content-GER.F.SG
> 'I fulfilled (lit. I did) for him (the King) the (office of) Overseer of Upper Egypt satisfactorily (lit. according to satisfaction).' (Urkunden I 106: 4)[18]

As has already been noted by Schenkel (1971: 303–304), Osing (1977: 166–168), Loprieno (1995: 77–78), Oréal (2010: 152–153), and others, the autobiographical genre of this period shows a tendency to resort to the Stative for first person singular narration, while the Perfect and, to a lesser extent, the Simple Past are used for the description of past events performed by the other interlocutors. In other words, the 1st person singular Stative can also be used to narrate the main course of events that are presented in temporal sequential order. In this case, the per-

---

18 A paradigmatic example for the transitive-active use of the light verb *jr(.j)* 'to do'; cf. Edel (1955/1964: 285 § 590α).

spectivizing function of the Stative is clearly related to the **foregrounded** parts of the discourse. The following three examples are meant to illustrate this point.

(22) Occurrence of first person singular Stative in foregrounded part of the discourse

   a. *s-hꜢ-k(j)*   *n=f*   *htp*
   CAUS-descend-STAT.1SG for=3M.SG offering.table.M.SG
   pn   *n*   *hrw-w*   *17*
   DEM.M.SG in day-M.PL 17
   'I transported for him (the King) this offering table in 17 days.'
   (Urkunden I 108: 1)

   b. *dꜢꜢ-k(j)*   *m* *nmj-w* *ḥnꜤ*
   cross.over-STAT.1SG in ship-M.PL with
   tʲz-wt   *ptn*
   troop-F.PL DEM.F.PL
   'I crossed over in transport ships together with these troops.' (Urkunden I 104: 14–15)

   c. *rdꜢ-k(j)*   *fꜢ-t(j)=f*   *jn* *tʲz-wt*
   give-STAT.1SG carry-PASS2=3M.SG FOC troop-F.PL
   n(j)-t   *pr*   *n(j)*   *dꜢt*
   LINK-F.SG house.M.SG LINK.M.SG eternity.F.SG
   'I arranged for him (the deceased father) to be carried by the troops of the House of Eternity.' (Urkunden I 136: 17)

The opposition between 1st person singular Statives on the one hand and 3rd person Perfect and Simple Past tense forms on the other hand signals different degrees of **empathetic involvement**, in the sense of Fleischman (1989: 24). In particular, narratively used 1st person singular Statives perform a function at the higher order of discourse structure: the affected subject viewpoint inherent to this verbal paradigm is metaphorically extended into a subjective mode for representing the major events in the life-time of the deceased speaker as having lasting effects in the present. This meaning component is not present in the narrative episodes relating to other discourse participants, which are represented from a more neutral retrospective perspective as historical events. Despite appearances, the perspectivizing function of the Stative in autobiographical discourse does not provide any conclusive evidence for its dynamic value. Even though I do not share Oréal's (2009: 192) skepticism about a discourse-based approach to analyzing this phenomenon, I would readily admit that it is very difficult to effectively render the affectedness connotation of first person singular Statives in this text genre.

4.3 The active syntax and use of transitive-based Statives

The focus of this section is on the syntactic and interpretational properties of transitive-active Statives. I shall first look at the different types of complements that Statives may select and then turn to the Eventive–Stative opposition in different lexical classes of verbs.

4.3.1 Direct object syntax

As is well known, transitive-active Statives are compatible with the same types of complements as their Eventive counterparts. In accordance with the Subject–Verb–Object (SVO) order of Stative sentences, the direct object must appear in postverbal position. Examples with direct object NPs and enclitic direct object pronouns are shown in examples (23a) and (23b), respectively.

(23) Transitive-active Statives with direct object NP and direct object clitic

    a.   *nḥm-kw*   *Rꜥ*   *m-ꜥ*   *ꜥꜣpp*

        save-STAT.1SG Re.M.SG from-arm.M.SG Apophis.M.SG

        rꜥ   *nb*

        day.M.SG each.M.SG

        'I save (the sun god) Re from (the god) Apophis every day.' (Coffin Text VII 403b/B12C)

    b.   *jw=tⁱn*   *rx-tjwn*   *wj*

        AUX=2PL learn-STAT.1SG CL.1SG

        'You (plural) know me.' (Coffin Text II 24b/B1C)

Subordinated clause with or without a complementizer may be used equally well as complements of transitive-active Statives. (Brackets demarcate the embedded clause.)

(24)   Transitive-active Statives with direct object clauses

    a. *j(w)=k*   *rx-t(j)*   *[ntt*   *ḏd-n*

       AUX=2M.SG learn-STAT.2SG COMP say-PERF

       Jdw   *r*   *sꜣ=f (...)]*

       Idu.M.SG about son.M.SG=POSS.3M.SG

       'You know that Idu said about his son(...)' (Letters to the Dead, Haskell Museum 13945: 1)

    b. *j-mr-k(j)*   *[nḏꜣ=k*   *jrt=k*

       AUG-love-STAT.1SG save.PFV=3M.SG eye.F.SG=POSS.2M.SG

       m-ꜥ   *jr*   *n=k]*

       from-arm.2M.SG do.PFV(-PTCP.M.SG) for=2M.SG

       'I have the wish to save your eye from him who acts for you.' (Coffin Text VI 220j/L2Li)[19]

It is also possible, though not very common, for transitive-active Statives to have an unspecified object argument, which is interpreted as inanimate. The content of the missing object can either be inferred from the extra-linguistic situation and world knowledge or is supplied anaphorically by the previous discourse. Thus, the understood object in example (25a) refers to goods that can be exported from the Wadi Hudi, such as precious stones, while it refers to previously mentioned activities of the 1st person singular narrator in example (25b).

(25)   Transitive-active Statives with elliptical direct objects

    a. *jn-k(j)*   *jm*   *r-ꜥꜣ-t*

       bring-STAT.1SG there PREP-be.great-PTCP.F.SG

       wr-t

       be.great-PTCP.F.SG

       'I used to import a lot from there.' (Wadi Hudi Inscription no. 14: 10)

---

19 Cf. also Edel (1955/1964: 278 § 579) for the prothetic yod form of the 1st person singular Stative *j-mr-k(j)*, translated by him as "Ich wollte" ("I wanted").

b. *jr-k(j)*   *mj-qd*   *r*   *ħz-t*
    do-STAT.1SG   altogether   to   praise-INF
    w(j)   *ħm=f*   *ħr=s*
    CL.1SG   majesty.M.SG=POSS.3M.SG   for=3F.SG
    'I used to act in every respect such that His Majesty would praise me
    for it.' (Urkunden I 106: 11)[20]

The above examples provide further illustration for the narrative use of 1st person singular Statives. The most natural interpretation of the entire clause is one of a Past Habitual, which, in the absence of information to the contrary, conveys the implicature that the recurrent events or activities reported in that clause no longer hold at the present moment. In this connection, it is interesting to note – as does Mittwoch (2005: 243–249) – that missing object pronouns are much commoner in habitual sentences than in episodic ones, as in the case at hand.

4.3.2 The Eventive–Stative opposition in transitive-active verbs

The Eventive–Stative opposition is attested in different lexical classes of transitive verbs, although the difference in meaning between the Eventive and the Stative alternant is often hard to pinpoint exactly. This is particularly the case in examples where the Eventive verb form contains the Perfect marker -*n*. As a first approximation, transitive-active Statives convey an object-oriented **possessive resultative** meaning. That is to say that the resultant state attained by the referent of the direct object has some positive or negative effect on the referent of the subject. As Nedjalkov & Jaxontov (1988: 25 § 3.3) put it, "in the secondary possessive resultative the state expressed by the form of the objective or, even, subject resultative (...) happens to be important for a person who is in some way involved in the resulting state. This person can be loosely called **possessor**". [Boldface in the original]. Consider in this regard the minimal sentence pair in (26), which involves the transitive verb *qrs* 'to bury'. This verb can be classified as a "verb of putting in a spatial configuration" (i.e., to place a dead body in the ground). The 1st person singular Perfect *qrs-n(=j)* 'I buried (my father)' in the a-example and the corresponding Stative in the b-example describe what is objectively the same situation (cf. also Edel 1955/1964: 285 § 590α). Yet the two inflected verb forms differ from each other with respect to the participant role of the subject.

---

20 The use of transitive-active Statives with omitted object pronoun has already noted by Edel (1955/1966: 285 § 590α), with particular reference to the above-cited passage.

In the Perfect, the completion of the event that is described principally affects the referent of the direct object, while the referent of the subject is presented as the initiator, agent, or effector of that event. Stative subjects, on the other hand, have a non-agentive interpretation. With transitive-active verbs, the subject denotes the entity on which the state of the direct object has a positive or negative impact. Thus, even though Stative subjects are non-agentive, their referent may be involved in the development of the state attained by the referent of the direct object. In sentence (26b), the lasting effects on the speaker by his own actions are explicitly stated in the following sentence, which gives a description of the impressive rewards allotted to him by the royal court.

(26) The Perfect–Stative alternation in "verbs of putting in a spatial configuration"

a. *jw*   *qrs-n(=j)*   *jt(=j)*   *pn*
    AUX   bury-PERF=1SG   father.M.SG=POSS.1SG   DEM.M.SG
    m   *jz=f*   *n(j)*   *χrt-nṯr*
    in   tomb.M.SG=POSS.3M.SG   LINK.M.SG   necropolis.M.SG
    'I buried this father of mine in his tomb of the necropolis.' (Urkunden I 139: 1)

b. *qrs-k(j)*   *z*   *pn*   *m*
    bury-STAT.1SG   man.M.SG   DEM.M.SG   in
    jz=f   *mḥj*   *Nxb*
    tomb.M.SG=POSS.3M.SG   north(-PTCP.M.SG)   Nekheb.M.SG
    rdꜣ-t(j)   *n(=j)*   *ꜣḥt*   *stꜣt*   *45*
    give-PASS2   to=1SG   field.F.SG   aroura.F.SG   45
    m   *tꜣ-mḥj*   *ʃmʕw (...)*
    in   Lower.Egyp.M.SG   Upper.Egypt. M.SG
    r   *ḥz-t*   *bꜣk*   *jm*
    to   praise-INF   servant.M.SG   there
    'I had this man buried in his tomb north of Nekheb. A field of forty-five arouras (of land) was given to me each in Lower and Upper Egypt (...) to reward this servant.' (Urkunden I 140: 8–11)

In a sense, then, the Eventive may be thought of as an **effective** and the Stative an **affective** verbal-inflectional paradigm. Klaiman (1991: 69–82) discusses comparable phenomena in Tamil, which are analyzed in terms of an active-middle voice contrast. Let us now turn to "verbs of creation", such as *jwr* 'to conceive, become pregnant' and *msj* 'to give birth, deliver'. As pointed out by Levin & Rappaport Hovav (1995: 247–248), members of this class describe the coming into existence of a new entity as the result of the very act of creation. For this reason, creation verbs in English are conventionally analyzed as having a complex event structure, which comprises a process sub-event through which an entity comes to exist, and a resultant state component, which asserts the existence of the newly created entity at some place, with its previous non-existence being presupposed. The Eventive–Stative alternation in Ancient Egyptian creation verbs is illustrated in examples (27a–b). The coordinated Simple Past Tense forms *jwr=s* 'she conceived' and *msj=s* 'she delivered' describe a previously occurring birth-giving event, whose resultant state (the existence of the reborn king in the hereafter) is not explicitly mentioned, although it is semantically implied. The corresponding 1st person singular Statives *j(w)r-kw* 'I have become pregnant' and *ms-kw* 'I have given birth' work in the opposite direction insofar as they highlight the resultant state without further specifying the causing event.[21] It therefore looks as if the selection of the Eventive and the Stative viewpoint correlates with the up- or downgrading of one component in the complex event structure of creation verbs.

(27) The Eventive–Stative alternation in "verbs of creation"

a. *jwr=s*   *sw*   *ms.j=s*   *sw*
conceive.PFV=3FSG CL.3M.SG give.birth.PFV=3F.SG CL.3M.SG
'She conceived and delivered him (the deceased king).' (Pyramid Text 1370a/P)

b. *j(w)r-kw*   *ʃdw*   *ms-kw*
conceive-STAT.1SG lower.sky.M.SG give.birth-STAT.1SG
pdꜣw
upper.sky.M.SG
'I have become pregnant with the lower sky andgiven birth to the upper sky.' (Coffin Text IV 51e–f/B3L)

The possessive sense of transitive-active Statives is, however, much more pronounced in the verb of knowledge and acquisition of knowledge *rx* 'to learn,

---

21 It may very well be the case that the affected subject is viewed more abstractly as the possessor and the direct object referent as the possessed item, as in Nedjalkov & Jaxontov's (1988: 25 § 3.3) analysis. According to this view, an appropriate semantic paraphrase of the conjoined first person singular Statives *j(w)r-kw* and *ms-kw* in sentence (27b) of the main text would be something like "I am the begetter of the lower sky" and "I am the mother of the upper sky", respectively.

understand'. The 1st person Perfect form *rx-n(=j)* 'I have learnt' in sentence (28a) makes reference to the acquisition of secret knowledge, while the possession of that knowledge is designated by the Stative counterpart *rx-k(j)* 'I know' in sentence (28b).

(28) The Perfect–Stative alternation in the "verb of knowledge and acquisition of knowledge" *rx*

a. *jw   rx-n(=j)   ħkʔ   nb*
   AUX   learn-PERF=1SG   magic.M.SG each M.SG
   ʃtʔ   n(j)   ynw
   secret.M.SG LINK.M.SG   residence.M.SG
   'I learned about every secret magic of the residence.' (Urkunden I 143: 2)

b. *jw   rx-k(j)   ħkʔ   nb*
   AUX   learn-STAT.1SG   secret.M.SG every.M.SG
   ʔx   n=f   m   yrt-ntʲr
   be.glorious(-PTCP.M.SG) for=3M.SG   in   necropolis.M.SG
   'I know (through learning) every magic by means of which one becomes glorious in the necropolis.' (Urkunden I 263: 14)

To conclude this section with a comparative note, the possibility of having transitive-active Statives in a language is unexpected under current analyses of the stative as a detransitivizing morpho-lexical operation that eliminates the agent and associates the patient or theme argument with the grammatical subject role. Dubinsky & Simango (1996) and Mchombo (2004: 98–102) present an analysis along these lines for the Chichewa [Bantu] Stative. As will become clear as we proceed, there are other problems with a detransitivizing voice analysis of the Old and Early Middle Egyptian Stative.

4.4 Statives formed from intransitive verbs

Having addressed the controversial issue of transitive Statives, I shall now turn to the contrastive semantic behaviour between Eventives and Statives in intransitive verbs, which is more transparent. Intransitive verbs seem to constitute a fairly homogeneous class of verbs with a single argument in subject position. Yet, there is an increasing body of evidence that the class of intransitive verbs is actually split up into two subclasses, which have come to be known as **unergatives** and

unaccusatives in the linguistic literature (see Perlmutter 1978 for the original proposal). According to the "Unaccusative Hypothesis", unergative and unaccusative intransitives are associated with distinct syntactic and semantic properties. In terms of argument structure, unergative verbs such as *laugh* and *dance* in English select an agent argument that corresponds in grammatical behaviour to the subject of a transitive verb. By contrast, the single argument of unaccusative verbs such *die* and *fall* displays many of the semantic and the coding properties of direct objects. The classification of intransitive verbs either as unergative or as unaccusative is complicated due to the fact that some verb classes show a variable behaviour. In any event, the unergative–unaccusative distinction should be established on language-internal grounds. In my dissertation (Reintges 1997: 222–230), I have shown that Old and Early Middle Egyptian impersonal passives can be derived from unergative but not from unaccusative verbs, with impersonal passives providing a crosslinguistically stable diagnostic for unergativity.

4.4.1 The Eventive–Stative opposition in unergative verbs

Here I shall concentrate on two classes of verbs that lexicalize motion and location in space – notions that are considered as central for the construal of events. The first class comprises "verbs of spatial configuration" and the second class "verbs of directed motion". The detailed study of spatial configuration verbs by Levin & Rappaport Hovav (1995: 126–133, 142–144, 163–164) reveals two basic senses of the non-causativized forms. The first sense is the "assume position" sense, which describes an animate subject obtaining a particular position under his or her control. With assume position verbs, the subject is typically a human, volitional agent. The second sense is the "simple position" sense, which is non-agentive and describes the position of the subject with respect to a particular location. Considering the case of the cardinal spatial configuration verbs ꜥḥꜥ 'to stand (up)' and ḥms 'to sit (down)' in Old and Early Middle Egyptian, it can be observed that the agentive and non-agentive senses are distinguished on a morphological basis. When appearing in the Eventive paradigm, the two verbs display an agentive "assume position" sense. This point is illustrated by examples (29a) and (30a). The corresponding Statives are used as simple position verbs, which describe simultaneously the at-rest position of the subject referent and its location with respect to some deictic reference point, to wit, the rising sun in example (29b) and the divine throne in example (30b).

(29) The Eventive–Stative alternation in the "verb of spatial configuration"
ʕḥʕ

    a.   *ʕḥʕ=k*   *r=k*   *m*
        stand.up.PFV=2M.SG   PCL=2M.SG   in
        jtr-tj   *ʔxt*   *ḥr*   *ʃw*
        chapel-F.DU horizon.F.SG on void.M.SG
        n(j)   *nwt*
        LINK.M.SG   sky.F.SG
        'You stand up in the two chapels of the horizon on the void of the
        sky.' (Pyramid Text 1992a/N)

    b.   *ʕḥʕ-tj*   *xft*   *Rʔ*   *pr=f*
        stand-STAT.2SG before Re.M.SG come.PFV=3M.SG
        m   *jʔbt*
        from east.F.SG
        'You are standing before (the sun-god) Re (when) he comes from the
        East.' (Pyramid Text 743b/T)

(30) The Eventive–Stative alternation in the "verb of spatial configuration"
ḥms

    a.   *ḥms*   *Nfr-kʔ-Rʕ*   *jr*   *rmn=k*
        sit.PFV Nefer-ka-Re.M.SG at shoulder.M.SG=POSS.2M.SG
        Ḥr
        Horus. M.SG
        '(King) Nefer-ka-Re takes a seat beside you, Horus.' (Pyramid Text
        2056a/N)

    b.   *j-ḥms-t(j)*   *ḥr*   *nst*
        AUG-sit-STAT.2SG on throne.F.SG
        jt=k   *Gbb*   *m-xnt*   *jtrt*
        father.M.SG=POSS.2M.SG Geb.M.SG   in-front chapel.F.SG
        ḥr *xnd*   *pw*   *n(j)*   *bjʔ*
        on chair.M.SG DEM.M.SG   LINK.M.SG iron.M.SG
        'You are seated on the throne of your father (the god) Geb before the
        chapel on this iron chair.' (Pyramid Text 1992b–c/N)

In connection with inherently directed motion verbs, Levin & Rappaport Hovav
(2010: 27–29) have pointed out more recently that members of this class conflate
the notions of motion and path. Furthermore, the direction of motion shares

important properties in common with results. The directed motion verb *descend*, for instance, specifies the direction of motion (downward) but not the manner in which the motion is effectuated. In addition, the lexicalized path component of this verb constitutes an ordered scale, in which the points on the path are ordered in the direction of gravity. Consider now the case of the Perfect–Stative alternation with the Egyptian equivalent *hꜣ(.j)* 'to descend'. In example (31a), the 1st person singular Perfect *hꜣ-n(=j)* 'I descended' asserts that the speaker has completed his/her trajectory, while the clause-final adverb *m spꜣt(=j)* 'from my district' specifies the starting point of that trajectory. The arrival of the subject at some location is not overtly expressed, even though it is semantically implied. As illustrated by example (32b), the displacement and the downward motion sense is backgrounded in the corresponding Stative form *hꜣ-k(j)* 'I have come down', which rather focuses on the presence of the subject at the terminus of the trajectory that he or she has travelled.

(31)   The Eventive–Stative opposition in the inherently directed motion verb *hꜣ(.j)*

    a.   *hꜣ-n(=j)*   *m*   *spꜣt(=j)*
        descend-PERF=1SG   from district.F.SG=POSS.1SG
        'I have descended from my district.' (Urkunden I 121: 12)[22]

    b.   *jw*   *hꜣ-k(j)*   *r*   *ꜣbdꜣw*
        AUX descend-STAT.1SG to   Abydos.M.SG
        ꜥr   *Rs*
        under Res.M.SG
        'I have come down to Abydos (i.e., I am now in Abydos) with Res.'
        (stele Metropolitan Museum NY 65.107:4)[23]

---

22 This formula occurs in the opening paragraph of late Old Kingdom tomb inscriptions. It is used as a metaphor describing the rite du passage from life to death – a process that involves two successive stages: the departure from the city of the living and the entry into the realm of the dead (i.e., the necropolis) (see Schenkel 1965: 61 footnote 2).

23 Although the end of the line is partially damaged, enough traces remain to reconstruct the word *rs* (Goedicke 1960: 290, note g, fig. 3). The following line *jw dj-n(=j) hꜣ=f r pr=f m hr-jb njwt* "I let him descend to his home in the middle of the city" (stela Metropolitan Museum NY no. 65.107: 5) seems to suggest that the primary purpose of Djemi's expedition to Abydos was to reinstate one of his followers in his former position (but cf. Goedicke 1960 : 290 notes g–k for an opposite view, which is based on his interpretation of *rs* as 'captured enemy').

The inherently directed motion verbs *jj* and *jw* 'to go, to come' do not fully lexicalize the direction of motion, which must rather be determined externally from the surrounding syntactic context. In particular, both verbs have a deictic orientation, whereby the points on the path are ordered according to whether they get closer to or further away from the deictic centre, i.e., the present location of the speaker. When inflected for the Stative, *jj* and *jw* no longer function as motion verbs "stricto senso", but rather show a more grammaticalized use as a locative auxiliary. The only extra contribution that they make is to add a presentative sense of appearing on stage. As pointed out by Levin & Rappaport Hovav (1995: 242) for the very similar case of English *come*, such a presentative sense is not part of the meaning of other existential auxiliaries.

(32)   The Perfect–Stative alternation in the deictic motion verb *jj*

a.   *jj-n*   *Wnjs*   *m*   *jw*   *nsjsj*
  come-PERF   Unas.M.SG   in   island.M.SG   fire.M.SG
  '(King) Unas has come into the island of fire.' (Pyramid Text 265b/W)

b.   *m*   *Wnjs*   *jj(-w)*
  INTERJ   Unas.M.SG   come-STAT.3M
  m   *Wnjs*   *jj(-w)*
  INTERJ   Unas.M.SG   come-STAT.3M
  m   *Wnjs*   *pr(-w)*
  INTERJ   Unas. M.SG   come.forth-STAT.3M
  'Look, (King) Unas has arrived! Look, (King) Unas has arrived! Look, (King) Unas has come forth!' (Pyramid Text 333a/W)

In summary then: when appearing in the Stative paradigm, verbs of spatial configuration and verbs of inherently directed motion display unaccusative behaviour, with the Stative subject being interpreted as the theme (i.e., the located entity). The Stative-inflected verb, on its part, comes very close in meaning to a positional or locative auxiliary.

4.4.2 The Eventive–Stative opposition in unaccusative verbs

It is a typologically well-established observation that statives display a close semantic affinity with unaccusatives. A particularly clear case in point is statives and unaccusatives in Chichewa, both of which have a patient/theme NP as a subject and may both undergo locative inversion. On such grounds, Mchombo

(2004: 100–102) proposes that the stative should then be subsumed under the phenomenon of unaccusativity. There is reason to believe that the Old and Early Middle Egyptian Stative cannot be so subsumed and that stativity–resultativity does not instantiate a genuine unaccusative category. Not only are there a considerable number of transitive-active Statives, it is also rather common to derive Statives from bona fide unaccusative verbs.

To explore the Stative–Unaccusative relation in this language, "verbs of quality, size, and colour", which denote physical characteristics of the subject referent, provide a convenient point of departure. Members of this class in English are based on adjectives and may form causative alternants, which are either zero-related to the adjectival base (e.g., *to clean, to empty*) or are marked morphologically by the derivational suffix *-en* (e.g., *to redden, to flatten*). In Levin & Rappaport Hovav's (1995: 95–96, 283) classification, deadjectival verbs that form the base for alternating verbs of change of state are characterized as externally caused. As shown by the contrast between examples (33a) and (33b), the adjectival verb *wʔdꝫ* 'to be green, fresh' can be found in the causative alternation, with the transitive alternant appearing in the Eventive. The Stative variant is always intransitive and describes the present condition or state of the subject. As already discussed in the introductory section, this kind of state is in principle reversible and can therefore be temporally restricted and transitory.

(33) The causative alternation in the colour verb *wʔdꝫ*

    a. *wʔdꝫ=j*   *n(j)*   *ꜥnx*
        pillar.amulet.M.SG=POSS.1SG   LINK.M.SG   life.M.SG
        m-ꜥ=j   *wʔdꝫ-jj=j*   *rxjjt=j*
        in-arm.M.SG=POSS.1SG   be.green-PROS=1SG   people.F.SG=POSS.1SG
        'My pillar amulet of life (is) with me. I shall refresh (lit. make green) my people.' (Coffin Text VII 165b–c/pap. Gardiner III)

    b. *jj*   *n=k*   *sn-t(j)=k*   *Ist*   *Nbt-Ḥr*
        come.PFV to=2M.SG   sister-F.DU=POSS.2M.SG   Isis Nephthys.F.SG
        s-wdꝫʔ=sn(j)   *kw (...)*
        CAUS-be.healthy.PFV=3DU   CL.2M.SG
        wʔdꝫ-t(j)   *wr-t(j)*   *m*   *rn=k*
        be.green-STAT.2SG be.great-STAT.2SG in   name.M.SG=POSS.2M.SG

n(j)   *wꜣḏꜣ-wr*
LINK.M.SG   be.great(-PTCP)M.SG-be.great(-PTCP)M.SG
'Your two sisters (the goddesses) Isis and Nephthys come to you to heal you (...), (and so) you are green (and) you are great in your name of the "Great Green One" (i.e., the Mediterranean Sea).' (Pyramid Text 628a–c/M)

Outside of the causative alternation, the Perfective-neutral aspect form of verbs of quality, size, and colour can be used to indicate inchoative aspect, which refers to the coming about of the state named by verb, without the agent. As pointed out by Smith (1995: 34–35), inchoatives often allow the inference that the resultant state continues, unless there is information to the contrary. The Stative provides a direct representation of the target state and denotes the physical condition or quality of the subject after the change of state has taken place. The minimal sentence pair in (34a–b) further illustrates this point.

(34)   The inchoative-stative alternation

     a.   *ꜣx-n=f*   *m*   *ꜣxt*
        be.glorious-PERF=3M.SG   in   horizon.F.SG
        ḏꜣd-n=f   *m*   *Ḏꜣdwt*
        endure-PERF=3M.SG   in   Djedut.F.SG
        'He has become glorious in the horizon (and) he has become enduring in Djedut (toponym).' (Pyramid Text 350c/T)

     b.   *ꜣx-t(j)*   *m*   *ꜣxt*   *ḏꜣd.t-t(j)*
        be.glorious-STAT.2SG   in   horizon.F.SG   endure-STAT.2SG
        m   *Ḏꜣdwt*
        in   Djedut.F.SG
        'You are glorious in the horizon (and) you are enduring in Djedut.' (Pyramid Text 1261b/N)

Even the most typical member of the unaccusative class, the verb *mwt* 'to die', participates in the inchoative-stative alternation. Levin & Rappaport Hovav (1995: 302–303 note 8) have classified unaccusative *die* as a "verb of disappearance". The Eventive variant of *mwt* refers to the process of dying, through which an entity comes to exist no more, while the Stative denotes the resultant dead state. Thus, compare example (35a) with example (35b).

(35) The inchoative-stative alternation with the "verb of disappearance" *mwt*

a. *n(j) m(w)t Nt   n- njswt n(j)*
   NEG die.PFV Neith.F.SG for- king   NEG
   m(w)t   Nt   n- rmt́-w
   die.PFV Neith.F.SG for man-M.PL
   '(Queen) Neith shall not die because of a king. (Queen) Neith shall not die because of people.' (Pyramid Text Neith 694 [plate 26])[24]

b. *jʔm-n   Nḥb-kʔw   mtwt*
   burn-PERF Nekheb-kau.M.SG semen.F.SG
   Hjw   mwt-tj
   Hiu–serpent.M.SG die-STAT.3F
   '(The god) Nekheb-kau burned the semen of the Hiu-serpent (such that it is) dead.' (Pyramid Text Neith 717 [plate 27])

The availability of unaccusative Statives in this language shows fairly clearly that stative aspect and and unaccusativity are two separate categories of verbal semantics, which should not be equated in the theoretical analysis.

4.5 The passive syntax and use of detransitivized Statives

Old Egyptian, and, to a lesser degree, Early Middle Egyptian, is a language with multiple passives, which all belong to the Eventive paradigm. As far as one can tell, there are no passive Statives in the morphological sense, whereby active and passive meanings are registered by changes in the inflectional morphology. The passive syntax of detransitivized Statives has long been acknowledged in Egyptological linguistics. Even so, as of yet little scholarly attention has been devoted to the contrastive semantic behaviour between morphological passives and passively interpreted Statives.[25] A comparable contrast between eventive passives

---

24 Quack (2003: 172) argues that the plene writing *mwt* is only sparsely attested in the Pyramid Texts. Moreover, the "mediae *y*" variant *mjjt* in *n(j) mjjt=k* "you shall not die" (Pyramid Text 657e/T) has to be taken into consideration (cf. Allen 1984: 557 § 736).

25 Edel (1955/1964: 284 § 589), for instance, claims that there are no semantic differences between passively interpreted Statives and morphological passives: "there is no difference in in meaning with respect to the passive *sḏm-f* form ("es besteht kein Unterschied in der Bedeutung gegenüber der passiven *sḏm–f* Form" [my translation from German].

and statives has been observed in the voice system of such diverse languages as English (Wasow 1977; Levin & Rappaport 1986), German (Kratzer 2000), and Chichewa (Mchombo 1993; Dubinsky & Simango 1996).

4.5.1 The contrastive semantic behaviour between morphological passives and detransitivized Statives

The evidence presented in §§ 4.1 to 4.3 reveals that the Old and Early Middle Egyptian Stative does not necessarily involve a valence-reducing operation. The referent of the affected, animate subject may, in fact, be acting upon an inanimate patient to induce a change of state. In many cases, however, Stative-inflected verbs appear in intransitive clauses whose affected subject is associated with the semantic role of patient, experiencer, and theme. Such detransitivized Statives run parallel to morphological passives, which align the NP bearing the patient or theme role with the grammatical subject function. In spite of these overlapping functions, the two grammatical voices differ in important respects. One such difference concerns the dynamic-stative contrast. In depicting dynamic situations from the viewpoint of the patient, morphological passives are eventive in a sense in which detransitivized Statives are not. The passive-stative opposition can conveniently be illustrated with examples of the kind in (36a–c).

(36) Morphological passives vs. detransitivized Stative

   a. *ḥz-t(j)(=j)*   *ḥr=s*
     praise-PASS2=1SG   for=3F.SG
     ꜥꜣ   *wr-t*
     be.great(-PTCP.M.SG) be.much-PTCP.F.SG
     'I was praised for it very much.' (Urkunden I 124:15)

   b. *ḥz-kw*   *ḥr=s*   *m*   *pr*   *njswt*
     praise-STAT.1SG for=3F.SG in house.M.SG king.M.SG
     'I was praised (lit. in a praised state) for it in the palace.' (Beni Hasan I, plate 8,northern jamb A3–4)

c. *ms-jj(=j)*   *m*   *grḥ*   *m-jj*
give.birth-PASS1=1SG at   night.M.SG   come-IMP.PL
ms-[k]j
give.birth-STAT.1SG
'I was born at night. Come! I am (in a) new-born (state).' (Pyramid Text 714a/P")[26]

Morphological passives such as *ms-jj=j* 'I was born' imply the presence of an agent even when it is not syntactically expressed. The identity of the implicit agent is either contextually given or inferable from pragmatic world knowledge. In the case at hand, the birth-giving event presupposes the involvement of a delivering female. The corresponding Stative *ms-kj* 'I am (in a) new-born (state)', on the other hand, describes the speaker's having entered a particular condition or state but such that there is no implication of agency responsible for this condition or state.

One might think, as I did in my dissertation (Reintges 1997: 191), that agentless passives represent the prototypical passive construction in this language. Viewed from this perspective, passive voice is a syntactic means for not revealing the identity of the agent or the instigator of the action that is described. However, all three morphological passive patterns allow the overt expression of the agent to yield a canonical passive construction in the traditional grammarian sense. As pointed out by Siewierska (1984: 35–36) and, more recently, by Ward et al. (2002: 1444–1445 § 10.2), canonical passives in English are only felicitous under certain pragmatic conditions. In particular, the passive subject must not represent information that is newer in the discourse than the demoted agent. In marking the demoted agent as the focus constituent of the passive sentence, the information structure of canonical passives has a morphological correlate in the presence of the focus particle *jn* on the sentence-final agent expression (for the syntax of the focus marker *jn*, see Reintges 1998 and Güldemann, this volume). The overt focus marking of the passive agent represents a conspicuous feature of the Old and

---

26 The vocative phrase *ms-jj-wt grḥ* '(oh) birth-givers of the night' in Pyramid Text 714a/T is in all likelihood original, since it is anaphorically related to the imperative plural *m-jj* 'come!'. In spite of maintaining the speaker-oriented point of view, the P" version must have undergone some editorial changes. The parallel versions in the Coffin Texts refer to dual entities, e.g., *ms-ty* (Coffin Text III 155c/B2Bo[b]) and *ms-jj-w(j)* (Coffin Text III 155c/B2L). The Passive 1 pattern recurs in the Coffin Texts parallels, e.g., *m ms-w=j* 'look I have been (re)born' (Coffin Text III 155d/B2Bo[a]). Perhaps, the resultative Stative *s-nxn-kwj* 'I am rejuvenated' in *sk ? ms–n=t͡n n.wj s-nxn-kwj* 'you have born me rejuvenated' (Coffin Text III 156c–157a/B2Bo[b]) is a reflex of the original first person singular Stative *ms-kj* 'I am (in) a newborn (state)'.

Early Middle Egyptian passive paradigm, as most of the world's languages resort to instrumental and locative prepositions for this purpose (see Keenan & Dryer 2007: 343–344).

(37)   Canonical morphological passive with *jn*–marked focus constituent

> *jwr(-w)=s*   *jn*   *Sxmt*   *ms(-w)*
> conceive-PASS1=3F.SG FOC   Sakhmet.F.SG bear-PASS1
> *Nt*   *tn*   *[jn]*   *ʃzmtt*
> Neith DEM.F.SG FOC   Shezmetet.F.SG
> 'She was conceived by (the goddess) Sakhmet. This (Queen) Neith (here) was born [by] (the goddess) Shezmetet.' (Pyramid Text/ Neith 7–8 [plate 8])

Detransitivized Statives, too, may be expanded by a focused agent phrase. The construction thus formed bears a close resemblance to canonical passive constructions, as many Egyptologists have observed (inter alia: Westendorf 1953: 49–51; Edel 1955/1964: 283 § 587aa; Schenkel 1971: 301; Allen 1991: 21–23; Loprieno 1995: 84–85). The situation with Old and Early Middle Egyptian Stative is therefore different from that of Chichewa, in which the addition of an agentive prepositional phrase renders the stative construction ungrammatical (see Dubinsky & Simango 1996: 751; Mchombo 2004: 95–96).

(38)   Detransitivized Stative with *jn*-marked focus constituent

> a.   *jw=j*   *j(w)r-kw*   *ms-kw*   *jn*   *ʃzmtt*
>   AUX=1SG conceive-STAT.1SG deliver-STAT.1SG FOC   Shezmetet.F.SG
>   'I was conceived (and) delivered through Shezmetet.' (Coffin Text VI 63d–e/B2L)

> b.   *ħz-k(j)*   *ħr=s*   *jn*   *nb(=j)*
>   praise-STAT.1SG because.of=3F.SG FOC lord.M.SG=POSS.1SG
>   'I was praised because of it (i.e., my vigilance) by My Lord.' (Urkunden I 255: 5)

Taken at face value, the presence of an agentive *jn*-phrase seems problematic for an analysis of detransitivized Statives as non-agentive, affected subject voice. Indeed, as I have demonstrated in previous work (Reintges 1997: 163–184, 1998: 211–219), the expression *jn* + NP for argument focus derives historically from a truncated cleft sentence "(it) is NP", which is added as a separate clausal unit to a preceding intransitive passive or detransitivized Stative sentence. Moreover, the focused argument may itself be an agent or a causer of the state of affairs denoted by the verbal predicate, thereby involving two different kinds of agency. The interested reader may refer to Doron (2005) for a more detailed discussion on the distinction between cause and actor. Consider in this regard the following example, in which the Stative–inflected *qʔ(-w)* 'is elevated' describes an externally caused change of state.

(39) Stative-inflected verb of quality and size with *jn*-marked argument focus

> *tʔ*   *qʔ(-w)*   *yr*   *Nwtj*   *jn*
> ground.M.SG   be.high-STAT.3M   under   Nut.F.SG   FOC
> *ʕ-w(j)=tʲ*   *Tfnwt*
> arm-M.DU=POSS.2F.SG   Tefnut.F.SG
> 'The ground under (the goddess) Nut is (in an) elevated state through your arms, (oh you) (goddess) Tefnut.' (Pyramid Text 1405a/P)

With detransitivized Statives, the clause-final argument focus designates the external causer or cause of the resultant state under consideration. The agentive *jn*-phrase is therefore related to the causing subevent of deadjectival verbs, as discussed in the previous section (§ 4.4.2).

4.5.2 The morphological non-distinctness of actively and passively interpreted Statives

In a thought-provoking paper, Kammerzell (1991) has considered the possibility that the active and passive uses of the Old Egyptian Stative may be distinguished morphologically by the presence of a preverbal augment *j-* traditionally known as the "prothetic yod". According to this proposal, prothetic yod-forms of the Stative are active voice, while detransitivized passives Statives lack this type of voice morphology (Kammerzell 1991: 177, 183). There are several theoretical and empirical problems with this approach. To begin with, when voice alternations are expressed by changes in the verbal morphology, it is generally the passive voice that receives additional coding material, while the active voice is left unmarked (see Haspelmath 1990 for the typology of passive voice markers and possible grammaticalization pathways). In the Pyramid Texts, both active and passive (imperfective and perfective) participles are attested with the prothetic yod (see Mathieu 1993: 318–329 for a survey of forms). There are also empirical concerns here, as the prothetic yod is not marked systematically on transitive-active Statives. None of the transitive-active Statives from the Pyramid Texts quoted in § 4.1 contains a prothetic yod. By contrast, there are also attested examples of detransitivized Statives from the Pyramid Text, which are, indeed, marked by a prothetic yod – contrary to the predictions of Kammerzell's proposal.

(40)　Prothetic yod-forms of detransitivized Statives in the Pyramid Texts

a.　*jzz-n=sn*　　　　*sw*　　*j-bḥn(-w)*
punish-PERF=3PL　CL.3M.SG　AUG-cut-STAT.3M
'They (i.e., the children of Horus) have punished him (so that) he is cut up (in pieces).' (Pyramid Text 643c/T)

b.　*ḏȝr　mȝȝ=sn　Tjtj　j-rnp-jj*
since　see.PFV=3PL Teti.M.SG　AUG-rejuvenate-STAT.3M
'Since they (the gods) see (King) Teti (in a) rejuvenated (state).' (Pyramid Text 715c/T)

c.　*j-s-mn-tj*　　　　　　*xntj*　　*pt*
AUG-CAUS-remain-STAT.2SG　in.front.of　heaven.F.SG
Ḥr　js
Horus.M.SG PCL
'You are established in front of heaven like (the god) Horus.' (Pyramid Text/ Neith 491 [plate 17])[27]

This leads me to conclude that the prothetic yod is not an active voice marker, but rather indicates an initial unstressed vowel, as argued by Mathieu (1996). As an affected subject voice, the Old and Early Middle Egyptian Stative enters into a paradigmatic opposition both with the active and with the passive voice. The active or passive denotation of transitive-based Statives is not registered by specific voice markers but rather depends entirely on argument realization. If the two arguments of a transitive verb are syntactically expressed as the subject and the direct object, respectively, the resulting Stative sentence will receive an active interpretation. On the other hand, if the agent is removed from the argument structure of the verb, the detransitivized Stative will have a resultative-pas-

---

27 Kammerzell (1991: 169) classifies the 2nd person singular Stative *j-s-mn-tj* "you are established" as a causative passive. The parallel version in Pyramid Text/ Neith 782 [plate 30] has the simplex form *mn-tj* 'you remain'.

sive interpretation. It would therefore be more correct to talk about the active or passive syntax of transitive-based Statives.

5 Concluding remarks

Earlier Egyptian is a language in which the morphological differentiation of event-denoting and state-denoting verbs is an essential part of the grammar. The language has at its disposal two finite verb paradigms, which present a given state of affairs from a more dynamic or more static point of view. The big picture that emerges from the present study is that the Old and Early Middle Egyptian Stative has a broad semantic distribution across various lexical classes of transitive, unergative, and unaccusative verbs. The possibility of forming Statives from bona fide unaccusative verbs generally shows that stativity and unaccusativity, in spite of their semantic affinity, are two different facets of verbal meaning. The syntactically encoded contrast between Eventive and Statives must therefore be distinguished carefully from the lexically encoded dynamic-stative contrast in different verb classes. The alternations in verbal meaning that we see with pairs of Eventive and Stative forms of the same root are highly systematic and predictable. This semantic regularity (predictability) follows from the uniformity of inflectional morphology, which leaves little or no space for lexical idiosyncrasy (for further discussion on the inflection-derivation divide, see Aronoff 1994: 125–127; Stump 2001: 14–19, among various others).

The Stative can be analyzed as an inflectional category of the verb, which is realized as an agreement paradigm. In spite of some remarkable person–gender and number–gender syncretisms, the Old and Early Middle Egyptian Stative manifests a morphologically uniform paradigm. I hope to have shown that the different person–number–gender inflections are never ambiguous between a grammatical and an anaphoric agreement function. In other words, these markers never acquire pronominal status themselves even when there is no independent subject in the sentence. The pattern of subject omissibility in Statives sentences could be shown to be a complex one. It represents a weak spot in the inflectional system that makes the Stative paradigm prone to morphological change – a topic that I have addressed in my *Folia Orientalia* 48 (2011a) paper "The evolution of the Ancient Egyptian Stative: Diachronic stability despite inflectional change".

The portmanteau analysis of the Stative paradigm that I have pursued here has broader implications for the theory of agreement. Most prominently, it provides potentially significant evidence against the commonly received wisdom that subject-verb agreement is devoid of semantic content and makes no contribution to the aspectual or temporal information of the clause. Corbett (2006: 26) proposes a general principle, according to which "canonical agreement is redundant rather than informative", but adds a precautionary note "it may be this principle which leads to canonical agreement being relatively rare among the world's languages" (pg. 27). This statement is well taken in view of the fact that it is not uncommon for grammatical agreement to intersect with aspectual and grammatical voice categories. The Semitic prefix and suffix conjugations are a prime example for the fusion of subject agreement with verbal tense and aspect. Classical Greek has separate agreement paradigms for active, passive, and middle voice. What makes the case of the Old and Early Middle Egyptian Stative special from a typological point of view is the synthesis of agreement, situation aspect, and affected subject voice in a single inflectional paradigm.

Abbreviations and symbols

1, 2, 3	first, second, third person
AUG	augment
AUX	auxiliary verb
CAUS	causative
CL	clitic pronoun
COMP	subordinating complementizer
COMP.NEG	negative complementizer
COMP.REL	relative complementizer
COP	pronominal copula
DEM	demonstrative pronoun
DU	dual number
F	feminine gender
FOC	focus marker
GER	gerund
IMP	imperative
IMPERF	Imperfective aspect
INF	infinitive
INTERJ	interjection
LINK	nominal linker
M	masculine gender
NEG	negation
PASS	passive marker
PERF	Perfect tense/aspect
PCL	particle
PFV	Perfective/neutral aspect
PL	plural number
PLUR	Pluractional
POSS	possessive pronoun
prosp	Prospective aspect
PTCP	participle

SG   singular number
(…)   left out for the sake of brevity
[…]   partly damaged passage
<…>   erroneous omission by the scribe

6 References

Allen, James P. 1984. *The Inflection of the Verb in the Pyramid Texts*. (Bibliotheca Aegyptia 2). Malibu: Undena Publications.

Allen, James P. 1991. Form, function, and meaning in the Early Egyptian verb. *Lingua Aegyptia* 1: 1–32.

Anderson, Stephen R. 1982. Where's morphology? *Linguistic Inquiry* 13: 571–612.

Anderson, Stephen R. 1992. *A-Morphous Morphology*. (Cambridge Studies in Linguistics 62). Cambridge: Cambridge University Press.

Aronoff, Mark. 1994. *Morphology by Itself: Stems and Inflectional Classes*. (Linguistic Inquiry Monograph 22). Cambridge, MA: Massachusetts Institute of Technology Press.

Baerman, Matthew. 2004. Directionality and (un)natural classes in syncretism. *Language* 80: 807–827.

Baerman, Matthew & Brown, Dunstan. 2005. Syncretism in verbal person/number marking. In: Haspelmath, Martin, Dryer, Matthew S., Gil, David & Comrie, Bernard (eds.), *The World Atlas of Language Structures*. Oxford: Oxford University Press, 122–125.

Baerman, Matthew, Brown, Dunstan & Corbett, Grevill G. 2005. T*he Morphology–Syntax Interface: A Study of Syncretism*. (Cambridge Studies in Linguistics 109). Cambridge: Cambridge University Press.

Baker, Mark C. & Hale, Kenneth. 1990. Relativized minimality and pronoun incorporation. *Linguistic Inquiry* 21: 289–297.

Bendjaballah, Sabrina & Reintges, Chris H. 2009. Ancient Egyptian verbal reduplication: Typology, diachrony, and the morphology-syntax Interface. Special Issue on Reduplication: Diachrony and Productivity. Ed. by Hurch, Bernhard & Mattes, Veronika. *Morphology* 19: 135–157.

Borer, Hagit. 1986. I–subjects. *Linguistic Inquiry* 17: 375–416.

Borghouts, Joris F. 2001. On certain uses of the Stative. *Lingua Aegyptia* 9: 11–35.

Borghouts, Joris. 2010. *Egyptian: An Introduction to the Writing and Language of the Middle Kingdom*. 2 vols. Vol. I: *Grammar, Syntax and Indexes*. (Egyptologische Uitgaven 24). Leuven: Peeters.

Bresnan, Joan & Mchombo, Sam A. 1987. Topic, pronoun, and agreement in Chicheŵa. *Language* 63: 741–782.

Carstairs-McCarthy, Andrew. 2001. Paradigmatic structure: Inflectional paradigms and morphological classes. In: Spencer, Andrew & Zwicky, Arnold M. (eds.), *The Handbook of Morphology*. (Blackwell Handbooks in Linguistics). Oxford: Blackwell, 322–334.

Chomsky, Noam. 1982. *Some Concepts and Consequences of the Theory of Government and Binding*. (Linguistic Inquiry Monograph 6). Cambridge, MA: Massachusetts Institute of Technology Press.

Chomsky, Noam. 2000. Minimalist inquiries: The framework. In: Martin, Roger, Michaels, David & Uriagereka, Juan (eds.), *Step by Step: Essays on Minimalist Syntax in Honor of Howard Lasnik*. Cambridge, MA: Massachusetts Institute of Technology Press, 89–155.

Comrie, Bernard 1976. *Aspect — An Introduction to the Study of Verbal Aspect and Related Problems*. (Cambridge Textbooks in Linguistics). Cambridge: Cambridge University Press.

Corbett, Greville G. 2006. *Agreement*. (Cambridge Textbooks in Linguistics). Cambridge: Cambridge University Press.

Corbett, Greville G. & Baerman, Matthew. 2006. Prolegomena to a typology of morphological features. *Morphology* 16: 231–246.

Cysouw, Michael. 2003. *The Paradigmatic Structure of Person Marking*. Oxford: Oxford University Press.

Cysouw, Michael. 2010. The expression of number and gender: A typologist's perspective. *Morphology* 21: 419–443.

Dahl, Østen. 1985. *Tense and Aspects Systems*. Oxford: Blackwell.

Doron, Edit. 1988. On the complementarity of subject and subject-verb agreement. In: Barlow, Michael & Ferguson, C.A. (eds.), *Agreement in Natural Language: Approaches, Theories, Descriptions. Papers Presented at a Conference held at Stanford University in October 1984*. Stanford, CA: Center for the Study of Language and Information Publications, 201–218.

Doron, Edit. 1996. The predicate in Arabic. In: Lecarme, Jacqueline, Lowenstamm, Jean & Shlonsky, Ur (eds.), *Studies in Afroasiatic Grammar. Papers from the Second Conference on Afroasiatic Languages Sophia Antipolis 1994*. The Hague: Holland Academic Graphics, 77–104.

Doron, Edit. 2005. The aspect of agency. In: Erteschik-Shir, Nomi & Rapoport, Tova (eds.), *The Syntax of Aspect: Deriving Thematic and Aspectual Interpretation*. (Oxford Studies in Theoretical Linguistics 10). Oxford: Oxford University Press, 154–173.

Doron, Edit & Heycock, Caroline. 2010. In support of Broad Subjects in Hebrew. *Lingua* 120: 1764–1776.

Dubinsky, Stanley & Simango, Silvester R. 1996. Passive and stative in Chicheŵa: Evidence for modular distinctions in grammar. *Language* 72: 749–781.

Edel, Elmar. 1955/1964. *Altägyptische Grammatik*. (Analecta Orientalia 34/39). Rome: Pontificial Biblical Institute.

Edel, Elmar. 1959. Beiträge zur ägyptischen Grammatik. 1. Zum angeblich geminierenden Pseudopartizip der Verben III. infirmae. *Zeitschrift für Ägyptische Sprache und Altertumskunde* 84: 105–108.

Embick, David. 2004. On the structure of resultative participles in English. *Linguistic Inquiry* 35: 355–392.

Erman, Adolf. 1889. Eine neue Art der ägyptischen Conjugation. *Zeitschrift für Ägyptische Sprache und Altertumskunde* 27: 65–84.

Erman, Adolf. 1919. *Reden, Rufe und Lieder auf Gräberbildern des Alten Reiches*. (Abhandlungen der Preußischen Akademie der Wissenschaften Jahrgang 1918. Philosophisch-Historische Klasse 15). Berlin: Verlag der Akademie der Wissenschaften.

Erman, Adolf. 1928. *Ägyptische Grammatik. Mit Schrifttafel, Paradigmen und Übungstücken zum Selbststudium und zum Gebrauch in Vorlesungen*. (Porta Linguarum Orientalium 15). Berlin: Reuther & Reichard.

Faulkner, Raymond O. 1969. *The Ancient Egyptian Pyramid Texts: Translated into English*. Oxford: Clarendon Press.

Fleischman, Suzanne. 1989. Temporal distance: A basic linguistic metaphor. *Studies in Language* 13: 1–50.

Frascarelli, Mara. 2007. Subjects, topics, and the interpretation of referential *pro*. *Natural Language and Linguistic Theory* 25: 691–734.

Franks, Steven. 1990. On the status of null expletives. *Lingua* 81: 1–24.

Gardiner, Alan H. 1957. *Egyptian Grammar. Being an Introduction to the Study of Hieroglyphs. Griffith Institute, Ashmolean Museum.* Oxford: Oxford University Press.

Goedicke, Hans. 1960. The inscription of Ḏmỉ. *Journal of Near Eastern Studies* 19: 288–291.

Greenberg, Joseph H. 1963. Some universals of grammar with particular reference to the order of meaningful elements. In: Greenberg, Joseph H. (ed.), *Universals of Language.* Cambridge, MA: Massachusetts Institute of Technology Press, 73–113.

Grimshaw, Jane. 1990. *Argument Structure.* (Linguistic Inquiry Monograph 19). Cambridge, MA: Massachusetts Institute of Technology Press.

Güldemann, Tom. 2014. How typology can inform philology: Quotative *jn* in Earlier Egyptian. This volume.

Harbour, Daniel. 2008. On homophony and methodology in morphology. *Morphology* 18: 75–92.

Harley, Heidi & Ritter Elizabeth. 2002. Person and number in pronouns: A feature-geometric analysis. *Language* 78: 482–526.

Haspelmath, Martin. 1990. The grammaticalization of passive morphology. *Studies in Language* 14: 25–72.

Holmberg, Anders. 2005. Is there little *pro*? Evidence from Finnish. *Linguistic Inquiry* 36: 533–564.

Huang, C.-T. James. 1984. On the distribution and reference of empty pronouns. *Linguistic Inquiry* 15: 531–574.

Huang, C.-T. James, Li, Y.-H. Audrey & Li, Yafei. 2009. *The Syntax of Chinese.* (Cambridge Syntax Guides). Cambridge: Cambridge University Press.

Jaeggli, Osvaldo A. & Safir, Kenneth J. 1989. The Null Subject Parameter and parametric theory. In: Jaeggli, Osvaldo A. & Safir, Kenneth J. (eds.), *The Null Subject Parameter.* (Studies in Natural language and Linguistic Theory 15). Dordrecht: Kluwer, 1–44.

Jaggar, Philip J. 1988. Affected-subject ('grade 7') verbs in Hausa: What are they and where do they come from? In: Shibatani, Masayoshi (ed.), *Passive and Voice.* (Typological Studies in Language 16). Amsterdam & Philadelphia: John Benjamins, 387–416.

Jansen-Winkeln, Karl. 1993. Das ägyptische Pseudopartizip. *Orientalia Lovaniensia Periodica* 24: 5–28.

Joseph, Brian D. 2009. Greek Dialectal Evidence for the Role of the Paradigm in Inflectional Change. *Morphology* 19: 45–57.

Kammerzell, Frank. 1990. Funktion und Form. Zur Opposition von Perfekt und Pseudopartizip im Alt- und Mittelägyptischen. *Göttinger Miszellen* 117/119: 181–202.

Kammerzell, Frank. 1991a. Augment, Stamm und Endung. Zur morphologischen Entwicklung der Stativkonjugation. *Lingua Aegyptia* 1: 165–199.

Kammerzell, Frank. 1991b. Personalpronomina und Personalendungen im Altägyptischen. In: Mendel, Daniela & Claudi, Ulrike (eds.), *Ägypten im afro-asiatischen Kontext. Aufsätze zur Archäologie, Geschichte und Sprache eines unbegrenzten Raumes – Gedenkschrift Peter Behrends.* (Afrikanistische Arbeitspapiere, Special Issue 1991). Cologne: University of Cologne, 177–203.

Kayne, Richard S. 2000. A note on clitic doubling in French. In: Kayne, Richard S. (ed.), *Parameters and Universals*. (Oxford Studies in Comparative Syntax). Oxford: Oxford University Press, 163–184.

Keenan, Edward L. & Dryer, Matthew S. 2007. Passive in the world's languages. In: Shopen, Timothy (ed.), *Language Universals and Syntactic Description*. Vol. V.1. 2nd ed. Cambridge: Cambridge University Press, 325–361.

Klaiman, Miriam H. 1991. *Grammatical Voice*. (Cambridge Studies in Linguistics 59). Cambridge: Cambridge University Press.

Kouwenberg, Norbert J.C. 2000. Nouns as verbs: The verbal nature of the Akkadian Stative. *Orientalia* 69: 21–71.

Kramer, Ruth. 2009. VSO and SVO order in Middle Egyptian. In: Häberl, Charles G. (ed.), *Afroasiatic Studies in Memory of Robert Hetzron: Proceedings of the Proceedings of the 35th Annual North American Conference on Afroasiatic Linguistics*. (NACAL 35). Cambridge, MA: Cambridge Scholars Publishing, 31–75.

Kratzer, Angelika. 2000. Building statives. In: Conathan, Lisa J., Good, Jeff, Kavitskaya, Darya, Wulf, Alyssa B. & Yu, Alan C.L. (eds.), *Proceedings of the 26th Annual Meeting of the Berkeley Linguistic Society*. (BLS 26). University of California, Berkeley: Berkeley Linguistics Society, 385–399.

Kuroda, Sige-Yuki. 1988. Whether We Agree or not: A Comparative Syntax of English and Japanese. *Linguisticae Investigationes* 12: 1–47.

Levin, Beth & Rappaport, Malka. 1986. The Formation of adjectival passives. *Linguistic Inquiry* 17: 623–661.

Levin, Beth & Rappaport Hovav, Malka. 1995. *Unaccusativityat the Syntax-lexical Semantics Interface*. (Linguistic Inquiry, Monographs 26). Cambridge, MA: Massachusetts Institute of Technology Press.

Levin, Beth & Rappaport Hovav, Malka. 2010. Reflections on manner/result complementarity. In: Rappaport Hovav, Malka, Doron, Edit & Sichel, Ivy (eds.), *Lexical Semantics, Syntax, and Event Structure*. (Oxford Studies in Theoretical Linguistics 27). Oxford: Oxford University Press, 21–38.

Lipiński, Edward. 2001. *Semitic Languages: Outline of a Comparative Grammar*. (Orientalia Lovaniensia Analecta 80). Leuven: Peeters.

Loprieno, Antonio. 1995. *Ancient Egyptian – A Linguistic Introduction*. Cambridge: Cambridge University Press.

Mathieu, Bernard. 1996. L'emploi du yod prothétique dans les textes de la pyramide d'Ounas et son intérêt pour la vocalisation de l'égyptien. *Bulletin de l'Institut Français d'Archéologie Orientale* 96: 313–337.

Mathieu, Bernard. 2004. La distinction entre Textes des Pyramides et Textes des Sacrophages est-elle légitime? In: Bickel, Susanne & Mathieu, Bernard (eds.), *D'un monde à l'autre: Textes des Pyramides et Textes des Sacrophages. Actes de la table ronde internationale «Textes des Pyramides versus Textes des Sacrophages». IFAO (24–26 September 2001)*. (Bibliothèque d'étude 139). Cairo: Institute Français d'Archéologie Orientale, 247–261.

McCloskey, James & Hale, Kenneth. 1983. On the syntax of person-number inflection in Modern Irish. *Natural Language & Linguistic Theory* 1: 487–533.

Mchombo, Sam A. 1993. A formal analysis of the Stative construction in Bantu. *Journal of African Languages and Linguistics* 14: 5–28.

Mchombo, Sam A. 2004. *The Syntax of Chichewa*. (Cambridge Syntax Guides). Cambridge: Cambridge University Press.

Mittwoch, Anita. 2005. Unspecified arguments in episodic and habitual sentences. In: Erteschik-Shir, Nomi & Rapoport, Tova (eds.), *The Syntax of Aspect: Deriving Thematic and Aspectual Interpretation.* (Oxford Studies in Theoretical Linguistics 10). Oxford: Oxford University Press, 236–254.

Nedjalkov, Vladimir P. & Jaxontov, Sergej Je. 1988. The typology of resultative constructions. In: Nedjalkov, Vladimir P. (ed.), *Typology of Resultative Constructions.* (Typological Studies in Language 12). Amsterdam & Philadelphia: John Benjamins, 3–62.

Oréal, Elsa. 2007. Fracture d'actance et dynamique morphosyntaxique: Le renouvellement du perfectif en Ancien égyptien. *Bulletin de la Société de linguistique de Paris* 102: 367–397.

Oréal, Elsa. 2009. Same source, different outcomes: A reassessment of the parallel between Ancient Egyptian and Akkadian 'Stative' conjugations. *Lingua Aegyptia* 17: 183–200.

Oréal, Elsa. 2010. Traces of a stative–eventive opposition in Ancient Egyptian – Rethinking pseudoparticiple as Old Perfective. *Zeitschrift für Ägyptische Sprache und Altertumskunde* 137: 145–156.

Osing, Jürgen. 1977. Zur Syntax der Biographie des *Wnj*. *Orientalia* 46: 165–182.

Perlmutter, David M. 1978. Impersonal passives and the Unaccusative Hypothesis. In: Jaeger, Jeri J., Woodbury, Anthony C. & Ackerman, Farrel (eds.), *Proceedings of the Fourth Annual Meeting of the Berkeley Linguistics Society.* (BLS 4). University of California, Berkeley: Berkeley Linguistics Society, 157–189.

Quack, Joachim Friedrich. 2003. Zum Charakter der "zweiradikaligen" Verben des Ägyptischen. In: Bender, M. Lionell, Takács, Gábor & Appleyard, David (eds.), *Selected Comparative-Historical Afrasian Linguistic Studies in Memory of Igor M. Diakonoff.* (LINCOM Studies in Afroasiatic Linguistics 14). Munich: LINCOM, 167–174.

Reintges, Chris H. 1994. Egyptian root-and-pattern morphology. *Lingua Aegyptia* 4: 213–244.

Reintges, Chris H. 1997. *Passive Voice in Older Egyptian.* (HIL Dissertations 28). The Hague: Holland Academic Graphics.

Reintges, Chris H. 1998. Mapping information structure to syntactic structure: One syntax for *jn*. *Revue d'Égyptologie* 49: 195–220.

Reintges, Chris H. 2004a. *Coptic Egyptian (Sahidic Dialect): A Learner's Grammar.* (Afrikawissenschaftliche Lehrbücher 15). Cologne: Rüdiger Köppe Verlag.

Reintges, Chris H. 2004b. The Older Egyptian *sḏm(-w)=f* passive revisited. *Folia Orientalia* 40: 51–70.

Reintges, ChrisH. 2005a. The correlation between word order alternations, grammatical agreement and event semantics in Older Egyptian. In: Kiss, Katalin É. (ed.), *Universal Grammar in the Reconstruction of Ancient Languages.* (Studies in Generative Grammar 83). Berlin: Mouton, 31–103.

Reintges, Chris H. 2005b. On passive participles and relative forms. *Lingua Aegyptia* 13: 103–139.

Reintges, Chris H. 2006. The Older Egyptian Stative revisited. *Lingua Aegyptia* 14: 115–134.

Reintges, Chris H. 2011a. The evolution of the Ancient Egyptian Stative: Diachronic stability despite inflectional change. *Folia Orientalia* 48: 7–97.

Reintges, Chris H. 2011b. The oral-compositional form of Pyramid Text discourse. In: Hagen, Fredrik N., Johnston, John J., Monkhouse, Wendy, Piquette, Kathryn E., Tait, John & Worthington, Martin (eds.), *Narratives of Egypt and the Ancient Near East: Literary and Linguistic Approaches.* (Orientalia Lovaniensa Analecta 189). Louvain: Peeters, 3–54.

Ritter, Elisabeth. 1995. On the syntactic category of pronouns and agreement. *Natural Language and Linguistic Theory* 13: 405–443.

Rizzi, Luigi. 1982. *Issues in Italian Syntax*. Dordrecht: Foris Publications.

Rizzi, Luigi. 1986. Null objects in Italian and the theory of *pro. Linguistic Inquiry* 17: 501–557.

Roberts, Ian & Holmberg, Anders. 2010. Introduction: Parameters in Minimalist Theory. In: Biberauer, Theresa, Holmberg, Anders, Roberts, Ian & Sheehan, Michelle (eds.), *Parametric Variation: Null Subjects in Minimalist Theory*. Cambridge: Cambridge University Press, 1–57.

Schenkel, Wolfgang. 1965. Beiträge zur mittelägyptischen Syntax III. Sätze mit Pseudopartizip. *Zeitschrift für Ägyptische Sprache und Altertumskunde* 92: 47–68.

Schenkel, Wolfgang. 1971. Das altägyptische Pseudopartizip und das indogermanische Medium/Perfekt. *Orientalia* 40: 301–316.

Schenkel, Wolfgang. 1990. *Einführung in die altägyptische Sprachwissenschaft*. Darmstadt: Wissenschaftliche Buchgesellschaft.

Schenkel, Wolfgang. 1994. ščm-Perfekt and śčm-Stative: Die beiden Pseudopartizipien des Ägyptischen nach dem Zeugnis der Sargtexte. In: Behlmer, Heike (ed.), ... *Quaerentes Scientiam. Festgabe für Wolfhart Westendorf zu seinem 70. Geburtstag überreicht von seinen Schülern*. Göttingen: Seminar für Ägyptologie und Koptologie, 157–182.

Schenkel, Wolfgang. 1997. *Tübinger Einführung in die klassisch-ägyptische Sprache und Schrift*. Tübingen: Pagina GmbH.

Sethe, Kurt. 1899. *Das aegyptische Verbum im Altaegyptischen, Neuaegyptischen und Koptischen*. 3 vols. Vol. II: *Formenlehre und Syntax der Verbalformen*. Leipzig: J.C. Hinrichs'sche Buchhandlung.

Shlonsky, Ur. 1997. *Clause Structure and Word Order in Hebrew and Arabic: An Essay in Comparative Semitic Syntax*. (Oxford Studies in Comparative Syntax 11). Oxford/New York: Oxford University Press.

Shlonsky, Ur. 2009. Hebrew as a partial null-subject language.Special issue on partial *pro*-drop. Ed. by Holmberg, Anders. *Studia Linguistica* 63: 133–157.

Siewierska, Anna. 1984. *The Passive: A Comparative Linguistic Analysis*. London: Croom Helm.

Siewierska, Anna. 2004. *Person*. (Cambridge Textbook in Linguistics). Cambridge: Cambridge University Press.

Smith, Carlota S. 1991. *The Parameter of Aspect*. (Studies in Linguistics and Philosophy 43). Dordrecht: Kluwer.

Spencer, Andrew. 1991. *Morphological Theory: An Introduction to Word Structure in Generative Grammar*. Oxford: Blackwell.

Stump, Gregory T. 2001. Inflection. In: Spencer, Andrew & Zwicky, Arnold M. (eds.), *The Handbook of Morphology*. (Blackwell Handbooks in Linguistics). Oxford: Blackwell, 13–43.

Thesaurus Linguae Aegyptiae. 2014. Arbeitsstelle Altägyptisches Wörterbuch. Berlin-Brandenburgische Akademie der Wissenschaften. Available at http://aaew.bbaw.de/tla/index. html.

Toivonen, Ida. 2000. The morphosyntax of Finish possessives. *Natural Language & Linguistic Theory* 18: 579–609.

Vainika, Anne & Levy, Yonanta. 1999.Empty Subjects in Finnish and Hebrew. *Natural Language & Linguistic Theory* 17: 613–671.

Vendler, Zeno. 1967. *Linguistics in Philosophy*. Ithaca, NY: Cornell University Press.

Vernus, Pascal. 1986. Aspect and morphosyntactic patterns in Middle Egyptian. In: Englund, Gerti & Frandsen, Paul F. (eds.), *Crossroad, Chaos or the Beginning of a New Paradigm. Papers from the Conference on Egyptian Grammar, Helsingør (May 1986)*. Copenhagen: The Carl Niebuhr Institute, 375–388.

Vernus, Pascal. 1996. La position linguistique des Textes des Sacrophages. In: Willems, Harco (ed.), *The World of the Coffin Texts. Proceedings of the Symposium held on the Occasion of the 100th Birthday of Adriaan de Buck, Leiden (17–19 December 1992).* (Egyptologische uitgaven 9). Leiden: Nederlands Instituut voor het Nabije Oosten, 143–196.

Ward, Gregory, Birner, Bety & Huddleston, Rodney. 2002. Information packaging. In: Huddleston, Rodney & Pullum, Geoffrey K. (eds.), *The Cambridge Grammar of the English language.* Cambridge: Cambridge University Press, 1363–1447.

Wasow, Thomas. 1977. Transformations and the lexicon. In: Culicover, Peter, Wasow, Thomas & Bresnan, Joan (eds.), *Formal Syntax.* New York: Academic Press, 327–360.

Wechsler, Stephen & Zlatić, Larisa. 2003. *The Many Faces of Agreement.* (Stanford Monographs in Linguistics). Stanford, CA: Center for the Study of Language and Information Publications.

Westendorf, Wolfhart.1953. Dynamischer Gebrauch des passivisch-intransitiven Pseudopartizips. *Mitteilungen des Instituts für Orientforschung* 1: 38–56.

Winand, Jean. 1992. *Études de néo-égyptien.* Vol. I: *La morphologie verbale.* (Aegyptiaca Leodiensia 2). Liège: Centre informatique de philosophie et lettres.

Zakrzewska, Ewa. 1990. Syntactic characteristics of the Old Perfective in the Coffin Texts. *Rocznik Orientalistyczny* 47: 123–145.

Andréas Stauder

A rare change: the degrammaticalization of an inflectional passive marker into an impersonal subject pronoun in Earlier Egyptian*

Abstract: The paper describes a rare change whereby an inflectional passive marker is extended to new uses as an impersonal subject pronoun. The change is analyzed as an instance of degrammaticalization, more specifically of deinflectionalization. The possibility for change is modeled in terms of formal equivocation and semantic conditions favouring alternative construals of the passive construction, without prior reanalysis of the latter. The change is further related to the spread of SV patterns, which had their origins in non-verbal constructions. Degrammaticalization is thus argued to have been rendered possible by a broad conjunction of independent conditions, none of which individually exceptional. The mechanisms of change are themselves ordinary ones, consisting in occasional reanalysis, pragmatic enrichment, and context generalization. A further case of deinflectionalization in second millennium BCE Egyptian is discussed in an Appendix.

1 Introduction

Old and Middle Egyptian (collectively known as Earlier Egyptian: ca. 2700–1300 BCE) display a rich variety of passive forms and constructions. Yet, in the course of the second and early first millennium BCE,[1] the language gradually lost all of

---

* My thanks are due to the organizers and editors of the present conference volume, Martin Haspelmath, Tonio Sebastian Richter, and Eitan Grossman. I further thank Petra Goedgebuure, Dmitry Idiatov, Salikoko Mufwene, Ilya Yakubovitch, and Gene Gragg for remarks on various oral presentations of the subject. Anna Siewierska and Chris Reintges kindly gave me access to (at the time) unpublished work of theirs. Research for the present paper was conducted at the Department of Near Eastern Languages and Civilizations and the Oriental Institute of the University of Chicago as part of a research project "From Earlier to Later Egyptian" funded by the Swiss National Science Foundation. The present paper was written in 2009 and revised in 2011; references to later publications could be integrated only marginally.
1 All periods in time are before the common era, and the siglum "BCE" is henceforth omitted

these. The present paper focuses on the central part of this overall process, the syntactic and semantic changes undergone by the passive morpheme {t}. In early times, {t}-marked constructions were promotional passives exclusively, fully aligned with other types of Earlier Egyptian inflectional passives. In the course of the second millennium, the morpheme {t} was extended to form new constructions, which are active impersonal in their syntax.[2] In these innovative uses, the morpheme {t} itself functions as a subject pronoun with non-specified reference (broadly similar in result to, but entirely different in origin from, for example, German *man*, French *on*).

While the change from a promotional construction (the passive) into a non-promotional one (the active impersonal) is found elsewhere, the rise of an impersonal subject pronoun out of an inflectional passive marker has apparently not been documented in other languages (Siewierska 2008) and therefore seems very uncommon. I describe here the evidence for this rare change as it can be traced philologically in the written record (§ 2–3, 7) and analyze how the change was made possible within the broader context of the changing grammar of early second millennium Egyptian (§ 4–6, 8–9).

As a contribution to the discussion of directionality in linguistic change, the change to be presented is submitted as an instance of degrammaticalization, and more specifically of deinflectionalization (§ 8; a further instance of deinflectionalization in second-millennium Egyptian is also introduced: § 10). The conditions for change are modeled in terms of formal equivocation and alternative construals of {t}-marked passives (§ 4–5), without prior reanalysis of the latter. I analyze how the present instance of degrammaticalization was made possible in relation to a whole series of largely independent dimensions (§ 4–6), some of which were entirely extraneous to passive voice itself (such as the gradual spread and semantic generalization of Subject-Verb patterns in the language: § 6). As with other rare changes, the possibility for change is thereby shown to have been with the conjunction of specific intra-linguistic circumstances – favorable conditions and motivating factors – none of which would have been sufficient alone, nor any exceptional in themselves (§ 9).

---

in the main text.

2 A more precise term for "active impersonal" would here be "desubjective" (as in e.g., Haspelmath 1990). The former label is nonetheless retained here, in keeping with common usage.

Part I. Describing the change in the written record

2 Before change: passive voice in third-millennium Egyptian

2.1 Background: a brief overview of passive voice in third-millennium Egyptian[3]

Third-millennium Egyptian has three different types of finite passive formations (i–iii). In all of these, passive morphology is fully inflectional and specialized solely for the passive function. In addition, a form otherwise used with stative/resultative semantics, the Resultative, provides the regular expression of the passive voice with positive, fully asserted perfective events (iv):

- (i) V-passives:[4] underlying morphology unclear; mostly unmarked in written form, rarely with a written ending -*w*;
- (ii) T-passives:[5] marked by {t} (*/-tv-/) after the stem; main allographs include -*t*, -*tw*, and -*tỉ* (the last only in early times);
- (iii) Reduplicating passives: a more marginal type, only with some inflectional classes; marked by the reduplication of the last root consonant;[6]
- (iv) Resultative.[7]

Among these formations, the T-passive type comprises a variety of individual forms, such as *sḏm-tw=f* (hear-PASS=3MSG), *sḏm-n-tw=f* (hear-ANT-PASS=3MSG), etc. (in more detail below, § 4.2). The V-passive probably consists of two forms.[8] The finite reduplicating passive is a single formal category.

Individual forms are complexly distributed in paradigms and in text. For instance, anterior passive events can be expressed by a V-passive, a T-passive, or

---

3 On Earlier Egyptian passive voice, Stauder (2014); Reintges (1997) (different analyses).

4 Stauder (2014: 21–44); also referred to in Egyptological discussion as "*sḏm(w)=f* passives".

5 Stauder (2014: 9–21); also referred to as "*tw*-passives".

6 The reduplicating passive is arguably a secondary morphological formation, and possibly only a sub-type of V-passives (Stauder 2014: 44–60; 2008; different interpretation by e.g., Reintges 2003); this formation is also referred to as "*sḏmm=f* passives".

7 Stauder (2014: 108–119, 235–250, 279–287); also variously referred to as "pseudoparticiple", "stative", or "old perfective".

8 Stauder (2014: 21–44); Schenkel (2004–2005); Allen (1984). Different view: Reintges (2004; 1997).

the Resultative, depending on polarity, information status, event semantics, and the nature of the subject.[9] Similarly, posterior passive events can be expressed by a V-passive, a T-passive, or the reduplicating passive, depending on modality, inflectional class, and written register.[10] Only relative present tense and imperfective aspect are the exclusive domain of one particular formation, namely T-passives (further discussion below, § 5.4).

All three types of passive formations (as well as the Resultative when used as a passive) can be followed by an agent phrase in syntactic periphery, introduced by *in* (§ 2.2.1). Moreover, both T-passives and V-passives are regularly derived from a variety of intransitive event-types, resulting in impersonal passives (§ 2.2.2).[11]

2.2 Third-millennium {t}-marked constructions as genuine passives

Among the various types of passive morphology introduced above, only {t} was extended to new environments in the second millennium, resulting in constructions which are active impersonal in syntax. In connection with this development, doubt has been raised as to whether {t} was a genuine passive marker in the first place, rather than, perhaps, an impersonal subject pronoun all along. A preliminary step therefore consists in establishing the nature of later third-millennium T-passives as genuine promotional passives, systematically on a par with V-passives[12] across all relevant passive constructions.[13] In order not to anticipate the result of the following conclusion, T-passives are provisionally referred to as "{t}-marked constructions". This terminological precaution is adopted only here, and T-passives will subsequently be referred to as "T-passives" again (from § 3 on).

---

9 Stauder (2014: 235–347).
10 Stauder (2014: 230–234).
11 No instances of impersonal reduplicating passives are found in the record, probably reflecting a gap in documentation (Stauder 2014: 75–76).
12 For the sake of expository economy, the more marginal reduplicating passive type is omitted from now on.
13 Major parts of the following argument are already in Reintges (1996), who reaches the same conclusion and provides references to the previous debate.

2.2.1 Promotion and demotion

Late third-millennium {t}-marked constructions display the very same promotional properties as V-passives do. Both {t}-marked constructions and V-passives are Verb-Subject (henceforth: VS) patterns. In the VS conjugation (active and passive), singular pronouns distinguish subject and object forms (in more detail, § 4.1). For the P argument,[14] {t}-marked constructions select subject clitics, just as V-passives do. The construction is therefore promotional with either passive type. Compare, respectively:[15]

(1) a. [T-pass.]

        n   *ms-n-t=i̓*   *i̓s*   *msyt*
        NEG give_birth-ANT-PASS=1SG.SBJ FOC birth
        'I was not born through regular birth.' (Coffin Texts I 344c)

  b. [V-pass.]

        n   *ms-w=i̓*   *i̓s*   *msyt*
        NEG give_birth-PASS.PFV=1SG.SBJ FOC birth
        'I was not born through regular birth.' (Coffin Texts II 3g G1T)[16]

---

14 The following labels are adopted for grammatical roles:
- A, the first core argument of a transitive event (subject in active clause);
- P, the second core argument of a transitive event (direct object in an active clause; subject in a passive one);
- S, the sole core argument of an intransitive event (subject in an active clause).

Only in the context of describing word-order patterns is S used differently, for denoting the grammatical relation of subject. In this usage, "S" is always adjacent to a "V" (e.g., SV, VS).

15 Glossing follows the Leipzig Glossing Rules. Two additional glossing conventions have been adopted. In Earlier Egyptian, linguistic function is often a feature of the overall constructional scheme rather than solely of an individual morpheme. For the sake of clarity, the gloss is nevertheless placed under the most characteristic morpheme of a given scheme. Moreover, glossing is "functional", rather than "etymological". This is justified by the synchronic formal and functional autonomy of various constructional schemes in which meanings have become fully grammatical rather than being inferred pragmatically.

16 The meaning of (1a) and (1b) is the same and the difference here only a diachronic one: (1a) represents a more innovative construction than (1b). This particular change is unimportant for the subsequent discussion and is not further developed here (see Stauder 2014: 250–263, 297–318, 334–343).

Compare, in the active:

c. *ms-n=i̯*   *i̯nw=s*
    give_birth-ANT=1SG.SBJ   ropes=3FSG
    'I have fashioned (lit. given_birth) its ropes (viz., of the Neshmet-bark [a sacred bark]).' (CG 20538 II, c, 4)

Late third-millennium {t}-marked constructions also display the very same demotional properties as V-passives do. With either formal type, the demoted agent can be expressed in syntactic periphery by a phrase introduced by *i̯n*[17] (henceforth: agent-expressing *i̯n*-construction). Compare, respectively:

(2) a. [T-pass.]

        šzp-t   *ʿ=f*   *i̯n   nṯr   ʿȝ*
        take\SUBJ-PASS   arm=3MSG   by   god   great
        'May his arm be taken by the great god!' (Mereri, east wall false door, l.1)

    b. [V-pass.]

        ṯ(ȝ)z   *mȝḵt*   *i̯n   rʿ   ḫft   wsir*
        knit\PASS.PFV   ladder   by   Re   before   Osiris
        'A ladder was tied together by Re before Osiris.' (Pyr. 472a[WNNt] [PT 305])

Moreover, V-passives and {t}-marked constructions license the very same range of demoted unexpressed or expressed agents. In particular, demoted agents can be singular and specific with passives of either morphological type (with expressed agents, compare (2a–b)). In "active impersonal" constructions on the other hand, implied agents are typically plural and/or non-specific in reference, and singular and specific agents are typically disallowed or uncommon (e.g., Blevins 2003).

---

17 On *i̯n*, Stauder (2014: 79–82, 95–108); Güldemann (in this volume); Reintges (1998; and in this volume).

2.2.2 Event types

Late third-millennium {t}-marked constructions are found with the very same range of event-types as V-passives are, and only with these. In Earlier Egyptian, passivization underlies a single semantic condition, namely that the event must have an (at least weakly) agentive participant (thus including, for example, verbs of perception):[18]

> *Semantic condition for passivization in Earlier Egyptian*
> The event to be passivized must have an (at least weakly) agentive participant.

Any transitive event that meets this requirement can be passivized, irrespective of the nature of the P argument (topicality, individuation, affectedness). Similarly, any intransitive event can be passivized, provided the above agentive-argument condition is met. These conditions apply to V-passives and {t}-marked constructions alike. With similar types of events, compare T- and V-passives in (3a–b) and (3c–d):

(3) a. [T-pass.]

       n   *pr-n-t*   *n*   *snd̠=f*
       NEG come_out-HAB-PASS for fear=3MSG
       'There was no coming out for fear of him.' (Moꜥalla II η 1)

   b. [V-pass.]

       spr   *r(=ỉ)*   *r=s*
       reach\PASS.PFV to(=1SG) about=3FSG
       'There was reaching to me about it.' (Moꜥalla II η 2)

   c. [T-pass.]

       mt̠n   *š3ꜥ-tw*   *grt* *m* *rd̠t* *p3* *ꜥqw (...)*
       COMP   start\SUBJ-PASS PTCL in give this food_provisions
       'Look ,one must now begin to give out these food provisions!' (Heqa-nakhte II, ro 31–32)

---

18 Stauder (2014: 71–79).

d. [V-pass.]

mtn	*š3ꜥ-w*	*m*	*wnm*	*rmṯ*	*ꜥ3*
COMP	start-PASS.PFV	with	eat	people	here

'Look, one has begun to eat people here!' (Heqanakhte II, ro 27–28)

Conversely, intransitive events that lack an (at least weakly) agentive participant are not found with V-passives. Nor are they found with {t}-marked constructions in late third-/very early second-millennium Egyptian either. Instead, a variety of other strategies are used whenever the non-agentive S of an intransitive verb is to be left unspecified. The following is illustrative of such alternative strategies, which include zero-subject active constructions (4a–c) and event-nominalization in presentative/existential patterns (4d). For the sake of the subsequent demonstration, examples have been taken from texts only slightly earlier than the ones in which innovative uses will be found (§ 3.1). Moreover, environments have been selected in which a {t}-marked construction is used with events meeting the condition for passivization. These include object clauses after governing *(r)dỉ* 'give, cause to' (4a, 4d), and general present tense state-of-affairs (4b–c):

(4) a.

n	*rḏ-n=f*	*ḥms-ø*	*ḥ3*	*ỉb=f*
NEG	cause-HAB=3MSG	sit\SUBJ	around	heart=3MSG

'He (viz., the king) does not allow one to rest around his heart.' (Sinuhe B 59 [literary, ca. 1950 BCE])

Contrast:

rḏ-ỉn	*sṯ3-tw*	*msw*	*nsw*
cause-PST	drag\SUBJ-PASS	children	king

'(He) had the royal children ushered in.' (Sinuhe B 263–264)

b.

sḏr-ø	*n=f*	*ḥdr*	*rꜥ*	*nb*
lie	for=3MSG	anguished\RES	day	every

'Because of it (viz., old age) one lies anguished every day' (Teaching of Ptahhotep 10 [literary, ca. 1950 BCE]

Contrast:

ỉw	*ḥsf-tw*	*n*	*sw3*	*ḥr*	*ḥpw*
COMP	punish-PASS	to	transgress\PTCP	on	laws

'There is punishment for the one who transgresses the laws' (Ptahhotep 90)

c. *ḥtp-ø*   *ḥr*   *bı͗n* (...)   [intr., S non-agentive]
be_content   about   evil
ı͗w   *ḥꜥdꜣ-tw* (...)   [intr., S agentive; event passivizable]
COMP   plunder-PASS
ı͗w   *šw-ø*   *m*   *ꜥḳ-ı͗b* (...)   [intr., S non-agentive]
COMP   lack   in   intimates
'(To whom shall I speak today:) There is contentment about evil (...)
(To whom shall I speak today:) There is plundering (...)
(To whom shall I speak today:) There is lack of intimates (...)' (Debate
of a Man and His Soul 108–124 [literary, ca. 1950 BCE])

d. *n-sp*   *ḏ(=ı͗)*   *ḥpr*   *m(w)t*   *n*   *ḥḳr*   *m*   *spꜣt*   *tn*
never allow(=1SG) occur die\INF for hunger in province this
'Never did I allow there to be starving in this province.' (Moꜥalla IV
17–18 [ca. 2150 BCE])

> [Event-nominalization in an existential/presentative construction with *ḥpr*
> 'occur'. In the same text, contrast with (3a) *pr-n-tw* (come_out-HAB-PASS).]

As the above illustrates, {t}-marked constructions in the late third and very early
second millennium underlie the very same semantic condition of passivization
as V-passives do:
– Both V-passives and {t}-marked constructions are regularly used with intransitive events that have an (at least weakly) agentive participant (3a–d).
– Neither V-passives nor {t}-marked constructions are ever used with intransitive events that do not have an (at least weakly) agentive participant. With
such events, alternative strategies are used whenever the non-agentive S is
to remain unspecified (illustrated in (4a–d) for environments that, in the
very same texts, display a {t}-marked construction with events that meet the
semantic condition for passivization).

In early times, {t}-marked constructions are therefore genuine inflectional passives, systematically on a par with V-passives on all three accounts: promotion,
demotion, and licensed event-types. Consequently, early {t}-marked constructions, such as the one discussed in the present section, are from here on again
referred to as "T-passives". The term "{t}-marked constructions" is henceforth
reserved for innovative usages of the morpheme {t}, in constructions that can not
be analyzed as passives anymore (§ 3).

3 Innovative constructions of {t} in second-millennium texts

Beginning in the early second millennium, {t} is extended to a series of new environments from which it was previously excluded. These include:
- (a) events that lack an agentive argument (§ 3.1);
- (b) subject-initial patterns, in which {t} is inserted into the pre-verbal subject-slot (§ 3.2).

In such environments, {t}-marked constructions cannot be analyzed as passives anymore, for semantic reasons (a) or for morpho-syntactic ones (b). Meanwhile, V-passives remained unaffected by either change. Both processes of extension are therefore specific to {t}.

3.1 Extension of {t}-marked constructions to event types and situations that cannot be passivized on semantic grounds

From the early second millennium on, {t}-marked constructions are found with event types and situations that do not meet the semantic condition for passivization, namely, that the event must have an (at least weakly) agentive argument (§2.2.2). Following the relative chronology of first occurrences in the written record, these innovative uses are the following:[19]

(i) Dynamic events lacking an agentive argument:

(5) a. sꜥnḫw   m   rḏ   mwt-tw
        life_giver NEG.IMP give die\SUBJ-DETR[20]
        sḥtmw   m   rḏ   ḥtm-tw
        destroyer NEG.IMP give perish\SUBJ-DETR

---

19 For each environment to be discussed, I give only the earliest examples in the written record. Note that the fine dating of several literary compositions only transmitted in later copies remains difficult to establish precisely (see Stauder 2013).

20 Innovative usages of {t} are henceforth glossed as "DETR" (for "detransitive"). The non-committal label is used in order not to anticipate on the analyses which follow. When {t} is used in the subject slot of Subject-Verb patterns and of non-verbal patterns (e.g., (7b), (8)–(12)), the morpheme is transcribed as =tw, reflecting its status as a clitic. In all other cases, {t} is transcribed as -tw.

'Life-giver, do not allow one to die! Destroyer, do not allow one to perish!' (Eloquent Peasant B1 252–254 [literary, ca. 1900–1850 BCE])

b.   *ỉw*   *ḫr-tw*   *n*   *ḥnt*   *w3*
      COMP   fall-DETR   for   greed   far
      'One falls far for greed.' (Eloquent Peasant B1 321–322)

c.   *n*   *wrd-n-tw*   *ḥr=s*
      NEG   become_weary-HAB-DETR   on=3FSG
      'There is no becoming weary through it.' (Graffito of Antef at Sehel, 8–9 [= JEA 39, 50–59; ca. 1800 BCE])

(ii) Non-dynamic events (perforce lacking an agentive argument):

(6) a.   *n*   *ḥḳr-tw*   *m*   *rnpwt=ỉ*
        NEG   be_hungry-DETR   in   years=1SG
        n   *ỉb-tw*   *ỉm*
        NEG   be_thirsty-DETR   therein
        ỉw   *ḥms-tw*   *m*   *ỉr-t-n=ỉ (…)*
        COMP sit-DETR   in   do\REL-FSG-CPD=1SG
        'There was no being hungry in my years, there was no being thirsty then; one was relaxed (lit. sitting) through what I had done (…)' (Teaching of Amenemhat § 11c–d [literary, dating debated, ca. 1850–1450 BCE])

b.   *nn*   *sḏr-tw*   *ḥḳr*   *n*   *mt*
      NEG   spend_the_night\SUBJ-DETR   be_hungry\RES   for   death
      'The night will not be spent fasting for death.' (The Prophecy of Neferti 9c [literary, dating debated, ca. 1850–1450 BCE]

c.   *nn*   *šw-tw*   *m*[…]
      NEG   lack\SUBJ-DETR   in
      'There will be no lack in […]' (The Lament of Ipuwer 10.6 [literary, dating debated, ca. 1800–1450 BCE]

(iii) With the Resultative, expressing a state:[21]

(7) a. ꜥḥꜥ-n=tw   ḥꜥ-w   ỉm   wr   r
　　　AUX-PST=DETR   rejoice-RES therein greatly more_than
　　　ḫt   nbt
　　　thing   any
　　　'One was in a state of rejoicing therein very greatly.' (Ameniseneb,
　　　Stela Louvre C13, 16–17 [funerary self-presentation, ca. 1700 BCE])

(7) b. tw=tw[22]   ḳb-w
　　　BASE=DETR be_fresh-RES
　　　'One is cool.' (Paheri, pl. 3 [caption to a pictorial scene in a tomb,
　　　evoking colloquial registers, ca. 1450 BCE])

(iv) In situational predicate constructions (a nonverbal pattern: Subject – Adverbial Phrase):

(8) a. ỉw=tw   m   ꜣḫt-ỉtn
　　　COMP=DETR in Akhetaten
　　　'One (viz., the king) was in Akhetaten' (Amarna Boundary Stela U, 4
　　　[ca. 1350 BCE])

(8) b. hrw pn   ỉw=tw   m   ꜥḥ (...)
　　　day this CIRC=DETR in palace
　　　'On this day, when One (viz., the king) was in the palace (...)' (Urk. IV
　　　2031, 15 [Tutankhamun's Restoration Stela, ca. 1325 BCE])

Such constructions of {t} are seen to be innovative when contrasted with only slightly earlier strategies for expressing unspecified reference of the S argument with the same, or similar, event-types: zero-subject active constructions and event-nominalization in presentative/existential constructions (§ 2.2.2). Among the examples quoted above, contrast:

21　This construction remains low in text frequency in all later times. This reflects the semantic unnaturalness of combining an expression of unspecified reference ({t}) with a stative/resultative gram which naturally displays a strong tendency to select highly topical subjects.

22　For the formation tw=tw (the Late Egyptian subject pronoun), see below, § 3.2.2.

- events of position:
    - *ḥms-tw* 'there is sitting' (6a):
        slightly earlier: *ḥms-ø* (4a);
    - *sḏr-tw* 'one is lying' (6b)
        slightly earlier: *sḏr-ø* (4b);
- physical and mental states:
    - *ḥḳr-tw* "there is being hungry" (6a), *ỉb-tw* 'there is being thirsty' (6a),
      wrd-n-tw 'there is becoming weary' (5c);
        slightly earlier: *ḥtp-ø* 'there is contentment' (4c);
- events of "disappearing":
    - *mwt-tw* 'there is dying' (5a), *ḥtm-tw* 'there is perishing' (5a);
        slightly earlier: *ḫpr m(w)t* 'there is dying' (lit.: 'death occurs') (4d);
- events of "lacking":
    - *nn šw-tw m* [...] 'there will be no lack of [...]' (6c);
        slightly earlier: *ỉw šw-ø m* (...) 'there is lack of (...)' (4c).

3.2 {T} extracted out of its inflectional position and accommodated into the subject slot of subject-initial patterns

Like V-passives, T-passives belong to the synthetic Verb–Subject conjugation. In T-passives, the passive marker {t} occupies an inflectional slot after the stem and before subject clitics:

[active:]   *sḏm-n=f*   (hear-ANT   =3MSG.SBJ)
[V-passive:] *sḏm-w=f*   (hear-PASS.PFV   =3MSG.SBJ)
[T-passive:] *sḏm-tw=f*   (hear\SUBJ-PASS =3MSG.SBJ)
                    sḏm-n-tw=f (hear-ANT-PASS   =3MSG.SBJ)
                    (etc., further illustration below, § 4.2)

In early second-millennium texts, {t} begins to be extended to subject-initial patterns. These cannot be passivized because they have the lexical verb in the infinitive and therefore lack an inflectional slot after the stem. {T} is then accommodated into the subject slot itself. Syntactically, the construction is non-promotional:

ỉw=f   r-sḏm=s (COMP=3MSG.SBJ FUT-hear\INF=3FSG.OBJ) ('He will hear her')
ỉw=tw r-sḏm=s (COMP=DETR   FUT-hear\INF=3FSG.OBJ) ('She will be heard')

3.2.1 {T} in the subject slot of *NP ḥr-sḏm* and *NP r-sḏm*

The early stages of the process are observed with the subject-initial patterns *NP ḥr-sḏm* and *NP r-sḏm:*

– *NP ḥr-sḏm* (a progressive tense in (9a), and as part of a past narrative construction in (9b)):

(9) a. | *wn=t* | *ḥr-ḳd* | *ḥnrt* | *pn (...)* |
| --- | --- | --- | --- |
| AUX.PST=DETR | PROG-build\INF | enclosure | this |

'This enclosure was being built (...)' (RILN 74, 6–7 [Antefiqer's Girgâwi rock inscription, Lower Nubia, ca. 1950 BCE])

Compare:

ḥr	*wn*	*Ḥr*	*ḥr-mr-t*	*grg=s (...)*
for	AUX.PST	Horus	PROG-wish-INF	found=3FSG

'For Horus had been wishing to restore it (...)' (Moʿalla I α 2)

b. | *wn-ỉn=tw* | *ḥr-rḏ-t* | *n=f* | *t3* | *10* | *ḥnḳt* |
| --- | --- | --- | --- | --- | --- |
| AUX.PST=DETR | PST-give-INF | to=3MSG | bread | 10 | beer |

ds	*2*	*rꜥ-nb*
jars	2	daily

'And one began giving him ten loaves of bread and two jars of beer daily.' (Eloquent Peasant B1 115-116 [ca. 1900–1850 BCE]).

Compare:

wn-ỉn	*sḫty*	*pn*	*ḥr-rm-yt*	*ꜥ3w-wrt (...)*
AUX.PST	peasant	this	PST-weep-INF	very-much

'And this peasant began weeping very much (...)' (Eloquent Peasant B1 55–56)

– *NP r-sḏm* (a future tense):

(10) a. | *ỉw=tw* | *r-rḏ-t* | *ꜥrk* | *p3* | *z* | *2* | *m-ḏd (...)* |
| --- | --- | --- | --- | --- | --- | --- |
| COMP=DETR | FUT-give-INF | swear | DEM | man | 2 | saying |

'The two men shall be made to swear as follows: (...)' (P. UC 32055, ro 9 [legal document, ca. 1800 BCE])

Compare:

iw=i   *r-ḏ-t*   *n=k*   *tp* (...)
COMP=1SG   FUT-give-INF   to=2SG amount
'I am to give you the amount (...)' (P. UC 32055, ro 4)

b.   *tw*   *r-šsp*   *ḫ°w*   *nw*   *°ḥз* (...)
    DETR FUT-seize\INF weapons of combat
    iw=tw   *r-ir-t*   *°ḥзw* *m* *biз* (...)
    COMP=DETR   FUT-do-INF arms in   copper
    'Weapons of combat will be taken up, (...);
    (And) arms will be made of copper (...)' (Neferti 8f–9a [literary, ca.
    1850–1450 BCE])

Compare:

sз   *n*   *s*   *r-ir-t*   *rn=f* (...)
son of man FUT-do-INF name=3MSG
iw   *°зmw*   *r-ḫr*   *n*   *š°t=f* (...)
COMP Asiatics FUT-fall\INF to massacre=3MSG
'(...) The son of a man will make his name (...);
The Asiatics will fall to his slaughtering (...)' (Neferti 14a–e)

In a similar fashion, {t} is later extended to two other subject-initial patterns: Subject – Resultative and Subject – Adverbial Phrase (situational predicate construction). These have already been mentioned for not being passivizable on semantic grounds (§ 3.1, (iii)–(iv)). As to the morphological issue, compare now:

–   Subject – Resultative:

    °ḥ°-n=tw   *ḫ°-w*   *im*
    AUX-PST=DETR   rejoice-RES therein
    'Then one was in a state of rejoiceing therein.' [= (7a), ca. 1700 BCE]

    °ḥ°-n=sn   *hr-w*   *ḥr=s*
    AUX-PST=3PL.SBJ be_content-RES on=3FS
    'Then they (viz., the priests of Wepwawet) were satisfied with it.' (Siut I 276).

– Subject – Adverbial Phrase (situational predicate construction):

iw=tw   *m*   *ȝḫt-itn* (...)
CIRC=DETR in   Akhetaten
'(...) when One was in Akhetaten' [= (8a), ca. 1350 BCE]

iw   *it=i*   *m*   *wʿw* (...)
CIRC [father=1SG].SBJ as   soldier
'(...) when my father was a soldier (...)' (Urk. IV 2, 10).

3.2.2 {T} as a component of the Late Egyptian subject pronoun

From the mid-second millennium on, {t} is accommodated into the paradigm of the newly developing Late Egyptian subject pronoun. In the first and second persons singular and plural, this pronoun is built on a (homograph, but entirely unrelated) base *tw=*, followed by the old subject clitics. The impersonal form of the new subject pronoun is analogical to interlocutive persons and accommodates {t} in the same slot as the old subject clitics:

Late Egyptian subject pronoun

– interlocutive persons: BASE + subject clitics

    tw=i (BASE=1SG) 'I';   *tw=k* (BASE=2MSG), *tw=t* (BASE=2FSG) 'you';

    tw=n (BASE=1PL) 'we'; *tw=tn* (BASE=2PL) 'you (pl.)';

– impersonal form: BASE + {t}

    tw=tw (BASE=DETR) 'one'.

The Late Egyptian subject pronoun is used in main clauses with some of the same subject-initial patterns illustrated above (§ 3.2.1): NP *ḥr-sḏm* (11, 22), Subject – Resultative (7b), Subject – Adverbial Predicate:

(11)   *ḥr*   *tw=tw*   *ḥr-ȝs=n*   *m*   *šmt*
        and   BASE=DETR PROG-hurry\INF=1PL   in   going
        'And they are hurrying us in our going.' (Paheri, pl. 3 [caption to a pictorial scene in a tomb, evoking colloquial registers, ca. 1450 BCE])

The first occurrences of *tw=tw* in the extant record (11, 7b) follow the first occurrence of the new subject pronoun itself only by a few generations. The difference in time is partly accounted for by the low density of less formal registers in the mid-second-millennium record compounded with the lesser text frequency of detransitive clauses in discourse. The chronological proximity of first occurrences therefore demonstrates that by the mid-second millennium, if not much before, {t} was freely used as an impersonal subject pronoun.

In the second part of the second millennium, {t} is further extended to all newly grammaticalizing Late Egyptian SV conjugational tenses (Conjunctive, Sequential (20b), Focusing tenses, Terminative, Negative Past, Negative Perfect, Negative Aorist); e.g., with the Terminative:

(12) *ỉmm=se*   *m*   *rmṯ-s3w*   *ỉỉrt=tw*   *gm*   *ỉṯ3w-rmṯ* (...)
     give\IMP=3SG as   prisoner   TERM=DETR   find\INF   thief
     'Make her a prisoner until a thief is found (...)' (P. BM 10052, XV.8–9 [ca. 1100 BCE; NB.: here not the earliest occurrence])

Compare:

ỉmm=sw   *n=s*   *ỉỉrt=ỉ*   *ỉỉ* (...)
give\IMP=3SG to=3FSG TERM=1SG   come\INF
'Give it to her until I come (...)' (P. Turin 1977, ro 7–8)

As with *tw=tw* just discussed, the first occurrences of these SV patterns with {t} shortly follow the first occurrences of the new patterns themselves. If need be, this further demonstrates the by then free use of {t} as an impersonal subject in SV patterns.

3.2.3 {T} doubled in the doubly inflected patterns *ḥr=f sḏm=f* and *k3=f sḏm=f*

Turning back in time, {t} was also extended to the doubly inflected patterns *ḥr=f sḏm=f* and *k3=f sḏm=f*, with earliest occurrences by 1800–1700 BCE. As with other SV patterns discussed above (§ 3.2), {t} is accommodated into the subject slot of active patterns. Moreover, {t} itself is replicated, thereby behaving differently from inflectional markers in Earlier Egyptian.[23] On both accounts, {t} aligns mor-

---

23 Doubling of inflectional morphemes is limited in Earlier Egyptian to patterns grammaticalized from erstwhile serial constructions such as the narrative past tense *ꜥḥꜥ-n sḏm-n=f* (AUX-ANT hear-PST=3MSG) '(Then) he heard' (< 'He stood up and heard' [stand_up-PST hear-PST=3MSG]).

phologically with pronominal morphemes rather than with inflectional markers of verbal categories. Compare:

– active, full noun subjects:

ḥr   *rmṯ*$_i$ *sḏm=f*$_i$ *NP*$_j$
(MOD[24]   man.SBJ   hear=3MSG.AGR   NP.OBJ)

– active, pronominal subjects:

ḥr=f$_i$ *sḏm=f*$_i$ *NP*$_j$
(MOD=3MSG.SBJ   hear=3MSG[25]   NP.OBJ)

– detransitive, with {t}:

ḥr=tw   *sḏm=tw*   *NP*
(MOD=DETR   hear=DETR   NP)

(13) a.   (...) *k3=tw*   *sḏm=tw*   *m*   *ḥs*   *ỉr-y*
          MOD=DETR   hear=DETR   in   return   to-ADV
          '(...) then there is to be news by return of it!' (lit.: 'then there shall be heard of it') (P. UC 32190A, ro, III.x+9, [business letter, ca. 1800 BCE])

    Compare:

    k3   *ṯ3ty*   *h3b=f*   *[wp]wtyw=f*   *r=s*
    MOD   vizier   send=3MSG.AGR   envoys=3MSG   about=3FSG
    'The vizier is to send his envoys for it (...)' (P. UC 32190A, ro, III.x+7–8)

    k3=k   *ꜥpr=k*   *p3y=k*   *bw-nfr*
    MOD=2MSG   provide=2MSG   POSS.ART=2MSG   goodness
    'You shall then provide your own goodness' (P. UC 32199, 8–9)

---

24 MOD for "modal". For a detailed analysis of the semantics semantics and diachronics of various *k3-* and *ḥr-* marked patterns, Vernus (1990: 61–99).

25 The second occurrence of the subject clitic, co-referenced to the first, can be analyzed here either as agreement (by analogy with the case of a full noun subject) or as a double realization of the pronominal subject in this particular pattern. The issue is inconsequential for the following discussion.

b. *ḫr=t*   *wbd=t=f* [26]
   MOD=DETR burn=DETR=3MSG
   'Then he shall be burnt.' (Abydenian boundary stela usurped by Neferhotep, 6 [ca. 1700 BCE])

Compare:

   ḫr=k   *ḏ=k*   *ỉnt*   *n=ỉ*   *ỉwt-n-ḥb*
   MOD=2MSG cause=2MSG bring to=1SG Iutenhab
   'You'll have to have Iutenhab brought to me.' (Heqanakht II, ro 40)

Part II. Analyzing the change

The change described in the preceding section consists of two roughly simultaneous processes of extension, to event types that cannot be passivized on semantic grounds (§ 3.1) and to patterns that cannot be passivized on morphological grounds (§ 3.2). Meanwhile, {t} continued to be used with passivizable event types in VS forms throughout the second millennium, just as it was in the third millennium. Such continued uses of T-passives are no less productive than they were before. Nor do second-millennium T-passives differ morphologically from third-millennium ones. Moreover, with T-passives the passive construction itself remains at first unchanged in both its promotional and demotional properties (in detail below, § 7). In analyzing the mechanisms of the changes described in the preceding section, one is therefore prevented from positing a reanalysis of T-passives *prior* to the extension of {t} to new environments.

Instead, the conditions for innovative constructions of {t} are analyzed here in terms of formal equivocation[27] and in terms of discourse contexts that favor alternative construals of T-passives. Alternative construals (§ 5.1), made possible by formal equivocation (§ 4) and encouraged in certain discourse contexts (§ 5.2–4), occur in the occasional representations of speakers. They provide sufficient conditions for the extension of {t} to new environments, without T-passives at this early point themselves undergoing any reanalysis, nor indeed, at first, any change at all.

---

26 On the formal realization of the P argument as a subject clitic, see the discussion below, § 7.2.3.

27 The term "equivocation" is inspired by Mufwene (1989).

4 Formal dimensions

Formal pre-conditions for the changes described here are on two levels: the means of overt coding of grammatical relations in Earlier Egyptian (§ 4.1), and the nature of T-passive morphology, as contrasting with V-passive morphology (§ 4.2).

4.1 Space for syntactic equivocation: the coding of grammatical relations in VS patterns

As previously discussed (§ 2.2.1), V- and T-passives are promotional constructions, i.e., constructions in which the P argument (the direct object in the active counterpart) is promoted to subject. On the other hand, the particular coding properties of grammatical relations in Earlier Egyptian result in considerable space for syntactic equivocation when it comes to passive constructions. This situation permits alternative construals of many passive constructions by language users as constructions in which the P argument is not necessarily promoted syntactically to subject.

The coding of core grammatical relations in Earlier Egyptian is primarily achieved by word order.[28] In SV patterns, coding is entirely determined at this level (S-V-O). In VS patterns (V-S-O), nominal morphology also comes into play, but only with singular pronominal clitics. Singular pronominal clitics distinguish two forms, which in VS patterns are associated with the roles of subject and object. The following Table illustrates those aspects of coding that are relevant to the present discussion:

- Nominal morphology (only relevant for VS patterns):

Singular clitics two sets of forms[29]					Plural clitics syncretic			Full nouns no case marking
1SG	2MSG	2FSG	3MSG	3FSG	1PL	2PL	3PL	
=ỉ	=k	=ṯ	=f	=s	=n	=ṯn	=sn	
=w(ỉ)	=ṯw	=ṯn	=sw	=s(ỉ)				

---

28 Intra-verbal agreement is limited to specific SV patterns, none of which are relevant to the present discussion.

29 Referred to in Egyptology as "suffix pronouns" (first line) and "dependent pronouns" (second line). Both behave as clitics. The longer forms (second line) are historically derived from the shorter ones (first line), e.g., 2MSG =ṯw (with the Old Egyptian alternant =kw) < =k + -w. In synchrony, the two paradigms are fully distinct, morphologically and functionally.

- Word order in VS patterns:

Rigid V-S-O; clitics precede full nouns; with singular pronouns, the first set of clitics is used with subjects, the second set with objects; e.g.:

sḏm nsw ḫrw	(hear king voice)	'may the king hear a voice'
sḏm=f ḫrw	(hear=3MSG.SBJ voice)	'may *he* hear a voice'
sḏm=sw nsw	(hear=3MSG.OBJ king)	'may the king hear *it*'
sḏm=f=sw	(hear=3MSG.SBJ=3MSG.OBJ)	'may he hear it'
sḏm=sn nsw	(hear=3PL king)	'may the king hear them' / 'may they hear the king'.

In VS patterns – to which Earlier Egyptian inflectional passives belong – both subject and object lie on the same side of the verb. On the other hand, passive constructions have only a single core argument, P, or none (in zero subject constructions of the passive and with impersonal passives).[30] In a language in which coding is mainly a feature of relative word order, equivocation as to the syntactic status of the P argument is then facilitated, extending to all cases in which the P argument is not a singular pronoun:[31]

Passives derived from transitives
  ('let it be eaten'; 'let them be eaten'; 'let bread be eaten'; 'let it be eaten'):
  – P sg. pronoun: *wnm-tw=f* (eat-PASS=3MSG.SBJ) [non-equivocating]
  – P pl. pronoun: *wnm-tw=sn* P subject, P object, or P indeterminate?
  – P full noun: *wnm-tw t3* P subject, P object, or P indeterminate?
  – Zero subject: *wnm-tw ø* no overt expression of P

---

30 Zero-subject passive constructions are constructions in which a subject low in individuation is left unexpressed as a strategy for inter-clausal cohesion (a kind of "anaphoric zero"; see Stauder 2014: 140–148). They are distinct from impersonal passives, which are derived from (primary or secondary) intransitives; in the latter, the construction is genuinely subjectless (Stauder 2014: 73–77; 158–178).

31 In comparison, the space for possible syntactic equivocation in Earlier Egyptian is even broader than in the Slavonic (Polish -to/-no and -się constructions) and Romance languages (Spanish *se* and Italian *si* constructions) in which a construction used as a promotional passive also went some way toward a non-promotional construction (for these, and other, changes, see Siewierska 2008; Haspelmath 1990: 57–58).

Impersonal passives, derived from (secondary or primary) intransitives
('let there be eating'; 'let there be coming'):
- P erased: *wnm-tw* no P
- no P: *ꞽꞽ-tw*   no P

4.2 Verbal morphology: the componentiality of T-passives

While the above equally applies to V- and T-passives, only the latter undergo the changes described in the present paper. In particular, only {t} is extracted out of its erstwhile exclusively inflectional position to be accommodated into the nominal subject slot of SV patterns. Among other things (see § 5.4 for semantic dimensions), this contrast relates to the different morphological nature of the two passive formations.

Earlier Egyptian verbal morphology can be broadly described as mildly synthetic, with a low degree of fusion and mostly singular exponence. Individual forms vary with respect to the above categories, as do inflectional passive formations. The morphology of (the) V-passive(s) remains difficult to reconstruct in any detail due to largely opaque graphemics. Yet, its fusional character is clear. Formally, V-passive morphology is characterized by a specific stem involving some distinctive vowel melody and/or stress pattern and syllable structure. Moreover, V-passive morphology codes passive voice and perfective aspect in a portmanteau fashion and is thus a rare exception to the aforementioned tendency of Earlier Egyptian verbal morphology to display singular exponence. Given such morphological and aspectual determinations, V-passive morphology is incompatible with any further inflectional marking of categories of Tense-Aspect-Mood.

By contrast, the morpheme {t} is mono-functional. It codes only the grammatical function of passive and is attached to the active stem after any Tense-Aspect-Mood markers there may be. T-passives are therefore componential, formally and semantically. Accordingly, T-passive morphology can be accommodated onto any active stem, provided the semantic conditions for passivization are met.[32]

---

32 As noted above (§ 2.2.2), this excludes events that lack an agentive argument in their semantic representation. In a related manner, passivization of imperatives is prohibited in Earlier Egyptian (recourse is made to periphrastic patterns instead). This is in conformity with a general pragmatic condition, observed in many languages, that the addressee of a strong manipulative speech act such as the imperative should be agentive in order to be able to carry out the orders given to him/her.

The contrast between the two morphological types is illustrated by the following Table:[33]

– V-passives: specific stems + subject

  – perfective passive: *ỉr=f* (passive counterpart to the anterior *ỉr-n=f* and to other forms)
  – future: *ỉr(w)=f* (passive counterpart to the prospective *ỉr(w)=f*)

– T-passives: active stem (+ TAM affixes) + {t} + subject

  – unaffixed stems:
    – OEg. past[34]   *ỉr=f*   *ỉr-t(w)=f*
    – unaccomplished[35]   *ỉr=f*   *ỉr-t(w)=f*
    – imperfective[36]   *ỉr~r=f*   *ỉr~r-t(w)=f*
    – subjunctive[37]   *ỉr(y)=f*   *ỉr(y)-t(w)=f*
    – prospective[38]   *ỉr(w)=f*   *ỉr(w)-t(w)=f*

  – affixed stems:
    – anterior   *ỉr-n=f*   *ỉr-n-t(w)=f*
    – past narrative   *ỉr-ỉn=f*   *ỉr-ỉn-t(w)=f*
    – sequential modal forms *ỉr-kꜣ=f*   *ỉr-kꜣ-t(w)=f*
                                         ỉr-ḫr=f   *ỉr-ḫr-t(w)=f*

As the above contrastive presentation of V- and T-passives directly suggests, a favorable condition for the extraction of {t} out of its erstwhile exclusively inflec-

---

33 Morphological paradigms are illustrated here with *ỉrỉ* 'do' rather than with *sḏm* 'hear' (as elsewhere in this paper). This is for expository purposes, because *ỉrỉ* belongs to an inflectional class that displays more alternations in written forms than the class to which *sḏm* belongs. Parentheses in transcription refer to segments that can be present or not in written form, with varying frequencies, depending on formal categories and parameters such as genre, time, and associated scribal traditions.

34 The morphology of the stem of the Old Egyptian past *sḏm=f* remains unknown.

35 Used as a relative present tense. Stem possibly realized as */'jv:rv-/ or the like (?? – evidence very scant).

36 Used in a variety of constructions, several displaying more or less strong shades of imperfective semantics (Stauder 2014: 324–330); the label 'imperfective' falls much short of a full synchronic description of the versatile functional profile of the form, and is to be understood as conventional. Stem probably realized as */jv'rv:rv-/, */jv'rvrrv-/, or the like.

37 Stem realized as */jvr'ja-/ (based on the form as preserved in Coptic *t*-causatives).

38 Stem probably realized as */jvrv:wv-/ or the like (Schenkel 2000).

tional position resides with the specific nature of T-passive morphology. The relevant dimensions – related to each other via a principle of "diagrammatic iconicity in stem-inflection relationships" (Bybee 1985: 11–12)[39] – are summarized below:

- singular exponence: {t} codes solely the function of passive voice;
- transparency: T-passives stand in a one-to-one relationship to active forms;
- no fusion: {t} is merely agglutinated to the active stem;
- position: {t} sits on the outer edge of the form, after any TAM markers that there may be.

5 Semantic and functional dimensions

5.1 Introduction

5.1.1 Passive constructions and active impersonal ones

The diachronic connection between passive and active impersonal constructions as two formal expressions of detransitive voice is well-documented cross-linguistically (e.g., Siewierska 2010; 2008; Givón & Kawasha 2006; Haspelmath 1990: 49–50). The phenomenon is interpreted as reflecting the considerable functional overlap between the two construction types.

Schematically, the passive construction re-maps arguments and syntactic functions (especially the one of subject) in the clause. With variation in individual languages, the passive is typically associated with functions determined by the relative topicality, individuation, and/or salience of core arguments in the clause. The passive, a functionally marked construction, is used in clauses that diverge from the prototypical discourse hierarchies (e.g., A is less topical than P, or A is unknown, irrelevant, or unexpected). The active impersonal, on the other hand, is a construction that allows an unspecified, and often non-specific, argument to fill the subject slot. Some argument other than the (here unspecified) agent is then the more topical one in the clause.

---

39 Note in particular that the position of the mono-functional {t} *after* any TAM markers is in conformity with principle (2): "The more relevant a category is to the verb, the closer its marker will occur with respect to the verb stem." By contrast, V-passive morphology, which synthesizes voice and aspect, consists in an altogether different stem, and is not compatible with any other marks of inflectional categories. This is in conformity with principle (3): "The more relevant a morphological category is to the verb, the greater will be the morpho-phonological fusion of that category with the stem."

In broader functional and cognitive terms, the difference, as well as the proximity, between the two construction types has been described by contrasting them as a prominence-based construction and a specificity-based construction (Langacker 2006; 2004). In discourse, reduced prominence often comes with lesser specificity. Lesser specificity in turn often implies reduced prominence.[40] Unsurprisingly then, active impersonal constructions are often used instead of passive ones, depending on discourse conditions and registers in languages that have both construction types (e.g., Sansò 2006), and in languages that lack passives altogether (as in the later stages of Ancient Egyptian itself, Demotic-Coptic).

Typical differences in extension between the passive and the active impersonal follow from the above. The passive is generally restricted to dynamic events implying an agentive argument of some sort (for Earlier Egyptian, above, § 2.2.2). On the other hand, the unspecified subject of the active impersonal typically has a human, non-specific, and non-singular referent:

Typical conditions

	events	reference of the unspecified participant
passive:	*implying an agent*	(no conditions)
active impersonal:	(no conditions)	*non-specific, or plural reference*

The active impersonal is therefore less restrictive in terms of the events it licenses (non-dynamic events, and even non-verbal situations, are often allowed) but is typically more restrictive in terms of the referents of the unspecified participant. This leaves considerable overlap.

Bearing the above background in mind, the change from a passive construction to an active impersonal one can be analyzed as a change from a prominence-based construction to a specificity-based one. Given the considerable functional overlap between the two construction types, alternative construals of a passive construction in terms of reduced specificity may easily occur in speakers representations under certain favorable conditions. I first examine how functional aspects of the Earlier Egyptian passive construction, including the broad use of impersonal passives, allow, and possibly even favor, alternative construals of the

---

40 In Langacker's (2006: 130) own words: "A participant not accorded its usual focal prominence (e.g., a passive agent) often remains unspecified. Conversely, failure to provide specific information about a participant renders it less salient. Absence of focal prominence and absence of specificity are mutually reinforcing strategies of defocusing. Each detracts from the optimal circumstances for viewing a given participant: the situation of a single, clearly delimited, fully identified individual put onstage as the specific focus of attention."

passive construction (§ 5.2–3). I then discuss how such alternative construals are more strongly favored with T-passives than with V-passives in relation to the differential aspectual correlates and preferred agent types, of either morphological type in text (§ 5.4).

5.1.2 Occasional written traces of alternative construals

Prior to such discussion, one phenomenon in Egyptian writing is noteworthy in the present context. By definition, alternative construals occur in (individual) speakers' representations and are therefore not directly visible in a sequence of speech, let alone in a written record. In a handful of cases however, the passive morpheme {t} is followed in writing by the <PLURAL> classifier. Such semographic complementation obtains at the written level only, with no correlates in the spoken sequence. Yet, the phenomenon opens a window on one individual scribe's linguistic representation of the construction: in terms of reduced individuation of the implied agent, and thereby going some way toward a construal as a specificity-based construction. Significantly, the few instances known are from expedition inscriptions outside of the Nile Valley, i.e., from contexts in which a less formal performance of written language was permitted than in most other occasions at the time:

(14)   a.   *ḥsbt   22   pr-t=ṯw*^{PLUR}   *r   ḥsmn   n*
            year   22   going_forth-INF=DETR   to   natron   for
            ḥr   ꜥnḫ-mswt (...)
            Horus   Ankhmesut
            'Year 22. Going forth (to fetch) natron for Horus Ankhmesut (...)'
            (Wadi el-Hudi 10, 1–4 [mining inscription in the Eastern Desert, ca. 1925 BCE])[41]

---

41 In this specific example, ongoing change is further evidenced by {t} being used in a slot that is not inflectional, after an infinitive. In accordance with a formal convention of the textual genre of expedition inscriptions, the infinitive introduces the short narrative to follow. The possibility for a an extension of {t} is given by the analogy with the fully regular construction of finite T-passives with similar events, as in (3a) *n pr-n-t* (...) 'there was coming out (...)'. The construction of the infinitive is here as if finite.

b. *ḥw-ꜣ*   *ir-t*[PLUR]   *smꜣ* *sfn*   *inrw*
   MOD-MOD   do\SUBJ-PASS   ramp be_lenient stones
   'May a ramp be constructed that will make soft (the way for) the
   slabs!' (Hammamat 19, 9 [inscription on a trade route to the Red
   Sea, ca. 1800 BCE])[42]

5.2 The specialization of Earlier Egyptian detransitive morphology on the sole passive function

Earlier Egyptian detransitive morphology, both V- and T-passive, never expresses any function in detransitive voice other than the passive itself.

This situation markedly contrasts with other Afroasiatic languages, notably Semitic ones, where detransitive morphology typically combines several functions such as the reflexive/reciprocal, the anticausative, and the passive, as well as imparting, or reflecting, medial semantics of various sorts (e.g., Retsö 1989; Kouwenberg 2010: 288–323, 355–437). In common to all these functions is a situation in which the event is oriented on an affected participant. Detransitive morphology is thereby "passive" in a *semantic* – rather than in a syntactic – sense.[43] When imparting, or reflecting, medial semantics, detransitive morphology variously interacts with lexical semantics in ways that, although following general trends, are not predictable in individual details. By contrast, passive voice, narrowly defined as a syntactic transformation, does not interact with lexical semantics.

The contrast between Earlier Egyptian and Afroasiatic detransitive voice is best illustrated by the morpheme {t} itself, also found in other branches of Afroasiatic (Semitic, Berber, Cushitic). With considerable variation in individual languages, {t} has a wide range of detransitivizing functions, which are often combined. The passive is only one of such, or may even not be present at all (e.g., Kouwenberg 2010: 360–375 [and fn.68], 380–382; 2005; Gragg 2001). {T}-marked stems are typically represented in the lexicon of individual languages, reflecting

---

42 Note that, just two clauses later, the innovative {t}-marked SV pattern illustrated in (9b) is found: *wn-in=tw ḫr-sfn nꜣ-n mnw* (...) (AUX-PST=DETR PST-be_lenient these monuments) '(A ramp was thus built,) and (the way for) these monuments one softened (...).'
43 Incidentally, this semantic notion of "passive" is the one underlying Dionysus Thrax's original notion of *páthos* (Andersen 1991: § 2.7). Note that Ancient Greek is a language in which, as in several Afroasiatic languages, passive voice in the narrower (syntactic) sense is often expressed by morphology that has more broadly middle and detransitivizing functions.

their position closer to the middle of the inflectional-derivational continuum. In Earlier Egyptian by contrast, {t}-marked forms are purely inflectional.[44]

The specialization of Earlier Egyptian detransitive morphology solely for the passive function may relate to the rigid word order of this language. Unlike in several other Afroasiatic languages, a constituent cannot be moved in the clause when the prototypical hierarchies of topicality are diverged from (e.g., when the A is less topical than P).[45] A passive construction is then necessarily made recourse to in order to place the more topical argument (the P) before the less topical one (the A) in the clause. This probably favored the use of detransitive morphology with passive functions and possibly could have favored its exclusive specialization on such.

With respect to the change analyzed here, it is proposed that the specialization of Earlier Egyptian detransitive morphology for the sole passive function could have been a facilitating factor. The functions of the passive have to do with the relative prominence of participants in the clause, and passive voice generally does not interact with lexical semantics. This semantic "simplicity" of the passive – a characteristic shared by the active impersonal – could have facilitated alternative construals of the construction as one based on the specificity of participants.

I emphasize that this is only a facilitating factor, not a necessary condition for change to happen. As the case of, for example, Romance *se/si* constructions demonstrates, a construction that has various combined functions in detransitive voice (including medial ones) may well develop usages that can be described as active

---

44 Another detransitive morpheme shared by Earlier Egyptian and Afroasiatic is {n} (Stauder 2014: 212–220; Vernus 2009; Edel 1955–1967: §§ 427, 431, 437, 445 [Earlier Egyptian]; Kouwenberg 2010: 288–323; 2004 [Akkadian, and references to Semitic more broadly]; Gragg 2001 [Cushitic]; Lieberman 1986 [Afroasiatic in general]). Like {t}-stems, {n}-stems in Afroasiatic languages display a wide variety of often combined detransitivizing functions; among these, the passive is but one (the detailed functional distribution of the {n}-and {t}-stems is a matter of considerable variation between individual languages). Just as {t}-stems, {n}-stems tend to interact with lexical semantics and to occupy a position toward the middle of the inflectional-derivational continuum. In Earlier Egyptian by contrast, {n} is a purely lexical derivation, reflecting or imparting intransitive or middle semantics, and is never used as a passive. Yet again, a formal category in common with Afroasiatic is functionalized differently in Earlier Egyptian. More generally, Earlier Egyptian detransitive morphology is either purely inflectional (T-passives), or purely derivational ({n}-stems). It never occupies a middle position on the inflectional-derivational continuum as is otherwise typical of many Afroasiatic languages.

45 This situation is described as a "pragmatic inverse" in Givón (1994). In many languages, pragmatic inversion is realized by a change in word order. In languages where this is not possible, the function of pragmatic inversion may then be realized as a sub-function of passive voice.

impersonal. This is because alternative construals operate on actual instances of a given construction in discourse, not on the total set of its possible functions.

What is proposed here, then, is that specialization for passive voice, as observed in Earlier Egyptian, provides a favorable background for change by making the cases in which alternative construals are possible all the more numerous.

5.3 Impersonal passives

Unlike many languages, Earlier Egyptian licenses, and productively uses, impersonal passives, that is, passives from intransitives – either from primary ones, e.g., *ỉwỉ* 'come', or from secondary ones, e.g., *wnm* 'eat' (under suppression of the P argument, 'eat (in general)').[46] Impersonal passives are used when the agent is unimportant or unknown, when discourse continuity bears on an oblique argument, or when the perspective is set on the event itself, often suggesting a thetic reading[47]. This broad use of impersonal passives provides another favorable condition for the chance under discussion.

5.3.1 The agent of impersonal passives

Passives from intransitives display a strong cross-linguistic tendency to disallow the expression of the demoted agent in syntactic periphery and to favor implied agents that are human and non-specific (e.g., Salvi 2008: 135–136; Shibatani 1985). The implied agents of impersonal passives thus come close to the ones typically associated with active impersonal constructions (see § 2.2.2, § 5.1.1).

In Earlier Egyptian, all passive constructions, from transitive and from intransitive events alike, are similarly limited to human agents (except for instances of personification). Impersonal passives therefore have no distinguished role in the change here analyzed on this particular level. Earlier Egyptian impersonal pas-

---

46 Among languages that have a passive construction, a great many allow for passive derivation only when some argument is syntactically promoted to subject (the "passive prototype", below, § 5.3.2). Within Afroasiatic itself, passives from intransitives are typically marginal in many languages, if licensed at all. This seems to relate to the fact that detransitive morphology in Afroasiatic languages is broadly defined in relation to the orientation of the event on some affected participant (§ 5.2).
47 On the discourse functions of Earlier Egyptian passives from intransitives, Stauder (2014: 158–178).

sives, however, have a distinguished role on the other levels mentioned above: the tendency to disallow an agent phrase in syntactic periphery, and the tendency to be used with implied agents that are generic or plural rather than specific and singular. While none of this manifests itself as a rule of grammar in Earlier Egyptian, both tendencies are strong in texts. Instances of impersonal passives with expressed agents are found, including cases with specific and singular agents,[48] but these remain uncommon and comparatively more rare than with passives derived from transitives.[49] In the vast majority of cases of impersonal passives, the agent of an impersonal passive is unexpressed and non-specific (compare above, (3a–d)).

5.3.2 Deviation from the passive prototype

Impersonal passives are non-prototypical because they lack a P argument that could be promoted to the position of subject. One immediate consequence is that impersonal passives are subjectless (except for dummy subjects in some languages, but not in Earlier Egyptian), and therefore often formally equivocating (compare § 4.1). Just as important, if not more, are the semantic correlates of the lack of a promotional component in impersonal passives. These can be expressed in terms of how impersonal passives deviate from the passive prototype.

The passive prototype simultaneously involves an orientation of the event on its Endpoint and a backgrounding of the agent, in various weightings, depending on individual constructions in individual languages and discourse contexts. Passives from intransitives, for their part, lack a P argument that could register a change of state. With passives from intransitives, the Endpoint orientation otherwise characteristic of passives can only be conceived of at a metaphorical level at best (e.g., with an oblique as the Goal of an event of directed motion). This diffuseness, or outright lack, of Endpoint orientation with impersonal passives in turn reinforces the relative weight of the agent backgrounding component (Comrie 1977; Shibatani 1985). Impersonal passives thus come closer to active impersonal constructions, which are themselves defined in relation to the agent (§ 5.1.1).

---

48 E.g., [V-passive:] *iw ng n=k in smn* (COMP gaggle\PASS.PFV for=2MSG by Nile_goose) 'There has been gaggled for you by the Nile goose' (Coffin Texts I 74b–c B1P); [T-passive:] *nis-t ir N in rˁ* (call\SUBJ?-PASS to N by Ra) 'There will be calling to king N by Ra' (Pyramid Texts § 346a).
49 For this, compare (2a)–(2b).

This is represented on the following schematic cline, which in the present case also has a diachronic interpretation. The cline is extended here in its topmost part in order to capture elements of the discussion in the preceding section (§ 5.2):

- (i) Endpoint orientation primary – *Middle voice, Stative/Resultative*
    (orientation of the event on an affected participant [*páthos*, [see § 5.2.1 and fn. 43];
    – often interacting with lexical semantics);
- (ii) Endpoint orientation *and* agent backgrounding – *Passive proper*
    (construction based on relative prominence of participants [*passivus*];
    – "semantic simplicity");
- (iii) Agent backgrounding primary – *Impersonal passives*
    (passive in syntax, but lack of a (syntactic) promotional component;
    – agent generally human, non-specific and plural);
- (iv) Non-specific agent – *Active impersonal*
    (active syntax; extension to events with no Agent in semantic representation;
    – unspecified participant generally human, non-specific, and plural).

In Semitic (more broadly, Afroasiatic) languages, detransitive morphology, and especially {t}-stems, typically have functions in both (i) and (ii) (§ 5.2). The functions in (i) are generally primary, in term of frequency and/or historically. The passive agent can only rarely be expressed in syntactic periphery, and impersonal passives (iii) are not regular, if licensed at all. In Earlier Egyptian by contrast, the functional domain (i) is realized by other formal means,[50] and V- and T-passives are exclusively passive in function (ii). The agent is commonly expressed in syntactic periphery (the *ỉn*-construction: § 2.2.1), and impersonal passives are fully regular (iii).

Beginning in the early second millennium, the Earlier Egyptian morpheme {t} was extended to environments that imply an analysis such as in (iv) (§ 3). As the proposed cline expresses, impersonal passives (iii) already diverge from prototypical ones (ii) because of their lack of a strong promotional component, the ensuing imbalance in favor of the agent backgrounding component, and the typically non-specific nature of the implied agent. They thereby provide a bridging construction

---

50 In most schematic terms, these include: (i) middle voice and intransitive events – specific lexemes, mostly based on particular roots, some of which are marked by {n} (in Earlier Egyptian a purely lexical derivation, [§ 5.2.1, fn. 44]); and morphologically unmarked transitivity alternations (P/S ambitransitives, such as *wˁb* "be pure, make pure": see Stauder 2014: 178–183); (ii) reflexive and reciprocal: use of the ordinary pronouns, coreferenced to the subject of the clause; (iii) stative/resultative voice: use of the Resultative form.

for {t} to be extended further down the cline. In VS patterns that do not meet the semantic condition for passivization, the gradualness of such extension is directly observed in the record: first to dynamic intransitive events that lack an agentive participant (5a–c), rapidly followed by non-dynamic events (6a–c), and eventually to statives (7a–b) and even non-verbal situations (8a–b) (§ 3.1).

5.4 The preferred aspectual correlates of T-passives in text

The dimensions discussed so far (§ 5.2–3) apply to V- and T-passives alike. Yet, only T-passives undergo the changes described here. Besides the morphological issues already evoked (§ 4.2), this is also due to the different aspectual correlates of the two passive types in discourse. In relation to these, T-passives are more commonly found with non-specific agents than V-passives are. This provides fertile ground for alternative construals of T-passives as a specificity-based construction.

5.4.1 V- and T-passives, and aspect

As already noted, {t} has singular exponence, coding voice only (§ 4.2). In T-passives, tense and aspect is expressed at the level of the stem to which {t} is appended; {t} itself is unmarked for tense and aspect. V-passive morphology, by contrast, synthesizes perfective aspect and passive voice. Perfective aspect is inherent to the passive nature of the form that is accordingly referred to as a "perfective V-passive".[51]

These general determinations of Earlier Egyptian passive morphology translate into the following (here simplified) distribution of morphological types in the passive paradigm.[52] The relative present tense is the exclusive domain of T-passi-

---

51 For the perfective aspect of the V-passive, Stauder (2014: 310–314); for V- and T-passives in contrast to one another, Stauder (2014: 308–310). Note that Earlier Egyptian conforms to the cross-linguistic prediction that whenever a language has multiple passives that do not differ in terms of the degree or nature of subject affectedness, they typically differ in terms of aspect (Keenan & Dryer 2006: 340–342; similarly observed in Reintges forthc.: § 6.2). The V-passive is thus an instance of the common "perfective skew" of passives (e.g., Comrie 1982). Diachronically, this may reflect a stative/resultative source of the Earlier Egyptian perfective V-passive, as is common in other languages.

52 The Earlier Egyptian passive paradigm is complex due to its sensitivity to the dimensions of polarity, information structure, and semantic transitivity. In addition, there is a diachronic component whereby in some environments T-passives tend to supersede V-passives. See Stauder

ves. Among forms and patterns to which the passive marker {t} can be appended, several are frequently interpreted as imperfective in text, and one (*irr=f*, below) is directly marked for such aspect. The anterior domain, on the other hand, displays a complex passive paradigm which involves both V- and T-passives as well as the Resultative form. Among these, anterior T-passives are used only in specific, functionally marked, environments. These include, most notably, negative and rhematically weakened events. Both have in common the fact that they deviate from the conditions of high semantic transitivity otherwise typically associated with perfective passives.[53] For the purpose of present discussion, anterior T-passives are thus mainly used in environments that are less common in discourse than the ones in which V-passives are used. Compare the following extracts of the Earlier Egyptian passive paradigm:

- Relative present tense: only T-passives – in particular:
    - *(iw) sḏm-tw=f*: covering the whole domain of relative present tense; often interpreted as a general or habitual aspect in text ((15c), (16a));
    - *n sḏm-n-tw=f*: commonly used as the negative counterpart to the above; commonly espresses habitual or general aspect (16c);
    - *irr-tw=f*: often conveying imperfective shades of meaning, commonly used notably in clauses in which the rhematicity of the verbal predicate is weakened ((16b), (16d)).

- Anterior tense: V- and T-passives, Resultative
    - main paradigm (positive, fully asserted events):
        Resultative (pronominal P) ~ V-passive (non-pronominal P [full nouns and subject complement clauses] and subjectless constructions] [impersonal passives]) (15d)[54]

(2014: 26–31, 250–263, 297–318, 334–343).

53 For the general notion of semantic transitivity, see Hopper & Thompson (1980). The tendency for anterior passives to be sensitive to semantic transitivity reflects the Endpoint orientation common to passive voice and perfective aspect (Comrie 1982; Woods 2008: 66–67, 285–301). For the case of Earlier Egyptian, see Stauder (2014: 235–348).

54 In the same environments, a {t}-pattern is found in Old Egyptian (*sḏm-tw=f*). The Old Egyptian past *sḏm=f* enters obsolesence in positive patterns already by the late Old Kingdom (ca. 2200 BCE), and the form is productively used only in a bound negative pattern in Middle Egyptian (below in the Table, *n sḏm-tw=f*).

– T-passives limited to functionally specific environments:
  – fully asserted negative events: *n sḏm-tw=f*;
  – rhematicity weakened:[55] *sḏm-n-tw=f* (15b), negative *n sḏm-n-tw=f ỉs*;
  – *sḏm-ỉn-tw=f*: a narrative tense (largely limited to some formal written registers).

5.4.2 Aspect and the agent of the passive

An alternative construal of the passive construction as based on the non-specificity of the agent is favored when the unexpressed agent of the passive is low in discourse topicality, and even more so when it is non-specific. Conversely, such an alternative construal is disfavored when the agent is specific, singular, and definite.

As far as grammar is concerned, both V- and T-passives are equally compatible with all types of agents, including singular and specific ones (2a–b). In discourse however, singular and specific agents tend to be more frequently associated with perfective events. Conversely, plural and non-specific agents tend to be more frequently associated with imperfective events. Given the distribution of V- and T-passives in the passive paradigm (§ 5.4.1), T-passives are then associated with plural and non-specific agents much more commonly than V-passives are. In a usage-based perspective on linguistic change, such issues of relative frequencies would have played an important role in the change here analyzed.

As an illustration of the preferential associations just outlined, compare:

– Perfective aspect, with a positive, fully asserted event [V-passive]:

(15) a. *ṯꜣz*   *mꜣḵt*   *ỉn* *rꜥ* *ḥft*   *wsỉr*
          knit_together\PASS.PFV   ladder   by   Ra   before Osiris
          'A ladder has been knotted together by Ra before Osiris.' (Pyramid Texts § 472a[WNNt] [ca. 2350 BCE])

---

55 In these constructions – which involve various other dimensions such as the presence or lack of certain discourse particles – the rhematic downgrading of the verbal event results in a correlative upgrading of some adverbial or circumstantial expression further down in the clause. These constructions have major functions in the domain of information structure (when the verbal event is pragmatically presupposed and/or for focusing upon an adverbial or circumstantial expression; see (15b) in the main text) and in the domain of inter-clausal cohesion (for establishing a tighter cohesion between the main clause and a following circumstantial clause).

- Anterior tense, in a functionally specific environment [T-passive]:

    b. *ms-n-t*   *NN pn*   *ḥr=ỉs*   *ȝḫt-ỉ=ỉs*
       give_birth-ANT-PASS NN this   Horus=as Horizon-ADJ=as
       'Like Horus, like the one of the Horizon, this (king) NN has been born.' (Pyramid Texts § 934b[PMN] [ca. 2300 BCE])

       (Contrasting with (15a), the rhematicity of the event is weakened: the birth of the king is here presupposed, and the scope of assertion is accordingly on the circumstances of such birth.)

- Relative present tense, with a reading as general/habitual aspect [T-passive]:

    c. *ỉn*   *ỉw*   *šd-tw*   *ḥnnw*   *m-ḫnw pr*
       INTR[56] COMP bring_up-PASS tumult within Palace
       ỉn   *ỉw*   *wbȝ-tw*   *mw*   *ꜥdd*   *gbb*
       INTR   COMP open_up-PASS water hack_up   earth
       s-wḫȝ-tw   *nḏsw*   *ḥr ỉryt=sn*
       CAUS-be_foolish-PASS commoners on doings=3MSG
       'Are people of tumult ever brought up in the Palace? Is water that destroys the fields ever let forth, and are commoners ever made into fools by their own actions?' (Teaching of Amenemhat 9b–d [literary, ca. 1850–1450 BCE]).

5.4.3 Imperfective environments

Among the various environments in which T-passives are used, imperfective ones are maximally favorable for alternative construals. In imperfective environments, the P argument itself is often plural or non-specific (see (16a), also (15d), (24b); pronominal P's remain rare in text).[57] Moreover, imperfective passives are

---

56 "Interrogative" (marking sentence questions).

57 E.g., *mw m ỉtrw swr-tw=f mr=k* (water in river drink-PASS=3MSG wish=2MSG), *ṯȝw m pt ḥnm-tw=f ḏd=k* (air in sky breathe~DETR=3MSG say=2MSG) 'Water in the river, it is drunk when you wish so; air in the sky, it is breathed when you say so' (Sinuhe B 233–234). In this passage, the two clauses are stylistically balancing. The balanced P arguments (*mw m ỉtrw* 'water in the river', and *ṯȝw m pt* 'air in the sky', respectively) are extraposed to the left of their respective clause, as extra-clausal topics. The anaphoric subject pronouns are resumptive within each clause (*swr-tw=f, ḥnm-tw=f*). Outside such particular conditions, pronominal subjects are uncommon in imperfective passive environments such as the ones discussed here.

not uncommonly subjectless, even if derived from syntactic transitives. Two constructions are involved in such subjectless passives that will be discussed briefly in the following.

In both the active and the passive, the P argument can be introduced by the preposition *m* 'in': V (...) P → V (...) *m* P. This construction – here referred to as "Mediate Object Construction" – has two, often combined, functions: setting P under narrow focus, and/or reducing the semantic transitivity of the event.[58] Whenever the latter function is at play, the Mediate Object Construction strongly correlates with imperfective aspect. When a passive is derived from a Mediate Object Construction, this results in a subjectless passive (16b).

In both the active and the passive, the P argument can be supressed, to express a generalization of the event. In this case – here referred to as "P-detransitivizing" – the construction strongly correlates with imperfective aspect. When a passive is derived from a P-detransitivized event, the resulting construction is subjectless (16c–d):

– P a full noun, plural or non-referential [very common]:

(16) a. *iw*   *in-tw*   *ꜥkw*   *wn*   *3k*
       COMP   bring-PASS   intimates   exist   ruin
       'Intimates are brought when there is ruin.' (Ptahhotep 349 P [literary, ca. 1950 BCE])

– Mediate Object Construction, P realized as an oblique: subjectless passive [not uncommon]:

     b. *snw*   *bin*   *in~n-tw*   *m*   *drdrw*   *r*
        brothers   bad\RES   bring~IMPF-PASS   MOC   strangers   for
        mtt nt ib
        honesty
        'Brothers have become bad; one brings only strangers for honesty.'
        (The Debate of a Man with his Soul 117–118 [literary, ca. 1950 BCE])

---

58 See Winand (this volume, in general); Stauder (2014: 173–188, for the interaction of the Mediate Object Construction with the passive). In much later times (beginning in Demotic, most clearly in Coptic), the construction evolved into a "Differential Object Marking" one (DOM), notably.

– P-detransitivized: subjectless passive [very common]:

c. *n*   *iwr-n-tw*

   NEG   conceive-HAB-PASS

   'There is no more conceiving.' (The Lament of Ipuwer 2.4 [literary, ca. 1800–1450 BCE])

d. *in~n-t*   *n=f*   *r-tnw*   *dbḥ=f*
   bring~IMPF-PASS   to=3MSG   whenever   ask\IMPF=3MSG
   sꜥr-t   *n=f*   *r-tnw*   *ibb=f*
   present\IMPF-PASS   to=3MSG   whenever be_thirsty\IMPF=3MSG
   'Whenever he asks, one brings to him; whenever he is thirsty, one presents to him.' (Coffin Texts V 11c–d [ca. 2100 BCE])

As the above illustrates, passives interpreted as, or marked for, imperfective aspect overwhelmingly either have full noun subjects (16a, 15c) or are subject-less constructions (16b–d). In texts, Earlier Egyptian imperfective passives are therefore formally equivocating in most cases (§ 4.1). In addition, imperfective passives typically have plural or non-specific agents (§ 5.4.2). Moreover, they select T-passives (§ 5.4.1), in which passive morphology has singular exponence and lies at the outer edge of the form (§ 4.2). A variety of factors thus conspires in making imperfective passives in Earlier Egyptian a maximally favorable environment for alternative construals of the passive as a construction based on the non-specificity of the agent.

6 Triggering factors: the rise and spread of SV patterns

As the innovative constructions of the morpheme {t} in SV patterns presented above (§ 3.2) imply, one triggering factor for the change discussed here lies with the rise of SV patterns themselves. The change of Ancient Egyptian from a VS language to a SV language, begun in the mid-third millennium, was a protracted process, not completed until Roman times some two and a half millennia later. The present section examines the earlier stages of this process as they bear on the change discussed here. It is argued that the initial rise of SV patterns at first did not trigger the change discussed (§ 6.1). Rather, it was only the subsequent spread of SV patterns to further domains of usage that eventually proved a powerful motivation for innovative constructions of {t} (§ 6.2).

6.1 The initial rise of SV patterns: counterpart relationships

6.1.1 The initial grammaticalization of SV patterns

In the mid-third millennium, two SV patterns mainly grammaticalize from situational predicate constructions:

– Situational predicate constructions:

$$NP_{subject} \qquad AP_{predicate}$$

– SV patterns grammaticalizing from the situational predicate construction:

NP ḥr-sḏm (NP on-hear\INF) 'NP is hearing' (progressive aspect)
NP r-sḏm (NP to-hear\INF) 'NP is bound to hear' (event necessarily to occur) (later weakening into a future)

In both patterns, the lexical verb is in the infinitive. In Egyptian, the infinitive cannot be inflected for verbal categories. Consequently, inflectional passive morphology can not be directly accommodated onto such patterns.

The patterns *NP ḥr-sḏm* and *NP r-sḏm* remain initially restricted to specific semantics, the former expressing progressive aspect, the latter an event that will necessarily occur. Passive counterparts are provided by various means, mostly through recruiting forms of the VS conjugation, which are passivized by appending {t} to the stem. The result is a series of non-isomorphic counterpart relationships between active and passive constructions (§ 6.1.2–3).

6.1.2 Active-passive counterpart relationships in the unaccomplished

The early (here simplified) paradigm in the unaccomplished can be summarized as follows:

	general/habitual events	ongoing events
active:	*N(P) sḏm=f*	marked progressive *NP ḥr-sḏm*
		/ unmarked N(P) *sḏm=f*[a]
passive:	⟵———————	*sḏm-tw NP*[b] ————————⟶

a) Ongoing active events can be expressed either by the unmarked unaccomplished *N(P) sḏm=f* or by the dedicated progressive pattern *NP ḥr-sḏm*. The latter has become more common in usage by ca. 2000 BCE but *N(P) sḏm=f* is still found with ongoing events, particularly in higher written registers.

b) The passive pattern *sḏm-tw NP* is based on the same morphological form of the verb as the active pattern *N(P) sḏm=f*. In the active, the subject is mostly anticipated in pre-verbal position. This anticipation does not occur in the passive. This difference between the active and passive patterns reflects the non-canonical nature of passive subjects (non-agentive and typically lower in discourse topicality than active subjects).[59]

In the passive, ongoing events are thus at first not expressed by a direct morphological counterpart to the dedicated active pattern *NP ḥr-sḏm*. Rather, the unmarked *sḏm=f* (as in the active *N(P) sḏm=f*, cf. n.a.) is recruited, and {t} is appended to it (*sḏm-tw NP*, cf. n.b.). This results in a situation in which the active distinguishes two categories while the passive does not (compare the Table above). The following example illustrates the counterpart relationship with ongoing events, first with two active ones, then with a passive one:

(17) *iw   srw   ḥr-rḏ-t   n=k*
     COMP officials   PROG-give-INF   to=2MSG
     iw=k   ḥr-iṯ-t   in   iw=k   m   ꜥwꜣy
     COMP=2MSG   PROG-take-INF INTR COMP=2MSG as   robber
     iw   stꜣ-tw   n=k   skw   ḥnꜥ=k   r   psšt   šdwt
     COMP   drag-PASS to=2MSG troops with=2MSG for division plots
     'Officials are giving to you, and you are still taking – so are you a robber? People are ushered in before you, and troops are with you for the division of land-plots!' (Eloquent Peasant B1 332–334 [ca. 1900–1850 BCE])

---

59 Stauder (2014: 223–226, 343–344).

6.1.3 Active-passive counterpart relationships in the future

With events that have future time reference, two successive stages must be distinguished.[60] Reflecting its origin in a situational predicate pattern with the preposition *r* 'to, toward', the pattern *NP r-sḏm* initially developed for expressing events that are bound to happen and/or to which the speaker is strongly committed. In relation to such semantics, the construction is not marked morphologically for voice, but is oriented semantically on the participant that is in some state entailing an event to come.[61] In a glossing translation: 'he is bound to hear', 'he is bound to be heard', both as *NP r-sḏm*. The earliest (here simplified) future paradigm, in the mid-/late third millennium, is thus as follows:

Future events, stage 1:

	future	events bound to occur (semantic orientation)
active:	*ỉr(w)=f*	$NP_{A/S}$ *r-sḏm*
passive:	*ỉr(w)=f, ỉr(w)-tw=f*[62]	NP_p *r-sḏm*

The following pair of examples is illustrative of how the same construction *NP r-sḏm* can have both passive and active readings when expressing events bound to occur:

(18)   a.   *ỉw=f*   *r-wḏꜥ*   *ḥr=s*   *ỉn   nṯr   ꜥꜣ*
             COMP=3MSG   to-judge\INF   on=3FSG   by   great   god
             'He is to be judged for it by the great god.' (Urk. I 122, 16 [ca. 2200 BCE])

   b.   *ỉw=ṯn*   *r-šd-t*   *n(=ỉ)*   *prt-ḫrw*
        COMP=2PL   to-recite-INF   for(=1SG)   invocation_offering
        'Your are to recite an invocation for me.' (Urk. I 119, 7 [ca. 2200 BCE])

Starting from such an initially highly restricted domain of use, the pattern *NP r-sḏm* gradually weakens into a future. When used as a future, *NP r-sḏm* is not

---

60 In more details, Stauder (2014: 230–234).

61 Stauder (2014: 119–122, 129–130).

62 The V-passive (*ỉr(w)=f*) is diachronically superseded by a T-passive formation *ỉr(w)-tw=f.* The first stages of the process can be observed by ca. 2200 BCE. See Stauder (2014: 26–31).

oriented semantically anymore, and passive voice must be marked morphologically. In a manner similar to the one just described for *NP ḥr-sḏm* (§ 6.1.2), a VS pattern that can also express the future, *ỉr(w)=f*, is recruited and passivized by appending the morpheme {t} to it. Around 2000 BCE, this resulted in the following counterpart relationships:

Future events, stage 2:

	future	(events bound to occur)
active:	$\longleftarrow$ *NP r-sḏm* (/*ỉr(w)=f*, obsolescent)$\longrightarrow$	
passive:	$\longleftarrow$ ————— *ỉr(w)-tw=f* ————$\longrightarrow$	
	(/NP_p *r-sḏm*)	

The following pair of examples is illustrative of the counterpart relationship:

[Passive: the king describing Sinuhe's future burial]

(19)   a.   *wḏꜥ-tw*   *n=k*   *ḥ3wy (...)*
  assign-PASS   to=2MSG   night_vigil
  ỉr-tw   *n=k*   *šms-wḏ3 hrw*   *sm3-t3 (...)*
  do-PASS   for=2MSG   procession day   burial
  'A night-vigil will be assigned to you (...); a funeral procession will be made for you on the day of joining the earth (...)' (Sinuhe B 191–193 [ca. 1950 BCE]).

[Active: Sinuhe's response to the king]

  b.   *ỉw*   *k3=k*   *r-rd-t*   *ỉry=ỉ*   *pḥwy ḥꜥw=ỉ*
    COMP   ka=2MSG   FUT-cause-INF   do\SUBJ=1MSG   end   body=1MSG
    m   *ḥnw*
    in   Residence
    'Your *ka*[63] will let me make an end with my body in the Residence.' (Sinuhe B 203–204)

---

63 A concept that is specific to the Egyptian cultural encyclopedia, with no equivalent in translation languages; roughly, the agentive force of the individual, also making him an individual.

6.1.4 The rationale for and initial stability of counterpart relationships

For centuries, the SV patterns *NP ḥr-sḏm* and *NP r-sḏm* therefore lacked direct morphological counterparts in the passive. Instead, complex indirect counterpart relationships obtain.[64] This situation, and it stability over centuries, reflect the following combined dimensions:

- Initial grammaticalization. Following a common trend, the new SV patterns initially grammaticalize with active, positive events.
- Morphology. SV patterns do not provide an inflectional slot onto which passive morphology could be directly accommodated (§ 6.1.1).
- Low text frequency. Two situations have to be distinguished:
  - (i) Initially restricted to events bound to occur, *NP r-sḏm* is then oriented semantically (18a-b). The weakened usages of *NP r-sḏm* as a plain future, which require morphological marking of voice, only gradually emerge during the late third and early second millennium (19a).
  - (ii) Progressive events tend to have a salient agent. With passive events, on the other hand, the agent is typically low in discourse salience. Passive ongoing events therefore tend to be uncommon in discourse.
- Availability of synthetic VS forms in the active. In the domains considered indirect passive counterparts to SV patterns could be formed by appending {t} to VS forms whenever needed ((17), (19a)).

6.2 The spread of SV patterns

During the first half of the second millennium, the SV patterns presented above spread in the language and came to be used in an ever-increasing number of functions. Also beginning in the early second millennium, one can observe the morpheme {t} being accommodated into the subject slot of these SV patterns (§ 3.2). As the compared chronology of developments suggests, it is the functional generalization and correlative spread of SV patterns – rather than their initial grammaticalization (§ 6.1) – that proved a strong motivating factor for the extraction of the morpheme {t} out of its erstwhile exclusively inflectional slot in VS forms.

---

64 Similar indirect counterpart relationships initially also obtain in the negative paradigm (Vernus 1990). The specific reasons, as well as the detailed chronology of developments, are partly different, but the general principle is similar.

6.2.1 Early stages of the spread

The following early developments are of major importance in providing the initial motivation for the innovative uses of {t} in the subject-slot of SV patterns:
- (i) Pursuing the development the early stages of which were sketched above (§ 6.1.3), *NP r-sḏm* continued weakening into a future and eventually superseded *ir(w)=f* as the sole expression of non-modal future events.
- (ii) The formal category *NP ḥr-sḏm*, initially only a progressive, was combined with narrative past auxiliaries:
  - (a) *wn-in=f ḥr-sḏm* (late third millennium), alongside older synthetic *sḏm-in=f* (rapidly confined to a few high-frequency verbs and/or with high-status subjects);
  - (b) *ꜥḥꜥ-n=f ḥr-sḏm* (early second millennium), alongside *ꜥḥꜥ-n sḏm-n=f*; by the mid-second millennium, the former has by and large replaced the latter, which is kept only in some elevated registers.
  - (c) *iw=f ḥr-sḏm*, a narrative sequential tense (securely documented by the mid-second millennium).

The role of these developments was in part illustrated by examples quoted above (§ 3.2):
- (i) *(iw=)tw r-sḏm* (COMP=DETR FUT-hear\INF): (10a–b);
- (ii.a) *wn-in=tw ḥr-sḏm* (AUX-PST-DETR PST-hear\INF): (9b).

Regarding (ii.b) and (ii.c), compare:

(20) a. *ꜥḥꜥ-n=tw*   *ḥr-iwꜥ=i*   *m*   *nbw*
      AUX-PST=DETR   PST-reward\INF=1SG with gold
      'Then I was rewarded with gold.' (Urk. IV 7, 16 [ca. 1500 BCE])

   b. (...) *iw=tw*   *ḥr-rd-(t)*   *iry=sn*   *sḏfꜣ-tryt*
        PST=DETR   PST-give-INF   do\SUBJ=3PL   oath_of_allegiance
        '(...) and One (viz., the king) had them swear an oath of allegiance.' (Urk. IV 1304, 2 [ca. 1400 BCE])

In the same period, a few early occurrences of {t} with *NP ḥr-sḏm* expressing the progressive are found as well. A detailed examination of these is revealing. The earliest instance (9a) is in a past progressive, providing a textual background. In such a discourse environment, the agent is naturally lower in salience than it usually would be in a present tense progressive (§ 6.1.4).

The second earliest instance (21), in a veterinary text, is equally revealing. The three parallel clauses are marked by the modal infix *-ḥr-*, relating the action to be carried out to the previously diagnosed symptoms. Contrasting with the synthetic *-ḥr*-infixed VS forms (*rḏ-ḥr-t=f*, *sỉn-ḥr-t=f*), the compound SV pattern in the second clause (*wn-ḥr-t=f ḥr-ntš*) combines these modal semantics with the progressive semantics of *NP ḥr-sḏm*, thereby emphasizing the continuous nature of the particular action of "sprinkling". Per se, a synthetic VS form (**ntš-ḥr-t=f*) could have been used as well, leaving the interpretation of the action as continuous to the reader/hearer's inferencing. In a technical treatise, a compound pattern is selected for higher explicitness:

(21) *rḏ-ḥr-t=f*   *ḥr*   *gs=f*   *wˁ*
place-MOD-PASS=3MSG.SBJ?   on   side=3MSG   one
wn-ḥr=t   *ḥr-ntš=f*   *m*   *mw*   *kb*
AUX-MOD=DETR   PROG-sprinkle\INF-3MSG.OBJ   with   water   fresh
sỉn-ḥr-t   *ỉrty=f*   *ḥnˁ*   *drw=f*   *ḥnˁ*
rub-MOD-PASS   eyes=3MSG   with   flanks=3MSG   with
ˁt=f   *nbt*
limbs=3MSG   all
'It (viz., the bull) is to be laid on its side; it is to be continuously sprinkled with fresh water, and its eyes are to be rubbed along with its flanks and all its limbs.' (P. UCL 32036, 20–22 [Kahun Veterinary Papyrus, ca. 1800 BCE])

6.2.2 SV patterns spreading yet further

The further spread of SV patterns led to an ever more common use of the morpheme {t} in the subject slot of these patterns. Schematically, two major developments are involved.

Beginning in the eighteenth century BCE, *NP ḥr-sḏm* was gradually extended beyond the marked progressive semantics for which it had initially grammaticalized. By the mid-second millennium, the old unmarked *N(P) sḏm=f* was obsolescent in all but formal registers, and *NP ḥr-sḏm* was left as the sole expression of present tense as a whole. Accordingly, *sḏm-tw NP* also entered obsolescence, and relative present tense events with a non-specified agent are all expressed by *X-tw ḥr-sḏm* patterns. Thus, with an event interpreted as habitual (note the adverbial temporal expression):

(22)   *ḥr   tw=tw*   *ḥr-šd*   *b3kw=f*   *m-dỉ=ỉ*
     and BASE=DETR PRS-request production=3MSG from=1SG
     rnpt   n   rnpt
     year   to   year
     'And one was requesting its production from me year after year.'
     (P. Cairo 58075, 8 = KRI I 238, 14–15 [ca. 1300 BCE, not the earliest
     example])

Beginning in the mid-second millennium, an entirely new layer of SV patterns develops. Rather than grammaticalized from situational predicate constructions (S-PRED > SV) (§ 6.1.1), these are directly derived from erstwhile VS conjugational forms, periphrased by means of an auxiliary *ỉrỉ* 'do'. The auxiliary is inflected, and the lexical verb (dependent upon *ỉrỉ*) is in the infinitive; e.g.: *sḏm-t=f* (do\REL-2FSG=3MSG) 'what he hears' > *(ỉ)ỉr-t=f sḏm* (AUX.REL-3FSG hear\INF). In these *ỉrỉ*-auxiliated patterns, events with non-specified agents are all expressed by placing the morpheme {t} in the subject slot (see above, (12)).

As a result of these combined developments, SV patterns of various origins become dominant in later second-millennium Egyptian. Accordingly, the majority of uses of the morpheme {t} are by then in the subject slot of such patterns. Old T-passives, although stable in themselves, have become limited to a constantly shrinking set of still productive VS patterns (§ 7).

Part III. The fate of T-passives in their original domains of use in the second millennium

7 T-passives and {t}-marked active impersonal constructions coexisting in synchrony

During the second millennium, SV patterns generalize their functional yield and become increasingly common in the language (§ 6.2). Such developments notwithstanding, several major VS forms remain fully productive, most notably the Late Egyptian past *sḏm=f*[65] and the subjunctive *sḏm=f*. With VS forms, T-passives themselves remain fully productive, no less than they were in the third millennium.

---

65 This is the functional, and probably also the morphological, successor to the Old and Middle Egyptian anterior *sḏm-n=f*.

The continued use of T-passives (in which {t} is an inflectional passive marker) alongside the innovative SV constructions (in which {t} is accommodated into the subject slot of an active impersonal construction) raises a series of descriptive issues (§ 7.1). Moreover, some change is ultimately observed with T-passives themselves, despite considerable formal stability (§ 7.2). In addressing these issues, it is proposed that a construction-specific approach is most appropriate here and that some syntactic indeterminacy in ongoing change has to be allowed for.

7.1 Construction-specific analyses

Throughout the second millennium, singular pronominal P's of T-passives are coded by the same set of personal clitics (23a; also 25) as in the third millennium (1a). In active VS forms, these clitics are associated with the grammatical role of subject. On a formal level, T-passives therefore remain promotional.

With the agent-expressing *ỉn*-construction, some change is eventually observed, but only centuries later (discussed below, § 7.2.2). In the earlier second millennium, the agent-expressing *ỉn*-construction is still productively used in all written registers (23b), like it was in the third millennium (2a). T-passives thus contrast with the {t}-marked SV constructions developing at the same time, which, in accordance with their active syntax, cannot accommodate the agent-expressing *ỉn*-construction.

The following examples are illustrative of both properties just discussed:

(23) a. *ỉnk*   *rḏ=ỉ*   *ỉr-tw=f*   *n=k*
          1SG.FOC cause\PROSP=1SG do\SUBJ-PASS=3MSG.SBJ to=2MSG
          'I will have it done for you.' (P. UC 32197, 13 [business letter, ca. 1800 BCE])

      b. *h3b*   *b3k-ỉm (...)*   *ḥr* *r[ḏt]* *ỉp-tw*   *r*
          send servant (...)   on   cause count\SUBJ-PASS   to
          dmỉ   *n* *pr-ḥny*   *ỉn* *nb* [...]
          quay   of   Perkheny   by   lord [...]
          'This humble servant (viz., the speaker) is writing (...) about having it counted to the quay of Perkheny by the lord [...]' (P. UC 32305, 17–18 [same corpus])

In the very same corpus of texts (Illahun business documents, ca. 1800 BCE), {t} is already being accommodated into the subject slot of SV patterns (10a). In the same period, {t}-marked VS forms are extended to events that are banned from passivization on semantic grounds (5a–c, 6a–c). These innovative constructions are non-promotional, with {t} itself functioning as an impersonal subject pronoun, at least in SV patterns. Yet T-passives still behave just as they did in the third millennium, as genuine promotional and demotional passives. If a uniform account of the syntax of earlier second-millennium {t}-marked constructions is sought in terms of constituency, one is faced with a contradiction.

This is solved if different analyses for different environments are allowed, i.e., if a perspective is adopted in which constructions, rather than their constituent parts, are considered as the primary objects of description and analysis. The two analyses then do not contradict each other, since they obtain in different environments. The morpheme {t} is defined in its function of expressing unspecified reference of the agent in either environment, and syntactic differences only emerge in relation to the broader constructional schemes in which the morpheme is used. All environments, innovative and older ones alike, involve a clear mapping of form and function: there was no functional pressure at this level for the language to change.

7.2 Formal retention and increasing syntactic indeterminacy

7.2.1 Background: the ultimate loss of all {t}-marked constructions

By the very late second millennium, {t}-marked constructions rapidly give way to active impersonal constructions with a non-anaphorically interpreted third person plural subject pronoun =w in the subject slot (also below, § 8.1.2). This development occurs with all {t}-marked constructions alike, both in SV and in VS patterns:

– SV patterns, e.g., negative past tense, 'he has not been heard':

> *bwpw-tw sḏm=f* (NEG.PST-DETR hear=3MSG.OBJ)
> > *bwpw=w sḏm=f*(NEG.PST=3PL hear=3MSG.OBJ)

– VS patterns, e.g., past tense, 'he has been heard':

> *sḏm-tw=f*   (hear\PST-PASS?,DETR?=3MSG.SBJ?)
> > *sḏm=w NP* (hear\PST=3PL   NP.OBJ)

In SV patterns, the impersonal pronoun {t} is merely replaced by the ordinary third person plural pronoun, and the overall syntax of the construction remains unchanged. With VS forms, the issue is more complex. On the one hand, T-passive constructions display little change over time, suggesting that they may have been construed as genuine passives even late in the second millennium. On the other hand, the ultimate replacement of the morpheme {t} by the 3PL-construction applies across the board, to VS and SV patterns alike and simultaneously. This could be taken as suggestive that by the later second millennium, T-passives were themselves increasingly construed as active impersonal constructions in speakers' representations. The present sub-section addresses this tension and more broadly discusses the later fate of T-passives.

7.2.2 Changes concerning the agent

A first set of observations suggests some change in the construal of the agent of T-passives during the second millennium.

Beginning in the early second millennium, instances are spotted in which a secondary predication is controlled by the unexpressed agent of a {t}-marked detransitive construction. Such complex constructions are found in innovative (24a = 6b, with a non-passivizable event) and in old environments alike (24b–c, with passivizable events):

(24) a. *nn sḏr-tw*   *ḥkr*   *n*   *mt*
NEG spend_the_night\SUBJ-DETR be_hungry\RES for death
'The night will not be spent fasting for death.' (Neferti IXc [ca. 1850–1450 BCE]

   b. *ỉw*   *pḥ-tw*   *mwt*   *ḥr-rḫ=st*
COMP reach-PASS death PROG-learn=3FSG
'One reaches death by trying to learn about it.' (Ptahhotep 288 [ca. 1950 BCE])

   c. *ỉr grt tw3-tw*   *ḥr-ḏd=st* (...)
if PCL complain-PASS PROG-say=3FSG
'If however one complains by saying it (...)' (P. UC 32200, 13–14 [ca. 1800 BCE])

No such constructions are found in any third-millennium texts, neither with T-passives nor with V-passives. Nor are these ever found with V-passives in any second-millennium texts. The development thus appears to be exclusive to second-millennium {t}-marked constructions, extending to all of these alike. Examples such as (24b–c) then provide evidence for an at least incipient, or occasional, interpretation of {t} in T-passives as itself standing for the unspecified agent rather than as merely signaling passive voice as a syntactic derivation.

Some change with the agent-expressing *in*-construction points in the same direction. While still used productively in all written registers in the earlier centuries of the second millennium (23b), the construction becomes increasingly obsolete by the mid-second millennium, being kept only in most formal registers. Significantly, the following fairly late instance of the agent-expressing *in*-construction is from an inscriptional register, the language of which harkens back to past textual – and hence linguistic – models (sim. (26)):

(25) *ḥs-tw=i*   *ḥr rḫ=i*   *m-ḫt rnpwt*
      praise\SUBJ-DETR=1SG.SBJ on knowledge=1SG after years
      in ntiw r-sn-t   *r ir-t-n=i*
      by REL FUT-pass-INF by do\REL-FSG-ANT=1SG
      'May I be praised for my knowledge after years by those who will imitate what I have done.' (Urk. 58, 2–3 [Ineni, funerary self-presentation, ca. 1450 BCE])

Slightly later than with T-passives, the obsolescence of the agent-expressing *in*-construction further extends to V-passives as well. By the last third of the second millennium, the *in*-construction had become restricted to a few stock formulae in administrative language, all with V-passives. As the relative chronology of developments suggests, T-passives had a leading role in the process by which the Earlier Egyptian passive construction evolved into one that increasingly disallowed the peripheral expression of the agent by means of *in*. I propose that this change is evidence for a partial reinterpretation of T-passives, under the influence of {t}-marked constructions in SV patterns. Being active impersonal in syntax, these {t}-marked constructions in SV patterns could not accommodate the agent-expressing *in*-construction.[66] The increasingly high relative frequency of {t}-marked SV patterns in the language would have played a role in speakers' changing representations of T-passives themselves.

---

66 A handful of cases of agent-expressing *in*-constructions with SV patterns can be found (Urk. IV 1281, 14–15; KRI IV 19, 8; KRI IV 155, 12). These are all from specific inscriptional registers, the hybrid language of which displays complex interferences between past layers of the language that are imitated or emulated, and more contemporary varieties.

On an altogether different level, a marginal graphic phenomenon is also noteworthy in the present context. Mostly in Late Egyptian literary registers, the graphic classifier for divine beings not uncommonly follows the morpheme {t} when the unspecified agent is the king. The use of T-passives with implied royal agents ("honorary passive") is documented from the third millennium on. However, written complementation by the classifier for divine beings is an innovation of later second-millennium scribes. Although merely a graphic phenomenon with no correlate in the sequence of speech, this scribal practice may be interpreted as further evidence for the ongoing reinterpretation of {t} in T-passives as itself standing for the unspecified agent.

7.2.3 Formal retention in doubly inflected patterns

As discussed above (§ 7.1, cf. (23a), (25)), the realization of singular pronominal P's in T-passives by subject clitics remains stable throughout the second millennium. A series of phenomena suggests that over time this formal stability becomes a mere formal retention, while the passive construction itself becomes increasingly indeterminate in its syntax.

Innovative uses of {t} include those in doubly inflected patterns (§ 3.2.3). In these, {t} aligns morphologically with (pro)nominal morphemes in the corresponding active pattern (i). This suggests an analysis of {t} as an impersonal subject pronoun, similar to other {t}-marked SV patterns. On the other hand, however, singular pronominal P's are still coded by subject clitics ((26), also (13b)), and {t}-marked doubly inflected patterns are compatible with the agent-expressing *in*-construction down to the mid-second millennium (26). These promotional and demotional properties suggest an analysis of the construction similar to that of T-passives (ii), thus conflicting with the one just made:

(26) *ḫr-t*   *nḏr-t=f*   *in*   *wpwtiw*
      MOD-DETR   seize-DETR=3MSG.SBJ?/.OBJ?   by   messengers
      n   *ṯзty*
      of   vizier
      '(...) then he shall be arrested by the messengers of the vizier' (Duties of the Vizier, R3 [formal register, ca. 1450 BCE]).

(i) doubly inflected patterns, detransitive and active:

- {t}-marked: *ḫr-tw   sḏm-tw NP* ('NP must then be heard')
- active: *ḫr NP$_i$ sḏm=f$_i$ NP$_j$* ('NP$_i$ must then hear NP$_j$')
(MOD NP.SBJ hear=AGR NP.OBJ)

(ii) singular pronominal P's and/or agentive *in*-phrase:

- *ḫr-tw sḏm-tw=f in N* ("He must then be heard by N")

Conflicting analyses:

→ based on (i), analysis of the {t}-marked construction as "active impersonal" (?!):

ḫr-tw$_i$	*sḏm-tw$_i$*	*NP$_p$*
MOD-DETR.SBJ	hear-DETR.AGR	NP.OBJ (?!)

→ based on (ii), analysis as a "genuine passive" (?!):

ḫr-tw	*sḏm-tw=f$_p$*		*in N$_A$*
MOD-PASS	hear-PASS=3MSG.SBJ	by	N (?!)

In a constituency-based approach, these conflicting analyses could be accommodated by describing the construction in (26) and (13a–b) as syntactically hybrid or gradient, conflating both "active impersonal" (i.e., non-promotional) and "passive" (i.e., promotional) syntactic properties. In an alternative approach, introducing no ad hoc exceptions, it is proposed that the construction should be considered in terms of the functionality of its form-function mapping. On the one hand, the innovative construction of the morpheme {t} in doubly inflected patterns relates to the broader process of the extension of {t} to new environments (§ 3.2), and is a token of a gradual evolution of {t} towards assuming features characteristic of pronominal morphemes. On the other hand, the continued coding of singular pronominal P's with subject clitics is in line with the fact that all constructions that have {t} in its old inflectional slot – as is also the case in doubly inflected patterns – maintain the inherited realization of singular pronominal P's with subject clitics. The continued acceptability of the agent-expressing *in*-phrase is accounted for along similar lines, in relation to a partial constructional commonality with the the still productively used T-passives:

	V-{t}=*SBJ.CLITICS* (*in* N)	(T-passives: § 7.1, § 7.2.4)
MOD-{t}	V-{t}=*SBJ.CLITICS* (*in* N)	

Although syntactically indeterminate, the construction results in no ambiguity for speakers. What would appear as the construction's syntactic "hybridity" is primarily a feature of descriptive frameworks.

7.2.4 Growing syntactic indeterminacy in mid-/late second millennium BCE T-passives

Pursuing the perspective just outlined (§ 7.2.3), it is proposed that some syntactic indeterminacy, growing over time, is more generally associated with mid- and late second-millennium T-passives.

The original possibility for the phenomenon has its roots in much earlier times. As discussed above (§ 4), syntactic equivocation – but not yet indeterminacy – is already found with late third-millennium T-passives and represents one pre-condition for the innovative usages of {t} that were to develop in SV patterns by the early second millennium. The very same dimensions that accounted for prior equivocation – the coding properties of grammatical relations (§ 4.1) and the componentiality of T-passive morphology (§ 4.2) – would also provide the conditions for later syntactic indeterminacy, as will be described now.

In the course of the second millennium, the innovative uses of {t} in SV patterns spread in the language and thereby became increasingly salient in speakers' linguistic representations. The two types of {t}-marked constructions, SV and VS ones, coexist in texts, and even occur side by side (for an early illustration of them alternating with each other, see (21)). Syntactically, {t}-marked SV patterns are active impersonal, and therefore non-promotional, in a fully non-equivocating manner. T-passives on the other hand are formally equivocating in most uses:

- SV-patterns: P direct object, in a non-equivocating manner:

   (by word-order: S-V-O):

(active)	X-NP$_A$	ḥr-sḏm	NP$_P$	(X-NP.SBJ PROG-hear NP.OBJ)
(detransitive)	X-tw	ḥr-sḏm	NP$_P$	(X-DETR PROG-hear NP.OBJ)

- T-passives: originally, P subject, but formally equivocating whenever not singular pronouns (in detail, § 4):

   sḏm-tw rmṯ$_P$ (hear\SUBJ-PASS men.SBJ?)

   (hear\SUBJ-DETR men.OBJ?)

In such conditions, it is proposed that the increasingly common (non-equivocating) {t}-marked SV patterns reinforce a representation in which the (often equivocating) T-passives become increasingly indeterminate as to the syntactic status of the P argument. In an informal dependency-based approach, the condition for such "attraction" of the syntax of T-passives to the syntax of {t}-marked SV patterns is represented as:

- (i) [SV patterns:] {t}-V ← P P direct object (non-equivocating)
- (ii) [T-passives:] V-{t} ← P P subject, often equivocating
  → P increasingly indeterminate

A full actualization, i.e., a formal mapping out (Harris & Campbell 1995: 77–89), of the incipient reinterpretation of T-passives as non-promotional constructions would consist in instances of *sḏm-tw=sw, with singular pronominal P realized as object clitics. Except for a handful of mostly late instances, all of which are philologically disputable, no instance of such is ever found in the record. The situation in mid- and late second-millennium Egyptian is therefore illustrative of a general principle in linguistic change whereby behavior is affected before coding (Haspelmath 2010; with detransitive constructions in particular, Siewierska 2010; Givón & Kawasha 2006; Givón 2006). In Egyptian, various changes in behavior relating to the unspecified agent are to be observed with second-millennium T-passives (§ 7.2.2) and may perhaps be interpreted as a partial actualization of ongoing change. On the other hand, the formal realization of singular pronominal P's as subject clitics remains stable (§ 7.1), even in constructions where {t} itself increasingly patterns as a pronominal morpheme (doubly inflected constructions, § 7.2.3).

This situation does not result in any interpretive ambiguity. In VS patterns, the single core argument of the detransitive clause is immediately identified as a P, regardless of how the morpheme {t} is analyzed syntactically[67] and independently of the fact that singular pronominal P's are realized morphologically with pronouns that are otherwise associated with the subject function in active VS patterns. With VS patterns becoming increasingly marginal, this formal retention, limited to singular pronouns, becomes a construction-specific idiosyncrasy, an island phenomenon within the overall syntax of the language. It would ultimately be solved by the overall replacement of {t}-marked patterns with the 3PL-active impersonal construction (§ 7.2.1).

---

67 Note that the situation is again easily represented in a dependency-based approach, informally as: V-{t} ← P. A constituency-based framework would have to assume rebracketing: $[V-\{t\}_{PASS}] \ P_{SBJ} > V-[\{t\}_{SBJ}] \ P_{OBJ}$. For other cases of changes that are more naturally described in a dependency-based approach, Haspelmath (1998: 330–332).

Part IV. Degrammaticalization; mechanisms and circumstances of a rare change

8 An instance of degrammaticalization

8.1 Preliminaries: what degrammaticalization in general, and the present change in particular, are not

Degrammaticalization does not refer to the literal reversal of a particular process, or path, of grammaticalization. In line with recent studies on the subject, degrammaticalization is a compound change that goes counter to certain dimensions associated with the general cline of grammaticality (for a more precise definition, see below, § 8.2). In particular, the term does *not* refer to the reversal of a change which previously happened in one particular language ("token reversal"). Nor does it refer to the reversal of a specific path of grammaticalization ("mirror-image reversal").

8.1.1 Token reversal

"Token reversal" has been described as "fantastically unlikely", and "token irreversibility", consequently, a "non-issue" (Norde 2009: 59, 61).[68] In Earlier Egyptian as well, the changes undergone by {t} do not constitute token reversal.

Although the origins of *{t} in Afroasiatic remain unclear in detail, they surely do not lie with an impersonal subject pronoun.[69] With considerable variation in individual Afroasiatic languages, {t} displays various, generally combined, reflexive, reciprocal, medial, anticausative, and/or passive functions (§ 5.2). Among these, the passive function is secondary, and the reflexive function is often salient. Earlier Egyptian T-passives may therefore represent the outcome of a classical grammaticalization path REFLEXIVE > ANTICAUSATIVE > PASSIVE (e.g., Heine & Kuteva 2002: 44). Alternatively, Afroasiatic *{t} may initially have been intransitivizing in a broad sense, and the development leading to Earlier Egyptian T-passives would then be of the sort INTRANSITIVIZING > ... > PASSIVE, with different bifurcations in the intermediary stages in individual languages.

---

68 Similar observations in Haspelmath (2004: 28), who coined the term "token reversal".
69 Stauder (2014: 220–221).

Either way, the original functions of Afroasiatic *{t} lie in imparting, or reflecting, reduced (semantic) transitivity. Reduction of (semantic) transitivity operates on the lexical semantics of the event. By contrast, active impersonal constructions have to do with the reduced specificity of the A/S argument and leave event semantics untouched.

In a long-term perspective, reaching back into prehistory, the general line of development is thus as follows (compare (i)–(iv) in the Table in § 5.3.2):

reduction of (semantic) transitivity [Afroasiatic *{t}]
→ various combinations of reflexive, reciprocal, medial, anticausative, or passive functions [individual historically documented AA languages]
→ *solely passive* [3d. mill. Egyptian, and some other AA languages]
→ *impersonal subject pronoun* [developing in 2nd mill. Egyptian]

8.1.2 Mirror-image, or type-reversal

Distinct from "token reversal", "mirror-image reversal" would consist in "type-reversal", i.e., in a gram moving up a given grammaticalization *chain* or *path*. No instance is known from the history of any language, and such development has been argued to "verge on the impossible" (Norde 2009: 123).[70]

At first sight, the change undergone by Earlier Egyptian {t} may seem to be a reversal of the well-documented development from active impersonal to passive (e.g., Siewierska 2010; Givón & Kawasha 2006; Heine & Kuteva 2002: 236–237; Haspelmath 1990: 49–50). Yet a closer look demonstrates otherwise. To begin with, the general development from passive to active impersonal is by no means exceptional, and the (so far very broadly phrased) active impersonal-to-passive connection is therefore bi-directional (Siewierska 2008; Haspelmath 1990: 57–58). The diachronic connection between the two broad construction types reflects their functional overlap and cognitive proximity (§ 5.1). The bi-directionality of possible change further reflects the fact that both directions involve a relaxation of restrictions and thereby context generalization (§ 5.1.1, *fine*). For the present purpose, it is mainly emphasized that no direction seems privileged.

---

70 Norde further recalls that degrammaticalization is defined as "a *single* change from right to left on the cline of grammaticality" (emphasis original) and argues that the "circumstances under which a degrammaticalization can take place are very rare, and it is quite unlikely that such circumstances would arise twice in the history of a given morpheme" (as would have to be the case in mirror-image reversal).

Moreover, the general development from active impersonal to passive does not in itself constitute a grammaticalization path.

It further appears that the respective source and target constructions for either direction of development are only superficially comparable. Passive constructions arising from active impersonal ones are often only incipient or emergent passives (Siewierska 2010; Givón & Kawasha 2006). Conversely, active impersonal constructions arising from passive ones are typically non-pronominal impersonal constructions (Siewierska 2008). Consequently, the two types of changes are not reversals of each other (Siewierska 2008):

(i) impersonal (3PL subjects) → *incipient/emergent* passives
(– generally not extended to all types of agents
– P often retaining a non-promotional coding)

(ii) passive (full-blown) → *non-pronominal* impersonal

Finally, cases of change from active impersonal to passive quoted in the literature seem to always, or at least very commonly, involve a specific path 3PL > PASS. The latter, now in a more restrictive formulation, constitutes a path of grammaticalization (Heine & Kuteva 2002: 236–237). In the present case, however, the passive marker {t} develops into an impersonal subject pronoun. This is remarkable against the general background of (ii) above, apparently remains unparalleled, and directly relates to the proposed interpretation of the change as an instance of deinflectionalization (below, § 8.3). Yet, the development is still not into a 3PL pronoun.

To be sure, all former uses of {t} would ultimately be taken over by a construction with a non-anaphorically interpreted 3PL subject pronoun (§ 7.2.1). However, {t} is then replaced by the 3PL pronoun rather than developing into such itself:

(i) the general grammaticalization path:

3PL > PASS (incipient, see above)

(ii) Earlier Egyptian {t}:

PASS	→	impersonal subject pronoun	(2nd mill.)

$\downarrow$

replaced by 3PL (=*w*)   (ca. 1100 BCE)

[→ "incipient passive" (cf. (i))[71]   (later 1st mill.)]

The rise of the 3PL-impersonal construction characteristic of first-millennium BCE Egyptian results from the extension of the (ordinary) anaphoric 3PL pronoun (=*w*) to non-anaphoric contexts. The development was probably eased by the fact that the language already had a widely used active impersonal construction, the one in which {t} acted as an impersonal subject pronoun. In being extended to non-anaphoric uses, the 3PL pronoun merely had to replace {t} in the very same environments (see § 7.2.1). Crucially, however, this is then a new construction formally speaking.

In sum, the Egyptian change from passive to impersonal subject construction is not a "mirror-image reversal" – nor is the overall, indirect process which ultimately led to a situation in which 3PL-active impersonal constructions are used in the first millennium in contexts in which passive ones were used in the third.

8.2 General conditions for qualifying as an instance of degrammaticalization

Following Norde (2009: 120), degrammaticalization is defined as:

> "a composite change whereby a gram in a specific context gains in autonomy or substance on more than on linguistic level (semantics, morphology, syntax, or phonology)".

---

71 Centuries later (first possible occurrence around ca. 500 BCE, very few cases before Coptic), the 3PL-active impersonal construction would be extended to accommodate agent-phrases in syntactic periphery, thereby itself going some way along the grammaticalization path in (i). The agent phrase is then introduced by variants of a compound preposition *n-ḏrt*, Coptic *ḥi-toot-* 'in/through/on the hand of' (entirely unrelated to the old *in*-construction (§ 2.2.1) which had fallen out of use for more than a millennium (§ 7.2.2)). Even in Coptic, the new agent-explicating construction remained fairly uncommon in text and apparently limited to third person (mostly plural) agents. The overall construction is therefore described as an "incipient passive", in broad conformity with similar developments observed elsewhere. An alternative qualification as "extended active impersonal construction" would perhaps be even more appropriate here.

For a change that goes against certain dimensions associated with the cline of grammaticality to qualify as a genuine instance of degrammaticalization, various conditions, all expressed in the above synthetic definition, have to be fulfilled.

The change has to happen "in specific contexts", i.e., fulfill a condition of "preserving (constructional) identity" (Haspelmath 2004: 27–28). Degrammaticalization is therefore distinct from various phenomena of lexicalization of affixes and other items of minor word-classes (such as *the pros and cons, isms,* etc.), which result in entirely new contexts of uses of these (Norde 2009: 9, 122–124; Haspelmath 2004: 27–33; Lehmann 2004: 174–177). In the present case, {t} is extended to new environments, but always for expressing the non-specified reference of the subject. The morpheme's function thereby remains within detransitive voice, and "constructional identity" is preserved. On the other hand, the ultimate replacement of {t}-marked impersonal constructions by 3PL impersonal constructions (§ 8.1.2., *fine*) does not belong to the process of degrammaticalization proper anymore since constructional identity is then breached on the formal level.

Secondly, the change has to involve some "gain". This distinguishes degrammaticalization from "retraction", i.e., a change in which a morpheme merely drops a more grammatical function and thus retracts to a less grammatical one that it had been used for all along (Haspelmath 2004: 33–35). The two types of changes contrast as in the following diagram. Only in degrammaticalization is the less grammatical function (A) innovated:

degrammaticalization: B → A (B) [the less grammatical function, A, is new]

retraction:[72]   AB → A [the less grammatical function, A, has been present all along]

That the change undergone by Earlier Egyptian {t} is not an instance of retraction has already been demonstrated in the context of previous discussions:
- By the early second millennium, {t} is extended to events that do not meet the semantic condition for passivization (§ 3.1). In earlier times, {t} was never

---

72 An illustration of retraction, in a related domain, is provided by English *man* (Haspelmath 2004: 34). In Modern English, *man* is used as a full noun only (like German *Mann*), while in Old English it was also used as an impersonal subject pronoun (like German *man*). However, the use as a full noun is also attested in Old English. Consequently, the change is in effect a loss, rather than a gain. In particular, the source construction – the full noun from which the impersonal had once grammaticalized – has remained present all along.

used with such types of events, while other formal strategies were demonstrably used instead with these (§ 2.2.2).

– By the early second millennium, {t} is extended to SV patterns (§ 3.2, § 6.2). In the later third millennium by contrast, passive counterparts to active SV patterns were never realized with {t}. Rather, they were then realized by recruiting VS patterns to which {t} was appended, resulting in indirect (non-isomorphic) active-passive counterpart relationships of various sorts (§ 6.1).

This is summarized as follows, in conformity with genuine degrammaticalization:

	3rd & very early 2nd mill. →	early-late 2nd mill.
VS, passivizable events:	{t}	{t}
non-passivizable events:	sḏm-ø, etc. (§ 2.2.2)	{t} (§ 3.1)
SV patterns:	counterpart relationships (§ 6.1)	{t} (§ 3.2, § 6.2)

Thirdly, the change must be "composite", i.e., involve "gain (...) on more than one level". This is demonstrated in the next sub-section.

8.3 An instance of deinflectionalization

I here consider the change undergone by {t} in terms of the reversal of primitive changes associated with grammaticalization. This demonstrates that among the three types of degrammaticalization identified by Norde (2009) – degrammation, deinflectionalization, and debonding – the Egyptian change qualifies more precisely as an instance of deinflectionalization.

Norde's (2009: 130–132, 228–231) parameters of degrammaticalization are indexed on Lehmann's (1995) parameters of grammaticalization which diversely apply to primary and secondary grammaticalization[73] (here symbolized as "1°" and "2°"). As argued throughout Norde (2009), the distinction is of relevance in

---

73 The terms "primary" and "secondary" grammaticalization (Norde 2009: 124) go back to Kuryłowicz (1975: 52) famous bipartite definition: "Grammaticalization consists in the increase of the range of a morpheme advancing from a lexical to a grammatical or from a grammatical to a more grammatical status." In a complementary fashion, primary and secondary grammaticalization may be thought of as associated respectively with the left and right parts of the "cline of grammaticality" (Hopper & Traugott 2003: 7): "content word > grammatical word > clitic > inflectional affix".

appreciating which primitive changes are reversed, and in identifying different types of degrammaticalization.

- (i) [Integrity:]
  - "*Resemanticization*":
    - (2°) √   {t} has gained the function of expressing non-specified reference in SV patterns and with non-passivizable events and nonverbal situations.

      (Compare also the occasional cases of graphic complementation (14a–b), [§ 7.2.2, *fine*]).
    - (1°) (no) [{t} does not develop full lexical semantics such as in e.g., *homo* or *Mann* (from which French *on* or German *man* grammaticalized in primary grammaticalization)].

  - "*Phonological strengthening*":
    - (2°) (no) [{t} is realized as *$/t(v)/$ in all environments.[74]]

  - "*Recategorialization*":
    - (1°) (no) [{t} remains limited to the syntactic position of subject[75] and cannot control subsequent anaphoric reference. It thereby contrasts with other Earlier Egyptian expressions used for expressing non-specified reference such as, most notably, *s* 'man' (below, (27a–b)).]

- (ii) [Paradigmaticity:] "*Deparadigmaticization*":
  - (2°) √   To be used in the subject slot of SV patterns, {t} has been extracted from its erstwhile exclusive inflectional slot and thus "discharge(d) from an inflectional paradigm".
  - (1°) (no) [{t} does not move "up" to an open class.]

---

74 Over time, the fuller writing of {t} as <*t+w*> becomes more common than the shorter one as <*t*>. This relates to more general changes in scribal conventions. Significantly, the distribution of fuller vs. shorter writings does not correlate in any meaningful manner with different environments of use of {t}. Differences that there may have been in the realization of {t} in different environments were phonologically conditioned. See Stauder (2014: 10–16).

75 One singular exception is found in (...) *r pзy=tw šm* (about POSS=DETR go\INF) '(...) about the fact that one has gone' (P. Salt 124 vso I.11 [ca. 1200 BCE]). The uniqueness of this expression – a hapax legomenon in a, by this time, relatively dense written record – suggests an exploratory, or non-standard, status of the construction. Moreover, {t} still stands for the agent in a construction in which the "possessed" noun is an infinitive, i.e., a nominalized action. Taken together, this suggests an analogical extension of use, exploratory or in a non-standard register.

- (iii) [Paradigmatic variability:] *"Deobligatorification"* (1° and 2°):
  - (no)   [In all its uses, including innovative ones, {t} remains an obliga-
            tory expression of non-specified reference. Moreover, it remains
            the sole grammatical expression of this category.[76] In particular,
            the construction with *s* 'man' (below, (27a–b)) is used in strict
            complementary distribution to {t}: when controlling anaphoric
            reference and/or in syntactic functions other than subject.]

- [(iv) Structural scope: This, a possibly problematic parameter in general
  (Norde 2009: 131), does not apply to the present change.]

- (v) [Bondedness:] *"Severance"*:
  - (2°) √   In T-passives, {t} is an inflectional affix (§ 3.2, introduction;
             § 4.2). When extended to SV patterns, it behaves as a clitic:
             (a) {t} is used in the slot otherwise occupied by subject clitics
             (compare the pairs of examples in § 3.2); (b) {t} can be attached
             to a variety of hosts: *iw=*, *nty=*,[77] *tw=*, *ḥr=*, *k3=*, *wn=*, etc.[78] The
             change is thus as: stem-{t} [T-passives] > host-{t} [SV patterns].[79]
             (Severance here does not entail "defusion": Already as an
             inflectional affix, {t} was agglutinated to the stem).

---

76 On another level, some very minimal paradigmatic variability is perhaps observed during the period around 1100 BCE when the 3PL pronoun gradually supersedes {t}, the two expressions shortly coexisting with each other for the same function (§ 8.1.2). As argued above, this part of the overall change does not belong to the process of degrammaticalization anymore and is therefore inconsequential for the present evaluation.

77 Not illustrated so far in the present paper; earliest instance: (...) *nt-t=tw r-irt* (REL-FEM=DETR FUT-do) '(...) what is to be done' (P. UC 32287, 2–3 [business document, ca. 1800 BCE]).

78 E.g., *iw=tw* (8a–b, 10a–b, 20b); *tw=tw* (7b, 11, 22); *k3/ḥr=tw* (13a–b, 26); *wn=tw* (9a); *wn-in=tw* (9b, fn. 42); *wn-ḥr=tw* (21); *ꜥḥꜥ-n=tw* (7a, 20a); *iirt=tw* (12); etc. In addition, a dozen cases are found in which {t} is not appended to any preceding host and stands at the beginning of the clause (e.g., (10b): *tw r-sḏm*); see Stauder (2013: 358–370, 376–390). These constructions remain limited to three literary texts and one personal name. In all cases, the lack of a preceding host reflects specific syntactic circumstances. Moreover, the position of {t} is uniquely determined even in clause-initial uses. Rather than as "debonding" (definition in Norde 2009: § 6), these clause-initial uses of {t} are therefore better interpreted as exceptional instances of a pro-clitic use, limited to specific textual contexts and syntactic environments (expressed in an exact transcription as *tw=r-sḏm*).

79 In the lack of objective criteria, the morphological status of {t} in VS patterns with non-passivizable events can be considered either as inflectional (as in T-passives), or, in a perhaps more cautious fashion, as indeterminate. Discussion above, § 7.2.

– (vi) [Syntagmatic variability:] *"Flexibilization"* (1° and 2°):
  – (no) [{t} is used in a variety of conjugational patterns and construc-
      tional schemes. In each of these, the position of the morpheme
      remains uniquely determined.]

[NB: *the s 'man'-construction*[80]
Full noun *s* 'man, *homo*', generically interpreted; used in cases when {t} cannot be used:

– non-specified subject controlling subsequent anaphoric reference:

(27) a. *s-ḫˁr*   *s*   *m*   *sp=f*   *bin s-sbt=f*   *bw-nb* (...)
         CAUS-rage man in occasion=3MSG bad CAUS-laugh=3MSG everyone
         'When a man causes anger by his bad deed, he makes everyone laugh (...)'
         (Debate of a Man and his Soul 110–111)

– syntactic position other than subject (here also controlling anaphora):

  b. *iw*   *rˁ*   *n s*   *nḥm=f=sw*
      COMP speech of man save=3MSG.AGR=3MSG.OBJ
      'A man's speech can save him' (Shipwrecked Sailor, 17–18).]

The innovative uses of {t} observed in the second millennium thus involve the reversal of multiple primitive changes: resemanticization (i), deparadigmaticization (discharge from an inflectional paradigm) (ii), and severance (v). The present change is a compound change, qualifying as an instance of degrammaticalization. No changes in expression occur (cf. (i), *sub* "phonological strengthening"), but this is unproblematic for the present analysis since changes in expression, "as in grammaticalization, may or may not occur" (Norde 2009: 233).

All observed changes are reversals of primitive changes associated with secondary grammaticalization, and no primitive changes associated with primary grammaticalization are reversed. Moreover, the specific types of primitive changes that are reversed correlate with each other in a meaningful way, leading to the description of the change discussed here as an instance of *deinflectionalization* specifically. Compare the following definition and typical correlation of primitive changes reversed:

"Deinflectionalization is a composite change whereby an inflectional affix in a specific linguistic context gains a new function, while shifting to a less bound morpheme." (Norde 2009: 152)

---

80 On this construction, Stauder (2014: 189–192). On active impersonal constructions more generally in Earlier Egyptian, Stauder (2014: 183–200).

"In deinflectionalization, the crucial parameter is paradigmaticity, because what is most characteristic of these cases is that inflectional suffixes cease to form part of inflectional paradigms (deparadigmaticization). Thus they develop into a less bound type of morpheme (severance), and they gain a new function or new meaning (resemanticization). However, they are not being recategorialized because they do not become members of a major word class." (Norde 2009: 231)

9 Summary: the mechanisms of, and circumstantial conditions for, a rare change

The change described in the present paper is a rare change, as can be seen from two, here equivalent, perspectives. The change from passive to active impersonal is otherwise documented, but not as leading to a *pronominal* active impersonal construction (Siewierska 2008). Moreover, the present change qualifies as an instance of degrammaticalization (§ 8.2), and more specifically of deinflectionalization (§ 8.3).

As noted by Norde (2009: 102), "(...) affixal degrammaticalization is admittedly rare, but in case of *favorable circumstances*, such as some kind of internal Systemstörung (Plank 1995) and a *possibility of* morphosyntactic reanalysis, it is by no means impossible [emphasis mine]." This concluding section summarizes the mechanisms and factors at work in the Egyptian change under discussion and the favorable circumstances that made it possible within the specific linguistic context of early second-millennium Egyptian.

9.1 Mechanisms of change

The mechanisms of change are threefold. The possibility for *occasional* reanalysis, by individual speakers, is given by ample formal equivocation (§ 4). This phrasing – different from "reanalysis" plain and simple[81] – is used in order to account for the fact that, even centuries after {t} had been extended to new environments, T-passives themselves remained unchanged in their morphosyntactic properties (§ 4, introduction). This implies that early second-millennium T-pas-

---

81 In many changes, reanalysis is considered a necessary mechanism (e.g., Harris & Campbell 1995: 61–96), including for grammaticalization (challenged by Haspelmath 1998). I submit that this is not the case in the change discussed here.

sives were still genuine passives (§ 7.1) only later to undergo some change themselves (§ 7.2). In the analysis advocated here, it is then the *possibility* for *occasional* reanalysis of T-passives – rather than *prior* reanalysis of such – that provides the condition for extending {t} to new environments.

The second mechanism for change – pragmatic enrichment – is observed in the passive marker {t} being associated with the referential properties of the non-specified agent itself (§ 5). In a passive construction, passive morphology codes a syntactic transformation and thereby only indirectly points to the agent. In its innovative uses, {t} itself stands for the non-specified, and often non-specific, agent. Following Langacker (2004; 2006), the condition for such change was described in terms of the alternative construal of a construction based on the relative prominence of participants (the passive) as a construction based on the (non-)specificity of the agent (the active impersonal) (§ 5.1). In Earlier Egyptian, T-passives were very commonly used in discourse-environments that not only permit but also often directly favor such alternative construals in speakers' representations (§ 5.2–4).

Finally, the change involves context generalization: to events that could not be passivized on semantic grounds (events and situations that lack an agentive participant (§ 2.2.2, § 3.1)) and to patterns that could not be passivized on morphological grounds (SV patterns originally grammaticalized from situational predicate constructions (§ 3.2, § 6.2)). The spread and functional generalization of these SV patterns language proved an important motivating factor for change. As in other instances of deinflectionalization,[82] an entirely unrelated process of change thus provided a specific intra-linguistic context for a rare change which otherwise may well not have happened.

The mechanisms of change (potential for reanalysis, pragmatic enrichment, and context generalization) are thus ordinary ones, and similar to ones found in grammaticalization itself.

9.2 The intra-linguistic context for the change

In Part II, I discussed a series of specific circumstances that not only made the Egyptian change here discussed possible but might even, in their cumulative effect, have favored it. These are briefly recapitulated here for a conclusive assessment (the siglum [T] signals those conditions that apply only to T-passives):

---

82 Compare the role of the demise of the case system in the deinflectionalization of the *-s* genitive in Scandinavian and Germanic languages (Norde 2009: 235).

Formal equivocation:

- (i) *Coding properties of grammatical relations* (§ 4.1):

  Coding of grammatical relations is mainly realized through relative word order in Earlier Egyptian. In a VSO language, both core arguments are post-verbal; word order is then nondistinctive for the sole core argument of a passive clauses (V-P, syntactically as V-S?/O?). In nominal morphology, only singular pronouns distinguish between subject and object cases, all other NP's being formally syncretic.

- (ii) [T] *T-passive morphology* (§ 4.2):

  Unlike V-passive morphology, {t} has singular exponence and is directly affixed to active stems (morphological transparency). Moreover, {t} is agglutinated to the stem (no fusion) and stands at the outer edge of the form.

Semantic conditions:

- (iii) *Specialization of voice morphology solely for the passive function* (§ 5.2):

  Earlier Egyptian voice morphology is purely grammatical in function and does not interact with the lexical semantics of the verbal event ("semantic simplicity" of the passive).

- (iv) *Broad use of passives derived from intransitives (impersonal passives)* (§ 5.3):

  Earlier Egyptian regularly uses impersonal passives. In such constructions, the agent backgrounding dimension is strongly reinforced over the Endpoint orientation otherwise prominent in passives. In addition, impersonal passives strongly favor non-specific and plural human agents.

- (v) [T] *Frequent association of T-passives with plural/non-specific agents in text* (§ 5.4):

  Although the morpheme {t} has no temporal-aspectual functions of its own, the overall distribution of V- and T-passives in the paradigm results in a situation in which T-passives are mostly used with relative present tense and/or imperfective aspect, and only rarely with anterior tense. Accordingly, the agent of T-passives itself is mostly plural or non-specific in texts.

- (vi) [T] *Only T-passives with events marked or interpreted as imperfective* (§ 5.4):

  Imperfectives passives, always realized as T-passives, typically have full-noun subjects or are subjectless altogether. Semantic conditions relating to the agent (v) are thus matched by formal conditions (i)–(ii).

[NB: While several of these favorable circumstances apply to V- and T-passives alike ((i), (iii)–(iv)), other ones are exclusive to the latter ((ii), (v)–(vi)). This accounts for the fact that only T-passives undergo change, although both morphological types are used in the exact same passive construction (§ 2.2). More precisely, morphological dimensions (ii) directly account for the fact that {t} is selected to be accommodated into SV patterns. Yet the issue is not solely a morphological one, as shown by the simultaneous extension of {t} – and only {t} – to events that are not passivizable on semantic grounds (§ 3.1). This demonstrates the importance of the additional semantic conditions in (v) and (vi).]

Motivating factor:
- (vii) *Semantic generalization and spread of SV patterns originally grammaticalized from situational predicate constructions* (§ 6):
  - The latter specification is important: it is because of such a source construction (a non-verbal pattern) that SV patterns present the lexical verb in the infinitive, i.e., in a form that cannot directly accommodate inflectional morphology.
  - The former specification is important as well: the original rise of SV patterns did not lead to any change in passive voice for centuries (§ 6.1), and it was only when SV patterns dramatically generalized their functional yield, spreading across the verbal system, that {t} was eventually accommodated to these (§ 6.2).

Some of the above dimensions are remotely related to each other. The broad use of impersonal passives (iv) and the specialization of voice morphology solely for passive functions (iii) may both relate to the rigid word order patterns of Earlier Egyptian (§ 5.2.), a dimension that in turn plays a major role in the particular coding properties of grammatical relations (i). On another level, the privileged aspectual correlates of T-passives (v)–(vi) result from the presence in the language of a perfective passive gram (the V-passive), with {t} (itself not inherently marked for tense-aspect) taking over all other functions in the paradigm. The singular exponence of {t}, more broadly its low semantic relevance, in turn relates to other morphological properties of the morpheme, notably its position at the outer edge of the stem (ii) (§ 4.2, with fn. 39). Such relations, however, are only partial and indirect, and their identification retrospective. The above dimensions can thus be considered as largely independent of each other.

I propose that it was the combined effect of the above, largely independent, favorable circumstances that made the change discussed here possible.[83] In a post-

---

83 "Combined effect" is here paramount. Several Semitic languages also witness the rise of

hoc account such as the present one necessarily is, it would almost seem that, given such conspiring of favorable circumstances, change "had" to happen. Yet no such functional teleology is permitted if this is understood in a strong, quasi-deterministic sense: for neither context to which {t} was extended was such an extension required. As regards events that are not passivizable on semantic grounds, other strategies, such as zero-subject constructions, were in use before the change began (§ 2.2.2, § 3.1, *fine*) and could have been kept later. As regards SV patterns, the active impersonal construction with a generically interpreted noun *s* 'man' – in use in VS patterns when the non-specific subject controlled subsequent anaphora (§ 8.3, with (27a–b)) – could have easily been generalized to cases in which it controlled no anaphora, and so made to provide the detransitive counterpart of innovative SV patterns. It so happened that for either environment Egyptian speakers selected another option, namely extending the uses of {t} itself.

Finally, none of the above circumstances are exceptional in themselves. As in other instances of rare changes, it is the contingent coming together of a series of ordinary circumstances that made an extraordinary change possible.[84] The mechanisms of change (§ 9.1), then, are themselves ordinary ones.

---

new SV patterns grammaticalizing from non-verbal constructions (e.g., Cohen 1984), yet none of them sees their respective T-stems undergo any change similar to the one here described in Earlier Egyptian. In contrast with Earlier Egyptian, this is accounted for by a variety of reasons. Morphologically, Semitic {t} is generally not at the outer edge of T-stems, and morphophonological processes, including some fusion, variously apply (contrast with (ii)). Semantically, Semitic T-stems display multiple, often combined, functions in detransitive voice, among which the passive is generally not the major one. Semitic T-stems thereby interact with lexical semantics and are broadly determined in relation to issues such as Endpoint-orientation and reduced (semantic) transitivity, contrasting with the solely passive functions of Egyptian T-passive (§ 5.2, contrast with (iii)). Moreover, Semitic languages in general – and Semitic T-stems in particular – tend to license passives from intransitives only marginally, if at all (§ 5.3.2, contrast with (iv)). In the lack of an equivalent of the Earlier Egyptian V-passive, Semitic T-stems do not show any preferential temporal-aspectual associations with imperfective events (contrast with (v)–(vi)). Finally, several Semitic languages have innovative SV patterns, but these do not undergo as dramatic a functional generalization as in Earlier Egyptian (contrast with (vii)).

84 For a similar line of analysis of typologically unusual structures more generally, Harris (2008).

10 From adverbializing -*w* to third person plural clitic =*w*

Although more instances will no doubt be found upon further investigation, degrammaticalization in general, and deinflectionalization in particular, seem to be uncommon phenomena. Haspelmath's (2004: 29) list comprises a mere eight cases of degrammaticalization[85], and only a few more are given in Norde (2009), including the one described in Idiatov (2008). As for deinflectionalization specifically, Norde (2009: § 5.3–6) analyzes four cases and mentions no more. In the context of the present discussion, it is therefore appropriate to briefly present yet another instance of deinflectionalization that occurred in second-millennium Egyptian.

10.1 The change in the record

Around the mid-second millennium, Egyptian sees the rise of a new 3PL clitic pronoun =*w* out of an erstwhile adverbializing affix -*w*.[86] The stages of the process (Edel 1959: 30–37; Kroeber 1970: 35–40) are summarized as follows:

(i) The Earlier Egyptian adverbializing ending -*w*[87]

Notably used for deriving adverbs from prepositions (so-called "Präpositionaladverbien"), e.g.:
– *ḫnt* 'before$_{PREP}$' → *ḫnt(-w)* 'before$_{ADV}$';
– *ḫft* 'according to' → *ḫft(-w)* 'accordingly';
– *n* 'to, for' → *n(-y)* 'therefore, for it'.

---

85 In Haspelmath's original wording, these are labeled "antigrammaticalization", while "degrammaticalization" is reserved for other phenomena which have in common the fact that they do not preserve constructional identity, such as lexicalization and conversion. The terminology is here harmonized with that in Norde (2009).

86 Ironically, this is the very same 3PL pronoun that was ultimately to replace {t} in all its uses by the end of the second millennium (§ 7.2.1, § 8.1.2). The two changes are unrelated: the rise of =*w* as a 3PL pronoun occurs by the mid-second millennium under circumstances that are described in the present section; the spread of =*w* to the environments in which {t} was used occurs only much later, by the very end of the second millennium.

87 Underlying morphology unclear; in written form, mostly <ø>, less commonly <-*w*> or <-*y*>; possibly a vocalic ending of some sort, with allomorphy not excluded.

(ii) (*N*) *sḏm-n(y)* (attested from ca. 2000 BCE on)

> In this construction, the *sḏm-n=f* accommodates the adverbializing ending in the slot otherwise reserved for personal subject clitics (=*f*). A full noun is generally anticipated to the left of the verbal form; e.g., (note that the referent is plural and generic):

> *ḥnmsw nw mîn   n   mr-n-y*[88]
> friends of   today NEG   love-HAB-X
> 'Friends of today, they do not love.' (Debate of a Man with his Soul 104)

> Following a cross-linguistically common process, the *sḏm.n=f*, an anterior tense, arose some time before 2800 BCE from a possessive perfective passive construction of some sort with the preposition *n* 'to, for', along the general lines of: *sḏm-n=f NP* (heard\PASS.PFV to=3MSG NP.SBJ) 'NP is heard to him' > *sḏm-n=f NP* (hear-ANT=3MSG.SBJ NP.OBJ) 'he has heard NP' (PERFECT) > 'he heard NP' (ANTERIOR).[89] Although -*n*- in *sḏm-n=f* is fully reanalyzed synchronically as a tense marker, its prepositional origin was probably still morphologically transparent enough by the time the construction (*N*) *sḏm-n(y)* arose.[90] The construction *sḏm-n(y)* thus results from the incorporation of the "Präpositionaladverb" *n(y)* into the *sḏm-n=f* form itself, replacing the tense marker -*n*- to which it was historically related.

(iii) Extension to the subject slot of *other VS conjugational forms* (ca. 1550 BCE)

> e.g., *ḏ=w* (give\PST=3PL.SBJ) 'they have given' (Kamose, Second Stela, 18).

---

88 The written form of the morpheme under discussion is <-*y*> in the present case. Other written realizations in stage (ii) include <ø> and <PLUR> (for the latter, see below, § 10.3). The formal identity of all these with the adverbializing ending in (i) is established in Edel (1959).

89 In itself, *sḏm-n=f* expresses anterior tense. When part of the bound negative pattern *n sḏm-n=f*, the form gradually specialized for the expression of negative habitual/general events, as in the example quoted above in the main text.

90 Note that (*N*) *sḏm-n(y)* may be older than its earliest attestation in the record, by ca. 2000 BCE. The written standard represented by Middle Egyptian (from ca. 2100 BCE) may be in part based on a different diatopic variety than the one on which Old Egyptian was based. Consequently, (*N*) *sḏm-n(y)* may have been in use in earlier times already, in varieties other than the ones represented in the extant Old Egyptian written corpus.

(iv) Extension to the subject slot of *non-verbal* patterns (ca. 1450 BCE)

e.g., (...) *ỉw=w r-ḫt=ỉ* (CIRC=3PL under_authority=1SG) '(...) while they were under my authority' (Urk. IV 54, 10).

(v) Extension to *non-subject* slots, and thus to all slots in which personal clitics are used (ca. 1350 BCE)

e.g., as a possessive marker after a noun: *fnḏw=w* (noses=3PL) 'their noses' (Edel 1959: 17).

(vi) Gradual replacement of the old 3PL clitic *=sn*, which ultimately disappears (ca. 1350–1000 BCE).[91]

10.2 An instance of deinflectionalization

The change presented here meets the conditions for it to be described as an instance of degrammaticalization (§ 8.2). The adverbializing *-w* is extended to new functions, and the change is therefore not an instance of retraction. The condition of constructional identity is less easily assessed since the functional extension is here ultimately to a new domain of grammar. Note however (ii) as a bridging context, in which the morpheme is extended to a verbal form that itself historically incorporates a preposition. Continuity in development is thus observed between stages (i) and (ii). Constructional continuity is further observed between stages (ii) and (iii), which both involve forms of the VS conjugation. A similar argument applies to subsequent stages of extension. By such continuity between each pair of successive stages, the change presented here differs from cases of "upgrading" that result in lexicalization, and qualifies as a genuine instance of degrammaticalization.

The change is a compound change and involves the reversal of the following primitive changes associated with grammaticalization:

---

91 The process proceeds at different paces depending on syntactic environments and written registers (with older *=sn* increasingly becoming an index of elevated language); detailed description in Winand (1995).

– Resemanticization (2°):	The morpheme gains new functions as a third person plural pronoun.
– Deparadigmaticization (2°):	The morpheme is extracted from its erstwhile exclusive affixal slot and is thus "discharge(d) from a (here derivational) paradigm".
– Severance:	As an adverbializing affix, -w was subject to lexical idiosyncrasies in derivation. The later status of =w as a clitic, on the other hand, is demonstrated by the following facts: (a) =w is ultimately used in all slots in which personal clitics are otherwise used; (b) =w can be attached to a variety of hosts, such as verbal forms (iii), clause complementizers (iv), and nouns (v).

On the other hand, =w does not develop full lexical semantics (no resemanticization, 1°), does not change in expression (no phonological strengthening), does not acquire morphosyntactic properties associated with a major word class (no recategorialization), does not "move up" to an open class (no deparadigmaticization, 1°), remains obligatory in each of its uses (no deobligatorification), and has a fixed position in each of these (no flexibilization).

In terms of the parameters of degrammaticalization, the change presented here scores exactly like the change affecting {t} (compare § 8.3). In this sense, both changes similarly qualify as deinflectionalization. The difference lies with the fact that the clitic {t} develops out of an inflectional affix, while the clitic =w develops out of a derivational affix. Strictly speaking, the change presented here would then be labeled a "de-derivationalization", in direct analogy to "de-inflectionalization". Alternatively, with the aim of avoiding terminological proliferation, the definition of deinflectionalization may be slightly extended to include a change in which the exact same processes that define deinflectionalization are made to apply to a morpheme that is originally derivational in nature.

10.3 Mechanisms and factors of the change

The mechanisms involved in the present change include pragmatic enrichment and reanalysis. Schematically:

Pragmatic enrichment:
- e.g., *ḫnt-w* 'before$_{ADV}$'
- interpreted as 'before *it*': with situational reference (i.e., reference to a state-of-affairs)
→ generic reference → PLURAL

> These successive stages of enrichment by pragmatic inferencing are directly evidenced by the increasing range of discourse contexts in which the morpheme comes to be used over time (§ 10.1). In addition, the morpheme is occasionally complemented by the <PLURAL> classifier, already with "Präpositionaladverbien" themselves and then increasingly so in all subsequent stages of its development.[92] Although merely a graphic phenomenon, this opens a window onto pragmatic enrichment at work in individual speakers' (/scribes') changing representations, even before reanalysis had begun showing any morphosyntactic effects in distributions. A similar graphic phenomenon was discussed above in connection with {t} itself (§ 5.1.2).

Reanalysis (sketch):
- *n-y* (to-ADV) 'therefore, for it' (i);
- used in *sḏm-[ny]*
  (§ 10.1, sub (ii): morphological transparency of *sḏm-n=f*, historically itself incorporating the preposition *n*);
- reanalysis of *sḏm-[ny]* as stem-subject: [*sḏm-n*]=*w*
  (by analogy to *sḏm-n=ỉ*, *sḏm-n=k*, *sḏm-n=sn* (hear-ANT=1SG, =2MSG, =3PL));
→ extension to other VS patterns (iii), e.g., *sḏm=w* (hear\SUBJ=3PL);
  [and thence, subsequent extension to all other clitic slots, (iv)–(v)].

Morphological reanalysis was no doubt facilitated by the fact that -*w* lay on the outer edge of "Präpositionaladverbien" and, subsequently, of *sḏm-ny*. A similar condition was observed with {t} in T-passives (§ 4.2) and seems more gener-

---

92 Also Vernus (fc.: § 5.2.1).

ally characteristic of a variety of cases of deinflectionalization and debonding (Idiatov 2008: 160). As the above discussion further implies, another major facilitating circumstance was the contingent co-presence of two formal categories in Earlier Egyptian: adverbs morphologically derived from prepositions ("Präpositionaladverbien") and a verbal form, the *sḏm-n=f*, that historically incorporates a preposition.

As described above in terms of pragmatic enrichment and ever-increasing extension, the change could have just proceeded by its own dynamics. In addition, one entirely independent, yet broadly simultaneous, change in the language may have acted as a motivating factor. By the mid-second millennium, the old 3PL clitic pronoun =*sn* (*/-svn/*) was reducing morphologically to */s$^{(v)}$/.[93] This resulted in increasing morphological syncretism with a series of other third person pronouns from either set of personal clitics (§ 4.1): set-I, 3FSG (=*s*); set-II, 3MSG and 3FSG (=*sw*, =*s(i)*), all > */s(^{v})/*. The extension of =*w* to most clitic slots from 1550 BCE on ((iii)–(v) in § 10.1) and its subsequent superseding of old =*sn* in all uses (vi) may in part have been in response to this situation of increasing syncretism, restoring formal distinctiveness.

10.4 Final consideration

A series of elements are in common to both cases of deinflectionalization presented here. Both morphemes undergoing deinflectionalization, {t} and -*w*, lay at the outer edge of their respective forms. In both cases, the possibility for change is given by the contingent conjunction of a series of independent favorable and facilitating circumstances, synchronic and diachronic, none of which is individually exceptional. Both changes involve context generalization and thereby, although going counter to some primitive changes associated with grammaticalization, conform with one very basic tendency in language change. Finally, pragmatic enrichment of affixes (passive and adverbializing, respectively) results in both cases in pronouns that are at the lowest end of the scale of discourse topicality: an impersonal subject pronoun (=*tw*) and a third person plural pronoun (=*w*).

---

93 The earliest signs of the process are manifest by the earlier second millennium (Uljas 2010). The detailed chronology remains difficult to assess, due to the generally conservative written standards of Earlier Egyptian.

11 References

Allen, James. 1984. *The Inflection of the Verb in the Pyramid Texts*. (Bibliotheca Aegyptia 2). Malibu: Undena Publications.

Andersen, Paul. 1991. *A New Look at the Passive*. (Duisburger Arbeiten zur Sprach- und Kulturwissenschaft 11). Frankfurt/M.: Peter Lang.

Blevins, James. 2003. Passives and impersonals. *Journal of Linguistics* 39: 473–520.

Bybee, Joan. 1985. Diagrammatic iconicity in stem-inflection relations. In: Haiman, John (ed.), *Iconicity in Syntax*. (Typological Studies in Language 6). Amsterdam: John Benjamins, 11–48.

Cohen, David. 1984. *La phrase nominale et l'évolution du système verbal en sémitique. Études de syntaxe historique*. Paris: Société Linguistique de Paris.

Comrie, Bernard. 1977. In defense of spontaneous demotion: the "impersonal passive". In: Cole, Peter & Sadock, Jerry (eds.), *Grammatical relations*. (Syntax and Semantics 8). New York: Academic Press, 47–58.

Comrie, Bernard. 1982. Aspect and voice: some reflections on perfect and passive. In: Tedeschi, Philip & Zaenen, Annie (eds.), *Tense and Aspect*. (Syntax and Semantics 14). New York: Academic Press, 65–78.

Cohen, Daniel. 1984. *La phrase nominale et l'évolution du système verbal en sémitique. Études de syntaxe historique*. Leuven/Paris: Peeters.

Edel, Elmar. 1955–1964. *Altägyptische Grammatik*. (Analecta Orientalia 34/39). Rome: Pontificium Institutum Biblicum.

Edel, Elmar. 1959. Die Herkunft des neuägyptisch-koptischen Personalsuffixes der 3. Person Plural –*w. Zeitschrift für Ägyptische Sprache und Altertumskunde* 84: 17–38.

Givón, Talmy. 1994. The pragmatics of de-transitive voice: Functional and typological aspects of inversion. In: Givón, Talmy (ed.), *Voice and Inversion*. (Typological Studies in Language 28). Amsterdam: John Benjamins, 3–46.

Givón, Talmy. 2006. Grammatical relations in passive clauses: a diachronic perspective. In: Abraham, Werner & Leisiö, Larisa (eds.), *Passivization and Typology: Form and Function* (Typological Studies in Language 68), 337–350.

Givón, Talmy & Kawasha, Boniface. 2006. Indiscrete grammatical relations: the Lunda passive. In: Tsunoda, Tasaku & Kageyama, Taro (eds.), *Voice and Grammatical Relations. In Honor of Masayoshi Shibatani*. (Typological Studies in Language 65). Amsterdam: John Benjamins, 15–41.

Gragg, Gene. 2001. Kuschitisch. In: Kienast, Burkhart, *Historische Semitische Sprachwissenschaft*. Wiesbaden: Harrassowitz, 574–617.

Harris, Alice C. & Campbell, Lyle. 1995. *Historical Syntax in Cross-linguistic Perspective*. (Cambridge Studies in Linguistics 74). Cambridge: Cambridge University Press.

Harris, Alice. 2008. On the explanation of typologically unusual structures. In: Good, Jeff (ed.), *Linguistic Universals and Language Change*. Oxford: Oxford University Press, 54–76.

Haspelmath, Martin. 1990. The grammaticalization of passive morphology. *Studies in Language* 14: 25–72.

Haspelmath, Martin. 1998. Does gammaticalization need reanalysis? *Studies in Language* 22: 49–85.

Haspelmath, Martin. 2004. On directionality in language change with particular reference to grammaticalization. In: Fischer, Olga, Norde, Muriel & Perridon, Harry (eds.), *Up and*

Down the Cline: The Nature of Grammaticalization. (Typological Studies in Language 59). Amsterdam: John Benjamins, 17–44.

Haspelmath, Martin. 2010. The Behaviour-before-Coding Principle in syntactic change. In: Floricic, Franck (ed.), *Mélanges Denis Creissels*. Paris: Presses de l'École Normale Supérieure, 493–506.

Heine, Bernd & Kuteva, Tania. 2002. *World Lexicon of Grammaticalization*. Cambridge: Cambridge University Press.

Hopper, Paul & Thompson, Sandra. 1980. Transitivity in grammar and discourse. *Language* 56: 251–299.

Hopper, Paul & Traugott, Elisabeth. 2003. *Grammaticalization* (2nd ed.). Cambridge: Cambridge University Press.

Idiatov, Dmitry. 2008. Antigrammaticalization, antimorphologization and the case of Tura. In: Seoane, Elena & Lopez-Couso, Maria José (eds.), *Theoretical and Empirical Issues in Grammaticalization*. (Typological Studies in Language 77). Amsterdam: John Benjamins, 151–169.

Keenan, Edward & Dryer, Matthew. 2006. Passive in the world's languages. In: Shopen, Timothy (ed.), *Language Universals and Syntactic Description. Volume I: Clause Structure* (2nd ed.). Cambridge: Cambridge University Press, 325–361.

Kouwenberg, Norbert J.C. 2004. Assyrian light on the history of the N-stem. In: Dercksen, Jan (ed.), *Assyria and Beyond: Studies presented to Mogens Trolle Larsen*. (PIHANS 100). Leiden: Nederlands Instituut voor het Nabije Oosten, 333–352.

Kouwenberg, Norbert J.C. 2005. Reflections on the Gt-stem in Akkadian. *Zeitschrift für Assyriologie* 95: 77–103.

Kouwenberg, Norbert J.C. 2010. *The Akkadian Verb and its Semitic Background*. (Languages of the Ancient Near East 2). Winona Lake/IN: Eisenbrauns.

Kroeber, Burkhart. 1970. *Die Neuägyptizismen vor der Amarnazeit. Studien zur Entwicklung der ägyptischen Sprache vom Mittleren zum Neuen Reich*. Tübingen.

Kuryłowicz, Jerzy. 1975. The evolution of grammatical categories. In: Kurilowicz, Jerzy, *Esquisses Linguistiques II*. München: Wilhelm Fink, 38–54.

Langacker, Ronald. 2004. Grammar as image: the case of voice. In: Lewandowska-Tomaszczyk, Barbara & Kwiatkowska, Alina (eds.), *Imagery in Language: Festschrift in Honour of Professor Ronald W. Langacker*. (Łódź Studies in Language 10). Frankfurt/M.: Peter Lang, 63–114.

Langacker, Ronald. 2006. Dimensions of defocusing. In: Tsunoda, Tasaku & Kageyama, Taro (eds.), *Voice and Grammatical Relations. In Honor of Masayoshi Shibatani*. (Typological Studies in Language 65). Amsterdam: John Benjamins, 115–137.

Lehmann, Christian. 1995. *Thoughts on Grammaticalization*. München/Newcastle: Lincom Europa.

Lehmann, Christian. 2004. Theory and method in grammaticalization. *Zeitschrift für Germanistische Linguistik* 32.2: 152–187.

Lieberman, Stephen. 1986. The Afro-Asiatic background of the Semitic N-stem: Towards the origins of the stem-afformatives of the Semitic and Afro-Asiatic verb. *Bibliotheca Orientalia* 43: 577–628.

Mufwene, Salikoko. 1989. Equivocal structures in some Gullah complex sentences. *American Speech* 64.4: 304–326.

Norde, Muriel. 2009. *Degrammaticalization*. Oxford: Oxford University Press.

Plank, Frans. 1995. Entgrammatisierung: Spiegelbild der Grammatisierung? In: Boretzky, Norbert, Dressler, Wolfgang & Oresnik, Janez (eds.), *Natürlichkeitstheorie und Sprachwandel*. Bochum: Brockmeyer, 199–219.

Reintges, Chris. 1996. The *sḏm.tw.f* as a morphological passive. *Göttinger Miszellen* 153: 79–99.

Reintges, Chris. 1997. *Passive voice in Older Egyptian. A morpho-syntactic study*. (HIL Dissertation 28). Den Haag.

Reintges, Chris. 1998. Mapping information structure to syntactic structure: one syntax for *jn*. *Revue d'Égyptologie* 49: 196–220.

Reintges, Chris. 2003. The reduplicative passive in Older Egyptian: description and typology. In: Bender, Lionel, Takács, Gábor & Appleyard, David (eds.), *Afrasian: Selected Comparative-Historical Studies in Memory of Igor M. Diakonoff*. (LINCOM Studies in Afro-Asiatic Linguistics 14), 175–186.

Reintges, Chris. 2004. The Older Egyptian *sḏm(.w)=f* passive revisited. *Folia Orientalia* 40: 51–70.

Reintges, Chris. (fc.) The diachronic typology of passive and stative voice in Ancient Egyptian. In: Kulikov, Leonid & Kittilä, Seppo (eds.), The Diachronic Typology of Voice and Valency-changing Categories. Amsterdam: John Benjamins.

Retsö, Jan. 1989. *Diathesis in the Semitic Languages. A comparative morphological study*. (Studies in Semitic Languages and Linguistics 14). Leiden: Brill.

Salvi, Giampaolo. 2008. Imperfect systems and diachronic change. In: Detges, Ulrich & Waltereit, Richard (eds.), *The Paradox of Grammatical Change. Perspectives from Romance*. (Current Issues in Linguistic Theory 293). Amsterdam: John Benjamins, 127–145.

Sansò, Andrea. 2006. 'Agent defocusing' revisited. Passive and impersonal constructions in some European languages. In: Abraham, Werner & Leisiö, Larisa (eds.), *Passivization and Typology: Form and Function*. (Typological Studies in Language 68). Amsterdam: John Benjamins, 232–273.

Schenkel, Wolfgang. 2004–2005. Das *sḏm(.w)=f*-Passiv, Perfekt vs. Futur, nach dem Zeugnis der Sargtexte. *Zeitschrift für Ägyptische Sprache und Altertumskunde* 131: 173–188; 132: 40–54.

Shibatani, Masayoshi. 1985. Passives and related constructions: a prototype analysis. *Language* 61: 821–848.

Siewierska, Anna. 2008. The impersonal to passive highway: an instance of bidirectional change. (Paper read at the 23th Scandinavian Conference of Linguistics, Uppsala, 1.–3.10.2008).

Siewierska, Anna. 2010. From 3pl to passive: incipient, emergent and established passives. *Diachronica* 27.3: 73–109.

Stauder, Andréas. 2008. Earlier Egyptian passive forms associated with reduplication. *Lingua Aegyptia* 16: 171–196.

Stauder, Andréas. 2013. *Linguistic Dating of Middle Egyptian Literary Texts*. (Lingua Aegyptia Studia Monographica 12). Hamburg: Widmaier Verlag.

Stauder, Andréas. 2014. *The Earlier Egyptian Passive: Voice and Perspective*. (Lingua Aegyptia Studia Monographica 14). Hamburg: Widmaier Verlag.

Uljas, Sami. 2010. Archaeology of language. A case study from Middle Kingdom/Second Intermediate Period Egypt and Nubia. *Studien zur altägyptischen Kultur* 39: 373–382.

Vernus, Pascal. 1990. *Future at Issue. Tense, Mood and Aspect in Middle Egyptian: Studies in Syntax and Semantics*. (Yale Egyptological Studies 4). Yale.

Vernus, Pascal. 2009. Le préformant *n* et la détransitivité. Formation $nC_1C_2C_1C_2$ versus $C_1C_2C_1C_2$. A propos de la racine √*gm* «notion de trituration». *Lingua Aegyptia* 17: 291–317.

Vernus, Pascal. fc. La non représentation segmentale du (premier) participant direct («sujet») et la notion de ø. In: Grossman, Eitan, Polis, Stéphane, Stauder, Andréas & Winand, Jean, *On Forms and Functions. Studies in Egyptian Syntax.* (Lingua Aegyptia 15). Hamburg: Widmaier Verlag.

Winand, Jean. 1995. La grammaire au secours de la datation des textes. *Revue d'Égyptologie* 46: 187–202.

Woods, Christopher. 2008. *The Grammar of Perspective. The Sumerian Conjugation Prefixes as a System of Voice.* (Cuneiform Monographs 32). Leiden/Boston: Brill.

Jean Winand

The oblique expression of the object in Ancient Egyptian*

Abstract: This paper deals with Direct Object Marking (DOM), a cross-linguistically well-known phenomenon. DOM is fully implemented in Coptic, but remains scarce in pre-Coptic Egyptian. This paper deals the emergence of DOM, relying mainly on Middle Egyptian and Late Egyptian data. I first give a brief overview of the rhematizing construction of the direct object and of the partitive construction(s), respectively. I then examine how the introduction of the preposition *m* with certain verbs can be explained as a detransitivizing, detelicising process, before coming back to the issue of DOM in pre-Coptic Egyptian. In my conclusion, I suggest that the circumstances that favoured the appearance of DOM in Egyptian differ in some significant ways from what is generally assumed in general linguistics.

1 Introduction

As is well-known, there is in Coptic a difference in the durative tenses between the pattern

V + DirObj and V + *n*- + NP (lit. 'in NP') or *mmo*= suff.pr.

(1) a. ⲉϥⲛⲉϫⲇⲁⲓⲙⲟⲛⲓⲟⲛ ⲉⲃⲟⲗ ϩⲛ̄ⲃⲉⲉⲗⲍⲉⲃⲟⲩⲗ
e-f-neč-daimonion *ebol* *hn-beelzeboul*
CIRC-3SGM-throw-demon out LOC-PN
'He casts out demons by Beelzebul.' (Luke 11:15 = Layton 2000: 132)

b. ⲉϣϫⲉ ⲁⲛⲟⲕ ⲉⲓⲛⲟⲩϫⲉ ⲉⲃⲟⲗ ⲛⲛⲇⲁⲓⲙⲟⲛⲓⲟⲛ
ešče *anok* *e-i-nouče* *ebol* *n-n-daimonion*
COND 1SG COND-1SG-throw out ACC-DEF.PL-demon
ϩⲛ̄ⲃⲉⲉⲗⲍⲉⲃⲟⲩⲗ
hn-beelzeboul
LOC-PN
'If I cast out demons by Beelzebul.' (Matt 12:27 = Layton 2000: 132)

* My sincere thanks to Eitan Grossman, Stéphane Polis, and Alessandro Stella for their remarks and comments on the draft of this article. The gathering of the data has been considerably facilitated by the use of the database *Ramses* (see Winand, Polis & Rosmorduc 2009).

The marked pattern (*n* + NP) is used when the object is high on the animacy scale or high on the scale of definiteness; in the other cases, the object is directly attached to the verb (the so-called 'Stern-Jernstedt Rule').[1]

Typologically, this phenomenon, known as Differential Object Marking (DOM) is very widespread.[2] Here is an example from Maltese:

(2) *spara*   *(lil-)l-kelb*
    fire\PRF.3SGM   (ACC-)DEF-dog
    'He shot the dog.'

(3) *spara*   *kelb*
    fire\PRF.3SGM   dog
    'He shot a dog.' (Bossong 1998: 253)

In this very minimal pair, the presence of an extra marker of accusative, the preposition *lil*, which is directly connected to Arabic *li-*, is triggered by the definiteness of the object. However, in this specific case, the preposition remains optional, for *kelb* 'dog', although an animate, is not human. For animals, some fluctuations can be observed in many languages that otherwise have a marked system for the object. In some cases, DOM seems to be used to convey a human emotion, so to speak, from the point of view of the speaker.

In Egyptian, DOM is also attested in Demotic, in circumstances that still await further investigation.[3] When going further back into the past, examples become exceedingly scarce. In Late Egyptian (LEg), only two, maybe three, certain occurrences surface.[4] The next three examples show how the DirObj of a very common Egyptian verb (*írî* 'do') is expressed. In the first example, the DirObj, which is

---

1 See Depuydt (1993), Layton (2000: § 171), Engsheden (2005). There are of course some fluctuations in the usage (see Layton 2000: 132). Ensgheden recently proposed that thematicity can play a significant role in the use of *n* in narrative constructions (see below). The distribution of the two patterns can also be affected by stylistic reasons, *lato sensu* (see Shisha-Halevy 1986 for some insightful comments on Shenoutian Coptic).

2 E.g., Spanish, southern Italian dialects, Slavonic languages, Caucasian languages, Uralic languages, Bantu languages, and of course some Semitic languages, both ancient and modern (see Lazard 1997; 2001; Bossong 1997). The case of Hebrew, both Biblical and modern, has been extensively studied (Givón 1978; Elwolde 1994; Danon 2001).

3 See Parker (1961), Simpson (1996: 151–156). For some consideration on Demotic data, see below, p. 550.

4 For a brief sketch of the history of Egyptian, see Loprieno (1995: 1–10), Winand (2006b), and Grossman & Richter (in this volume).

preceded by the possessive article, is introduced by the preposition *m* 'in', in a syntactic environment that has much in common with what can be observed in Coptic. In the second one, the DirObj is left undefined; and in the last one, the noun is preceded by the possessive definite article *t3y.sn* 'their'. Regarding the last two examples, one can observe that there is no syntactic variation: the DirObj immediately follows the verb. Obviously enough, the marked pattern has not been grammaticalized in LEg. Of course, there is a difference between the two examples that have a definite object, thus between ex. 4 and 6, as the first sentence has a progressive aspect and the last one has what I have called elsewhere an *inaccompli général*.[5] Although the special marking of the DirObj, at first glance, seems rather exceptional, the situation in LEg deserves a closer look.

(4) sw   ỉr   m   p3y-f   shn
3SGM do\INF LOC POSS-3SGM job
'He is doing his job.' (LRL 32,13)

(5) twn   ỉr   shn-w
1PL do\INF job-PL
'We are working (lit. we are doing jobs).' (P. BM 10375, v° 11)[6]

(6) st   hr   ỉr-t   t3y-sn   ỉp.t   <n>   db.t   m-mn.t
3PL PROG do\INF POSS-3PL count <of> bricks every_day
'They do their amount of bricks every day.' (P. An. III, v° 3,2)

Two questions immediately arise:
−   how did DOM appear?
−   why is it limited to the durative tenses?

In pre-Demotic Egyptian, there are a number of patterns involving the preposition *m* 'in'. Together with *n* 'to', *r* 'towards' and *hr* 'on', *m* constitutes the basic stock of the Egyptian prepositions as shown, among many features, by their high degree

---

5 See Winand (2006a: 271–286). In what follows, I stick strictly to my terminology, strongly distinguishing between the perfective/imperfective, for expressing semantic classes, and the accompli/inaccompli, for expressing a grammatical opposition in a tense system.
6 In this papyrus, the word *shn* 'order, mission' is used 4 more times in various configurations: with a demonstrative (r° 20, *m p3y shn* 'in this mission'), with the universal quantifier *nb* (r° 28, *twn ꜥr shn nb n p3y.n nb* 'we are accomplishing all the missions of our lord; cf. r° 28–29), with the indefinite article *wꜥ* (v° 4, *hn.n <r> ỉr.t n.i wꜥ shn* 'let's go to do a job for you [lit. for me]').

of polysemy and, above all, by the fact that they quickly undergo a process of grammaticalization by entering some verbal (or non-verbal) predicative patterns (Middle Egyptian *iw.f n X* 'it belongs to X', *iw.f r sḏm* 'he shall hear', *iw.f ḥr sḏm* 'he is hearing').[7]

The preposition *m*, which is the focus of this paper, immediately caught the grammarians' attention due to its polysemy. According to the standard grammar of Gardiner (1957), the preposition has 9 main uses.[8] Recently, scholars have tried to understand the functions of the preposition by using semantic maps.[9]

In Egyptian, two constructions display the surface structure V + *m* + NP: one for rhematizing the DirObj in the so-called 'emphatic' constructions and another one for expressing the partitive.[10] To these, one can add some valency patterns involving the preposition *m*.

In §§ 2 and 3, I give a brief overview of the rhematizing construction of the direct object and of the partitive construction(s) respectively. In § 4, I examine how the introduction of the preposition *m* with certain verbs can be explained as a detransitivizing, detelicising process. In § 5, I come back to DOM in pre-Coptic Egyptian. In my conclusion, I will suggest that the circumstances that favoured the appearance of DOM in Egyptian seem at odds with what is generally assumed in general linguistics.

2 The emphatic construction V + *m* + NP

In the literature, some attention has been paid to a construction that puts emphasis on the DirObj (Silverman 1980): it mainly consists of using a restricted set of verbal forms, called 'emphatic', whatever this means at a morphological level (Winand 2007), and transforming the DirObj into a PrepP using the preposition *m*. The next two examples show such a contrast. In the second example, the verb *rdi* 'give' takes a particular form (signalled by gemination); what was a DirObj in the first example (*pʒ it* 'this barley') has become a PrepP headed by *m*:

---

7 See Vernus (1998), with previous literature, to which one can add Shisha-Halevy (2003: 263–265) for a typological comparison between Egyptian and Celtic languages.

8 Gardiner (1953: 124–125).

9 See Werning (2012); and Grossman & Polis (2012).

10 See Winand (2006a: 137–149) for some typological considerations.

(7) *h̲3*   *d̲i-t̲n*   *p3*   *it*   *n*   *p3y-tn*   *h̲ry-kn*
     please   give\SBJV-2PL   this   barley   to   POSS-2PL   porter
     'Please give this barley to your porter.' (P. Westcar 11,7)

(8) *dd-k*   *n-f*   *m*   *it*   *h̲q3t 8 n*   *ibd*
     give\THMZ-2SGM   DAT-2SGM   LOC   barley   heqat 8 per   month
     'It's 8 heqat of barley that you should give him each month.' (P. Heqa-nakhte I, 17)

The pragmatic intention is particularly clear in textual variants, as for instance in this excerpt from *Ptahhotep*, where the textual tradition splits, with variant (a) have an 'emphatic' form and variant (b) having a non-emphatic form. In this particular case, as the emphatic construction has been passivized, the subject has been demoted to a PrepP:

(9) a. *iw*   *in-tw*   *ˤk-w*   *wn*   *3k̲*
         AUX   bring\INACC-PASS   friend-PL   be   misfortune
         'One brings friends when there is misfortune.' (Ptahhotep, 349 P)

     b. *inn-tw*   *m*   *ˤk-w*   *wn*   *3hw*
         bring\THMZ-PASS   LOC   friend-PL   be   need
         'It is friends who are brought when there is need.' (Ptahhotep, 349 L²)[11]

The contrast is also very sharp in some balanced phraseological sentences, where a situation is alternatively presented in the affirmative and negative:

(10) *d̲d-t(w)*   *n(-i)*   *bin*   *d̲d(-i)*   *m*   *nfrw*   *(n?)nb(-i)*
      say-PASS   DAT(-1SG)   bad   say\THMZ(-1SG)   LOC   good   to lord(-1SG)
      'Even if bad is said to me, I say only good to my lord.' (Siut IV, 64–65)[12]

---

11 The version of L² is undoubtedly the revised version; significant in this respect is the loss of the pun present in the P. Prisse (*ˤk.w* 'friends' vs. *3k̲* 'misfortune'). Other well known examples are *Ipwer* 12,13–14 (*ir šm z 3 h̲r w3.t, gmm.tw m z 2, in ˤš3.t sm3 ˤnd̲.t* 'if three people walk on the road, only two are found, for it is the majority that kills the minority'); *The Dispute between a Man and his Ba*, 117–118 (*snw bin.w, inn.tw m d̲rd̲r.w r mtt n.t ib* 'brethren have become evil, it is foreigners who are brought for the sake of affection'). See Winand (2006a: 141–142).

12 Due to the relative opacity of the hieroglyphic spelling, *d̲d(.i)* could also be analysed as a prospective *sd̲m(.w).f*.

The last example is of course a distant although not exact precursor of the well-known LEg expression:

(11) *ỉ-ḏd-n*   *m*   *mꜣꜥt bn*   *ḏd-n*   *ꜥḏꜣ*
      THMZ-say-1PL LOC   truth NEG   say\SBJV-1PL lie
      'We'll say only the truth, we won't say a lie.' (KRI II, 802,13)

To sum up, the emphatic construction of the DirObj
- is attested from very early on in our documentation, already in the Old Kingdom,
- is used in the first stage of Egyptian with all forms that can have an emphatic function (*mrr.f, sḏm.n.f, sḏm.w.f*). This notwithstanding, in the vast majority of the cases, the *mrr.f* form, that is, a tense of the inaccompli, is found,[13]
- is used with count nouns (singular and plural) and mass nouns,
- can also be passivized, as shown by the *Ptahhotep* example.

3 Partitive construction

The argument structure with preposition *m* is rather well documented for expressing the partitive, from Old Egyptian onwards. The second example nicely contrasts both constructions, the direct one and the oblique one, in a very rare minimal pair. The partitive construction is most probably the consequence of the polarity inversion, the second part of the sentence being negative (see below examples 19 and 32):

(12) *swr-w*   *m*   *ỉrp*
      drink\PTCP-PL) LOC   wine
      'Those who drink wine.' (Pyr. 440)

---

13 It might not be a coincidence that the unique example of a perfective known to me involves the verb *rḫ* 'to learn', which takes on the meaning 'to know' in the perfective (cf. *gignoskô* vs. *egnôka* in Greek); see Winand (2006a: 242–244).

(13) *ir p3 w3ḥ nb ḏr.t.f ḥr ḏr.t.î îm.w*
'As for the one among them who laid his hand on mine,

îw-î	*r*	*dî*	*n-f*	*3ḥ-t-i*
FUT1-1SG	FUT2	give\INF	DAT-3SGM	goods-F-1SG

I will give him my goods

ir p3 nty bwpw.f dî.t Ø n.î
as for he who did not give to me

bn	*îw-î*	*r*	*dî*	*n.f*	*m*	*3ḥ-t-i*
NEG	FUT1-1SG	FUT2	give\INF	DAT-3SGM	LOC	goods-F-1SG

I will not give him of my goods.' (KRI VI, 238,1–2)[14]

At this stage, some observations can be made: as is only to be expected, this partitive construction is exceedingly common with consumption verbs (*wnm* 'eat', *swr* 'drink') and mass nouns (this term being understood *sensu lato*):

(14)

îw	*swr-f*	*m*	*mw*	*šnš*
CIRC	drink\PRF-3SGM	LOC	water	putrid

'After having drunken putrid water.' (LEM 26,12)

(15)

îmy	*tw*	*wnm-î*	*m*	*t3*	*mîs-t*	*n*	*p3y*	*îḥ*
give:IMP	2SGM	eat\SBJV-1SG	LOC	DEF.FSG	liver-F	of	this	ox

'Let me eat from the liver of this ox.' (LES 26,3–4)

The construction with *m* never became the only way for expressing partitivity, even in Coptic[15]. Actually, the DirObj remains the most widely used construction, as shown by the next two examples (from the New Kingdom and Early Demotic respectively).[16] In the third one, the tradition splits into a DirObj and an oblique object. In this case, it is difficult to ascertain whether the direct expression implies the total consumption of the bread:

(16)

r3	*n*	*swr*	*mw*	*m*	*ḥr.t-nṯr*
formula	of	drink\INF	water	LOC	Necropolis

'Formula for drinking water in the Necropolis.' (LdM 61)

---

14 Cf. *înn bn îw.k dî.t n.î îm.w* 'if you do not give (any) of them to me' (KRI VI, 515,10–11).

15 Partitive can be expressed by a DirObj, a PreP headed by *n-/mmo=* or *(ebol) hn-*, the latter being quite common (E. Grossman, p.c.).

16 Examples from the Coffin Texts are numerous: *îw.f wnm.f t m s.t nb.t rww.t.f r.s* 'he eats bread in every places he goes' (CT VI,273f).

(17) *ḫpr rmṯ nb nty m tȝy.w-ḏȝy iw.w*   *swr*   *ḥnḳ-t*

          CIRC-3PL   drink\INF   beer-F

'It happened that everyone who was in Teudjoi was drinking beer.' (P. Rylands IX, 2,9–10)[17]

(18) a. *wnm-k*   *t-k*

          eat\SBJV-2SGM   bread-2SGM

          'You shall eat (from?) your bread.' (CT I,11e B2Bo)

    b. *wnm*   *PN pn*   *m*   *t-f*   *pn*

          eat\SBJV PN this LOC bread-3SGM this

          'This N shall eat of this bread of his.' (CT I,11e T9C)

When found, the partitive construction is most widely used with the tenses of the *inaccompli*, or with a negative. The correlation of partitive and negative is typologically well attested:

(19) *bn*   *st*   *ḥr*   *dỉ.t*   *m*   *nkt*

      NEG   3PL   PROG   give\INF   LOC   something

      'They are not giving anything.' (KRI III, 557,13)

As was to be expected, even with a negation, the partitive marking was never obligatory. The next example shows an accumulation of features (verb of consumption, mass object and negation) that normally would safely predict the use of a marked partitive expression. Nevertheless, a DirObj was here preferred:

(20) *rȝ*   *n*   *tm*   *wnm*   *ḥs*   *swr*   *wsš-t*

      formula   of NEG eat\INF excrement drink\INF urine-F

      m   *ḫr.t-nṯr*

      in Necropolis

      'Formula for not eating excrement nor drinking urine in the Necropolis.' (LdM 53,1)

---

17 For the absence of DOM in this example, see below, p. 552.

The partitive *m* cannot be easily passivized. Instead, Egyptian has a strategy for avoiding DOM in a passive context. In the first example, the adopted solution is a dummy object, the noun *nkt* 'something':[18]

(21) *ìr*   *dì-k*   *ìn-tw*   *nkt*   *ìm-sn*
      COND   give\SBJV-2SGM   bring\SBJV-PASS   something   LOC-3PL
      'If you let something of them be brought.' (O. Berlin 11239, 8–9)

In the second example, the noun used in the partitive phrase (*ḥḏ* 'silver') has been extracted to play the role of a DirObj:

(22) *ì-ḏd*   *n-ì*   *rmṯ*   *nb* *dy*   *n-w*   *ḥḏ*
      IMP-say\   DAT-1SG   people   all   give\PTCP.PASS   DAT-3PL   silver
      m   *pȝy*   *ḥḏ*
      from   this   silver
      'Tell me all the people which were given some silver from this silver.'
      (P. BM 10052, r° 5,18)

The marked pattern is only attested with mass nouns or indefinite nouns. Exceptions are rare and they can be explained for semantic reasons. In the next example, the definite article is easily explained by the fact that the liver is no longer an a-morphic substance, but a well defined piece of meat belonging to an identified animal:

(23) *ìmy*   *tw*   *wnm-ì*   *m*   *tȝ*   *mìs-t*   *n*   *pȝy*   *kȝ*
      give\IMP   2SGM   eat\SBJV-1SG   LOC   this   liver-F   of   this   bull
      'Let me eat from the liver of this bull.' (LES 26,3–4)

---

18 Those examples nicely contrast with ex. 19, where *nkt*, used in an active construction, is introduced by *m*.

4 *m* as a detransitivizing, detelicizing process

The constructions of the type V + *m* + NP once more raise the crucial issue of what transitivity (or intransitivity) actually means. In the literature, there is now general agreement for not considering transitivity and intransitivity as clear-cut, discrete categories.[19] They are better viewed as two ranges of a continuum. Egyptian is of course no exception. There are Egyptian verbs that always construct their object intransitively. The prepositions can be *m* 'in' (*mḥ m* 'to grasp') or *r* 'towards' (*nw r* 'to look at').[20] Another category allows different valency patterns. Statistically transitive verbs sometimes take an oblique object using the prepositions *m*, *r*, or *n* 'to'. This usually entails a shift in meaning:

(24)   *ỉw*   *mdw-k*   *n-ỉ*   *nn*   *wỉ*   *ḥr*   *sḏm*   *st*
       AUX   speak\INACC-2SGM   DAT-1S   NEG   1SG PROG   hear\INF   3SGF
       'You speak to me, but I am not listening to it.' (Shipwrecked Sailor, 73–75)

(25)   *sḏm*   *r-k*   *n-ỉ*
       hear\IMP   to-2SGM   DAT-1S
       'Listen to me, you!' (The Dispute between a Man and his Ba, 67)

In what follows, I shall of course focus on verbs that allow both a DirObj and an oblique object introduced by the preposition *m*. I would like to build my case by studying more closely a very common verb in LEg, namely *bꜣk* 'work'. I will then examine the verb *thỉ* 'transgress', which seems to display a nice case of split transitivity.

The mediate construction of the object can also be viewed as a strategy of detransitivizing, detelicizing transitive telic verbs. Following many scholars, I would like to suggest that there is no clear boundary between transitivity and intransitivity by examining some striking examples in Egyptian. I will consider in some detail three lexemes : *bꜣk* 'work', *ỉṯỉ/ṯꜣỉ* 'take' and *thỉ* 'transgress'.

---

19 Cf. Hopper & Thompson (1980).

20 Interesting variations in the lexicon undoubtedly deserve some scrutiny; for instance, in LEg: *mḥ m* 'to grasp, to seize' vs. *ṯꜣỉ* 'to take', or *nw r* 'to look at' vs. *ptr* 'to see'.

4.1 The case of *b3k* 'work'

The constructions in which *b3k* appears can be arranged according to an increasing degree of transitivity. In the first example, *b3k* is used intransitively as an activity verb:

(26) *iw*   *h3m*   *hr*   *b3k*   *n*   *h3y*
     CIRC   Kham   PROG   work   for   PN
     'As Kham is working for Hay.' (O. CGC 25517, r° 8)

The place where the activity takes place can be specified by a PrepP introduced by *m* 'in':

(27) *iw*   *rmt<is.>t*   PN   *hr*   *b3k*   *m*   *t3y-f*   *mʿhʿ-t*
     CIRC   workman   PN   PROG   work\INF   LOC   POSS-3SGM   room
     'As the workman PN is working in his room.' (O. BM 5624, r° 1–2)

The same PrepP can be used for expressing an object one is working on:

(28) *nty*   *hr*   *b3k*   *m*   *n3*   *bnš-w*
     REL   PROG   work\INF   LOC   DEF.PL   door-jamb-PL
     m   *hwt-ntr*   *n*   PN
     LOC   temple   of   PN
     'Those who are working on the door-jambs in the temple of PN.' (P. Turin B v° 3,10)

Now, *b3k* can also be used transitively. In example 29, the DirObj is a mass noun, *it* 'barley'. As usual in LEg, mass nouns are zero-defined (Groll 1967; Winand 2009). In examples 30 and 31, the DirObj is a count noun: in the first one, *mrkbt* 'chariot' is preceded by a plural definite article (*n3*), in the second one *wt* 'coffin' is preceded by a singular definite article (*p3*):

(29) *sw*   *hr*   *b3k*   *n-f*   *it*   *m*   *pr*   *nbt-htp*
     3SGM   PROG   work\INF   DAT-3SGM   barley   LOC   house   Nebet-Hotep
     'He is working barley for him in the domain of Nebet-Hotep.' (P. Anastasi VI, 29–30)[21]

---

[21] One can also work the land (*b3k p3 t3*: P. Brooklyn 47.218.35, 6,7), work the gold (*b3k p3 nbw*: P. BM 10053, 2,6). One also has a very interesting example with an internal object: *twn hr b3k p3*

(30) n3   ḥmw-w   ḥr   b3k   n3   mrkbt
      DEF.PL craftsman-PL   PROG work\INF DEF.PL chariot
      'The craftsmen are working on the chariots.' (P. Anastasi III, v° 1,2)

(31) iw.f   dy   ḥms   ḥr   b3k   p3   wt
      CIRC-3SGM here sit\STAT.3SGM PROG work\INF DEF.MSG coffin
      'As he is now working on the coffin.' (O. CGC 25504, v° II,7)[22]

In example 29, it is difficult to decide whether the intended expression has something to do with the transformation of the grain (cf. French 'travailler le bois') or if it simply means an activity related to barley. But in the next example, the DirObj is clearly treated like a patient: the *mrkbt* 'chariot' is undoubtedly the intended result of the work in progress. The same can be said of the next example, where the DirObj *wt* 'coffin' is countable, definite, and singular.

When used transitively, *b3k* can be in the so-called 'Pseudo-Participle' form, a stative-resultative form, which entails a shift of diathesis; in this case, the DirObj becomes the subject of the stative construction.[23] The PrepP introduced by *m* here has an instrumental meaning:

(32) iw   n3y-sn   ibrḏ   b3k   m   nbw
      CIRC POSS-3PL   ibrḏ   work\STAT.3SGM with gold
      'And their *ibrḏ* are worked out with gold.' (P. Koller, 4,4)

Now I would like to come back to example 28, which could be interpretated as a possible instance of DOM. When considering the material available for *b3k*, I am more inclined to analyse *b3k* as an intransitive in this specific case. If so, the very *raison d'être* of the PrepPhrase *m n3 bnš.w* 'LOC the doorjambs' is clearly to restrict the scope of the process *b3k* is applied to. In this respect, there is a semantic difference between a DirObj, which implies that the object is totally affected by the

---

r3-ꜥ-b3k ꜥ3 n pr-ꜥ3 'we are working on the great work in progress of Pharaoh' (O. Gardiner 59, 2–3).

22 On the use of a verb of position, like *ḥmsi* 'sit', as an aspectual auxiliary to mark the progressive, see Winand (2006a: 311–313).

23 The form here called Pseudo-Participle is known in Egyptology under different names (Pseudo-Participle, Stative, Qualitative, Old Perfective); Stative is now widely used, but it does not come without problems of its own, for it puts too much emphasis on one, albeit important, meaning of the form. I stick to the very old appellation Pseudo-Participle, because it clearly identifies the form at the morphological level while being now completely void of any semantic or syntactic meaning, which has its advantages too. For the meaning of this form in Egyptian, see Kruchten (1984), Winand (2006a: 337–338). See also Reintges (this volume).

process, and a PrepP, which rather suggests that the object is partially affected, in which case *m* is used.

As already stated above, the presence of a negation can trigger an oblique construction as shown in the following example with the verb *ḳd* 'build', which is closely semantically related to *bꜣk* in the texts. The intended meaning of the second part of the sentence is probably that the man who is criticized did not even take part in the building:

(33) *ı̓nk ı̓-ḳd*   *pꜣ*   *ḥnw*   *n*   X
       1SG PTCP-build\ACCOM   DEF.MSG   abode   for   X,
       ı̓w   *bwpw.f*   *ḳd*   *ı̓m-f*   *ı̓rm-ı̓*
       CIRC   NEG.PST-3SGM build\INF LOC-3SGM with-1SG
       'I built the abode for X, and he did not build in it with me.' (KRI VI,252,9)

4.2 The case of *thı̓*

In LEg, *thı̓* 'violate, transgress, harm' displays two main argument structures with respect to the second argument: DirObj and PrepP. In the latter case, the preposition *r* 'to' is the most frequent one; *m* 'in' is comparatively much less common. Here are some examples:

(34) *thı̓*   *sw*   *nꜣ*   *ı̓ṯꜣw*
       harm\ACCOM 3SGM DEF.PL.   thieves
       'The thieves did him some harm.' (P. Abbott r° 2,6–7)

(35) *m-ḫt gm-tw-w*   *ı̓w*   *thı̓-w*   *tꜣy st-nfrw*
       after find\PASS-3PL   CIRC violate\PRF-3PL this place-perfection
       'After they were found to have violated this place of perfection.' (P. BM 10068, r° 1,4)

(36) *ı̓w*   *bw*   *ı̓r*   *pꜣ*   *wr*   *n*   *ḫtꜣ*
       CIRC   NEG   AUX.INACC   DEF.MSG   lord   of   Khatti
       thı̓   *r*   *pꜣ*   *tꜣ*   *n*   *km.t r*   *nḥ*
       violate\INF to   DEF.MSG   land   of   Egypt to   eternity
       'As the lord of Khatti won't ever attempt to violate the land of Egypt.' (KRI II, 227,15)

(37) *sḏm-i*   *r-ḏd* *tw.tn* *ḥr*   *thỉ*   *r*
      hear\PRF-1SG that   2PL   PROG violate\INF to
      n3   *rmṯ*   *n*   *p3*   *nṯr*
      DEF.PL people of   DEF.MSG god
      'I have heard that you are molesting the people of the god.' (KRI I,
      322,5–6)

(38) *mtw-tn*   *tm*   *ỉy*   *r*   *thỉ*   *m*   *t3*   *n*   *kmt*
      CONJ-2PL NEG come\INF to   violate\INF LOC land of   Egypt
      'And you should not come to do harm in the land of Egypt.' (KRI VI,
      521,7–8)

Some observations ought to be made:
- First, *thỉ* does not seem to use a PrepP before New Kingdom LEg. In Old and
  Middle Egyptian, *thỉ* always takes a DirObj. In LEg, both constructions, the
  direct and the indirect one, are used in parallel. This suggests that the two
  constructions cannot be viewed in a diachronic relation, as is the case, for
  instance, with *pḥ* 'to reach'.[24]
- From a semantic viewpoint, the term under the scope of the verb is totally
  affected when construed as a DirObj. When the PrepP with *r* 'to' is preferred,
  the object is not totally affected. It is more or less a question of contact. In
  many cases, a conative effect can be observed. With respect to actionality
  actionality, the PrepP can be analyzed as a kind of detelicizing process.
- Now, and this is more striking, there is a correlation between the choice of
  an argument structure and the grammatical tenses (Figure 1). The immediate
  object has a statistically demonstrable connection with the tenses associated
  with the accompli, whereas the oblique construction, with *m* or *r*, tends to
  be used exclusively with the tenses of the inaccompli.[25] This is thus a case
  of split accusativity according to an aspectual distribution. Typologically,
  complementary distributions of this kind can be observed elsewhere. A well-
  known case is Hindi which knows a similar split along aspectual lines with
  respect to the way the second argument is construed.[26]

---

24 This verb always has a DirObj as its second argument in Earlier Egyptian; from LEg onwards,
the DirObj is replaced by the PrepP *r* + NP 'to NP', most probably by analogy with the verbs of
movement (Winand 2003).
25 For an exhaustive overview of the aspectual system in Egyptian, see Winand 2006a (with a
complete bibliography).
26 Lazard (1994: 179). For a possible case of split transitivity in Egyptian involving the verb *3ṯp*
'to load', see Winand (2012).

– According to the available data, *r* seems to the preferred preposition when the noun phrase is definite, while *m* tends to be used with non-definite substantives, which is of course the mark of a partitive construction.

EarlierEgyptian[27]	DirObj			
Later Egyptian	*Accompli*		*Inaccompli*	
	DirObj	*r* NP	DirObj	*r* NP
	X	rare	rare	X

Figure 1: Distribution of the grammatical tenses used with *thỉ* 'transgress' according to the argument structure

5 The V + *m* + NP patterns in Egyptian

In LEg, three distinctive patterns exhibit the same external configuration V + *m* + NP: the emphatic construction, the partitive, and the differential marking of the DirObj (DOM). The purpose of this section is to examine whether those constructions are in some way interrelated.

The emphatic and the partitive postulate two very different kinds of operation at the cognitive level. The partitive is an operation of extraction, where an entity x, devoid of any clearly defined shape, is a sub-part of X, whose referent is the global entity. When an element is given emphasis, there is an operation of identification / specification / selection of an X among many possible X's.[28] In this case, the X's referent is an entity in a set.

---

27 Egyptian is traditionally subdivided into five phases: Old Egyptian, Middle Egyptian, Late Egyptian, Demotic and Coptic. From a typological viewpoint, Old and Middle Egyptian are parts of one main stage (Egyptian I), while Late Egyptian, Demotic and Coptic constitute the second stage (Egyptian II). Egyptian I and Egyptian II are deliberately very neutral labels that correspond to what Loprieno (1995: 5–7) calls Earlier Egyptian and Later Egyptian, respectively.
28 Cf. Depuydt's (1991) notion of isolating emphasis.

The two operations can be conveniently contrasted in the two figures below:

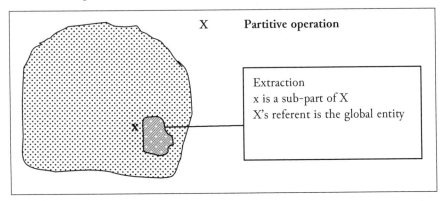

Figure 2: The partitive extraction

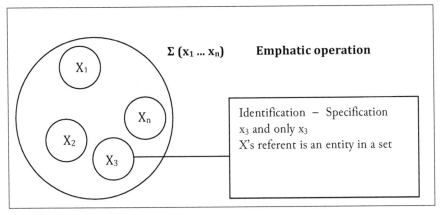

Figure 3: The emphatic selection

Elaborating on previous research in this field,[29] I'd like here to suggest some strong connections between partitivity and the progressive aspect. There is now a wide consensus for considering that the progressive should be conceived as a sub-part of something else; as is well known, its limits are vague – or rather, they lack any cognitive salience – which puts the progressive on the mass side, so to say.[30]

In Egyptian, it is probably not a coincidence that the preposition *m*, which is closely associated with DOM, is first of all used to express a localisation: x *m* Y "x (is) in Y"

---

29 Carlson (1981: 47–48).
30 Cf. Winand (fc.).

(39) *nn*   *sj*   *m*   *ib-i*
NEG   it   LOC   heart-1SG
'It was not in my heart.' (Sinuhe, B 223–224)

The preposition *m* is also found in the progressive, in alternation with the preposition *ḥr* 'on':[31] in both cases, the progressive is thus conveyed in Egyptian, as in other languages[32], by means of prepositions specialized in expressing the localisation:

(40) (and I saw eleven ships) *iw-w*   *m*   *iw*   *m*   *p3*   *ym*
                               CIRC-3PL   PROG   come\INF   PROG   DEF.MSG   sea
'As they were coming from the sea.' (LES 73,10–11)

(41) *iw*   *ḥr(j)-ḥb(.t)*   *ḥr*   *ir-t*   *ḫt*
AUX   lector priest   PROG   do\INF   things
'The lector priest is performing the ritual.' (Mereruka, II, pl. 109, l. 1)

As shown in figure 4, the progressive is cognitively very close to the partitive; it can be conceived as a segment out of a dense process, with underspecified boundaries that cannot be co-extensive with the limits of the process. In the progressive, the limits of the process lack any cognitive salience, which is somewhat reminiscent of the undefined shape of a mass noun.

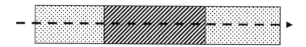

Figure 4. The selection of the progressive

---

31 Cf. Winand (2006a: 311, n. 44), with some bibliography on the formation of the progressive in Old English, Irish, Finnish, and Creoles.

32 In Old English, the progressive is expressed by a locative (Comrie, 1976: 99). This is also the case in some Celtic languages (Bybee & Dahl 1989: 78; Macaulay 1992: 46, 217–220, 279–281, 408). One can also mention the progressive in Creoles for using the auxiliary *stay*, which is very close to what can be observed in LEg and in several African languages (Givón 1982: 124). Generally speaking, African languages show a predilection for locative constructions (Bybee, Perkins & Pagliuca 1994: 129–131). Cf. also Cohen (1989: 125–127), who cites numerous examples from different Semitic languages.

6 Conclusion

The preposition *m* 'in' is found in several constructions in Egyptian: partitive, emphatic, DOM, and also in some valency patterns. In the partitive, *m* is never obligatory; it is mostly associated with the tenses of the *inaccompli*. For rhematizing the direct object, Egyptian can use the so-called emphatic constructions, which trigger a recategorization of the DirObj as a PrepP introduced by *m*. It is also possible to use a cleft sentence (Neveu 1994: 203–205). Interestingly enough, the emphatic construction seems to be preferred with the tenses of the *inaccompli*, whereas the cleft sentence is usually found with the tenses of the *accompli*:

(42) a. *irr-k*   *m*   *ḥrt-îb-k*
          do\THMZ-2SGM   LOC   desire-2SGM
          'It is only your desire that you do.' (Shipwrecked Sailor, 20)

  b. *bt3*   *ˤ3*   *p3w*   *î-îr-f*
      crime big that   REL-do\ACCOM-3SGM
      'It is a big crime that he did.' (RAD 52,2–3)

This apparent restriction on the use of the emphatic constructions does not apply for rhematizing an adverbial adjunct, for which they remain the most widely used constructions. In LEg, for instance, the emphatic form *î.îr.f sḏm* is predominantly found with past tenses.

The first undisputable cases of DOM are found in LEg. In this stage, it clearly remains exceptional. Its use does not seem to be conditioned by a scale of animacy or by the degree of definiteness. As shown in the example below, DOM can be found with inanimate, indefinite nouns:

(43) *iw-î*   *ḥr*   *îr-t*   *m*   *i3wt* *nb* *ˤ3* *n*   *pr-ˤ3*
      CIRC-1S   PROG do\INF   LOC task all big of   Pharaoh
      'As I was engaged in doing all kinds of important work of Pharaoh.' (P. Leyde I 371, r° 10)

It is also striking that the LEg examples are linked to progressive aspect. In Demotic, the rules governing the use of DOM seem to be very close to what can be observed in Coptic. In P. Rylands IX, an early Demotic document, DOM is only found with durative tenses in the following circumstances:[33]

---

33 See Parker (1961). On the use of DOM in Demotic, see also Simpson (1996: 151–156).

- personal pronoun, both animate (5) and inanimate (5)
- definite article + substantive, both animate (1) and inanimate (3), both singular (2) and plural (2)
- demonstrative + inanimate singular substantive (1)
- possessive article + inanimate singular substantive (1)
- Ø + geographic name (2)

The contrast with the non-durative tenses is very clear, as shown in the next pair of examples:

(44) a. Ahmose stayed in Hnes, *ỉw-f*   *mnk*   *m*
          CIRC-3SGM   finish\INF   LOC
          t3y-f mdt
          POSS-3SGM   affair
          'finishing his business' (P. Rylands IX, 2,4–5 = Parker 1961: 181, ex. 7)

      b. *mnk-f*   *n3*   *mdt*
          finish\PRF-3SGM   DEF.PL   affairs
          'He finished the affairs.' (P. Rylands IX, 19,4 = Parker 1961: 181)

In Coptic, DOM is obligatory with durative tenses when the object is definite and high on the scale of animacy. It later becomes optional with narrative tenses. Referentiality seems to play a role in the use of DOM, but also thematicity in the sense used by Engsheden (2005). DOM can also be correlated with the transitivity scale as defined in Hopper & Thompson (1980): the higher an element is on this scale, the more it can be expected to have a differential marking.[34]

It is difficult to escape the conclusion that DOM is a means, among many others, for distinguishing the two basic meanings of the *inaccompli*: the progressive and the non-progressive ones. This can explain why DOM appeared in LEg. In Middle Egyptian, there are two distinct constructions for expressing the progressive and the non-progressive *inaccompli*, as shown in the following Table:

---

34 See most recently Aissen (2003), Kamper (2006), de Swart (2007).

Table 1: The opposition of non-progressive vs. progressive within the inaccompli domain (Middle Egyptian)

	non-progressive	progressive
positive	*iw.f sḏm.f*	*iw.f ḥr sḏm*
negative	*n sḏm.n.f*	*nn sw ḥr sḏm*

In later Middle Egyptian, *iw.f sḏm.f* became obsolete; as a result, *iw.f ḥr sḏm* took over the whole domain of the inaccompli, at least in the positive. In negative constructions, Egyptian maintained an aspectually-founded opposition. This remains so in LEg, at least as long as one considers only the constructions that are part of a regular and grammaticalized system of oppositions (Table 2).

Table 2: The opposition of non-progressive vs. progressive inside the inaccompli[35] domain

	non-progressive	progressive
positive	*iw.f ḥr sḏm >*	
	sw ḥr sḏm	
negative	*n sḏm.n.f >*	*nn sw ḥr sḏm >*
	bw sḏm.n.f >	*bn sw ḥr sḏm*
	bw sḏm.f >	
	bw ir.f sḏm	

The loss of a dedicated pattern for expressing the progressive undoubtedly prompted LEg to use other means when ambiguity had to be avoided. The most widely used expression was a combination of one of the posture verbs (*ʿḥʿ* 'stand', *ḥmsi* 'sit', and *sḏr* 'lie') conjugated in a resultative form, usually the Pseudo-Participle (a resultative form), followed by the auxiliated verb in the infinitive:[36]

---

35 The broken brackets suggest the evolutionary steps from Middle Egyptian to Late Egyptian. They do not necessarily correspond to a morphological evolution from one form to another. For the diachronic process, see Winand (2006a: 313, n. 48, with previous bibliography).
36 See references given in footnotes 22 and 32.

(45) *ỉw-ỉ   sḏm   m-dỉ-w   ỉw-w   ꜥḥꜥ*
      SEQ   hear\INF   from-3PL CIRC-3PL stand\STAT.3PL
      ṯtṯt   *ḥr   wꜥ   ḥḏ*
      quarrel\INF   on   one   silver
      'I heard it from them as they were quarrelling about one (quantity of) silver.' (KRI VI, 821,13–14)

The following figure shows how LEg can positively mark the progressive with respect to the non-progressive, when needed[37]. The default pattern is the so-called Present I, *sw ḥr ỉr.t* '3SGM on do\INF', which may equally mean 'he does' or 'he is doing'. The progressive can be positively marked by using special devices (Table 3):

- a posture verb conjugated in a resultative tense (cf. example 45),
- the preposition *m*, in place of *ḥr*: this occurs only with verbs of movement,[38]
- the adverb *dy* 'here' to anchor the process in the moment of speaking, which, as a side effect, generally entails a progressive meaning,[39]
- DOM
- in the negative, as already said, LEg has two specialized constructions, one for the non-progressive, the other one for the progressive; this opposition is fully grammaticalized,
- in the participial and the so-called relative forms, LEg uses a periphrastic form with the verbs of up to three radicals for expressing the non-progressive. This contrasts with the simple form of the participle (or the relative), which has a perfective meaning, and the converted form of the Present I (introduced by the relative *nty*), which has a progressive meaning.[40]

---

37 It should be stressed that the marked forms remain outside the regular system of morphological oppositions. They are only used when the speaker feels the need to do so, for whatever pragmatic reasons.

38 Cf. Winand (2006a: 303–311).

39 Cf. Winand (2006a: 313; 400–402), Grossman (2008: 26, and n. 52).

40 See Winand (1992: § 567–574).

Table 3: The marked patterns of the progressive resp. non-progressive in LEg

	non-progressive	**progressive**
unmarked pattern	sw ḥr ỉr.t	
	he does / he is doing	
marked patterns	*sw ḥr ỉr.t*	*sw ꜥḥꜥ.w ḥr ỉr.t*
	he does	he is doing (lit. he is standing on doing)
	sw ḥr ỉy.t	*sw m ỉy.t*
	he comes	he is coming
	sw ḥr ỉr.t	*sw dy ḥr ỉr.t*
	he does	he is doing (lit. he is here on doing)
	sw ḥr ỉr.t	*sw ḥr ỉr.t ỉm.f*
	he does it	he is doing it (DOM)
	bw ỉr.f ỉr.t	*bn sw ḥr ỉr.t*
	he does not do	he is not doing
	ỉ.ỉr ỉr.t	*nty ḥr ỉr.t*
	(one) who does	(one) who is doing
	ỉ.ỉr.f ỉr.t.f	*nty sw ḥr ỉr.t.f*
	(that) which he does	(that) which he is doing

These complementary constructions were never fully grammaticalized. The oblique expression most probably was originally a way, among many others, to force the progressive reading. In the course of time, it was progressively grammaticalized.

When considering the pre-Demotic data, constructions with preposition *m* are found with the partitive and the emphatic construction. With the partitive, in the majority of the cases, the object is directly attached to the verb; the oblique construction with the preposition *m* remains an exception. Now, when this latter one is used, there is a strong tendency to do so when the tense is an *inaccompli*, or when the object is under the scope of a negation. With the emphatic construction, in the vast majority of the cases, tenses of the *inaccompli* are found. As already noted, the object seems to be insensitive to the opposition ± definite, ± animate. When other tenses are used, LEg tends to favour another construction, i.e., a variety of cleft sentences. In the examples gathered by Neveu (1994), there is only one example of a progressive tense; it might be no coincidence that the verb is wḫꜣ 'seek', a verb known to avoid the oblique construction in Coptic (Depuydt 1993).

The construction with *m* probably has its origin in the partitive construction.[41] The choice of the preposition *m* 'in' is obvious enough. The first examples of it go back to the Old Kingdom. As already noted (see footnote 11), it was never fully grammaticalized; the normal way of expressing partitivity in Coptic is to use a direct object. It was used in the so-called emphatic construction to convey a rhematic force to the direct object. This is already attested in Egyptian I, probably as early as the Old Kingdom. Later on, in the New Kingdom, the use of *m* was extended to what would eventually become DOM in Demotic. In LEg, examples are exceedingly rare. The objects are inanimate, and either definite or indefinite. In Demotic, DOM became fully grammaticalized. It is tempting to say that DOM was a means of distinguishing between the two possible meanings of the Present I, which does not distinguish in the positive between a progressive and a non-progressive meaning. Clearly enough, the *m*-Phrase is also a detransitivizing, detelicizing process, as is shown by the continuum in the argument structure of verbs like *bꜣk* 'work'.

The demarcating line between partitive meaning and DOM can sometimes be extremely fuzzy as is only to be expected if the derivational process suggested here is correct. A nice case is offered by this excerpt from the Battle of Qadesh:

(46) *iw-i*   *ḥr*   *ḥdb*   *im-sn*   *r*   *mr-n-i*
   CIRC-1SG PROG kill\INF LOC-3PL to   wish-PRF-1SG
   'As I was killing among them as much as I wished.' (KRI II, 140,7)

In the general literature, one often pushes forward the argument that DOM is used to clearly mark the object when it displays properties typically attributed to subjects (e.g., definiteness, animacy)[42]. This argument clearly does not hold for the LEg data, however scarce they are. More than a generally speaking, it should also probably be relativized when one comes to languages where the relative places of subject and object are not a matter of dispute, as is the case in Egyptian II.[43]

The restriction of DOM to the progressive aspect in Egyptian has prompted some Egyptologists to advocate a parallel with Finnish.[44] The understanding of how the progressive works in Finnish is notoriously a tricky matter, even for

---

41 This link was already suggested by Spiegelberg one century ago (1904), and never really challenged, with the notable exception of Engsheden (2006).
42 See Aissen (2003).
43 I use such a periphrasis to avoid tags like S–V–O, which are a bit arbitrary and reductionist.
44 E.g., Polotsky (1990: 221), as I did myself (Winand 2006a: 266, 312). Another possible candidate is Palau (Western Malayo-Polynesian, cf. Hagège 1986).

Finns, it seems. Since such a comparison has been vigorously challenged in a recent contribution by Engsheden (2006: 215–216), it is perhaps appropriate to dwell on this topic here with some details. The following lines mainly reflect the presentation that Sami Uljas kindly gave me.[45]

In Finnish, there are four possible cases for object marking: nominative, genitive, accusative and partitive. The first three cases form a group with which the partitive contrasts. The partitive is chosen if the effect of the verb on the object is somehow unlimited. Basically this is the case if
- the clause has a negative implication,
- the clause is 'aspectually unlimited',[46]
- the object is a mass noun or somehow quantitatively imprecise.

Otherwise one uses one of the other cases, all of which potentially imply 'total effect' on the object. The variation is extremely complex. In principle, the nominative is used (or in some instances, can be used) in instances where there is no real or implicit willing actor involved. This is the case in the 1st and 2nd person imperative, single person passives and necessive constructions. The genitive is used when the object is a singular noun and the verb has (or could have) a willing actor.[47]

Now, the progressive is formally a so-called third infinitive with an inessive case-suffix after a conjugated auxiliary 'be'.[48] It is rarer than simple 'present' in the expression of progressive. Its object is typically partitive. However, the genitive (or accusative with personal pronouns) is also possible with punctual verbs, but then the idea is that of anticipation of completion. In the progressive, the partitive is the default case for the object.[49]

---

45 It is my pleasure here to thank Sami Uljas very warmly for what appeared to me to be a clear and convincing picture. For the sake of brevity, the examples given by him have been dropped.

46 According to Bossong (1998: 243–244), it is probably more correct to give a progressive meaning to the sentence as a side effect of the use of the partitive, than the other way around.

47 In some grammars the genitive is called "accusative", but this is misleading because the form is identical to genitive case. The accusative is better reserved for the case used to mark "totally affected" personal pronouns.

48 See Heinämäki (1995), Tommola (2000). This construction is morphologically derived from the locative expression, which is fairly common typologically.

49 With the genitive there is potential for confusion, because this case is in some grammars called "accusative". It is also possible with the progressive, but only with punctual verbs, and then the sense is future. For personal pronouns there is a special case called "accusative". This is functionally the same as the genitive with nouns, and can be used in the progressive with the same (future) sense. In short, partitive, genitive and the personal pronoun accusative can all be used with the progressive, but the last two do not have a strictly progressive sense but rather a

It must be noted that the use of the progressive is never obligatory. For expressing something like the English "be doing X", one most commonly uses just the simple "present" with adverbs such as "now", "at this moment", etc. This is also the commonest strategy with intransitives. The progressive is quite marked and less common overall than the simple present even in case genuine progressive sense is intended in spite of its unambiguous sense.

As already noted, Egyptian sometimes shifts to a partitive expression when the sentence is negated. The preposition *m* is also used in this case. The use of a partitive expression in a negative context is typologically well attested, and has sometimes been fully grammaticalized. Finnish, once again, is a case in point. One can also recall the use of the genitive in Russian, and, to a lesser extent, the use of the prepostion "de" in French ("je lis un livre" vs. "je ne lis pas de livre").[50]

Finally, it would be interesting to study if Egyptian has differential subject marking (DSM).[51] Typologically, DSM is much less widespread than DOM. Due to the lack of space, it is impossible even to broach this topic here. However, Egyptian has a large array of features that point to a DSM system (e.g., types of personal pronoun in the non-verbal predicative system, strategies to avoid an indefinite subject in initial position, etc.).

Abbreviations

The glossing conventions, as well as the glosses, are adapted from the Leipzig Glossing Rules and the proposal made by Di Biase-Dyson, Kammerzell, & Werning (2009). The following are language-specific glosses:

ACCOM	accompli
CIRC	circumstantial
CONJ	conjunctive verb form
INACC	inaccompli
SEQ	sequential verb form
STAT	stative verb form
THMZ	thematizing verb form

---

future, and they cannot be used with durative verbs with which only the partitive is possible.
50 See Christol (1998: 476).
51 For DSM in Coptic, the latest stage of the Egyptian language, see Grossman (this volume).

7 References

Aissen, Judith. 2003. Differential Object Marking: Iconicity vs. Economy. *Natural Language & Linguistic Theory* 21: 435–483.

Bertinetto, Pier Marco, Bianchi, Valentina, Higginbotham, James & Squartini, Mario (eds.). 1995. *Temporal Reference, Aspect and Actionality*, vol. 2. Torino: Rosenberg & Sellier.

Bossong, Georg. 1997. Le marquage différentiel de l'objet dans les langues d'Europe. In: Feuillet, Jack (ed.), *Actance et Valence dans les langues d'Europe*. (Eurotyp 20–2). Berlin: De Gruyter, 193–258.

Bybee, Joan & Dahl, Østen. 1989. The Creation of Tense and Aspect Systems in the Languages of the World. *Studies in Language* 13: 51–103.

Bybee, Joan, Perkins, Revere & Pagliuca, William. 1994. *The Evolution of Grammar: Tense, Aspect and Modality in the Languages of the World*. Chicago: University Press.

Carlson, Lauri. 1981. Aspect and Quantification. In: Tedeschi, Philip & Zaenen, Annie (eds.), *Syntax and Semantics* 14. *Tense and Aspect*. New York: Academic Press, 31–64.

Christol, Alain. 1997. Marquage oblique des actants. In: Feuillet, Jack (ed.), *Actance et Valence dans les langues d'Europe*. (Eurotyp 20–2). Berlin: De Gruyter, 457–523.

Cohen, David. 1989. *L'aspect verbal*. Paris: PUF.

Dahl, Østen (ed.). 2000. *Tense and Aspect in the Languages of Europe*. ([Eurotyp 20–6). Berlin: De Gruyter.

Danon, Gabi. 2001. Syntactic definiteness in the grammar of Modern Hebrew. *Linguistics* 39: 1071–1116.

Depuydt, Leo. 1991. On Distinctive and Isolating Emphasis in Egyptian and in General. *Lingua Aegyptia* 1: 33–56.

Depuydt, Leo. 1993. For the Sake of ογωϣ, 'love': an Exception to the Stern-Jernstedt Rule and its History. *Journal of Egyptian Archaeology* 79: 282–286.

Di Biase-Dyson, Camilla, Kammerzell, Frank & Werning, Daniel A. 2009. Glossing Ancient Egyptian. Suggestions for adapting the Leipzig Glossing Rules. *Lingua Aegyptia* 17: 343–366.

Elwolde, John. 1994. The Use of 'et in non-biblical Hebrew Texts. *Vetus Testamentum* 44.2: 170–182.

Engsheden, Åke. 2006. Über die Markierung des direkten Objekts im Koptischen. *Lingua Aegyptia* 14: 199–222.

Feuillet, Jack (ed.). 1997. *Actance et Valence dans les langues d'Europe*. (Eurotyp 20–2). Berlin: De Gruyter.

Gardiner, Alan H. 1953. *Egyptian Grammar*, 3rd ed. Oxford: Clarendon.

Givón, Talmy. 1978. Definiteness and referentiality. In: Greenberg, Joseph (ed.), *Universals of Human Language*. Stanford, CA: Stanford University Press, 291–330.

Givón, Talmy. 1982. Tense-Aspect-Modality: the Creole prototype. In: Hopper, Paul (ed.), *Tense-Aspect: Between Semantics and Pragmatics*. Amsterdam: Benjamins, 115–163.

Groll, Sarah Israelit. 1967. *Non-verbal Sentence Patterns in Late Egyptian*. London: Griffith Institute.

Grossman, Eitan. 2008. Nucleus-Satellite Analysis and Conjugation Mediation in Coptic and Later Egyptian. *Zeitschrift für Ägyptische Sprache und Altertumskunde* 135: 16–29.

Grossman, Eitan & Polis, Stéphane. 2012. Navigating Polyfunctionality in the Lexicon. Building a Semantic Map of Allativity. In: Grossman, Eitan, Polis, Stéphane & Winand, Jean (eds.),

Lexical Semantics in Ancient Egyptian. (Linguae Aegyptia – Studia monographica). Göttingen: Seminar für Ägyptologie und Koptologie.

Grossman, Eitan, Polis, Stéphane & Winand, Jean (eds.). 2012. *Lexical Semantics in Ancient Egyptian*. (Linguae Aegyptia – Studia monographica). Göttingen: Seminar für Ägyptologie und Koptologie.

Hagège, Claude. 1986. *La langue palau, une curiosité typologique*. München: Wilhelm Fink Verlag.

Haspelmath, Martin (ed.). 2001. *Language Typology and Language Universals*. (Handbücher zur Sprach- und Kommunikationswissenschaft 20.2). Berlin: De Gruyter.

Heinämäki. Orvokki. 1995. The progressive in Finnish: pragmatic constraints. In: Bertinetto, Pier Marco, Bianchi, Valentina, Higginbotham, James & Squartini, Mario (eds.), *Temporal Reference, Aspect and Actionality*, II. Torino: Rosenberg & Sellier, 143–154.

Hopper, Paul (ed.). 1982. *Tense-Aspect: Between Semantics and Pragmatics*. Amsterdam: Benjamins.

Hopper, Paul & Thompson, Sandra. 1980. Transitivity in Grammar and Discourse. *Language* 56: 251–299.

Kamper, Gergely. 2006. *Differential Object Marking*. (The Even Yearbook 7). http://seas3.elte. hu/delg/publications/even.

Khan Geoffrey A. 1984. Object Markers and Agreement Pronouns in Semitic Languages. *Bulletin of the School of Oriental and African Studies* 47.3: 468–500.

Lazard, Gilbert. 1994. *L'actance*. Paris: PUF.

Lazard, Gilbert. 1997. Definition des actants dans les langues européennes. In: Feuillet, Jack (ed.), *Actance et Valence dans les langues d'Europe*. (Eurotyp 20–2). Berlin: De Gruyter, 11–146.

Lazard, Gilbert. 2001. Le marquage différentiel de l'objet. In: Haspelmath, Martin. (ed.), *Language Typology and Language Universals*. (Handbücher zur Sprach- und Kommunikationswissenschaft 20.2). Berlin: De Gruyter, 873–885.

Layton, Bentley. 2000. *A Coptic Grammar*. Wiesbaden: Harrassowitz.

Loprieno, Antonio. 1995. *Ancient Egyptian, A Linguistic Introduction*. Cambridge: University Press.

Macauley, Donald (ed.). 1992. *The Celtic Languages*. Cambridge: Cambridge University Press.

Neveu, François. 1994. Vraie et pseudo-cleft sentence en néo-égyptien. *Lingua Aegyptia* 4: 191–212.

Parker, Richard A. 1961. The Durative Tenses in P. Rylands IX. *Journal of Near Eastern Studies* 20: 180–187.

Polotsky, Hans Jakob. 1990. *Grundlagen des koptischen Satzbaus*. (American Studies in Papyrology 29.2). Atlanta: Scholars Press.

Shisha-Halevy, Ariel. 1986. *Coptic Grammatical Categories*. Rome: Biblical Institute Press.

Shisha-Halevy, Ariel. 2003. Celtic Syntax, Egyptian-Coptic Syntax. In: Hasitzka, Monika, Diethart, Johannes & Dembski, Günther (eds.), *Das Alte Ägypten und seine Nachbarn: Festschrift zum 65. Geburtstag von Helmut Satzinger*. Krems: Österreichisches Literaturforum, 245–302.

Silverman, David. 1980. An Emphasized Direct Object of a Nominal Verb in Middle Egyptian. *Orientalia* 49: 199–203.

Simpson, Robert S. 1996. *Demotic Grammar in the Ptolemaic Sacerdotal Decrees*. Oxford: Griffith Institute.

Spiegelberg, Wilhelm. 1904. Koptische Miszellen. *Recueil de Travaux* 26: 34–35.

de Swart, Peter. 2007. *Cross-linguistic Variation in Object Marking*. Utrecht: LOT.

Tedeschi, Philip & Zaenen, Annie (eds.). 1981. *Tense and Aspect*. (Syntax and Semantics 14). New York: Academic Press.

Tommola, Hannu. 2000. Progressive aspect in Baltic Finnic. In: Dahl, Østen (ed.), *Tense and Aspect in the Languages of Europe* .(Eurotyp 20–6). Berlin: De Gruyter, 655–692.

Vernus. Pascal. 1998. Processus de grammaticalisation dans la langue égyptienne. *Comptes rendus de l'Académie des Inscriptions et Belles-Lettres*, 191–210.

Werning, Daniel. 2012. The Semantic Space of Topological Prepositions in Ancient Egyptian. In: Grossman, Eitan, Polis, Stéphane & Winand, Jean (eds.), *Lexical Semantics in Ancient Egyptian*. (Linguae Aegyptia – Studia monographica). Göttingen: Seminar für Ägyptologie und Koptologie.

Winand, Jean. 2003. A Dictionary between Lexicon and Grammar. Interplay of Verbal Aktionsart and Grammatical Aspects. In: Hafemann, Ingelore, *Wege zu einem digitalem Corpus Ägyptischer Texte*. Berlin: Achet, 252–270.

Winand, Jean. 2006a. *Temps et aspect en ancien égyptien. Une approche sémantique.* (Probleme der Ägyptologie 25). Leiden: Brill.

Winand, Jean. 2006b. La prédication non verbale en égyptien ancien. *Faits de langues* 27: 73–102.

Winand, Jean. 2007. Les formes nominalisées en égyptien ancien. *Faits de langues* 30: 69–82.

Winand, Jean. 2009. Zero(s) in Ancient Egyptian. In: Müller, Matthias & Uljas, Sami (eds.), *Proceedings of the Crossroads IV Conference (Basel, March 19–22, 2009)*. *Lingua Aegyptia* 17: 319–339.

Winand, Jean. 2011. Le verbe et les variations d'actance. Les constructions réversibles. In: Grossman, Eitan, Polis, Stéphane & Winand, Jean (eds.), *Lexical Semantics in Ancient Egyptian*. (Linguae Aegyptia – Studia monographica). Göttingen: Seminar für Ägyptologie und Koptologie.

Winand, Jean. fc. *Quelques réflexions sur l'actionalité des procès en égyptien ancien*.

Winand, Jean, Polis, Stéphane & Rosmorduc, Serge. 2009. An Annotated Corpus of Late Egyptian. In: Kousoulis, Panagiotis (ed.), *Proceedings of the Xth International Association of Egyptologists Congress (Rhodos, May 2008)*. Leuven: Peeters (in press).

Index of authors

Index of Languages

General index